'Just the kind of book I like: discursive, varied, relaxed, dealing with literature, art, theatre and social life as well as politics'
Paul Johnson, *Sunday Telegraph* Books of the Year

'This is a compelling, splendidly researched biography of a city'
Clive Aslet, *Country Life*

'As richly stuffed as a *boudin truffé* . . . Mansel writes well and arranges his material with skill and lightness of touch'   *The Economist*

'This gripping and delightful book . . . Never have the revolutions of 1830 and 1848 been so vividly conveyed . . . Mansel's book is full of wonderful characters, deftly sketched . . . All the wit, sexuality, greed and intrigue of Paris is magnificently portrayed'
Simon Sebag Montefiore, *Sunday Times*

'Deserves nothing but praise for its readability, its erudition and its entertainment'   Robert O'Byrne, *Irish Times*

'Part of the fascination of Mansel's story lies in the picture of Paris as the key not just to France but to Europe and to twentieth-century European history . . . Both a fine history and an historical guide book that any reader who loves Paris will learn from and enjoy'
Patrick Marnham, *Daily Mail*

'This excellent book is full of insight and revealing detail'
Richard Vinen, *Financial Times*

'Philip Mansel's absorbing and admirable history . . . he has an eye for the good story and the telling detail'   Philip Hensher, *Spectator*

'A work of admirable enthusiasm, detail, intelligence . . . Mansel's book is vastly instructive and entertaining'
Gillian Tindall, *Times Literary Supplement*

Philip Mansel, who has lived and taught in Paris, is the author of several books on the history and monarchies of Europe and the Middle East. He has written for numerous newspapers and periodicals, and is the editor of *The Court Historian*, newsletter of the Society for Court Studies. *Paris Between Empires* was long-listed for the Samuel Johnson Prize, 2002.

Also by Philip Mansel

Louis XVIII

Pillars of Monarchy

Sultans in Splendour: Monarchs of the
Middle East 1869–1945

The Court of France 1789–1830

Constantinople: City of
the World's Desire, 1453–1924

Prince of Europe: The Life of
Charles-Joseph de Ligne 1735–1814

PARIS BETWEEN EMPIRES

1814–1852

Monarchy and Revolution

Philip Mansel

PHOENIX

To Paris friends

A PHOENIX PRESS PAPERBACK

First published in Great Britain
by John Murray (Publishers) Ltd in 2001
This paperback edition published in 2003
by Phoenix Press,
a division of The Orion Publishing Group Ltd,
Orion House, 5 Upper St Martin's Lane,
London WC2H 9EA

A CIP catalogue record for this book is
available from the British Library.

Set by Servis Filmsetting Ltd, Manchester

Printed and bound in Great Britain by
Clays Ltd, St Ives plc

ISBN 1 84212 656 3

Contents

Illustrations

(between pages 274 and 275)

The author and publisher would like to thank the following for permission to reproduce illustrations: Plates 1, 2, 23, 24, 25, 27, 28, 29, 35, 43 and 47, Réunion des Musées Nationaux; 3, 8, 9, 10, 11, 19, 31, 36, 37, 38, 40, 44, 45, 46, 49 and 50, Musée Carnavalet; 4, 5, 6, 7, 13, 17, 18, 21, 26, 32, 33, 41, 42 and 48, Private Collection; 12, Hazlitt, Gooden and Fox; 14, Musée du Louvre; 15, National Gallery of Ireland; 16, Agnew's; 20, 22 and 30, Musée de l'Ile de France; 34, Musée des Beaux-Arts, Chambéry; 39, Heinrich Heine Institut Düsseldorf; 51, 52 and 53, Roger Viollet. The illustration reproduced in Appendix II is from a Private Collection.

Acknowledgements

The author would like to thank all those who have helped him with this book, in particular:

Olivier Aaron, Robert Alexander, Sheila de Bellaigue, Zeenie Bonifacio, Micheline Boudet, Anthony Bourne, Prince Gabriel de Broglie, Marie-Françoise Brizay, Caroline Butler, François Callais, Cirillo Camara, Baron de Cassagne, Edward Corp, William Dalrymple, Frédéric Didier, Fram Dinshaw, Jane Dormer, Emmanuel Ducamp, Olivier Gabet, René and Béatrice de Gaillande, Jean-Louis Gaillemin, Didier Girard, the Knight of Glin, Pat Gomer, David Higgs, Niall Hobhouse, Mira Hudson, Anne Hurley, Eardley Johnson, Sue, Ossama and Nur Kaoukgi, Manuel Keene, Neil Kent, Randal Keynes, Caroline Knox, Mrs Laing, Richard and Daphne Lamb, Katherine de Leusse, Mrs Bulwer Long, Maxwell Lowe, Thomas de Luynes, Jacques Mallattier, Mlle Marchant, Pippa Mason, Giles McDonogh, Bernard Minoret, Shaaker Mohamed, Joy Moorhead, Mrs R.S. Mortimer, Laure Murat, Gay Naughton, André Nieuwazny, Constantine and Nicola Normanby, Patrick O'Connor, Dr Sylvia Ostrova, Jacques Perot, Daniel-Georges Polliart, Michel Poniatowski, Alexandre Pradère, Jane Preston, Vicomte de Rohan, Comte Jean de Rohan-Chabot, Baronne Elie de Rothschild, Gérard Rousset-Charny, Francis Russell, Ian Scott, Dr H. Smiskova, The Hon. Mrs Townshend, Bruno Villien, Christopher Walker, Adam Zamoyski, and the staffs of the Bibliothèque Nationale, the London Library and the British Library.

He is particularly grateful for their comments on the manuscript to Roger Hudson, Caroline Knox, Metin Münir, Fouad Nahas and, above all, Howard Davies.

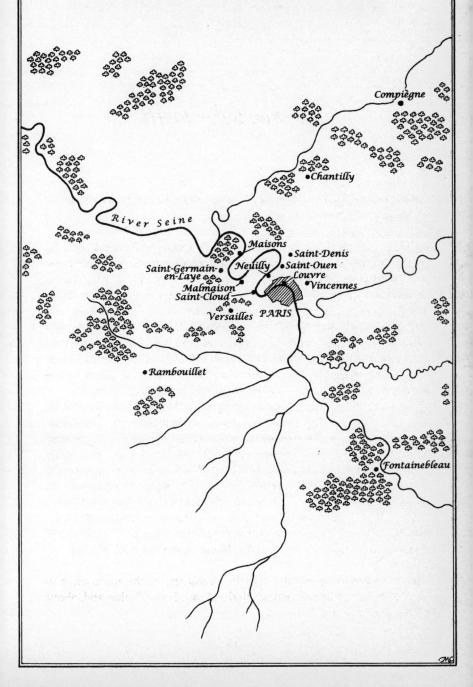

THE ILE DE FRANCE

Compiègne

Chantilly

River Seine

Maisons

Saint-Denis

Saint-Germain-
en-Laye

Neuilly

Saint-Ouen

Louvre

Malmaison
Saint-Cloud

Vincennes

Versailles

PARIS

Rambouillet

Fontainebleau

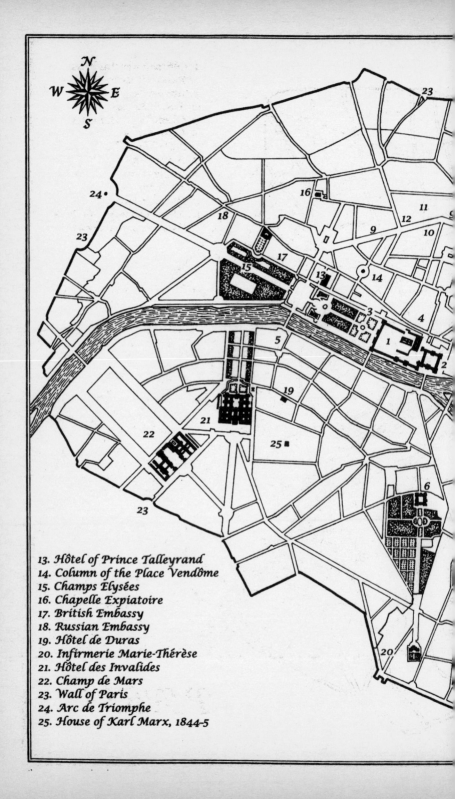

13. Hôtel of Prince Talleyrand
14. Column of the Place Vendôme
15. Champs Elysées
16. Chapelle Expiatoire
17. British Embassy
18. Russian Embassy
19. Hôtel de Duras
20. Infirmerie Marie-Thérèse
21. Hôtel des Invalides
22. Champ de Mars
23. Wall of Paris
24. Arc de Triomphe
25. House of Karl Marx, 1844-5

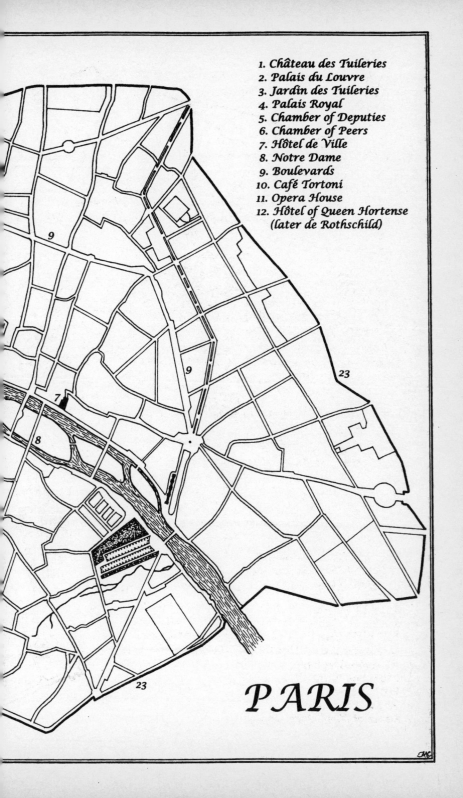

1. Château des Tuileries
2. Palais du Louvre
3. Jardin des Tuileries
4. Palais Royal
5. Chamber of Deputies
6. Chamber of Peers
7. Hôtel de Ville
8. Notre Dame
9. Boulevards
10. Café Tortoni
11. Opera House
12. Hôtel of Queen Hortense
    (later de Rothschild)

PARIS

Nous nous estimerons heureux d'avoir présenté au Voyageur tous les objets dignes de son admiration ou de sa curiosité dans une Cité dont la magnificence rivalise avec celle de l'antique Thèbes; le luxe, le goût pour les sciences et les arts avec Athènes; et qui domine sur l'Europe, comme Rome, lorsqu'elle eût conquis l'empire du monde!

F.-M. Marchant, *Le Conducteur de l'étranger à Paris*, March 1814

I

Death of an Empire:
Europe takes Paris

March–June 1814

C'est à la Ville de Paris qu'il appartient dans les circonstances actuelles d'accélérer
la Paix du Monde . . . l'Europe en armes devant vos murs s'adresse à vous.
Proclamation of Marshal Prince Schwarzenberg, 31 March 1814

THE NIGHT WAS clear and still; there was little movement in the streets. From the heart of the city Parisians could see the campfires of the enemy army on the surrounding hills and listen to the strange sound of Russian music.[1] For the first time in its eight centuries as capital of France, Paris was besieged by a foreign army. The shock was all the greater given that, in the previous twenty years, under the Republic and the Empire, French soldiers had marched in triumph into almost every city in Europe, from Lisbon to Moscow. In 1811 the French Empire, under Napoleon I, had covered half the continent, from Hamburg to Rome, from Brittany to Dalmatia.

The buildings of Paris reflected its European empire. The Musée Napoléon in the Louvre was filled with the spoils of war, seized from churches and palaces in Italy, Belgium and Germany, or extracted from France's vanquished foes on the grounds that their rightful place was not with 'slaves' but in 'the bosom of a free people'. Among the loot were Rubens' *Descent from the Cross*, removed from Antwerp cathedral; Raphael's *St Cecilia* from Bologna; Veronese's *Marriage at Cana* from Venice; and statues such as the Venus de' Medici and the Apollo Belvedere, taken from Florence and Rome respectively.[2] The four ancient Greek bronze horses from the façade of St Mark's cathedral in

Venice adorned the summit of the Arc de Triomphe du Carrousel, built in 1806–7 in front of the Tuileries palace to honour the French victories over Austria and Russia in 1805. The sword and decorations of Frederick the Great, and the Victory quadriga from the top of the Brandenburg Gate in Berlin, had been placed in the Invalides.[3] Archives from Vienna, Simancas and the Vatican had been removed to the Archives Impériales in the rue du Faubourg du Temple. The Cardinals too had been taken from Rome to Paris, after the imprisonment of the Pope and the annexation of the Papal States in 1809.

But the retreat from Moscow in 1812 and, even more, the Emperor's defeat by an army of Russian, Austrian and Prussian soldiers at the 'Battle of the Nations' outside Leipzig in October 1813 had been the beginning of the end. Since Leipzig Paris had been filled by dread of impending cataclysm. The only news that could be trusted was the location of the Emperor's headquarters, as reported in his war bulletins, while he darted across the plains east of Paris at the head of an army of 50,000, trying in vain to block the advancing torrent of Russian, Austrian and Prussian soldiers. The Russian troops, enraged by the French invasion in 1812 and the burning of Moscow (in reality ordered by their own government), were said to know only two words of French: *brûler Paris*.[4]

At the end of March the streets of Paris had been made impassable by the arrival of peasants fleeing the fighting, bringing their cattle and carts laden with relations and possessions. The shouts and groans of frightened animals and people were deafening. Soldiers and cannon leaving for the battlefield crossed more files of carts piled with allied prisoners. Wounded French soldiers crawled haggard and emaciated through the streets of Paris demanding money, or simply lay down to die.[5]

Lunatics were driven out of asylums, patients out of hospitals, to make way for the wounded. So many died that they had to be buried in mass graves to avoid a typhus epidemic. Other corpses were thrown in the Seine. According to Thomas Richard Underwood, an English artist who had lived in Paris as a prisoner on parole since the resumption of war between Britain and France in 1803, 'the number of dead bodies seen, either floating down the river or stranded on the banks was immense and exhibited an appalling spectacle'. To reassure Parisians that the soldiers' corpses had not contaminated the Seine, which was the city's main source of drinking water, two professors and the Dean of the Paris Faculty of Medicine were persuaded to publish a statement 'that the continued fluctuation and change of water destroyed all putrescence and that the fluid was consequently harmless'.[6]

The Napoleonic Empire had internal as well as external enemies. One of the most influential was the celebrated former bishop and revolutionary politician Charles-Maurice de Talleyrand, Prince de Bénévent. Although in personal disgrace with the Emperor owing to his opposition to French expansion in Europe, as Vice-Grand Electeur he remained at the summit of the Empire's official hierarchy. On 6 March he had sent a royalist, the Baron de Vitrolles, to allied headquarters in the east of France, with a letter written in invisible ink. Vitrolles' mission was to reveal the strength of hostility to Napoleon in Paris and to urge an allied advance on the city.

Both the British and Russian governments had long helped finance the activities and propaganda of the exiled Bourbon pretender Louis XVIII, younger brother of Louis XVI. In his efforts to find a haven safe from the advancing French armies, he had spent the last twenty-three years on an odyssey around Europe – from Germany to Verona, back to Germany, on to Mittau in Russia, Warsaw and finally England, where he lived from 1807 to 1814. Britain and Russia encouraged the distribution in France of his printed Declaration of Hartwell (his residence near Aylesbury in Buckinghamshire between 1809 and 1814), promising peace, stability, freedom and an endorsement of the post-revolutionary administrative settlement and property distribution. Madame de Marigny, sister of the great writer Chateaubriand whose works *Le Génie du Christianisme* (1801), *Les Martyrs* (1809) and *Itinéraire de Paris à Jérusalem et de Jérusalem à Paris* (1811) had spearheaded the Catholic revival in France, wrote in her diary on 17 and 20 March that the King's declaration was being thrown into streets and shops, that the police were tearing it off the walls, that the Bourbons were talked of 'more than ever' and that there was no news from the Emperor. He was leading a last desperate campaign to the south and east of Paris, hoping to split the advancing allied armies and defeat each section in turn.[7]

'For the first time', so Underwood wrote, 'I heard the people openly dare to venture complaints against the Emperor as the sole cause of the impending calamity; but I witnessed no patriotic feeling to repulse the enemy.' Patriotism had been weakened by the demands of the Empire's relentless wars. Moreover, since his seizure of power by a military coup in 1799, many Parisians had doubted Napoleon's claim to represent France. Madame Reinhard, the wife of a senior official, recorded: 'The *dénouement* is approaching and is desired to put an end to the anguish oppressing all hearts.'[8] The interception of a despatch from the Minister of Police to Napoleon, revealing fears of a royalist uprising in Paris, finally persuaded the allies to advance directly on the capital, ignoring Napoleon's army south of the city.[9]

Not only royalists and foreigners were gathering for the kill. Another enemy was emerging from below. Like all governments of the day, the Napoleonic Empire based itself on property; only the richest men had the vote in elections to the Corps Législatif and the Senate. The plebiscite, based on universal male suffrage, had not been used since it ratified the proclamation of the Empire in 1804. Conversely the regime despised what was called *la plus vile populace*, the unpropertied poor who composed three-quarters of the population, and it lived in fear of what one police report called 'the overthrow of the entire social system'.[10] Class tension governed or affected most human relations. In March, according to one Parisian, 'the dregs of the people . . . individuals with no religion, no morals and leading an abject and degraded life' terrified bourgeois Parisians by pointing out the houses they planned to pillage with the help of the Cossacks in the Russian army. On 27 March Talleyrand wrote to his mistress the Duchesse de Courlande, who had retreated to the safety of the countryside, that dread of pillage, famine and catastrophe tormented Paris. He himself feared 'social breakdown . . . no one obeys and yet no one dares to give orders.'[11]

The principal protection against the 'populace', and the main lawkeeping body in the city, was the Paris National Guard. Founded in 1789 as the military arm of the Paris bourgeoisie, it had played a crucial role in the early years of the revolution, both advancing its cause and preventing the poor from taking it over. In 1814 it was composed of 12,000 bourgeois property owners serving – in turn and equipped at their own expense – as guards and policemen outside public buildings throughout the city. On 23 January 1814, after Sunday mass in the Tuileries palace, the Emperor had entrusted the protection of the city of Paris, of his wife the Empress Marie Louise, born an Archduchess of Austria, and of their son the King of Rome, to 'the courage of the National Guard'. With tears in their eyes and cries of *Vive l'Empereur!* nine hundred officers in new uniforms had sworn their loyalty. However, fear of *la plus vile populace* had led the Prefect of Police, Baron Pasquier, to admit known royalists as officers.[12]

The ceremony had taken place in the Salle des Maréchaux of the Tuileries palace, the long grey palace, now destroyed, built by Catherine de Médicis in 1561–4, west of the Louvre. It was situated between a courtyard, the Cour du Carrousel, and the Jardin des Tuileries, the largest and most fashionable public garden in the city and one of its centres of life and movement. Well-dressed Parisians, including ministers and ambassadors, spent hours walking every day in the garden – among orange and chestnut trees, fountains, flowerbeds and marble statues of gods and goddesses – eyeing each other, talking or sitting and reading newspapers.[13]

After the National Guard had escorted Louis XVI and the royal family from Versailles to the Tuileries on 6 October 1789, the palace had become famous throughout Europe as the seat and symbol of sovereignty in France. It was from the Tuileries that Louis XVI had fled to Varennes in 1791, and to the Legislative Assembly in 1792 – the palace walls still bore the marks of the cannon shot fired against it by the national guards on 10 August 1792, the day they helped a Parisian mob overthrow the monarchy.[14] It was in the Tuileries that the Convention had sat in 1793–4, and there that, since 1800, Napoleon had lived and ruled. It symbolised both the power and the fragility of the French monarchy.

The continued presence in the Tuileries of the Empress Marie Louise had been considered the capital's best protection against allied vengeance, and had given courage to its defenders. However, throughout 29 March, according to Underwood, the ladies of her court had been seen through the windows of the palace 'running from apartment to apartment; some were weeping, and in a state of distraction; whilst servants were hurrying from place to place in like confusion'. At half past six in the evening fifteen carriages, including the gilt coronation coach of Napoleon I covered in green canvas, left with the crown jewels and the imperial archives, escorted by cavalry. Sentries kept the stunned and silent spectators at a distance. Finally at 10.32 p.m. the Empress herself, in a brown cloth riding habit and holding the three-year-old King of Rome, dressed in a blue jacket and screaming that he did not want to leave his house, departed from the palace in a coach surrounded by fifty horse guards, followed by fifteen or twenty other coaches. According to the novelist Stendhal, then an official in the furniture department of the imperial household, the spectators 'showed no sign of emotion'. The Empress's procession drove along the quay on the right bank of the Seine, heading south-west for the château of Rambouillet. She never saw Paris again.[15]

*

Paris sheltered behind its brown stone wall, three metres high and twenty-four kilometres long. The wall, which had been built in 1784–7 to incorporate the massive expansion of the city under Louis XVI, separated the city from the fields and farms which then came right up to the first houses of Paris. The wall was pierced by fifty-four iron gates, or *barrières*, flanked by railings, where all goods entering the city, even carts of hay, were examined by municipal officials and obliged to pay internal customs duties. (Surviving *barrières* can be seen at, for example, Place Denfert-Rochereau and Place de la Nation.)[16] These barriers had recently been blocked and fortified with wooden palisades – more to impress the Parisians with evidence of government resolve than to provide a serious defence.

Under the supreme authority of the Emperor's brother King Joseph-Napoleon, former King of Spain, Marshals Marmont and Mortier were in charge of the defence of the city, at the head of approximately 20,000 soldiers and 6,000 national guards: the other national guards, with the Paris garrison and the gendarmes, were kept back to maintain law and order in the city. The French forces faced an allied army of about 100,000 covering the plains north and east of the city. Its commander was the great Austrian Marshal Prince Schwarzenberg, victor at Leipzig in 1813.[17]

At 5 a.m. on 30 March allied forces began their attack. They were impressed by the vigour and volume of the cannon and musket fire from the French.[18] For four hours the roar of artillery could be heard, and the smoke from cannon shot be seen, from Vincennes in the east of the city to Montmartre in the north. Montmartre was then an isolated hill, renamed Montnapoléon, riding high above the plain of the Seine outside the city walls. It was covered by windmills where flour for the city's bread was ground, and situated on its summit was the celebrated telegraph machine whence Napoleon had transmitted orders to his armies and news of his victories to Paris. Pupils of the Ecole Polytechnique and some French and Polish soldiers fought bravely. The Prussian guards suffered 'monstrously', according to one of their officers the seventeen-year-old Prince Wilhelm of Prussia, who wept over the deaths of 'so many dear good people'. In all about 9,000 allied soldiers died, compared to only 3,000 French.[19]

However, further resistance against overwhelming numerical superiority was pointless. The National Guard was unenthusiastic; the police, who normally arrested soldiers running away from the battlefield, were invisible. At 10 a.m., from his position beside the telegraph on

Montmartre, King Joseph gave the order to the marshals to start negotiations for a ceasefire when they thought fit. To the indignation of the Parisians, he then left the city with the remaining members of the imperial family and the ministers, as fast as their coaches could carry them, to join the Empress at Rambouillet.

Some Parisians had been watching the battle through telescopes from high points in the city or from their own rooftops.[20] Others, as usual, spent the day in the centre of the city on the boulevards. Whereas Vienna kept its fortified ramparts until 1853, as early as 1670 Louis XIV had ordered streets to be laid out on the site of the old city bulwarks (= boulevards) built by King Philippe-Auguste around 1200. The boulevards were wide tree-lined streets stretching from the Madeleine to the Bastille and, although completely transformed, are – like the Boulevard des Italiens stretching east from the Place de l'Opéra – still in existence today. In contrast to the boulevards, the heart of Paris, which was one of the few cities in Europe to have been a metropolis since the Middle Ages, was full of winding streets, some of which were so dark, damp and narrow that they gave the impression of a subterranean city; houses had to burn lamps throughout the day for much of the summer as well as in winter.[21] Receiving the *ordures* of 200,000 households as well as countless workshops, butchers' shops and horses, these streets were, in addition, covered by 'a black mud' which stank of 'pestilential miasmas'.[22]

The boulevards, on the other hand, were made for strolling by day and – since they alone were well lit – by night. As Underwood noted: 'During the battle the Boulevard des Italiens (now Coblentz) and the Café Tortoni were thronged with fashionable loungers of both sexes, sitting, as usual, on the chairs placed there and appearing almost uninterested spectators of the number of wounded French and prisoners of the allies which were brought in.' However, at 2 p.m. a cry of *sauve qui peut* on the boulevards caused a 'general and confused flight, which spread, like the undulations of a wave, even beyond the Pont Neuf'.[23]

That evening one Parisian took a route of his own. By prior arrangement Talleyrand ensured that, at about 7 p.m. on 30 March, leaving to join the Empress later than most other dignitaries, his carriage was stopped at the Barrière de la Conférence in the west of the city by national guards commanded by a friend, the Comte de Rémusat. They implored him not to abandon Paris. Talleyrand then returned to await events in his house on the rue Saint-Florentin off the Place de la Concorde.

Meanwhile at 3.30 p.m., Montmartre having fallen to Russian troops under the émigré general Comte de Langeron, the marshals had ordered a ceasefire. Discussion of capitulation terms began with allied commissioners at a small *cabaret* called *Au Petit Jardinet* outside the Barrière de Saint-Denis.[24] Details were finalised that night in the house of Maréchal Marmont, in what is now 51 rue du Paradis, between Montmartre and the boulevards. Among those packing the salons were Marmont himself, covered in mud and blood, with his arm in a sling, exhausted after hours of combat; the leading Paris banker, Jacques Laffitte; the Prefects of Paris and the Police; and Talleyrand, who asked an aide-de-camp of the Tsar, Count Michael Orlov, to convey to his master the expression of his profound respect. Opposition between soldiers and civilians was evident, as it would be in many crises in Paris in the ensuing century. While Laffitte, then a violent royalist, was blaming the Emperor for the catastrophe, Comte Hulin, military governor of Paris, cursed *vos bourgeois enrégimentés et endimanchés*. However, like most other officers, Hulin considered it more important to save the city than to fight on – even at the risk of disobeying the Emperor himself.

Napoleon had ordered the main Paris powder-store to be blown up, intending like Count Rostopchine in Moscow in 1812 to unleash a volcano of destruction on the capital. Its commander, however, refused to obey.[25] The same day the chief of staff Marshal Berthier, the Foreign Minister the Comte de Caulaincourt and General Belliard had also refused to obey the Emperor. Napoleon had hoped to advance on Paris from the south-east to make it 'the foreigners' graveyard'. His command, 'My carriage, Caulaincourt. Let us go to Paris', had been greeted by silence. Paris, he was reminded, had already capitulated; he had no troops and would only expose it to pillage if he advanced. Paris itself was thus a political factor. Its buildings and people weakened Napoleon's ability to fight on. Napoleon took up residence in the palace of Fontainebleau, forty miles south-east of the city.[26]

Terms were finally agreed at 2 a.m. on 31 March: Marmont and Mortier, with their troops and weapons, were permitted to evacuate Paris to the south, thereby retaining an army for the Emperor. The capitulation document concluded by recommending the city 'to the generosity of the allied powers'. The French evacuation began that morning. At the same time, posted on the walls of Paris was a declaration by the Tsar, which his royalist aide-de-camp Count Charles-André Pozzo di Borgo had helped to draft. Like Bonaparte Pozzo came from

Corsica. As young men, these two equally ambitious and impoverished nobles had become implacable enemies. Their natural antagonism had been sharpened by their struggle for the favour of the Corsican national hero Pasquale Paoli, who was supported by Britain. Pozzo had won, and after 1793 had entered the service of first Britain, then Russia: Bonaparte had chosen the French Republic and become an Emperor. Pozzo did not win a throne. However, for the twenty years after his enemy's fall, as Russian ambassador in Paris Pozzo would be one of the uncrowned kings of the city. Vivacious, red-faced, speaking French with a marked Italian accent, while others were called by their titles – *Monsieur le duc, Son excellence, Madame la vicomtesse* – this handsome cosmopolitan bachelor was known simply as *Pozzo*.[27]

On the last occasion European allied armies had approached Paris, at the beginning of the French revolutionary wars in August 1792, a declaration by their commander-in-chief the Duke of Brunswick, written in violent language, in part by royalist émigrés, had threatened the city with 'military execution and total subversion' if the royal family was harmed. In 1814 many allied soldiers also wanted to raze the city: the Prefect of the Seine the Comte de Chabrol saw Russian soldiers throw the ash of their campfires in the air shouting *Paris! Paris!*[28] However the allied leaders, the French émigrés and Parisians themselves were wiser and less bloodthirsty: and as a deputy to the Legislative Assembly in 1792, Pozzo had personally witnessed the effect of the Declaration of Brunswick. The Tsar's declaration promised protection for the city; he would no longer treat with any member of the Bonaparte family, but wanted a large and strong France with a new government and constitution. On the morning of 31 March, to a delegation of mayors and officers of the National Guard come to pay him homage at his quarters at the château of Bondy outside Paris, the Tsar declared that Napoleon was his only enemy; the French were his friends; the city of Paris was promised his 'special protection'. They should give themselves a government which would procure them and Europe peace.[29]

That same morning, as French troops evacuated the city to the south-west, crowds of Parisians streamed outside the barriers to the east to see the Tsar. Others only learnt the news that Paris had capitulated from the milkmaids walking in as usual from the countryside with their morning milk. At 11 a.m., riding a grey horse, the Tsar entered the city through the Barrière de Pantin. Preceded by Cossacks of the Guard in red jackets and baggy black trousers, he had Prince Schwarzenberg

9

on his right and King Frederick William III of Prussia on his left. They were surrounded by 2,000 officers and princes, the great names of the European coalition against the French Empire, including the Russian general von Osten-Sacken, appointed military Governor-General of Paris; Count Radetzky, the pillar of Austrian military power in Europe until his death in 1857; the Prussian generals Blücher, Gneisenau and Kleist; Platov, the Hetman or commander of the Cossacks; the Crown Prince of Württemberg; and Prince Leopold of Saxe-Coburg, then an officer in Russian service, later first King of the Belgians.

After the sovereigns and their staffs came the Grand Duke Constantine with an élite force of Russian, Prussian and Baden guards and Austrian grenadiers, followed by the rest of the army, about 50,000 men in all. Many allied troops wore French uniforms taken from the bodies of their enemies, since their own uniforms had been reduced to shreds in the previous weeks' fighting. In order to avoid being shot from their own side, they also wore white armbands and sprigs of oak or laurel in their helmets. The advancing allied troops thus looked like a forest on the move.[30]

One eye-witness called the procession *la fête de l'Europe*, the reunion of the European family. It was the start of a period when Europeans played as prominent a part in French politics and culture as Frenchmen did in European politics and culture. The hero of the hour, the Tsar, believed in a great European family of peoples and sovereigns: the peace of Europe mattered more to him than the expansion of Russia. In a proclamation widely distributed in Paris, and again written or influenced by Pozzo, Prince Schwarzenberg consciously appealed to Parisians' European feelings. Echoing the Tsar, he promised to preserve the city of Paris and called on Parisians to form a government 'which could cement the union of all nations and all governments with itself'. As the allied sovereigns and soldiers advanced in perfect order through one of the poorest and unhealthiest areas of the city, the Faubourg Saint-Martin, down the boulevards to the Champs Elysées, they generated a surge of public emotion. Joy replaced fear. Conquering enemies were greeted as angels from heaven.[31]

Relief that the battle for Paris was over was universal. Parisians' cheers were a form of propitiation, and a way of defusing the desire for revenge; moreover royalists had organised cheer groups along the allies' route.[32] As a Russian officer wrote, 'Windows, roofs and pavements were filled by a seething mass, shouting, waving handkerchiefs as we went past.' According to the official Russian campaign journal, the joy and hope of the vast crowd made it 'the most touching and brilliant scene in all history'. For the Crown Prince of Prussia, unable to believe his eyes, 'the Berliners' joy on our return from Prussia* was restrained compared to the joy of these Parisians'.[33] In an age which considered manners as important as birth or wealth, popular exaltation was heightened by the punctuation of the allied officers' words of command to their troops, in German or Russian, with smiles, bows, outstretched hands and words of assurance to Parisians in French – *Vive la Paix!*, 'Frenchmen, we come to deliver you from your tyrants', and, from the Tsar himself, 'I should have been here sooner but for the bravery of your troops . . . you will have peace, I have come to bring it to you.'[34]

'It was the finest moment which a sovereign can have enjoyed since the world began,' so a Russian officer Count Bulgakov recorded. Other officers agreed; it was the greatest moment in their lives, a whirlwind of happiness which avenged the many defeats their respective countries had suffered in the previous years, and compensated for the horrors of cold and mud experienced on the march to Paris. Their joy was not simply the joy of victory. It was also, as many remarked, the joy of witnessing a great people beginning to breathe freely.[35] Many Parisians shouted *A bas le Corse! A bas le tyran!* and, referring to Alexander I, *Vive notre libérateur!*[36]

A British officer attached to the Tsar's staff, Lord Charles Stewart, in Underwood's words 'conspicuous by his fantastic dress, evidently composed of what he deemed every army's best', described the entry of the European army into Paris for his brother Lord Castlereagh, the Foreign Secretary who had done so much to create and finance the last anti-Napoleonic coalition:

> Already was the crowd so enormous, as well as the acclamations so great, that it was difficult to move forward; but, before the monarchs reached the Porte de St. Martin, there was, to those on the Boulevards, a moral impossibility of proceeding. All Paris seemed to be assembled and concentrated on one spot. One animus, one spring evidently directed all their movements. They thronged in such masses round the Emperor and the King that with all their condescending and gracious familiarity, extending their hands on all sides, it was in vain to attempt to satisfy the populace; they were positively devoured amidst the cries of *Vive l'Empereur Alexandre! – Vive le roi de Prusse! – Vivent les*

---

*The Hohenzollerns returned to Berlin on 23 December 1809, after a three years' absence following the Prussian defeat by the French at Jena in 1806.

rois libérateurs! Nor did the air alone resound with these peals; for, with louder acclamations, if possible, they were mingled with those of *Vive le roi! – Vive Louis XVIII! Vive les Bourbons! A bas le tyran!* The white cockade appeared very universally, many of the National Guards whom I saw wore them. The clamorous applause of the multitude was seconded by a similar demonstration from all the houses along the line to the Champs Elysées; and the waving of handkerchiefs as well as the fair hands which waved them, seemed in continued requisition – in short my lord, to have an idea of such a manifestation of electric feeling as Paris displayed, it must have been witnessed.[37]

Caulaincourt reported to Napoleon that royalist cries were much stronger once the allies reached the Boulevard des Italiens and entered the richer area of the city. These Parisians seemed like another people. Their fervour may have been increased by the mistaken belief that the allied soldiers' white armbands were a sign of support for the Bourbons, whose colour was also white.[38]

Women were particularly 'electric'. They retained much of the independence, in daily life, which they had enjoyed in the eighteenth century. Foreign visitors were surprised to see them enter restaurants or the theatre 'unattended by gentlemen', and found them 'very agreeable and polite to strangers'.[39] 'Day and night they are seen in continual bustle and tumult: they form the major proportion in all place of public resort and take part in every conversation and transaction.'[40] Most women were hostile to Napoleon, as one waitress told an English visitor, 'because he had all our lovers killed' – and husbands, sons, brothers, too. As the allies marched past, women did not limit their acts to waves and cheers: some climbed on to rooftops, seized the hands of foreign soldiers, knelt on the ground, or mounted on their horses in order to have a better view of the *Tsar libérateur*. An Austrian officer wrote of women 'electrifying opinion in the intoxication of emotion and joy, by the passionate élan of their royalism'. Some read out proclamations by Louis XVIII promising peace and freedom, or gave money to passers-by to make them cry *Vive le roi!* When told that Paris had capitulated, Madame de Marigny was so overjoyed that she kissed her maid.[41]

Between 11 and 3, 'like an unending flood' the allied army passed through Paris to the Champs Elysées, then a large, thickly wooded park west of the Place de la Concorde. Most of the army was then housed in the many French barracks in and around Paris vacated by the retreat of Napoleonic soldiers. Others camped on the Champs Elysées and in the Bois de Boulogne; for weeks afterwards the toothmarks from the

Cossack horses tethered to the trees could be seen on their bark. Rations were allotted to the allied soldiers and their horses by the Conseil Municipal, in the same way that they had been to French troops under the Empire. The city of Paris was divided into three military districts, under a Russian, an Austrian and a Prussian officer, with von Osten-Sacken in over-all command.[42]

Throughout the next month the National Guard, rapidly raised to 35,000 men, with three to five thousand on duty at a time, was the main law-keeping force in the city. Their commander General Dessolles was an able officer who, like many future royalists, had served on the staff of General Moreau, Napoleon's greatest rival in the French army prior to 1804, when Moreau was exiled for royalist contacts.* The Paris National Guard even had the right to arrest foreign soldiers.[43] Public places and buildings were patrolled by mixed bands composed of Russian and Prussian guards, Austrian grenadiers and Paris national guards.

One building, however, was guarded solely by the Tsar's company of the Preobrazhenski Guard Regiment.[44] For after the Tsar and the King of Prussia had reviewed their troops that afternoon, Alexander I took up residence on the first floor of the magnificent neoclassical *hôtel*, on the corner of the rue Saint-Florentin and the Place de la Concorde, where Talleyrand, almost alone in Paris, maintained the *train de vie* of an eighteenth-century *grand seigneur*, surrounded by servants, relations, dependants, supported by *une richesse aristocratiquement dépensée.*[45]

The Tsar spent the rest of the day discussing the future of France, and of Napoleon I and Louis XVIII, with the King of Prussia; Princes Schwarzenberg and Liechtenstein; Pozzo and the Russian Secretary of State Count von Nesselrode; and a group of Talleyrand's advisers, including the Abbé de Pradt, the financier Baron Louis and a noble from the Rhineland, the Duc de Dalberg. Former servants of Napoleon I, after his defeat they had suddenly covered themselves in the insignia of royalism, white cockades and Croix de Saint-Louis.

When they heard the news of the welcome Paris had given to the allies, Napoleon I and his supporters at Fontainebleau were incredulous. Some called Paris *la Grande Cosaquie* and Parisians *les monstres cosaques.*[46] Back in Paris, however, royalists kept the initiative. On 31 March, while Parisians were cheering the allies, small groups of royalists, mainly nobles and bankers who had held aloof from the Empire, led by

---

* He was killed by French gunfire on 27 August 1813, during the Battle of Dresden, while serving in the Russian army.

the Duc de Fitzjames and Sosthènes de La Rochefoucauld, were walking or riding along the boulevards, the rue de Rivoli (then just a row of arches, begun in 1807 and covered in scaffolding and blocks of stone)[47] and the rue Saint-Honoré, distributing white cockades, waving fleurs-de-lys flags and shouting *Vive le roi! Vive Louis XVIII! Vivent les Bourbons! A bas le tyran!* If they received little support, except from some national guards, they encountered no opposition. Other royalists, led by the Comte de Sémallé, an agent of the Comte d'Artois, took over newspaper offices, installed royalist editors and distributed royalist proclamations and fleurs-de-lys flags and white cockades made by Madame de Sémallé. After a tumultuous meeting at the house of a fervent royalist Madame de Morfontaine, a deputation was sent in the evening to ask the Tsar to restore the Bourbons.[48]

Next day a much larger royalist demonstration at the opera house on the rue de Richelieu, opposite the Bibliothèque Impériale, provided further proof that, contrary to a widely held view, the Bourbons were not forgotten in 1814. In the early nineteenth century the opera and the theatre were not only places of entertainment; they were also arenas for the élite and, in cheaper seats in the 'gods', the people to meet, to hear news and to display their clothes, their status and their politics. Many Parisians lived for and in the theatre, going two or three times a week, transfixed by actors' performances and personalities.[49] The public was both emotionally closer to the actors (Napoleon himself had instructed the great tragedian Talma, the idol of the Parisian public, how to play an emperor), and physically closer to the stage, than today. Moreover the theatre had a political role. In a period of strict newspaper censorship, it was the principal forum for comment on public events – a play representing the fall of the Bastille, in which some of the assailants appeared as actors, had been performed in a Paris theatre on 15 July 1789.

At 7 p.m. on 1 April 1814, the orchestra at the Paris opera house began by playing a royalist song *Vive Henri IV!*, celebrating the most popular of Bourbon kings, who had become a living presence in French minds and hearts since Voltaire, in his poem *La Henriade* of 1723, had started a cult of him in books, songs and pictures. The words were sufficiently familiar for the audience to join in. When the Tsar and the King appeared in the central box at the opera, after dining with Talleyrand, it seemed as if the theatre would collapse under the weight of the enthusiasm. The entire audience stood up and cheered for half an hour, shouting *Vive Alexandre!*, waving hats or handkerchiefs, and throwing white cockades in the air. Men and women climbed on the edge of their boxes in order to get a better view of the Tsar, who smilingly acknowledged their cheers. The opera *La Vestale* (1807),* Spontini's masterpiece, could not begin until 9 p.m. In an *entr'acte* an actor sang:

> *Vive Alexandre!*
> *Vive ce roi des rois!*
> *Sans rien prétendre,*
> *Sans nous dicter des lois,*
> *Ce prince auguste*
> *A le triple rénom*
> *De héros, de juste,*
> *De nous rendre un Bourbon.*[50]

Royalism also erupted elsewhere in the city. Paris had no independent administration. Throughout this period, in order to forestall the return of an independent and active Commune like that which had functioned in the Hôtel de Ville in 1789–94, the Conseil Municipal (consisting of twenty-four notables) and mayors of Paris were nominated by, and under the continuous surveillance of, the central government. Nevertheless, on 2 April, through the energy of a lawyer called M. Bellart, most of the municipal council of Paris, meeting in the Hôtel de Ville in the east of the city, agreed to sign the first of the many anti-Napoleonic diatribes printed in Paris that year. Although it called for the restoration of Louis XVIII, it was driven primarily by loathing of Napoleon I. He was attacked for his imprisonment of the Pope, dissolution of the Corps Législatif, high taxation, destruction of commerce, industry and agriculture; above all for his wars. 'Which of us has not lost a son, a brother, relations, friends? For whom have all these men died? For him alone and not for the country . . . What good have these fatal victories done us?' The proclamation concluded with 'the most ardent wish that the government should be re-established in the person of Louis XVIII and his legitimate successors'.[51] It was posted on walls and sold throughout the streets of the city.

On 5 April 1814 appeared Chateaubriand's famous pamphlet *De*

---

* At the Tsar's insistence, *La Vestale* had been substituted at the last moment for *Le Triomphe de Trajan*, in which the references to an emperor's generosity might have seemed boastful.

Buonaparte et des Bourbons et de la nécessité de se rallier à nos princes légitimes pour le bonheur de la France et celui de l'Europe. It denounced Bonaparte's 'empire of deceit', his execution of the Duc d'Enghien, imprisonment of the Pope and invasion of Spain as 'impious, sacrilegious, odious and above all anti-French acts'. Napoleon was *un faux grand homme* who combined 'the sword of Attila and the maxims of Nero'. The allies were not conquerors but liberators who were displaying unique moderation in victory. The Bourbons will 'heal the wounds of the world'. He ended with the 'cry of peace and happiness: *Vive le roi!*' The pamphlet sold 16,000 copies in two months.[52]

Meanwhile, at the centre of the political whirlwind, Talleyrand's *hôtel* in the rue Saint-Florentin was called a mixture of madhouse and magic lantern. French politicians, allied officers, ex-revolutionaries, bishops, journalists, royalists, Bonapartists like Caulaincourt – the Minister of Foreign Affairs representing the fallen Emperor – argued among themselves in the gilded salons on the first floor where the Tsar was staying, and in the six-room *entresol* below, which Talleyrand had kept for himself. In the constant agitation the only people to remain calm were the Cossacks of the Russian Imperial Guard sleeping on straw in the courtyard. An exchange, overheard at Talleyrand's by the Prefect of Police Baron Pasquier, revealed the clash of loyalties in Paris in April 1814, and contemporary awareness of the role of money in politics. An ally of Talleyrand, the Abbé de Pradt, who had been Napoleon's Premier Aumônier, called out to Caulaincourt:

> – Monsieur le Duc, go and tell your master that government stock which was quoted at 45 francs on 29 March is now at 63.
> – Yes, and I will add that he who was always the most eager of his flatterers is now the first to insult him. Nobody is surprised.[53]

The Tsar could be seen by Parisians every morning and evening walking from the rue Saint-Florentin across the street to the Russian Orthodox chapel temporarily established in the Ministère de la Marine on the Place Louis XV (the original name of the Place de la Concorde, to which it had just reverted). His modest smiles, flattering remarks about the French and, above all, thousands of well-disciplined troops, made him the idol of Paris. 'The intoxication inspired by Alexander', Madame de Marigny wrote, 'is constantly increasing. He is kind, affable, generous.' When he appeared on the balcony of the Tuileries, he was cheered by an 'immense crowd'. He discussed with Caulaincourt, who claimed that 'Paris did not represent all France', the idea of a regency by the Empress Marie Louise in favour of Napoleon II. This apparent hesitation, after so many proclamations hostile to the Bonapartes, may however have been a ruse to encourage Napoleon I to abdicate.[54]

For meanwhile, with the Tsar's agreement, Talleyrand, who was determined to replace the Napoleonic Empire by a constitutional monarchy, had taken the political initiative, declaring himself President of a Provisional Government. It met in his bedroom and was composed of three of his intimates, the Marquis de Jaucourt, the Comte de Beurnonville and the Duc de Dalberg, and a royalist politician, the Abbé de Montesquiou; its secretaries were a former secretary of Napoleon, Louis-Antoine Fauvelet de Bourrienne, and Dupont de Nemours, founder of the American industrial dynasty. The irresistible appeal of peace and of the word 'Paris' at the head of the Provisional Government's orders ensured that it rapidly replaced the Napoleonic administration, now based in Blois, as the central government of France.[55] Thus, if Talleyrand did not make the Restoration, he did destroy the Empire.

Yet Napoleon still had an army under his command. At a review in the courtyard of Fontainebleau on 3 April he was acclaimed by his soldiers with cries of *Vive l'Empereur! A Paris! A Paris!*[56] However the desire to save Paris from fighting in the streets, which had encouraged the allies to be merciful on 31 March, may also have encouraged Napoleon to abdicate in favour of his son on 6 April. Meanwhile, on 4 April, the Provisional Government had acquired its own army when, at Talleyrand's urging, the troops under Maréchal Marmont, who might have acted as Napoleon's vanguard in an attack on Paris, switched allegiance to the Provisional Government. For the only time in French history the senior chamber, the Senate – housed in a seventeenth-century royal palace, the Palais du Luxembourg, in the south-east of the city – took the political initiative. Under Talleyrand's presidency on 2 April it pronounced the overthrow of Napoleon and on 6 April the adoption of a liberal constitution, recalling 'Louis-Stanislas-Xavier' to the throne. He was deliberately referred to as 'brother of the last king', rather than as Louis XVIII, successor of Louis XVII who had died as a prisoner in the Temple in 1795, in order to prove that the new monarchy would be based on a constitutional contract between the King and the representatives of the French people, rather than on the hereditary right of the Bourbons.[57]

*

The victory of Europe in Paris received ceremonial consecration at an Easter service on 10 April: by coincidence, 1814 was one of the few years when the Catholic and Orthodox Easters have fallen on the same day. The altar for the service was erected on the Place Louis XV. So many people, including Louis XVI and Marie Antoinette, had been guillotined there that, as some Parisians remembered, cows driven to slaughter in the Halles at the centre of the city had refused to pass, from revulsion at the human blood spilt on the paving stones.[58] Indeed Alexander I regarded the ceremony, which he personally organised, as a purification of the square and the city. The entire length of the boulevards, from the Bastille to the Madeleine, was occupied by allied troops, who then marched past the Tsar and the King of Prussia into the Place Louis XV. Under a blazing sun, watched by thousands of Parisians, squares of bareheaded allied soldiers stood in perfect order and silence, 'as if composed of one person and one soul', during the Orthodox Te Deum, mass and benediction. At the end of the service a hundred Russian cannon were fired. The soldiers fell to their knees. The Tsar embraced the King of Prussia, Marshals Schwarzenberg and Wrede and, in a gesture of Christian reconciliation, Marshals Oudinot, Ney, Marmont, Lefebvre and Sérurier.[59]

The same day the Austrian Foreign Minister Metternich arrived in Paris. A cosmopolitan who regarded Europe as his fatherland, Metternich knew Paris intimately: he had spent three years there as Austrian ambassador in 1806–9, and six months in 1810 as Austrian Foreign Minister, after the marriage of Marie Louise and Napoleon I. Metternich observed the rapidity with which the outward signs of Napoleon and his dynasty, which the Emperor had scattered throughout his capital with unprecedented profusion, were now disappearing. Busts of Napoleon had been taken down from above the entrances to the Louvre and the Corps Législatif (the present Chamber of Deputies opposite the Place de la Concorde). On 8 April, the statue of Napoleon I dressed as a victorious Roman emperor, with a figure of Fortune in his hand, was pulled off the summit of the Colonne de la Grande Armée, which had been inaugurated on 15 August (Napoleon's saint's day) 1810 in the middle of the Place Vendôme, on the site of an equestrian statue of Louis XIV, destroyed in 1792. Modelled on Trajan's column in Rome and made from 1,200 melted-down Austrian cannon, the column is decorated with scenes from the triumphant French campaign of 1805 culminating in the victory of Austerlitz.

The rue Impériale was renamed rue de la Paix, the Lycée Napoléon the Lycée Charlemagne, the *Journal de l'Empire* the *Journal des débats*. Suddenly it seemed to many visitors as if Napoleon had never existed.[60] In Metternich's words:

> People speak of him as if he had ruled in the fourteenth century. All the eagles have disappeared. There are no more of those innumerable N's . . . Everywhere the royal arms [are] in all the shops; all the theatres – nothing but white cockades. All the lackeys, all the coachmen, all the postilions wear fleurs-de-lys . . . Everything is as peaceful as if there had been no war.[61]

The noise of Paris – *mouvant-remuant-riant-insouciant-criant* – had also revived, so Metternich noted. The loudest sounds were *les cris de Paris*, the vendors on the boulevards advertising wares to satisfy every kind of human want, from rabbit skins to chair cane, potatoes to dream books:

> *Ah les pommes de terre! les pommes de terre!*
> *Petits pains au lait, chaud! chaud! chaud!*
> *Voilà le plaisir, mesdames! voilà le plaisir!*
> *J'ai bon fromage de Champaigne.*
> *Au lait, au lait sans eau!*
> *Avez-vous rêvé de chien, avez-vous rêvé de chat?*[62]

A common cry was that of the sellers of old clothes, *Vieux habits! Vieux galons!* ('Any old clothes? Any old trimmings?') Pierre-Jean de Béranger, a poet whose easy rhymes and popular nationalism would make him as famous as Chateaubriand, used this cry as the title of a poem written in 1814, with the subtitle *Réflexions morales et politiques d'un marchand d'habits de la capitale*. The poem mocked the importance Parisians attached to clothes, and the ease with which in April 1814, from ministers to coachmen, they were literally changing coats, as they ordered new uniforms or liveries for use under the Bourbons.

> *Tout marchands d'habits que nous sommes,*
> *Messieurs nous observons les hommes,*
> *D'un bout du monde à l'autre bout*
>   *L'habit fait tout.**

---

* Indeed the republican General Malet had been able briefly to seize power in Paris, on 23 October 1812 while Napoleon was in Russia, partly owing to the respect inspired by the sight of his Lieutenant-General's uniform.

De m'enrichir j'ai l'assurance:
L'on fêtera toujours en France,
En ville, au théâtre, à la cour,
   L'habit du jour.

Gens vêtus d'or et d'écarlate,
Pendant un mois chacun vous flatte:
Puis à vos portes nous allons
   Vieux habits! Vieux galons!

Talleyrand was the archetype of such men. Created by Napoleon Prince de Bénévent in southern Italy, he was known as the *prince à tout vent* or *l'homme girouette*, since like a weathervane, or *girouette*, he turned the way the wind blew. A bishop who had renounced his vows, a politician with the reputation of betraying everyone who had purchased his support, as Foreign Minister of the French Republic and Empire in the years 1797–1807 he had conducted a vendetta against the Bourbons, hoping to kidnap or degrade Louis XVIII, and justifying the execution of the kidnapped Bourbon prince the Duc d'Enghien in an official circular. In the opinion of the wife of one of his most trusted officials, Comte Reinhard, he was, for the Bourbons, 'an object of horror'. Some royalists called him 'the mitred monster'.[63]

In Paris in April 1814, however, Talleyrand welcomed the first French Bourbon whom Parisians had seen since the last, fatal journey of Louis XVI, on 21 January 1793, from the Tower of the Temple in the east of the city (demolished on Napoleon's order to stop it becoming a royalist shrine) to the guillotine on the Place de la Concorde. The Comte d'Artois, younger brother of Louis XVI and Louis XVIII, had left France three days after the fall of the Bastille and had spent the last eighteen years in Edinburgh and London. He was distinguished by the charm of his manner and the exaggeration of his royalism. He had left London in January 1814 and since the end of March, in accordance with the instructions of the allied powers, had been approaching Paris from the east. On the morning of 12 April, he entered the city riding a white horse. In a tactful gesture, he wore the uniform of the National Guard and was preceded by some of its soldiers, as well as by Marshals Ney, Marmont, Kellermann, members of the old nobility, and a band playing the inevitable *Vive Henri IV!* In tribute to the role of Britain in sheltering the exiled Bourbons, financing the European coalition and fighting the Napoleonic army in the Iberian peninsula, Lord Castlereagh and the members of his mission were the only foreigners in the procession.[64] At the Barrière de la Villette Talleyrand welcomed Artois with a few words in praise of constitutional monarchy, including the phrase 'you can only be supported by what resists'. With tears in his eyes, flashing his characteristic wide smile that showed off his teeth, the prince replied: 'Thank you, Messieurs, I am very happy. Let us advance', possibly adding a phrase, later famous, 'Nothing has changed. There is merely one Frenchman the more' – an oblique echo of the Provisional Government's attempts to dissociate 'Buonaparte' from France by insisting, in its proclamations, that *le Corse* was 'not even French'.[65]

Artois rode through the streets to Notre Dame, stopping at churches on the way for priests to offer him incense. Underwood recorded:

> the count was received with more enthusiasm than I had ever seen the French evince on any occasion . . . Many persons shed tears . . . Monsieur is a very handsome man; and no one ever gave me a higher idea of a dignified and accomplished cavalier. It is impossible to have saluted a mixed multitude in a manner more flattering to them or to himself; his animated looks were directed to all and all seemed to sympathise with the delight which radiated from his countenance . . . the windows were crowded with elegantly dressed women waving their handkerchiefs.

Inside Notre Dame, according to Wellington's niece Lady Burghersh, the first of the thousands of Englishwomen who would visit Paris that year, 'every creature shouted "*Vive le Roi!, vive Louis*" etc and waved handkerchiefs, clapped hands etc with a degree of enthusiasm which I never saw in England for anything.' In her eyes Artois was more dignified, because less eager to court popular adoration, than the Tsar. That evening, only fourteen days since the departure of the Empress Marie Louise, Artois slept in the Tuileries.[66] On the same day in Fontainebleau Napoleon, having abandoned plans for fighting on in Italy or the Loire valley, abdicated unconditionally for himself and his dynasty. Oppressed by the desertion of some of his most trusted followers, he then swallowed the poison capsules he had carried since 1812. His servants and Caulaincourt rescued him and subsequently kept the incident secret.[67] Thereafter he started preparations to leave for Elba, the island off Tuscany which he had been granted by the Treaty of Fontainebleau of 11 April.

When Artois' second son, the Duc de Berri, also wearing the uniform of the National Guard, visited the theatre the evening of his arrival in Paris from Normandy on 16 April, the entire audience rose and sang three times in succession, in a delirium of royalism, *Vive Henri*

IV! Vive ce roi vaillant! On 20 April there were similar scenes. When the allied commander of Paris General von Osten-Sacken appeared in the pit, cries were raised of *Vivent les alliés! Vive Alexandre! Vive la paix!* The great actress Mlle Mars, 'a beautiful woman with fine, dark and expressive eyes which spoke to the very heart', known as 'the diamond of the Comédie Française' and considered by many the finest comic actress in Europe, then sang couplets praising the allies and the Bourbons. At the line 'To be happy all we needed was one Frenchman the more', the audience turned to Monsieur, waving hats and handkerchiefs, weeping tears of joy.[68]

Outside the theatres, Paris was divided. While the Provisional Government was eliminating Napoleon from the buildings of Paris and the constitution of France, Bonapartists in the poorer districts of the faubourgs – whom Madame de Marigny called *la canaille . . . fort insolente et fort audacieuse* – were tearing down royalist proclamations and terrorising people wearing the white cockade.[69] On 19 April, a British MP, W.F. Mackenzie, reported from Paris that, although many were glad 'to have got rid of Bonaparte', he had 'a strong party in the army and in the mob of Paris'. Most observers agreed. According to the son of Madame de Staël, the most famous woman writer of the age, Auguste de Staël, who was serving in the Swedish army, 'the spirit of the army is detestable.'[70] There were fights between French and allied troops over women, or over attempts by French soldiers to tear off the allied soldiers' victory medals and sprigs of oak-leaves. 'A look of blasted glory, of withered pride and lurking revenge' could be seen on the faces of French soldiers in Paris.[71] The commander of the Paris National Guard, General Dessolles, felt obliged to issue an *ordre du jour* to try to calm his men:

> the mistakes which opened France to the allies are foreign to the French army. The allied powers admit this . . . it is a prejudice to think that a dry and hard tone or acts of violence give a military air. On the contrary a thousand examples prove that nothing is more often associated than extreme gentleness and extreme courage.[72]

The spirit of outraged nationalism aroused by these events in some Frenchmen can be felt in the letters of a brilliant twenty-nine-year-old lieutenant-general, Charles de Flahaut, who had joined the army at the age of sixteen and had won the reputation, even among the able and ambitious courtiers of Napoleon, of being *un homme fait pour aller à tout*.[73] Flahaut was the charmer of the Grande Armée. One of his many mistresses, Comtesse Anna Potocka, wrote of him: 'No one has ever better realised the ideal of a hero of romance and true *chevalier* . . . he understood the art of conversation like a true Frenchman, never exhausting one's interest, passing from one subject to another smoothly yet not too slowly.' He had learnt the art of pleasing – he was a good singer and dancer as well as a brave general – in part from his mother, a woman from a similar, cultivated Parisian *milieu* to Madame de Pompadour (whose brother had married her sister). Madame de Flahaut, like Madame de Staël, was one of Talleyrand's many ex-mistresses: Talleyrand rather than the old Comte de Flahaut, Intendant du Jardin du Roi, who had died on the guillotine in 1793, was almost certainly Flahaut's father. As an émigré in London and Hamburg in the years 1793–7, while her son learnt English and German, Madame de Flahaut had earned her living by writing novels (and had enjoyed a brief affair with the Duc d'Orléans).[74] In 1802 she had taken as her second husband Don José Maria de Souza Botelho, a Portuguese diplomat who enjoyed life in Paris so much that he remained there after ceasing to be Portuguese ambassador, refusing all inducements to return. The Souzas lived in a large house in Grande rue verte no 6 (now the rue de Penthièvre, running between the rue du Faubourg Saint-Honoré and the Champs Elysées) in one of the most fashionable districts of Paris. Flahaut occupied the first floor. While claiming to be warm, simple, sentimental, Madame de Souza was considered by another Napoleonic general, General Foy, 'the most cunning and intriguing woman I know. She has perfected the art of displaying a sensitivity in which she knows that nobody believes.' Her love for her son, however, was not affected: friends joked that all she could say was *mon fils, mon fils.*[75]

Appointed an aide-de-camp of Napoleon I in 1813, Flahaut had become sufficiently trusted to conduct peace negotiations with the allies in February 1814. On the morning of 31 March, just before the allies' entry into Paris, he had been sent by Napoleon to the Tuileries, to burn secret papers and remove personal treasures and trophies.[76] With Berthier and Caulaincourt he had helped to restrain Napoleon I from attacking Paris that day and during the following week, and to persuade him to abdicate. In 1814 Flahaut was as typical of the Bonapartist, nationalist and military spirit as Pozzo was of the spirit of 'European union'.

Flahaut's letters to his mother from Fontainebleau in April 1814 reveal his importance in Napoleon's entourage; they show, too, the Bonapartists' loathing for foreigners, at a time when Parisians were cheering Alexander I, and the intensity of French family ties in the early nineteenth century – in contrast to the coolness, or worse, of the previous century. Some children, among them Talleyrand himself, claimed never to have slept under the same roof as their parents; grandparents had been said to get on with grandchildren because they were their enemies' enemies.[77]

> *7 April* Having persuaded the Emperor to make the greatest sacrifice which a man can make, we bow our heads beneath the yoke of the foreigner and dishonour the nation. My poor mother, one can no longer say 'I have the honour to be French'. So I am firmly decided only to keep my French birth but not to occupy any position in my degraded country. I am resigning [from the army] and will live entirely for you.

> *8 April* The Emperor has given me complete freedom to serve the new government but how can one serve when a black crêpe covers our flags and we have added, to the hatred foreigners felt for us, their well-deserved contempt?

> *9 April* I have not tendered my resignation and despite the mourning which covers our flags, despite the shameful degradation of the fatherland, I will still wear my uniform and will serve my country . . . I contributed to saving it from a civil war although that was against my personal interest . . . I am not going to visit you, those foreign armies are odious to me, I cannot bear to set eyes on them . . . Mon Dieu! are we no longer French?[78]

Flahaut refused to follow Napoleon to Elba on the grounds that 'I owed myself to you [his mother] before everything'. Indeed Napoleon I himself asked him to stay, perhaps with a view to reorganising support in France.[79] On 16 April he adhered to the Provisional Government. On 18 April, the day before the Emperor's departure, he wrote of his horror at newspaper insults directed against Napoleon, ending, 'I embrace you with all my heart and truly love you with all my soul my very dear and good *maman*.'[80] He then returned to Paris.

The conflicts between nationalism and Europeanism, Bonapartism and royalism, soldiers and civilians, expressed in Flahaut's letters, conditioned the history of Paris and the lives of Parisians in this period. They were made visible and audible at the entry of Louis XVIII into Paris. On 2 May, at the château of Saint-Ouen, at the gates of Paris, he had signed the Declaration of Saint-Ouen guaranteeing a 'liberal constitution' and a two-chamber legislature with control over taxation, freedom of the press and access to government positions for all. At 10 a.m. the next morning, on a hot cloudless day, seated in one of the Emperor's carriages hastily painted over with Bourbon colours and insignia, he drove into the city. On his way he passed mounds of earth covering the corpses of soldiers, buried in haste so that the farmers could begin ploughing and sowing. Along his route from Calais to Paris, his carriage had been unhorsed and pulled by civilians delirious with happiness. In Paris, to please the army, Louis XVIII's route was lined and his carriage escorted by the soldiers of the Garde Impériale, the famous corps familiar to Parisians by its victories and its long residence in the capital.

The King, although obese and sixty, looked dignified and gracious, and frequently bowed to the crowd, smiling and putting his hand to his heart. The houses along the rue Saint-Denis were festooned with wreaths of flowers and flags; curtains, carpets and tapestries were hung out of windows which were packed with people waving handkerchiefs. According to Chateaubriand, however, the guards lining the route showed their rage by baring their teeth like tigers, or letting their busbies slide down over their eyes in order not to see the King. Chateaubriand had never seen human faces express such menace.[81] Despite the efforts of the marshals riding beside the King's carriage, no soldiers and few members of the crowd on the rue Saint-Denis joined their cries of *Vive le roi! Vivent les Bourbons!* At the rear of the column, indeed, many soldiers and spectators boldly shouted *Vive l'Empereur* or *Vive la garde!* In the King's carriage sat his niece, the Duchesse d'Angoulême, daughter of Louis XVI, and two elderly cousins, the Prince de Condé and the Duc de Bourbon. According to Underwood, 'The astonishment at the little English bonnet worn by the Duchess, which presented a remarkable contrast with the very large ones then the fashion at Paris, seemed to overpower every other feeling.'[82]

When the King descended from his carriage to enter Notre Dame, Parisians could see for themselves that he was a semi-invalid who, owing to gout, could hardly walk. However they greeted him with what W.F. Mackenzie called a 'delirious cry'. During the service the thunder of the organ was frequently drowned by more thunderous cries of *Vive le roi!* from every part of the cathedral.[83] In contrast to the reaction in the rue Saint-Denis, after the Te Deum the enormous crowd covering roofs, windows and streets on the way to the Tuileries, as well as the national guards standing by, cheered with enthusiasm, clapping and crying *Vive le roi!*[84] The King and his cousins took off their hats to a statue of their ancestor Henri IV on the Pont Neuf, which had been hastily reconstructed in plaster. A hundred young girls dressed in white, with lilies in their hair, threw flowers in front of the royal carriages. Two orchestras in temples erected on either side of the statue, dedicated to *la concorde des français* and *la paix des nations*, played *Vive Henri IV!* and another royalist song: *Où peut-on être mieux qu'au sein de la famille?* The latter owed its popularity to its association of the royal family with the family feeling which, after what Louis XVIII called 'the demon of property', was the strongest force in French society.

At 4 p.m. the royal family finally reached the Tuileries, appearing afterwards on the balcony facing the Jardin des Tuileries to receive more applause.[85] Foreign soldiers had been consigned to barracks to ensure that the King's entry was a national occasion. However within a few days a caricature was being sold in secret, showing an obese Louis XVIII entering Paris clinging to a Cossack, whose horse was galloping over the corpses of national guards while villages burnt in the distance.[86]

The rivalry between the Bourbon and Bonaparte dynasties was the crux of French history at this period. The rivalry had a European dimension since the two dynasties had different views of France's place in Europe. Until his fall Napoleon had insisted that France retain Antwerp and the 'natural frontiers' (all land west of the Rhine), whose annexation had been written into every French constitution since 1795. Since the mid-eighteenth century, on the other hand, the Bourbon kings and their servants had believed, as the foreign minister Vergennes had written in 1777, that 'France constituted as it is should fear expansion rather than desire it.' This commitment to what they called *les véritables intérêts de la France* was reaffirmed by Louis XVIII both before and after his restoration – despite the increase in territory and population of France's rivals Austria, Prussia and Russia over the last twenty years.[87] The allies had backed the Bourbons in 1814 not because of their right to the throne, but because of their commitment to France's pre-1792 frontiers. They were more interested in strategy than legitimacy.

Talleyrand shared the Bourbons' moderation. A disciple of Vergennes, he too could think and behave as a European. Under Talleyrand's administration, in accordance both with traditional Bourbon policy and with the facts of allied victory, on 23 April Artois as Lieutenant-General of the Kingdom had signed a convention ceding to the allies all French conquests, including fifty-three strongholds still occupied by French troops such as Antwerp, Hamburg, Mainz and Mantua and much war equipment. By the Treaty of Paris of 30 May

1814 France returned to the frontiers of 1792, with a few changes: the loss of Tobago and Mauritius to England and the gain of 650,000 inhabitants in Savoy and on the Belgian frontier. As Metternich wrote:

> We could have destroyed France – have made her pay dearly for the evils she has brought Europe for twenty years; we preferred a state of things which does not leave cause for well-founded discontent. But it will happen of this peace as of all human things. It will be found too harsh in France and too soft beyond their frontiers.

Allied troops began to leave. On 2 June the barriers round Paris were handed back to French soldiers. On 3 June an uninterrupted line of wicker vehicles – the Austrian baggage trains – was seen departing down the boulevards.[88]

The other issue around which French and much of European politics would revolve for the next forty years was the nature of the French constitution. On 4 June the King drove in state to the Corps Législatif. He ascended the steps of the throne leaning on the arm of his Capitaine des Gardes du Corps, the Duc de Gramont, the only court official who had accompanied him throughout the emigration. In his first speech from the throne, Louis XVIII referred to Europe, and the arts, before the French constitution. If war was universal, he boasted, 'reconciliation is also . . . the masterpieces of the arts henceforth belong to us by rights more stable and more sacred than those of victory.'[89] (In fact he willingly returned to the King of Prussia and the Duke of Brunswick archives and works of art, such as the Brandenburg Gate quadriga, if they were in storage and not visible to the French.)[90] The Chancellor of France Comte Dambray then read out the text of the new French constitution, the *Charte constitutionelle des Français*.

Drafted in the last two weeks of May by the Abbé de Montesquiou, Comte Beugnot and Comte Ferrand (a moderate royalist, a former Napoleonic official and an ultra-royalist) in consultation with representatives of the Senate and the Corps Législatif, and based on the Declaration of Saint-Ouen, the Charte was both monarchical and liberal. On the one hand, in contrast to the Senatorial Constitution imposed as a condition of the King's return to power, it was 'granted' 'by the free exercise of our royal authority' by the King in the 'nineteenth year of our reign', a formula which, by implicitly delegitimising all intervening regimes, offended much of public opinion. Under its provisions judicial, executive and legislative authority was stated to reside in the crown alone. The franchise was restricted by stringent property qualifications to about 80,000 voters – far fewer than in the United Kingdom. Alexander I, who had personally recommended the Senatorial Constitution to the King, was offended. Until his departure on 4 June he had spent more time with the ex-Empress Josephine and her daughter Queen Hortense at her private paradise at Malmaison west of Paris, where she had assembled the finest collection of exotic plants in Europe, than with the royal family in the Tuileries.

On the other hand the Charte endorsed the post-revolutionary settlement, guaranteed equality before the law, religious toleration, freedom of the press and of petition, irrevocability of judicial appointments, and oblivion for all previous political acts. The sales of national lands were guaranteed. Confiscation of private property was abolished. The budget had to be approved by the two Chambers – of Peers of France nominated by the King, and of Deputies elected by the wealthiest taxpayers of each department of France. It was the most liberal constitution in Europe, providing greater religious freedom than England; the secretary-general of the Minister of the Interior, François Guizot, and two members of the commission drafting the Charte, were Protestants, members of a religious minority, at a time when all non-Anglicans were barred from public life in England. The Charte rapidly achieved the miracle, given the political divisions among educated Frenchmen, of winning their acceptance.

Pozzo di Borgo, on Alexander I's behalf, had advocated the Senatorial Constitution to Louis XVIII and urged the case for giving the Chambers the right to propose laws. Nevertheless, he wrote, 'every party finds something to criticise and everyone has submitted to it.'[91] Indeed the Charte would be the battlefield on which disputes over the nature of the French monarchy and the relations of the crown and the Chambers would be fought during the next thirty-four years.

The defeat of the Napoleonic Empire led to changes in the population of Paris as well as in the French constitution. For twenty years Paris had been the capital of Belgium and the Rhineland, as well as France, and for four years the capital of *le grand Empire*, including north-west Germany, the Netherlands and north-west Italy. The fall of the Napoleonic Empire made Paris the setting for human dramas comparable to those which would occur a hundred years later in Vienna and Constantinople, after the fall of the Habsburg and Ottoman empires. As imperial administrators and soldiers (among them General Hugo, the last French general to leave Madrid and father of Victor Hugo) returned to the former imperial capital from the territories recently lost, natives of these territories left the city to start new lives in their birthplace. Thus when the former Archichancelier de l'Empire, Cambacérès, met Charles-Emmanuel de Rivaz, a former deputy from a Swiss canton to the Corps Législatif, in the Tuileries palace, he showed his amazement: 'Ah! You are still here? I thought you had left a long time ago.' On 30 May, the day of the Treaty of Paris, a stilted circular from the Vice-President of the Corps Législatif signalled the formal end of the Napoleonic Empire in Europe, and of Rivaz's reason for being in Paris: 'Monsieur and former colleague, We have felt profound regret in realising that circumstances were depriving us of a large number of our former colleagues, deputies of departments which did not form part of the territory of France.' Rivaz wished to secure a job in Paris, but lacked patrons. He returned to live in Switzerland.[92]

Meanwhile, for the first time in twenty-five years, royalists were converging on the palaces and ministries of Paris. They came from abroad, from the country – 'the provinces are flooding Paris,' the word went in June 1814[93] – and from a separate royalist world based on the Faubourg Saint-Germain. The most splendid aristocratic quarter in Europe, soon to be a political force in its own right, it was situated to the left and right of the Chamber of Deputies, and was pierced by streets of triumphal arches – the elegant portes cochères leading into the courtyards of the town palaces on which, in the eighteenth century, many French nobles had spent the money which English nobles had devoted to country houses. In Paris, royalists confronted resentful Napoleonic soldiers and administrators who were convinced that they alone were qualified to run the country.[94]

The old royal household revived without orders from the Bourbons. The Marquis de Dreux-Brézé, for example, the Grand Master of Ceremonies whom Mirabeau had insulted when told to leave the States-General in Versailles in June 1789, resumed his duties at court in April 1814. A royalist officer called Monsieur de Marsilly returned to Paris from Reims and, for the first time since the fall of Louis XVI, put on his uniform of an officer of the Cent-Suisses, a royal guard unit founded in 1484, went to the Tuileries, and was presented to the Comte d'Artois. He wrote in his diary: 'To be recognised by the brother of the unfortunate Louis XVI, the grandson of Louis XV, whom I have also served, in this defiled palace, now sanctified by the presence of a Bourbon! These sweet moments made me shed tears – so twenty-five years of misfortunes are obliterated!' The conflicts brewing in Paris are suggested by the emotion in his language: most Parisians would have been infuriated by the description of the revolution and the empire as 'twenty-five years of misfortunes'.[95]

Not only the Bourbons and their followers but also many other enemies of Napoleon I were returning to Paris. The celebrated liberal politician and writer Benjamin Constant, who had not been in Paris since his expulsion from the Tribunate by Bonaparte in 1803, arrived on 15 April; his former mistress Madame de Staël, who had also been exiled by Napoleon since 1803, on 14 May. She moved into a rented apartment in the Hôtel de Lamoignon, 105 rue de Grenelle, in the Faubourg Saint-Germain.[96] An English visitor noted that Madame de Staël 'is not vulgar' but had 'a complexion not far removed from that of a white Mulatto', with 'her eyebrows dark and her hair quite sable, dry and crisp like a negro's though not quite so curling'. Her clothes, which recalled the fashions of the Directoire, revealed large areas of dilapidated flesh. She always wore a turban. Speaking fluent English, she expressed distaste for both royalists and Bonapartists and claimed, with characteristic exaggeration, that the people in Paris who truly desired a free constitution were 'not enough to make a dinner party'.[97]

A figure even more characteristic of the cosmopolitan Paris of the period than this wealthy, intelligent, independent woman was Pozzo. When he had been appointed Russian ambassador in Paris in May, his letter of accreditation had praised him for 'twenty years of perseverance in the purest principles and his zeal, his activity, above all the services he rendered the good cause in the late events'. In the new era of peace, the replacement of Napoleonic marshals and ministers by European ambassadors as the dominant figures in Paris was reflected in the change of occupancy of its principal mansions. Pozzo rented the *hôtel* formerly used by the most devoted and influential minister of Napoleon I, Maret Duc de Bassano;[98] whilst Louis XVIII received him in the evening, alone in his study, 'every time I desire such a favour'.[99] Similarly, two of the finest houses in Paris, in the rue du Faubourg Saint-Honoré and the rue de Bourbon (now de Lille), became in 1814 the British and Prussian embassies respectively. Both enjoyed similar histories. Built in the eighteenth century for the Ducs de Charost and de Villeroy respectively, they had been sold during the revolution after the Dukes' execution. The first had subsequently become the Paris residence of Napoleon's sister Princess Pauline, the second that of his stepson Eugène de Beauharnais. Both had been refurnished and redecorated in the most majestic Empire style. With the fall of Napoleon they had to be resold in haste: witnessing many of the dramas of French relations with Britain and Germany in the subsequent centuries, these two *hôtels*, their Empire furnishings intact, still house the British and German embassies today.[100]

Echoing Béranger in *Vieux habits! Vieux galons!*, Pozzo di Borgo wrote, of the city he had not seen since he had been a radical young deputy from Corsica to the Legislative Assembly in 1792: 'Paris now offers a spectacle of completely unprecedented interest and curiosity; it is the change of roles among people who for years have played only one and the way they watch, judge and tear each other to pieces . . . like a play by Beaumarchais.' Everyone, he noted, *'without a single exception* is discontented'; the main problems arose from the overbearing pretensions of the army and 'the lack of unity and solidarity in the conduct of the ministry'.[101] The latter included three representatives of the Napoleonic army, Marshals Oudinot and Moncey and General Dessolles; two reactionary royalists, the Chancellor Dambray and Comte Ferrand; Talleyrand and the members of the Provisional Government; and the three princes of the royal family, Artois, Angoulême and Berri.[102]

The central role of the royal family and the ministers was a sign of Napoleon's concentration of power and authority in the monarchy. In 1814 Paris was not only a parliamentary capital with two chambers housed in the Palais Bourbon and the Palais du Luxembourg. More than at any time since the early years of the reign of Louis XV, it was a court city. An outward and visible sign of this role was the multiplication of royal *brevets* for tradesmen, like the royal warrants in modern London, awarded not only by each member of the royal family but also by each department of the Maison du Roi. Tradesmen often displayed a royal coat of arms on their stationery as well as their shopfront. In one year alone fifty-six tradesmen would receive *brevets* from the department of the Menus Plaisirs du Roi (in charge of the fêtes and ceremonies of the court).[103] In addition the decision was taken to 'allow the King's arms to be multiplied on tradesmen's shop signs, considering that one cannot attribute evil intentions to a person who adopts this emblem'.[104] Badges with the royal coat of arms were also worn by men not directly connected to the court such as *huissiers, notaires* and coachmen in the Messageries Royales which ran the coach routes throughout France.

Since 1789 confiscations and the introduction of compulsory divisions of inheritance among children (the reason why so many French châteaux are sparsely furnished today), by reducing great private fortunes, had made positions in government service more appealing, both to royalists and revolutionaries. Thus, more than in the eighteenth century, and in the opinion of the Duke of Wellington 'far greater even in proportion to the size and population of France than in any other country', careers, wealth, honours depended on the patronage of the monarchy and the central government.[105] In 1814 petitioners demanding jobs and honours pursued the Ministre de la Maison du Roi, the King's confidant, a forty-two-year-old émigré called the Comte de Blacas, 'like a wild beast'. He worked until 3 or 4 a.m. every morning, in his small *entresol* above the King's study in the Tuileries, where the ministers met every Sunday.[106]

The careers of even the most important writers depended on the government. Benjamin Constant, who admitted 'I have every pettiness of vanity', spent the year after his return to Paris in a whirlwind of visits and petitions, in the search for orders, jobs, introductions. *Servons la bonne cause et servons-nous* was his programme.[107] In her writings Madame de Staël denounced 'the courtier spirit, the most insipid of all'. In reality she too went to court and flattered and petitioned the King – as he had flattered her, when he needed her pen, in England before the Restoration.[108] In France she called him, several times, 'an angel', 'the greatest and most just and admirable king in the world'. One motive for her royalism was the wish to recover the two million francs owed to her father by the French government. Only thus could she provide a dowry large enough for her daughter by Benjamin Constant, Albertine de Staël, to marry the young Duc de Broglie. Broglie was in particular need of a rich wife since his family, like many other French nobles, had lost its fortune during the revolution.[109]

Royal and ministerial favours were also hunted by the only other writer of comparable fame in France, Chateaubriand. Having formed part of Artois' escort into Paris on 12 April, on 5 May 1814 he wrote with irony: 'I am now a courtier; I am always in antechambers; I want to make my way and I consider literature far beneath the great role I play.' Well connected at court through his passionate friendship with the Duchesse de Duras, wife of a Premier Gentilhomme de la Chambre du Roi, he was keen to obtain money from the King's Civil List. He became ambassador to Sweden (a post which he never occupied), asked the King for a gratuity of 100,000 francs, and received the rank of honorary colonel. Until his death in 1848, the conditions of his existence in Paris would be decided – and in part paid for – by the Bourbons.[110] The future poet of the Romantic movement Alphonse de Lamartine, who arrived in Paris from the provinces in May, also depended on the court. His father arranged for him to enter a recently reformed royal guards unit, the Gardes du Corps, in the company of the Prince de Poix, with whom Lamartine *père* had defended the Tuileries palace on 10 August 1792. Service in the Gardes du Corps, 'in order simply to have a position', would be Lamartine's first prolonged experience of Paris.[111]

Most men of the élite, French and foreign, battle-scarred Napoleonic marshals and royalists who had never seen a shot fired in anger, ministers, bishops, even regicides who had voted for the death of Louis XVI in 1793 (such as Carnot), went to pay their respects to the King in the Tuileries on Sunday morning (women paid court separately on Monday evenings).[112] First they attended mass in the palace chapel, where the orchestra of the imperial, now royal, chapel played the best music in the capital, much of it composed by the two directors of the orchestra, the former Napoleonic director Le Sueur and the anti-Bonapartist Cherubini. The ceremony was accompanied by military pomp. At midday, according to Edward Stanley, a cultivated English visitor who later became Bishop of Norwich:

> drums in the church rolled a loud peal to announce the approach of the King. A crimson velvet curtain was drawn aside, the door opened and a man advanced to the front and cried out *Le Roi* in a voice that shook the building. All this time the gentry in the great saloon [beside the chapel] kept walking backward and forward talking aloud with the most profound indifference as if they had been in the street.

At the elevation of the host, however, 'everyone ceased speaking at the same moment and dropt on his knee. There was a profound silence for about two minutes.'

After the service, watched by Parisians and tourists, the King and his courtiers moved from the chapel through the central public room, known as the Salle des Maréchaux from the eighteen marshals' portraits hanging there – so famous that Edward Stanley called it 'a room of which I had heard much and wished above all things to see'. There the King was greeted with showers of petitions and cries, especially from the women, of *Vive le roi! Vive notre bon père!*[113] When the King appeared on the balcony above the Tuileries garden, 'he was received with universal and loud applause. *Vive le roi* was heard as loud as heart could wish, hats, sticks and handkerchiefs were flying in all directions.'[114] He then entered the state apartments. There courtiers could pay their respects to the King and royal family, talk to ministers, marshals and other potential patrons, and hear the latest news.

Sunday at the Tuileries in 1814 was described by the King's cousin Louis-Philippe Duc d'Orléans – son of the regicide prince Philippe Egalité, whose enthusiasm for the most extreme aspects of the revolution of 1789–93, and vote for Louis XVI's death, had aroused especial horror among French royalists. The House of Orléans, descended from the younger brother of Louis XIV, had adopted radical views at a time when the growing number of princes in the elder branch of the Bourbon dynasty was reducing the Orléans' chances of succeeding to the throne. Louis-Philippe had last seen Paris as a young republican general in 1792. Since his desertion from the French army while on active service in 1793, he had lived in Switzerland, America, Cuba, England, and most recently Sicily under the protection of his father-in-law King Ferdinand IV. When he arrived in Paris on 16 May 1814 he was still wearing Sicilian uniform. On 1 June, Orléans sent the mistress of the Duke of Kent in London a long letter which demonstrates both an émigré's delight in his return and the brilliance of the art of letter-writing in nineteenth-century Paris.

Like Metternich, Orléans was seduced by the city's 'imposing grandeur'.

It is greatly improved, it is almost too beautiful for one to be able to convey an idea of it to someone who has not seen it . . . One of my first visits was to the opera, and I must say that in my capacity as a spectator I was struck with admiration . . . What magic in the orchestra, what violin strokes, what unity, how well it plays and what an effect it produces! . . . I jumped for joy in my chair. And when the curtain rose, what décor, what costumes, what skill in every kind of theatrical effect! Nothing can give you an idea of the décor, the scenery is admirable, with a richness, a sense of colour which leave nothing to be desired and much superior to anything we saw before the revolution. Then there are the delights of the theatre, the dances – and what a *corps de ballet*! What a collection of performers – anywhere else they would be *premières danseuses* . . .

Orléans was also captivated by the court:

But I must describe for you an opera of another kind, the Thuilleries. What grandeur, what splendour, what magnificence! I was overwhelmed by it. And what a strange gathering of people you see there! What matter for reflection on human oddity and vicissitudes! I accompanied the King to mass. Nothing is finer than this mass which is sung by all the actors and actresses of the opera and is celebrated in great pomp and you know, Madame, that nowhere are pomp and ceremony so well understood as in France. The terraces and gardens are always full of people who fill the air with cries of *Vive le roi* the moment the King appears, he stops, salutes the people and then the hats of the men, the handkerchiefs of the women wave in the air and the cries redouble to the point of fury: *Vive le roi, vivent les Bourbons, vive notre ancienne famille!* and note this remark, truly French and even Parisian, of a woman of the people who, seeing the King salute the crowd, cried, 'Ah, you can tell that this one is French, he is polite; in the fifteen years of his reign the other did not bow to us once.'

Orléans spent the next few months ordering new uniforms, recovering old properties, renewing old acquaintances and making new ones. In the park of Le Raincy outside Paris, a family estate partly ruined by demolition and plundering Cossacks, he met an old keeper, bent with age, wearing his old Orléans livery: the keeper had kept it in secret like a holy relic throughout the years of the Republic and the Empire. Another family retainer greeted him with the words, 'Ah Monseigneur, Monseigneur. I saw you being born and I will die happy since I am again in the service of the Maison d'Orléans.'[115]

If one factor united the returning Parisians of 1814 – Louis XVIII, Orléans, Talleyrand, Pozzo di Borgo, Madame de Staël and Constant – in addition to their participation in the struggle against Napoleon, it was, like the Parisians cheering the allies' entry on 31 March 1814, their feeling for the identity and common interests of Europe. In part this was due to the political accident that, like thousands of other enemies and supporters of the French revolution, they had been obliged since 1789 to spend years outside France. It was also in part conscious policy. Throughout his reign, Louis XVIII maintained his renunciation of territorial ambitions and his policy of peace and union with the other European powers. His official instruction in September to Talleyrand as France's representative at the Congress of Vienna confirmed this determination: 'France is a state so powerful that other peoples can be reassured only by the idea of its moderation.' A later Président du Conseil would reaffirm: 'The King is and remains a stranger to all ideas of ambition.'[116] His cousin Orléans, during much of his time abroad, had regarded himself as a British agent. 'I am a cosmopolitan', he wrote, 'who takes root nowhere and the place I inhabit is indifferent to me . . . Palermo, Paris, Twick [Twickenham, where he had resided in 1800–8], the Seine, the Thames *are all one to me*' (the last five words are in English in the original).[117]

Talleyrand was distinguished by his belief in a Franco-British alliance and a strong Austria; his secret communications, since 1808, with Alexander I and Metternich had been designed to limit Napoleonic expansion. The *true* interests of France, he wrote at the end of his life, were never in opposition to the *true* interests of Europe.[118] Pozzo di Borgo had chosen Europe when, and partly because, Bonaparte chose to serve the French Republic: he believed in what he later called 'the European union'. Since 1803 Madame de Staël, whose father, Louis XVI's finance minister Necker, had been a citizen of Geneva, had lived in Geneva, Rome, Weimar, Vienna, Berlin, St Petersburg, Stockholm and London. She considered the struggle against Napoleon 'the European cause' and, despite occasional outbursts of French patriotism, recorded on 16 May, 'I have become a European.'[119]

Benjamin Constant came from a European background (his family had French Huguenot, Swiss and Dutch roots). He knew Germany and its literature intimately (he had been a *kammerjunker* at the court of Brunswick in 1787–94, had translated Schiller, married a German and lived in Hanover before 1814) and occasionally felt that his foreign roots were an 'insurmountable' barrier to his desire to 'niche' himself in France, although he did buy a house in Paris in late 1814.[120] His pamphlet *De l'esprit de conquête et de l'usurpation dans leurs rapports avec la civilisation européenne*, published in January 1814 in Hanover in French, denounced Napoleon for making Europe 'one vast prison', supported monarchy as the best defence of liberty, and condemned the tricolour as 'a blood-stained standard drenched in blood and crimes'.[121] Calling France 'the soul and heart [of Europe] by its genius and its position', Chateaubriand also justified the Bourbon restoration for the peace it brought to Europe.[122]

The sense of a common interest in being both French and European was not limited to well-travelled members of the ruling élite. Many thousands of Parisians had cheered the Tsar and the allied army on 31 March 1814, and continued to regard the occupation as a liberation. Like Americans in 1944, Russian officers entering cafés might be greeted with cries of *Vivent les Russes!* and offers of free drinks. Bashkir tribesmen in the Russian army were called, from the bows and arrows slung over their backs and their many conquests, *les Cupidons du Nord*.[123] If such behaviour was not in itself a sign of cosmopolitanism, it suggests that nationality, for many Parisians, was a flexible commodity. Formerly a violent Jacobin, Baron Gérard had become drawing-master of the Empress Marie Louise and painter of such Napoleonic scenes as

Count Rapp presenting the flags of the Russian Imperial Guard to Napoleon at Austerlitz, which adorned the ceiling of the hall beside the Tuileries chapel. In 1814, while receiving a stream of foreign visitors, this 'little man with a sharp intelligent countenance', whom contemporaries compared to Tintoretto and Raphael, painted in rapid succession portraits of the leaders of Europe: the Tsar, the King of Prussia, Louis XVIII, Artois, Wellington and Schwarzenberg.[124] The Tsar's discontent with Louis XVIII's policies showed in his expression in his portrait.[125] The lucidity of Baron Gérard's style and the mobility of his convictions are characteristic of many other Parisian artists and writers in this period.

Another Parisian European was the fifty-four-year-old Comte de Saint-Simon, a precursor of socialism who divided society into 'producers' and the 'idle'. Called 'a madman' by the First Surgeon of the King, the disreputable Père Elysée, Saint-Simon was an outsider who challenged the bases on which French society was built. For him 'present-day society is the world turned upside-down': industrialists should rule. He was also one of the few Parisians who, not content with European sentiments, advocated European institutions. In a pamphlet published in Paris in 1814, *De la réorganisation de la société européenne ou de la nécessité de rassembler les peuples de l'Europe en un seul corps politique en conservant à chacun son indépendance nationale,* he advocated, in addition to national parliaments, 'a general parliament which decides the common interests of European society', with, above it, a European Chamber of Peers. European deputies should acquire 'the habit of thinking of the interests of Europe instead of national interests'. He feared that Germany was destined to play the first role in Europe and that a German revolution would be more violent than the French. Only in a united Europe, he felt, would mankind enter the golden age.[126] Most Frenchmen, however, were more interested in recovering European hegemony than in creating European unity.

2

Paris takes Europe

July 1814–March 1815

London now is out of town,
Who in England tarries?
Who can bear to linger there,
When all the world's in Paris?

Words sung by the clown Joseph Grimaldi,
on stage in London, October 1814

AFTER MAY 1814, the city of Paris was no longer, as it had been under Napoleon I, the political centre of the continent. As Parisians constantly complained that year,[1] the Treaty of Paris of 30 May had ensured that, both absolutely and relatively, the three eastern monarchies of Austria, Prussia and Russia increased in territory and population while France reverted, with few exceptions, to the frontiers of 1792. France had lost approximately 916,000 soldiers (not counting civilian losses)[2] and gained little but the hatred of Europe. The shift of power from France to the three 'northern courts' (St Petersburg, Berlin, Vienna) was symbolised by the opening, in September 1814, of the congress of monarchs, ministers and diplomats gathered to regulate the peace of Europe, in Vienna.

However, Paris was soon to recover through the arts the hegemony which it had lost through arms. In the century before 1789, 'Europe', so an Italian living in Paris had written, 'takes its tone from Paris ... One is astonished to see Paris spread across frontiers, to find its customs, and to hear its language on the banks of the Vistula as well as of the Seine.'[3] To Parisians Paris was the capital, while the rest of the world composed the provinces. 'Parisians believe that they have not only the

38

best customs in the world but the best appearance, manner and behaviour, to such an extent that the most respectful compliment that can be paid a foreigner consists in these exact words: Monsieur, you do not behave at all like a foreigner, let me congratulate you on it,' wrote one Russian visitor in 1778.[4] Foreign monarchs like Catherine II and Gustavus III kept correspondents in Paris, in addition to ambassadors, to inform them of the latest developments in literature and fashion.

But the eighteenth century had also been an Italian century. The Italian language, and Italian artists, architects and musicians (such as Tiepolo, Rastrelli, Canaletto, Casanova and Goldoni), had been employed throughout Europe: Italians had designed the Royal Palace in Madrid and the Winter Palace in St Petersburg, while the Grand Tour had reinforced the position of Venice and Rome as European capitals of arts and pleasures. Venice, however, had lost its spirit with the extinction of its independence by the French army in 1797. Under Austrian rule, according to Thomas Macgill, 'gaiety has given place to melancholy; and to the serenades of the lover, to the voice of pleasure and merriment have succeeded the groans of indigence and misery.' Byron called it an 'empty oyster shell'.[5] Rome, once the entrepôt of Europe, 'universal capital of the arts', had been traumatised by the Napoleonic occupation in 1809 and the removal of the Pope and the Cardinals. Its population had fallen from 170,000 in 1798 to 113,000 in 1814.[6]

In the years between 1792 and 1814 when war, terror, emigration and censorship castrated French creativity, Vienna had replaced Paris as the cultural, social and intellectual capital of Europe. In the words of one of its English visitors, Vienna was 'the only capital fit for a gentleman to live at . . . The number of people of fashion who reside here, the ease with which we were introduced and the many places of public lounging are beyond those of any town we have seen on the continent.'[7] Once peace returned to Europe, however, Vienna could no longer compete with Paris. Size alone ensured the hegemony of Paris in the nineteenth century. With a population of 650,000 in 1814, it was, after London (one million), the second largest city in Europe: Naples had about 435,930 inhabitants, Vienna 247,000, Berlin 172,000.[8] No other city, apart from London, had the population to sustain so many shops, theatres and cafés, or such a variety and intensity of intellectual, artistic and social life.

The French language also reinforced the pre-eminence of Paris. Even more than English today, it was the common language of the European élite. Already widespread in the seventeenth century, regarded as 'universal' by the 1780s, in the last thirty years its use had been extended both by the royalist emigration and by the Republican and Napoleonic conquests. Since they had few other marketable skills, many émigrés – including, for a time, Orléans and Chateaubriand – had lived by teaching French. Emigrés had taught French to Heine in Düsseldorf, to the poet Leopardi in Ancona, to Robert Peel in London and to George Borrow in Norwich; the main teacher in the Corps des Pages in St Petersburg under Nicholas I was an émigré, as were some teachers of the Greek élite in Constantinople.[9] In 1798 Mahmud Raif Efendi, author of a book of artillery regulations published in Constantinople in 1798, *Tableau des nouveaux règlemens de l'Empire ottoman*, wrote in French, so he recorded, *cette langue étant universelle.*

Members of the British Cabinet often spoke in French among them-selves in London if foreigners were present. Hearing ladies speaking French at a reception at Carlton House, Chateaubriand commented to Wellington: 'at least there are some conquests which Europe has not taken from us, our language and our fashions.' According to the American envoy, 'there is scarcely a well-educated person in England who does not speak French.'[10] French was also, until the second half of the nineteenth century, the language of the Prussian and Russian diplo-matic services. Thus the Russian Foreign Secretary Nesselrode, a German from the Rhineland, wrote to the Russian ambassador in London, Count Lieven, from Paris on 7 April 1814, as always in French: *voilà le monde délivré et à jamais.*[11] The former Napoleonic Marshal Bernadotte, Crown Prince and then King of Sweden from 1810 to 1844, never learnt more than a few words of Swedish; all Swedes with whom he had frequent contact knew French. At the same time Republican and Napoleonic conquests had ensured that for at least ten years the lan-guage of most French satellite governments had been French. Thus Charles de Lacretelle, President of the Institut (the body grouping the five learned academies including the Académie Française), was able to boast to Alexander I and Frederick William III, at a special session on 21 April, that the French language had extended its conquests to the banks of the Danube, the Oder and the Neva.[12]

Paris was also the capital of pleasure, a role which helped defuse the Francophobia caused by the horrors of the recent wars. The pleasures of Paris, of which British travellers had been starved for eleven years since the end of the Peace of Amiens in 1803, were the reason for the arrival of so many of them in the summer of 1814. Disproving Dr Johnson's claim that 'there is in London all that life can afford', their arrival was a sign of the cultural, social and intellectual intimacy which, despite years of war since 1689, had developed between members of the British and French élites. Metternich wrote to his wife: 'It is raining English here – five to six hundred a day and the prostitutes of the Palais Royal cry "Long live the little hats!"* You should see the unbelievable appearance and costumes of some of these English women.' As early as 14 May rents in Paris were said to have doubled owing to the arrival of so many foreigners.[13]

Paris became not just an adjunct, but a focus, of British life, as it would be of Polish, Italian and German life. Indeed the descriptions of Paris in British guidebooks, diaries, letters and novels of this period form the richest portrait of one city ever drawn by writers of another nation.[14] In span, if not in genius, it is comparable to, and in some domains (such as politics) more informative than, the portrait of Paris in Balzac's *Comédie humaine*. British visitors often recorded aspects of daily life which Parisians took for granted. Underwood's diary, for example, already cited, is an important source for opinions in Paris in March 1814, as are those of the English radical Helen Maria Williams, who had lived in Paris since 1790, and Byron's friend John Cam Hobhouse, for Paris during the summer of 1815. Family and friends of British Parisians demanded every scrap of information about the city known as 'Babylon the great', which enjoyed the reputation of being 'the most interesting place on earth'.[15]

The variety of pleasures available in Paris drew visitors in increasing numbers. They came, of course, for the physical pleasures – of shopping, eating, love; the social pleasures available in the salons and the boulevards; and the visual pleasures found in museums, theatres, the city itself. The focus of these pleasures lay north of the Tuileries in the Palais Royal. Built by the Cardinal de Richelieu in the 1630s, given by Louis XIV to his brother the Duc d'Orléans in 1692, the Orléans family palace had been extended by his great-great-grandson, Louis-Philippe's father, in 1781–4. In the largest urban development of the day, he built an oblong quadrangle north of the palace, enclosing a garden of lime trees and gravelled walks. On the street the façades of the Palais Royal quadrangle look like other white-plastered eighteenth-century houses in Paris: from the inside its sober grey-brown columned façade, five storeys high, and its long arcades, make it seem like a larger, neoclassical version of the Piazza San Marco in Venice. Today it is an oasis of

---

* A reference to the diminutive size of Englishwomen's bonnets.

calm in the heart of Paris, the haunt of schoolchildren and old ladies. In 1789 it housed, as well as the Paris Bourse, the most celebrated concentration of shops, cafés, casinos and brothels in the world.

Not only a focus of pleasure and luxury, it was a building which accelerated, and occasionally created, history. In 1789 it had been the birthplace, the propaganda-centre and the barometer of revolution. There radicals had exchanged news, declaimed speeches, cheered, paid and feasted mutinous soldiers, paraded heads on pikes and organised the attack on the Bastille of 14 July and on Versailles of 5 October.[16]

Since the Consulate, however, the Palais Royal had been devoted to pleasure not revolution. 'The capital of Paris', the 'rendez-vous of Europe', 'the salient point of the world', visitors hurried there on their first evening in the city.[17] A Russian engineer reported: 'We arrive towards midday in Paris. I see the Palais Royal, the Jardin des Tuileries and the Café Montansier.'[18] A world in itself, some people were said to spend not days but years there.[19] In the words of a guidebook:

> There you can see everything, hear everything, know everything . . . everything one wants is to be found there . . . All the senses are aroused, all the passions are excited and a general intoxication of pleasure may be said to prevail in this enclosure of luxury; it is the centre of trade, the meeting-place of rogues and swindlers, the abode of idleness and festivity; it is the Palais-royal.[20]

The Palais Royal stood out as an island of light as well as pleasure. It was more brilliantly lit than ordinary Paris streets, which boasted only the occasional lantern hanging from a rope slung between houses.

In 1814 a typical cross-section of the Palais Royal contained a restaurant in the basement; a shop on the ground floor; a café on the first; a brothel on the second floor; and rooms for single people, frequently prostitutes, in the attics.[21] Even more than today, Paris shops were richer, more 'unspeakably elegant', open at more convenient hours, better lit, above all better stocked, than shops in other capitals. A Russian officer, Baron Löwenstern, ADC of the Russian Minister of War, was 'stunned by the richness and elegance of the shops and boutiques'.[22] Prince Clary, a Viennese *grand seigneur* who kept a diary of a pleasure trip in 1822, was impressed by an 'incredible' shop in the Passage des Panoramas selling papers, paints, boxes and screens: indeed 'everything needed to write and draw. One almost finds ideas there, there is so much of everything.'[23] In addition to ordinary commodities, shops stocked luxury items like gold, enamel and pearl-set pistols firing not bullets but perfume – *articles de Paris* – which were never of such elegant craftsmanship elsewhere. In a gesture indicative of both the city's supremacy and the nature of monarchy in the nineteenth century, the first shop Alexander I had visited in Paris was that of the famous watchmaker Abraham-Louis Bréguet – to buy not Bréguet watches, which he already possessed, but pedometers, to help the soldiers of the Russian Imperial Guard march in time.

Metternich too, if he despised Paris politicians, respected Paris crafts-men. In the few moments in April and May when he was not discussing peace terms in the Hôtel de Talleyrand, he went shopping in the Palais Royal. For his office and his palace in Vienna he bought, often at the famous shop *Le Petit Dunkerque*, furniture by Jacob, gold and silver objects by Biennais, bronze ornaments by Thomire, porcelain, books and fabrics. In the end his Paris purchases filled several transport wagons. He also hired the great court artist Isabey to draw the states-men of the forthcoming Congress of Vienna, and organise its fêtes.[24]

As contemporaries pointed out, if Britain had won the empire of the seas, France retained the empire of fashion.[25] According to Lady Charlotte Bury, 'The variety and beauty of all materials for ladies' dress far surpasses our wares and Lady Westmoreland says they are far cheaper.' The Emperor of Austria himself bought lace, gloves and stockings for his wife in Paris.[26] Reflecting the temptations of Parisian shops, a famous after-dinner toast in Britain ran: 'London and Liberty! – Edinburgh and Education! – Paris and Pocket-Money!'[27]

The best chefs and restaurants in Europe were also to be found in Paris. For the Tsar one attraction of staying with Talleyrand was that he had 'the only regular table of the old school kept up in France', run by the most celebrated *chef de bouche* in Europe, the great Carême, and a large staff including a *rôtisseur*, a *saucier*, a *pâtissier* and an *officier* (superin-tending desserts, ices and *confitures*).[28] Carême was a philosopher of the kitchen who believed that good food stimulated good social relations, although even he found *pâtisserie* 'a continuous battle'. Pozzo's chef was so good that when Lord Lonsdale dined there he called it 'the best dinner I ever sat down to'. Restaurants, which had first appeared in the 1770s, had become more numerous and lavish since the revolution, although cooks from royal and noble households, like Antoine Beauvillier, a former *officier de la bouche* of the Comte de Provence, were already opening restaurants in the Palais Royal before 1789.[29] The most expensive restaurant in Paris in 1814 was Véry Frères in the Palais Royal (founded as Les Quatre Nations in 1788). Its brilliantly lit salons, granite tables, gilt bronze candelabra and mirror-lined walls provided almost as much enchantment as dishes such as *caille à la financière* (three francs) or *filet mignon en chevreuil* (one franc ten sous).[30] On his first evening in Paris, on 31 March 1814, Baron Löwenstern enjoyed 'the best dinner possible', oysters, fish, champagne and Clos Vougeot, at the Rocher de Cancale in the rue Mandar: another restaurant in the Palais Royal, the Trois Frères Provençaux, was famous from the Tagus to the Neva for *poulet à la Marengo* (one franc fifteen sous), *fricassée de poulet à l'Austerlitz aux truffes* (four francs ten sous), *blanquette de veau de Pontoise* (one franc). At one time Stendhal dined there every day.[31]

There were some 3,000 restaurants of all kinds in Paris.[32] Less wealthy visitors found that they could enjoy an excellent dinner with soup, fish, two dishes of meat, dessert and a bottle of wine in a Palais Royal restaurant like Le Caveau – which also dated from before the revolution – for two to three francs (about five shillings) a head.[33] Even the bread rolls seemed 'finer' than elsewhere.[34] Such a dinner in London was four times more expensive, and by no means so good.[35]

Indeed the relative cheapness of Paris for British visitors was one of its main attractions. A 'small but perfectly clean' apartment in a hotel in the rue de Richelieu could be rented for five guineas a week. It was said that a single man could live as well in Paris on £200 a year as in London on £500.[36] People who needed to make further economies, however, often chose to live in Brussels, in order to avoid the temptations of Paris: hence the large number of British civilians at the Duchess of Richmond's ball on the eve of Waterloo.

Paris was a city of cafés as well as restaurants. There were between three and four thousand cafés in the city,[37] of which perhaps about half were considered respectable. The following description of a Paris café from an often-reprinted guidebook, *Galignani's Paris Guide*, shows that cafés provided, in addition to refreshments, freedom from solitude.

> Strangers converse with each other *sans cérémonie*; some play at dominoes, others read the newspapers and periodical publications which are chained or locked to boards adapted for that purpose; others again sip their coffees, drink their sugar and water or enjoy their glass of lemonade or liqueur with haply now and then a sly glance at the goddess of the scene (in vulgar English the Bar Maid) who is generally chosen for that distinguished post for her charms and graces . . . everyone who enters is greeted by her with a 'witching smile' of welcome.[38]

Cafés were patronised by people of every class. The former governor of Moscow, Count Rostopchine, spoke to strangers in cafés in the

Palais Royal about their families, the future of Haiti or the retreat from Moscow. He heard many witty remarks, so he said, but no swearing.[39]

The role of cafés as temples of sociability had grown in importance following the revolution, which had destroyed or deconsecrated so many of the city's churches (200 out of 290) and closed trade guilds and fraternities. The poor patronised those cafés outside the barriers known as *goguettes* or *guinguettes*, often with dance halls attached, which, in Balzac's phrase, circled the city like a wall of mud: the most famous included the Jardin de la Gaieté at the Barrière du Maine or the Ile d'Amour at Belleville. Their prices were cheaper as goods consumed there did not pay Paris customs dues, and they would often be patronised by people from a particular trade or province, for example soldiers or Auvergnats. Having been paid on Saturday, their clients danced, ate and drank, often throughout the day on Sunday and Monday: some establishments had rooms for six or seven hundred customers at a time.[40] On those days such cafés functioned as 'the parliament of the poor', where they could sing songs of love and war, celebrate French victories, forget the miseries of their daily life – and, occasionally, as in July 1830, plan action to improve it.[41]

Other establishments were the preserve of students – such as Le Père Bonvin, a mile beyond the Barrière de Montparnasse, in countryside dotted with chalk pits, wooden shanty towns and grazing land.[42] The rich also had favourite cafés, such as the royalist Café de Foy in the Palais Royal, whose waiters were said to be the most dignified and to earn the biggest tips; Stendhal breakfasted there every day with friends, even in a crisis such as that of 29 March 1814, the day the Empress Marie Louise left Paris.[43] Other famous cafés were the Café Anglais on the Boulevard des Italiens, preferred by Mérimée, who described a circle of his friends as *le gang du café Anglais*. Full of dancers, officers, journalists, drinking, smoking and shouting until 4 in the morning, it was called by the critic and novelist Barbey d'Aurevilly 'the sanhedrin of the devil'.[44] Berlioz corrected proofs for hours on end at a table in a café in the rue de Richelieu.[45] Delacroix thought it best to work alone in the evening, and not to frequent *le grand monde* or the company of other artists. However he did talk to people in cafés, writing in his diary: 'the evening in the café agreeable. Good conversation of the Italian.'[46] The most fashionable café in Paris, Tortoni's on the Boulevard des Italiens, had been founded by a Neapolitan in 1798 in order to supply Paris with good ices. An English visitor in 1815, James Simpson, described it as 'a very elegant suit of rooms, well lighted and always full of company. The ice creams and water ices certainly excell any I had ever seen before ... with your ice is brought iced water in a neat carafe, which is lined with a shell of ice.'[47] Until the 1830s it remained the most fashionable café in Paris, the place to show yourself after the opera or, 'with the serene air of a man who has just solved a tiresome problem', after fighting a duel.[48] Stockbrokers, too, continued their speculations there at night when the Bourse was closed.[49]

The Café des Mille Colonnes, on the first floor of the right-hand arcade of the Palais Royal, was so popular that clients had sometimes to queue to enter its four large mirrored salons, hung with 'magnificent chandeliers' and supported by Corinthian columns of green marble. In what was called the 'throne room' the cashier, known as *la belle limonadière*, plump and attractive though *un peu passée*, richly dressed with diamonds in her hair and 'a complexion like Parian marble', exhibited 'her charms as in the early part of her life she had done at the corners of the streets of Paris', while receiving the compliments and the francs of the customers. The chair on which she sat was a circular gilded throne formerly used by Napoleon's youngest and most incompetent brother, Jerome-Napoleon King of Westphalia, who had auctioned the furniture before abandoning his palace at Kassel in 1813.[50]

Some men also went to the Palais Royal to gamble: 'the most brilliant company in Paris among men' lost and won fortunes every evening at the luxurious gambling-house called the Cercle des Etrangers, nearby in the rue de la Grange Batelière.[51] For many male visitors, however, as before and since, Paris meant women; and in 1814 women meant the Palais Royal. More women were sold in Paris than in Constantinople.[52] As one guidebook recounted, the Palais Royal was the haunt of 'very sweet and very accommodating women', of 'all shades of temperament', available at any price and any time. They bore names like Balzamine, Palmire, Virginie (sic), Belle-Cuisse,[53] and their trade was strictly controlled by the police: once a woman had been inscribed on 'the registers of infamy', she had to submit to two years' police surveillance to be able to have her name removed.[54] According to police statistics, there were about 3,000 prostitutes inscribed at any one time (rising to 4,285 by 1847).[55]

Their attractions were not overlooked by allied soldiers. Cartoons such as *Le premier pas d'un jeune Officier Cosaque au Palais Royal* and *L'embarras du choix ou les Anglais au Palais Royal* show English or Russian officers ogling well-dressed women in the Palais Royal. Independent operators would entice customers with the invitation, if sitting on chairs in the garden – *Monsieur, voulez-vous vous asseoir?*; or, if walking in the arcades: *Allons, voyons; voulez-vous monter?* or *Monsieur, me voulez-vous? me voilà!* [56] They would then take their customers to a room in the attics or to 'infernal cellars' or *cabinets noirs* where, according to one guidebook *The Englishman's Mentor*, there were scenes 'such as no Englishman can conceive . . . of frightful and unimaginable sensuality'. [57] In addition there were officially licensed brothels called *maisons de tolérance*, and unlicensed ones known as *maisons clandestines*. [58] In the cartoon *Les Adieux au Palais Royal ou les suites du premier pas* Russian officers visit an apothecary to buy a treatment for the venereal disease subsequently caught [59] (although the obligatory monthly visit of prostitutes to the Dispensaire de Salubrité established in 1810 in the rue Croix des Petits Champs should have prevented such mishaps). [60] Hence the gleam in the eyes of elderly officers in St Petersburg, thirty years later, when they asked the young Turgenev, on his return from his first visit to Paris: 'Well, and how is our grand old Palais Royal?'

A young officer in the Russian Garde à Cheval, Boris Uxkull, described in his diary the girls whose company he enjoyed in Paris that April and May: 'I was unable to resist their provocations and went to see a few of them, especially the negroes and Creoles whose nature is so different from our own and whose ways are so piquant and curious . . .' He soon settled down with three 'enchantresses' whose mothers had been 'very helpful': three houses had become homes for him.

> I have pretended to love each one of them without feeling anything . . . Marie has a slender figure, eyes *à la madeleine* and a sweet voice of admirable timbre. It is costing me a lot of money but there is no risk of catching some fatal sickness here as many of my comrades have done . . . I can understand how the life of a Paris dandy must have great charms. You run from one conquest to another, from one amusement, one dinner, one show to another, and you do that every single day without stopping. [61]

Among senior allied officers, the Crown Prince of Bavaria found Parisian ladies 'pretty and very unrestrained'. One of the handsomest men of the age, Prince Leopold of Saxe-Coburg, wrote that there was no need to force oneself on *les nymphes de la capitale*, 'for here when you ask a woman to sit down she lies down'. [62]

Attractions of another kind were also available in Paris. Homosexuality, a crime in every other country, for which men could still be executed in England, had been decriminalised in France since 1790.

Paris was its centre. The former Director Barras, Bonaparte's one-time patron who had been expelled from office by the *coup d'état* of Brumaire 1799, according to a police report received few visitors in private carriages in the evening but many soldiers *en fiacre* (the cheap one-horse vehicle used by people who could not afford carriages). The politician Fiévée lived *en ménage* with the dramatist Théodore Leclerq. After a play-reading in their apartment, one guest commented: 'Oh Fiévée has found a way to render all that almost respectable!'[63] There was also, under the bridges, *la sodome des quais.*[64]

For some visitors to Paris its greatest attraction was its physical appearance. Napoleon I had wanted Paris to be capital of the universe. He had not only stamped his personal and dynastic emblems on its buildings, but also spent much of the money won from conquests in Europe on improvements in Paris. In addition to the Colonne de la Grande Armée in the Place Vendôme and the Arc de Triomphe du Carrousel, he had begun the Arc de Triomphe de l'Etoile; the Ponts d'Austerlitz and d'Iéna, named after his victories over Austria and Prussia; the Bourse, the façade of the Corps Législatif and the Temple de la Gloire (now the Madeleine). Work had also started on, among other projects, palaces for the King of Rome and the imperial archives, the University and new markets, a military hospital, prisons and slaughterhouses. The Emperor also planned a new city between Paris and Saint-Cloud. So much construction was in progress that, according to one commentator, Paris looked as if it had been taken by assault by architects and would need a hundred years to be finished.[65]

The 'embellishments' to Paris fascinated Europe. Lady Burghersh, no admirer of Parisians themselves ('so vulgar, such *mauvais ton*'), was lost in wonder: 'As to the town of Paris, the beauty and magnificence of it surpassed anything I could form an idea of. All the Arcs de Triomphe, pillars etc which Buonaparte has erected are perfect.'[66] Another English visitor, Augustus Foster, wrote: 'It requires to recollect all Bonaparte's tyranny not to regret him; his works and improvements are so magnificent.'[67] London would soon provide the most telling tribute to Napoleonic Paris. Within a few months of assuming the regency in 1811, the Regent had boasted that he would 'quite eclipse Napoleon'. His architect John Nash visited Paris in 1814. In the following fifteen years Carlton House Terrace was built on the model of the buildings on the Place de la Concorde; Regent Street, with interiors 'in the richest Parisian style imaginable', on that of the rue de Rivoli. The columns commemorating Nelson and the Duke of York were intended to surpass the column in the Place Vendôme, whilst the Marble Arch was inspired by the Arc du Carrousel.

Alexander I, too, when he first visited the Tuileries, already knew his way around: since 1808 he had received a monthly bulletin on Paris building projects from the principal exponent of neoclassical architecture in France, and Premier Architecte de l'Empereur, Pierre Fontaine. The Alexander Column, honouring the triumph of the Russian armies over Napoleon I, dedicated on the Emperor's name day, 30 August 1834, on the square in front of the Winter Palace, would be intended to surpass, by its height, its simplicity and its Christian symbolism, the column in the Place Vendôme. Made of plain granite, instead of bronze sculpted with scenes of military triumphs, it was surmounted by a statue of an angel with the features of Alexander I, holding a cross while crushing a serpent.[68]

The greatest attraction in Paris, however, was the museum of paintings and sculpture in the Louvre. 'The first thing I did when I got to Paris', William Hazlitt recorded, 'was to go to see the Louvre', and many others shared his priorities.[69] No other capital possessed a museum which could rival the Louvre: neither the Prado nor the National Gallery nor the Kunsthistorisches Museum then existed. France's recent imperial past, and Paris's role as a court city, were again decisive. The Louvre was a royal museum, founded by Louis XVI and administered by the crown: liveried royal footmen admitted visitors. The collection, originating in that of the French crown, expanded by revolutionary and Napoleonic confiscations, now contained, according to official lists, 1,321 pictures divided into French (112), Dutch, Flemish and German (638) and Italian (561) schools, and 400 pieces of classical sculpture.[70] Edward Stanley wrote:

> words cannot describe the coup d'oeil. Figure to yourself a magnificent room so long that you would be unable to recognise a person at the other extremity, so long that the perspective lines terminate in a point, covered with the finest works of art all classed and numbered so as to afford the utmost facility of inspection; no questions asked on entering, no money to be given to bowing porters or butlers . . . It is noble and grand beyond imagination.[71]

All agreed, however, that away from the court end of the city – the Palais Bourbon, the Tuileries, the Louvre and the boulevards – the streets of Paris, compared to those of St Petersburg, Berlin, even London, were 'in general narrow and irregular'. Moreover they were a vortex of noise, dirt, people colliding, mingling, being showered by mud and filth from gutters running down the middle of the street: there were no pavements. At night they looked like dark, narrow mountain passes.[72]

The artist Benjamin Haydon, however, although in Paris to study the pictures in the Louvre, found the moving picture of life in the streets even more fascinating: 'Why stay poring over pictures when we were on the most remarkable scene in the history of the world?' For Haydon the attractions of Paris included the sight of troops from 'all the nations in the world', the studio of Baron Gérard, and the reverberations from the city's recent past: 'At that time every step in Paris excited mighty associations. Every church, every palace, every street and every corner was remarkable for some slaughter or struggle, or some wonder connected with revolution and blood; yet everywhere a sense of despotism pressed on your mind.'[73]

Of all the streets in Paris the most fascinating were the broad tree-lined boulevards, down which the allied troops had so often paraded in April and May 1814. Lined with shops, cafés and theatres, the boulevards were like a perpetual fair. In addition to street-sellers hawking their wares, there were dancing dogs, puppet shows, sword-swallowers, ballad singers, jugglers, actors, conjurors, and 'raree-shew men', 'who have each their distinct audiences'. A young girl in a turban, so the English scholar and bibliophile the Reverend Thomas Frognall Dibdin noted, 'seems to have no mercy either upon her own voice or upon the hurdy-gurdy on which she plays'.[74] In the afternoon and evening and on holidays it was difficult to move along the boulevards, such were the crowds who had come out to lounge and stare. In comparison to Londoners, Parisians walked in a slow, nonchalant fashion.[75] Under the trees people hired chairs on which they sat drinking lemonade or beer – there were 'incessant reports from drawing the corks of beer bottles' – or eating ices. Carriages crowded around the entrances to cafés. 'Between these loungers and the entrances to the cafés', wrote Dibdin, 'move on, closely wedged and yet scarcely in motion, the mass of human beings who come only to exercize their eyes, by turning them to the right or to the left.'[76] So full of life were the boulevards, according to one proverb, that 'when the good Lord is bored in heaven, he opens the window and watches the boulevards of Paris'.[77]

Amid the bustle of the Paris streets, the manners of Parisians were also admired, in terms which suggest the coarseness of other cities. Haydon praised 'the intoxicating gaiety of French manners . . . the lowest servant took your hat and gloves as if you did her a favour.

Nothing struck us English more in the manners of the French than the sweetness of address in all classes.'[78] The gentleness of the Parisians, their 'amenity of manners', 'absence of all disgusting excesses' and lack of 'insolent puppyism' were remarked on by many English visitors. At a time when London had no police force, Edward Mangin, an English tutor visiting the city, noted that 'The French are a very civil kindly people among themselves and tender towards children . . . and in these points are certainly the very reverse of the British: one meets here no street brawls, no fighting as in London and the lash is hardly ever applied in France to child, dog or horse.' Parisians, moreover, were 'delicate in their deportment' towards foreigners, even when met at the same *table d'hôte* in a hotel during the allied occupation.[79] During the annual celebrations of the King's feast day, the Fête de Saint-Louis, every 25 August, when there were free distributions of wine, bread and sausages in the Champs Elysées, an American visitor was astonished to note 'not a single instance of drunkenness or of quarrelling, not withstanding the eager strife of the very lowest classes'. In general there was little drunkenness on the streets of Paris.[80] The Paris public could be admitted to the national botanical garden, the Jardin des Plantes; in London however, one English general wrote, if the public had been admitted, the garden would have been trampled on and 'knives would operate in all directions'. Even beggars in Paris 'conduct themselves with a modesty and decency of manner not to be surpassed'.[81]

The behaviour of Parisians was also admired at another of the principal attractions of the city, the theatre. The audience was considered better mannered, and the actors more skilled, than in other cities, including London.[82] On the night of their arrival, many foreign visitors went not to the Palais Royal but to the theatre. The seventeen-year-old Prince Wilhelm of Prussia, serving as a captain in the Prussian guards, went every night in May 1814. 'We live at the play here,' Lady Bessborough wrote.[83] Horace Walpole's friend, Miss Berry, enthused to a correspondent:

> . . . what a *perfect* thing is French comedy! The representation of *their* life and *their* manners are so perfectly natural that all idea of a theatre vanishes; and as they admit of much more conversation, and less action and bustle on the stage than we do, one often feels oneself admitted into the interior of a private house and listening to their family arrangements.[84]

The social charms of Paris were not restricted to the boulevards and theatres. Society was then a European institution, defined by letters of introduction, presentation at court (which automatically gave access to other courts) and a shared culture. It incorporated in the same world people of different nationalities and professions. One of the distinguishing freedoms of Paris was the looseness of class barriers. Since the second half of the eighteenth century, if not before, talent and conversation could count, at certain hours in certain salons, as much as birth and rank. Men and women of letters could talk, as nowhere else, as near-equals of princes and dukes. At least in foreign eyes, the barriers of manners, accent and dress between the different classes were less elevated than in London or Vienna: all had *le vernis parisien*.[85]

One salon which mixed the classes was Madame de Staël's: indeed, since it contained representatives of every human type, however curious, it was compared by a young officer Boniface de Castellane – author of one of the best diaries of the period – to Noah's ark.[86] Madame de Staël admitted that 'the pleasure of conversation and conversation in Paris . . . has always been for me the most piquant of all'. So important was her salon that the Director-General of Police described it to Louis XVIII, in one of his daily bulletins, as 'a power in the opposition'. *The Times* called it 'the central point of the literary, political and fashionable world'.[87]

One particularly impressive assembly, representative of the cosmopolitan Paris of 1814, had taken place on 25 May, after dinner, between 9 and 12 at her salon in the rue de Grenelle, in the Faubourg Saint-Germain. Her guests included, among others, the Tsar, Talleyrand, La Fayette, Benjamin Constant; August Wilhelm von Schlegel, her intellectual guide to Germany and literary adviser, and a celebrated critic and translator of Shakespeare; and her most trusted French friend Mathieu de Montmorency, a former revolutionary who had become leader of a royalist secret society, the Chevaliers de la Foi. With characteristic modesty the Tsar, who behaved in society like a private gentleman rather than a sovereign, insisted that Madame de Staël and her daughter – who had come out of the apartment to greet him at the top of the stairs – precede him into the salon. With Constant and La Fayette he discussed the new French constitution and, according to a Swiss guest Pictet de Richemont, 'appeared to place the greatest importance on it being liberal. The interest this Prince shows for the happiness of the French people is really admirable and can hardly be imagined. He then talked of the museum [the Louvre] which he regards as the finest collection in the world.' The Tsar admitted, 'This collection is too magnificent, too well arranged to alter anything in its ensemble.' Madame de Staël replied: 'Sire, not everyone thinks like you, and M. Schlegel who is here would like some of these beautiful statues to return to Rome.' Conversation then turned to the burning of Moscow. The Tsar said: 'although we are called the barbarians of the North, we are slowly acquiring gentler habits.'[88] For Constant, however, as he reveals in his *Journal intime*, the purpose of the evening had been advancement of his own career rather than discussion of the constitution: 'Soirée with Alexander. Great benevolence. Shall I not profit from it?'[89]

Thanks to the mechanism of international society, many foreigners soon came to feel at home in Paris. On 26 September 1814 Lady Dalrymple Hamilton, for example, arrived in Paris with her husband Sir Hew, a Member of Parliament, their daughter Henrietta and her maid Miss Whicker, having left Calais on 23 September and slept on the way at Abbeville and Amiens. On 27 September they rented an apartment in the Hôtel de Noailles on the rue du Faubourg Saint-Honoré – another building which had changed ownership with the change of regime since the old Duc de Noailles, who had spent the revolution and the Empire on the banks of Lake Geneva, had recently recovered his family house from a Napoleonic dignitary, the Architrésorier Lebrun. The Dalrymple Hamiltons visited sights such as Notre Dame, the royal palaces and the Louvre, where they were 'confused' by the number of pictures. Thereafter they became part of the social hurricane of Paris in 1814 – it was said that there had never been so many balls, or carriages in the street, as in the winter of 1814–15.[90] They went out to dinner or the theatre almost every night, meeting court officials, Napoleonic marshals, members of the old nobility, the royal family and Madame de Staël.

Lady Dalrymple Hamilton's diary is packed with entries such as:

Nov 2d Dined at Clichy with Madame de Stael a delightful party. Talma [the greatest French actor of the day] was there and in the evening recited parts from Hamlet, Macbeth and the Cid most incomparably, afterward went to the Duke of Wellington's, a small party and excellent music.

Nov 3d Dined at the Duke of Wellington's to meet Macdonald Duc de Tarente, Soult Duc de Dalmatie, Victor Duc de Bellune and Gouvion St Cyr. Mme Soult and Mme Victor were there, Macdonald handed me to dinner. In the evening we went to the Duchesse d'Aumont very good music, but the party rather formal.

Dec 7 The Duchesse of Orléans Drawing Room, this was the first night of the Palais Royal* being opened, it is nearly finished and magnificent. The great Gallery is purple silk with gold fleurs de lys, the bedroom scarlet satin embroidered with gold. The furniture is beautiful and the whole suite of rooms very fine.

Feb 7 1815 Ball at the Princesse de Wagram's very fine indeed, the rooms magnificent and the entertainment superb in every respect.

By 27 February she could write: 'My ball. The Duc and Duchesse d'Orléans and Mademoiselle were there, the Duc de Berri sent his apology. There were 600 persons.'[91] To be able to give a ball for six hundred, five months after arriving in Paris for the first time, was a miracle, which today only the very richest foreigner – as opposed to the wife of an undistinguished MP – could perform. It shows not only the lady's charm and wealth but also the eclectic nature of Paris social life.

The prominence of the English in Paris was encouraged by the Anglophilia of the King and the royal family. Louis XVIII had returned from England committed, as he had told a delegation from the City of London, in English, 'to promote the utmost cordiality between the two nations' – sentiments often repeated by members of his family and household. In a speech at Carlton House much criticised in France, he had attributed 'the restoration of our house on the throne of its ancestors', after divine providence, 'to the counsels of Your Royal Highness, to this glorious country and to the steadfastness of its inhabitants'.[92] In Paris Louis XVIII continued to consider the interests of the French and British governments as one and the same.[93] He invited the Prince Regent to Paris for the signing of the peace treaty, assuring him that 'all France' yearned to express its gratitude to the English nation. He ensured that English visitors, however badly dressed, had privileges of access and seating at court and the Chapel Royal over French visitors. They were admitted whenever they wished. He himself bowed, took off his hat or kissed his hands to them when he saw them at court or on his daily carriage ride through the streets of Paris.[94] He wore the Garter round his knee more often than the Légion d'Honneur on his chest – and displayed it with pride to English visitors.[95]

Many in Paris and France welcomed constitutional monarchy and

---

*That is, the apartments of the Duc and Duchesse d'Orléans on the first floor of the main section of the palace, south of the quadrangle of shops and cafés.

European peace. Whereas Napoleon I had felt obliged in January to dismiss the Corps Législatif for its opposition to his war policy and refusal to make peace, that autumn the Chambers' sessions went smoothly: laws introduced by the government were voted without difficulty. Trade was booming, there were not enough workers for the jobs available and the price of bread had gone down.[96]

For many Frenchmen the principal cause of discontent was not the internal situation in France but France's situation in Europe. They considered Europe not a fatherland but an enemy. Louis XVIII's Anglophilia would prove as unpopular, in Paris, as Louis XVI's commitment to his Austrian wife and alliance had been in the 1780s.[97] In contrast to the feeling of exhaustion in France after the wars of Louis XIV, after the even more sanguinary wars of Napoleon many Frenchmen wanted to start again. They, rather than the Bourbons, had learnt nothing and forgotten nothing. Ignoring the allied military superiority paraded on their streets that April and May, many Parisians reacted like Germans after 1918. In conversations at the theatre, in coaches, in cafés, they claimed that France had been defeated only because Napoleon and Paris were 'betrayed, much betrayed'. If the 'traitor' Marmont had held out one day longer, Napoleon would have arrived in time to defeat the allies.[98]

Loss of empire heightened feelings of outraged nationalism. Many Frenchmen, particularly soldiers, felt a passionate (but unreciprocated) desire to recover the German and Belgian departments on the left bank of the Rhine which had been French for twenty years: 'at least Belgium will be ours in two years,' said one Parisian to Haydon.[99] Marshal Suchet told Lord Buckingham that the only way to keep peace was for France to have the Rhine frontier. Schoolboys from the old imperial *lycées*, brought up to love the Emperor and to attend lessons in uniform to the roll of drums, told returned émigrés that France must have the Rhine frontier: 'it is a natural limit.'[100] The fact that Louis XVIII had abandoned these conquests – although in early May he had tried for an extension of the French frontier, from Dixmude to Sarrelouis, in order to please the army – confirmed the equation between French nationalism and anti-royalism. Since 1789 the word *la nation* had often been used to mean not France but the revolutionaries in the Palais Royal. *National* denoted support for the revolution, and *biens nationaux* those properties of the Church, émigrés and other assumed enemies of the revolution which had been sold by the revolutionary government, and whose possessors, in 1814, felt such apprehension for the security of their purchases.[101]

Loss of pre-eminence in the state exacerbated the discontent festering in the army. The aspirations of the army and in particular of the Garde Impériale had alarmed even Napoleon, who had confided to Caulaincourt in 1812: 'you need a very strong will to keep it in check.' The Directeur-Général de la Police Comte Beugnot, addressing himself to Louis XVIII on 9 July 1814, denounced 'the army which has all too great a tendency to form an entirely distinct corps within the state and there assume for itself an absolute supremacy'.[102]

Both the Provisional Government and Louis XVIII, however, had made it a 'fundamental principle', as Pozzo noted, not only to renounce French conquests in Europe but to reduce the importance of the army in France. 'Europe in my opinion should be grateful to him for a policy on the success of which its peace and happiness depend,' wrote Pozzo prophetically.[103] Moreover the state of French finances required a reduction in the size of the army. As Louis XVIII announced at one council meeting, 'he [the King] is aware of the importance of the army but it is indispensable to make reductions.'[104] The army was left smaller but otherwise essentially the same in spirit, organisation and appearance as under Napoleon. Its resentment was heightened by the promotion of émigré officers: Chateaubriand, who had not fought since the émigrés' invasion of France, with the Austro-Prussian forces in 1792, became a Colonel; the Comte de Bruges, an ADC of Monsieur who had served twenty years in the British army, was appointed Lieutenant-General and, incredibly, Grand Chancelier de la Légion d'Honneur.

Like most royalists, and most of his fellow monarchs, Louis XVIII believed that the security of his throne rested on the loyalty and effectiveness of the guard. The desertion of the Gardes Françaises in July 1789 was to many the reason for the success of the revolution. The first measure the King proposed at the first meeting of his council on 5 May 1814 – having reviewed the Russian and Prussian guards in front of the Tuileries the day before – was the revival and expansion of the pre-1775 Maison Militaire du Roi (household troops), including *mousquetaires*, *gendarmes* and *chevau-légers de la garde* and *gardes du corps*: 'the preservation of the monarchy', so Artois said, depended on the creation of these corps. Although two companies of gardes du corps under Marshals Berthier and Marmont were added by Louis XVIII 'to prove to the army that his confidence is equal in all Frenchmen', and many guards in other units had served in the Napoleonic army, the new units proved both unpopular and ineffective in Paris.[105] Marmont's company of gardes du corps was nicknamed *la compagnie de Judas*.

On 24 June the gardes du corps replaced the national guards on duty inside the Tuileries, while the latter, who had not been informed, were at lunch. Their pride wounded, many national guards refused to turn up for the duties which they were still required to perform outside the palace. The subsequent banquet offered by the Gardes du Corps to the National Guard was 'more official than friendly . . . the groups formed during coffee were composed of men of each force without fusion.'[106] Similar resentments surfaced at the banquet offered by the city of Paris to the King and the royal family at the Hôtel de Ville on 25 August to celebrate the feast of St Louis. Since the King was present, the gardes du corps alone were on duty: Beugnot feared physical violence between them and the National Guard, who were aggrieved that the interest of 'only one class' had been consulted.[107] An *ordonnance* praising the National Guard for its role in the defence of Paris, the King's boast that with such troops he feared no enemy, the award of special flags and the right to be the sole guard of the King on the anniversary of his entry into Paris on 3 May, were not enough to soothe the National Guard's feelings of irritated vanity.[108]

The disputes over the King's guard showed that Paris itself was to be a cause of problems to the monarchy. Since the signature of the Concordat in 1802, religious processions had returned to other French cities. Their reappearance in Paris, beginning with the Fête-Dieu procession of 12 June 1814, the first since 1790, was not unpopular. It was the grandest public religious commemoration of the year, to honour the real presence of Jesus Christ in the Host, and took place in other Catholic capitals throughout Europe.* Princes and officials in full dress, religious confraternities and young girls in white followed the consecrated Host which, held under a canopy by priests and acolytes, was carried through streets lined with troops and tapestries, past images of the Virgin and busts of the King, triumphal arches and flower-decked altars especially erected for the occasion.[109] It was free theatre: few spectators needed to be told by the gendarmes to take off their hats as the procession went past.[110]

However, until midday on Sunday cafés and shops, with the exception of pharmacies, were instructed to close by a new *ordonnance*. Shopkeepers threatened to have the King's head cut off, and defiantly

---

* Until 1914 the procession through the streets of Vienna, attended by the Emperor, the Archdukes and the authorities and corporations of the capital, was several hundred metres long.

kept their shops open. A caricature was soon on sale entitled *Le Déjeuner du dimanche*. It showed a famished man, repeatedly refused breakfast in cafés, who in the end can only obtain nourishment by means of a *lavement* in his posterior, administered through the door of a pharmacy.[111]

Another cause of discontent in Paris was the King's plan to spend half the year, from May to October, at Versailles. The restoration of the melancholy, denuded palace, its courtyards overgrown with weeds – begun in 1808 by Napoleon, who had also intended to live there – was praised as a means of providing employment for hundreds of workers. The work was paid for out of the funds left in Napoleon's Domaine Extraordinaire – the money he had extracted from the countries he conquered. The haste with which the restoration proceeded, however, was considered by some to show a repugnance for Paris and an eagerness to leave it. According to one police report, 'it disturbs and displeases everyone.'[112]

The role of Paris as capital of both France and Europe, the abundance of public spaces – the Tuileries, the Palais Royal, the theatres and cafés – their juxtaposition of people from different nations, parties and classes, bred other tensions. The British stood out not only by their clothes, their voices and their wealth but also by their height: the French were, until the late twentieth century, considerably smaller.[113] A popular play about English visitors to Paris, *Les Anglaises pour rire ou la Table et le Logement*, which ran from December 1814 to May 1815, is relatively friendly and celebrates Paris's religion of pleasure:

> *Des jeux et des plaisirs*
> *Paris seul est l'asile.*
> *. . . le Plaisir est le seul dieu*
> *Qu'on adore en ce lieu.*[114]

However, on 2 November a police agent reported: 'Hatred for the English is growing daily. They are regarded as the destroyers of French industry* . . . it is said that the King and the princes do not like the French.' Quarrels over Bonaparte took place between French and English at the opera and in cafés. 'The greatest misfortunes' were foretold. On 18 December, according to a police report, some English were

---

*Following the proclamation of peace in 1814, cheap British products flooded the French market, which had been closed since the renewal of war in 1803.

obliged to leave the Tuileries garden after being 'surrounded by a crowd of strollers who, while showing a foolish and impertinent curiosity, addressed to them rude and insulting remarks'.[115]

The prominence and unpopularity of the English in Paris was symbolised by the change in attitude towards the most famous Englishman of his day, the Duke of Wellington. When Wellington had passed through Paris in May, on his way from Spain to England, he had been cheered at the opera.[116] When he returned as ambassador in August he incurred widespread odium. The choice, as British ambassador to France, of the general who had spent the previous six years defeating French armies, was hardly tactful. Moreover 'Monsieur le duc de Vilainton', as he was sometimes called, was too casual for Paris. Even in London he was famous for his 'nonchalance and coolness of manner'.[117] In Paris James Mackintosh, a Whig historian come to consult the French archives, condemned the 'great coat and boots bespattered with mud' in which, late from a royal hunt, Wellington had attended a dinner given by Maréchal Berthier: 'the negligence of the Duke of Wellington's manner and the familiarity of his nods are quoted in every company as proofs of his insolence . . . he has neither courtesy nor display enough to be popular at Paris.'[118] Although Napoleonic marshals attended his entertainments, some felt more resentment than gratitude. Elizabeth Duchess of Devonshire wrote that she would not easily forget a dinner at the Duke of Wellington's on 3 November. Marshal Gouvion Saint-Cyr was 'very sore on the subject of the last campaign and the preponderance of England, saying it is your country that has won. See if you are not masters of the sovereign state of Belgium.' Wellington replied: 'it is quite against our wishes that we have an army on the continent [in Belgium] but it was stipulated and asked for by the sovereigns when they were in England.'[119] Evidently the crowned heads of Europe had been alarmed by the discontented Frenchmen they had noticed in Paris in April and May, and so required a reliable army on the French frontier.

The open manner in which Wellington neglected his wife and conducted an affair with Giuseppina Grassini, former Première Cantatrice de Sa Majesté l'Empereur and one of Napoleon's many mistresses, was considered shocking.[120] Moreover he was regularly seen to be consulted by the King and his ministers – Britain and France having allied themselves against Russia and Prussia at the Congress of Vienna – and was a favoured visitor at the Tuileries.[121] General Foy, who had fought in the French army for most of the Peninsular War, went to court and to the British embassy, where he and Wellington talked over their recent campaigns. Yet he wrote in his diary of his regret for the end of what he called 'twenty-five years of glory and struggle', his horror of the Bourbons – *de vieilles bêtes* rushing to their ruin, 'the very humble valets of England' – and his 'execration' of the English: he also discussed with Caulaincourt the possibility of the Emperor's return.[122] On 28 November the Whig MP, James Mackintosh, wrote – and his opinion is confirmed by police reports: 'the feeling is now so strong and so general against us as to make the residence of Paris really unpleasant.' On 14 January the British government, concerned for Wellington's safety, sent him to attend the congress in Vienna.[123]

Whereas the British had plenty of money to enjoy themselves in Paris, the loss of the Empire had deprived not only France of European supremacy but individual Frenchmen of money. Napoleon had given some 5,000 people, including most of the marshals, estates or incomes worth a total of 30 million francs a year, based on properties or government bonds held outside the old frontiers of France, in order to bind them to his monarchy and his conquests. Marshal Ney, for example, had been given estates in Italy, Germany and Poland producing about 500,000 francs a year.[124] By the Treaty of Paris of May 1814 they lost their estates and incomes outside France, and so had to reduce their standard of living in Paris.

In April, after the fall of the Empire, Marshal Ney – Duc d'Elchingen and Prince de La Moskowa, who had won the epithet *le brave des braves* for his heroism during the retreat from Moscow – had been happy to give a ball. His wife Adèle danced with the Tsar, as she did at other balls that spring: she became the Tsar's favourite waltzing partner. Napoleon I had considered a splendid residence in Paris a definition of rank and so had given large sums to help his relations, marshals and ministers buy one: the ball took place in Ney's magnificent *hôtel* at 74 rue de Bourbon in the Faubourg Saint-Germain.[125] By September, however, Ney was so disillusioned with the new regime that Beugnot reported him to Louis XVIII as saying that Wellington's presence in Paris was 'an insult to the nation', and as threatening an act of revenge: 'Marshal Ney since the loss of his *dotation* is not rich and owes a lot; that is the principal reason for that spirit of bitterness which is apparent in him even more than in most of his comrades. He has already been obliged to dismiss three-quarters of his household.'[126] Although invited, his wife had not attended the 25 August banquet at the Hôtel de Ville, on the pretext that she was spending summer in the country.

Another discontented Napoleonic grandee was Savary Duke of Rovigo, Napoleon's tyrannical former Minister of Police. In part encouraged by the authorities, who preferred him to leave Paris, he decided to let his splendid *hôtel* in the rue d'Artois near the Champs Elysées, decorated with portraits of the Bonapartes.[127] His wife, a leader of fashion said to change her shoes five times a day, had to show potential tenants round their house. One English viewer, Frances Burgoyne, remarked that 'she acquitted herself as well as possible in the novel situation of a Duchess become a *Lodging letter*.'[128]

Few Napoleonic grandees were more discontented than the Emperor's favourite ADC, the Comte de Flahaut. Once Napoleon and his few remaining courtiers and guards had left, Flahaut returned from Fontainebleau to a life of leisure in Paris. Like almost all Bonapartists in 1814, he went to court in the Tuileries – in his case once a month. He also played a lot of tennis.[129] His mother Madame de Souza pretended that she only enjoyed sitting by her fireside and playing patience. A police spy reported, however, that Madame de Souza's house 'is frequented by many people particularly by foreigners, English as well as Spaniards and Portuguese . . . General Flahaut openly expresses his attachment for King Murat [brother-in-law of Napoleon and still King of Naples] and there seems to be no doubt about his ill-will towards the present government.' By December 1814 her house had become, according to James Mackintosh, a headquarters of the Napoleonic party.[130] Flahaut could be heard singing 'old National Songs' such as *Le vaillant guerrier français*, promising that soon French eagles would fly over the Tower of London and French soldiers would have 'English guineas in their pocket and English beauties in their arms'.[131] His mother revered the memory of Napoleon, and claimed, at a time when three Napoleonic marshals (Soult, Moncey, Oudinot) were ministers, and two others (Berthier, Marmont) were captains of companies of gardes du corps, that 'Anyone who has been at all prominent in the last ten years is relegated to their lair.'[132] At the end of the year the Minister of War exiled Flahaut, who had defended his intimate friend General Exelmans against a charge of corresponding with Murat. Alleging ill-health, Flahaut refused to leave Paris. Fear of displeasing his assumed father Talleyrand prevented the Minister of War ordering his arrest, while Exelmans was acquitted by a military tribunal on 23 January.[133]

Another headquarters of the Napoleonic party was the salon of Napoleon's stepdaughter Hortense, who had married his brother Louis, former King of Holland. Like many Parisians, she returned to the city in

October after a summer in the country. On 30 May the King, at Alexander I's request, had made her Duchesse de Saint-Leu. On 14 October she obtained an audience of Louis XVIII in order to request his intervention in her lawsuit with her separated husband over custody of their two sons. While a few members of the Napoleonic élite complained of the coldness of their reception at the court of Louis XVIII, Queen Hortense remembered that courtiers behaved to her with as much deference as if Napoleon had still been on the throne – as indeed he appeared to be, since Ns and bees (the heraldic symbol of the Bonapartes) still decorated the throne room. The King, who rose to receive her and asked her to return whenever she wished, praised her manners so highly that the Duc de Gramont joked that she should hurry her divorce so that he could marry her.[134] A second audience with the King in January left her, as she wrote to her brother, 'enchanted: it is impossible to have been more amiable towards me, and to my lawsuit, or to have shown me more interest.'[135]

In her large and elegant *hôtel* at 15 rue Cerutti (now rue Lafitte), running north of the Boulevard des Italiens, Hortense spent much of her time looking after her sons and taking drawing and music lessons. Having been selected by Napoleon to 'do the honours of Paris' before 1814, she was also used to entertaining on a large scale.[136] Frequent visitors to her house included the Emperor's trusted officials, the Duc de Bassano, the Comte de Lavallette and 'many English': one of them, Michael Bruce, who became Maréchale Ney's lover, described it as 'by far the most agreeable House I have seen in Paris'. It was Queen Hortense who started the fashion for placing in the centre of the salon a round table at which women sat, read or sewed, while men stood nearby or played billiards.

Her most frequent visitor was the Comte de Flahaut, Queen Hortense's lover since 1807. 'My entire life belongs to her,' he told his mother. Madame de Souza acted as the intermediary in their correspondence and brought up their illegitimate son, known as Auguste Demorny, who had been born in secret in Savoy, far from Parisian eyes, on 6 October 1811.[137] Hortense protested that she only wanted peace, that it was the first period of happiness in her life, but admitted that her guests, especially Flahaut, talked in her house of what she called 'their plans and hopes'.[138] Her neighbour the Vicomtesse de Noailles, a rival in politics and love – she defined the wars of the Empire as *une guillotine en permanence*, and tried to win Flahaut, with whom she also was in love, for her royalist salon – was correct in thinking Queen Hortense an active

Bonapartist.[139] On 16 October she wrote to her brother Prince Eugène: 'the soldiers are still very discontented, the faults of the Emperor Napoleon have been forgotten and at present he is more beloved than ever.'[140] Pozzo was so infuriated by her guests' mockery of the allies and the émigrés, that he never returned to her salon after his first visit: he had already had one argument with Flahaut in May, at a soirée at Talleyrand's, over Napoleon's talents as a general. To Pozzo the Emperor's last moves in the campaign of France were those of a madman: for Flahaut they made the campaign a masterpiece. The subsequent exchange epitomised the conflicts then dividing Parisians. Pozzo replied:

– He ought to have known the people were against him.
– To be sure he did think Paris would have stood true to him. He did not take treachery into account.

Another Bonapartist sympathiser who had remained in the French army and lived in Paris *en cosmopolite*, Comte Dedem de Gelder, also claimed that the houses of the Duchesse de Bassano and Queen Hortense were 'the centre from which all the tentacles spread'.[141]

Bonapartist hopes and plans were also discussed by officers and soldiers meeting at, among many other haunts, the Café de la Gaieté and Café Chinois on the Boulevard du Temple, the Café Bodineau in the rue du Bac and the Tabagie de la Comète in the Palais Royal. According to police reports, 'Bonaparte seems to be everything' to them – Louis XVIII a fat pig.[142] On 18 October at the Restaurant de la Citerne opposite the Palais de Justice on the Ile de la Cité, a lunch of eighty officers ended with cries of *Vive l'Empereur! Mort pour le roi!* A police agent reported that 'public spirit is bad'; Blacas was 'universally detested'.[143]

Yet there were also demonstrations of popular royalism. On their many visits to the theatre and the opera in the autumn, the King and the royal family were cheered with frenzy, and greeted with calls for *le roi, le roi, notre bon Louis!* 'I have never seen enthusiasm more marked, more unanimous and above all more sincere,' wrote the Swiss diplomat Pictet de Richemont after the King's visit to the Odéon on 24 November.[144] In all quarters but the army, Louis XVIII's emphasis on the need for peace was well received. On 13 December applause of lines such as *Nos peuples désolés n'ont besoin que de paix* in the play *Rhadamiste et Zénobie* by Crébillon, which attacked the tyranny of the Roman Empire, was so deafening that the performance had to be stopped: all eyes turned to the King, the entire audience cheered.[145] According to a police report, the King was 'loved, much loved', as 'he governs constitutionally, he has liberal ideas, the King is good' – and he had started to wear the Légion d'Honneur again.[146]

Louis XVIII corrected the proofs, and publicly praised the principles, of *Réflexions politiques*, a pamphlet by Chateaubriand published at the end of November which stated that the King did not 'separate those who have served the King from those who have served the fatherland'.[147] Much of the public, accustomed to the tyranny of the Empire, was bewildered by the new freedom. A disapproving police agent reported that 'the freedom to speak and express yourself openly has never been so bold' – even during mass at the Chapel Royal.[148] Chateaubriand, however, and through him Louis XVIII, praised the fact that there was 'the most complete liberty of opinions in the two Chambers, in books, in newspapers and speeches . . . people come and go and do what they wish.' The throne found its security and splendour in the Charte, the liberal bicameral constitution which guaranteed the rights of all Frenchmen. France needed no further territory, for 'France finishes where French is no longer spoken': no mention was made of French-speaking areas in the southern Netherlands.[149]

On 17 January 1815, however, the burial of Mlle Raucourt of the Comédie Française brought politics on to the streets of Paris. The curé of Saint-Roch, in accordance with Catholic tradition but contrary to the laws of France, refused to bury an actress on consecrated ground (although previously happy to accept the alms she gave for the poor of his parish). When a protest from a group of actors to the Director-General of Police and the Duc de Duras – as Premier Gentilhomme de Service the court official responsible for actors – produced no effect, a crowd of about 4,000, led by actors in the uniform of the National Guard, acompanied this popular actress's funeral procession from her house in the rue du Helder, broke open the main door of the church and installed the coffin in a makeshift funeral chapel. Along the way, people appeared at windows, crying 'To the church! To the church!' 'The most insulting remarks' against the clergy and the government were mixed with cries of *Vive le roi!* when a priest appeared to say prayers. For days nothing else was talked of in salons, cafés and cabarets in Paris; the curé was universally blamed, as was the government for its weakness and failure to prevent the riot.[150] The Comte de Jaucourt, replacing Talleyrand at the Ministry of Foreign Affairs while the latter was attending the Congress of Vienna, felt the government was daily losing respect and would have preferred a united ministry with a real opposition, 'as in England', to the system of having ministers in the government to represent different opinions, which he called 'this artificial union which gives [only] an appearance of agreement'.[151] Marshal Soult, with Artois' backing appointed Minister of War in December, was described by Jaucourt as 'vain, gross, cunning, supple and a flatterer'; like many military men, he was nostalgic for autocracy. He had told an English officer 'that the new constitution would never do, the French require a despotic government'.[152] He installed a chapel in the ministry of war and was considered more sympathetic to émigrés than to his former Napoleonic comrades.[153]

On 21 January, anniversary of the execution of Louis XVI, a more imposing funeral than that of Mlle Raucourt took place on the King's orders in the traditional royal burial-place of the abbey of Saint-Denis, five kilometres north of Paris (where, on 6–8 August 1793, fifty-one royal tombs, the work of centuries, had been destroyed in three days):[154] this was the reburial of the remains of Louis XVI and Marie Antoinette, exhumed from the cemetery of the Madeleine. The soldiers of the Maison Militaire were seen for the first time in their splendid uniforms, as they escorted the hearse in freezing weather from Paris to Saint-Denis. In the Gothic abbey, hung with black cloth and lighted by thousands of tapers, the solemnity of Cherubini's requiem mass was heightened by 'the occasional clang of the gong and trumpets'. It was cold enough to remind Maréchal Ney of the retreat from Moscow. However, according to an English witness, the ceremony 'is blamed by the majority of Paris as tending to inflame past recollections'. Fontaine, former Premier Architecte de l'Empereur, who as one of the King's official architects had helped organise the ceremony, wrote in his diary that the funeral spread 'consternation in all spirits'.[155]

Tensions between Bonapartists and royalists, foreigners and Parisians; disputes over interpretations of the Charte and the revolution; reactionaries' fury over the licence unleashed in Paris, and liberals' belief that, as Benjamin Constant wrote, 'everything is leading towards full-scale counter-revolution';[156] alarm at the state of near-war between Britain, France and Austria, and Russia and Prussia, over the future of Saxony and Poland, questions which agitated even stallholders in the markets, *les forts de la halle*; and the proximity of Napoleon on Elba, as threatening to France as that of Vesuvius to Naples – all contributed, by early 1815, to a feeling of impending catastrophe almost as widespread as that which had preceded the fall of the Empire a year earlier. Paris was so insecure that the Tuileries courtyards were kept illuminated at night and the palace was guarded like a fortress in wartime.[157]

While the King remained popular, his family was, in many quarters, detested.[158] With an uncontrollable temper, the Duc de Berri often insulted officers or soldiers at the many military reviews he held.[159] Since both her uncles had lost their wives during the emigration, the Duchesse d'Angoulême, daughter of Louis XVI, was the most important woman at court. She was childless. In May 1814 at the Comédie Française Mlle Mars had celebrated her return in words that expressed the hopes of the French people that the lily, if it had not flourished on foreign soil, would flower in France. The Duchess rose and acknowledged the audience's cheers. However the lily did not flower. The Duchess bore no heir. In other cities like Warsaw, where she had lived in 1801–5, and Bordeaux, which she visited in 1815, her dignity, simplicity and charity made her beloved. In Paris, however, her red eyes, harsh crow's voice, lack of interest in clothes and pleasure, political extremism, above all what one English witness, Dr William Roots, called her 'air of despondency' and 'wretched dejection', made her unpopular.[160] Pozzo admired her force of character, but lamented her lack of intelligence and 'that unfortunate austerity which drives so many people away from her, her whom the slightest feeling of kindliness would render the idol of this nation'.[161]

The royal family never spoke in support of the Charte, while some of their courtiers spoke against it. In her journal a writer and noblewoman, Victorine de Chastenay, reflected many Parisians' fears: 'thanks to the clumsy and unintelligent courtiers around Monsieur people are convinced that he will try to destroy [the Charte] ... the priests above all are feared ... the Duc de Berry is forgotten and the Duc d'Orléans selected for a revolution like that of 1688.'[162] Police agents observed the number of carriages outside the Palais Royal and noted that some people were talking about the possibility of Orléans ascending the throne: 'the poison spreads in the most subtle manner.'[163] Other people, however, looked to Elba rather than the Palais Royal. The Duc de Rovigo prophesied on 13 February: 'We will see Bonaparte again and it will truly be their fault.'[164] On 1 March Bonaparte landed at Fréjus on the southern coast of France, with the 1,000 men of the Garde Impériale whom he had been permitted to take to his island empire.

3

War

March–December 1815

La guerre est un état de tranquillité comparée aux intrigues de cette Babylone.
Pozzo di Borgo to Nesselrode, Paris, 8 July 1815

THE CONTEST IN Paris between Bourbons and Bonapartes was expressed in symbolic as well as human form. The Bourbons took as their emblems the lily, which adorned the royal coat of arms, and in popular prints dogs, for fidelity; the heraldic symbols chosen by the Emperor in 1804, the eagle and the bee, stood for the Bonapartes. But in early 1815 another symbol was added to those representing Napoleon: the violet, the favourite flower of Queen Hortense. *Père la violette*, as some began to call Napoleon, would return in the spring when the violets flowered. Even before news of his landing at Fréjus arrived by telegraph in Paris on 5 March, violets had begun appearing in the buttonholes of 'young people of all classes' strolling in the Palais Royal and the Jardin des Tuileries.[1]

As Napoleon and his small force of imperial guards marched north in the direction of Paris, the core of his appeal, in his proclamations to the French people and army, was French resentment of the allied victory. In March 1814, Napoleon proclaimed, 'the French' had been on the verge of even greater triumphs. The allies had been in a disastrous position. Only the treason of Maréchal Marmont had thrown the French army into confusion and opened the gates of Paris. Napoleon denounced the 'shameful yoke' of the foreigners and 'the anti-national party', and the ambitions of priests, émigrés (although some of his own followers, like Flahaut and his chamberlain and later propagandist Comte Emmanuel de Las Cases, had been émigrés) and former landowners eager to recover their *biens nationaux*. Abandoning his role of dynastic autocrat, he recreated himself as a radical. All power, he urged, should come from 'the people'. He renounced all conquests since 1792 and denounced the royal government's alleged intent to re-establish feudal rights and the tithe. Capitalizing on the significance of Paris to the French imagination, he prophesied that 'the eagle with the national colours will fly from steeple to steeple until it alights on the towers of Notre Dame.'[2]

The royal government reacted by bluffing. Louis XVIII asked the ambassadors at their weekly audience in the Tuileries to inform their courts that he was in good health, but for an attack of gout, and that he was not alarmed by 'this event. I hope it will trouble neither Europe's repose nor mine.'[3] Court society rallied to the King. The numbers of women attending court were recorded by royal officials as a way of measuring loyalty to the King; in addition to the normal Sunday reception for men, on 8 March 450 women, on 9 March 578, went to his evening reception in the Tuileries (among them Madame de Staël who, having received Blacas' formal promise of repayment of her two millions, had just announced her daughter's marriage to the Duc de Broglie).[4] The long and fatiguing ceremony obliged women in full court dress to move sideways across the immense throne room, following each other at the distance of their long court trains. Curtsying first to the King – while trying to prevent their trains from causing them to overbalance – they moved on at once, hardly giving him time to say a few words. They then had to climb up and down the different staircases of the Tuileries palace, traverse ill-heated corridors and basements, and repeat the process in the reception room of each member of the royal family. The princes' apartments being smaller than the King's, women had at times to battle with their elbows to reach the Duchesse d'Angoulême. The sole benefit obtained was a few seconds in the royal presence.[5]

While the élite may have been loyal, it was soon clear that no French soldiers would fight against Napoleon I. On 7 March, outside Grenoble, a cousin of Flahaut and guest in Queen Hortense's salon, Colonel de Labédoyère, made the critical first move. Having distributed tricolour cockades hidden in a drum to his troops, and taken a bronze eagle from his pocket and embraced it before them, he became – to cries of *Vive l'Empereur!* – the first commanding officer to lead his regiment over to Napoleon.[6] The decision to maintain the Napoleonic army in 1814 was, as Napoleon later said, the 'unpardonable mistake' of the First Restoration, but for which he would never have reached Paris in twenty days without a shot being fired. On 10 March he entered Lyon in triumph, at the head of the troops sent to oppose him.[7]

Back in Paris a wealthy Cambridge Fellow John Bowes Wright wrote on 11 March: 'Paris as yet is tranquil but one cannot but see there is a troubled ferment below the smooth surface.' Even among royalists, hatred for the British was so general that there were rumours that Britain had allowed Napoleon to leave Elba in order 'to promote confusion and civil war' in France.[8] A fourteen-year-old schoolboy Emile Bary, son of a government archivist, reflected the views of the royalist bourgeoisie. He noticed that in the garden of the Tuileries fewer people were wearing lilies on their coats and that 'consternation is spread on all faces.' Using an image often invoked in 1815 by those Parisians for whom Napoleon represented not 'the people' but the army, he denounced Napoleon's followers: 'are we not now slaves of these soldiers, of these new Praetorians, these other Janissaries who sell the Empire?'[9]

Until 19 March royalist crowds thronged the garden and the courtyard of the Tuileries, often asking for arms. Much of the Paris middle class as well as the court nobility and even part of the 'people' was royalist. Crowds round the Tuileries were described by a Russian diplomat replacing Pozzo, who was attending the Congress of Vienna, as *le peuple* or *la populace* – the poor: 'the people does not leave the courtyard of the château and shows much devotion for the King.' Among them, reported an officer of the Gardes du Corps, were 'many workers and people of the lower class'. Two men who cried *Vive Bonaparte!* in the Tuileries garden were murdered by women walkers *à coups de parapluie*. At the same time, however, 'from all sides comes news of troops defecting'.[10]

Unable to rely on regular soldiers, the royal government decided to raise volunteers. In the antechambers of the Tuileries hundreds inscribed their names in registers to serve in the Gardes de la Porte, the Cent-Suisses or a new force called the Volontaires Royaux. The Restoration having introduced a new era of constitutional freedom, many liberal students from the two great faculties of the Sorbonne, the Ecoles de Droit and de Médecine, also enrolled. Cannon were placed round the palace, while the Maison Militaire camped on the Champ de Mars and in the courtyard of the Tuileries. The National Guard also appeared devoted to the King; but M. de Marsilly of the Cent-Suisses wrote in his diary: 'Can it resist, above all if it sees its homes, its commerce, its properties under threat?'[11]

Moreover, many officers on active service in the French army, and many peasants in the countryside, were Bonapartists. There were rumours, and some evidence, of a Bonapartist conspiracy in Paris. Napoleon later said that Flahaut had sent him word on Elba of the date of the arrival of Labédoyère at Grenoble:[12] Labédoyère and Flahaut had discussed, in Queen Hortense's salon, the possibility of his regiment taking 'national' colours and the eagle many weeks before he led it over to Napoleon at Grenoble. If he had not planned his actions, Labédoyère would not have had bronze eagles and tricolour cockades with him for distribution to the troops.[13] Napoleon's former Minister of Police Rovigo and other Bonapartists were also in communication with Elba; Caulaincourt later admitted that he had suggested Elba as his master's retreat, with an eye to the future.[14] In addition, what Hortense called 'a thousand different plots' revolved around Fouché.[15] The former regicide, organiser of mass murder at Lyon and Nantes in 1793–4, and Napoleon's Minister of Police from 1799 to 1809, had by 1815 emerged as the ex-Republicans' unofficial leader. The plots have never been elucidated, but may have been in favour of the Duc d'Orléans. On 11 March the former Chasseurs à Cheval of the Garde Impériale marched on Compiègne. The conspiracy ended in no more than the arrest of a few generals, but that evening guests at Madame de Souza's prophesied that 'not a shot will be fired in the defence of the Bourbons.' On 12 March Benjamin Constant noted: 'Fouché. Sébastiani. The Buonapartists are enticing me.'[16] Queen Hortense, Caulaincourt, Flahaut and Napoleon's former Directeur des Postes Antoine-Marie Comte de Lavallette already assumed that Napoleon's arrival in Paris was a certainty.[17] French political fantasies, as well as realities, had a European dimension. That March, if royalists blamed Britain for Napoleon's escape from Elba, Queen Hortense and other Bonapartists claimed to believe that he was supported by Austria – as the Emperor himself, in private conversations, also implied.[18]

In secret interviews the King's confidant Blacas and Chancellor Dambray had tried to win Fouché, and through him the ex-Republicans, for the royal government. On 15 March, after Fouché's refusal of the Ministry of Police had shown that he believed the royal government was doomed, an attempt was made to arrest leading Bonapartists in Paris. Its failure proved the feebleness of the royal government, and the ease with which Paris could defy as well as display royal power. Flahaut hid in the house of his friend Comte Alexandre de Girardin. Fouché climbed a ladder leaning against his garden wall and escaped into the garden of

Queen Hortense's house next door in the rue Cerutti, hiding thereafter with a former police agent. Caulaincourt found refuge with a cook; Lavallette in the servants' quarters of the house of Queen Hortense. She herself left her house in disguise, to avoid police spies outside, and took refuge in a fourth-floor apartment near the boulevards belonging to a trusted old black servant from Martinique called Madame Lefebvre. There, watching volontaires royaux parading through the streets shouting *Vive le roi!*, she awaited events.[19]

In Fontainebleau the concierges were preparing the palace for Napoleon's arrival; in Paris more young people could be seen wearing bouquets of violets. Soldiers muttered: 'it is the right weather for violets to grow.'[20] In the same spirit as Orléans' footman under the Empire had preserved his former royal livery, soldiers under the Restoration had kept their Napoleonic eagles and tricolour cockades. They felt no love for a King who, as they said, 'needs six of us to carry him'.[21]

A rush to leave the city revealed, and heightened, the sense of panic: Madame de Staël fled on 10 March, the Duchess of Wellington on 11 March, the Duchesse d'Orléans on 14 March, the same day that, on the King's orders, his Premier Valet de Chambre Baron Huë set out for England with the crown jewels. Lady Dalrymple Hamilton, who found there was 'not a horse to be had', wrote in her diary that day: 'all hope was at an end. Macdonald returned alone in the afternoon [from Lyon], all his troops having joined Buonaparte, very general confusion amongst the people, some calling *Vive le roi*, others *Vive la violette* the pass word of Buonaparte.' On 15 March she recorded: 'the news still as bad as possible'; on the 16th: 'I found the dislike to the English getting so great that I hired a French carriage and only went out with foreign servants.' French carriages were clumsier and heavier than the 'light and genteel' carriages of the English, which had the reputation of being the best in the world. The next day she left for Brussels.[22]

Against the advice of his right-wing ministers Blacas, Soult and Chancellor Dambray, the King sought to invoke the founding document of his reign: the Charte. On 16 March, with Monsieur, Orléans and Berri in his carriage, drawn by eight horses and surrounded by guards, he drove through steady rain to the Chambre des Députés for a *séance royale*. Most of the crowds along his route, though the Cour du Carrousel, along the *quais*, over the Pont Royal to the Chambre des Députés, shouted *Vive le roi!* The faces of the troops, however, although they had been given extra brandy rations, expressed disapproval.[23] Inside the Chamber, having taken his place on the throne with difficulty owing to an attack of gout, the King spoke in his simplest style, stressing that he represented Europe and peace:

> I returned to my fatherland; I reconciled it with all the foreign powers, who will, have no doubt about it, remain faithful to the treaties which have given us peace . . . I fear nothing for myself, but I fear for France: he who comes to reignite among us the fires of civil war also brings the scourge of foreign war.

He concluded with praise for the French people: 'Could I at nearly sixty years better terminate my career than by dying for its defence?' From every corner of the hall he was interrupted by the cheers of peers and deputies: *Vive le roi! Mourir pour le roi! Le roi à la vie et à la mort!* With tears in their eyes, all present swore loyalty to the Charte. The King called it 'our sacred standard', 'my finest title in the eyes of posterity', around which all Frenchmen should rally. Artois, who on the pretext of illness had not attended the *séance royale* promulgating the Charte on 4 June 1814, said, too late, that the King's sentiments were shared by all the royal family, kissed the King's hand and then embraced him. The royal family departed to a torrent of applause.[24]

Paris was the focus of the conflict. An attempt to establish a government elsewhere (as recurred in 1870, 1914, 1940) would be futile, according to the Duc de Feltre, who had replaced Soult as Minister of War: he had personal experience of the fiasco of the Napoleonic government's attempt to rule France from Blois in April 1814.[25] Maréchal Marmont, the famous anti-Bonapartist Joseph-Henri-Joachim Lainé, President of the Chamber of Deputies, and Chateaubriand thought the King should barricade himself in the Tuileries palace with the two Chambers, sitting on his throne with the Charte in one hand and the will of Louis XVI in the other. Protected by the National Guard and the Maison Militaire, he would overawe Bonaparte – or at least perish in a fashion worthy of his rank.[26]

However, royalist fervour among peers, deputies and Parisians was less decisive than Bonapartist fervour among the troops. On 18 March, news arrived in Paris that Marshal Ney, who had promised the King to bring back Bonaparte in an iron cage, had led his army over to Napoleon. Like many of his contemporaries, Ney oscillated between royalism and Bonapartism according to the pressures and needs of the moment. In a scene of which similar versions were played throughout Paris, General Ameil told the King of the Emperor's ecstatic reception at Lyon. 'How could you have violated your oaths and joined the usurper?' the King inquired. 'Sire, we soldiers are libertines,' Ameil replied: 'if you are our legitimate sovereign the Emperor is our mistress.' The King laughed but, to stop him spreading disaffection in Paris, ordered him confined to barracks.[27]

The army assembled south-east of Paris under Maréchal Macdonald was the next to desert: if he had not fled, his troops would have lynched him. On 19 March, despite pouring rain, there were cries of *Vive le roi!* from the crowd surrounding the Tuileries when, as every Sunday, the King appeared on the balcony after mass. However that day the King left Paris. He had no desire for martyrdom. Louis XVI's experiences as a prisoner there were not encouraging; and the desire to preserve the city from fighting may also have affected his decision.[28] His departure was not announced until the Capitaine des Gardes in waiting, the Prince de Poix, gave the password at 9 p.m. that evening, either because the decision was not reached until the last moment or for fear of arousing opposition in the crowd surrounding the palace. Ministers and foreign ambassadors were not informed until after the King's departure. He left in such haste that some of his snuffboxes and other personal possessions and papers were later found in the Tuileries.[29] In the afternoon, while the luggage was being packed, the King passed a last review of the Maison Militaire on the Champ de Mars. He then issued an order to its commander *mon cousin le Maréchal duc de Raguse* to take it and the remaining volontaires royaux 'with all the speed compatible with good order' over the Pont d'Iéna to Saint-Denis. Despite torrential rain, high winds and a sea of mud, the royal troops did not stop until they reached Beauvais, eighty kilometres north of Paris; many royal guards then decided to go home.[30]

At 9 p.m. an officer in the Gardes du Corps, Monsieur d'Arblay, who was stationed in the Tuileries, wrote to his wife the novelist Fanny Burney, whom he had married during the emigration: *Ma chère amie, tout est perdu! – je ne puis entrer en aucun détail, de grâce partez – le plutôt sera le mieux. A la vie et à la mort!*[31] National guards, gardes du corps and servants waited in silence on the staircase of the Pavillon de Flore. Suddenly at 12.30 a.m. on the morning of 20 March a door opened and the King appeared, supported by Blacas and Duras and preceded by a footman bearing torches. In a spontaneous movement the national guards and gardes du corps present fell on their knees. Some kissed the King's hands or clothes in tears, begging him not to leave. With unusual prescience, a few assured him that they would meet again in three months' time. Saying 'My children, I beg you, spare me; I need strength.

I will see you again soon. Return to your families . . . my friends, your attachment touches me', the King descended the stairs with difficulty, got into a carriage and, escorted by gardes du corps, drove off into the night.[32]

The next morning Paris appeared to be the capital of a different country. Shopkeepers calmly replaced Napoleonic for Bourbon titles and eagles for lilies on their shop signs, often simply by turning them round. On the boulevards and elsewhere there was general gloom; few people shouted Napoleonic slogans, even when urged to do so by his soldiers.[33] An Italian Parisian, the Bonapartist historian and literary critic Sismonde de Sismondi, wrote to his mother in Tuscany: 'Everyone was looking after their own affairs, little was said, people looked worried. I walked in the most populous quarters of the city, I only heard one cry of *Vive Napoléon* there, to which everyone seemed afraid to reply.' In the Jardin des Tuileries at the beginning of the afternoon some people still wore a white cockade and cried *Vive le roi!*, others wore a tricolour; by 5 p.m. the white cockade had disappeared.[34]

On the other side of the palace, however, on the Cour du Carrousel, another crowd began to cry *Vive l'Empereur!* The sight of royal courtiers and servants leaving the palace with their masters' possessions excited the crowd's anger and greed. At 2 p.m. they forced open the gates in the railings, despite the opposition of the national guards on duty, and, bent on pillage, surged into the palace. However, at the sight of smoke rising from a chimney, where a servant was burning the papers of the Grand Aumônier, the crowd, thinking the palace was on fire, ran away in panic.[35]

Later in the afternoon Napoleon's former ministers, councillors of state, maîtres d'hôtel and valets began to arrive at the Tuileries, wearing the Napoleonic liveries and uniforms which they had kept, as soldiers had kept their eagles and tricolours, since the fall of the Empire. 'Calmly and quietly they resumed their duties as if Bonaparte had made only a short journey,' wrote Alexandre de Laborde, son of one of the great bankers and developers under Louis XVI, who was on duty that day as an officer of the Paris National Guard. According to his account, several hundred officers gathered outside the palace. At 9.30 p.m., like a fantastic apparition, Napoleon arrived, his eyes half closed, a fixed smile on his face, at the exact spot where the King had said farewell to weeping national guards twenty-one hours earlier. Caulaincourt and Flahaut were with him. In April 1814 they had dissuaded Napoleon from advancing from Fontainebleau to Paris; on 20 March 1815 they had ridden halfway from Paris to Fontainebleau to escort him back to the city. The Emperor was carried up the stairs by ecstatic officers, weeping for joy and crying *Vive l'Empereur!* 'The scene had something gigantic and out of proportion with human events,' Laborde recorded.[36]

At the top of the stairs the Emperor was greeted by his ministers and ladies of his court, among them Queen Hortense, who had been cheered on her arrival at the Tuileries, and the Duchesses de Bassano and de Rovigo. They noticed that he looked more ungainly and squat than before. In the palace, too, the change of regime had brought a change of decoration. While waiting for the Emperor's arrival, officers and ladies had unpicked the Bourbon lilies sewn on the carpet in order to reveal the Bonaparte bees underneath. The following day the Emperor found time, between working with ministers and generals, to see Queen Hortense in private. He reproached her for, alone of the former imperial family, choosing to remain in France in 1814: 'Your behaviour was that of a child. When one has shared the elevation of a family, one should also share its misfortune.' She resorted to the usual tactics: tears; pleas of helplessness; a dash for the moral high ground. Forgetting her own and Flahaut's love of Paris, she claimed that she had merely wanted her sons to remain in their fatherland.[37] The Emperor forgave her, and she remained the leading lady at his court during the Hundred Days.

In the following weeks many Parisians, in particular soldiers and what Sismondi called *la très petite bourgeoisie*, gathered around the Tuileries, shouting *Vive l'Empereur!* whenever he appeared at the window. In the Palais Royal vendors cried: 'Buy tricolour cockades. They are less likely to get dirty than white ones.'[38] Part of the Théâtre Montansier in the Palais Royal (originally the marionette theatre of a younger brother of the Duc d'Orléans) had been transformed into a café, which became 'the rendez-vous of the friends of national glory'. Before the laurel-crowned bust of the Emperor, crowds sang songs in favour of Napoleon and liberty. French soldiers were going to liberate the world:

> *Napoléon, Gloire et Patrie!*
> *Ah, répétons ces mots si chers!*
> *Napoléon, Gloire et Patrie!*[39]

On 26 March Napoleon told a deputation from the Conseil Municipal that he would halt the restoration of Versailles and reside only in Paris.

The royal throne had been imposed by foreigners, he informed the Paris National Guard on 16 April; he, on the other hand, returned 'armed with all the force of the people and the army'.[40] To appeal to former revolutionaries, Fouché and Carnot, the 'organiser of victory' in 1793–4, were appointed Ministers of Police and the Interior respectively – although Carnot was made a Count. Detachments of *fédérés*, volunteers from the suburbs and the provinces, paraded through the streets of Paris singing *Ça Ira* and the Marseillaise, songs which praised liberty and the fatherland rather than the Emperor.[41]

While Napoleon courted popularity in Paris, Louis XVIII established his residence in Ghent in Flanders. He was joined there by many politicians, among them Chateaubriand, who had left Paris in his carriage four hours after the King, and Pozzo, who arrived from the Congress of Vienna. Chateaubriand became Minister of the Interior *par intérim*. Resolutely royalist, Pozzo defended the King's record on the grounds that in the First Restoration he had been dealing with all the demons of the revolution; the individual acts of his administration were irreproachable. The responsibility for Napoleon's return lay with the French army.[42]

Orléans, despite the King's orders to come to Ghent, preferred his second home, Twickenham, to which he now returned. Throughout 1815, like previous Ducs d'Orléans, he maintained a private foreign policy, corresponding with, among others, Fouché, Wellington and Alexander I, taking the opportunity to criticise the King and present himself as an alternative. Another active correspondent was Madame de Staël, from her refuge at Coppet, her château near Geneva. For her the fundamental issue was nationalism. The King was loved and his regime had been liberal; but 'the nation hates foreigners'.[43]

The behaviour of Benjamin Constant was an extreme case of the combination of mobility and lucidity typical of Parisians in this period. On 19 March, in part spurred by his love for Madame Récamier, who was a royalist, he wrote a famous article in the *Journal des débats* in which, damning Napoleon as Attila and Genghis Khan, and praising Louis XVIII for allying himself with liberty and the people, he asserted: 'I am not the man to crawl, a miserable traitor, from one seat of power to another. I am not the man to hide infamy by sophisms, or to mutter profane words with which to purchase a life of which I should feel ashamed.' On 20 March he fled west from Paris. On 28 March, after much hesitation and indecision, he returned. His acts then betrayed his words.

On 4 April, at the house of Lord Kinnaird, a Scottish Whig living in Paris, Constant dined with Fouché and made 'offers of services'. On 14 April he wrote in his diary: 'Interview with the Emperor, long conversation, he is an astonishing man. Tomorrow I will bring him a plan for a constitution. Will I finally arrive? Should I desire it?'[44] On 19 April he became a salaried councillor of state. Thereafter he frequently saw the Emperor in private audience and at *levers*: 'so here I am part of the new court.' A week later: '*Lever*. Nothing is being achieved and opinion remains bad. Dinner at Caulaincourt's. Soirée at Madame de Souza's.' On 13 May he wrote, of the Emperor, 'he understands liberty very well.' In reality Constant laughed as much as anyone when reading out the government newspaper, the *Moniteur*, to his liberal friends. It is difficult to disagree with Madame de Staël who, with the venom of a discarded lover, wrote to him on 28 May: 'money alone decides your political and private conduct.'[45] Yet could he not have written the same to her, at least in 1814–15 while she was trying, with his help, to secure two million francs from the French government so that her daughter could marry a duke? Politics was a game. Men who had been royalists even before the end of the Empire in 1814, like the deputy Flaugergues or the banker Jacques Laffitte, could be Bonapartists in 1815. Louis XVIII's Minister of War, Marshal Soult, swore to lay all the King's enemies at the foot of his throne in March, but became Major-General of the Grand Army a month later. Parisians could switch from Bonapartism to royalism and back again, or like Fouché play with both sides at the same time, depending on their changing moods and needs, and the political circumstances of the moment. Retribution was unlikely from insecure governments in need of popularity.

If Constant was one of the Emperor's councillors in internal politics, Flahaut was vital in military matters. After Napoleon's return, when asked if he thought he was dreaming, he replied: 'On the contrary, I think I have woken up.' He was despatched on a mission to Vienna with letters from the Emperor for Talleyrand and Marie Louise (there to secure her future as Duchess of Parma) but had only reached Stuttgart when, on 4 April, he was sent back to France: Europe stuck to the policy of no peace with Napoleon. On 18 April Flahaut was placed in charge of all matters of military personnel, in order to act as the Emperor's personal check on the Minister of War Marshal Davout.[46] Napoleon summoned Madame de Souza to the Tuileries, to express his satisfaction with her son's dignity and disinterestedness during the First Restoration. Throughout the Hundred Days she entertained constantly in an attempt to win friends, English as well as French, for the Emperor.[47]

Much of Paris however remained royalist, as was revealed by voting figures in the plebiscite held in May, to approve the new more radical version of the Napoleonic constitution, the *Acte Additionnel*, guaranteeing freedom of the press and the abolition of confiscation of property by the government. It had been prepared with the help of Benjamin Constant – hence its name *la benjamine* – although he himself was the first to deride it. By turning radical the Emperor had lost the élite. Only 12 per cent of electors in Paris (compared to 15 per cent in Lyon, 3 per cent in Bordeaux, 1 per cent in Marseille and 21 per cent in all France) voted in favour, a decline of almost 50 per cent compared to the plebiscite of 1804 that had legitimised the Empire.[48] In the opinion of the schoolboy Emile Bary,

> For the Emperor [were] the purchasers of national lands. Soldiers and officers. Young men who were about to enter the army. Former Jacobins. Workers. The Emperor's employees. Doctors for whom a war provides jobs and wounded to take care of . . . For the King émigrés and nobles, priests. Mothers and children who fear conscription. Prostitutes and ladies whose lovers, brothers etc are taken by the war. The King's officials. Generals tired of fighting. Shopkeepers.[49]

Bary himself, like many Parisians, idolised the absent Louis XVIII: 'Poor Louis XVIII! Such a good and such an honourable man.' Another unknown Parisian referred in a private letter to the King's 'angelic kindness', in contrast to the 'bellicose and factious people' over whom he reigned. For the Duchesse d'Abrantès, widow of one of Napoleon's favourite marshals, Junot, Napoleon had become 'the tiger'; Louis XVIII was 'always noble, always the most loyal and dignified Frenchman in his kingdom'.[50] Boniface de Castellane, a former officer of the Napoleonic army who remained loyal to Louis XVIII in the Hundred Days despite his resentment at the medals and promotions awarded to royalist officers, wrote in his diary: 'Paris is sad; there are few carriages, almost everyone being in the country. Workmen cannot find employment; everyone is hoarding their money while waiting to see what will happen.'[51] Displaying his class's hatred and contempt for the poor, he called the Emperor's review on 14 May in the courtyard of the Tuileries of 15,000 *fédérés* from the Faubourgs Saint-Antoine and Marceau, wearing working clothes and crying '*Vive l'Empereur!* Down with the nobles! Down with the priests! Down with the rich!', 'at once pitiable and laughable'.[52] In fact the Emperor put the interests of the social order before those of national defence and his own dynasty. He refused to give the *fédérés* weapons with which to defend Paris in case they used them against the rich.[53]

Not all the poor were Bonapartists. 'Why is bread dearer and meat cheaper since 20 March?' went one popular riddle. 'Because the baker has left and the butcher has returned.' According to all observers, from the English diarist Helen Maria Williams to Queen Hortense herself, women were 'unanimously royalists', and 'formed the force of the royalist party'. Lainé said that women had done much for the Restoration: 'only they can do something for us now.'[54] However, failing to realise the originality of their cause, royalists could not conceive of organised female action in Paris in 1815. Songs and clothes were their weapons. Paris was inundated with royalist songs, pamphlets and shawls printed with royalist slogans.[55] The song 'Give us back our pair of gloves' honoured Louis XVIII.* Since white flowers were suspect, women wore blue, 'the royal colour and the symbol of constancy'.[56]

Beneath Napoleon's populist façade, he remained the autocrat he had been before 1814. He tried to confiscate the property of a number of royalists and to banish thirty leagues from Paris all émigrés who had returned in 1814; members of the King's government, and his civil and military households; and volontaires royaux.[57] In fact the Emperor's officials were now sufficiently independent to choose whether or not to enforce such measures. On 1 June a ceremony called the Champ de Mai, held for the benefit of soldiers and members of the electoral colleges, to commemorate the proclamation of the *Acte Additionnel*, was the Emperor's riposte to the *séance royale* of 16 March 1815. A vast pentagonal amphitheatre of painted wood, decorated with clusters of wooden poles crowned by eagles, was erected on the largest open space in Paris, the Champ de Mars in front of the Ecole Militaire. Within the amphitheatre there was 'a plain of soldiers'. After mass the Emperor distributed new eagles to each regiment. John Cam Hobhouse, who had come over from London to observe Paris and Napoleon, 'the world's wonder', during the Hundred Days, noted with disgust, however, that many spectators 'drank brandy and gave into other plebeian amusements', and that the cries of *Vive l'Empereur!* were not very animated.

'Emperor, soldier, consul, I hold everything from the people,'

---

* Pair of gloves = *paire de gants* = *père de Gand* = father of Ghent.

Napoleon had proclaimed before distributing the eagles. In reality he was contemptuous of *la canaille de Paris*, telling his sister-in-law Queen Julie, wife of his brother Joseph, ex-King of Spain: 'they are cowards who change their sovereign as they change their shirt.'[58] Moreover, even at this public ceremony, he insisted that, like himself, his court and government officials wear elaborate ermine and velvet court costumes, cloaks and feathered bonnets. He made his Chamber of Peers hereditary, which Louis XVIII had not, and, in an act of *hauteur* indicative of his imperial pretensions, employed chamberlains rather than ministers as his messengers to the Chamber of Representatives – as, at the beginning of the revolution, Louis XVI had employed his Grand Maître des Cérémonies. Many of the representatives had served in the revolution. According to Hobhouse, they burst out in 'the most violent murmurs . . . many members rose at once; some spoke from their places, others struggled to reach the tribune. At last a member declared a chamberlain to be a very unfit channel of official correspondence between the Emperor and the representatives of the people.' The Emperor had to change his messengers.[59]

In June, as allied forces massed on the frontier, Napoleon expanded the French army, and organised the defence of Paris. About 1,000 workers, in addition to national guards, were employed strengthening fortifications and digging bastions from Montmartre to Vincennes. Sometimes, in fits of enthusiasm, they carried busts of Napoleon – easily available as they had been carved in great numbers before 1814 – decorated with violets and laurel leaves to work, and burnt white flags, Bourbon cockades and proclamations. Two hundred cannon were taken off ships and placed around Paris. However, the Emperor admitted to Fontaine, who remained an official architect through all changes of regime, that Paris could not stand a siege; Fontaine himself, although a Bonapartist, considered such efforts a waste of money.[60] On 12 June the Emperor left Paris to lead his army in a sudden attack on the allied troops assembled in the southern Netherlands under Wellington.

On 18 June Napoleon's army was defeated by British, Netherlandish, Hanoverian and Prussian soldiers under Wellington and Blücher at Waterloo. On the battlefield Pozzo, serving as Russian commissioner with Wellington, had caught his first and last glimpse of Napoleon since they had chosen to serve different masters – the French Republic and Britain – in Corsica in 1793. At 6 p.m. on 21 June the Emperor drove back into the courtyard of the Elysée palace in a humble post-carriage.

For many Frenchmen his prestige evaporated with his flight from the battlefield of Waterloo. Fontaine wrote in his diary: 'he came back to Paris like a fugitive, thinking only of his own person . . . the magic is gone. We can no longer regard him as someone extraordinary.'[61] In the opinion of Hobhouse, 'the effect of this fifth retreat from his armies . . . is an entire abandonment of him and his cause . . . Even in the army he has lost his best partisans.'[62] Napoleon's lack of solid support in the élite, and the Empire's lack of credible institutions, became evident. The Paris Bourse rose on the news of Waterloo.[63] Generals immediately began to think of Orléans, the only Bourbon prince who had appointed Napoleonic officers to his household. On 22 June Soult wrote to Napoleon: 'the name of Orléans is in the mouths of most of the generals and commanders.'[64] At a last meeting with his ministers on 22 June Napoleon again appealed to their nationalism: 'are we or are we not a nation?'[65] However, on the same day, possibly in order to forestall deposition by the Chamber of Representatives, Napoleon I abdicated in favour of his son.

The Chamber of Representatives declared itself in permanent session and obtained its own security force of national guards. La Fayette, the hero of 1789, made a famous speech claiming that three million (in reality about 1,400,000) Frenchmen had died fighting for Napoleon, from the sands of Egypt to the snows of Russia. He asked Frenchmen to rally round 'the standard of 1789, the standard of libery, equality and public order' – fraternity was forgotten. Despite protests from Bonapartists, a Commission of Government of five public figures, including Caulaincourt, was established under the presidency of Fouché, now the master of Paris, and installed itself in the supreme symbol of nineteenth-century French monarchy, the Tuileries palace. In the Chamber of Peers a few loyal Bonapartists such as the Emperor's brothers, as well as Bassano, Labédoyère and Flahaut, who had ridden with the Emperor 'knee to knee' from the battlefield of Waterloo, made speeches in favour of Napoleon II. Flahaut, who blamed Napoleon's defeat on treachery, denied that the French army had been destroyed. Moreover, 'he [Napoleon I] has abdicated, he is politically dead. Why should his son not succeed him?'[66] Fouché, however, who had corresponded with Louis XVIII and Artois in Ghent, and with Metternich and Talleyrand in Vienna, had made other plans.

Napoleon retained support in the masses. Until 25 June many poor Parisians thronged the Avenue de Marigny outside the Elysée palace to cheer and talk to him, and scramble for the coins thrown to them by his chamberlains the Comtes de Montesquiou and de Beauvau. They were easily dispersed by Fouché's police.[67] Other Parisians, to the cry of *Vive la nation! Vive la France! Vive la patrie!*, helped dig moats in front of the city walls.[68] However, on 25 June, on the Commission of Government's orders, Bonaparte moved to Malmaison, where Hortense acted as his hostess. Flahaut went on missions to Paris on his behalf, hoping to prevail on the government to provide boats to take them to America. On 30 June Bonaparte retreated to Rambouillet and thence to the west coast. On 7 July, having failed to arrange for a boat to take him to the United States, he finally gave himself up to the Royal Navy. Flahaut took up his post as commander of the ninth division of cavalry around Paris; Hortense returned to her house in the rue Cerutti.[69]

Meanwhile Wellington's armies, and Prussian forces under Marshal Blücher, were racing towards Paris. On 28 June the city was placed under a state of siege. By 29 June the allied armies were outside the walls. At the same time Louis XVIII and his court were drawing closer. If the King returned, according to a famous phrase, 'in the baggage train of the foreigners', the foreigners also returned in the King's baggage train. As Wellington often stated, he could not have reached Paris so quickly if French fortresses and towns on his route had not capitulated when summoned to do so in the King's name.[70] For the French army had been defeated at Waterloo, but not annihilated, and it still took orders from the Minister of War, Marshal Davout, in Paris.

Talleyrand, now the King's chief minister, and Metternich, the Austrian Foreign Minister, wanted the King to reside in the palace of Compiègne north of Paris, in Lyon, or any location far from foreign bayonets.[71] However Louis XVIII insisted on Paris. He had never been ashamed to present himself as Europe's candidate for the throne of France. Moreover he was alarmed by the popularity of Orléans; Pozzo di Borgo had advised the King to return to Paris before another took his place.[72] In addition he was a Parisian concerned for the city he had loved as a young prince living in the Palais du Luxembourg in the 1780s. Sir Charles Stuart, the new British ambassador, reported on 30 June that 'he flatters himself he shall save Paris from pillage.'[73] Indeed Prussian soldiers outside Paris were out of control. Captain Cavalié Mercer of the Royal Artillery was sickened by the 'gutted and disfigured' houses in villages outside Paris, and the 'ruin and havoc' created by Prussian soldiers at one château. Oriental manuscripts were found in the pond, silk curtains were hanging on bushes, while the quantity of broken glass outside created the effect of a valley of diamonds. On 2 July Prussian troops even sacked the headquarters of their own commander Marshal Blücher.[74]

Early in the morning of 30 June Parisians again heard the sound of allied cannon coming from Belleville and Montmartre, as in 1814. The next day the shops and barriers were closed. Dread of massacre, pillage, starvation returned. Peasants again streamed in from the countryside, with their cattle and carts loaded with mattresses, furniture and children.[75] The city was split between Bonapartists and royalists. According to Helen Maria Williams, the Boulevard des Italiens was divided into two sections, the Boulevards de Gand and de l'Ile d'Elbe. The former was 'brilliant with a thousand wreaths of fresh blown lilies twined round every hat while the latter is abandoned to the faction of the scarlet pink [its first appearance as a Bonapartist symbol] and the violet'.[76]

On all sides Parisians could hear the sound of drums, and troops marching to cries of *Vive l'Empereur!* A wounded officer was borne on a plank along the Boulevard des Italiens, crowded as usual, groaning 'Finish me off, my friends, finish me off – you see that I am dying. *Vive la patrie!*' However, Helen Maria Williams noticed: 'no tender tear from any female spectator – no interest but that of simple curiosity.' Fighting to the west of the city, at Nanterre, Meudon and elsewhere, was watched by Parisians through their telescopes. The battle was evenly balanced; on 2 July French forces defeated Prussians near Versailles. The army defending Paris was 60,000 strong, more than in 1814, and many soldiers were so anti-royalist that they would have preferred, so they said, the Duke of York or the Duke of Wellington as king rather than a Bourbon.[77] However, no one, either in the Commission of Government in the Tuileries, or the army command in the Place Vendôme, or the Conseil Municipal in permanent session in the Hôtel de Ville, had the will to continue fighting. On 3 July Fontaine wrote: 'resigned to submission the city awaits a master.'[78]

That day a Convention was signed by the Commission of Government and representatives of Blücher and Wellington. In accordance with its terms the French army at once began to evacuate the city and move south to the Loire.[79] Their guard posts in the city were taken over by national guards, who, in their turn, at midday on 7 July handed over their posts at the barriers of Paris to allied troops. More disappointed by the simplicity of the ceremony than the prospect of foreign occupation, Parisian spectators at the Barrière des Champs Elysées were heard to comment: 'Is this all?'[80]

Until the last moment there had been fears of tumult or massacres in the capital. But the gendarmes and the national guards, who conducted house to house searches to remove arms, maintained order as thousands of Prussian and British troops, avoiding the formal entry of 1814, moved into the city in the course of the afternoon. The streets were deserted.[81] Many Parisians, royalist and Bonapartist alike, wrote in their letters: 'France is finished.' In the salons people talked of 'the late France', or prophesied that it would be partitioned like Poland, or become an English colony.[82]

British forces controlled the right bank, Prussians the left. The military governor of the city, in charge of food supplies and security, was the Prussian General Müffling.[83] On the morning of 8 July a detachment of the Prussian army surrounded the Chamber of Representatives and refused entry to its members, thereby dissolving it.[84] The city resembled an army camp, full of the sights and sounds of war. Twenty thousand of Wellington's troops, including Foot Guards and Household Cavalry, camped in the Bois de Bologne and the Champs Elysées. Trees were cut down for firewood or to make huts for the troops. Allied monarchs and statesmen moved into the best houses in and around the city. Lord Stewart requisitioned the Hôtel de Montesquiou, Lord Cathcart the Hôtel d'Abrantès, the Emperor of Austria the *hôtel* of Maréchal Berthier on the Boulevard des Italiens, Metternich that of Duc Décrès in the Faubourg Saint-Germain, Prince Schwarzenberg that of Queen Hortense, the Tsar the Elysée palace, Lord Combermere Malmaison, Blücher Saint-Cloud – the Versailles of the nineteenth-century French monarchy. Built for the Duc d'Orléans, brother of Louis XIV, it enjoyed a superb situation set in a park on a hill overlooking Paris from the west. Walking through its great Galerie d'Apollon, where Napoleon I had accepted the Senate's offer of the French throne on 18 May 1804, now 'very elegantly and tastefully furnished' with embroidered Lyon velvet hangings, porphyry and malachite candelabra, Sèvres vases and pictures of Napoleonic victories, Blücher told Metternich that Napoleon was a madman to have left such a paradise to go to Moscow.[85]

At the same time as negotiations over the entry of allied troops, parallel negotiations for the return of the King and the formation of a new government had been conducted at Wellington's headquarters at Neuilly by the inner circle of kingmakers, Wellington, Pozzo, Fouché and Talleyrand. Wellington considered Fouché, despite his regicide past, indispensable in the King's government.[86] On 2 July Louis XVIII had arrived at Arnouville, fifteen miles north of Paris. Thousands of Parisians streamed out to greet him, 'laughing, chatting and even singing'. Since they had not seen any fighting, the King's gardes du corps, 'radiant with joy' in their blue and silver uniforms, looked smarter than the British soldiers camped nearby.[87] On 5 July the King moved to the abbey of Saint-Denis, where Louis XVI and Marie Antoinette had been buried six months earlier. Late on 7 July Fouché was admitted to an audience with Louis XVIII to kiss hands on his appointment as the King's Minister of Police – the post for which he had been intriguing for the last eighteen months. Chateaubriand, an eye-witness, recorded the scene in one of the most celebrated passages of French prose:

> Suddenly a door is opened: vice leaning on the arm of crime silently enters, M. de Talleyrand walking supported by M. Fouché: the infernal vision passes slowly before me, enters the King's study and disappears. Fouché had come to swear allegiance and fidelity to his lord; the loyal regicide on his knees put the hands which condemned Louis XVI's head to fall between the hands of the brother of the martyr king; the apostate bishop stood guarantee for the oath.

Like most contemporary French memoirs, Chateaubriand's belong to literature rather than history: they are the best novel he ever wrote. Despite his righteous rhetoric, Chateaubriand was at the time a supporter of Talleyrand. Nor, a few weeks later, did he refuse an invitation to dine with 'crime' himself in the house of a former mistress, Madame de Custine. Even though her husband had been guillotined, Madame de Custine was one of many nobles in the Faubourg Saint-Germain who considered Fouché the saviour of King and country, for having helped to organise the peaceful transition from the Empire to the Restoration.[88] The pressures of the moment were more important than memories of the past. On 2 August Fouché would marry a beautiful if impoverished noblewoman, Gabrielle-Ernestine de Castellane-Majastres – one of the many unions across barriers of class and allegiance which took place in Paris at this period. In accordance with French custom, in order to connect the royal family with the families of their servants, the King signed the marriage contract.

The question of the French flag was also debated at Saint-Denis. In 1814 most national guards had wanted to retain the tricolour; in 1815 this sentiment was even stronger. On 6 July the *chefs de légion* of the National Guard declared that they would keep the 'national colours' 'for ever'. At the barriers a mob cried *A la lanterne!* to royalists returning from Saint-Denis wearing the white cockade. There were also shouts of *Pas de Bourbons! Vive la représentation nationale! Vive la liberté et le pain blanc!*[89] However, Paris was not the sole motor of events in France. In March 1814 Bordeaux' proclamation of Louis XVIII had strengthened royalism in Paris; in July 1815, in another surge of provincial royalism, most other French cities, from Lille to Marseille, and most villages around Paris, had already accepted the King's authority and the white flag. This made it almost impossible for the King, even if he had so desired, to retain the 'national colours' in Paris. Moreover, as a sign of the growing importance of the military factor in French politics, the King's guards, perhaps even his family, threatened to return to Ghent if he adopted the tricolour.[90] The white flag, with three golden fleurs-de-lys in the centre, remained the French flag.

At 3 p.m. on 8 July, only a few hours after Prussian troops had occupied the Chamber of Representatives and half an hour after the National Guard had discarded the tricolour, the King made his entry into Paris in a closed carriage, escorted by gardes du corps, cent-suisses, national guards both of Paris and the northern departments, and volontaires royaux. The Prefect of the Seine the Comte de Chabrol greeted him at the Barrière de Saint-Denis with a short speech. 'A hundred days have passed since the fatal moment when Your Majesty left his capital,' he began, coining the phrase 'a hundred days', which thenceforth described this period. The King replied:

> I only left Paris with the most poignant sorrow and an equal emotion. Accounts of the fidelity of my good city of Paris have reached me. I return there with tenderness; I had foretold the evils with which it was threatened; I desire to prevent and repair them.[91]

He then drove down the rue Saint-Denis along the boulevards to the Tuileries. Accounts of his reception differ, but he himself considered it finer than that of 3 May 1814. The Marquis de Clermont-Tonnerre, a former Napoleonic officer who had become a fervent royalist and rode in the King's escort, wrote to his wife:

> I have witnessed the finest and most touching reception of which history can boast. Nothing is comparable to the joy, the intoxication, the emotion which could be seen on all faces; the crowd along the entire length of the boulevards surpassed any that I ever saw in other pompous [i.e. Napoleonic] ceremonies.[92]

Helen Maria Williams thought 'the very windows spoke' – they were crowded with women dressed in white and 'white handkerchiefs floated from thousands of fair hands'. Both accounts, with their emphasis on 'faces' and 'hands', suggest that there was little cheering. According to an English officer, Captain George Bowles, '*Vive le roi* was not very enthusiastically repeated by the people but no dissatisfaction was in any way manifested . . . The bugles are now playing the downfall of Paris' – an Austrian march composed to celebrate the allied victory.[93]

That evening the pro-allied and pro-Bourbon mood of April 1814 was again evident, mainly for the same reason: to propitiate the enemy, and the new government, and to avert disaster from Paris. The King appeared on the balcony of the Tuileries, gestured to the thousands in the courtyard for silence and made a short speech of which the only recorded words were 'my friends'; some national guards then fell to their knees and kissed his hands.[94] Often wiping tears from his eyes, 'in a state of great emotion and exultation at the reception he had met with from his subjects', he yielded to the cheers of the crowd below and descended into the garden. Accompanied only by a few national guards, he endured a *bain de foule*, as women sang, danced for joy or knelt at his feet. Later in the evening, according to Lord Castlereagh,

> during the long audience to which we were admitted, it was almost impossible to converse, so loud were the shouts of the people in the Tuileries garden, which were full of people, though it was then dark . . . Candles were then brought which enabled the people to see the King, with the Duke by his side. They ran from all parts of the garden, and formed a solid mass, of an immense extent, rending the air with acclamations. The town is very generally illuminated.[95]

French nationalism was clearly very flexible if, three weeks after Waterloo, Parisians could cheer the Duke of Wellington. For the next few weeks, possibly paid by the government or royalist organisations, groups of people danced for joy every evening below the windows of the Tuileries, singing *Rendez-nous notre paire de gants*. Spontaneous popular demonstrations were then considered so disagreeable, as evidence of political activity by the people, that some royalists were shocked.[96]

At the same time, in by now customary fashion, footmen changed their livery from green to blue, and stonemasons converted Ns into Hs (for Henri IV); Napoleonic names were painted over with royalist replacements. The former could often be seen through the new coat of paint, or by the protrusion of the suffix *-ial* (*impérial* being a longer word than *royal*).[97]

The allied monarchs and the King passed July in negotiations, reviews and returning each other's visits. On 12 July at a banquet in the Tuileries, Louis XVIII himself poured his royal guests' wine; some Parisians called him *le regretté*, others *l'impossible*, *le préfet de l'Angleterre* or, from his taste for that delicacy, *Louis des huîtres*. The Emperor of Austria told the Crown Prince of Bavaria that he was *l'inévitable*.[98] 'Thinking people', according to Hobhouse, predicted that he would not last six months.[99] For the allied occupation was much harsher than in 1814. For a time Prussian troops bivouacked in the courtyard of the Tuileries. Prussian cannon were trained on the palace; Prussian soldiers hung their clothes out to dry on the Tuileries railings.[100] Prussian forces' demands for money and lodgings, their seizure of government-owned tobacco and salt, shocked the Duke of Wellington. On 15 July only the personal intervention of the Tsar and the King, who threatened to go and sit on the bridge himself, prevented Blücher blowing up the Pont d'Iéna, named after the French victory over the Prussians in 1806. It was hastily renamed the Pont des Invalides.[101] Since the British army, in contrast, generally paid for what it took, Parisians fought to have British soldiers billeted on them.[102]

The King also preferred the British army. On 14 July, as British officers were retiring from their formal presentation to Louis XVIII in the Tuileries, one of the company, General Augustus Frazer, commander of the Royal Horse Artillery, recorded that the King paid tribute to their troops 'in a very slow, dignified, audible voice':

> 'Gentlemen, I am very happy to see you here. I have wished to see you all together, to felicitate you on your valour and to thank you for your humanity to my poor subjects. Many fathers and many children thank you for your humanity.' At concluding the address His Majesty's voice faltered a little and he was visibly affected: so were all that heard him. I never witnessed a more interesting scene.[103]

Since the allied occupation prevented the usual seasonal labourers from Burgundy from reaching the farms around Paris in order to reap the harvest, British soldiers were authorised to help bring it in, making their own bargains with the farmers.[104]

Meanwhile the occupation was tightening its grip. Soon there were over one million allied troops in France. There were more brawls and duels, often with fatal casualties, between the French and the hated

Prussians than with any other occupying army. These clashes took place, often on the slightest pretext, in the Palais Royal, the Ile de la Cité, along the *quais* lining the Seine. On 18 August the Prussian military governor of Paris issued orders to fire on *attroupements* and anyone who insulted his forces.[105] The occupation of 1814 had cost the Paris municipality according to its own remarkable statistical service, only 5,100,000 francs; that of 1815 cost 51,200,000.[106]

The horror of the occupation began to erode the popularity of the King, who was seen to be losing his effectiveness as a propitiator. On 16 July after attending Sunday mass in the Tuileries, Robert Peel wrote:

> The garden of the Tuileries was absolutely full of people and nothing can exceed or describe the enthusiasm of the women and children in favour of the King. If shouts – and applause and *Vive le roi* – and white handkerchiefs could contribute to his strength – his throne would be on solid foundations, but I do not see that men – fighting men – partake so much of the general joy.

Gardes du corps, the shock troops of royalism, had already sacked the Bonapartist Café Montansier (renamed Café de la Paix), threatened Queen Hortense in the rue Cerutti, and started fights in the Jardin Turc and the Café de la Gaieté. On 17 July on the boulevards some gardes du corps attacked people wearing red pinks, which had replaced violets, temporarily proscribed, as the chosen sign of the Bonapartists. A crowd of two or three thousand gathered and drove them off with cries of *A bas les gardes du corps!* Finally the ultimate arbiters of Paris, the national guards, restored order: thenceforth gardes du corps were forbidden to appear on the boulevards in uniform, while the National Guard had orders to arrest anyone who refused to remove their pinks. According to John Cam Hobhouse, 'the hyacinth of the duke of Orleans is equally proscribed' – a perplexing mention of its political role (in July hyacinths are not in flower). A large hog was paraded through the Faubourg Saint-Marceau with flowers around its ears and tail and forced to stop at wine houses and drink the health of *gros papa*: the King. By late July, the King could hear for himself, on his daily drives through Paris, that cheers were 'not universal'.[107] On 1 August Wellington gave a ball. There were 400 men present, including Metternich, Pozzo, Fouché, Talleyrand and the King of Prussia, but only forty women. A niece of Talleyrand, Comtesse Juste de Noailles, when asked how she was feeling, replied, 'As well as one can, after having danced on the tomb of one's country.'[108]

*

One of the first tasks of the royal government had been to draw up a list of proscribed Bonapartists. On 17 July Queen Hortense had left Paris for Switzerland.[109] Probably protected by Talleyrand, Flahaut withdrew to the Lyon area. His mother, who had had Prussians billeted on her, had been 'half crazed' by the defeat of Napoleon.[110] She protested that she had never been a Bonapartist: 'alas I have been only a Flahautiste' – as if the two had not been synonymous. Carnot left for Prussia, after an exchange with Fouché which Castlereagh reported back with glee to Lord Liverpool. 'Traitor, where do you want me to go?' Carnot had asked. 'Wherever you wish, imbecile,' had been Fouché's reply.[111]

The Emperor's Premier Peintre David, and many other Bonapartists, moved to a traditional refuge for discontented Frenchmen, Brussels, which became, for the next five years, the capital of the Napoleonic emigration. Benjamin Constant, who had the horses of an entire English commissariat stabled in his house, had been going round Paris looking like someone condemned to death, as much because of his unrequited passion for Madame Récamier as for Napoleon's defeat. He submitted a written justification of his conduct to the King which, as he said, 'almost convinced myself'. He was removed from the list of proscribed Bonapartists on the personal intervention of the King and his new favourite Elie Decazes, the thirty-year-old Prefect of Police of Paris. Like Lainé, Dessolles, Marshals Macdonald and Gouvion Saint-Cyr and many others, Decazes was a liberal non-noble whose royalism had been reinforced, rather than weakened, by the Hundred Days. Constant felt grateful but wrote in his diary on 3 August: 'Where to go? Visit to Decazes. No action possible. The country lost. *Sauve qui peut.*'[112]

On 19 August, crying *Vive le roi!*, Labédoyère, condemned for leading his regiment over to Napoleon in March, was shot on the Plaine de Grenelle, west of the Champ de Mars. His wife had refused to see him during the Hundred Days on account of his Bonapartism. But she had thrown herself at Louis XVIII's feet on his way to mass, begging for her husband's pardon. The King had replied that his heart was sorry that he could not grant this request, but the safety of the throne and the interest of his people demanded an example.[113] To the Duchesse de Duras, who had expressed pity for Labédoyère, Chateaubriand wrote that no one had shown pity for royalists, including one of his cousins, who had been shot as a spy during the Empire on the same plain. Moreover he felt no sympathy for an officer guilty of the most abominable crime, whose actions had helped bring 600,000 foreigners into France.[114]

Labédoyère was buried in the cemetery of Père Lachaise, a former Jesuit property and garden (hence its name – Louis XIV's Jesuit confessor Père Lachaise had lived there), on a hill-slope beyond the Barrière de Vincennes, with a striking view of Paris from the east. Since 1804 it had been transformed into a cemetery where wealthy Parisians were buried in a variety of urns, obelisks, pyramids, temples, funerary mansions and Gothic chapels, arranged in winding avenues among cypresses, weeping willows, orange trees, lilacs and roses.[115] Poorer Parisians had anonymous graves. The cemetery received on average about 10,000 corpses a year, many of whose funerals were paid for by the city of Paris itself.[116]

After 1815 it became a place of pilgrimage for Bonapartists. The inscription on Labédoyère's simple stone memorial – *Ici repose Charles Angélique François Huguet Comte de la Bédoyère. Enlevé à tout ce qui lui était cher le 19 août 1815* – is a masterpiece of tact. When Madame de Labédoyère went to pray there, she found flowers left with messages like *Honneur aux braves! Les Français reconnaissants*.[117] For while anti-Napoleonic caricatures 'of the most cutting and often of the most indecent description' were on sale in Paris (such as *Entrée triomphante de Buonaparte dans son nouveau royaume*, showing him riding a cat being greeted by fleeing rats on his arrival in St Helena), many Parisians continued to excuse Napoleon. His only fault, according to an often used phrase, was that 'he had too much ambition'.[118] For forty years after the humiliation of Waterloo, for many Frenchmen, dynasties and political systems were less important than their desire for revenge. Many prints on sale in Paris bore the legend, based on General Cambronne's reply to a call for surrender at Waterloo: *La garde meurt mais ne se rend pas* ('the guard dies but does not surrender'), or *Aux braves morts le 18 juin 1815*.[119] The young liberal poet Casimir Delavigne expressed Parisians' disgust at the occupation:

Faut-il, muets témoins, dévorer tant d'outrages?[120]

The Palais Royal was both the meeting-place and the epicentre of the embittered city. British and Prussian troops stood guard outside with loaded cannon and piled muskets. In *Paul's Letters to his Kinsfolk*, the most popular novelist in Europe, Walter Scott, called it 'this central pit of Acheron . . . this focus of vice and treason'.[121] A famous London editor John Scott wrote, in his book on Paris in 1815, the numerous passages leading into it were choked with a living stream of all nations, ages, ranks, costumes and physiognomies, driven as if by some irresistible impulse towards its fatal vortex . . . The Prussians seemed to live in it . . . the fashionable lounge and bold stare of Bond Street were to be recognised in the carriage of the young men of our hussar regiments.

Soldiers strolling through its arcades included fair-haired Prussians, 'fine boys' neatly dressed in blue, brown or green coats with dark brown or dark green trousers (many wore stays and used padding in their jackets to swell out their chests). Austrians wore white coats and tight light blue pantaloons 'often heavily embroidered'. In addition there were tight-waisted and black-helmeted officers of the Russian Imperial Guard 'carrying themselves with a swagger'; Highlanders with bagpipes, bonnets and 'swinging kilts'. Nassau troops in 'bottle green faced with orange' were, according to Haddy James, Assistant Surgeon to the First Life Guards whom he had accompanied to Paris, 'the finest-looking body of men in the Duke of Wellington's Army'.[122]

Already, as is clear from the popularity of the Palais Royal, some Parisians had found that the occupation was good for business. On allied pay days much of the money extracted by the occupying forces returned to Parisian pockets: the Bonapartist writer Béranger wrote a poem attacking shopkeepers' fondness for *nos amis les ennemis*.[123] In the clubs of the Palais Royal, Blücher himself could be seen gambling on August evenings: 'He was in a plain blue frock[-coat], and seemed quite intent on the game. He hardly ever looked up, or spoke a word, but put in money, or took it out, as he lost,' wrote an English general, Sir John Malcolm.[124] The parties of Bonapartist officers who had frequented Véry Frères in late June had been replaced, the night of the King's return, by Prussian, English and royalist officers. The next night Wellington invited all his general officers to dine there to meet Blücher.[125] Another night Wellington, Sir Charles Stuart, Metternich and his secretary Gentz, had dinner at Véry Frères. The female guests were Mlle Mars, although she had appeared on stage during the Hundred Days smothered in violets, and Lady Caroline Lamb, who had descended on Paris, according to her cousin Lady Granville, 'in a purple riding habit . . . ready primed for an attack upon the duke of Wellington and I have no doubt but that she will to a certain extent succeed as no dose of flattery is too strong for him to swallow or her to administer'.[126] In the Café Beauvilliers Etonians present in Paris gave a dinner to their former headmaster Dr Keate, who ate as if he had never eaten before. After listening to their rendering of *Floreat Etona*, Dr Keate said that, if he had one regret, it was that he had not flogged them more.[127]

The occupation provided animation as well as profit for Paris. Crowds of Parisians assembled in the evening to enjoy the celebrated band of the Emperor of Austria playing outside his residence on the Boulevard des Capucines, and what a police report called 'the foreign but harmonious and expressive music' of Prussian bands in the Jardin du Luxembourg.[128] At night British army camps in the Bois de Boulogne and the Champs Elysées appeared to be cities of light and music, for surrounding the white tents of the soldiers, erected among the trees, were temporary restaurants, dance halls, wine and brandy shops, cafés and *guinguettes* established by enterprising Parisians. 'Our soldiers seem to agree very well with the inhabitants,' wrote a visiting Englishman Major Frye.[129] An aged beauty called the Marquise de Coigny (once known as the Queen of Paris – Marie Antoinette was Queen of Versailles) said of the British in the Bois: 'it is so like a *fête* that it is a pity that it is a conquest.'[130]

While Parisians were adapting to the occupation, one last blow to their city was organised from London. On 15 July the Prince Regent proposed the removal of the 'plundered' pictures and sculptures from the Louvre. He and his Prime Minister Lord Liverpool intended both to weaken 'the military spirit and vanity of the nation', and to prevent Paris being 'in future the centre of the arts'.[131] To this end, although there was no direct benefit to Britain, the British government paid the travel expenses from Rome of Canova, whose colossal naked statue of *Napoleon as Mars the Peace-Maker* was, that summer, removed from the Louvre stores and presented by Louis XVIII to Wellington himself. (It now stands in the stairwell in Apsley House in London. Other statues of Napoleon were given at this time to the King of Prussia and Marshal Blücher.) Canova, who had reluctantly visited Paris from Rome in 1810, in order to sculpt the *Empress Marie Louise as Concord*, returned in a new capacity, as Director of the Vatican Museums, to remove works of art for the Pope from what he called 'this great cavern of stolen goods'.[132]

The operation was supported by a memorial from thirty-nine foreign artists working in Rome, also organised by the British government, which attacked Paris in terms anticipating the dislike for the capital which was to become, for some foreigners and many Frenchmen, a passion. The artists included Germans, Belgians, Dutch, Danish, Spanish, Russians, the Prussian sculptor Wilhelm Schadow, the English architect C.R. Cockerell, the Danish neoclassical sculptor Bertel Thorvaldsen. For them Paris had not yet supplanted Rome as 'capital of the arts for all peoples'. Paris, the memorial continued, with its 'spirit of system and fashion', its 'false and petty manner', was bad for artists. 'It is in Rome that a religious repose and a truly patriarchal simplicity of life, by saving the artist from the distraction, the tumult of Paris, assure him a pure and tranquil enjoyment of the arts.'[133]

The loss of so many treasures from the Louvre infuriated some Parisians more than the French defeat at Waterloo. Throughout August and September the museum was visited by Parisians come to bid farewell to favourite paintings and sculptures. At the same time there were so many foreign soldiers that the long gallery 'exhibits a moving picture of all the nations of Europe in their military dresses'. At moments the Louvre resembled Bond Street: 'the ladies sit on the benches which are placed opposite the chief pictures and look sideways at the gentlemen: the gentlemen walk up and down in long uncivil rows, and look full at the ladies.' From 23 August the Dutch pictures were the first to go, removed on the orders of the Duke of Wellington, in his capacity as commander-in-chief of the Netherlands army.[134] Soon Prussian soldiers, then those of Austria and other German states began to remove pictures. Jacob Grimm – author, with his brother, of the renowned collection of fairy tales and formerly librarian to Jerome-Bonaparte, King of Westphalia – came to Paris as chargé d'affaires of the Elector of Hesse, to organise the return of four crates of pictures to Kassel. The Louvre began to show 'blanks on the walls'.[135]

The French authorities, from the King down, felt a mixture of resentment and indignation. There was no justification for restitution, so they believed: in theory the allies had made war on Napoleon not France, certainly not on Louis XVIII, whose property the works of art had been recognised to be in 1814.[136] One pamphlet published in September by a bookseller in the Palais Royal expressed the reverence of Parisians for their museum:

> But what a loss for the arts! Collected at the same point in the most magnificent palace of the Universe, these pictures, these vases, these statues, these bas-reliefs provided a unique assembly of the talents of all ages and all civilised peoples. Neighbouring nations could admire and study these immortal masterpieces easily and without effort since France by its fortunate position is placed almost at the centre of Europe.

They were better there than under the 'eternal fog' of England.[137] At a large dinner given by Talleyrand on 19 September there were 'the most stormy scenes' between him and Wellington.[138] So great was French fury at the sacrilege being committed in the Louvre that Wellington took the precaution of distributing soldiers of the Rifle Brigade, two by two, along the staircases and the length of the great gallery. Their long rifles and dark green uniforms formed, according to John Scott, 'a marked contrast to the tranquil dignity of the Raphaels and Titians on the walls'.[139] For a time, to prevent disturbances, Frenchmen were forbidden to enter the Louvre. As Scott recorded: 'Parisians stood in crowds around the door looking wistfully within it, as it occasionally opened to admit Germans, English, Russians etc ... Every Frenchman looked like a walking volcano ready to spit forth fire.' As the packages of works of art came out, the crowds gave vent 'to torrents of *pestes*, *diables*, *sacrés* and other worse interjections'.[140]

On 29 September came the cruellest blow. Parisian workers having refused the task, Austrian soldiers began to remove the four bronze horses of St Mark from the top of the Arc de Triomphe du Carrousel. The King was outraged at what he considered an indignity committed against himself in front of his own palace. That night gardes du corps drove the Austrians away.[141] The next day Austrian soldiers returned in overwhelming numbers, surrounded the arch and began to remove the horses, watched at a distance by immense crowds of Frenchmen 'grinning with rage and muttering curses'. The windows of the gallery of the Louvre overlooking the Cour du Carrousel were crowded with spectators. When the first horse appeared suspended in the air, according to an English eye-witness Henry Milton, the English in the gallery continued to stare. Most French, however, 'drew back from the windows or quitted the gallery unable to suppress or disguise their feelings ... In a short time the three horses were removed and the dismantled arch has ever since been surrounded by the populace in sorrowful and astonished groups.'[142] In the streets of Paris, people stood in doorways to watch the horses go by, lying on their sides in separate carriages, escorted by drum-beating foreign troops.[143] On 1 October Marshal Schwarzenberg, who had organised the operation, wrote: 'I have now had the inexpressible pleasure of turning my back on this city and for that let God be praised.'[144]

Paris vented its spleen not on Schwarzenberg but on Wellington. From the former Hôtel Grimod de la Reynière on the Champs Elysées, his residence as commander-in-chief of the allied army of occupation, he exercised a powerful influence on the royal government.[145] On 1 October he went to the Opéra Italien to hear Madame Catalani's debut in *Sémiramis* by Charles-Simon Catel. Apparently by mistake, he was shown to the large royal box to the left of the stage, instead of to his normal seat behind a grille in a smaller and more discreet royal box. The sight of Wellington and his ADC Frederick Lamb in the King's place outraged both the propriety and the patriotism of the audience. There were cries of 'Down with the English! Let them be shown out, *les insolents!* Show them the door!' The noise was so great that the opera had to be stopped. More intimidated by a Paris audience than by a French army, the Duke retreated in haste. Even court society was exasperated. At one of the evening receptions of the Duchesse de Duras, wife of the Premier Gentilhomme in waiting, as Wellington was looking for his hat on his way out, her fifteen-year-old daughter Félicie remarked, assuming that he would remove all the visitors' hats as he had removed the treasures of the Louvre: 'Do not trouble yourself, M. le Duc. Here as in the rest of Paris there is nothing left to take.'[146]

In reality, as Schwarzenberg knew since he had had to leave Veronese's *Marriage at Cana* in Paris – it was too difficult to move – many foreign pictures remained in place, while others were sent by the Louvre to provincial museums. Almost half of the 506 pictures removed from Italy after 1796, for example, still hang in French museums.[147] As the King said after a tour of the Louvre in 1816: *Allons, nous sommes encore riches!* Moreover in the following years the Restoration government, determined to compete with its predecessor, organised the purchase for the Louvre of such treasures as the Venus de Milo, seized by a French diplomat from the island of Melos in 1820, and a collection of Egyptian antiquities acquired in 1826–8.

The Talleyrand–Fouché ministry lost office at the same time as the Louvre lost its works of art. As master of the largest army occupying France, Alexander I remained a dominating figure in French politics, as in 1814, but this year he was a changed man. In June 1815, under the influence of a Baltic baroness called Julie de Krüdener, this waltzing womaniser had been reborn as a mystical Christian. A novelist who spoke perfect French and, like many Europeans, regarded France as 'my real fatherland', Madame de Krüdener had been reconverted to Christianity by her horror at the slaughter and suffering she witnessed during the Napoleonic wars.[148] From June 1815 she convinced Alexander I – *notre Ange* – that he was the second Abraham, the elect of the Lord, the hope of the Peoples, destined to found the Kingdom of Christ on earth. In August and September 1815 her simple salon in a hired apartment at 35 rue du Faubourg Saint-Honoré, not far from the Tsar's residence at the Elysée, with nothing to sit on except a few straw chairs, became one of the power centres of Paris.[149] Between visions, prayers, readings from the Bible and discussions on the immortality of the soul, she received a stream of Parisians who hoped to persuade her to speak to the Tsar on their behalf: politicians in need of a job, like Bergasse, Fiévée, Roux Laborie; Mlle Cochelet, a lady-in-waiting of Queen Hortense; Madame Récamier, now a devout Catholic; Madame de Labédoyère, trying to save her husband; the Duchesse de Duras.[150]

One visitor was Benjamin Constant. Madame de Krüdener persuaded him not to commit suicide over Madame Récamier, promising to create a 'bond of soul' between them. Constant wrote on 6 September: 'her conversation did me good, I would like to place myself totally under her control.' Like many Frenchmen in 1815, he felt 'a sudden need of religion'; he even wrote a prayer – although he also admitted: 'those people go too far, talking of paradise as if it was their bedroom.'[151] Another visitor was Chateaubriand. In the elections held that August for the Chamber of Deputies the Talleyrand ministry had tried to avoid 'pure' royalists being elected as much as, if not more than, Jacobins.[152] However outside Paris, as Chateaubriand, who was presiding over the electoral college of Orléans, informed the Duchesse de Duras, a wave of royalism was sweeping the country.[153] Ultra-royalists won an overwhelming majority in the elections, and Chateaubriand himself, abandoning his previous moderation, had become one of the most ardent of them. He wrote to Madame de Krüdener:

> France will finally be represented by Christians and by that ancient breed of Frenchmen who enjoyed the esteem of all Europe . . . What glory for the magnanimous prince whom you certainly do not admire more than I do if . . . after having dethroned our oppressor he also dethrones our revolution.

On his return to Paris, Chateaubriand paid court to the Tsar in her apartment on 15 September. He counselled both continued allied occupation of France and his own appointment as Ministre des Cultes (the ministry of public instruction, which he was offered that month, he considered beneath him).[154] The Talleyrand–Fouché ministry was about to fall. That day Louis XVIII, influenced by the refusal of the Duchesse d'Angoulême to receive one of the men who had voted for her father's death, dismissed Fouché.

Talleyrand was also doomed. The Tsar's role in his fall is suggested by the following newspaper account of the events of 22 September at the Tuileries: 'The Emperor of Russia stayed a very long time with the King; he went to see Mme la duchesse d'Angoulême. The visit lasted very long.' The King, so regular in his habits, delayed the hour of his lunch by half an hour. At 3.30 Talleyrand could be seen limping down the staircase from the King's apartment. On 24 September, to Talleyrand's surprise, the King accepted his offer of resignation. In compensation he received the great court office of Grand Chamberlain. That was the end of his political career – though not of his political ambitions – for the following fifteen years. On 28 September the Tsar left Paris.

The incoming ministry had what Castlereagh called 'a strong Russian tinge'.[155] Louis XVIII had ordered the new Président du Conseil, the Duc de Richelieu, a descendant of the Cardinal's brother, to take the position both in his own name and in the Tsar's.[156] In Talleyrand's famous phrase he was 'the man in France who knows most about the Crimea'. For he was an émigré who had returned to France only in 1814, having spent the previous twenty-four years in Russian service. Yet in 1815 his years in Russia strengthened his usefulness to France: they had won him not only the confidence of the Tsar but also, as governor of Southern Russia in 1802–14, a reputation as an honest statesman. Like many other members of the European élite, he changed service, as a modern football player changes team, without loss of reputation or nationality. Even the ultra-Bonapartist Madame de Souza called him 'an object of hope to everyone'.[157] Service abroad contributed to reputation in France.

One of the first acts of the new Richelieu ministry was also the principal reason for its selection: the signature of a peace treaty. During the Hundred Days it had been alleged by the Napoleonic government that the foreign powers wanted to efface France from the map of Europe; and indeed some in the Prussian camp wanted to annex the two German-speaking provinces of Alsace and Lorraine.[158] In reality, since Richelieu was more trusted by foreign powers than Talleyrand, he obtained relatively good terms for France. The second Treaty of Paris of 20 November 1815 deprived France of the additional territory kept in 1814, and imposed an indemnity of 700 million francs and an army of occupation, subsidised by France, for seven years.[159] Concern for the stability of Europe, however, deterred allied statesmen from treating France with the same harshness with which Napoleon I had treated his defeated enemies. In comparison, the main losers in the territorial rearrangements of 1814–15, Napoleon's allies Denmark and Saxony, each forfeited a considerably greater proportion of their territory.

In 1815 a sense of European union was apparent both on the streets of Paris and in the minds of some of its inhabitants. The Emperors of Austria and Russia and the King of Prussia often wore the uniforms of each other's army, and were guarded in rotation by each other's troops, to show both to French troops and their own what Walter Scott called 'the close and intimate union of the sovereigns in the common cause of Europe'.[160] At one review, the Emperor of Austria and the King of Prussia, wearing the uniform of the regiment of the Russian Imperial Guard of which each had been made Colonel, led it past the Emperor of Russia and the Duke of Wellington.[161]

In addition to the French government, there was a second, in some ways more powerful, certainly more European, government in Paris. A conference of allied ministers and generals – Wellington, Castlereagh, Hardenberg, Humboldt, Razumovsky, Nesselrode, Metternich and Schwarzenberg – met daily at the British embassy to regulate details of the occupation.[162] There were even attempts to give institutional form to Europe. At the instigation of the Tsar the four great powers signed a Holy Alliance, to which France adhered on 19 November 1815. Its inspirer, Madame de Krüdener, considered it 'the Declaration of the Rights of God'. Castlereagh, however, called it a 'piece of sublime mysticism and nonsense'. Few except the Tsar believed in it, and it soon sank without trace.[163]

The Quadruple Alliance between Russia, Austria, Prussia and Britain, signed on 20 November 1815, the same day as the Treaty of Paris, was more serious. The four powers promised 'to renew their meetings at fixed periods . . . for the purpose of consulting upon their common interests' and upon measures 'for the maintenance of the peace of Europe'. Individual allied statesmen were enthusiastic. The most European of British foreign secretaries, Lord Castlereagh, wanted 'free intercourse between the Ministers of the Great Powers *as a body*'; and to give what he called 'the European Commonwealth' 'the efficiency and almost the simplicity of a single state'. Richelieu could suggest to Metternich that they act not as ministers of two different powers but as 'two honest and well-intentioned Europeans who discuss together the ways of preventing our poor Europe from returning to chaos'.[164] The Tsar and Pozzo di Borgo called Europe and 'the

99

European association' 'a general alliance for the happiness of all'.[165] Pozzo even felt, at times, that 'the union of Europe is a truth which is beginning to establish here [in Paris] all its empire.'[166] Some writers also shared a European outlook. The political analyst C.L. Le Sur considered that 'the European association' should function as 'one vast machine'.[167] Victor Cousin, then famous as a liberal philosopher, wrote that 'civilised Europe today forms no more than one family.'[168] From St Helena Napoleon himself, reflecting the mood of the period, presented himself as a proto-European; under his rule Europe could have been one country, with one supreme law court, one currency, one people.

However, perhaps because allied statesmen felt sufficiently united by their recent struggle against Napoleon, and because none could think of surrendering control of their armies, the 'European association' developed no institutions. Saint-Simon's dream of European Chambers of Peers and Deputies did not materialise. European statesmen did not adopt Pozzo's suggestions for 'a central and permanent point of contact' or 'a sort of permanent federal European diet' – nor Gentz's proposal for a 'European office' in Vienna, run by himself.[169] For lack of institutions and popular support, the Europeanism of 1814–15 withered away.

The Tsar helped establish a new French institution as well as a new French ministry. The Napoleonic army had been dissolved on 13 July. A new army based on departmental legions was formed thereafter by the Minister of War, Gouvion Saint-Cyr. At the same time a new royal guard was clearly necessary to replace the old Maison Militaire. Gouvion Saint-Cyr proposed one of 12,000 men, but Louis XVIII, contrary to his normal practice, refused to sign the ministerial *ordonnance* prepared to this effect. Following the advice of his fellow monarch Alexander I, who urged the political and military advantages of a large guard with extensive privileges, Louis XVIII created one of 26,678. Its four major-generals were four Napoleonic marshals who had stayed loyal to the King during the Hundred Days: Marshals Oudinot, Victor, Macdonald and Marmont. No precautions were avoided to make the new guards reliable. They were chosen not only for height and strength but also for loyalty: from former volontaires royaux; soldiers who had served before 1814; and the sons of rich farmers and artisans who had certificates of 'good conduct' and 'devotion to the King' signed by three notables. In accordance with French royal tradition, 3,700 of the 26,678 soldiers were Swiss: their red uniforms stood out against the blue of the other regiments. With its splendid men and uniforms (white trousers, blue coats, red epaulettes, white-plumed busbies), the Garde Royale became one of the ornaments of Paris.[170] By 25 January 1816 the last foreign troops had left the capital and the Garde Royale had taken over garrison duties. Calm returned to the city.[171]

The need felt for a large and devoted royal guard in and around Paris underlines the achievement of the National Guard in keeping order throughout the upheavals of 1815. During the change of regimes in late June and early July 1815 (as on 20 March between the departure of Louis XVIII and the arrival of Napoleon I) they had been – as most Parisians acknowledged[172] – the crucial, though unpaid, force which protected lives and property and prevented riots. From 23 June there had been, in theory, 3,000 national guards on duty at any one time. On 8 July General Dessolles recovered command of the Paris National Guard from Marshal Masséna.[173] Fontaine, who himself served in the National Guard, wrote: 'everyone is convinced of the importance of their duties, the general spirit is excellent and all that is due to the wisdom and the influence of General Dessolles who commands us.' The men insisted on guarding the Tuileries even when not obliged to do so. Surgeon James of the Life Guards admired the National Guard as 'a soldier-like and well-disciplined body of men. They are well armed and numerous, many of them fine stout fellows, particularly in the Grenadiers. Their uniform is a blue coat faced with white, white breeches and long black gaiters' and red epaulettes: 'it must be allowed that they always appear remarkably clean and *comme il faut*.'[174]

With the combined forces of the Garde Royale and the National Guard, in addition to the gendarmerie and the line regiments garrisoning the city, Paris after 1815 appeared as much a military capital as Berlin or St Petersburg. There was at least one barracks in each arrondissement and six in the first, often built on the sites of former monasteries and convents.[175] At least 500 soldiers and 200 national guards were posted to guard the Tuileries palace at any one time, in addition to 1,500 troops and 1,264 national guards on duty every day elsewhere in the city.[176] An English visitor called Sutton Sharpe, a lawyer and friend of Stendhal and Mérimée, was once taken to a National Guard guardhouse when he did not reply to a sentry's *Qui vive?* at night. He wrote of the experience:

Paris is really like a camp. Guard is mounted in all the quarters of Paris both day and night and at night sentries are placed in various parts of the town after the night watch. They challenge everybody that passes them on the quays, through all the gates and about the environs of the palace and public buildings . . . The public gardens and places that are shut up at night are cleared by beat of drum and the morning and evening drum is beat through the streets of Paris every day. You can go nowhere without meeting detachments of soldiers – changing guard at the different guard houses, and [marching] from barracks to the palace etc. besides the review that there is every morning in the Place de Carousel before the Tuileries. In addition to all this there is the National Guard of about 30,000 strong of whom one 28th is always on duty, as it comes to every man's turn for 12 hours every fortnight, sometimes oftener; if expecting anything they double the guard.

In addition there were gendarmes in military uniform 'mounted on horseback and riding through the streets, either singly or in pairs, in all directions, to see that everything is going on right. They are astonished when I say we have none of these in London.'[177]

The militarisation of Paris, combined with what one police official called the disgust of the poor – and many rich – for the 'chimaeras with which they had been tricked', that is to say the ideals of the French revolution, had created a different city from the cauldron of 1789–95.[178] At every level of society Parisians were determined to prevent blood on the streets. In their decisions not to fight for Paris, both Napoleon I in April 1814 and Louis XVIII in March 1815 were probably guided as much by a desire to save the city as by fear of defeat.

Despite occasional riots and brawls, political and class hatreds were restrained. In March 1815, as Napoleon approached the city, Paris remained as calm as in the previous twelve months. On 29 June 1815, in the interval between the departure of the Emperor and the return of the King, General Foy, a Bonapartist and a nationalist, wrote with evident disappointment: 'I have never seen a people so calm, an immense city so tranquil at the approach of such great events.'[179] This calm had helped Paris survive two invasions, two foreign occupations and three changes of regime in sixteen months. By the end of 1815 it was ready to resume its reign as capital of Europe.

4

Chambers and Salons

1815–1820

O Torys! O Whigs! Où êtes-vous?
> Louis XVIII to his Président du Conseil, Elie Decazes, December 1819

O N 6 OCTOBER 1815 the King had driven in state from the Tuileries, escorted by the old Maison Militaire – its last appearance in public before its replacement by the new Garde Royale – to open the new parliamentary session in the Palais Bourbon across the Seine. The Palais Bourbon, built in the 1720s for the Duchesse de Bourbon, an illegitimate daughter of Louis XIV, had been given by Louis XV to his cousin the Prince de Condé in 1764, as a reward for Condé's part in the Seven Years' War, and had been restored to him by Louis XVIII in 1814. Until his death in 1818 Condé, almost blind and very deaf, lived not in the main palace but in a separate wing. He served 'perfect' food and 'exquisite' wine, according to one of his guests Maréchale Oudinot, but sometimes forgot in which century he was living and informed them: 'I will speak of your interests to Madame de Polignac who will explain your matter to the Queen.'[1]

The main part of the Palais Bourbon, however, had since 1797 housed the principal legislative body of France. It was, and remains, a blend of old and new, Napoleonic and Bourbon. The façade we see today – statues of four celebrated legislators of the old French monarchy, Sully, L'Hôpital, Colbert and D'Aguesseau; an impressive flight of steps leading to twelve Corinthian columns supporting a massive pediment – dates from 1806–10. The sculptures within the pediment, however, date from the winter of 1815–16. Figures of Napoleon I presenting enemy flags taken during the Austerlitz campaign to a deputation of the Corps

Législatif were replaced by a more peaceful scene, revealing the Restoration's image of itself. In the centre, one giant female figure, Law (by some accounts France with the features of Minerva), is seated on a throne, holding the tablets of the Charte, and supported by figures of Force and Justice. On one side Peace brings back Mercury, God of Commerce; on the other Abundance, under the auspices of the Law, is followed by the Arts and Sciences. In the corners are statues of the rivers Seine, Marne and Rhône.[2]

Inside the entrance, spacious corridors and vestibules, draped in 1815 with green baize cloths masking pictures of Napoleon's triumphs,[3] led to the large and handsome semicircular assembly hall, lit from a large glass ceiling, where French deputies still debate today. The principal wall was lined with statues of classical legislators* in the centre of which was the President of the Chamber's chair, placed in front of a recess decorated with busts of Louis XVI, Louis XVII and Louis XVIII. In front of the president's chair were tables for journalists and the focus of parliamentary life in France, the rostrum – *la tribune*. Coloured red, it was raised to dominate the Chamber and decorated with white marble figures of the Muse of History and Fame.† From the rostrum the deputies spoke, facing a front row of government ministers and eight semicircular rows of deputies, raised as in a theatre. Above the rows of deputies, in the equivalent of opera boxes behind an Ionic colonnade, 200 places were available for members of the public who had procured tickets from deputies or the government; separate areas were reserved for *conseillers d'état*, peers, members of the Corps Diplomatique and of the household of the Prince de Condé. Thus instead of speaking from their seats as in Westminster, members had to walk across the floor and mount the steps to the tribune, like actors on a stage: indeed they often read from prepared speeches.[4] The President of the Chamber controlled debates, and secured silence, by rapping on his table with an ivory hammer or, if that did not work, by ringing a bell.[5]

On 6 October 1815, from a throne erected in the space normally occupied by the tribune, surrounded by princes, peers and marshals in full uniform, with Talleyrand and Richelieu sitting on stools at his feet, Louis XVIII read out the third speech from the throne of his reign. Reaffirming his devotion to 'this Charte on which I have meditated with

---

* Lycurgus, Solon, Demosthenes, Brutus, Cato and Cicero.
† Originally 'History writes the word Republic and Fame publishes the great event of the Revolution'.

care before granting, and to which reflection attaches me more every day', he warned of the sacrifices France would have to make to the allies. According to the Speaker of the House of Commons, Charles Abbott, who had travelled from London to give the French government advice on British parliamentary procedure, he spoke 'not from a written paper, well and clearly and distinctly, without hesitation and with a paternal dignity'. Like many Parisians the Speaker was impressed by the elegance of the peers' and deputies' costumes, which they wore for formal cere-monies and for speaking from the tribune. Their 'blue coats with white waistcoats, breeches and swords' asserted loyalty as well as status. The peers' high capes and broad cuffs were 'embroidered with fleurs-de-lys in gold, the deputies' in silver'. After the King's speech the princes, including Condé and Orléans, followed by the peers and deputies, one by one, swore, with outstretched hands, 'loyalty to the King, observa-tion of the constitutional Charter and obedience to the laws'. Then, accompanied by 'the loudest acclamations within the house and in the streets', the King returned to the Tuileries.[6]

The Restoration not only marked the resumption of Paris's role as a parliamentary capital: it was the first time parliamentary debates had taken place in France without fear of interruption by armed mobs or soldiers, as had often occurred since the opening of the States-General in 1789. The Chambers of Peers and Deputies rapidly came to play as important a part in the life of the city as the court. Debates there enabled Parisians to overlook the presence of foreign soldiers on their streets. Lord Liverpool was told: 'Now the Chambers occupy the public mind . . . exclusively . . . Every one is running to the tribune to hear debates, and these alone are talked of.'[7]

Debates in the Chamber were considered one of the best spectacles in Paris: for the next thirty years both foreigners and Parisians com-peted for tickets to the Chamber's public galleries as eagerly as for seats at the opera or theatre. It was the fashion to make appointments to meet friends there.[8] Since parliamentary monarchy and freedom of speech were novelties, there was, after 1815, a vigour and enthusiasm in debate which later, more cynical epochs often lacked. In 1819 the debates on the censorship laws were of a particularly high standard. The young liberal Charles de Rémusat heard Parisians remark: 'it is really too much of a feast for the intelligence to hear M. de Serre in the morning at the tribune and Talma in the evening in *Athalie*.'[9] Ten years later an English visitor, a Mrs Allen, found debates more stimulating than at home: 'There is a great deal of good speaking if it could be heard from the uproar that continually goes on[:] it reads better in the journals. It is not that frothy wordy stuff which serves to little purpose in England but short and pithy leading to a direct purpose.'[10]

Spectators came from every background and country. Still excluded at Westminster, ladies, even fashionable actresses, were admitted, and did not have to queue for tickets with other members of the public.[11] During one debate, with the insolent familiarity of the *ancien régime*, Madame de Balbi, who had been Louis XVIII's mistress before the revolution, maintained a running commentary, took off her hat, bonnet and shawl, asked a deputy for a pinch of snuff, and during a speech from the liberal deputy Monsieur d'Argenson, snorted: 'Ah! Monsieur d'Argenson would do much better to cultivate his estates.'[12] The wife of the Russian Foreign Secretary, Countess Nesselrode, was said to live in the Chamber. She considered a morning spent there more enjoyable than an evening at the opera, and tried never to miss a sitting.[13]

Another Russian, Princess Bagration, known as *la chatte blanche* for her alabaster skin, famous both for her *connaissances pratiques* in matters of love and for wearing nothing in the evening but 'white muslin, clinging to her form and revealing it in all its perfection', was also said to attend every session from beginning to end, sitting in the ambassadors' box. She was said to write an account of the day's debate for the Tsar himself.[14] The Comte d'Artois, no admirer of parliamentary government, told his old friend Elizabeth Duchess of Devonshire, on her arrival in Paris: 'I expect you would like to attend our Chamber of Deputies as you like our country. You can hear and enjoy the entire show.' He instructed his favourite aide-de-camp Prince Jules de Polignac to procure her tickets.[15]

As in London, the parliamentary session dominated the movements of the élite. 'When the session is finished', noted the Duc de Luxembourg, notwithstanding that he was a senior court official, 'Paris will be completely empty.'[16] The wife of another courtier peer, the Duchesse de Duras, had to change her summer plans on account, not of the movements of the court but of the 'prolongation of the session'.[17] When re-elected a deputy in 1819, Benjamin Constant returned to Paris from the provinces only for sessions of the Chamber.[18]

In comparison to the Chamber of Deputies in the Palais Bourbon, the Chamber of Peers in the Palais du Luxembourg (built by Marie de Médicis in the 1620s) aroused less interest. The existence of a hereditary second chamber is evidence that the political élite was more conservative than at any time since 1788. There was disagreement over personnel and policies, but agreement on the necessity of a strong monarchy and a bicameral legislature. Even the principle of the heredity of the peerage, established by Napoleon in June 1815, was welcomed on both left and right as a defence against the concentration of power in the hands of the government and the Chamber of Deputies. The Chamber of Peers inherited the semicircular chamber of the Napoleonic Senate, similar to the Chamber of Deputies, although each peer, instead of sitting on a bench, enjoyed a chair of his own. In the Luxembourg in 1815, as in the Palais Bourbon, pictures of Napoleonic victories on the wall were hidden by green baize cloth, tightly nailed down. The public was not admitted to debates, but could read accounts of them in the newspapers.[19]

The peers were described by Chateaubriand, one of their most eloquent members, as *restes désséchés de la vieille monarchie, de la Révolution et de l'Empire*. Coming from such diverse backgrounds, they confronted each other, in their early sessions, much like strange beasts. A future Prime Minister, Count Molé, who had the reputation of being one of the most intelligent young politicians of the day but had served Napoleon I in the Hundred Days, felt royalists staring at him as if he had a club foot. So many peers were old and deaf, reported Chateaubriand, that speeches were interrupted by the sound of their ear-trumpets dropping to the floor as they fell asleep.[20]

However, through the system of committees, the ample revenues and political independence of the Chamber of Peers, and the conscious policy of the Grand Référendaire the Marquis de Sémonville, an institutional *esprit de corps* almost as strong as in the pre-1789 Parlement de Paris (in which Sémonville had served, as he had every subsequent regime), soon developed. Moreover, as the supreme law court in the kingdom, the Chamber of Peers in 1815 became the scene of one of the dramas of French parliamentary history: the trial of Marshal Ney. Demanded by Richelieu in the name not only of France and the King but of Europe, it began on 21 November. The prosecution was led by Bellart, the Paris bourgeois who had been the inspiration behind the proclamation of the Conseil Municipal against Napoleon in 1 April 1814. Evidence was contradictory, but in the end most peers decided that Ney had left Paris on 16 March 1815 with the intention of betraying the King. On 6 December they voted his condemnation to death.

At performances of *Cinna* in the Théâtre Français the audience applauded allusions to clemency.[21] However, in the mood of ultra-royalist rage sweeping the court and the Chambers, the King could have granted a pardon only at the request of his niece the Duchesse d'Angoulême, whom no ultra-royalist would have criticised. In 1804, the Empress Josephine and Queen Hortense had interceded with Napoleon I for the life of royalist conspirators such as Jules de Polignac. The Duchesse d'Angoulême, however, was convinced that mercy had weakened the monarchy. On a cold and sombre morning on 7 December, while Maréchale Ney and their children waited in an ante-chamber of the Tuileries in the hope of making a last plea for mercy to the King, *le brave des braves* was shot by a firing squad on the Place de l'Observatoire, south of the Palais du Luxembourg. In his diary entry that day Boniface de Castellane, an officer in the new Garde Royale, remembered only the marshal's heroism during the retreat from Moscow: *au feu le plus vif il était sublime.*[22]

The Hundred Days had undermined moderation on both right and left. The Chamber of Deputies soon distinguished itself by the aggression of its ultra-royalism. Deputies passed a battery of laws reimposing censorship, creating special courts, imposing harsher penalties for every sign and sound of Bonapartism, and banishing regicides who had supported the Hundred Days (including a Swedish regicide who had assassinated Gustavus III in 1792). The Richelieu ministry soon came under attack, since many deputies considered government moderation responsible for Napoleon's return from Elba. To the King's dismay they felt obliged 'to defend the King against his own clemency', and asked for a 'few drops' of blood to be shed now, to prevent 'torrents' of blood in the future. On 18 December Pozzo reported that the King had said to him: 'if these Messieurs had complete liberty, they would end by purging him himself.'[23]

Ambassadors enjoyed particular prominence in Paris after 1815. Chateaubriand lamented that France had exchanged a garrison of Cossacks for a garrison of ambassadors. The son of the Duc d'Orléans complained of their 'intolerable' insolence and their attempts to take precedence over the princes of the blood: the Congress of Vienna had been as great a victory for them as the Battle of Austerlitz had been for Napoleon.[24] Indeed, while the Chamber of Deputies was becoming a synonym for extremism, the French government suffered the humiliation of having its measures watched and criticised by the conference of the four allied ambassadors in Paris, who inherited the role of the conference of allied ministers during the occupation in 1815. Representing a form of European supervision of French internal affairs, it met in the

British embassy on Wednesday and Sunday mornings at 11 (its reports were copied by a French police agent and read by Richelieu and Decazes). Wellington, who also attended the conference when he was not at his headquarters in Cambrai, acted as counsellor and critic of both the royal family and the French ministers.[25]

The British ambassador in Paris from 1815 to 1824, and from 1828 to 1831, Sir Charles Stuart later Lord Stuart de Rothesay, was considered by Richelieu to be hostile to France and to lack even basic good manners; his letters were so harsh and dry that Richelieu found it hard to reply to them politely.[26] He also chased actresses. In the words of Lady Granville (whose husband, Lord Granville, would succeed Stuart as British ambassador in 1824), he was '*le moins mari que possible*, affiche-ing the worst company and lowest connections' – although his wife Lady Elizabeth, 'a charming amiable agreeable woman whom everyone likes', appeared 'perfectly satisfied'.[27]

In contrast his rival for diplomatic influence, the Russian ambassa-dor Pozzo di Borgo, an old friend of Richelieu since their years as French émigrés in Russian service, was more sober and more influen-tial. Pozzo had not obtained a ministry as he had hoped, since even in 1815 the roles of Russian ambassador and French minister were consid-ered incompatible.[28] However, he considered himself as much French as Russian and Corsican, and planned to end his days in France. As a reward for his services to the royal cause (he successfully worked to diminish allied financial demands on France), he had requested and obtained from the King 1,500,000 francs and the promise of the title of Duke. Hence the King's alleged comment: 'I pay for everything I owe him and for all the good he has done France.'[29]

Count Molé, whom Pozzo helped to his post as Minister of Marine in 1817 (without his having seen any boats other than the barges on the Seine – hence the phrase *marin comme Molé*),[30] described Pozzo in these years:

> Endowed with consistent good health, and prodigious physical strength, having no taste other than politics, no passion other than ambition, he kept us all out of breath: he had finished, without having been asked to do so, by giving his advice on everything, on the least important appointment, the slightest detail of administration.

As a personal friend of Richelieu, Pozzo enjoyed easy access to the King, the royal family and the ministers. It was said that France had exchanged the government of one Corsican for that of another.[31]

Pozzo was a mentor and confidant of the King's favourite, Decazes, a former officer in the Paris National Guard and volontaire royal, who since September 1815 had been Minister of Police. The career of Decazes illustrates the strength of the court system in nineteenth-century France. Through looks, charm and ability, this bourgeois from Libourne had won the favour first of Napoleon's mother, Madame Mère, then of Louis-Napoleon King of Holland, finally of Louis XVIII. Between 1815 and 1820 the King loved him as a favourite son, wrote to him several times a day, followed his advice and saw him alone most evenings after 9.[32] At times Decazes ruled France.

While the Chamber bayed for blood, government repression contin-ued. On 27 July 1816, for example, three men accused of participation in a Bonapartist conspiracy suffered the punishment reserved for parri-cides (the King being father of his subjects): first their right hands were cut off, then at 8 p.m on the Place de Grève in front of the Hôtel de Ville they were guillotined before a huge crowd.[33] Nevertheless minis-ters were attacked so violently in the Chambers for not being harsh enough, not purging the bureaucracy, and not giving greater powers and wealth to the clergy, that Richelieu believed that, if there was another parliamentary session like that of 1815–16, France and the royal family would be finished.[34] During the summer recess, the ministers, pushed by Decazes and Pozzo, aided by a letter from Alexander I and their own threat to resign, persuaded the King to dissolve the Chamber and call new elections.[35] By this step he resolved in effect to be King not of a party but of France. When he asked an émigré general the Comte de Vioménil for his opinion of the *ordonnance* of 5 September dissolving the Chamber, the reply sped round Paris. 'Sire, Your Majesty can see by the joy shining in the faces of his enemies and the consternation of his loyal subjects what he should think of this *ordonnance*.'[36] The number of roy-alists cheering Louis XVIII on Sundays in the Tuileries garden began to diminish.[37]

In Chateaubriand's opinion France was lost if the course of modera-tion, which he had once supported, was pursued.[38] In September 1816 Decazes, on his own initiative, tried to prevent publication of Chateaubriand's pamphlet *De la monarchie selon la Charte*, since it sug-gested that the King's public commitment to his government's moder-ate policy did not express his private feelings; the pamphlet's failure to fulfil all the formalities of registration with the police, the national library and the chancellery was made the pretext. Decazes had forgot-ten that Chateaubriand was, in the words of a former minister, 'devoured by the demon of publicity'.[39] On 18 September, wearing his peer's costume, Chateaubriand assembled the printer's assistants at the press of M. Le Normant, 8 rue de Seine, and removed copies before the eyes of the police, to cries of *C'est M. de Chateaubriand! Vive le roi quand-même! Vive la liberté!* (Hundreds of copies had, in any case, as Chateaubriand pointed out, already been despatched to the provinces.)[40] Although permitted to retain the pension he had been granted on the funds of the Chamber of Peers, Chateaubriand, whom the King now considered a personal enemy, lost the title and salary of a Minister of State.[41]

Chateaubriand feared a new Convention. The elections however returned a government majority of ninety in the Chamber. Most of the 9,677 voters in Paris, paying the required 300 francs a year in direct taxes, took part. Deputies included a mixture of royalists and liberals: Bellart, who had led the Conseil Municipal against Napoleon in 1814; Pasquier, a former official of Napoleon now a minister of Louis XVIII, known as *l'inévitable*; and one of the richest men in France, originally a lawyer from Champagne, Comte Roy, who had made a fortune out of land during the glut on the market caused by the sale of church and émigrés' property during the revolution.[42] Two non-noble deputies were more hostile to the government: the wealthy banker Casimir Périer, and an even wealthier banker Jacques Laffitte, who received the largest single number of votes. The son of a poor carpenter of Bayonne, Laffitte had come to Paris in 1788 at the age of twenty-one: first a clerk, then an associate of the banker Perregaux, he had risen to be a governor of the Banque de France. Having been royalist in 1814, he had turned Bonapartist during the Hundred Days. It was said of him that Paris was his rotten borough and that the Maison Laffitte behaved like a firm in competition with the Maison de Bourbon.[43]

During the next four years Paris appeared calm. Despite a bad harvest in 1816, leading to a dramatic rise in the price of bread in 1817, there were no serious riots: the soldiers of the Garde Royale, given 5 centimes a day extra pay from the funds of the Civil List, ensured the maintenance of order.[44] Louis XVIII personally intervened with the Prefect of the Seine to ensure that the city of Paris should subsidise the bread supply not only of the indigent but also of *toute la classe mal-aisée dans les tems de disette*.[45] Richelieu boasted that elections in Paris were so calm that a stranger walking through the city would not have known that citizens were voting.[46]

As in 1814–15, political passions were more easily expressed at the theatre than on the street. A 'battle' took place at the Théâtre Français on 22 March 1817 over the first night of a play. *Germanicus* was a tragedy set in Imperial Rome by A.V. Arnault, a Bonapartist deputy for Paris during the Hundred Days, who had subsequently been excluded from the Académie Française and exiled to Brussels. Despite pleas from the King himself, who had read and passed the play, half-pay Bonapartist officers and royalist gardes du corps and officers of the Garde Royale seized the opportunity for a fight. They could identify each other in the theatre since royalists wore black waistcoats and white ties, Bonapartists white waistcoats and black ties. Both sides carried long sticks weighted with lead at one end. Despite the presence of the King's nephew the Duc de Berri, Richelieu, Decazes and Wellington, when the author's name was called for at the end of the play, men in the audience began to shout, whistle and exchange blows. Women fainted. Neutral theatre-goers took refuge in the orchestra. One member of the audience was Lady Dalrymple Hamilton.

After her flight in March 1815, she had returned to Paris in October 1816, renting the *hôtel* of the former Grand Chambellan of Napoleon the Comte de Montesquiou on the rue Monsieur for 'a very moderate price'. Of that evening she wrote: 'parties ran very high . . . at length from words they came to blows. The confusion was excessive and was only concluded by the Gens d'armes jumping into the pit and taking up the ringleaders.' The Bonapartists in the audience were more numerous but in the end order was restored by soldiers commanded from his box by Marshal Victor Duc de Bellune. The next day gardes du corps and officers of the Garde Royale, with large white ribbons in their button-holes, and half-pay Napoleonic officers, wearing bunches of violets and the cross of the Légion d'Honneur in theirs, walked round the Tuileries garden and the Palais Royal exchanging threats and insults, in some cases snatching each other's flowers or issuing challenges to duels.[47] The Bonapartist actress Mlle Mars was jeered by gardes du corps in the Tuileries garden: she turned round and asked what Mars could have in common with the gardes du corps.[48] An *ordonnance* was issued forbidding the presence of sticks and guns in theatres, and all future performances of the play.

On the surface French politics continued peaceful. In the autumn of 1818, after the last payment of the allied indemnity and of the French subsidy to the costs of occupation, which had been the principal pre-occupation of the French government since 1815, allied troops left

France earlier than planned. The partial elections of 27–29 October 1818, in which electors selected deputies for a fifth of the seats in the kingdom, took place as peaceably as the others. The principal issue dominating political life in France in 1814–48, after the choice of dynasty, was the franchise: how many Frenchmen should be allowed to vote in elections to the Chamber of Deputies? A new electoral law had been passed on 5 February 1817. Partly in order to reduce the influence of ultra-royalist landowners, and to increase that of prefects, the location of electoral colleges had been moved from the main towns of cantons to those of departments; in order to avoid violent political change, elections every year to one-fifth of the seats in the Chamber had been substituted for total renewal of the Chamber every five years.[49]

In Paris, however, the government candidate Guillaume Ternaux, an industrialist who employed about 20,000 in his textile business, defeated Benjamin Constant by only eighty votes. After his volte-face during the Hundred Days, Constant could no longer hope for honours or office under the Bourbons and, like Laffitte, had become their enemy in a way he had not been in 1814. A constitutional royalist, Ternaux was one of the members of the Paris bourgeoisie who hesitated between support for and opposition to the Bourbons. He had emigrated in 1792, had detested the Empire, and followed Louis XVIII to Ghent. Although an enemy of the court and courtiers, he also held the Charte to be 'the most solid foundation of the Restoration as well as the first guarantee of the liberty, the repose and the happiness of France'. He would remain a deputy for Paris until 1823 and again from 1827 to 1833.[50]

In the thirty-five years after 1815 the influence of Paris as a parliamentary capital would be as great as, in the previous century, that of Versailles as a court. With the exception of the continued application of the Code Napoléon in parts of Germany and Italy, and the introduction of *gendarmeries*, the Napoleonic Empire had left no permanent legacy in Europe: not one Napoleonic monarchy, constitution or frontier survived. However, the Charte of 1814 was the principal model for the constitutions which were, as in France, freely 'granted' by the monarch in Poland in 1815, in Bavaria and Baden in 1818, in Württemberg in 1819, Hesse-Darmstadt in 1820, Brazil in 1824, Portugal in 1826, and (after the revision of the Charte in 1830) Spain in 1837, Greece in 1844, Piedmont in 1848 and Prussia in 1850: often clauses in these constitutions were translated directly from the French texts of 1814 or 1830.[51]

Either because Britain did not have a written constitution or because

Paris was more familiar than London, the Houses of Parliament in Westminster had few imitators in Europe. In Karlsruhe and Stuttgart, the capitals of Baden and Württemberg, chambers of peers and deputies were constructed according to the hemicycle model of Paris rather than the rectangular model of Westminster.[52] In Munich, according to the French ambassador, in the first budget debate in Bavarian history, deputies used ideas and phrases they had found in the Paris newspapers.[53]

Stendhal loved Italy and hated the Bourbons: he never went to court after 1814. Yet without the two chambers Italy seemed to him, as he wrote in 1817, politically, culturally and linguistically dead.[54] Debates in the Chamber of Deputies occupied the salons and shopkeepers of St Petersburg and Berlin – according to French ambassadors posted in those cities – almost as much as those of Paris.[55] Many Russians, including future members of the Decembrist conspiracy of 1825, and Greeks such as Alexander Mavrocordato, a leader of the War of Independence, acquired their first knowledge of revolutions, liberal ideas and parliamentary practices from visits to Paris after 1814, or from reading the pamphlets published there by Benjamin Constant or the liberal intellectual and future Prime Minister François Guizot.[56]

Nevertheless, below the surface there was little confidence in the future of the constitutional monarchy. The legacy of past bloodshed and instability was exacerbated by conflicts of two kinds: on the dynastic level, between the three families of Bourbon, Orléans and Bonaparte, and their followers; on the political level, between the rival creeds of autocracy, Catholicism, militarism, nationalism, parliamentarianism and revolution, each of which appealed to sections of public opinion. Such conflicts added to the sense of dislocation and scepticism felt in France as a result of the convulsions experienced since 1789, compounded by the need to master a new parliamentary system. As Count Molé said in the Chamber of Peers: 'Nothing in our history resembles what we are seeing. We have never been as we are now. We must to a certain extent create ourselves.'[57]

A further source of instability came from the opposition of Talleyrand and his followers in the Chambers of Peers and Deputies. In the words of a visiting Irish liberal Lady Morgan, Talleyrand normally looked 'like the shell of a human frame', 'no tint varying the colourless hue of his livid complexion'. The American author Fenimore Cooper referred to his 'unearthly aspect'.[58] After drinking at dinner, however, Talleyrand became less reserved. When Pasquier, Minister of Interior in

1815 under Talleyrand, became an ally of Decazes and was selected by the King as President of the Chamber of Deputies, Talleyrand felt betrayed. On 17 November 1816, after a dinner in his honour at the British embassy, possibly to show that the British government supported his return to office, Talleyrand denounced the ministers as ruining the state, drew Pasquier alone into a corner of the salon and, in a torrent of abuse, attacked Decazes as nothing but a pimp: the Chamber dishonoured itself by its relations with him.[59]

After the scene at the British embassy, the King not only banned Talleyrand from court but inflicted a public humiliation on him. At the annual memorial service for Louis XVI at Saint-Denis on 21 January 1817 Talleyrand was ordered by the Grand Master of Ceremonies the Marquis de Dreux-Brézé to leave the group of court officials in which he was standing. In front of a congregation composed of delegations from the principal institutions of France, he had to limp over to a bench reserved for peers.[60]

Talleyrand riposted with remarks, repeated around Paris, which reflected the political fears of those years. When the King teased him about the return from England of his wife, a former *demi-mondaine* whom he had just divorced, he replied, 'Yes Sire, her return is for me a 20 March' (an allusion to Napoleon's return from Elba).[61] To a lady who, like many others, complained that the King was no royalist, Talleyrand replied: 'How can you say that? He did not sign the *Acte Additionnel*, he went to Ghent and he is ready to return there.'[62] When guests expressed concern about the King's health, Talleyrand retorted that he looked so healthy, and could walk so well, that he would live to bury the monarchy.[63] Many Parisians shared his views.

In April 1817, assuring Louis XVIII that he was resolved to be noticed as little as possible, Orléans had returned from Twickenham to Paris with his family. At their New Year reception in the Palais Royal in 1818, the royalist deputy Maine de Biran noted: 'this family has something attractive about it; its horoscope seems to several people highly favourable.' Courtiers were heard complaining that 'royal authority is vanishing every day and democracy gaining in proportion.'[64] Indeed some deputies said that the Chamber should be mistress of the government, rather than the other way round, with the power to regulate the army and decide on peace or war.[65] On 28 August 1818, three days after the grandiose inauguration by the King of the equestrian statue of Henri IV which still adorns the Pont Neuf – cast in part out of the melted-down bronze from the statue of Napoleon on the column in the

Place Vendôme – Madame de Souza wrote to Flahaut in England: 'Everyone who has experienced a revolution agrees that there is a distant sound of thunder portending a crisis.'[66] Count Molé remarked in private conversation on 1 November 1818, 'France is anti-Bourbon.' Maine de Biran commented in his diary: 'So much the worse for France, for France cannot live without the Bourbons; outside legitimacy I see only anarchy and despotism.'[67]

In January 1819, facing fundamental disagreement inside the ministry over whether to turn right or left, feeling that the King preferred Decazes to himself, and yearning to leave politics, Richelieu resigned. There had been talk of his replacement by Pozzo.[68] However, until 1848, despite the power of the Chambers, the King and his family remained at the centre of politics. The composition of a majority in the Chamber of Deputies could reflect not only the wishes of voters and deputies, but also those of the King, his ministers and relations. Backed by the King, Decazes became the leading minister. The government turned to the left. Allied ambassadors and the majority of the Chamber of Peers, hitherto government supporters, were alarmed. At a performance in the court theatre in the Tuileries, Pozzo accused Decazes, whom he now regarded as a personal enemy (Richelieu had been an intimate friend of Pozzo and the Tsar himself), of disturbing Europe.[69] In a despatch which shows that Pozzo could be as much a fantasist as Benjamin Constant, he claimed that Decazes wanted a dictatorship, and that the King planned to dethrone his own dynasty.[70]

In 1819 the remaining censorship laws were removed; liberal newspapers like *Le Censeur européen*, *La Minerve française* and *Archives philosophiques* were published again, with frequent contributions by Benjamin Constant; most Bonapartist exiles, including A.V. Arnault the author of *Germanicus* (but not David), returned to Paris from Brussels. Some Parisians agreed that, while Napoleonic tyranny had been 'rapidly ruining the French mind', France was now 'the most truly free of any country in Europe'. The Chambers assumed such importance that, for the first time in French history, ministers began to be selected not because of administrative ability, royal favour or, like Talleyrand and Richelieu, European reputation, but because of their parliamentary skills. One of the best speakers in the Chamber of Deputies, a former émigré Comte Hercule de Serre, became Minister of Justice in 1819. Another politician famed for his parliamentary talents was the Comte de Villèle, the ultra leader from Toulouse whose 'fluency and perspicuity' in speaking on the 1818 budget, despite a Midi accent and undistinguished appearance, impressed the English banker Francis Baring.[71] Pasquier was said to have the talent of satisfying his audience without telling it anything, and was described by the King as 'indispensable to the tribune'.[72] The best liberal speaker, General Foy, who had fought in Napoleon's army in Spain, was one of the many former Napoleonic satraps who – with a hypocrisy which disgusted many of their contemporaries – after the Emperor's fall developed a passion for freedom.[73] The ultra-royalist Duchesse d'Escars commented to her daughter: 'We have seen the brutes become chamberlains: so judge what value the word liberty has in their mouths.'[74] (Only the Duc de Broglie, recalling the reign of terror which he had helped enforce as a junior official in Spain, was honest enough to express in his memoirs his 'profound sentiment of regret and humiliation'.)[75] Since 1815 Paris had replaced Europe as outlet and stage for what Madame de Staël called 'that devouring activity which had consumed it [France] itself as well as Europe'.[76] The French élite had turned from conquest to constitutionalism.

In March 1819, when the Chamber of Peers begged for a new electoral law that accorded more influence to landowners, the King shocked many royalists by creating sixty new peers, including prominent Bonapartists like Marshal Suchet, in the hope of attaching them to the regime. He also agreed to be crowned in Paris, rather than at Reims as Bourbon tradition decreed, although the state of his health was to prevent this.[77] Even Decazes, however, could not persuade Louis XVIII, in the interests of efficiency and economy, to reduce the pay and privileges of the Gardes du Corps or to dismiss the Swiss regiments of the Garde Royale, whose broad shoulders, high pay and foreign nationality aroused resentment in the French army and the Chambers. The King told the liberal Minister of War, Maréchal Gouvion Saint-Cyr, never to mention the subject again. He valued his Gardes du Corps as much as his crown and considered the Garde Royale the security of the monarchy or, as Richelieu had put it, 'the safeguard of our existence . . . the pupil of our eyes'.[78]

If the government relied on the King, the ultra-royalists, in the opinion of Richelieu, Pozzo and Wellington, and many others, owed much of their power to the support of the heir to the throne the Comte d'Artois. Despite his extreme political views, and lack of realism, Artois had confidence, charm and a taste for political activity: even his opponents said that he had the best manners in the kingdom.[79] A Napoleonic officer hostile to Artois' political views like Boniface de Castellane

wrote, after a private audience: 'it is impossible to be better, more obliging and more gracious than this excellent prince.'[80] When Wellington
had tried to persuade him to support the ministry, in June 1817, Artois
had refused, preferring the role of an opposition leader: 'you foreigners
do not know men; I am better informed and my party is certainly the
strongest.'[81] To Pozzo, who had urged him in the name of Europe to
support the government, he replied that he approved of the Charte, but
only if executed by 'pure and honest royalists', in other words by 'my
party'. In reality he dreamed of an autocratic monarchy, resembling the
Napoleonic Empire rather than the *ancien régime*: in private conversations with courtiers he called Napoleon I 'our master'.[82]

Some of the most virulent ultra speakers in the Chambers, like
Fitzjames and Sosthènes de La Rochefoucauld, derived part of their
impact from their positions as members of Artois' household. One of
his Capitaines des Gardes the Comte de Puységur, an elderly émigré
with hair and eyebrows dyed jet-black, detested Decazes. Known for his
pursuit of actresses, he also made remarks which went the rounds of
Paris. When Artois had been cheered at a theatre soon after Ney's execution: 'two or three more men hanged and France will be at your feet'.
To people who feared a return of the old regime with its abuses, he said
that he wanted the abuses above all. He once announced: 'I am not
French, I am from the Pavillon de Marsan' – the wing of the Tuileries
overlooking the rue de Rivoli, where Artois and his household resided,
and where he often received ultra politicians like Chateaubriand in
private audiences in the evening.[83]

Chateaubriand was in continuous correspondence with, and received
financial support from, Artois and friends in his household, to whom
he referred in letters, with proud familiarity, as *Jules* (de Polignac) and
Mathieu (de Montmorency). Always in financial difficulties, after 1816 he
had to sell not only his carriages but also his house in the Vallée aux
Loups: it was bought by Mathieu de Montmorency. Thereafter,
Chateaubriand lived in an apartment at 27 rue Saint-Dominique in the
Faubourg Saint-Germain.[84] When he went to court, as he did once a
month, like many ultras he paid his respects to Artois in the Pavillon de
Marsan but not to the King in the state apartments.[85] In 1818 Artois, in
protest against the loss of some of his power over the National Guard,
threatened to separate himself from the King and to publish a manifesto attacking 'the moral [as opposed to the material] interests of the
revolution'. Only the intervention of the Austrian ambassador and
several ministers persuaded him to remain silent.[86]

Louis XVIII told Pozzo that he hoped to live long enough 'to calm and destroy by [his government's] success the errors which now dominate him [Artois]'.[87] Yet the fear that the King did not have long to live was another destabilising factor. Aged sixty-three, increasingly confined to his wheelchair, he was no longer strong enough to attend Sunday mass in the royal chapel. He heard it in his private apartments, after which the doors of the Grand Cabinet were opened and he emerged in his wheelchair to say a few ritual words – omitted if he wished to indicate disfavour – in the same order of precedence, to his family, his ministers and the marshals of France. Every time he had an attack of gout, government stocks fell. Ultra-royalists rejoiced: some were even heard to remark, so friends of Decazes alleged, 'we are hoping for gangrene.' In the afternoon, partly to test the reaction from passers-by, partly to demonstrate that he was in good health, the King was in the habit of driving through Paris – particularly the centre of insurrection in 1792 the Faubourg Saint-Antoine, which he called *notre faubourg* – or the surrounding countryside. His carriage was always escorted by large numbers of gardes du corps and gardes royaux. If he did not go out, people feared the worst.[88]

After 1815, popular discontent was such that, even when he went in state from the Tuileries to the Palais Bourbon to open the parliamentary sessions of 1816 and 1817, there were few cheers in the streets.[89] On 3 May 1819 few private houses in Paris, as opposed to government buildings, bothered to place candles in their windows at night to celebrate the anniversary of the King's return in 1814.[90]

Discontent was not limited to Paris. Touring provincial France in the summer of 1819, Richelieu, who now believed that freedom of the press made monarchy in France impossible, echoed the feelings of Artois and of foreign statesmen like Metternich and even Alexander I: 'the revolutionary spirit has made immense progress. What rage and what frenzy in the newspapers! Good God, can it be true that Bonaparte with his iron hand was alone capable of governing our poor country?'[91] In September 1819 thirty-five liberals were elected to the Chamber, including two declared enemies of the Bourbons: a former *conventionnel*, the Abbé Grégoire, and La Fayette. Grégoire, who believed that a good Christian should be a good democrat, had welcomed Louis XVI's condemnation to death in 1793, denouncing him as 'the greatest criminal', and had been one of the few to attack the Charte in 1814; La Fayette, a personal enemy of Louis XVIII since before the revolution and the gaoler of Louis XVI in 1791, had in July 1815 asked the allies for a king from any dynasty other than the Bourbons. The election of Grégoire to the Chamber of Deputies of Louis XVIII showed the detestation of the government felt by both liberals and the ultras who had voted for him in accordance with their party's *politique du pire*. Grégoire, however, was excluded from the Chamber to cries of *Vive le roi!*[92]

The government, surrounded by malevolence, contempt and distrust, as the King had acknowledged in his speech from the throne, alarmed by the ferocity of the ultras and the disloyalty of many liberals, decided to move to the right. On 19 November 1819 Gouvion Saint-Cyr, who had helped create a national army based on selective conscription, was replaced as Minister of War by the less radical Latour-Maubourg, and Decazes became Président du Conseil.[93] Decazes, now denounced on the left as *le Séjan libournais*, prepared to introduce a new electoral law, substituting total renewal of the Chamber every seven years for the system of partial annual elections. Even Monsieur promised support.[94]

If the Chambers were one centre of power in Paris, the salons were another. Although the former were public and institutional, and the latter private and informal, their influence was considered comparable. A young liberal, Charles de Rémusat, could report: 'neither Chambers nor salons are functioning any longer, therefore there is no news.'[95] The Duc de Broglie remarked of the Chamber of Peers in 1819: 'In its present state the Chamber of Peers is a salon' – hence the King's reference to it, in a letter intended to be shown to Broglie, as *le salon de la rue de Vaugirard*.[96] Far more than in the eighteenth century, when salons had been dominated by literature and largely excluded from politics, many salons after 1815 functioned as extensions of the Chambers. Indeed many peers and deputies spent their evenings, and discussed and read their forthcoming speeches, in salons. One factor heightening political tension after 1815 was what Pozzo called 'the petulance of the salons of Paris'. Indeed, as many contemporaries remarked, disputes in the Chambers both dominated, and were dominated by, discussions of even greater violence in salons.[97] In 1815 the sister of the Duc de Richelieu Madame de Montcalm noted that 'the salons already form a deliberating power in the government': her own salon confirmed the truth of her assertion.[98] A Piedmontese diplomat wrote to his government of 'the salons which here have so much power over public affairs'.[99]

Liberals like Guizot, and two intellectual enemies of the Empire Royer-Collard and Camille Jordan, met in the houses of Pasquier or

Molé; ultra-royalist peers and deputies, like Chateaubriand, Bonald, Villèle and Corbière, dined together several times a week, and planned their strategy, in a house in the Faubourg Saint-Germain on the corner of the rue de Ventadour and the rue Thérèse, hired for the purpose by an obscure provincial lawyer called Monsieur Piet, deputy for the Sarthe. Different deputies would contribute game and food: Artois paid the remaining expenses. One of the deputies attending was a former royalist conspirator called M. Hyde de Neuville: hence their epithet *les hideux*.[100]

Ternaux, the moderate deputy for Paris, held an evening salon in his *hôtel* in the Place des Victoires, near the Palais Royal, most of the wall-hangings of which were made in his own factories. *La société Ternaux* or *la réunion Ternaux* was a synonym for the group of about fifty centre-left deputies whom he led and entertained.[101] Of Laffitte, the deputy for Paris who lived in the rue de Montblanc and led another, more left-wing group of fifty deputies, Rémusat wrote: 'He almost never went out and stayed at home every evening. Anyone who wanted to could come.' The two groups were known as *les Ternaux* and *les Laffitte*.[102]

Pozzo di Borgo was an ornament of the salons of the Duchesse de Duras, Madame de Montcalm, and the Princesse de Poix, the matriarch of the younger branch of the Noailles family.[103] George Ticknor, a young American scholar of German and Spanish literature who arrived in Paris in 1817 at the age of twenty-seven, described Pozzo as having 'that facility and grace in making epigrammatic remarks which in French society is valued above all other talents'.[104]

Even in salons whose basis was not overtly political, politics was the principal topic of conversation. According to Madame de Montcalm, men and women who had hitherto thought of little but horses and novels, suddenly, after 1814, began criticising the budget or the administration of the wheat trade.[105] 'Society is still in a terrible state,' the Duchesse de Broglie reported, 'politics invades everything, no one has time any more to read, to please or even to make love.'[106] Madame de Genlis called a dinner party at the Comte de Valence's, after which the men sat in a circle discussing politics to the exclusion of the female guests, 'a veritable representation of the Chamber of Deputies'. Like Puységur and many others, she mourned the new seriousness and the end of the *galanterie française* – the attention paid to women – she had known before 1789.[107]

Women could not be deputies or peers or speak in public. A salon, however, could give them a power base of their own and an opportunity to debate political issues. That is one reason why a salon was, in the words of the writer Madame d'Agoult, 'the supreme ambition of the Parisienne, the consolation of her maturity, the glory of her old age'. Thus politics was 'the taste, the constant occupation' of the Princesse de La Trémoïlle, who held a violently ultra-royalist salon in the rue de Bourbon.[108] Although Madame de Montcalm complained of the nullity of women's lives, her salon at 37 rue de l'Université, the *hôtel* she bought from Maréchal Macdonald in 1817, gave her the opportunity to play a political role. Her brother Richelieu used it as a place to meet ministers and deputies, and explain policy. Owing to ill-health she rarely left the chaise longue whence, draped in a shawl, she directed the conversation of the guests sitting in a circle of chairs around her. Intelligent, intimidating, demanding and frequently ill-tempered, she was a source of information for Pozzo, helped Molé become a minister and tried to reconcile Chateaubriand with her brother, both in 1817 and 1821; political feelings ran so high, however, that in 1816, after a friendship of twelve years, Chateaubriand had ceased to visit her.[109]

In her salon guests were not allowed to talk independently of the general conversation. One younger visitor the Comte d'Haussonville was so intimidated that he never opened his mouth; another, Madame de Sainte-Aulaire, never returned after she was asked by her hostess to explain to the other guests a joke she had been sharing with a neighbour.[110] One day the guests in her salon were discussing the social position of writers before the revolution. Some claimed they were received in the best society. The Abbé de Montesquiou disagreed and said they were invited to dinner *par tolérance*, but without intimacy. Finally Comte Charles de Damas announced: 'yes, men of letters were the dregs of society' (*la crasse de la société*). A young middle-class writer, Abel-François Villemain, who taught French literature at the Sorbonne, later remarked that, as he left the salon, he understood the French revolution.[111] When Madame de Montcalm died from cholera in 1832, however, Lamartine bestowed on her the highest praise for which a hostess could wish: 'Paris is nothing to me without her . . . I do not know where to spend the evening.'[112]

The political character of Paris social life was heightened by the frequency of government and court receptions. They were considered a necessary part of royal and ministerial duties. Thus, in addition to seeing petitioners every day between 6 and 8 p.m., ministers held evening receptions on different days of the week: the Minister of Foreign Affairs on Thursdays, that of the Interior on Wednesdays, that of Finance on

Mondays and Thursdays.[113] Once inscribed on the ministry's books, visitors needed only to present their cards to be admitted. One Russian resident of Paris, a retired diplomat called Piotr Kozlovski, noted that the minister's wife generally sat in the chair nearest the fire, surrounded by a circle of chairs for her female visitors. No refreshments were served, nor was gambling permitted. The atmosphere was like a court, although ministers spoke less to their visitors than did members of the French royal family, contenting themselves with nods and brief remarks to a chosen few. Kozlovski was struck by the 'universal idolatry of transitory power'.[114] Speaking of a later period, the English traveller James Silk Buckingham wrote: 'a great deal of personal communication passed between the minister and his visitors on topics of public interest, of which he would sometimes make a note in his tablets, for reference on the following day.'[115]

Talkative, indiscreet, with a need to do everything and intervene everywhere, Decazes allowed his house to become a political café, full of people throughout the day. Richelieu, in contrast, a solitary man with dishevelled hair, smelling of tobacco, whose wife lived in the country, regarded social life as torture. Yet even he felt obliged to give two dinners and two receptions every week, and attached importance to the presence at them of a leading deputy such as Villèle.[116]

In the nineteenth century social life was considered not only, or primarily, a human need and a method of government, but also a duty, a means to maintain the social order and the particular status of a family, a ministry or a court.[117] Balzac writes of *les obligations du monde*.[118] A crisis could be caused by a prince's or ambassador's failure to invite all the King's ministers to a ball. Social life could also be considered part of a good education. Books such as *Manuel de l'homme de bon ton, ou Cérémonial de la bonne société* (1823), *L'Art de briller en société ou le Coryphée des salons* (1824, by P. Cuisin) and *Nouveau Manuel complet de la bonne compagnie ou Guide de la politesse et de la bienséance destiné à tous les âges et à toutes les conditions* (new edition 1845, by Madame Celnart) taught the behaviour necessary for occasions such as visits, meals, balls, church services and duels. The Duchesse de Luynes *douairière*, who ran a celebrated salon in the Hôtel de Luynes, advised her grandson: 'above all, search for good society, you will educate yourself by its conversation, you will learn to know men.'[119] The young Comte de Carné called the salons of Madame de Montcalm and the Duchesse de Duras *un champ inépuisable de jouissances et d'observations*.[120] The alternative of solitude, or staying at home, Lady

Granville and the Duchesse de Broglie agreed, was 'injudicious, ostentatious and cowardly.'[121]

The King and the royal family also considered it part of their royal duty to hold receptions – in Louis XVIII's case four times a week. Unlike Bourbon practice before 1789, they also attempted to address a few words to some of the people attending them.[122] In addition, on Louis XVIII's instructions, his court officials regularly entertained court society on his behalf. The wife of the Premier Gentilhomme in waiting, in a large apartment on the first floor of the Pavillon de Flore by the Seine, and the Duchesse d'Escars, wife of the Premier Maître d'Hôtel du Roi, in attics at the top of the Tuileries, were paid to 'do the honours of the court' once a week.[123] Thus an Irish visitor, Mrs Calvert, wrote in her diary on 18 August 1817, after her presentation at court: 'we went last night to the Duchesse d'Escars. She lives at the Tuileries perched up so high that we were quite out of breath getting to her apartments which are very low and rather like the cabin of a ship. All the fine people were there.' A few days later, on the Feast of Saint-Louis, she went to a concert given by the Duchesse d'Aumont, wife of the Premier Gentilhomme in waiting: 'we met the King of Prussia, the Duke of Wellington and all the fine world.'[124] Sometimes the Duchesse d'Escars counted as many as 230 at her reception.[125]

Many of her guests, such as the Irish novelist Maria Edgeworth, found the Duchesse d'Escars 'perfectly well-bred', despite her ultra-royalist views and contempt for what she called, in private letters to her children, 'names which the revolution has saved from oblivion'. Madame de Souza, her political and social enemy, however, claimed that Madame d'Escars believed herself to be 'floating between heaven and earth and of a completely different substance from the rest of the human race'.[126]

A conversation recorded at the Duchesse d'Escars' confirms the dominance of Parisian conversations by politics. Enough Russians were living in Paris for Pozzo to call them 'the colony': they had the reputation not only of spending lavishly but also of paying their bills.[127] One of the most celebrated was Count Rostopchine, the governor who had burnt Moscow at the time of the Napoleonic invasion. He had a love–hate relationship with what he called *ce coquin de Paris*. Like many others, he believed that it should have been destroyed by the allies in 1815: Paris was a monster which devoured and corrupted France. In time, he hoped, grass would grow in the rue de Richelieu and he would go rabbit shooting in the Palais Royal. Parisians were the vainest people in the world, with no common sense.[128] Yet he lived there from 1816 to 1824, later remarking that 'every foreigner who has lived in Paris becomes more or less its advocate.'[129] His daughter, who married the Comte de Ségur, became the most famous of all writers of children's stories in French.

Madame de Staël had returned to Paris in October 1816, after spending a winter in Pisa, where her daughter married the Duc de Broglie, and a summer at Coppet entertaining what were called 'the States-General of European opinion'. Although in bad health, she had presented the new Duchesse de Broglie at court and reopened her salon.[130] Rostopchine did not accept her invitations. One evening they met at the Duchesse d'Escars'. Defending Constant's remark that Russia was not a nation, and alluding to Rostopchine's Tartar features, she said that he looked as if he had been born before the dawn of civilisation. He said that she was nothing but a conspiring magpie – *une pie conspiratrice*. Increasingly angry, she replied that the Russians ought to revert to what they had formerly been. He went for her weak point, her banker father Necker:

> to that I retorted that, descending from the Tartars who are a nomadic people, I would be perfectly happy to do that, if she set the example;
> – and what example?
> – I will take my cattle to pasture once you return to the shop counter of your ancestors where you will keep accounts in duplicate and I am not certain that you will make as much at it as Monsieur your father.
> That caused a roar of laughter and following the example of the country, after this thrust I left.

Next day all the old royalists who hated Madame de Staël, but were too timid to challenge her in conversation themselves, called on Rostopchine to congratulate him.[131]

For some Parisians society was a matter of life and death. Madame de Staël said that she always felt a start of joy at the sound of the bell in her courtyard announcing a visit. In June 1817 she fell ill after attending a reception at Decazes' house. Even on her deathbed, 'pale, feeble and evidently depressed in spirits', she continued to receive visitors and give dinners, although they took place in a room beside her bedroom, and her daughter acted as her hostess, as well as her nurse.[132] Talleyrand too had not only *la maladie du ministère* but also *la rage de dîner en ville*. He would die from the effects of twisting his club-foot in the folds of the dress of Princess Lieven, whom he was taking in to dinner at the British embassy.[133] Chateaubriand claimed to live 'absolutely' alone. In a Paris salon, with his 'folded arms and abstracted look', this former pilgrim to Jerusalem struck Lady Morgan as affecting an 'air of Arabia Deserta'.[134] Yet in addition to the celebrated salons of the Duchesse de Duras and Madame Récamier, he regularly visited Madame d'Aguesseau and Madame de Montboissier, the daughter of Malesherbes, minister and defender of Louis XVI.[135] Louis XVIII himself would hasten his death by insisting, despite ill-health, on returning from Saint-Cloud to hold receptions in Paris.

Another reason for the intensity of social life in Paris, in addition to its political role and the number of court and ministerial receptions, was the possibility it offered the host of entertaining without the organisation, constrictions and cost of a meal. With no recommendations other than charm, intelligence and an enthusiastic letter of introduction from the French ambassador in Madrid, the American scholar George Ticknor soon had an open invitation to dine with the Comtes de Sainte-Aulaire and de Pastoret, and the Ducs de Duras and Broglie. Nevertheless he wrote: 'Dinner is not so solemn an affair at Paris as it is almost everywhere else. It is soon over; you come into the salon, take coffee and talk and by nine o'clock you separate.'

In London social life was 'vitally interwoven' with the dinner party; in Paris it was based on after-dinner visits, at around 9.30 p.m. Many married couples expected to spend the evening not at home, or with friends, but on separate visits to different salons.[136] Whereas morning visits were reserved for intimates, the purpose of evening visits was general conversation.[137] Lady Morgan, who claimed to have twenty houses to visit in the evening in Paris in 1816, wrote that they were 'soirees given without expense and resorted to without form': there was 'no gambling, no full dress', no lavish refreshments. Parisians laughed at the size, the 'bustle and motion of an English rout'. One British ambassadress, Lady Granville, was surprised by the absence of refreshments in Paris: 'The French . . . are easily satisfied; talk and a little syrup is all they want.'[138]

Once the hostess had issued a general invitation to spend the evening on a certain day or days of the week, guests did not need further invitations. In 1819 the English barrister Sutton Sharpe, for whom Paris was *une seconde patrie* which he visited nearly every year for his own amusement, met a Parisian Englishman called Sir John Byerley, whom he described as 'more French than English being a *Chevalier de la Légion d'Honneur* and a *membre de l'Institut*'. He was immediately introduced to

Byerley's circle of Parisian liberals, including Benjamin Constant and Stendhal, and was soon visiting three or four houses a week: 'the more regularly you go, the greater the attention.'[139]

The physical process of attending a salon was also fairly easy. Since most salons were in the same relatively small districts, the Faubourgs Saint-Germain or Saint-Honoré, many men, even ministers, walked rather than going by carriage.[140] They would mount the stairs, usually to the first floor, passing through antechambers where servants were waiting, often reading or playing cards. (In London, in contrast, whatever the weather, servants were usually compelled to wait in the doorway, the street or in carriages.) They would then generally be announced at the door of the salon by the maître d'hôtel of the person visited.[141] The rooms were furnished with sofas and armchairs, more informally and with greater concern for comfort than they had been in the eighteenth century, when stools and chairs had been arranged in formal rows or circles.[142]

When a guest arrived, the hostess did not rise from her armchair, but merely said *bon soir*, or *bonjour*: you could then move around and talk or remain silent as you wished.[143] While ladies sat talking in a circle, or sewing round a table, men stood in groups known as *petits pelotons*, or leant on the backs of the chairs of the ladies to whom they were talking. In some salons they were permitted to lounge, to put their feet on the fender or their elbows on the table.[144] Ticknor wrote of such evenings:

> They are the most rational form of society I have yet seen . . . You come in without ceremony, talk as long as you find persons you like and go away without taking leave, to repeat the same process in another salon . . . the general tone of these societies . . . is brilliant, graceful, superficial and hollow.[145]

Departure could be as casual as arrival. According to an Irish visitor Harriet Edgeworth, cousin of Maria Edgeworth, who passed the summer of 1820 in Paris:*

> it is the fashion for gentlemen to endeavour to get away with the least possible observation from the lady of the house. For this purpose he always looks around till he sees she is engaged in interesting conversations and then out he slides and happy he who gets the door shut without any remarks from Madame whose business it is to catch and regret him before he escapes.[146]

---

*The Edgeworths had an automatic entrée to royalist society, their cousin the Abbé Edgeworth having been confessor to Louis XVI at the time of his execution in 1793.

This was informal Parisian society. Despite years in the service of the Republic and the Empire, Talleyrand's manners remained those of the *ancien régime*, when rank had been revealed by whether a guest was greeted in the middle of the salon, at the door, on the landing or at the foot of the staircase. After his dismissal from the ministry in 1815, having painted *Hôtel Talleyrand* in golden letters on the porte cochère, he opened his house to everyone in Paris with a European reputation, in addition to his normal circle of diplomats, cronies and old ladies, hoping to win support for what was called *le parti Talleyrand*.[147] Despite his age and club-foot, the prince was described as 'constantly moving, limping backwards and forwards through the crowd in the different rooms, and to and from the door of entry from the anteroom, conducting those of mark who arrive and acompanying them when they retire'.[148]

Accessibility as well as political intensity distinguished the social life of Paris from that of every other European capital. In Vienna, 'town of pride and ceremony and etiquette', the nobility was 'unbelievably exclusive', and refused to receive 'all Merchants, Bankers, in fact a large proportion of truly respectable and highly educated people', according to Martha Wilmot, wife of the British embassy chaplain. The different classes lived such separate lives that they did not even make jokes about each other. In London a gentleman might be embarrassed to acknowledge his own father in the street: 'Almacks peers' did not care to know peers who were not admitted to that Olympus.[149]

In Paris on the other hand, according to a later traveller, 'the deference shown to talent, whether literary, political or artistic, in preference to mere rank or wealth without this qualification, furnishes a striking contrast to an English party in high life'.[150] 'The most agreeable house in Paris', in the words of a rival hostess Madame de Boigne, was that of the Duchesse de Duras in her spacious *hôtel* at 31 rue de Varenne. Yet it was more accessible than the aristocratic salons of 1900 described by Proust in *A la recherche du temps perdu*. She received every evening between 9 and 12 in 'an attractive *cabinet* full of books, pictures, prints, globes, vases, bibelots in good taste and from every corner of the globe. She rests an elbow on a large desk on which is the book of the moment, many English books etc.'[151] She was an intellectual, a writer of novels and *pensées* whom some found pretentious and difficult; just as Madame de Staël had held a sprig of laurel between her fingers if she felt especially eloquent, for hours at a time the Duchesse de Duras 'rolls little bits of paper between her fingers'. One day she gives you a smile, noticed a Polish visitor Count Raczynski; the next asks you a question; and the following day refuses you both. After she had married her daughters in 1819, she stopped paying visits to other ladies.[152]

An enemy of what she called 'stupidity, gossip, frivolity', her *petit cercle* included, in her view, 'most of the distinguished men who are in Paris'.[153] Alexander von Humboldt, author of a classic account of Spanish America, an unofficial observer for the Prussian government in Paris from 1806 to 1827, and 'equally indefatigable in science as in society, having studied everything, seen everything', called her friendship 'a luminous point in my life'. With a fierce face and a strange smile, he was described by the poet Fontaney as a 'robust' talker.[154] Baron Cuvier, the inventor of palaeontology, professor of anatomy at the Jardin des Plantes and president of the Commission for Public Instruction, Talleyrand, Pozzo and Villemain were other regular visitors. In 1825 Baron Gérard and the American writer Washington Irving were invited to come any evening in the week between 9 and 11.[155] Politicians and courtiers like Villèle, Molé, Mathieu de Montmorency, the Ducs de Lévis, de Doudeauville, de Maillé, and many others, also attended. Indeed so many important people met in her salon that Richelieu once wrote to ask for her 'indulgence' for his government.[156]

In 1817 George Ticknor was immediately made welcome. Soon, in his own words, he was 'positively bewitched'. The Duchesse de Duras' visitors formed 'as interesting a society as could well be collected . . . I liked her very much and went to her hotel often, in fact sometimes every day.' On Sundays he dined there; on Tuesday evening he went when 'she received at home and all the world came'. He also attended what she called *mes petites cinq heures* when she received four or five intimates in the library before dinner at 6. Her intelligence and literary culture were combined with passionate belief in the Bourbons and 'the European alliance'. Once during the political crisis at the end of 1818 (when Richelieu was about to leave office) Ticknor found her and Talleyrand alone in the library, arguing about the meaning of a phrase in the Charte. Talleyrand was trying to convince the Duchess that the King should recall him to power: *un petit moyen* had not yet been tried – himself. Their conversation was so confidential that the Duchess sent a secretary to summon Ticknor back, as he was walking out of the courtyard, to request him not to mention it.[157]

A talented young noble with wealth and literary ambitions, a former officer in the Mousquetaires Gris, the Marquis de Custine, noted that her salon, like Madame de Montcalm's, was her career. She had 'the will-power of a conqueror;* but as she has no army at her orders, this faculty torments her uselessly'.[158] Convinced that she never made mistakes about people, she also used her salon to try to wean former Bonapartists like Cuvier and Gérard from their admiration for the Emperor. Benjamin Constant came once. So many people were present that the Duchess could not talk to him. He did not return.[159]

Inside the *grande dame*, however, was an unhappy woman. The Duchesse de Duras was not only honest, direct, intelligent and relatively unprejudiced, but also dominating, susceptible and apt to regard her own desires as decrees of providence. She admitted that 'one cross look, one mark of forgetfulness, one little wrong from those I love and I am demoralised for a week.'[160] Moreover she had never been pretty. After the first years of marriage, her husband, a Premier Gentilhomme de la Chambre of such arrogance that Madame de Boigne called him *plus duc que feu monsieur de Saint-Simon*, was unfaithful. He rarely attended her salon and is rarely mentioned in her letters.[161] Her epigrams reflected her situation:

– If you have never been pretty, you have never been young.
– How many times one dies before the real moment of death.
– Everything is bearable in life except to look back on regrets which nothing can soften, errors which nothing can repair.
– There are beings from whom one feels separated by those walls of crystal described in fairy stories: one sees them, one speaks to them, one is near them; but one cannot touch them.[162]

She loved her two daughters Félicie and Clara with a passion as fierce as that of Madame de Souza for Charles de Flahaut. After the younger daughter Clara married the silent, caustic Henri de Chastellux on 30 August 1819, she continued to live with her parents, and to lavish as much tenderness and devotion on her mother as on her children. When her husband went to Lisbon as French ambassador, she stayed in Paris. The Duchesse de Duras called her 'an angel', 'the glory and the consolation of my life'.[163]

However, she felt betrayed by her elder and favourite daughter Félicie who continued, after her first husband's death, to live with her

---

* As he knew well, having barely managed to resist the Duchess's commands to marry her daughter Clara, whom he did not love, whom he knew he would make unhappy and whom his own mother considered too poor.

former mother-in-law the ultra-royalist Princesse de Talmont. Money was a motive: the princess had made Félicie her heir.* The Duchesse de Duras refused to see her daughter and called the princess *la femme fausse et méchante à laquelle elle m'a sacrifiée* and her relations *une famille de gens factices et égoïstes*. On 14 September 1819, against her parents' wishes, Félicie married again, to an ultra-royalist provincial noble from the Vendée, M. de La Rochejaquelein. The Duchesse de Duras suffered the torments of one of the rejected lovers in her novels. She regarded her daughter as no longer the same person. Chateaubriand consoled her with the remark that she was 'in the same position as the rest of us: deceived in what we love most'.[164]

Chateaubriand was both the genius in her salon and the man in her life. She told him that she loved him more than anyone in the world; his mind and his heart pleased her more than any other. The year of Félicie's betrayal, however, he had a *coup de foudre* for Madame Récamier. He began to visit her celebrated *cellule* on the third floor of the Abbaye aux Bois, at 16 rue de Sèvres (a nunnery which also contained a school and flats for ladies), as often in the afternoon as he did the Duchess in her *hôtel* in the rue de Varenne in the morning. He was so regular in his times of arrival – 11 a.m. at the latter, 3 p.m. at the former – that neighbours set their watches by him.[165] When he was away, the Duchess wrote: 'I have had all the clocks stopped in order no longer to hear the hours striking when you will no longer come.'[166]

The Duchesse de Duras detested sharing. She called him a *tyrannique enfant gâté*: his selfishness was such that everyone who had loved him had been unhappy. Yet Chateaubriand remained the friend to whom she could talk about 'all the horrors which fill our lives'. In his notes he assured his *chère soeur* – although, as she frequently complained, his acts did not bear out his words – 'You are all I miss about Paris'; 'My life will not be very long but what is left of it is yours'.[167] Her letters are at least as eloquent as his, and considerably more sensible: she was appalled by the 'folly' and 'unreason' of his ultra friends, and, on several occasions, like Madame de Montcalm, tried to reconcile Chateaubriand with the government.[168]

For Chateaubriand the salons of both the Duchesse de Duras and Madame Récamier were political bases as well as emotional outlets. The Duchesse de Duras was his link to the royal family, the court and leading

---

* Félicie inherited her *hôtel* at 77 rue de Grenelle, and other properties, on her death on 8 May 1831.

politicians. Madame Récamier was a link to her old friend the leading ultra Mathieu de Montmorency and a means, through the writers attending her salon, of reinforcing his literary glory. While away from Paris serving as French ambassador in Berlin, hearing of a brief indisposition of the Duchesse de Duras, Chateaubriand ordered: 'Get better in order to open your salon and have me recalled.'[169] Four years earlier, during another crisis, he had written: 'I can do nothing without you.'[170]

Her salon was a European institution; in addition to all her other visitors, a school friend Madame de Sainte-Maure called on the Duchess every day.[171] Yet the Duchesse de Duras felt a sentiment of isolation and uselessness – perhaps due to her husband's preference for others, lack of good looks, an innate insecurity. Her novels, which pleased Goethe as well as the Parisian public, reveal a pure style and an original mind. They were about *isolés*, barred from happiness by race, class or sex:[172] the hopeless passion for a French noble of a black girl *Ourika* (1823, published by the Imprimerie Royale), destined to be 'alone, always alone, never loved';[173] a bourgeois in eighteenth-century noble society in Paris, *Edouard* (1825); and an impotent man, *Olivier ou le Secret* (1826). In the opinion of Chateaubriand she combined in her writing the force of Madame de Staël with the grace of Madame de La Fayette.[174]

The salon of the Princesse de Vaudémont was another neutral meeting-ground for people from different classes, countries and political parties. Born a Montmorency, widow of a prince of Lorraine, she came from the highest court nobility and, although small, plain and fat, retained a *grand air*. Lady Granville described her as 'uncommonly agreeable, full of new thoughts and strong opinions, cordial and good-natured and as natural as her monkey'. Administering her own fortune, she could afford a *salon de permanence*. Both in her château in Suresnes outside Paris and in her flower-filled *hôtel* in the rue de Provence near the boulevards, where every room was a garden, she kept open house every day of the year, except on the day she gave a ball for the poor. Her guests, whom she called her conscripts, included – as well as the Corps Diplomatique – Wellington, Richelieu, Pasquier and Count Rostopchine. Talleyrand often sat in a corner, playing with his cane, breaking his silence only to lash out with a well-prepared epigram against the enemy of the moment.[175]

Rostopchine found the conversation of the scientists and writers in her salon particularly instructive. He wrote to his wife:

I was talking yesterday with one of these gentlemen at the Princesse de Vaudémont's, and he surprised me by his knowledge ... he demonstrated by deductions made from several excavations in the surroundings of Paris from the different layers of soil that the earth cannot have lasted longer than Genesis says and he made a terrible outburst against those who have used physics to support their disbelief and as a basis for their erroneous opinions. We enjoy complete liberty of conversation here. Everyone is at liberty to talk with everyone else or separately [unlike Madame de Montcalm's guests]. While this gentleman was explaining his system to me, Madame de Coigny was arguing about Racine with Belmonte, two Frenchmen were talking of war with the Prussian minister, the Princesse de Vaudémont was proving the antiquity of the breed of *Charlots* [King Charles spaniels] and two ladies were telling anecdotes of London.[176]

In contrast to London, there was no talk of hunting or shooting or racing. Perhaps for that reason, in the opinion of Lady Blessington, the English did not shine in Paris salons; they lacked Parisians'

lightness and brilliancy, a sort of touch and go ... Never dwelling long on any subject and rarely entering profoundly into it, they sparkle on the surface with great dexterity, bringing wit, gaiety and tact into play ... Conversation is with the French the aim and object of society ... Such is the tact of the Parisians that even the ignorant conceal the poverty of their minds.[177]

Like those of Madame de Montcalm and the Duchesse de Duras, the princess's salon had a political role. Seeing so many people every day, she was often better informed about a minister's or an ambassador's plans than were his own colleagues.[178] Moreover she was a liberal with friends in the Napoleonic nobility, on whose behalf she was prepared to intervene. In December 1815 she had inspired three Englishmen, Douglas Kinnaird, John Hely-Hutchinson and Michael Bruce, to help an old friend, Napoleon's Directeur des Postes the Comte de Lavallette, to escape from prison disguised in his wife's clothes.[179] She was a friend of Fouché and helped put him in touch with royalists in July 1815. Nor did she abandon him after his disgrace: in 1827 she gave the reception after the marriage of his daughter Joséphine-Ludmille to Adolphe de La Barthe, Comte de Thermes – one of many marriages which, like the salons themselves, united nobles and non-nobles.[180]

The seductive power of her salon is described by a young doctor from the Balearics, Joseph Orfila, who had come to Paris in 1807 at the age of eighteen. Paris was the medical, as well as the cultural, capital of Europe, a leader in research and treatment (including treatment of venereal disease).[181] In part because so many men wounded in the revolutionary and Napoleonic wars needed treatment, the medical profession was rising in prestige. To keep this able young Spanish doctor in Paris, Orfila was made a member of the newly created Académie de Médecine, *médecin par quartier* of the King and finally Professor of Chemistry. By 1814 the princess regarded him as a son and he was going to her salon twice a week. 'I have met in her house several doctors and other personalities', Orfila wrote, 'whose acquaintance has already helped me and could still be useful to me on occasion. In this country men are regarded from a different point of view than in ours: talent is considered to be the true nobility.' Like many salon 'conscripts', he concluded: 'I have obtained more advantageous decisions for the Faculty, I have succeeded in more projects relative to research, in salons than in the proceedings of commissions and in government offices.'[182]

For a salon could be an employment agency for guests as well as a career for their hostess. Indeed Stendhal claimed that people attended them only to obtain advancement: 'everyone knows perfectly well that you only obtain fame and fortune through *les relations de salon*.'[183] In 1820 Lamartine, who had left the Gardes du Corps in 1816, received his first post in the diplomatic service, as an Attaché d'Ambassade in Naples, with the help of the Duchesse de Broglie and Madame de Sainte-Aulaire, who had spoken on his behalf to ministers attending their salons.[184] The Duchesse de Duras was also known for advancing the careers of young diplomats.[185] For his part the richest banker in Paris, James de Rothschild, informed his brother in London: 'if I attend a society party I go there to become acquainted with people who might be useful for the business.'[186]

The Princesse de Vaudémont served tea, ices, and at the end of the evening punch.[187] On some evenings she also provided music, sung by such celebrated performers as Judith Pasta and Louis Lablache – although the music was often interrupted by the noise of fighting among the princess's dogs. Orfila wrote of her salon, as Ticknor did of the Duchesse de Duras', with the intensity of love: 'The attraction which this salon had for me was such that it completely absorbed me and I almost never left my home except to go there.'[188]

Not all salons were run by women. In his four-room apartment on the rue des Beaux-Arts (now Bonaparte), or occasionally in his studio, the most fashionable painter in Europe, François Gérard, helped by his wife and a favourite pupil Mlle Godefroid, for over thirty years received a variety of artists, diplomats and royalists: Pozzo,* Rossini, Meyerbeer, Ingres, Delacroix, Stendhal. Alexander von Humboldt felt like one of Gérard's family. General Foy described the artist as 'always witty, always brilliant, always excellent to listen to'. Lady Morgan noticed that his salon was 'always open to young and rising talent'. One of Balzac's definitions of happiness was to have a salon as 'astonishing' as that of Gérard.[189]

In 1817 Gérard's painting of the *Entry of Henri IV into Paris in 1594*, commissioned by the Maison du Roi, was the sensation of a salon of another kind, the salon of paintings held every two years in the Louvre. The picture, which the King himself came to admire, depicted scenes of reconciliation between warring Frenchmen, appropriate to the King's current policy.[190] Saying 'I am happy that such a fine work has been executed under my reign', Louis XVIII, to the fury of ultra-royalists, appointed this former Jacobin and drawing-master of the Empress Marie Louise Premier Peintre du Roi.[191] Known as the painter of kings and the king of painters, Baron Gérard, as he became in 1820, was said to consider that the political opinions of a painter should be like his palette, on which every colour should be found.[192] Indeed while painting portraits and historical pictures for Louis XVIII – and a picture of *Ourika* for the Duchesse de Duras – Gérard was at the same time painting a picture of Napoleon in his study for the British Bonapartist Lady Holland, and after his death in 1821 would paint a picture of his tomb on St Helena.[193] (Talleyrand likewise, while serving Louis XVIII as Grand Chamberlain, would plan his overthrow.) Gérard also provided the illustrations for the first correct edition of the national epic of Portugal, Luis de Camões' *Lusiads*, prepared by the Comte de Souza and printed with special Portuguese characters, which Louis XVIII himself declared to be 'the finest work which has been printed by a French press'. At a dinner given by Gérard in February 1818 to celebrate publication, guests included another court artist Isabey, *le terrible Rostopchine, un tigre blafard devenu gris*, in the words of Madame de Souza, and the Bonapartist writer Etienne de Jouy, who read excerpts from his play *Bélisaire* in praise of the law-giving Emperor Justinian – Napoleon.[194]

Baron Gérard was the most Parisian of painters. The Duc d'Orléans, Pozzo, Decazes, General Foy, the British ambassador Sir Charles Stuart,

---

* Pozzo owned, in addition to several portraits by Gérard, Gérard's pictures of *Les Six Amours*: *L'Arrivée*, *L'Attaque*, *Le Succès*, *Le Regret*, *Le Repos*, *Le Départ*.

the Duchesses de Dino and de Broglie, Madame Récamier and Mlle Mars (whose house he decorated) were among the celebrities who commissioned a portrait from him. Gérard's salon operated every Wednesday evening. Even during the summer the family returned from their house at Auteuil to receive guests, until one day a servant was obliged to announce to those arriving: 'Monsieur le Baron died this morning.' On 13 January 1837 the vast abbey church of Saint-Germain des Prés was not large enough to contain all those who came to his funeral. Balzac wrote: 'he was a man full of exquisite qualities and sincerely loved by his friends which is very rare in the world of gold and iron called Paris.'[195]

The salons of Baron Gérard, Madame de Montcalm, the Princesse de Vaudémont and the Duchesse de Duras favoured the Restoration. However Paris contained a separate Napoleonic society, hostile to the Restoration, whose centre was the house of Maréchal Suchet, Duc d'Albuféra, at 31 rue du Faubourg Saint-Honoré. Son of a Lyon silk manufacturer, Suchet had been one of the most successful of Napoleon's marshals, in Italy, Spain and the defence of France in 1814 and 1815. Maréchale Suchet's guest list begins with the Comtesse de Gotland – the name adopted by her aunt Désirée Clary, wife of Marshal Bernadotte Crown Prince of Sweden, who, on account of her dislike of Sweden and passion for the Duc de Richelieu, remained in Paris while her husband reigned in Stockholm. If she did not see Richelieu at the opera, *ma folle de reine*, as he called her, hunted for him on the streets, or in the Jardin des Tuileries.[196] Others on the Suchets' list included Marshals Oudinot, Gouvion, Masséna, Pérignon, Lefebvre and Marmont's wife, but not Marmont himself: in that world he would have been considered a traitor.[197] There are no royalist names. Madame de Souza wrote of 'Marshal Suchet who receives every Sunday, to whose house we [the Bonapartists] all go, where not a word of politics is mentioned; for only music is performed; but his salon is a true salon of the Emperor and it displeases the government.'[198] The fact that 'not a word of politics' was mentioned was itself political. Marshal Suchet was so Bonapartist that, by his own insistence, the peerage he received in 1819 was dated from that year, rather than from his first nomination as a peer in 1814, in order to commemorate his exclusion from the peerage in 1815 for serving the Emperor during the Hundred Days.[199]

For General Foy, a frequent visitor who would not have known royalist salons, 'the salon of Marshal Suchet is the most brilliant in Paris'.[200] Foy also enjoyed balls in the house of another Napoleonic marshal,

Soult. Despite Soult's exile from France in 1815–19, he had maintained the magnificent *hôtel* which he had bought in 1803 in the Faubourg Saint-Germain at 69 rue de l'Université – formerly the property of Talleyrand's émigré cousin the Prince de Chalais – as a Napoleonic enclave in Restoration Paris. It was furnished with Jacob Desmalter furniture, Thomire bronzes, a Salon de l'Empereur and a Salon Militaire decorated with trophies and the marshal's coat of arms on the walls: the marshal's bed and bedside table were adorned with carved wooden axes, shields, spears and helmets. The glory of the *hôtel* was Soult's gallery of sixty Spanish pictures looted – according to the marshal, saved from destruction – during the Peninsular War from the monasteries of Seville and the Spanish royal collection: Delacroix would find the Murillos 'admirable'.[201] When Soult asked Marquess Wellesley if his brother the Duke of Wellington had such fine Spanish pictures at Apsley House, the Marquess replied: 'No, you had the first choice.' According to Baron Denon, who had been the Emperor's chief adviser on which foreign works of art to take for the Louvre, Soult's pictures were worth seven million francs. Denon's own house at 7 quai Voltaire, in addition to containing his splendid collection of pictures and antiquities, was another shrine to *Napoléon le Grand* in Restoration Paris, with pictures of the Emperor in every guise, old, young, Roman, modern.[202]

Politics decided not only the conversation but also the composition of Paris salons. In addition to the royalist salons of the Duchesse de Duras and Madame de Montcalm, and the Napoleonic salons of Maréchal Suchet and Baron Denon, there was a liberal society, which had been severed from the royalists by the political passions of 1815 and 1816.[203] In 1817 the Duchesse de Broglie inherited her mother's salon – although her father Benjamin Constant, discredited by his volteface in the Hundred Days, came less frequently, preferring to spend his evenings in the gambling clubs of the Palais Royal or the salon of Jacques Laffitte. Not a good speaker in the Chambers – he had a monotonous delivery and was unable to stand still – Constant once said that winning at cards interested him more than anything in the world.[204]

Warmer-hearted than Madame de Staël, and unlike her a devout Protestant, the Duchesse de Broglie was described by Ticknor as possessing 'great simplicity and frankness, not a little personal beauty and an independent original way of thinking'. For Castellane she was 'charming: the most beautiful eyes in the world, tall, a very *svelte* figure, very pretty hands and feet, a sweet and benevolent smile, supple in all her movements, sometimes gauche, graceful because she is simple'. The

Duke her husband was agreeable, erudite and distinguished, although 'rather a teaser like all the Broglie'.[205] For the next twenty years the *doctrinaires*, as such high-minded liberals were called – Rémusat, Guizot, Villemain, Barante, Royer-Collard, Sainte-Aulaire and their wives – liberal deputies and celebrities like Talma, met around the table in her salon at 74 rue de Bourbon, the sumptuously decorated former *hôtel* of Maréchal Ney, into which she had moved in 1819.

With the arrogance of other intellectual aristocrats, such as their contemporary equivalent in London the Holland House set, or a later Edwardian counterpart the Souls, the *doctrinaires* considered themselves the most brilliant society of their time. Madame de Rémusat wrote that it was the only house in Paris where people conversed *d'une manière solide*. At Madame Récamier's, royalists joked that they were a small self-regarding group. An anonymous verse described them as

> *assemblés sur ce canapé,*
> *autour d'une jeune beauté,*
> *qui vous parle de premiers principes,*
> *et vous enivre avec du thé.*[206]

According to Flahaut: 'there never was a coterie so well made to inspire dislike and appear ridiculous . . . suffisance, conceit, a look of contempt for all those who don't belong to their half dozen is indescribable . . . the manner of Rémusat in particular is quite beyond description.'[207] Even the Duchesse de Broglie herself admitted that most *doctrinaires* lacked the easy charm of, for example, the Prince de Montmorency-Laval, a *grand seigneur* hardly aware that a revolution had taken place: 'he has very good manners and when one lives among *doctrinaires* . . . one is not displeased to relax from time to time in a very gentle politeness. They are self-indulgences to which one should not treat oneself for too long, for fear of weakening, but *en passant* they do one good.'[208]

For some Parisians, a salon was not only a power base, an employment agency, an education or a substitute home, but also a place to look for a wife or a mistress. People attending salons could be very free in their behaviour. The Duc de Chevreuse warned his son, the young Duc de Luynes, in 1819: 'the most terrible diseases are the result of libertinage and unfortunately shameful diseases can sometimes be found in salons and almost always with women of the street.'[209] After dinner, according to Count Molé, Talleyrand might behave with his beloved niece Dorothée in such a fashion as to 'make even the most hardened warriors lower their eyes'. She also had younger lovers. After her husband was made Duc de Dino by the King of Naples in 1815, Parisians remarked on the inappropriateness of her new title. The new Duchess of Dino was not accustomed to say no.[210]

The salons of the Duchesse de Duras, Madame de Montcalm, the Princesse de Vaudémont, Baron Gérard, Maréchal Suchet and the Duchesse de Broglie were the most prominent in Restoration Paris. There were many others. The Sundays of Madame de La Briche, mother-in-law of Count Molé, in her house in the rue de la Ville l'Evêque in the Faubourg Saint-Honoré, or during the summer in her magnificent neoclassical château of Le Marais south of Paris, were said to be the only permanent institution in France (never having been interrupted, since their inception in 1786, except by the reign of terror).[211] A mediocre liberal poet and playwright, an enemy of the Romantics called Jean-Pons-Guillaume Viennet, never worked in the evening. He frequented, among other salons, the Napoleonic salon of the Comtesse de Ségur (*de la bonne et vieille causerie parisienne où l'on apprend toujours quelquechose*); the military salon of Maréchal Gouvion Saint-Cyr; the literary salons of the Princesse de Salm-Dyck (formerly Madame Pipelet) and Madame Dufrenoy; the musical salon of Madame Thayer (whose husband, an American shipowner, had built the fashionable covered shopping arcade, the Passage des Panoramas, in 1799); the aristocratic salon of the Vicomtesse de Ruolz; and the semi-official salon of the politician Comte Roy.[212] Viennet was one of the many people for whom salons were primarily an escape from solitude. Twenty years later another author, Prosper Mérimée, would write: 'at last there are some salons reopening and one knows where to go to spend the evening.'[213]

The freedom and brilliance of Paris social life – royalist, Napoleonic, liberal, political, literary and musical – contributed to its status as the capital of Europe almost as much as the freedom and brilliance of its parliamentary life. According to the Cambridge don John Bowes Wright, who often resided in Paris:

> Of all the cities I have been in none certainly is comparable to it for variety of character, society and amusement; and on no former occasion have I witnessed such a display of these as at present. The extraordinary combinations which the various reunions present and the still more extraordinary scenes and sentiments to which they give rise are well calculated powerfully to excite and agitate the mind . . . [London] appears triste and stupid after the lively scenes of Paris . . . I would not leave Paris . . . for all the Carnivals of Italy combined.[214]

Wright was a bachelor in search of women. The wife of a Protestant pastor from the city of Geneva, however, was equally emphatic: 'It is not the beauty, the arts, the monuments, the pictures, it is the society, the spirit which reigns, full of amenity, indulgence [unlike her native city] and in addition so many objects of interest.'[215] Lady Morgan judged that 'the society of Paris taken as a whole, and including all parties and factions, is infinitely superior in point of taste, acquirement and courtesy, to that of the capital of any other nation.'[216]

Whether royalist, liberal or Bonapartist, salons were generally a woman's domain. Lady Blessington noted that in Paris there was 'a strict observance of deferential respect from the men towards the women while these last seem to assume that superiority accorded to them in manner, if not entertained in fact, by the sterner sex' . . . Young men would pick up the fans, and listen to the anecdotes, of old women. A man 'takes off his hat in France to every woman whom he has ever met in society, although he does not address her, unless she encourages him to do so'; in England the woman had to bow first. 'The mode of salutation is also much more deferential in France than in England. The hat is held a second longer off the head, the bow is lower and the smile of recognition is more *aimable*.' English 'glumness' or 'nonchalance' were almost unknown.[217] Hence the saying that Paris was the paradise of women, the purgatory of men and the inferno of horses.[218]

5

The British Parisians

1814–1830

We have met with a surprising number of our acquaintances since we came to
Paris, not less than six in the first day; and this gave us a very English feeling.
Emma Allen to Elisabeth Wedgwood, Hôtel de Tours,
rue Notre-Dame-des-Victoires, 16 September 1815

O NE FACTOR UNITING both the Chambers and salons of Paris was
the paramount influence of Britain. In political and economic life,
in society, literature and the arts, the British were everywhere. Like the
United States since 1945, Britain was the 'indispensable nation'.
Powerful, liberal and innovative, it was an inevitable point of reference
and source of inspiration. Politics was the basis of this Franco-British
symbiosis.

France was learning to operate a parliamentary monarchy. The
bloodshed of the French revolution still made it an object of revulsion
to most French politicians. Britain was thus their principal model and
inspiration. At the very beginning of the Restoration, Talleyrand – after
Guizot, the French politician who most appreciated Britain – presenting the Senate to Louis XVIII at Saint-Ouen on 2 May 1814, had said:
'institutions well tried by a neighbouring people give support and not
barriers to monarchs who love the law and are fathers of their people.'[1]
Liberals admired the strength of Parliament and the freedom of the
press, royalists the power of the crown and the nobility. The Parliament
in Westminster, 'the mechanism of the English government' and its perfection, was one of the main topics of discussion in Paris.[2]

Louis XVIII himself often referred to English political practices as
precedents to follow in France. In 1815 he accepted Talleyrand's offer

of resignation with the words: 'Ah well, I will be obliged to behave as in England and to charge someone to form a new cabinet.' During the crisis of November 1819, when the government was about to move right, he wrote to Decazes, alluding to English crises in 1783 and 1806: 'That is not what happens in England . . . When the King changes his ministry he does not charge two people but one individual to form one for him.'[3]

The Princesse de Poix was dominated by 'a fanatical admiration for England brought back from the emigration', as well as a passionate interest in parliamentary debates in both Paris and London.[4] Madame de Souza had a cult of *l'heureuse et constitutionelle Angleterre*, and believed that Frenchmen returned better for having tasted 'the freedom of spirit and conversation which one enjoys in England and that love of justice which animates all classes there'.[5] The son of Louis-Philippe Duc d'Orléans, who was taken to the United Kingdom by his father in 1829 in order to finish his education, called its organisation 'one of the masterpieces of the human spirit', and returned for another visit to *cet admirable pays* in 1833.[6] The oppression of Ireland and the Roman Catholics; what Byron called Britain's 'cant and hypocrisy' and growing Puritanism; the unprecedented harshness of Lord Liverpool's ministry, shown in the Peterloo Massacre in 1819 (when eleven civilians were killed by militia during a mass meeting), the suspension of *habeas corpus*, the imprisonment of radical MPs and writers like Hobhouse and Leigh Hunt; and the near-revolutionary situation in London, when the Regent was booed on his way to open Parliament and the guards themselves showed signs of revolt during the trial of the popular heroine Queen Caroline, did not disturb Parisian Anglophilia.[7]

For many Parisians, royalist and liberal, old and young, London was the natural alternative to Paris. Louis XVIII himself, after the Hundred Days, kept over £200,000 in Coutts bank in London, as a precaution against upheaval in his kingdom. When Chateaubriand was disgusted with politics in France, he considered retiring to England – whose language he knew and whose 'noble hospitality' he had appreciated as an émigré: when he had returned from London to Paris in 1802, like many other émigrés he had felt 'half-English' in manners and mentality.[8] During the ultra-royalist reaction, Constant lived there from September 1815 to June 1816 – and found conversation less 'discreet', since less subject to police surveillance, than in Paris. In order to show similar disapproval of ultra-royalism, from September 1815 until April 1817 the Duc d'Orléans had also lived there, in the house in

Twickenham where he had lived from 1800 to 1808 – to the relief of the French government, which considered that he did less harm in London than in Paris. More Anglophile than even Louis XVIII and Artois, he continued to forward copies of his correspondence with the King of France to the British government.[9] When Decazes wanted to attack Monsieur, even suggesting that the Duc d'Angoulême directly succeed Louis XVIII, he did so through articles by senior civil servants published in *The Times* or the *Morning Chronicle*, and then translated back into French newspapers.[10]

Ordinary Frenchmen and women also visited London, to observe the sessions of the Houses of Parliament, the functioning of the jury system, or the progress of the Industrial Revolution. In 1822, for example, Auguste de Staël, who later wrote *Lettres sur l'Angleterre* (1825), the Duc de Broglie, and Ternaux returned desolated by England's industrial and social superiority over France.[11] Indeed between 1800 and 1850 the gap between the British and French economies, particularly in such modern sectors as iron production and cotton spinning, grew even wider.[12] By its industrial, commercial and maritime preeminence, not Paris but London, the largest and wealthiest city in the world, deserved the title of 'capital of the nineteenth century'. Between 1800 and 1850 the population of Paris grew by 86 per cent, from 565,000 to 1,053,000; that of London by 136 per cent, from 948,000 to 2,236,000. Impressed by the multitudes of ships on the Thames and of carriages on the streets, Alfred de Vigny called London 'the image of modern civilisation'. For Chateaubriand, annoyed by the French habit of calling themselves the first nation in the world, the approach up the Thames, past thousands of ships moored in the largest port in the world, 'surpasses all images of power'.[13]

As leader of the Industrial Revolution, Britain influenced the economy, as well as the political life, of Paris. In 1816 a British resident, F.A. Winsor, organised the first lighting by gas of a public place in Paris, the Passage des Panoramas. Slowly thereafter gas lighting spread from public places to streets; the first Paris street lit by gas was the rue de la Paix in 1829.[14] On 29 March 1816, the first steamboat to appear on the Seine, watched from the *quais* by admiring Parisian crowds, was a British boat, the *Elise*. The same year the first French steamboat, called *Le Charles-Philippe* after the Comte d'Artois, was launched near Paris. By 1823 twenty-two steamboats were operating on the Seine; soon they were a popular means of public transport.[15] Many of the steamboats were constructed by a British firm, Manby & Wilson, in its factory at

Charenton east of Paris: the many British workers they employed were often involved in fights with French workers.[16]

When the French government needed loans with which to pay off the final allied indemnity in 1816–18, it turned not to French bankers but to the great London bank of Barings – more accustomed to funding the British government's war effort against France than the French government itself. British investment in the Paris stock market was such that during the depression of 1819 a banker called Haldimand complained: 'Few gentlemen return from Paris without having made a small investment in French stock.'[17] The Prefect of the Seine himself, the Comte de Chabrol, visited London in 1823, to study its systems of gas lighting, drains, water supply, pavements. He admired the latest machinery and returned with 'a fine collection of plans to execute'.[18]

At the same time as the French found inspiration in Britain, the growing number of British visitors reflected the continuing attraction of Paris. On 20 July 1816 *The Times* thundered:

> The emigration from England to France continues to be indeed alarming . . . They take the bread from the mouth of the slaving workman in England and lavish it on French luxuries and French amusements . . . The words *national bankruptcy* begin to be familiar to our ears.

There were said to be 29,000 British living in Paris: 68 per cent of foreign visitors in Paris hotels were British.[19] Revisiting Paris in 1816, Edward Stanley, who had been there in 1814, asked: 'where are the French? Nowhere, all is English. English carriages fill the street.'[20]

Perhaps because the Regent held no more than four Drawing-rooms a year in London, British ladies turned to the court in Paris as an alternative route to social recognition. In some years more British than French ladies were presented at the court of the Tuileries; the royal family often talked to them in English.[21] If a request for presentation was refused, as it was to the Whig Earl and Countess of Oxford in 1816, the applicant's fury was unbounded.[22] By 1816 so many British ladies were being presented that the Premier Gentilhomme began to demand, from the British ambassador, certificates of prior presentation at the court of St James's, signed by two British ladies who themselves had already been presented there. The British ambassador replied that, given 'the exceptional number of English ladies in Paris', he did not have time to check.[23] Nervous British ladies' efforts to dash from one door to another of the throne room, having curtseyed at a distance without approaching Louis XVIII, obliged the Premier Gentilhomme in waiting to rush after them, shouting in English, 'The King! The King!'[24]

Since Paris offered a unique combination of luxury, pleasure, freedom and cheapness, many wealthy British set up house there with family, servants, carriages and plate. The British Parisians soon developed their own charities, literature and slang: they talked of 'doing a little Tuileries' and walking in the 'sham Elizas' (Champs Elysées).[25] The centre of British Paris was a broad new street running north from the Palais Royal, the rue Vivienne. Now drained of life and elegance, in these years it was packed with shoppers. General Mercer could write: 'Here is to be seen all the beauty and fashion of Paris.' (It was in this street that Dumas fils placed the first meeting of Armand Duval and *la Dame aux Caméllias*.) British visitors compared it to Bond Street, although a visit to its rich and substantial shops* could be unpleasant, as the street was filthy and there was no pavement.[26] For the British the most celebrated address was number 18, Galignani's, at once a bookshop, publisher and reading room. Galignani came from Brescia. Having spent part of the French revolution in London, he opened a shop in Paris during the Peace of Amiens in 1803. James Simpson, an advocate and author of an account of his visit to Paris in 1815, wrote:

> for about three shillings a fortnight one has access to all the principal London papers, besides everything of the kind published in Paris damp from the press. Information of all public matters, sights, fetes etc. etc. is to be obtained here; and hardly anything can occur to puzzle an Englishman but he will have it here unravelled. Galignani was long in London and thoroughly understands the relation between the two cities. He sells books exceedingly cheap.

In 1819 another English visitor Edward Mangin could enjoy in Galignani's reading room a choice of 43 French newspapers, 14 German, 6 American, 7 Swiss and Italian, 5 Dutch and 17 British.[27]

From 14 July 1814 Galignani published one of the most popular guidebooks to Paris, *Galignani's Paris Guide*, and his own newspaper, first weekly then daily, *Galignani's English Messenger*: Byron read it in Venice, to learn what was happening in England. In 1823 Galignani took over the *Paris Monthly Review of British and Continental Literature*, founded by a former Napoleonic prefect, Louis-Sébastien Saulnier, which was henceforth

---

* Such as Braquenié, the celebrated fabric firm, selling carpets, silks and cottons, which moved there in 1823 and stayed until 1959.

called *Galignani's Magazine and Paris Monthly Review*.[28] Many of Stendhal's articles on Paris life and French literature were translated into English by a friend called Stritch, director of the *Germanic Review* in London, for periodicals such as the *New Monthly Magazine*, the *Athenaeum* or the *Paris Monthly Review*. They were later translated back into French to appear in another Anglo-French review, the *Revue britannique*.[29] If British Parisians bought books at Galignani's, they cashed bills of exchange and letters of credit at the bank of Perregaux and Laffitte in the rue du Mont-Blanc. One office in the bank was 'exclusively appropriated to the English and the business is done in a very easy and satisfying manner'.[30]

After 1815 thousands of English also visited Italy, but in Byron's words, they 'Florenced and Romed – and Galleried – and Conversationed it for a few months', keeping 'the infection of their society' to 'lazzarettos'.[31] Many English in Paris also remained in a national ghetto, attending English churches, reading the English newspapers at Galignani's, eating English food, drinking ale and sherry, and rarely meeting French people. A couple called Vavasour, for example, according to their acquaintance Anne Lister, 'have never occasion to speak French but in the shops'.[32] Despite her extensive French acquaintance, Lady Morgan once dined at different British houses in Paris eight nights running.[33] For their part many Frenchmen retained the Anglophobia of the past. For example in 1819 some lancers of the Garde Royale called out to a visiting Englishman: 'god dam god dam'. The man in question Edward Mangin wrote: 'I made a slight bow with a grave face and walked away.'[34] Popular plays and sketches, sometimes performed in front of the Duke of Wellington himself, mocked English visitors' clothes, 'brusque' manners, *tournure guindée*, 'bizarre, savage, laughable' accent, and love of beer and *rosbif*.[35] Smart Paris ladies might remark: *Lady une telle est bien: on ne la prendrait pas pour une Anglaise*.[36]

At the same time, however, the similarities between the two monarchies and cultures, and the common use of French, helped both British and French in Paris to escape the prison of their nationality. More than at any time before or since, Britain and the British were part of Paris life, as Paris was of British life. The Franco-British symbiosis was helped by the number of meeting-places in Paris: the court, the salons, the cafés, Galignani's. Thus in 1816 Lady Dalrymple Hamilton recorded in her diary: 'I had a party in the evening which turned out very well, indeed all the foreign Ministers and most of the French and English of distinction were with me.' That year the Duchesse d'Escars wrote: 'My Sunday was superb, there were many ugly Frenchwomen and a lot of charming

Englishwomen.' In a letter of 1823 Talleyrand reversed the order of the two nationalities: 'All the elegance of Paris is at Saint-Germain: it is there that all the parties of the smart young English and French take place.'[37] After a month in Paris in 1826, planning Franco-British cooperation over the Greek War of Independence – the first joint naval action since the 1670s – the Foreign Secretary George Canning felt at home: he had many French friends since the emigration, had paid long visits to Paris in 1816 and 1825, and received the exceptional honour of an invitation to dinner in the Tuileries with the King himself. Lady Granville found him 'in spirits that I had never seen'. He himself considered the location so convenient for couriers that the entire Foreign Office should consider moving there.[38]

On 2 March 1829 the grandest court ball of the Restoration was also Franco-British. Inspired by the novels of Walter Scott, it recreated, using costumes inspired by old drawings in the Bibiliothèque Royale, an imaginary visit of Marie of Lorraine Queen Mother of Scotland to her daughter Marie Stuart Queen of France. Lady Stuart de Rothesay, wife of the British ambassador (in 1828 Stuart had returned, replacing Granville after the death of Granville's patron Canning), represented the Queen Mother of Scotland, the Duchesse de Berri the Queen of France. The processions and quadrilles were magnificent. Guests consisted of almost equal numbers of British and French.[39]

The ways individual British residents enjoyed and used Paris show its range of attractions. Lord Herbert (known to unkind Parisians as *l'air bête*), later Earl of Pembroke, was famous both for his extravagance and his wig; it was said to be the best in Paris. Lord Malmesbury wrote: 'I never saw a handsomer equipage . . . Lord Pembroke lives in great state in Paris and is as famous for his cook as for his horses. He is a very handsome man.'[40] The Earl of Thanet was said to have broken the bank twice in one night, at the Salon des Etrangers, the luxurious gambling club in the Palais Royal, with a famous kitchen and cellar, where other gamblers might include Benjamin Constant, Marshal Blücher or Monsieur de Souza.[41] Lord Fife spent a fortune on Mlle Noblet of the opera, whose debut in November 1818, as the violet in *Flore et Zéphire* by Didelot, had been described by Lamartine as *l'infini de la danse et de la volupté*.[42] Her virginity – she was only eighteen – was offered by her mother to the Grand Duke Constantine for 22,000 francs – four thousand times the cost of a good dinner.[43]* According to the leading

---

* He refused, saying that he could have the greatest ladies of Paris and St Petersburg for that sum.

memorialist of British Paris, Captain Gronow, a retired officer who lived there from the 1820s until his death in 1862, and himself married a dancer,* Lord Fife would carry Noblet's shawl, hold her fan, run after her with her scent bottle in his hand, admire the diamond necklace someone else had given her. Another British admirer of Paris beauties, Lord Lonsdale, wrote in his diary: 'Fife is a public nuisance. He shocks the moral by his public exhibition with his women and he defeats the designs of the immoral and profligate in raising the price of all the bitches.'[44] In fact Mlle Noblet remained faithful to a Napoleonic general, the Comte Claparède, until his death in 1842.[45]

It was said that, at any one time, a third of the House of Lords was in Paris. The journey took no more than fifty hours and on important issues they would set out for London to vote in the House of Lords.[46] Many peers and peeresses felt sufficiently at home in Paris to remain there until they died. Most were Irish or Scottish, because they tended to be either poorer, or more Francophile, than English peers, and surely found Paris society less condescending and more accessible than that of London. Among the peers were the Earl of Devon, Beckford's former lover, who came to live in Paris, like Lord Dudley in Balzac's *La Fille aux yeux d'or*, *afin d'éviter les poursuites de la justice anglaise qui, de l'Orient, ne protège que la marchandise*, and died there in 1835.[47] The Countess of Aldborough, who used to give *matinées dansantes* in her garden beneath a banner proclaiming *la France et l'Angleterre seront toujours en paix*, and requested to be buried in France in order to be further from her husband, died in Paris in 1846; the Earl of Blessington and his Countess, the famous writer, died there in 1829 and 1849 respectively. The senior Scottish peer, the Duke of Hamilton, died from a fall on the Boulevard des Italiens in 1863, at the age of fifty-two, after a lengthy supper with two ladies at the Maison Dorée.[48]

In contrast to such wealthy peers and peeresses, other British residents (for reasons of economy) chose to live in towns and villages outside Paris. The actress Mrs Jordan, former mistress of the Duke of Clarence (later William IV), died alone and in poverty, abandoned by her lover and their children, at Saint-Cloud in 1816. Another discarded royal mistress, Mrs Clarke, formerly attached to the Duke of York, died

---

* Perhaps the lady of whom an unsigned and undated letter to Lord Stuart de Rothesay stated: 'Gronow's woman is better dressed and paid than any Duchesse and gave a dinner last week to all the flash men in Paris.'

at Boulogne, in more prosperous circumstances, in 1852.[49] Life was cheaper in the suburbs, especially in Versailles, which, since the departure of the court, contained a large number of empty houses. Hence the complaint of the Irish poet, and friend of Byron, Thomas Moore, who lived in a cottage in Sèvres between 1820 and 1822 in order to escape his debts in London, that a ball in Paris was attended by 'Versailles English and bad French'. Moore had already visited Paris in 1817, and written a poem mocking the vulgarity and ignorance of English visitors, *The Fudge Family in Paris* (1818). In Paris he loved the boulevards, the theatres, the Café des Mille Colonnes. Flahaut talked to him of Napoleon, Madame de Souza of Paris publishers; the Duchesse de Broglie invited him to dinner to meet Lamartine.[50] Galignani's cheap English editions of Moore's poems were often closer to the original texts than London editions: French translations of *Lalla Rookh* and *Irish Melodies* won him many admirers.[51] Other friends of Byron who lived in Paris, in addition to Thomas Moore, were John Cam Hobhouse, author of a famous diary describing Paris during the Hundred Days; the liberal Lord Kinnaird, who introduced Constant to Fouché, in 1815–16; and the disgraced gambler Scrope Davies, who could be seen every day in the Tuileries gardens, sitting on a bench talking to his acquaintances.[52]

So many English were living in Paris that novels about them became a distinct sub-genre, like novels about Americans in Paris a hundred years later. *Six Weeks in Paris; or a Cure for the Gallomania* (1817), 'by a Late Visitant', is a denunciation of 'the metropolis of Europe' and of French 'hatred – deceit – rapacity'. Its message is in its prefatory quotation: 'their appetite for unusual pleasure is in proportion to their former ferocity'.[53] David Carey's *Life in Paris* (1822), with illustrations by Cruikshank, describes orgies in cellars in the Palais Royal, where John Bull behaves like 'Jean Brute', as well as the more respectable behaviour of Sir Humphrey and Lady Halibut MP who visit the Invalides, the Gobelins and the opera and are presented at court. Its message is:

> If Life to view should be your wish,
> And pockets overflow,
> To catch a sight
> Of true delight,
> To Paris you must go, must go, must go,
> To Paris you must go.[54]

Other 'tales of two cities' were *The English in Paris* (1819), a satire on 'the Paris set' 'of inveterately incurable rakes, gamblers and swindlers'; and

Paris Lions and London Tigers (1825) by the celebrated courtesan Harriette Wilson, who often 'strolled in the Tuileries or down the Champs Elysées' while living in Paris. Her philosophy was: 'It won't do to play the game of hearts in Paris and wherever we may be we must take the world as we find it.'[55] In *The English in France* (1828), Lord Normanby praised 'the youth, the freshness of the French mind', and the 'true social enjoyment' found in France, in contrast to England.[56]

Between 1831 and 1835 Thackeray lived much 'in a little den in the rue des Beaux-Arts', trying to learn to be a painter by copying old masters in the Louvre: he later called a painter's life in Paris 'the easiest, merriest, dirtiest existence possible'. Having failed as a painter – but become a confirmed gambler during evenings at Frascati's – he turned to writing: his first novel, *The Memoirs of Mr Charles J. Yellowplush* (1838), described the life of a footman attending an English resident in Paris after Waterloo.[57] In his articles about Paris for *Blackwood's Magazine*, he said that there was 'a thousand times more life and colour' in Paris than in London. Thinking of the crowds of 'mechanics' visiting the Louvre, he expressed admiration for French love of art, 'social happiness and manly equality. If to our freedom we could but add a little of their happiness!'[58]

Ethel (1839), a love story set in London, Paris and Ireland, largely about Lady Odile Macnally the convent-educated daughter of an Irish peer who becomes 'the most elegant doll in Paris', is the only such novel by a Frenchman, the Marquis de Custine. Yet Custine was one of the few French authors of this period to attack England. He considered London more disagreeable than any other large city in Europe, like a damp and sombre prison cell, and described himself as 'the born enemy of this sordidly greedy nation, hypocritically governed in the name of humanity and liberty'.[59] In *Greville; or, A Season in Paris* (1841), Catherine Gore, a British diplomat's wife with a salon in the Place Vendôme, wrote: 'it is admitted by candid persons of all nations that, after a long residence in Paris, the society of all other capitals produces the impression of provinciality': she also repeated the famous saying that 'Paris is the spot on earth where it is easiest to dispense with happiness.'[60] The best of such novels is *Hargrave, or the Addiction of a Man of Fashion* (1843) by Fanny Trollope, who had visited Paris on several occasions over the previous twenty years. The reasons that lead its central character, a banker with criminal tendencies called Charles Hargrave, to live in Paris underline its attractions of cheapness and freedom. He 'preferred Paris to London for the display of his wealth because he fancied not only that it went farther and distinguished him more, but also that its origin was less likely to be inquired into'.[61]

The symbiosis between the French and British élites was reflected in an unprecedented number of marriages and liaisons. British dowries, generally larger than French, were particularly appreciated after the ravages of the French revolution. To marry a rich Englishwoman, Balzac wrote, was the dream of young Frenchmen.[62] From his eighteen years' residence in Edinburgh and London between 1796 and 1814, the Comte d'Artois retained only the habits of shaking hands and playing whist.[63] The Duc de Berri, however, brought back an English mistress called Amy Brown, and their two daughters, whom he installed in a house in the rue Blanche in Montmartre.[64] On 17 June 1816 he was compelled to make a dynastic marriage to the sixteen-year-old Marie Caroline of the Two Sicilies. In order to provide Parisians with a public spectacle, it was celebrated in splendour in the cathedral of Notre Dame, rather than in a palace chapel like the marriages of his uncles Louis XVI and Louis XVIII, his father Artois, and Napoleon I in 1810. Berri revealed his private Anglophilia to his cousin the Duc de Bourbon, son of the Prince de Condé, who continued to live in London with a former prostitute thirty-three years younger than himself, called Sophie Dawes: 'I consider you very lucky still to be able to live as a private person . . . in that good country where one can think at one's ease and where I have been so happy.'[65] Finally, even the Duc de Bourbon returned to Paris, to attend his father's spectacular military funeral at Saint-Denis on 26 May 1818, thereafter remaining in France. 'Totally enslaved' by Sophie Dawes, Bourbon gave her a dowry which enabled her to marry, in London on 6 August 1818, another of her lovers, an officer called the Baron 'de' Feuchères (temporarily deceived into believing that he was marrying the prince's illegitimate daughter, and promoted to be one of his Gentilshommes Ordinaires). Although Bourbon greatly preferred hunting on his domains at Chantilly and Saint-Leu to entertaining in Paris, he later created for the Baronne de Feuchères, in his wing of the Palais Bourbon, one of the most luxurious Parisian interiors of the period. There she reigned, 'dominating and triumphant', mistress of the prince's household as well as the prince, for the following twelve years.[66]

Paris contained more conventional Franco-British households. In 1816 Jules de Polignac married Miss Campbell, an heiress with 200,000 francs a year.[67] Miss Dalrymple Hamilton, whose mother's diaries have already been quoted, married the Duc de Coigny on 15 June 1822, the same year that Lady Frances Seymour Conway, daughter of the Marquess of Hertford, married the Marquis de Chévigné, an officer in the Gardes du Corps. That year another Franco-British *ménage* began when the Marquis de Custine met Edward Sainte-Barbe – *mon ami anglais* – with whom he lived for the next thirty-five years and to whom he left his fortune.[68] Two French writers of the new Romantic school of literature not only owed much of their inspiration to English and Scottish writers but also married Englishwomen. Alphonse de Lamartine married Eliza Birch in 1820, Alfred de Vigny Lydia Bunbury in 1825: hence remarks in de Vigny's letters, during his in-laws' visits to Paris, that he was dining *en Angleterre* or receiving *toute l'Angleterre*.[69]

The most unexpected of Franco-British households, however, which would play a considerable role in Paris for the following fifty years, was that of the Comte de Flahaut. The collapse of the Empire had led to the end of his affair with Queen Hortense. In October 1815, while Queen Hortense was in Switzerland and Flahaut temporarily in Lyon, she opened letters forwarded for him from Paris. They were love letters from Mlle Mars. The liaison may have flourished when Queen Hortense was out of Paris in the summer of 1814. Although she herself had rejected Flahaut's offer of marriage – probably in order to preserve her independence as the mother of a potential Bonaparte heir – she was grief-stricken – *dans le plus grand anéantissement*. Refusing his pleas for forgiveness, she ended their affair.[70] When she asked for the return of her letters kept in two little boxes (with those of others) in the rue Verte, Flahaut wrote to his mother: 'Ah my poor mother, what misfortunes this fatal year 1815 has piled on my head!' The misfortunes which, partly as a result of his own actions, had been piled on France, were not mentioned.[71]

In 1814 Flahaut had declared his hatred of all foreigners. However, for Flahaut, as for his contemporaries, nationality was a flexible commodity. In November 1815, he moved to England. Like Benjamin Constant, he was fêted by those Whig aristocrats whose cult of Napoleon was inflamed by their hatred of Napoleon's enemies in the Tory government. Flahaut lived in Holland House (his mother arranged Lady Holland's lodgings and shopping on her visits to Paris),[72] and later in Thayer Street, the same street in which the Duc de Berri and other royalist émigrés had lived before 1814.[73] The Duke of Bedford called him *le noble, le galant, enfin l'idéal chevalier français* and invited him to Woburn.[74]

Madame de Souza congratulated herself on having been 'a *barbarian* mother' who had sent Flahaut to boarding school in England, when they were émigrés during the reign of terror, and he did not understand a word being said there. Madame de Souza had an emigration strategy. She advised Flahaut to perfect his English, attend debates in Parliament and nurture the cult of Napoleon by telling stories of his kindness to his staff. Flahaut should use his time in England, as Richelieu had his in Russia, to win a reputation as a man of honour and a statesman in order to become, like Richelieu, 'an object of hope for everyone'.[75]

When the Duchesse d'Orléans met Flahaut in London in 1816, she wrote: 'he is tall, well built, with an agreeable face, although a little faded. He is very *soigné* and amiable in society, but one can see that he is too pleased with himself, having been spoiled by the ladies.'[76] On 20 June 1817 at St Andrew's Church, Edinburgh, Flahaut married a twenty-nine-year-old Scottish heiress whom he had met at Woburn: the Honourable Margaret Mercer Nairne. A women of independent mind and means, having inherited a fortune from her mother, she was one of the few female friends who had remained loyal to Byron after the collapse of his marriage in 1816. Having spent most of his career fighting the French navy – and having received the surrender of Napoleon himself in July 1815 – her father Admiral Viscount Keith forbade her to marry his enemy's favourite aide-de-camp. Her financial independence enabled her to defy her father's wishes. The Flahaut marriage created a sensation: the Duke of York wrote to Madame de Souza that it was as if the Pope was marrying the daughter of the Grand Turk. Lord Bathurst suggested that Flahaut should change his name to MacFlahaut.[77] At the request of Lord Keith, the French Minister of War refused Flahaut permission to marry. Flahaut resigned from the French army and decided to settle in Scotland and England.[78] News that the gates of Paris were closed to him for ever would not cause him the least pain, he assured his wife – although he knew she wanted to visit it and he would have liked to present her to his mother.[79] Madame de Flahaut, who had a passion for politics, came to share her husband's love of Napoleon. For his part he received letters of denization in Scotland, in order to help him to administer or inherit his wife's estates.[80]

Madame de Souza was overjoyed by the marriage. In her letters differences of nationality and religion are hardly mentioned, and never as obstacles. In Paris more English friends than French came to congratulate her on the birth of Flahaut's first daughter – among them the Dalrymples, who considered themselves part of her family.[81] She was delighted when, as early as August 1817, she claimed to detect the first mistakes of French in Flahaut's letters.[82] Once threatened by royalist vengeance, by 1819 Flahaut felt that Paris was calm enough for him to take his wife there. His mother and his wife, however, did not get on. Madame de Souza had once wanted to be buried with her son's letters; she now told him that she had cried every day 'to be neglected, forgotten by the son whom I have loved tenderly all his life'.[83]

As well as French wives and mistresses, British Parisians acquired French pictures and furniture. After 1814 Paris was the centre of the art market, as Amsterdam had been before 1789. The upheavals of the revolution and Empire had led to the dispersal of most French art collections. The contents of the palace of Versailles, for example, had been sold in 17,182 lots between August 1793 and August 1794, much being bought at low prices by Paris dealers.[84] Returned émigrés, like the Duc de Richelieu or the Comte d'Orsay, whose father had owned the most celebrated collection in Paris, could see objects from their family collections on display in the Louvre or other French museums. Alone of the returned émigrés, by special favour of Louis XVIII, the Prince de Condé recovered a few of his pre-revolutionary collections of pictures, furniture and statues, including the famous statue, now at his country seat of Chantilly, *Vénus aux belles fesses*.[85]

After 1815 members of the former imperial family, obliged to leave Paris, also put their collections up for sale. The pictures of the Empress Josephine, bought in Paris in 1816 by the Tsar, are now in the Hermitage. That year Lady Morgan attended the sale of part of one of the largest art collections of the century, assembled by the ex-Emperor's uncle Cardinal Fesch.[86] British nobles were the main buyers. By 1814 they had developed a taste for French eighteenth-century art, possibly out of a subconscious feeling that they had replaced the French nobility as the principal models of luxury, wealth and arrogance in Europe. Stendhal reflected a common view when he wrote: 'there are no more *grands seigneurs* except in England.'[87] A cosmopolitan Scot called Quentin Craufurd, who had helped arrange the French royal family's flight to Varennes in 1791 and the British government's purchase of the Hôtel de Charost in 1814, lived in a luxurious house at 21 rue d'Anjou, surrounded by a celebrated collection of historical French portraits.[88] In her journal of her visit to Paris in 1814, the Duchess of Rutland described one of the principal activities of wealthy English visitors: 'We passed the day in visiting various shops with a view to the purchase of articles of ancient furniture.'[89] The British taste for eighteenth-century Sèvres drove prices so high (10,000 francs for an entire service) that Madame de Souza wrote that it was cheaper to order a new service from Sèvres, *sur les vieux dessins*, than to buy an old one.[90] In 1815 the Duke of Devonshire boasted that he had bought 'all Paris': he later had a room at Chatsworth decorated like a café in the rue de Richelieu.[91] In order to assert his semi-royal status as a cousin of the Stuarts, the Duke of Hamilton bought, on a massive scale, furniture and pictures formerly in the collections of members of the Bourbon and Bonaparte dynasties. In 1817 Wellington himself bought Boulle cabinets and Empire tables from the Fesch sale. The collections of the Beauchamp family at Madresfield, the Earls of Mansfield at Scone, and in many other country houses in Britain and Ireland, also contain trophies of these forays to Paris.

The British ambassador Sir Charles Stuart collected French books and furniture as well as actresses. In 1816 he bought armchairs and *tabourets*, made by the famous firm of Jacob, which worked without a break throughout the period 1765–1828, from the widow of Maréchal Ney who, after the marshal's execution, sold his *hôtel* and left Paris. Some of his furniture can be seen in the Victoria and Albert Museum. Stuart liked French art so much that he later incorporated part of a Normandy château into Highcliffe, his house in Hampshire.[92]

Even during the Napoleonic wars the Regent had continued, as he had since the 1780s, to buy furniture and porcelain in Paris. After 1815 his chief agents in Paris were, for pictures, Sir Charles Long, later Lord Farnborough, a Trustee of the British Museum and the National Gallery, which was then being founded in imitation of the Louvre and, for furniture and textiles, a French servant called Nicolas Morel. In Parliament government spokesmen asserted the King's determination to patronise only British artists and craftsmen. In reality he imported crates of French furniture, porcelain, silks and tapestries, including many objets d'art which had once been in the royal apartments at Versailles, such as the opulent Sèvres service commissioned by Louis XVI at the end of the American War of Independence:[93] hence the array of Sèvres vases, gilt bronze clocks and candelabra, Boulle *armoires*, *boiseries* and Gobelins tapestries which still impart a note of Parisian elegance to the interiors of Windsor Castle and Buckingham Palace.[94] In all George IV's official portraits by Thomas Lawrence he had himself painted standing beside the *Table des Grands Capitaines*, decorated with profiles of the great captains of antiquity. Executed at Sèvres for

Napoleon I in 1806–12, it had been given in 1817 by Louis XVIII to the Regent *comme une marque de souvenir et d'amitié* (and because the Regent had asked for it), and now adorns the Blue Drawing Room in Buckingham Palace.[95] Such gestures and purchases – and similar purchases by Metternich, the King of Prussia and the Tsar – are in part triumphalist, demonstrating their owners' desire to decorate their palaces with trophies of victory over France.[96] They are also another sign that, having lost its political empire in Europe, France had reinforced its artistic pre-eminence. Few conquerors have shown such determination to acquire the art and majesty of the conquered.

The greatest English collector of French art was the fourth and last Marquess of Hertford. His father, then known as Lord Yarmouth, had been an intermediary between Talleyrand and the British government after being caught in Paris by the outbreak of war in 1803. Lady Yarmouth remained in Paris, living first in the rue Cerutti, and after 1827, with her younger son Lord Henry Seymour, in the former Hôtel de Brancas on the corner of the rue Laffitte and the Boulevard des Italiens, above the fashionable Café de Paris: like many foreign residents, her favourite occupation was to sit at her window and watch the boulevards. Her elder son, having served as an attaché at the British embassy in 1817–19, also began to live in Paris. He preferred living 'like a fallen angel' in Paris, generally avoiding 'good company', to running the family estates and political interest in England. From the salerooms and art dealers of Paris he assembled one of the great collections of Europe: a combination of eighteenth-century French pictures, many by Boucher and Fragonard, and objets d'art, often of royal provenance; some of the finest works of Titian, Rubens and Velázquez; Dutch 'cabinet pictures'; and contemporary Parisian pictures by Ary Scheffer, Horace Vernet and Bonington. It is today called the Wallace Collection, after the surname taken by Richard Wallace, one of his illegitimate sons. The frequency of revolutions in Paris led to the decision to move it from the Hertfords' Paris houses to their London residence in Manchester Square, and to leave it to the British rather than the French nation. Since much was left to Wallace's secretary, what the public sees today is only a portion of the original collection. Nevertheless, one of the greatest collections of works of art from Paris is in London.[97]

In contrast many Parisians dismissed eighteenth-century works of art, even those they themselves had owned before the revolution, as, in the words of Madame de Souza, *ces vieilles et vilaines formes*.[98] Louis XVIII turned down an offer to buy back, in 1814, a desk made for him, in 1774, as a young prince at Versailles.[99] Parisians of all ages and allegiances preferred the latest neoclassical style: 'nothing but sphinxes, caryatides and tripods meet the eye in every direction,' wrote William Playfair, editor of *Galignani's English Messenger*, in 1818.[100]

British Parisians bought books and manuscripts as well as pictures and furniture – as is evident from the libraries of British country houses, filled with the works of Guizot and Chateaubriand, as well as Voltaire and Rousseau. The eighth and last Earl of Bridgewater bought the Hôtel de Noailles, 335 rue Saint-Honoré, as Napoleon was marching on Paris in March 1815. He lived there surrounded by cats and dogs, which he sent every day in two carriages to be walked on the Champ de Mars. When he died in 1829 the Egerton collection of manuscripts, mainly of French and Italian literature, which he had assembled was left to the British Museum.[101] John Wilson Croker, a political adviser of the Marquess of Hertford, made frequent visits to Paris to assemble his unrivalled collection of manuscripts and pamphlets on the French revolution, which was also acquired by the British Museum. On 17 June 1818 – the day before the anniversary of the Battle of Waterloo – there was a dinner in Paris of the Roxburghe Club of British book-lovers, attended by French guests like Baron Denon and Monsieur Van Praet, chief librarian of the Bibiliothèque Royale (the staff of which was renowned for its 'extreme kindness and civility'). At the dinner one of the founders of the club, the Reverend Thomas Dibdin, gave toasts *A la gloire de la France! A l'union perpetuelle de la France et de l'Angleterre!* Thinking of the qualities and defects of London and Paris – too much commerce and dirt in the first, too little comfort in the second – he pleaded: 'we should *approximate* a little towards each other.'[102]

Paris clubs as well as London art collections reflected the Franco-British interaction. Hitherto Paris had contained few men's clubs. In 1816 a Cercle Anglais, formed 'for the Comfort and accommodation of the English Nobility and Gentry in Paris', was opened by a Mr Woodthorpe: its subsequent history is unknown, but a second club of that name opened in 1826.[103] In 1822 the Cercle des Etrangers, later known as the Cercle de l'Europe, opened on 104 rue de Richelieu, but soon became yet another gambling club.[104] The most elegant club in Paris, the Cercle de l'Union, specifically dedicated to union between France and the United Kingdom, was established in 1828 on the corner of the rue de Gramont and the Boulevard des Italiens near Galignani and the Palais Royal. In order to fulfil its mission there was a club rule that half its members had to be foreign: diplomats posted in Paris were automatically admitted. Members included ten Dukes, three Greffuhles, two Noailles, two Rothschilds, Pozzo, Talleyrand, Flahaut, Lord Henry Seymour, Lords Pembroke, Sligo and many others. Its founder and first president was a former British officer the Duc de Guiche, Premier Ecuyer of the Duc d'Angoulême, 'beautiful as an angel' and in the opinion of Lady Blessington 'the *beau idéal* of a nobleman'.[105] That embodiment of British nationalism, Lord Palmerston, described it as 'a great convenience to a casual visitor at Paris, and gives one a *Pied à Terre* immediately for news and society and knowledge of who is here and what is going on' – although 'the Frenchmen have not yet learnt patiently to endure the mortification of being *blackboulé* '.[106] With 108 members in July 1828, it had 252 permanent and 150 honorary members in 1837.[107] Men of 'all parties and all nations' met there. There was a good library; according to the diarist of British Paris, Thomas Raikes, conversation was generally 'very interesting', in contrast to 'the trivial *commérages*' of St James's.[108]

Lord Hertford's younger brother, Lord Henry Seymour, was an idol of Parisians who was English only in name: born in Paris in 1805, his father may have been the Comte de Montrond, the most dissipated of Talleyrand's friends, known in London gambling clubs as 'old French'. His carriage was always the most magnificent, his largesse the most profuse, at the orgiastic procession down into the heart of Paris from the hill of la Courtille during the carnival.[109] Short, but extremely muscular – according to the journalist Hippolyte de Villemessant he had the largest biceps in Paris – Lord Henry Seymour founded a gym and a fencing school in the family *hôtel*, becoming the best fencer in Europe, the terror of boxers. In 1833 he was first president of the Société d'Encouragement pour l'Amélioration des Races de Chevaux en France, established to improve French bloodstock by importing British studs and mares. In another reflection of the switch of French energy from conquest to pleasure, other founders of this society included the sons of four Napoleonic marshals (Berthier, Bessières, Davout and Ney). In 1834 the society was renamed the Jockey Club, and acquired premises on the Boulevard des Italiens: it rapidly became, and remains to this day, one of the most aristocratic clubs in Paris.[110] Hitherto Paris had been one of the least equestrian of capitals. Few men went about their daily business on horseback: fewer horses were tethered outside the Chambre des Députés than outside the House of Commons.[111]

Henceforth, however, the British influence in Paris affected horses as well as humans. Gentlemen began to pay visits on horseback rather than by carriage or on foot, followed by a servant also on horseback.[112] Horse races, begun by Artois in Paris in 1776, suspended during the revolution and Empire, began again on the Champ de Mars in the autumn of 1819 under the patronage of the Duc d'Angoulême and the Duc de Guiche. Lord Henry Seymour's horse often won. However, some bloodstock did not improve. In the 1840s, to British eyes, most cab-horses in Paris looked like 'old worn-out animals', which proceeded at a very slow pace.[113]

Artists as well as writers, collectors and horse breeders reflected 'the Franco-British moment'. For the first time many British artists came to paint the streets of Paris (in the previous century they would have chosen Rome or Naples). Among them were Thomas Shotter Boyes (1823, 1829–36); the son of an émigré, Augustus Pugin (1821 and 1828); and David Cox (1829–32).[114] Delacroix, in 1816 an eighteen-year-old student at the Ecole des Beaux-Arts on the Left Bank, also reflected the French switch from conquest to creativity. He was son of a prefect, and brother of a general, of Napoleon I. Delacroix himself was a liberal Bonapartist who earned his living, in part, by selling caricatures of the King, Artois, the allied troops and English visitors – invariably represented, in contrast to the elegant and decorous French, as gluttonous, lustful and ill-bred.[115]

Yet even this Bonapartist became a British Parisian. He learnt English from the son of an émigré, and shared a studio in the Place Saint-Germain-des-Prés, and his model and mistress Mlle Rose, with his contemporary Bonington. Bonington had arrived in Paris in 1818, when his father opened a shop to sell Nottingham lace in the rue des Tournelles. Bonington and Delacroix met in the long gallery in the Louvre; the former was making watercolour sketches when Delacroix stopped to admire his technique. Delacroix later remembered him as 'a tall young man in a short jacket silently painting studies in water colour usually after Flemish landscapes'. Bonington was a student of Baron Gros, Gérard's rival as a painter of the Napoleonic Empire. By the salon of 1824 he himself had acquired many 'converts and imitators' in Paris. As an artist he was neither French nor British but Parisian. Constable's work was also exhibited at the salons of 1824 and 1827 and had a lasting impact on French artists such as Delacroix and Géricault. The artist and critic Délécluze, a pupil of David who visited England and admired

Shakespeare, called contemporary French artists 'this modern school modelled on that of England'.[116]

The Franco-British moment was reflected in literature as well as paintings. Although so many of his friends lived in Paris, Byron himself, when he left England in 1816, refused to do so. His main reasons were hatred of the Bourbon Restoration – which he considered 'the triumph of tameness over talent' – and fear of sounding a fool. He spoke bad French: 'I know nothing of French, being all Italian. Though I can read and understand French, I never attempt to speak it; for I hate it.'[117] If Byron did not love Paris, however, Paris loved Byron. Galignani, to whom he sold the right to publish his works in France in 1818, published them in Paris in English the same year, and twenty-one more such editions before 1847; in addition there were innumerable translations into French. As a result, Byron became one of the most famous poets in France. Stendhal wrote in 1818: 'I am a furious romantic, that is to say that I am for Shakespeare againt Racine, and for Lord Byron against Boileau.' Lamartine, who wrote a poem to Byron, thought him the incarnation of genius. The *Journal de Paris* of 10 April 1820 called him 'the greatest poet of the nineteenth century'.[118]

If Byron was the 'great poet' in France, Walter Scott was the great novelist. At least 20,000 copies of each of his novels were sold in translation in France; in some circles it was fashionable to discuss them the same week they were published in London.[119] When Scott visited Paris in November 1826, staying at the Hôtel Windsor to research his life of Napoleon, he was 'eaten up with kindness' in all quarters, from the Tuileries to the Halles.[120] Reading rooms and lending libraries known as *cabinets de lecture* were then becoming popular: there were about 460 in Paris in 1830, to some of which admission cost only 10 centimes.[121] In these *cabinets de lecture* Scott was by far the most popular novelist. The French translations of his novels developed their own influence. The translations of *Ivanhoe*, *Kenilworth*, *The Bride of Lammermoor* were adapted by the famous Parisian playwright Eugène Scribe as librettos for operas of the same name.[122] If some Frenchmen went to Britain to see Parliament, others went to see – and praise in further French travel books on Britain – Walter Scott. His visitors included an early Romantic Charles Nodier in 1821; a literary critic and professional Anglophile Philarète Chasles in 1825; and the Duc de Lévis, a royalist philosopher whose maxims include *noblesse oblige*, in 1828.[123] Scott's popularity reflected that of British literature in general. Until 1842 a third of all novels published in France were English. In the peak year 1830, 111

English novels were published in France, compared to only 109 French.[124] Historical and horror novels were particularly popular. However, *Raison et sensibilité* (1815), *La Nouvelle Emma* (1816), *Orgueil et prévention* (1821) and *L'Abbaye de Northanger* (1824) appeared in Paris soon after they did in London.[125]

The most industrious translator from English was a former émigré A.-J.-B. Defauconpret, who between 1815 and 1828 translated 422 volumes: he also wrote books such as *Londres en 1817*, *Une année à Londres*, *Six semaines à Londres*. Another was Philarète Chasles, who lived in London from 1815 to 1818, partly out of hostility to the Restoration, and spent his life fighting what he called 'this stupid animosity. This nation which formerly we were so resolved to despise we now respect and even imitate with a fervent friendship.' When asking for invitations to the British embassy he called himself *un half-English*. He wrote many articles on English poets for the *Revue britannique*, founded in 1825 by the former Napoleonic prefect Louis-Sébastien Saulnier, in the belief that England was so advanced that France needed to know everything about it:

> moreover at a time when part of the French public, avid for new emotions, accuses the forms of our literature of timidity and monotony, the analysis of publications of a foreign literature which had freed itself from the rules which almost all our writers impose on themselves, should present a particular degree of interest.

Scott, Fenimore Cooper, William Hazlitt and Charles Lamb were published in the *Revue britannique*, as well as articles from the most famous British reviews such as the *Edinburgh* and *Quarterly Reviews*, and economic articles likely to be of interest to French industrialists.[126] The aim was, as the first editorial stated, to learn from the British example to 'improve gradually, without upheavals and without violence, civil and political institutions'.[127]

In the autumn of 1827 the plays of Shakespeare, already the subject of Guizot's *Essai sur la vie et les oeuvres de Shakespeare* (1821) and Stendhal's *Racine et Shakespeare* (1823), were performed in an English-language Shakespeare season at the Théâtre de l'Odéon. (An earlier attempt in 1822 to bring Shakespeare to Paris had failed in the face of nationalist demonstrations.) Kemble and a beautiful blue-eyed actress called Harriet Smithson took Paris by storm in *Hamlet*. The theatre was full to the roof every night; the Shakespeare season became 'quite a political event'.[128] To the young Alexandre Dumas it seemed like a glimpse of the Garden of Eden. Berlioz, who married Harriet Smithson five years later, felt he had seen 'the whole heaven of art'. Delacroix, who took many of his subjects from Shakespeare (and Byron and Milton), wrote: 'the most obstinate classics are lowering their flag.' Mlle Mars was jealous and, to some, began to appear outdated. A year later de Vigny's translation of Othello, *Le More de Venise*, was a success at the Comédie Française.[129]

Education as well as literature, politics and the economy reflected British influence. The first 'Lancaster schools', based on an English model where older children helped teach younger pupils, were established in Paris after 1815. Ten years after the first infants' schools for children under six were founded in Scotland in 1816, they were started in Paris by a committee of wealthy women.[130]

The intimacy of the connections – political, artistic, literary and personal – between the British and French in Paris was demonstrated by a widespread feeling that Britain was a model for France's future, as well as its present. At this time the French élite knew British history almost as well as its own. In the eighteenth century David Hume's *History of the Stuarts* had been more popular in France than in England: its admirers included the future Louis XVI and his brothers.[131] Many Frenchmen, including speakers in the National Assembly in 1789–91 and in the Chamber of Deputies after 1815, considered the French revolution and Restoration not new beginnings but re-enactments of seventeenth-century British history.[132] Madame de Staël, a lifelong friend of the English, called 'the entire English nation the aristocracy of the rest of the world by its enlightenment and its virtues'.[133] In her last work *Considérations sur la Révolution française*, published in London and Paris in 1818, she tried to separate *les bons principes de la révolution* from subsequent horrors: it was said to have sold 60,000 copies that year. She devoted one-sixth of the book to English history and parliamentary practice (and an entire chapter to the influence of salons in 1814–15). Like most French liberals – and unlike Byron and Shelley – she had an idealistic view of England as the land of liberty and justice: in her view *tout est empreint d'un sentiment de noblesse en Angleterre*. She also described the English and French revolutions and restorations as 'symptoms of the same disease':[134] a revolution (in 1642 and 1789 respectively), followed by a regicide (Charles I in 1649, Louis XVI in 1793); a military dictatorship (Cromwell in 1653–8, Bonaparte in 1799–1814); a restoration (Charles II in 1660, Louis XVIII in 1814); finally the usurpation of the throne by a cadet member of the royal family (William III in 1688, the Duc d'Orléans at an unknown date in the future), although she also, like Chateaubriand, considered Louis XVIII to be both Charles II and William III.

Thus there was a British 'alternative reality' running in parallel to the daily reality of French politics. Innumerable books, private conversations and letters, as well as speeches in the Chambers, compared the fates of the Stuarts and the Bourbons and the course of the English and French revolutions.[135] Villemain, the friend of the Duchesse de Duras and Madame de Montcalm, published a two-volume *Histoire de Cromwell d'après les mémoires du temps et les recueils parlementaires* in 1819 (which helped Victor Hugo with his verse drama *Cromwell* eight years later). Guizot, who felt that he had two fatherlands, England and France (although he also called Geneva 'my intellectual cradle'), published the first and only French translations of English seventeenth-century memoirs, in twenty-five volumes, in 1823–5 and a two-volume *Histoire de la révolution d'Angleterre depuis l'avènement de Charles Ier jusqu'à la restauration de Charles II* (1826–7).[136] Chateaubriand revered Shakespeare, wrote a history of *Les Quatre Stuarts* (1828), an *Essai sur la littérature anglaise et considérations sur le génie des hommes, des temps et des révolutions* (1836), and translated Milton's *Paradise Lost*.[137]

A physical reminder of seventeenth-century British history in Paris were the Scottish Catholic college and the convent of English Augustinian nuns established in that century by exiled supporters of the Stuarts, and revived after 1814.[138] Another tribute to this period of British history was the reburial on 9 September 1824, on the orders and at the expense of George IV, of an urn containing parts of the intestines of James II* in the parish church of Saint-Germain-en-Laye, beside the palace where he had died in 1701. Like the tombs of their Bourbon cousins, and for the same reasons, during the revolution the tombs of the exiled Stuarts had been violated, and their remains disinterred. The ceremony was conducted by the Bishop of Edinburgh and British and Irish Catholic priests of Paris, and attended by Jacobite descendants residing in Paris, including Maréchal Macdonald, the Duc de Fitzjames and the Abbé-Duc de Melfort. It was an equivalent, for them, of the reburial of Louis XVI in 1815. The King's remains received sovereign honours from the company of gardes du corps stationed in the town.

* In accordance with French and British royal tradition, his body had been ceremonially disembowelled on his death in 1701.

The Sardinian ambassador, representing the heir to the Stuart claim, was present; on the grounds that he represented a Protestant monarch, the British ambassador was not.[139]

The reburial of James II preceded by only seven days the accession to the throne of the Comte d'Artois, who many believed was destined for a similar fate. Thus when Molé had paid Madame de Staël a morning visit in 1816, it had been natural for her to say to him, after denouncing the follies of the court and the émigrés:

> We are starting the history of England again . . . fortunately the King to whom I am personally attached, will die in peace on the throne but surely you do not believe that his brother will succeed him? Monsieur will have the fate of James II.

Like many others, she felt that the Duc d'Orléans would be the William III of France – *notre Guillaume*.[140] On the day she died, 14 July 1817, she received Orléans in her bedroom.[141] Benjamin Constant, while comparing Louis XVIII favourably to Charles II, warned 'those tempted to imitate James II' that when the moment came the throne would fall without a sword being drawn in its defence.[142] Richelieu too warned Artois, in a private conversation, of 'a fate comparable to that of the Stuarts'.[143] While more sympathetic to Artois' politics, in 1818 the Duke of Wellington expressed similar forebodings: 'The descendants of Louis XV [the royal family as opposed to the Orléans] will not reign in France and I must say and always will say, that it is the fault of Monsieur and his adherents.' Artois should 'read histories of our Restoration and our revolution'.[144]

Thus for many Frenchmen, in part because of the intimacy of the Franco-British connection, the Bourbons were not a dynasty with a future, but a dynasty with a revolution foretold.

6

Murder at the Opera

1820–1824

Nuit d'épouvante et de plaisir, nuit de vertus et de crimes!
Chateaubriand, *Mémoires . . . touchant la vie et la mort de S.A.R.*
[*le*] *Duc de Berri*, May 1820

CARNIVAL WAS AN annual period of revelry before Lent – the six weeks of abstinence and mourning that precedes the celebration of the Resurrection at Easter. Carnival was a European celebration. In Venice Byron did not have a wink of sleep for a week.[1] In Rome there were races of riderless wild horses down the Corso and an 'almost total levelling of all classes and even of all inhabitants' in its delirium of pleasure.[2] In Vienna, during one carnival 772 balls took place.[3] Until 1914 Paris too had its carnival. At night the boulevards were filled with processions of carriages, masked revellers and a special model of a prize ox, the *boeuf gras*, prepared by the corporation of butchers. On one night in the carnival of 1815 the King himself had joined the procession.[4]

Forbidden during Lent, dancing dominated the last week of carnival. Dancing was especially popular during the Restoration, perhaps in reaction to the wars of the Republic and the Empire. Reflecting the cosmopolitan character of the era, and the role of émigrés as cultural transmitters, there was a fashion for the *polka*, *mazurka* and *polonaise* from Poland, the *valse* from Germany, *écossaises* and *anglaises* from across the Channel. *Bals publics*, such as the Bal de l'Opéra, or the Prado dance hall on the Place du Palais de Justice, were open to anyone who paid (generally about one franc fifty for men, fifty centimes for women): the young Thackeray, on an escapade from Cambridge, was entranced by the 'demoniacal frantic yells and antics' he witnessed at one of them.[5]

The poor danced at the *guinguetttes* and *cabarets* which circled Paris outside the barriers, where the wine served was free of the tax imposed on it inside the city.

The élite, however, danced in private houses. During the carnival of 1820 there was an especially large number of balls: a diplomatic ball given by the Prussian ambassador; a *bal costumé* for the *beau monde* at the house of the banker the Comte Greffulhe, where Madame Decazes went *en Livonienne*, her sister-in-law Madame Princeteau *en Péruvienne*; a ball for Napoleonic society given by the Duc de Plaisance; balls for court society in the Elysée palace given by the Vicomtesse de Gontaut, Gouvernante des Enfants de France, and the Duc and Duchesse de Berri. Even the Duchesse d'Angoulême came to the Berris' ball on 29 January, which, like many Paris balls, lasted until 6 the next morning. Guests ranged in rank from ambassadors to army captains, and in political views from La Bourdonnaye, an ultra-royalist known as 'the white Jacobin', on the far right, to Casimir Périer on the left. The Duchesse de Berri seemed to communicate her gaiety and ardour for pleasure to all around her.[6] The Berris were the youngest and only pleasure-loving members of the royal family: they enjoyed watching boulevard entertainments like dwarves, conjurors, fairground slides (known as *montagnes russes*). Since both Louis XVIII and Artois were widowers, and the Duchesse d'Angoulême was childless after twenty-one years of marriage, they were also the only Bourbons likely to produce a male heir. After three and a half years of marriage, however, the Duchesse de Berri had had many miscarriages and only one daughter.[7]

Another carnival pleasure, much appreciated by the Berris, was the theatre and the opera. On the evening of Sunday 13 February 1820 the Duc de Berri took his young wife to the opera on the rue de Richelieu, beside the Palais Royal, to see two ballets, *Le Carnaval de Venise* and *Les Noces de Gamache*, and an opera, *Le Rossignol*. The theatre was open that Sunday since it was the last Sunday before Lent, when theatres closed.[8] In an *entr'acte*, since she had been up late the previous night at the Greffulhes' costume ball, the Duchess decided to leave: Berri escorted her to their carriage, waiting in the rue Rameau, which runs off the rue de Richelieu, at about 10.58 p.m. Taking their right hands, the Duke handed his wife and her lady-in-waiting Madame de Béthisy up into the carriage; her Premier Ecuyer, the Comte de Mesnard, handed them up by their left hands. With the words 'Goodbye Caroline, we will see each other again soon',[9] he turned back towards the opera, to see the last act. He may also have stayed behind for another purpose: one of his mistresses, since his arrival in Paris in April 1814, was an actress called Mlle Virginie, 'pretty as an angel and stupid as a cabbage'.[10]

At the moment the Duke was turning back to the opera house, a man coming from the rue de Richelieu rushed between the sentry on duty, the footman folding up the carriage steps and two courtiers, the Comtes de Choiseul and de Mesnard, and stabbed the Duke above his right breast with a sharp flat dagger about seven inches long. At once Berri said: 'I am assassinated! This man has killed me!' A few seconds later, having pulled out the dagger: 'I am dead, I am dead, I have the dagger!' Assisted by his courtiers, he was taken to the guardroom of the opera house, followed by his wife and her lady-in-waiting. He sat on a bench, bleeding heavily, leaning his head against a wall. He asked for a priest and was then moved to the salon of the royal box. There, in the words of a celebrated memoir by Chateaubriand, based on eye-witness accounts and published within three months of the murder, 'the young princess threw herself on her husband and in an instant her *habits de fête* were covered in blood'.[11]*

Berri's death agony in the following six hours was the next step in the *danse macabre* of love and hate, fear and need, performed between Paris and the Bourbons since 1789. Drifting between unconsciousness and agony, having increasing difficulty in breathing, Berri knew he was dying. Nevertheless doctors bled him, operated on him and applied leeches, and soon afterwards moved him to an office with enough space for him to lie on a mattress on the floor. Before long the mattress was drenched in blood, sweat and vomit.[12] Meanwhile the number of bystanders grew and grew, drawn by the magnetism of a royal death.

The first of the royal family to arrive had been the Duc d'Angoulême. In floods of tears he kissed his brother's wound. He was followed by his wife and Artois. The panic of the moment led to a momentary suspension of class barriers. Artois' Premier Gentilhomme on duty, the Duc de Maillé, rushed after his master and jumped up among the footmen standing behind the carriage. A stunned contemporary called this gesture 'sublime', and 'an act no doubt unique and which honours the gentleman who performed it no less than the prince who was able to inspire it'.[13] Artois was soon followed by the Berris' daughter Mademoiselle, the Orléans family, also at the opera that night, and the Duc de Bourbon.

---

* Pieces of her bloodstained dress were later distributed among royalists as relics.

The wound, made by a long dagger contrived by the assassin himself, was visible to all. The dying Duke recommended the doctors and his household to his father, remarking that 'it is cruel to die by the hand of a Frenchman.' More and more people were arriving: Chateaubriand in his peer's costume; royalist revellers still wearing the costumes they had worn to Madame de La Briche's masked ball; Berri's two daughters by his English mistress, to whom he addressed a few words in English and whom the Duchess immediately called 'my children'; all the Duchess's ladies-in-waiting; the marshals of France; the ministers; Richelieu.

Meanwhile gendarmes, servants and soldiers had rushed after the murderer: he was caught in the Arcade Colbert near the rue de Richelieu by Jean Paulmier, a waiter from the Café Hardy on the Boulevard des Italiens, and taken bound hand and foot to the guard post of the opera. Louis-Pierre Louvel was his name – 'a small man', so Chateaubriand described him, 'with a sly, dirty face like thousands whom one sees on the streets of Paris'. So intense was the hatred between royalists and Bonapartists that Louvel maintained that he was proud of his act. Since Decazes at first interrogated him in a low voice, ultra-royalists around the deathbed – a majority of those present – murmured that he was the murderer's accomplice.[14] For her part, the Duchesse de Berri, shielding her daughter from Decazes, shouted that Decazes could have had them all murdered.[15]

Since news of the assassination had not reached the stage of the opera, the show went on. Chateaubriand later wrote: 'On one side you heard the sound of music, on the other the sighs of the dying prince.' Finally the opera ended. Berri recommended his weeping servants to his father, confessed in public, forgiving his murderer and asking forgiveness for his own sins, and received the last rites. He begged his wife to preserve herself for the sake of the child she was bearing, and gave his blessing to his daughter with the words, 'Poor child! I hope you are less unfortunate than the members of my family.' He was tormented by thirst: 'I am suffering horribly! Ah how slow death is in coming!'[16] While the foyer and passages leading to the room were packed with people, the streets outside became quiet. Angoulême held his brother's hand; Artois, in tears, knelt at the foot of the bed.[17] The prince bade farewell to the members of his household and talked to his wife. Finally, at 5 a.m., in the first light of dawn, the sound of horses could be heard, indicating the approach of gardes du corps escorting the King's carriage.[18]

When the King arrived, Berri asked him to grant the murderer's pardon:

– Uncle, I ask you as a favour to spare the life of the man.
– Nephew, you are not as badly hurt as you think, we will talk about it.
– The King does not say yes. Forgiveness at least for the life of the man so that I can die in peace.

The King was immovable. At 6.35 in the morning Berri died. Despite her ladies' efforts, the Duchess had pushed back through the crowd to her husband. She knelt down, felt one of his hands and uttered a terrible cry: 'Good God! This hand, this hand is cold!!! Ah! Charles is no more!!!' In a state of indescribable despair, she screamed that she wanted to die, threw herself on his body, covered his hand with kisses, then asked the King's permission to leave with her daughter for Sicily. She was led away to a carriage which took her, the Duchesse d'Angoulême and two of their ladies to the Elysée. All present fell to the ground, wept and prayed. Then followed the silence of fear: no one was certain that Louvel was not part of a larger conspiracy. Finally, after most people had gone, leaning on Dr Dupuytren, the King closed Berri's eyes, kissed his hand and left.[19]

Louvel's interrogation by the police and subsequent trial by the Chamber of Peers showed that he was not, as ultras claimed, part of a conspiracy, nor was he inspired by liberal ideas. He was a solitary nationalist fanatic, driven by a desire to avenge Waterloo and exterminate the Bourbons. He considered them the cruellest enemies of the fatherland. Their rule dishonoured France; he blamed them, not his hero Napoleon I for whom he had worked on Elba, for the invasions of France in 1814 and 1815. Louvel, who was thirty-six, had lived a solitary life in Paris, working as a saddler in the royal stables, and had recently made a pilgrimage to Père Lachaise, to the tombs of Marshals Lannes and Masséna (the latter an obelisk inscribed with the names of the marshal's victories – *Rivoli, Zurich, Gênes, Essling. Masséna mort le 4 avril 1817*). Berri was his chosen victim, since Berri was considered the only Bourbon capable of producing heirs. Having long planned the deed, Louvel had been walking near the opera house at 8 p.m. when he had heard an officer ordering the prince's carriage for just before 11.[20]

In the following days Paris was swept by hurricanes of emotion – what Pozzo called 'this whirlwind of tumults and vociferations' – familiar to anyone who has lived through the aftermath of a violent royal death. Some liberals, delighted by Louvel's deed, sneered that dying was the only thing the Bourbons knew how to do well.* Faced with the prospect of the possible extinction of the Bourbons, according to Pozzo, 'the former servants of Bonaparte no longer know how to contain themselves and betray at every moment the hope of recovering their influence and their past grandeur.'[21] Delacroix made a romantic engraving of Louvel. The future historian Michelet, then a law student in Paris, wrote in his diary: 'Louvel has avenged Ney.'[22] At *guinguettes* outside the barriers, some workers drank and sang 'in the most scandalous manner and very often seditious songs'.[23]

Many Parisians, however, spent days in tears. Some wrote of their shame of being French, of their fear that, in the absence of male heirs among the elder branch, the Orléans were destined to inherit the throne. Madame de Nansouty, a friend of Madame de La Briche and mistress of Baron Pasquier, wrote to a friend: 'Ah my dear, what a country, what a misfortune to be born there and to await death there, and what kind of death?' The Duchesse de Duras wrote: 'we are in a state of sorrow which it is impossible to shake off; no one can talk of anything else.'[24]

When he had heard the news, Decazes had warned his colleagues: 'we are all assassinated.'[25] The murder was indeed blamed by enraged royalists on Decazes' moderation, his favour with the King, and what was called 'this odious liberty of the press', instead of the real cause, Bonapartist nationalism – and Berri's own refusal to be accompanied in Paris by large numbers of soldiers.[26] The King himself was not spared. As in 1814 and 1817, quarrels and duels erupted between royalist and Napoleonic officers in the cafés of the Palais Royal. The ultra Café de Valois was closed; the gardes du corps were confined to barracks to stop them sacking the Bonapartist Café Lemblin.[27] Some talked of trying to assassinate or kidnap Decazes.[28] The Duchesse de Bellune, wife of the Major-General of the Garde Royale in waiting, said that there was no reason to hesitate between the life of one man and the fate of a dynasty.[29] When the Duchesse de Broglie defended Decazes, she was accused of being his mistress.[30] Pozzo reported that it was difficult to describe 'the irritation of the parties and public excitement in the midst of this mixture of atrocity and weakness'. Baron Séguier, Premier Président de la Cour Royale de Paris, presenting its condolences to the King, requested the re-establishment of torture.[31]

---

* Another sneer, referring to Berri's death in the opera house where he had found many mistresses, was that he had died on the field of honour.

In the Chamber of Deputies Decazes was accused by an ultra and friend of Chateaubriand, Clausel de Coussergues, of being the assassin's accomplice. A general cry of dismay and *A l'ordre! A l'ordre!* forced Clausel de Coussergues to descend from the tribune. The King was heartbroken, but resolved to defend his minister and his system of moderation. The royal family moved over to the attack. On 15 February, after consultations with ultra politicians, Artois promised to force Decazes' resignation from the King. On 16 February Parisians learnt that the Duchesse d'Angoulême had refused to lunch with the King, as she normally did, and had left the room in tears. On 18 February, in 'a very bitter scene' after dinner, Artois and the Duchesse d'Angoulême begged the King on their knees for Decazes' dismissal. Among their weapons were the threat to leave Paris – and by implication establish a rival court in the provinces – and the threat, masked as a plea to save his life, of Decazes' murder by the gardes du corps. *Sire, c'est pour éviter une victime de plus*, the Duchesse d'Angoulême pleaded. All Paris knew that she had again left the King's study in tears.[32]

Chateaubriand also went over to the attack. He revised articles by other ultras and, in a famous article of his own, would write of Decazes that 'his feet have slipped in blood.' On 17 February he and Villèle spent all evening, from 9 to midnight, in Monsieur's apartment in the Tuileries. On 19 February a police agent reported to Decazes that Chateaubriand had been working since 7 in the morning with Clausel de Coussergues, and others, on the act of accusation against Decazes: 'Madame de Duras sent [a servant] to look for M. de Chateaubriand at half-past four, telling him that he was awaited, and the Viscount went there at once.' He stayed until it was time to return home to dress for dinner with Talleyrand – who was so convinced of his imminent return to office that he was discussing his choice of ministers as he left the royal mass in the Tuileries.[33] The King, however, was determined above all to avoid the necessity of asking Talleyrand to form a ministry.[34]

The government's fate was decided not at court but in the Chambers. Both right and left withdrew their support: liberals because, in the reaction to Berri's death, the ministry was preparing to introduce repressive laws reimposing censorship (as much against ultra-royalist as against liberal newspapers), limiting individual freedom and changing the electoral law; ultras, even those who had been prepared to support Decazes' modification to the electoral law before Berri's death, out of loathing for Decazes. Party spirit was stronger than desire to support the King's government. Since Decazes' majority had slipped away, he would not be able to get the laws passed.[35] Far from being, as his former admirer Pozzo alleged, 'a degraded instrument in the hands of a pupil of the police',[36] Louis XVIII put his desire for the passage of the new electoral and censorship laws before his love for Decazes and on 20 February, in tears, accepted his resignation.[37] His replacement by the Duc de Richelieu was indispensable.

Under pressure from the King, Artois and the Duchesse d'Angoulême – Artois paid a visit to Richelieu in his *hôtel* in the Place Vendôme and promised to be his 'first soldier' – Richelieu, who had refused in November 1819, was finally persuaded to accept the Présidence du Conseil again. Since, despite the growing power of the Chambers, France also remained a court system, Decazes' departure from Paris, where he might have been able to influence the King, was one of Richelieu's conditions of acceptance: Decazes was made a Duke and ambassador to London.[38] Finally on 20 February, a week after Berri's murder, Parisians could see Decazes' possessions leaving the Ministry of the Interior, 122 rue de Grenelle, for the Hôtel de Soyecourt, the magnificent residence of his parents-in-law the Comte and Comtesse de Sainte-Aulaire nearby at 43 rue de l'Université.[39] He left Paris on 26 February.

Meanwhile the body of the Duc de Berri had been lying in state in the Louvre, in the same room as the body of Henri IV had lain after his assassination in 1610 – a room which had also recently displayed the Exhibition of the Products of French Industry which had been one of the triumphs of Decazes' ministry. On 22 February, watched by a huge crowd, the corpse left the Louvre for burial in Saint-Denis. Proving again the underlying strength of the monarchy, Berri's funeral became a national event. Just as almost all deputies, even La Fayette, had paid their respects to the corpse, so a large number of army officers, including many Napoleonic officers, as well as beggars, the *confrérie des charbonniers*, the coal-porters of Paris, followed the procession, escorted by national guards and soldiers and watched by a crowd of thousands, the ten kilometres from the Louvre to Saint-Denis. In an unprecedented infraction of royal etiquette, the King himself, mortified by accusations of indifference to his nephew's death, as well as the royal family, the two Chambers and deputations of state and military institutions, attended the funeral. Reflecting the obsession with statistical precision characteristic of the period, one estimate by a Spanish resident of Paris, D. Cabello Felix, put the total number of people, including soldiers and peasants from the surrounding countryside, escorting or watching the funeral procession at 272,744.[40] After being closed for nine days the theatres finally reopened. The opera however, considered defiled by the prince's murder, was moved from the rue de Richelieu to the Salle Favart on the Boulevard des Italiens. It did not reopen until 19 April.[41]

In the next six months France moved right. By 15 March the laws on press censorship and individual freedom had been passed. Even some liberal deputies had been disgusted by the experience of speaking in the Chamber 'under the whip of the newspapers'.[42] Finally there remained the electoral law: it re-established the principle of the double vote beloved of royalists, which gave the richest quarter of the already minuscule electorate of 90,000 two votes, and enabled them to vote in the chief town of each arrondissement rather than of each department.

Hitherto the lack of popular disturbances in Paris, even in 1815, had led many to believe that the people were indifferent to political disputes: Benjamin Constant's remark in 1819, 'the sovereign people had handed in its resignation', was much repeated.[43] In reality this was only half true. The people did show interest in the electoral law, even though they had no prospect of voting themselves. In speeches against the law of the double vote in the Chambers, implicitly threatening to use their contacts among the people, Constant, who now looked like a Protestant pastor with white hair and upraised right arm,[44] La Fayette and General Foy prophesied a 'terrible' resistance and a new revolution. Some liberals claimed that the ministry intended to re-establish the feudal system and serfdom. A deputy who refused to stand at the *séance royale* opening the parliamentary session when all other deputies rose to their feet with the cry *Vive le roi!*, General Foy thought that the dynasty was about to fall and in one celebrated outburst in the Chamber praised the *glorieux cocarde tricolore*. Going for the nerve, he appealed to French nationalism by attacking ultras for ruling through foreigners and émigrés: 'Do you believe that without the foreigners we would have basely endured the outrages, the insults of a handful of wretches whom we had despised, whom we had seen in the dust for thirty years?' After fighting a duel with one former émigré M. de Corday, a relation of Charlotte Corday, the assassin of Marat, Foy later apologised and even praised the dignity of some émigrés.[45]

The past remained toxic. On 27 May, during discussion of the electoral law, there was a confrontation between the Minister of Justice de Serre and La Fayette, in which the former condemned the latter for his role in leading 'the furious bands' in their attack on the château of Versailles on 6 October 1789. Like Foy, La Fayette declared war on the regime. He praised the tricolour, blamed the emigration rather than the revolutionaries who stormed the Tuileries for the fall of the monarchy in 1792 and the reign of terror in 1793–4, and threatened that the French people, unable to resign itself to the new laws, would seize 'the sacred *fasces* of the principles of eternal truth and sovereign justice'.[46] De Serre was correct when he claimed that liberals like La Fayette used the word 'nation' as a synonym for insurrection and revolt.[47]

Again events in Paris and Europe were intertwined. Shocked by Berri's death, many European rulers blamed Paris and a mythical 'central committee' as the source of the 'impiety and anarchy' spreading across the continent. In 1820 Alexander I called France 'a country lost, demoralised and the cause of the disorganisation of European society'.[48] In reality, as Alexander I learnt for himself from a mutiny that year in his favourite Semenovsky guards regiment, France was far from being the sole cause of 'disorganisation' in Europe. Indeed the success of a military coup in Spain, and the restoration by Ferdinand VII on 7 March 1820 of the ultra-liberal Spanish constitution of 1812 – the first European constitution with adult manhood suffrage – was an inspiration for similar events in southern Europe. It was followed by coups and the proclamation of versions of the Spanish constitution in Naples (7 July), Lisbon (15 September) and Turin (13 March 1821). It also inspired hopes of a similar military coup in France: 'in the salons people talk only of Naples and Madrid,' wrote General Foy.[49]

A new phenomenon appeared in Paris to support the liberal deputies: student militants. Since the thirteenth century Paris, home of the Sorbonne, had been a great university town as well as a royal capital. The first book printed in France, the *Epistolae* (1470) of Barzizius, dedicated to Paris, hailed it as *capitale du royaume, nourisse des muses*, pouring knowledge on the world.[50] By the end of the Empire the two main faculties of the Sorbonne, the Schools of Law and Medicine, had been transformed into artillery schools. Many students had been conscripted and had fought bravely in the defence of Paris on 30 March 1814. The Sorbonne returned to life only with the Restoration.[51] The number of students in Paris rose from 2,300 in 1814 to about 4,500 in 1821 – among them the young Balzac in the Ecole de Droit (1816–18) and the young Berlioz in the Ecole de Médecine (1822–3).[52] They were concentrated in one of the oldest and dirtiest quarters of the city, the Quartier Latin between the Luxembourg, the Panthéon, the Jardin des

Plantes and the river. It was full of what contemporaries called sombre and tortuous streets, filthy gutters and pestilential smells – as well as the bookshops and student restaurants described in Balzac's *Illusions perdues*.[53]

After 1815, partly under the influence of the writer Victor Cousin, most students espoused a rational radical philosophy opposed to Catholicism and nostalgic for the nationalism – and rapid promotion prospects – of the Empire.[54] Many students came to loathe the Bourbons and the introduction of compulsory religious observance: they hissed royalist plays, refused to write compositions on royalist themes, fought duels over the price of lilies.[55] At the Lycée Louis-le-Grand, schoolboys leapt on the chapel altar shouting *Pas de Dieu! Vive Royer-Collard!* and, inspired by Cambronne's remark at Waterloo *La garde meurt et ne se rend pas*, 'French pupils die and do not surrender.' For a few days in 1819 the Quartier Latin had resembled a city under siege.[56]

In May and June 1820 Paris students from the Schools of Law and Medicine, the majority still in their early twenties – severed from their families and their provincial backgrounds before, in the words of their historian Alan B. Spitzer, falling back after the age of thirty 'behind the ramparts' of their social class – provided leadership for the liberal opposition.[57] The debates on the electoral law in the Chamber of Deputies aroused such passions that queues for places in the public galleries began forming outside the Chamber at 2 in the morning.[58] Debates were particularly intense, since right and left appeared almost equally balanced; some deputies were still undecided; one speech could affect the destiny of the law or the government. Debates acquired what Molé called 'a character of boldness and frankness in political opinions which had not yet been seen at the tribune'.[59] Moreover, with the introduction of newspaper censorship, the Chambers were the last outpost of free public debate. As the Duchesse de Broglie remarked, 'all French wit, all the weapons of ridicule have passed to the tribune.'[60] Sometimes the uproar among deputies, from both right and left, was so violent that spectators were reminded of an episode of the revolution – or a schoolroom in revolt. Pozzo compared the Chamber to an erupting volcano.[61]

In the first fortnight of June political passions took to the streets of Paris. The right was, for once, as well organised as the left. Despite formal orders from Richelieu and the Minister of War to stay in barracks, gardes du corps in civilian clothes, recognisable by their height and the white ribbons in their hats, attacked members of the crowd between the Chamber and the Pont Louis XVI and on the *quais* – many of them students – with canes and truncheons weighted at one end with lead. The guards shouted *Vive le roi!*, the students *Vive la Charte!*[62] On 3 June voting began on the first article of the electoral law. There were 'violent altercations' between deputies of opposing views in the Chamber itself. Briefly standing in as President of the Chamber, Villèle received blisters on his hand from the number of times he had to ring the bell to maintain order.[63] As they left the Chamber at the end of the day's session, the liberal deputies Kératry, Courcelles and Chauvelin were insulted by royalists. La Fayette was threatened. Chauvelin was obliged to cry, through the windows of the sedan chair which he was using on account of ill-health, *Vive le roi!* Casimir Périer and Benjamin Constant were chased as far as the rue de Bellechasse. Only the speed of their horses prevented them being hit as well as their servants. While the gardes du corps remained masters of the area around the Chamber, a crowd of students and workers marching down the rue de Rivoli shouted 'sinister cries' outside the Hôtel de Talleyrand and *Vive la Charte!*, in opposition to *Vive le roi!*, under the windows of the Pavillon Marsan: they were soon dispersed by a cavalry charge.[64]

The Garde Royale and the Paris garrison, increased to a strength of 40,000, were under the command of Maréchal Macdonald, as loyal and energetic in June 1820 as he had been in March 1815. Since the guard's formation in September 1815, regular rotation to Lille, Rouen and Orléans (the Gardes Françaises who had helped revolutionaries win control of Paris in July 1789 had been Parisians quartered in Paris) had prevented any regiment acquiring, through long residence in the capital, what one Minister of War called 'a hostile attitude due to their contacts with the bourgeoisie'.[65] The gendarmes were also effective. In the political destiny of Paris, as of other great European capitals, the military factor was paramount. Pozzo wrote: 'the attitude of the Garde Royale, from its first appearance on the scene of the drama, decided the issue.'[66]

However, on 3 June a soldier of the Garde Royale, acting without orders but possibly under provocation, opened fire in the rue de Rohan near the Tuileries. A twenty-three-year-old law student, Nicholas Lallemand, son of a Paris grain merchant, was killed.[67] He was the martyr for whom the organisers of the demonstrations had been hoping: according to Pozzo they had even arranged for boys to leave school in order to encourage a dramatic death.[68] The fourth of June, a Sunday, was quiet. The processions of the Fête-Dieu were able to take place as usual. On 5 June demonstrations by students and bourgeois started again, aimed at intimidating the government, testing the temper of the troops and preventing the passage of the new laws.[69] For the first time they left the centre of Paris and reached the Faubourg Saint-Antoine, the stronghold of revolution in 1789. On 6 June a funeral procession accompanied Lallemand's coffin from his father's house in the rue du Petit-Carreau to the church of Bonne-Nouvelle and then on to the cemetery of Père Lachaise. The simple funeral monument, erected that year and paid for by a national subscription, had four inscriptions, indicating the origins of his Parisian mourners: *A Lallemand mort le 3 juin 1820. Ecole de droit. Ecole de médecine. Ecole des beaux-arts* and, last but not least, *le commerce*.[70] On the same day one of the most brilliant and anti-Bourbon liberal deputies, Jacques-Antoine Manuel, claimed that all France opposed the new law and caused a sensation by calling the soldiers and policemen 'assassins'. Recently dismissed as Director of the Banque de France on account of his liberal opinions, Laffitte accused soldiers of 'knifing' innocent citizens.[71]

On 7 June, Louvel, calm and unrepentant, was guillotined on the Place de Grève. Both on 7 and 8 June, in the evening after the day's work, renewed student demonstrations were joined by thousands of workers, shop assistants and ex-soldiers – what the military authorities called 'people of the most common class'. On 9 June a crowd of almost 30,000 left the Faubourgs Saint-Antoine and Saint-Marcel, shouting *Vive la Charte!* It occupied the boulevards, particularly the area between the Portes Saint-Denis and Saint-Martin, reached the site of the Bastille and threatened to march on the Tuileries. Soon some of the crowd were also shouting: *A bas les chambres! A bas les émigrés! A bas les cuirassiers! A bas les dragons!*, even *Vive l'Empereur!*, *Vive Napoléon! Vive la liberté!* and *Vivent nos frères de Manchester!* – an allusion to the 'Peterloo Massacre' of August 1819, in which eleven people had been killed by the local militia.[72]

Torrential rain, however, dispersed the crowd. The police were well aware that there was collusion between demonstrators and liberal leaders in the Chambers, especially La Fayette and Laffitte, and Bonapartist officers. There was even a plan for a provisional government drawn up by La Fayette, with himself as President. An eye-witness the Baron d'Eckstein, a Danish Jew who had become a French royalist, swore that money had been distributed to demonstrators and soldiers.[73] However, the government, having learnt the lessons of 1815, feared the publicity of a trial and a possible acquittal – or an executed martyr.

On 10 June Laffitte denounced the bloodshed in the capital, claimed that the Chamber was not free, and demanded that the Garde Nationale as well as the Garde Royale be used to maintain order. However he also said that he was not making an apology for 'demonstrations' – 'given my wealth, I am clearly interested in order.' De Serre replied with a denunciation of the 'systematic organisation' of sedition. Constant blamed the demonstrations on 'the occult government' of the Comte d'Artois: 'the root of the evil is in the counter-revolutionary faction.'[74] From 10 June, following Laffitte's speech, patrols of the Garde Nationale joined those of the Garde Royale. On 12 June the law of the double vote, further amended to placate *les Ternaux* (*les Laffitte* were irrevocably opposed), was finally passed by a majority of only five votes. In its final form, voted even by General Foy, it kept the 258 deputies already in existence, but added 172 deputies chosen by the 23,000 richest voters.[75] After the law was passed, as if by magic, the demonstrations ceased.

Three factors had helped the government: the bourgeoisie was more frightened of revolution than of the right and did not move. The favourable economic situation meant that there was plenty of work available for what the Prefect of the Seine called 'the class least favoured by fortune, those estimable artisans who nourish their families by the fruit of their daily labour'[76] – that is, the poor – and little economic motive for them to listen to liberals' pleas for insurrection. Above all the Garde Royale had displayed a winning combination of loyalty and restraint. Unlike the Household Cavalry in London, nicknamed 'the Piccadilly butchers' by radical journalists, it was skilled in avoiding pointless deaths. On 15 June Maria Edgeworth, who had been staying at 93 Place du Palais Bourbon opposite the Chamber, wrote: 'All is now perfectly quiet in Paris and will I think continue so till the death of the King and then! Heaven knows what will happen – *the duc d'Orléans – Prince of Orange or little Napoleon* with Beauharnais.'[77] She did not mention Artois.

Throughout this tumultuous period the King and the royal family had remained in the Tuileries. After Sunday mass on 11 June the King thanked the commanders of the Garde Royale for their zeal. He chose to ignore the demonstrations. On 18 June, referring to the Faubourg Saint-Antoine, which he called 'my' Faubourg and on whose bread supply and loyalty he often checked, he thanked the Corps Municipal for the attachment of 'this populous faubourg where I often receive such touching marks of love for the laws and, if I dare say so, for my person'.[78] On 22 July the parliamentary session came to an end.

Parisians had demonstrated their doubts about the Restoration. However, events began to prove the resilience as well as the fragility of the regime. A rash of military conspiracies failed, including one called *le Bazar français* after the name of a shop in the rue Cadet run by three Bonapartists. The dynasty also recovered its biological base. With his dying words Berri had revealed that his wife was pregnant. Having moved from the Elysée to the Tuileries, the Duchesse de Berri could be seen that summer, draped in black crêpe, walking on the terrace above the Seine like an ambulating tragedy. On some occasions she was cheered by passers-by; on others, even if guards and courtiers were present, insults were yelled at the pregnant widow. Having dreamt that St Louis had covered her daughter and a son with his royal robes, she was convinced that she would bear a male heir.[79] A boy, Henri-Dieudonné Duc de Bordeaux, was born in the Tuileries at 2.35 in the morning of 29 September.

As leader of the Bonapartists in Paris, Maréchal Suchet had been chosen to be one of the witnesses to the birth, along with a former émigré the Maréchal de Coigny. In the climate of distrust prevailing in Paris, the former was more likely to be believed than court officials and gardes du corps. The birth was so rapid that it was only with great difficulty that the Duchess kept the umbilical cord attached to the child long enough for Suchet to be able to see with his own eyes that her son was attached.[80] According to Sir Charles Stuart, with the words *Prenez, M. le Maréchal, tirez,* the princess urged the marshal to pull the cord himself: 'Upon the Marshal showing some repugnance to do so, she repeated *Mais tirez donc, Mr. le Maréchal.*'[81]

Despite such presence of mind, enemies of the royal family claimed to entertain suspicions that the prince was a changeling. In front of the King and the royal family, who were dazed with joy, both the Duc and Duchesse d'Orléans, furious with disappointment (since the Duc d'Orléans would otherwise have remained heir to the throne after Angoulême), asked Suchet, and three national guards who had also been witnesses, if they had indeed seen the cord attached to the child. In her diary, clearly intended to be read by others, the Duchesse d'Orléans repeated her doubts for the benefit of the 'impartial reader'.[82] The Orléans' loss of the prospect of eventual succession to the throne deprived the legitimate monarchy of a liberal future – and the Orléans of part of their incentive to remain loyal. As royalist crowds gathered in the Jardin des Tuileries and the bells of the churches of Paris pealed in joy, Pozzo remarked that they were sounding the death knell of the House of Bourbon.[83]

Nevertheless the birth of Bordeaux temporarily added force and popularity to the dynasty. Thousands of Parisians filed through the palace to glimpse the child. Reading the message of congratulation from the Corps Diplomatique to the King in the Tuileries, the Papal Nuncio hailed the Duc de Bordeaux as *l'enfant de l'Europe*, a guarantee of peace. Speaking from the palace balcony, the King announced to a crowd in the Tuileries garden: 'My children, your joy increases mine a hundredfold. A child has been born to us all [*cheers*]. This child will one day be your father, he will love you as I love you, as all my family loves you.'[84] Bordeaux' birth was celebrated with a magnificent christening in Notre Dame: wise cat-owners locked them up for fear they might end in some of the 37,000 pâtés distributed free by the government to the poor.[85] Parisians grew to like the Duchesse de Berri. Unlike the Duchesse d'Angoulême, she was young and graceful, with a natural Neapolitan manner.[86] Parisians watching the Fête-Dieu procession in June 1821 could be heard saying: 'how young she is, how beautiful she is, and how well dressed!'[87]

Another sign of the strength of the monarchy was the indifference with which, at first, Parisians received the news of Napoleon's death on St Helena on 23 May 1821. Lady Bessborough wrote of the 'perfect Apathy of everyone high and low here'.[88] In the salons people talked about the news for a few minutes before moving on to other topics.[89] Suffocated by memories, General Foy was shocked that in the Chamber of Deputies 'people talked about it as if it was a matter of indifference. They were much more interested in the speeches by de Serre and Pasquier.' Maréchal Suchet talked of Napoleon as if he had been Emperor of China.[90] Other Parisians were more shaken. Talma never again acted on the anniversary of the Emperor's death.[91] The Duchesse de Broglie claimed that 'The impression which this death has produced on the people is much stronger than I first told you. They gather in crowds around the print shops. Many young people wear mourning bands on their arms.' She felt that some regretted his despotism more than his glory.[92] The Napoleonic legend was already potent. Among the prints executed soon after Napoleon's death was one by Horace Vernet, whose studio in the Nouvelle Athènes was by day a Bonapartist propaganda factory and by night a rendezvous for those who 'maintained their loyalty to the Emperor'. It showed the

Emperor, like Jesus Christ at the Resurrection, stepping laurel-wreathed out of his tomb.[93]

In December 1821, the Chamber of Deputies had voted a hostile address, which had indirectly accused the Richelieu ministry of favouring Russia. Both an increase in the number of ultra deputies and the growing influence of the King's new favourite Madame du Cayla had strengthened the ultras' position. Although personally insulted in the address and at first reluctant to see Richelieu and his colleagues resign, in the end Louis XVIII had insisted, 'with many examples taken from England', that all leave together. They resigned and were replaced by a new ultra-royalist ministry headed by Villèle.[94]

The new ministry proved unexpectedly successful. Villèle, an impressive leading minister and able parliamentary manager, spoke well from the tribune.[95] The Princesse de Vaudémont was reported by Sosthènes de La Rochefoucauld, a friend of Villèle and Madame du Cayla, as saying: 'I am not biased, I hate politics and I am not *exagérée*; but we have at this moment a very clever man; no one can be compared to him. His system reattaches many people [to the regime]; long may he remain in power!'[96]

Chateaubriand's correspondence is a window into the hearts and minds of Paris in these years. As part of the long-anticipated rapprochement between the government and the ultras, he had been appointed ambassador first in Berlin, then in London, in 1821–2. He could now afford his own carriage and servants and play a leading part in European politics. The Duchesse de Duras, who told him that no one – that is, not even Madame Récamier – worked better for his interests than herself, wrote: 'This is the culmination of all my efforts and all my hopes.'[97]

However, he ordered both the Duchesse de Duras and Madame Récamier to arrange as soon as possible for him to end his days of 'exile' from Paris.[98] The Duchess talked to Villèle in her salon frequently, and at length, about the advantages of employing Chateaubriand in an even more influential position, saying that he would be 'an adornment for France'.[99] Chateaubriand was interested in serving not only himself and the monarchy, but also his party. Finding *les affaires* easier than he had anticipated, he wanted to prove that, despite royalists' lack of experience, they could govern France better than the 'valets of Bonaparte'.[100] He wrote to Pasquier that only legitimists should be employed: 'when France realises that there is no hope of favour except for those who faithfully serve the Bourbons, all France will be *Bourbonienne*.'[101]

In January 1823 he finally had to, as he wrote, *passer les ponts* – that is, to leave his apartment in the rue Saint-Dominique, on the left bank of the Seine, for the Ministry of Foreign Affairs in the former *hôtel* of Maréchal Berthier on the Boulevard des Capucines on the right bank. As a reward for her hard work, the Duchesse de Duras' son-in-law, Henri de Chastellux, Duc de Rauzan, followed him, becoming Under-Secretary of State for Foreign Affairs. *Quel tripotage!*, commented the Duchess's friend Alexander von Humboldt to Baron Gérard.

Chateaubriand understood the European nature of French politics, the correlation between the strength of France in Europe and the strength of the monarchy in France – recently underlined by the fall of the Richelieu government on the imputation of being pro-Russian. In Chateaubriand's opinion the external humiliations of France under Louis XV had helped destroy Louis XVI, as Louis XVIII's return with the foreign armies in July 1815 had weakened the Second Restoration. It was essential, he later wrote, 'to give the Bourbons an army capable of defending the throne and emancipating France . . . legitimacy was dying for lack of victories after the triumphs of Napoleon.' The means he chose was a French invasion of Spain to liberate Louis XVIII's Bourbon cousin Ferdinand VII from liberal control.[102]

On 23 January 1823, in his speech from the throne at the state opening of parliament, Louis XVIII announced to the Chamber of Deputies that the Duc d'Angoulême, at the head of 100,000 'sons of St Louis', would cross the Pyrenees and restore a descendant of Henri IV to his throne. Invoking 'the dignity of my crown', 'the honour and security of France', he ended with the words, 'We are French, *messieurs*, we will always agree to defend such interests.' But his speech also referred to the need to reconcile Spain with Europe: Chateaubriand had already secured the other powers' consent to the Spanish expedition at the last of the great European congresses of monarchs and statesmen, at Verona. The French expedition was seen by them, and represented by Chateaubriand, as serving *la bonne cause, la cause commune des monarchies*.[103]

Echoing many liberals, General Foy called the expedition 'a mad and culpable enterprise'. Talleyrand and the Duchesse de Dino saw in it the chance of an anti-Bourbon revolution in Paris, and conspired with members of the liberal opposition – Maréchal Soult, Generals Foy and Sébastiani, Molé and Stanislas de Girardin – in the house of a Parisian cosmopolitan, the Comtesse Bourke. The Neapolitan widow of a Danish ambassador to Spain, living at 49 rue du Faubourg Saint-Honoré, she was, according to Molé, a 'totally vulgar person but [one] who did not lack a certain finesse . . . no one was afraid to compromise her.' Her guests discussed their hopes and plans for *un grand mouvement* in the corners of her salon. In June 1823 she was asked by the police to leave Paris for a few months.[104]

In reality the Spanish expedition stabilised the Restoration. As they crossed into Spain, French soldiers fired on a band of former Napoleonic soldiers waving the tricolour; Cadiz, which had resisted the forces of Napoleon, fell to those of the Duc d'Angoulême. On 13 November Ferdinand VII re-entered Madrid in triumph, sitting in a chariot twenty-five feet high drawn by a hundred men in green and pink livery. When the Duc d'Angoulême returned to Paris for his own, more modest triumphal entry, Parisians noted that, for once, his wife was radiant with joy. To honour his victory in Spain, work was resumed on the Arc de Triomphe at the top of the Champs Elysées.

The success of the war, and the proven loyalty of the army, foiled the hopes and prophecies of the liberals and the 'Talleyrand opposition'. Contemporaries felt that it royalised 'everything'.[105] For the only time in the Restoration, in 1824 Paris voted right. Laffitte, Delessert and Ternaux were defeated; as were, outside Paris, such celebrated liberals as La Fayette and Manuel, who had been expelled from the Chamber on 4 March 1823 for excusing the execution of Louis XVI and speaking of French 'repugnance' for the Bourbons. The only remaining liberal deputies for Paris were Foy, Constant and Casimir Périer.* A new law in March 1824 made the entire Chamber renewable every seven years.[106]

Even after the fall of his friends in the Richelieu ministry, Pozzo had continued to act not only as Russian ambassador to France but also as a major European statesman. From Paris he had a watching brief over Russian diplomats in Spain and the Italian peninsula. In 1820–1 he had gone on special missions to Troppau and Naples, to help organise the restoration to absolute power of Ferdinand IV of Naples, to whom he was temporarily accredited. In 1823, alone of foreign ambassadors in Paris, he had actively encouraged French intervention in Spain, going on a special mission to Madrid, with the similar purpose of restoring

---

* Playing on the names of liberal deputies, it was said in Paris that *pour être bon patriote, il faut s'habiller en Casimir, boire du Laffitte, lire son Manuel, y ajouter Foy et lui rester Constant.*

Ferdinand VII to power. After the successful French invasion, his view was: 'you are finished for twenty years, *messieurs les libéraux*.'[107]

At the same time, swayed by the spirit of the age, many younger writers were turning to royalism. As early as 1819 Pozzo had written of 'the favourable movement of opinion which is beginning to show itself'.[108] The liberal Duchesse de Broglie admitted that the best writers and newspapers were royalist.[109] Instead of being seduced by liberal certainties and deifying Napoleon, many of the younger generation modelled themselves on Chateaubriand and preferred the emotionalism, cosmopolitanism and Catholicism associated with royalism. Among their number was Lamartine, whose *Méditations* (1820) revived the tradition of religious poetry in France. Selling 10,000 copies in the first year, and changing literary tastes overnight, it won the author compliments from the King, Talleyrand, Molé, Pasquier – everyone except Chateaubriand, who felt supplanted.[110]

Victor Hugo, unlike most other Paris law students a convinced royalist, dedicated *Le Génie* to Chateaubriand in 1820 and wrote, among other royalist works, odes on the Vendée, the death of the Duc de Berri and the birth of the Duc de Bordeaux.[111] The new trend was given institutional expression by the Société Royale des Bonnes Lettres, founded in 1821 specifically in order to 'turn all the Muses royalist and make them the interpreters of monarchical France' – and to help preserve young students from 'the dangers of Paris'. Its motto was *Dieu, le Roi et les Dames*. Its meetings, which took place on Tuesday and Friday evenings in the Hôtel de Gesvres, 17 rue Neuve-Saint-Augustin, in the student quarter near the Place Saint-Michel, offered poetry readings by, among other members, Hugo and Alfred de Vigny, as well as courses on history, geography, astronomy and physics. The premises contained a lecture hall, a reading room and a library. Chateaubriand became president soon after its foundation; other members included then famous writers such as Lacretelle *le jeune*, Bergasse and Bonald, as well as an array of prominent royalists, the Ducs de Fitzjames, de Doudeauville and de Blacas, Villèle, Corbière and Jules de Polignac.[112]

Sosthènes de La Rochefoucauld, an aide-de-camp of Monsieur and Colonel of the fifth legion of the Garde Nationale de Paris, seemed vain and ridiculous to most observers. However, after he had been appointed Directeur-Général des Beaux-Arts in 1824, he tried to make the monarchy, as in the reign of Louis XIV, the main patron of the arts: in his opinion nothing contributed more to the glory of a reign. Writers and musicians given state pensions at his instigation included an early

Romantic Charles Nodier; two non-royalists Augustin Thierry and (temporarily) Casimir Delavigne; Cherubini, Boieldieu and many other musicians.[113] In order to stop the most famous composer of the day, Gioachino Rossini, from settling in London, he was lured to Paris in 1824 by a contract engaging him, in return for 40,000 francs a year, to live in Paris and compose exclusively for its opera; the idol of the Paris public – his operas guaranteed successes at the Théâtre Italien of which he was made director – he later became Premier Compositeur du Roi et Inspecteur-Général du Chant.[114] On the grounds of his talent and his poverty, Victor Hugo had already obtained a pension, through his own efforts and the recommendations of the Duchesse de Berri and Chateaubriand; 1,000 francs a year had been awarded him in September 1822, on the fund assigned to *pensions et gratifications aux artistes et gens de lettres*.[115]

Meanwhile an economic boom was giving the monarchy the aura of prosperity. Peace was finally enabling France to resume the rate of economic growth which it had enjoyed in the decade before 1789. In 1822 one Parisian royalist, the Comte de Moré, who himself had been a businessman in Trieste during the emigration, wrote:

> all thoughts are turning towards the rise and fall of shares. There is frenzied speculation by foreigners as well as French, peers of France, dukes, marquesses, barons; the streets around the Bourse are frequently blocked by their carriages; ladies wait in their carriages for their husbands to come and inform them of the latest prices. That and the theatres, *voilà Paris*. The Chamber arouses little interest except for the influence the violence of debates could have on government stocks.[116]

A few years later General Foy was to say that people talked of nothing but business deals and railways.[117]

The boom received architectural expression. In 1808 the architect A.T. Brongniart had designed a magnificent new Bourse in the form of a rectangular Roman temple, in accordance with Napoleon's wish for a building 'worthy of the grandeur of the capital and which suits the volume of business which will one day be transacted there'. It was built during the subsequent fifteen years at the end of the rue Vivienne, in a a large new square laid out on the site of a former convent. The new building, into which stockbrokers finally moved in 1825 from temporary accommodation nearby in the rue Feydeau, contained a vast arcaded central hall, and was surrounded on the outside by sixty-six Corinthian columns, raised above sixteen steps. People noticed the contrast between the classical purity of 'this admirable temple', 'worthy of the greatest age of Greece', and, within, the activities of the multitude of 'veritable black devils shouting and stealing'.[118]

Land remained the basis of most of the largest French fortunes. However, stock-market speculation was so intense that it led one government agent to write: 'landed wealth no longer exists . . . All wealth is in portfolios, they are the lever and magnet of Democracy.'[119] Some people, including the Castellane family and Maréchal Marmont, lost fortunes. Pozzo, who had already estimated his fortune in 1820 at four million francs, speculated on a large scale in French and Spanish government bonds during the crises of 1820–3, in which he played such a prominent role: he gained a fortune but lost part of his reputation. When Metternich visited Paris in March 1825, the greatest change since his visit in 1815, he observed, was that Pozzo was simply the Russian ambassador.[120]

Such was the power of the Bourse that in June 1824, when the Villèle administration tried to lower the rate of interest on government stock in order to defray an indemnity to émigrés, there was a political crisis. Not only thousands of small *rentiers* in Paris and their deputies, but also the Archbishop of Paris and senior court officials, opposed the measure. The new law was rejected in the Chamber of Peers. However, in the Faubourg Saint-Antoine the people said: 'they voted against it only because they have it.' Despite his post as Foreign Minister, Chateaubriand had failed to speak in favour of the law in the Chamber of Peers and was said to have attacked it in the salons. On Sunday 6 June 1824, while waiting in an antechamber of the Pavillon de Marsan to pay his court to Monsieur, Chateaubriand was told that he had been dismissed as Minister of Foreign Affairs; he was to leave the palace and the ministry at once. 'The court and the city' rushed to write their names in a show of sympathy at the door to his apartment in the rue de l'Université. It was said that he told his two favourite cats: 'my good friends, the time for playing at being great ladies is over. Now you must think of catching mice.' Indeed, to the horror of most of his friends, he began a campaign of violent and systematic attacks on the Villèle ministry, accusing it in the *Journal des débats* of being against 'the spirit of the Charte'.[121]

The rise of the Paris Rothschilds – who frequently collaborated with the Villèle ministry – was another manifestation of the economic boom in these years. Like many other Parisians of the period, like Pozzo and the

Bourbons themselves, they owed their success to their support of the European coalition against the French Empire. The founder of the dynasty Meyer Amschel Rothschild had been *Hoch-fürstlicher Hoffaktor* (based in Frankfurt) to, among others, the Elector Wilhelm I of Hesse-Kassel and the Emperor Franz I of Austria. His son James arrived in Paris in 1811, at the age of nineteen, and through the secret family network across Europe helped to supply the British army invading France with French coin, and to convey Britain's subsidies to its European allies. After the victory Lord Liverpool wrote: 'Mr Rothschild has been a very useful friend. I do not know what we should have done without him last year.'[122] The family philosophy was expressed in a letter of Amschel Rothschild to his younger brother James on 8 February 1816: 'A court is always a court and it always leads to something.'[123] Bankers to the monarchs of the Holy Alliance, with brothers and branches in London (since 1803), Paris (1811), Frankfurt, Vienna (1816) and Naples (1821), the Rothschilds had become an economic force on a European scale. In 1817 they were ennobled with the title of Baron, and the magic particle *von* or *de*, by the Emperor of Austria.

Although he had constantly visited Richelieu, to whom he talked in German,[124] James de Rothschild had been excluded from participation in the French loans of 1817–18. However by 1820 he had become sufficiently powerful to be able, by his network of couriers, to convey news of the Duc de Berri's assassination to Vienna and Berlin over twenty-four hours before the arrival of official diplomatic couriers.[125] That summer he helped raise a loan of a million francs to enable the Richelieu government to increase the strength of the Paris gendarmerie during the June riots.[126] The offices of his bank were in the two wings between the street and his town house, Fouché's impressive *hôtel* at 19 rue Laffitte, purchased in 1818; they remained there until the building's demolition in 1967.[127] Although a friend of Decazes, James de Rothschild found many liberals disdainful. Flahaut, after dining with him in 1820, wrote: 'the dinner was execrable and smelt of the synagogue.'[128]

But the royalist nobility, and a group of fashionable ladies known as *le château* – since they tried to recreate *la vie de château* in Paris, and banned politics as a subject of conversation – were more appreciative.[129] The first ball given by a Rothschild in Paris took place on 2 March 1821. Comtesse Juste de Noailles, niece of Talleyrand, Dame d'atours of the Duchesse de Berri, 'perhaps the first *élégante* in Paris and quite certainly the most amiable', drew up the guest list (as she would for other foreign hosts eager to conquer Paris, such as the Anglo-Dutch millionaire William Williams Hope in 1826).[130] Louis-Martin Berthault, who had organised balls for the Comte d'Artois before the revolution and redecorated Compiègne for Napoleon I, erected a neo-Gothic ball-room overlooking the garden and supervised practical arrangements.[131] It was said that each lady at the ball received a diamond ring or brooch as well as a bouquet of flowers.[132] General Foy recorded: 'We have just returned from Rothschild's ball. It was an enchantment . . . More than fifteen hundred people. All the ladies of the court and all the ultras on earth.'[133] Rothschild, who in 1818 was made Austrian Consul-General in Paris, had become part of court society. Madame de Béthisy complained that she was the only lady-in-waiting of the Duchesse de Berri not to be invited to Rothschild's ball.[134] Rothschild helped arrange the French government's communications with, and payment of, French troops in Spain in 1823.[135] He was seen at a concert at the Duchesse de Duras', where Pozzo, Talleyrand and Chateaubriand were also present. The Duc de Duras, the Duc and Duchesse de Maillé, the Duke of Devonshire, the Foreign Minister, Pozzo and the Diplomatic Corps attended his dinners: by now the great chef Carême, who had previously worked for Talleyrand, the Prince Regent and Alexander I, was working for Rothschild.[136] By 1825 the combined capital of the Rothschild brothers was eleven times larger than that of James de Rothschild's principal rival in Paris, the liberal banker Laffitte, and exceeded the capital of the Banque de France itself.[137]

Rothschild's rise was a sign of the growing size, confidence and prosperity of the Jewish community in Paris. The last remaining discriminatory laws lapsed in 1818; the Chief Rabbi went to court to present his respects to the King at the same time as the chief pastors of the Lutherans and Calvinists. Among other prominent Jewish families settling in Paris between 1810 and 1830 were the Péreire, the Fould and the Worms. In Paris Jews lived mainly around the rue Saint-Martin. There were five synagogues in the area in 1818: at the inauguration of another, on 5 March 1822, Louis XVIII was hailed as *un nouveau Cyrus*.[138] When compared to the restrictions and anti-Semitism of Berlin, Vienna,* St Petersburg, and the vicious anti-Jewish riots in Frankfurt in 1819, such acceptance confirms Paris's reputation as the metropolis of liberalism.

---

* James de Rothschild's brother Salomon, while running the Vienna branch, also lived beside his brother in Paris, at 17 rue Laffitte, former residence of Queen Hortense. He did not have the right to acquire a house of his own in Vienna until 1842.

Another result of French economic growth was the biggest building boom in Paris since the reign of Louis XVI. Contemporaries were astonished. Flahaut reported to his wife: 'You have no notion of the number of speculations going on here – Ground bought a few years ago for 5 or 10 thousand Pounds has been sold for 50,000 . . . It is a sort of mania which must end in the ruin of the speculators.'[139] One new quarter being built west of the boulevards (north of the present Opéra) in what was still almost countryside was baptised by a journalist *la nouvelle Athènes*: among other artists Talma, Mlle Mars, Géricault and Horace Vernet lived there. The house of Mlle Mars, built in 1820–4 by an Italian Parisian Louis Visconti, was one of the sights of Paris. Designed like an Italian villa, surrounded by greenhouses, it resembled on the inside a white marble classical temple with columns, statues, bas-reliefs, fountains, 'an infinity of luxury, magnificence and good taste which resembles magic'.[140]

An Austrian, Prince Clary, grandson of the famous courtier and writer the Prince de Ligne, visited Paris in 1822. Coming from an absolute monarchy where there was no parliamentary life, he seemed to Frenchmen the epitome of the *ancien régime*, frivolous, childish, ignorant of his own country, talking of nothing but novels, theatres and actresses.[141] In Paris, so he wrote, there were 'enormous white stones everywhere as houses were going up'. Near the Tuileries the rues de Castiglione and de Rivoli, now approaching completion, struck him as 'beautiful, immense, magnificent, animated, elegant'.[142] Further new areas were being developed in the west of Paris, near the Parc Monceau, between the Champs Elysées and the Seine and on the Plaine de Grenelle to the south-west of the city.[143] Madame de Souza, by now an old lady made wretched by her husband's bad health and temper (he died in 1825), was indignant: 'the rage of building is so general that all those small gardens belonging to every house are disappearing to build mean little hovels . . . it will all go to make Paris *une véritable ville boutiquière.*' In her view Paris was becoming *mesquin.*[144]

The creation of covered shopping galleries or *passages* was a sign of the building boom. Some of the most luxurious shops in Paris could be found in the elegantly decorated Passage de l'Opéra, the Galerie Vivienne, the Galerie Véro-dodat, the Grand Bazar Saint-Honoré, which opened near the Boulevard des Italiens and the Palais Royal between 1822 and 1825. Their attraction was that they were cleaner, safer and better lit than the streets of Paris, many of which still lacked pavements.[145]

The building boom gave physical expression to Paris's role as capital of Europe as well as France. Paris is the only city in Europe to have a district called by that name: the *quartier de l'Europe*.* An area west of the boulevards, on the site of the Jardin de Tivoli – since 1770 the largest pleasure garden in Paris – it began to be laid out after 1821 as a commercial speculation. At the centre of the *quartier* was, and still is, the Place de l'Europe, into which ran the rues de Londres, de Constantinople, de Vienne, de Saint-Pétersbourg, de Naples, de Rome, de Berlin and de Madrid.[146]

In these years Paris also reaffirmed its role as a court city. The centre of the city was already dominated by the physical mass of the royal palaces – the Tuileries, the Louvre and the Elysée; their stable buildings; the barracks of the Gardes du Corps and the Garde Royale; the royal theatres (Théâtre Français, Théâtre Italien, Théâtre de l'Odéon, Opéra-Comique, Académie de Musique), each of which contained not only royal boxes but also two or three boxes reserved for senior court officials; the royal tapestry and carpet factories of Gobelins and Savonnerie; the mint; and many other *hôtels* and *dépendances* belonging to the Maison du Roi.[147] A splendid new royal opera house with seating for 2,000 – partly paid for by the Civil List, and built to replace the old one demolished after the murder of the Duc de Berri – opened in the rue de La Grange Batelière by the Boulevard des Italiens on 16 August 1821 with the anthem *Vive Henri IV*, the opera *Les Bayadères* by Charles-Simon Catel, and a ballet, *Le Retour de Zéphire*.[148]

Royal statues returned to Paris. On 25 August 1818 the statue of Henri IV (made in part out of the melted-down bronze of the statue of Napoleon I formerly surmounting the column of the Place Vendôme) had been re-erected on the Pont Neuf. On 22 August 1822, a statue of Louis XIV by the King's Premier Sculpteur Baron Bosio, was inaugurated on the Place des Victoires, on the site of the previous statue, toppled in 1792.[149]

The centuries-old process of finishing the Louvre and linking it to the Tuileries, in a complex even larger than the Winter Palace and the Hermitage in St Petersburg, continued. Houses between the two palaces were purchased and transformed in order to accommodate different court offices and the Garde Royale. The function of the Louvre as a royal palace was reaffirmed when it became the site of the

---

* Although a promenade along the banks of the Elbe in Dresden was known as 'the balcony of Europe'.

state opening of parliament. By 1820 the King's legs, long afflicted by gout, gangrene and diabetes, had become paralysed: he had had to be lifted, by a special chair designed by the great furniture-maker Georges Jacob and carried by eight men, to the Pavillon de Marsan to congratulate the Duchesse de Berri on the birth of the Duc de Bordeaux. Largely to spare him the physical effort of entering the Palais Bourbon, from 1820 the *séance royale* opening the parliamentary session was held in the great hall on the first floor of the Pavillon de l'Horloge in the Louvre: the King arrived by wheelchair, through the long gallery of the museum, directly from the Tuileries.[150]

Louis XVIII also made two personal additions to the city of Paris. Aggrieved that the Conseil Municipal had not seen fit to acquire the château of Saint-Ouen at the gates of Paris where, on 2 May 1814, he had signed the Declaration guaranteeing the country's liberal constitution – indeed the château had since been demolished by building speculators[151] – the King ordered the site to be acquired in 1820. Under the direction of the architect Jean-Jacques-Marie Huvé, whose father had worked for his sister Madame Elisabeth before the revolution,[152] and from a plan first sketched by the King himself, a new château was begun for his new favourite the Comtesse du Cayla. Born in 1785 into a family of Paris *noblesse de robe*, despite a close friendship with her old school friend Queen Hortense, she had been one of the royalist women who cheered the allies' entry into Paris on 31 March 1814. Married to a disagreeable eccentric, she had asked for an audience with the King in 1817 in order to facilitate the then audacious process of separation. It is said that she first caught his attention by being able to continue his quotations from Racine's *Esther*. Gradually she became a regular visitor to the King, often with her children, on Wednesday afternoons. She wrote him letters whose content was discussed in advance with Villèle and Sosthènes de La Rochefoucauld.[153] In March 1821 Boniface de Castellane had written in his diary that she was 'beautiful, witty, extremely intriguing and very affected'. The King was said to sniff snuff from her bosom; hence her epithet *la tabatière royale*, and the loud sniffs from the gardes du corps when she went through the Salle des Gardes on her way to see the King: she was also known as *la du Barry de la Charte*.[154] No one else was allowed to enter his study during her visits: she was soon used as an intermediary with the King by ministers, court officials and the royal family itself.[155]

The new château was a perfect cube, with five windows on each side, in a simple neoclassical style. The interior was richly decorated with panels by Baron Gérard showing flowers, animals and mythological scenes, silk upholstery, Sèvres china and four sets of chairs made by Pierre-Antoine Bellangé, of appropriate degrees of opulence, for the salon, the music room, the billiard room and the dining room. Following the latest Paris fashion, Madame du Cayla later installed in her private apartments on the first floor a neo-Gothic library, as well as a sumptuously furnished bedroom.[156] The thirty-hectare park which went down to the Seine contained a farm breeding merino sheep and dovecotes with room for 26,000 pigeons.

A fête for over 400 people, organised by Isabey, inaugurated the château on 2 May 1823, the anniversary of the Declaration of Saint-Ouen nine years earlier. In the morning the Archbishop of Paris blessed a chapel in the basement. If the King himself, who may have been expected, did not come, all the ambassadors, including the Papal Nuncio, were present. Lunch was served in a tent: since it was a Friday, when Catholics were supposed to eat only fish, it was *en maigre*. In a small theatre there was a prologue in honour of the King, followed by a play and a specially commissioned *vaudeville* performed by court actors. Cantatas were sung in the main salon until a telegram arrived announcing the fall of Saragossa to the French army.[157]

Then, in the *petit salon* next to the billiard room, a life-size portrait of the King by Baron Gérard, commissioned and 'composed' by the King himself, was unveiled. Surrounded by a massive gilt frame decorated with fleurs-de-lys, surmounted by a large crown and the royal coat of arms, it shows the King in his study in the Tuileries on 3 May 1814, the day of his arrival in Paris. He is sitting at the simple wooden desk at which in 1803, during the emigration, he had written his refusal of Bonaparte's offer of money in return for giving up his claim to the throne of France: he continued to use the desk in France, in preference to the elaborate gilded desks of his predecessors. He is meditating on the institutions he will give his people. In one hand he holds a copy of the Declaration of Saint-Ouen, which guaranteed constitutional government: on the desk are his books and a copy of the will of Louis XVI, which promised forgiveness. The portrait commemorates not only the King's liberalism but also his confidence in his own legitimacy. It records a moment which had impressed even Talleyrand: when he arrived in the Tuileries, after his triumphal entry into Paris, Louis XVIII's desk and books were already installed in what had been the Emperor's study, and the King sat down to work without showing any astonishment at his return to Paris after twenty-three years in exile.[158] No other portrait was believed to capture the King's expression so well.

Many guests found the occasion slightly ridiculous. Clearly, however, the King's intention at Saint-Ouen was to commemorate his parliamentary monarchy, as the Galerie des Glaces at Versailles commemorates the reign and conquests of Louis XIV. The foundation stone of the Château de Saint-Ouen, containing documents and medals and sealed by the King himself in his study in the Tuileries, had been laid on 8 July 1821 – anniversary of his entry into Paris in 1815 – in the presence of Madame du Cayla, her brother Vicomte Talon, Colonel of the Lancers of the Garde Royale, and Sosthènes de La Rochefoucauld.[159]

So often accused of living in the past, at Saint-Ouen Louis XVIII was clearly looking to the future. On the wall opposite his portrait, in letters of bronze inserted in a large marble plaque on the spot where he had signed the Declaration, is the inscription, composed by the King: 'Here on 2 May 1814 a new era began.' Madame du Cayla later wrote: 'in fact everything was done by his orders and according to his plans. His Majesty wanted to leave a great memorial to himself . . . in fact everything here speaks of him and has become, from this moment, posterity. A sort of cult should here remain consecrated to his memory.' Saint-Ouen was 'the only place in the world about which he cared'; he hoped that its view of Saint-Denis would encourage her to pray for him. The King's decision to memorialise himself and his reign in a private house, rather than a royal palace, suggests a fear that his family would destroy his legacy. Perhaps, as Madame du Cayla later claimed in her efforts to obtain even more money than Louis XVIII had already given her, he intended the possessor of Saint-Ouen to be a Duke, endowed with a large sum to maintain the château as a permanent, and accessible, memorial to himself at the gates of Paris.[160]

If the Château de Saint-Ouen looked to the future, Louis XVIII's other monument in Paris, the Chapelle Expiatoire, commemorated the past. Designed by Fontaine, the chapel was built by the western boulevards, on the site of the mass grave where the bodies of Louis XVI and Marie Antoinette, and hundreds of other victims of the guillotine, had been interred. The King personally approved of, and modified, the design. The chapel is a circular domed Roman-style basilica, preceded by a rectangular arcaded courtyard. Inside the chapel are life-size statues of Louis XVI in prayer and Marie Antoinette rising to heaven, consoled by Religion with the features of Madame Elisabeth. Buried under arches around the courtyard are the Swiss guards who had died defending the

Tuileries on 10 August 1792. In the middle of the courtyard are the graves of more than a thousand victims of the guillotine, irrespective of class or beliefs (including enemies of the royal family such as Madame Roland). Begun in 1816, using stones from the palace started by Napoleon I for his son on the hill of Chaillot, the Chapelle Expiatoire was consecrated on 21 January 1824. The Duchesse d'Angoulême, daughter of the royal victims, often visited it alone.[161]

With so many recent dramas to commemorate, commemoration was a fashionable occupation in Restoration Paris. The Chapelle Expiatoire was one of many memorial chapels and gardens in Paris being founded by relations of the revolution's victims. If Bonapartists went on pilgrimages to the tombs of Ney, Labédoyère and Masséna at Père Lachaise (corners of which resemble a shrine to the Empire), royalists paid their respects in the commemorative chapel created on the King's orders in 1816 (and marked by an inscription composed by the King himself), in the prison cell of the Conciergerie on the Ile de la Cité where Marie Antoinette had spent her last night; at a monument to the Duc d'Enghien in the chapel of the Château de Vincennes, beside which the Duke had been shot in 1804; and in the Jardin de Picpus in eastern Paris, a quiet convent garden transformed since 1796 by victims' relations into a cemetery for a further 1,300 victims of the reign of terror. An annual memorial service there is still attended by descendants of the victims today.[162] In 1818 the Duchesse d'Orléans visited the seventeenth-century Carmelite convent at 70 rue de Vaugirard, where around 160 priests had been massacred on 2 September 1792, by men organised and paid by the Commune of Paris. It contained, so she wrote, 'bloody and awesome remains' (bones and skulls are still visible in a crypt wall today) in a martyrs' chapel 'completely coloured with their blood'.[163] Princesse Louise de Condé, sister of the Duc de Bourbon, established a memorial convent on the site of the tower of the Temple where the royal family had been imprisoned. At the same time, on the King's orders, the remains of members of the royal family were brought back from their burial places abroad (in the case of the King's aunts Mesdames Adélaïde and Victoire), or from museums and other churches in France, and relocated in the abbey of Saint-Denis. Saint-Denis' role as the Bourbon necropolis was reaffirmed every year at grandiose memorial services in honour of Louis XVI and Marie Antoinette: their statues, finished in 1819, are the last royal effigies placed in the abbey.[164] At the same time the King's cousin the Duc d'Orléans was building a separate

Orléans family necropolis at Dreux, west of Paris, where he, his wife and their children were to be buried.

Indeed Paris was a court city to such an extent that it could contain two courts: the King's court in the Tuileries and the subordinate but rival court of the Duc d'Orléans in the Palais Royal. After his return in 1817, Orléans had three principal occupations: complaining about the royal family, with what some considered real aversion, to liberals like Broglie, Foy, Guizot, Laffitte, and offering himself as a 'patriotic' alternative;[165] reorganising and running his estates;* and building. He was said in his household to have 'the building disease', *le mal de la pierre*, and rapidly extended the country house of Neuilly near the Bois de Boulogne which the King had given him in 1817 in exchange for the stables of the Palais Royal.[166] A rambling one-storey house surrounded by a 220-hectare park, it stretched from the banks of the Seine almost to the walls of Paris.[167] Concerned to further his popularity, against the King's wishes he sent his eldest son the Duc de Chartres to the Lycée Henri IV in 1819, rather than giving him a princely education in his palace.[168]

The art collection he created in the Palais Royal, like his fury on the night of the birth of the Duc de Bordeaux, revealed his dynastic ambitions. Considering modern French painters the equals of those of Renaissance Italy, he asked Baron Gérard's advice on the choice of artists to paint pictures which would replace, in the galleries of the Palais Royal, the celebrated Orléans collection of old masters, sold at Christie's in London between 1793 and 1800. Using the liberal code word 'national', Orléans wrote that he wanted to create 'a national monument to console us in part for the losses we have made in this domain'.[169] This was the beginning of his gallery of pictures of revolutionary and Napoleonic battles, such as the massive canvases painted by Horace Vernet between 1821 and 1826 of the Republican victories of Valmy and Jemappes in 1792, in which Orléans himself was proud to have fought, and the Napoleonic victories of Hanau (1813) and Montmirail (1814). In such pictures Orléans was able to advertise his sympathy for French nationalism and the Napoleonic Empire, and to display – if relatively discreetly – the tricolour flag, which was outlawed both from the Salon de Peinture (from which, in 1822, Vernet's *Battle of Jemappes* was

---

*Thanks to his management the Orléans family remained the largest landowners in France until the 1960s.

excluded) and the streets of Paris.* This gallery was as much a political statement as Orléans' complaints about the royal family, and his employment in his household of officers who had served in the Hundred Days. His past as the most pro-British of émigrés, eager to serve the British government against France between 1800 and 1814, was consigned to oblivion (except in the memories of certain Foreign Office officials, who kept his letters as weapons for the future). Although there were many French royal portraits from the seventeenth century, no recent royalist subjects were represented in the galleries of the Palais Royal, just as no revolutionary or Napoleonic subjects were represented in the equally large and politically oriented picture collections, dominated by scenes from the lives of Henri IV and Louis XVI, then being assembled by the Duchesse d'Angoulême and the Duchesse de Berri.[170]

At this stage – in part because of his obvious ambitions and relentless exploitation of his property claims in Paris – Orléans inspired little love or respect. 'Nature', Pozzo claimed, 'has given him no noble or elevated sentiment and his education has given a false and petty veneer to the mediocrity of his mind.' An Irish visitor, Fanny Edgeworth, considered him 'rather English in his manner but not high bred or the least dignified – short and fat'.[171] At a fête in the Théâtre de l'Odéon to celebrate the baptism of the Duc de Bordeaux, the Duchesse d'Orléans noted that they were received by the commanders of the Gardes du Corps and Garde Nationale with insolence.[172]

As the political health of the monarchy had improved, the physical health of the King had deteriorated even further. At the service of thanksgiving in Notre Dame for the success of the Spanish campaign on 12 September 1823, he had fallen asleep; part of one boot had come off and there had been 'an inundation' on the cathedral floor.[173] He continued to decline but, having often said that a King could die but should never be ill, tried to maintain his routines.

Preferring Paris to any other residence, he insisted, against his doctor's advice, on returning from Saint-Cloud, where he normally went for one to two months in the summer, in time for the Fête de Saint-Louis on 25 August 1824. He was very thin, almost blind, and barely audible; his head was resting on his knees and his hands resembled those of a skeleton. Yet he managed to say a few words to everyone in the Grand Cabinet, as if taking his leave. The long and exhausting

---

*These four pictures, bought by Lord Hertford after the revolution of 1848, now hang in the National Gallery, London.

reception continued all day.[174] To the Prefect of Paris, presenting the city's congratulations, he replied: 'I am very touched by the sentiments expressed to me by my good city of Paris; it knows all my love for it. I am truly convinced that when it celebrates my feast-day it does so from the bottom of its heart.'[175]

The illness of the King interrupted the life of the city. On 12 September, the Bourse, the theatres and places of public entertainment were closed. Since none of his family dared mention the subject of his taking the last sacraments, Artois asked Madame du Cayla to use her influence. She finally persuaded him to take them on 13 September. According to all observers, the looks and words of the people in the crowd outside the palace in the Tuileries gardens indicated real sorrow. They were impressed by the fortitude with which he had borne his illness. Moreover some remembered with gratitude the King's efforts in 1814 and 1815 to spare Paris the worst horrors of foreign occupation. So silent was the crowd that people inside the palace were not aware of its presence unless they looked out of the window.[176]

On the other side of the Tuileries the courtyard was filled by the carriages of court officials, ministers, marshals, ambassadors and princes, including Orléans, who spent day and night in the state apartments. The King finally died on 16 September at 4 a.m. The King's younger brother Artois, now Charles X, and the royal family, suffocated by tears, withdrew to Saint-Cloud. For days the body of Louis XVIII lay in state in the throne room. As many as 40,000 Parisians in one day, according to one newspaper, filed past to pay their respects. 'Never for any event has such a crowd been seen,' wrote a former chamberlain of Napoleon. A young liberal journalist and protégé of Talleyrand, Adolphe Thiers, who had arrived in Paris from Marseille in 1821, noted: 'The entire population of Paris is wearing mourning . . . all week the Tuileries has been besieged with people wanting to see the throne room.'[177]

On 23 September, as church bells tolled throughout the city and artillery fired ceremonial salutes every five minutes, a funeral cortège more magnificent, and more admired, than those of either Louis XIV or Louis XV proceeded through the streets of Paris to Saint-Denis. An aide-de-camp of the Duc d'Orléans noted: 'All the windows were packed and the streets crowded. Outside the city on the road to Saint-Denis there was an even greater crowd.'[178] Thus if some Parisians had rioted against the monarchy at the time of Lallemand's funeral in 1820, there were more of them who respected, or at least tolerated, the monarchy in 1824.

Receiving the deputations of the Chambers and the law courts at Saint-Cloud on 18 September, the new King, Charles X, made solemn assurances of his determination to maintain the Charte. The left-wing deputy Casimir Périer was distinguished, and complimented for his parliamentary talents, by the King at the first reception of the reign, which was attended by approximately 1,500 people. Even Benjamin Constant, to the astonishment of all observers, including the King, had joined in the general cry of *Vive le roi!*[179]

Whereas all kings of France since Louis XIV in 1660 had made their state entry into Paris in a carriage, on 27 September Charles X rode into his capital on horseback, thereby displaying to best advantage his air of youth and grace and what the artist Sir Thomas Lawrence called 'his peculiarly benevolent expression'.[180] He was also the first monarch to make his state entry from the west. At the Barrière de l'Etoile at the entrance to the Champs Elysées, he was presented with the keys of the city by the Corps Municipal and the Prefect of the Seine, the Comte de Chabrol. He said: 'Proud to possess its new king, Paris can aspire to become the queen of cities by its magnificence, as its people aspires to be foremost in its fidelity, its devotion and its love.' Riding along the rue du Faubourg Saint-Honoré, the boulevards and the rue Saint-Denis to Notre Dame for a Te Deum, then back along the *quais* to the Tuileries, escorted by his household and, at his special request, all the senior army officers in Paris, despite a steady drizzle, Charles X was received with enthusiasm by 'every class of the People'.[181]

7

King and Country

1824–1829

THE TRIUMPH OF the Bourbon monarchy could be seen, and its weakness heard, at Charles X's next state entry into Paris, on 6 June 1825, after his coronation in the traditional site, the city of Reims sixty miles north-east of Paris. On a hot summer day, seated in the wedding carriage of Napoleon – transformed into a Bourbon vehicle bearing a royal crown, gilded fleurs-de-lys and four trumpet-blowing goddesses – the King advanced through the streets of Paris, from the Barrière de La Villette in the east to Notre Dame in the heart of the city. His procession was accompanied by ambassadors' carriages and 'a horde of aides-de-camp, of adjutants, of valets wearing the King's livery'. Both figuratively and literally the monarchy was at the height of its authority. Charles X towered above the Prefect and mayors of Paris, when he leaned out of the carriage window to receive the keys of the city and listen to an address of welcome.[1]

In the eight months since the King's triumphant reception by Parisians on 27 September 1824, however, his government had alienated much public opinion. In early 1825 laws had been passed to provide financial indemnities for properties confiscated by the French Republic from émigrés and other enemies and victims of the revolution, and to impose the death penalty for profaning the host in Catholic churches. The latter measure, clearly infringing the principle of equality between religions, was designed to appeal to the Catholic clergy. The former had long been favoured on both left and right, even by Laffitte, in order to remove uncertainties from the property market. However, in 1825 many people believed, or claimed to believe, that it was a humiliation for all those who had not emigrated, a step towards counter-revolution and the destruction of the Charte: 'priests and nobles are at the moment totally triumphant,' wrote the liberal art critic Délécluze.[2] 'The émigré nobility', backed by the Holy Alliance, occupied every job and every ministry, lamented the royal architect Pierre Fontaine: indeed the Minister of War, the Baron de Damas, was a former émigré who before 1814 had fought in the Russian army against the French.[3]

In reality beneficiaries of *le milliard des émigrés*, as it was soon called, included prominent liberals such as Orléans and La Fayette, as well as the families of many who, by staying in France, had proved their acceptance of the revolution. Nevertheless, there was, by all accounts, 'very little enthusiasm' as the King's carriage advanced at a slow regal pace towards Notre Dame. Although there had rarely been so many people in the streets of Paris or watching from windows, Délécluze commented: 'except for the noise which I heard at the moment when the procession was beside us, I heard very few cheers or vivats. People were moved rather by a vague curiosity.' According to General Foy, although there were few cries of *Vive le roi!* the people were reaccustoming themselves to the Bourbons and 'the idiocies of the monarchy'.[4]

In celebration of the coronation there was a round of magnificent receptions and balls at the court, the Hôtel de Ville, the ministries and embassies, and gala nights at the royal theatres and the opera – Rossini's *Il Viaggio a Reims* was written especially for the occasion – entertainments which inspired in Talleyrand, attending on the King by virtue of his office of Grand Chamberlain, the celebrated comment: 'Life would be bearable if there were no pleasures.'[5]

If the Parisians were silent, the élite showed greater support for the regime. Most of the senior army officers in Paris chose to accompany the King's entry on horseback, including General Exelmans, one of the leaders of the Bonapartist opposition in 1814–15, who had only returned to Paris from exile in 1819. Among opponents of the regime there was talk of 'transactions' and 'reconciliation', particularly after the abolition of censorship in October 1824. The King and the Dauphine – as the Duchesse d'Angoulême became on the accession of Charles X – made special efforts to be gracious to General Foy when he went to court.[6] The ultra-Bonapartist artist Horace Vernet attended the ceremony in the Louvre at which the King awarded prizes to artists – while continuing, for private clients, to paint Napoleonic subjects such as *The Emperor's Farewell to the Guard at Fontainebleau* (1826).[7]

One reason for the good relations between the monarchy and the élite was the popularity of the Chamber of Peers in the Luxembourg palace. In 1815 and 1816 it had had the reputation of blindly following government policy.[8] By 1819 it had become sufficiently independent to assist in persuading the government to move right and change the electoral law. To the Duchesse de Broglie it provided 'a fine example of conscientiousness and impartiality'. A speech there by her husband gave her one of the greatest moments of happiness in her life.[9] In 1824 opposition in the Chamber of Peers had obliged the Villèle government to drop its law on the conversion of government stocks. After the session of 1827, when the Chamber of Peers debated and modified government laws on the composition of juries, on military jurisdiction, the slave trade and censorship, its debates were praised by one Paris newspaper as 'models of parliamentary discussion . . . powerful, calm and rational, soothing by its very moderation the exalted passions of the Chamber of Deputies'.[10]

The debates of the Chamber of Peers were permitted to take priority over the functioning of French foreign policy: in order to attend its sessions, peers who were French ambassadors could obtain permission to leave their embassies and return to Paris.[11] In preparation for speaking in the Chamber, peers' sons visited Westminster to study the workings of the House of Lords, and took lessons in declamation from professional actors in Paris.[12] A peerage could be the decisive factor in determining a marriage: it was said to be the equivalent, for a man, of a dowry of a million francs for a woman.[13] According to Madame d'Agoult, wife of an officer in the Garde Royale: 'the peerage under the Restoration was the dream, the ambition, the subject of ardent rivalry among families: they were overwhelmed by it and thought of nothing else.'

A further reason for the appeal of a peerage was that peers could create *majorats*, entailed property which was inherited by the peer's eldest son. Other parents in contrast had to divide 80 per cent of their property equally among all their children (daughters had a right to only half a son's share). Balzac expressed the views of many conservatives when he said that the Code Civil implanted the revolution in the soil:

in wanting to be a nation the French have renounced being an empire. By proclaiming the equality of rights to paternal inheritance, they have killed family spirit, they have created fiscality! But they have prepared the weakness of the upper classes and the blind strength of the masses, the extinction of the arts, the reign of personal interest and paved the way for Conquest![14]

Nevertheless on 12 April 1826 the peers rejected the government's attempt to change the inheritance law, and overturned a proposal that, unless there were written dispositions to the contrary, the eldest son should automatically receive the 20 per cent share hitherto left to the father to allocate as he wished. The peers' vote was greeted in Paris with joy: popular demonstrations, fireworks and illuminations.[15] *Le Constitutionnel* saw it as a victory over counter-revolution and wrote: *Honneur à la Chambre des Pairs!*[16] Thus, even for the most aristocratic institution in the country, equality took precedence over liberty. The freedom to dispose of your property as you wished was considered less important than the principle of equality among heirs.

Moreover much public opinion was convinced that equal division among heirs – which in some provinces, including Paris, pre-dated the revolution – was not only a question of justice, and the basis of modern French society, but also encouraged the growth of agriculture and industry.[17] In reality the consequences, which have lasted to this day, were to encourage the perpetual division of properties and to create obstacles to the establishment of substantial and durable agricultural estates, family businesses and art collections in France.[18] Moreover, in order to avoid the sale and subdivision of family properties, the principle of equal division in effect encouraged voluntary birth control. As contemporaries pointed out, other countries' birth rates began to exceed by a very large proportion that of France, thereby, with the losses incurred during the revolution and the Empire, helping to undermine the basis of French power in Europe. The rate of increase of the population of Prussia was five times that of France. In 1789 the populations of France and Germany were 27 and 20 million respectively; in 1814 about 35 and 32 million; in 1848 about 37½ and 45 million.[19]

The popularity of the Chamber of Peers was a sign of the reviving strength of the nobility. The new nobility founded by Napoleon in 1808 – to which even the painter David, a non-noble regicide, had been raised – had rapidly assumed habits of marriage, inheritance and display not very different from the old nobility's: indeed almost a quarter of the *noblesse d'empire* came from the *noblesse d'ancien régime*. The military successes of Napoleonic nobles, two-thirds of whom were army or navy officers, helped ease their absorption into the old nobility, which prized military virtues above all others. Certainly after the successful French intervention in Spain in 1823, the *noblesse d'empire* no longer remained a world apart. Napoleonic celebrities such as Marshals Soult and Suchet, and the Duchesse de Bassano, now vied as to who could have more royal ministers and court officials at their balls.[20] Before inheriting their titles of Duc de Dalmatie and Duc d'Albuféra, their sons assumed the *ancien régime* title of Marquis, unknown under the Empire. The non-noble Napoleonic Marshal Oudinot, who had rallied to the Restoration and become one of the four major-generals of the Garde Royale, was called, after one of the heroes of the old royal army, *le Bayard de la Grande Armée*. His wife, born Eugénie de Coucy, was Dame d'Honneur of the Duchesse de Berri.

For their part most peers, court officials and officers supported the refusal of Napoleonic marshals to attend receptions at the Austrian embassy when the ambassador decided, during the carnival balls of 1827, no longer to announce them by those titles – for example Maréchal Soult *Duc de Dalmatie*, Maréchal Marmont *Duc de Raguse* – taken from provinces or towns which had passed from French to Austrian rule. The Marquis de Sémonville, Grand Référendaire de la Chambre des Pairs, who devoted himself to raising the Chamber's prestige, announced that any peer who visited the Austrian embassy should feel himself dishonoured.[21] For his ode on the coronation of Charles X Victor Hugo had been rewarded with a Sèvres service, a large and luxurious edition of his work printed by the Imprimerie Royale – of which 200 copies were bought by the Ministère de la Maison du Roi – and an audience with the King (*M. Victor Hugo! il y a déjà longtems que j'admire votre beau talent. Je relirai votre ode avec le plus grand intérêt, et je vous en remercie!*).[22] Nevertheless, in reaction to the insult by the Austrian embassy, Victor Hugo wrote an *Ode à la colonne de la Place Vendôme*, to the most celebrated monument to Napoleonic glory in Paris, praising the giant who had enslaved Europe.

Attitudes to the nobility remained complex. Bourgeois hostility to nobles remained strong enough to be used, when convenient, as a political or a conversational weapon. Thus the Bourbons' enemy the banker Laffitte, sitting at dinner in his splendid château of Maisons overlooking Paris – one of the many residences of the Comte d'Artois before the revolution, subsequently the property of Maréchal Lannes Duc de Montebello, whose widow had sold it to Laffitte in 1818 – responded with bourgeois pride to a guest who told him: 'Do you know that you have here the residence of a *grand seigneur*?' 'No, Monsieur,' Laffitte replied, 'it is the residence of a citizen proprietor.'[23]

General Foy (himself a Napoleonic count) claimed in a speech in the Chamber of Deputies that the French were two different peoples on the same territory, nobles and non-nobles. In his pamphlets and courses at the Sorbonne the liberal politician and historian François Guizot represented recent French history as a war between two peoples, Franks and Gauls, nobles and bourgeois.[24] In July 1821 Baron Ternaux, ennobled in 1819 as a reward for his contribution to the Industrial Exhibition that year in the Louvre, boasted in the Chamber of Deputies that he had never formally accepted his title, in protest against the insult to commerce implied when an ennobled merchant called Hervier de Charrin had, at his own request, been given official *lettres de relief* from his family's commercial past by the titles office in the Ministry of Justice.[25] Ternaux moved left; on 2 May 1823 he gave a party, for liberals, in the petit château at Saint-Ouen, in deliberate rivalry to the reception held on the same day, in honour of the King, by Madame du Cayla at the main château.[26] They carried their rivalry even into the wool trade. A member of the Société Royale de l'Agriculture, as well as the Conseil Général des Manufactures and the Société d' Encouragement de l'Industrie Nationale, Ternaux imported goats from Tibet, Madame du Cayla merino sheep from Spain, to graze their parks at Saint-Ouen, in order to produce wool sufficiently soft and luxurious to be used by Paris clothes-makers for the production of cashmere shawls and dresses.

Popular anti-noble caricatures available at print-sellers – of Messieurs de la Jobardière, de Fièrenville or d'Argentcourt – made capital of the contrast between nobles' pretensions and their poverty.[27] In a play of 1827 *Les Trois Quartiers* by two popular playwrights Picard and Mazères, describing the different classes inhabiting the rue Saint-Denis (the poor), the Chaussée d'Antin (bankers), and the Faubourg Saint-Germain (nobles), a banker called Martigny complains of nobles 'proud of their birth, despising everyone who is not a noble'.[28]

Yet in reality there was no gulf of hatred between nobles and non-nobles. The composition of the court, the Chambers, the salons, and the attraction of Parisian fortunes made bourgeois–noble differences less marked than in other European capitals or most provincial French cities. As Chateaubriand had written in 1820, what divided the French élite was less important than its shared commitment to monarchy, aristocracy and property.[29] In *Les Trois Quartiers*, although there is tension between nobles and bankers, they go to each other's balls, as they did in reality, and are united by a common lust for money, and by intermarriage: 'there is no nobility which can resist a million' (there were equally few millions which could resist a noble title).[30] In 1790 noble titles had been abolished with little opposition; in 1830 a proposal to abolish them would be dropped as too unpopular.[31] If there had been vehement anti-noble feeling in France, La Fayette, Chateaubriand and Lamartine would not have been among the country's most popular politicians.

Like nationality, nobility was a flexible commodity. Individuals could renounce, acquire or assume the label of 'noble', according to their wealth or personal wishes. In matters concerning his family and inheritance Benjamin Constant used the noble particle, to which his ancestry entitled him: in politics or on the title page of his books Benjamin de Constant became Benjamin Constant. In 1829 it was the fashion among some young nobles to omit titles on their visiting cards – the brilliant young liberal journalist called himself Charles de Rémusat rather than M. le Comte Charles de Rémusat.[32] The young Alexandre Dumas showed no interest in claiming the noble rank of his grandfather the Marquis de Davy de La Pailleterie, a *gentilhomme* of the Prince de Conti. He worked as a librarian for the Duc d'Orléans, who combined pride in his rank as *premier prince du sang* with satisfaction in presenting himself as a bourgeois *père de famille*.

On the other hand, the importance of a noble title as an emblem of status and wealth led to many cases of self-ennoblement. Bernard François Balzac was a civil servant who adapted to every change of regime between 1776 and 1814, and lived in the 'antipodes of the mode', the cheap if respectable quarter of the Marais in the east of Paris. He used the noble particle *de* when it suited him. In reality in 1746 he had been born Balssa, son of a peasant in the Tarn.

After 1831 his son Honoré also called himself *de Balzac* – an assertion both of his contempt for the bourgeois revolution of the previous year, and of his success as a novelist. He claimed descent from the ancient, but long extinct, noble family of Balzac d'Entragues, and had its coat of arms engraved on his books, his watch and the pommel of his cane.[33] He could be realistic, admitting that 'Nobility today consists in an income of 500,000 francs or personal celebrity.' However, when angered by being beaten by a Noailles for a seat in the Académie Française, he boasted that the Balzacs were older than the Noailles, who were mushrooms grown from the manure of Louis XIV's stables.[34] He was ambitious to be a *grand seigneur* as well as a great writer. He boasted of the relationship of his Polish wife to Marie Lesczynska, wife of Louis XV, and prepared for them in Paris a house which he filled with objects of royal provenance, as well as the exceptional status symbol of a private chapel.[35]

Victor Hugo, hitherto plain Monsieur Hugo, used the title of Baron in official documents and stationery after the death in 1828 of his father, who claimed to have been made a Count in Spain by King Joseph-Napoleon. Other self-created nobles during the Restoration included the writers Victor d'Arlincourt and Charles de Lacretelle. The Pastoret family whose head, the Marquis de Pastoret, became Chancellor of France in 1829, claimed to be of ancient nobility in their *lettres patentes* of 11 September 1818, and awarded themselves the noble particle, as Castellane noted, 'no one knows why'.[36] In reality they were bourgeois from Marseille.

In Prussia noble *mésalliances* remained in theory illegal; in France, in order to 'manure their land' by marrying money, it was an established tradition for impoverished nobles to marry non-noble heiresses. The Comte d'Osmond, brother of Madame de Boigne and a favoured aide-de-camp of the Duc d'Angoulême, married on 25 November 1817 Mlle Destillières, daughter of one of the richest Parisian financiers who owned, among many other properties, the celebrated Paris café Frascati.* Richelieu's nephew the Comte de Rochechouart married on 3 January 1822 Mlle Ouvrard, whose father had made a fortune supplying munitions to the French army.[37]

Another example of bourgeois acceleration into court society under the Restoration was the Greffulhe family. The wealthy banker Monsieur Greffulhe, a Protestant of French stock born in Amsterdam, had married a lady of an ancient Provençal family, Marie Françoise Célestine Gabrielle du Luc de Vintimille, in 1811; his sister Cordélia, subsequently mistress of Chateaubriand and Molé, among others, had married Boniface de Castellane in 1813. Greffulhe had won royal favour by following the King to Ghent during the Hundred Days and, during the near famine of 1816, distributing large sums of money among the poor of Paris. Madame de Souza, whom he had visited daily under the Empire but had since dropped, saw him one day in 1818 sitting in a carriage in Paris, wearing the green and gold uniform of Monsieur's hunt with 'an air of jubilation [sufficient] to make one weep'. That year he

---

* Remembering Adèle d'Osmond's marriage in 1798 to the similarly wealthy General de Boigne, Talleyrand remarked: *Il faut en convenir, en mariant leurs enfants, les d'Osmond ne s'appauvrissent pas.*

was ennobled, made a Count and a Peer. His wife was one of the most fashionable women in Paris. The Duc and Duchesse de Berri had attended a ball at their house on 12 February 1820, the day before the Duke's murder.[38]

All France's key institutions contained nobles and non-nobles. In the Chamber of Deputies 58 per cent of members in 1821, 49 per cent in 1827, were nobles.[39] Of the Chamber of Peers about a third were Napoleonic nobles, while two-thirds came from the pre-1789 nobility.[40] Although over 85 per cent of its officials were noble, the court, after its reform by the Richelieu ministry in November 1820, had non-noble officials. When Generals Rapp, Coutard and Mermet were made Gentilshommes de la Chambre, the Bonapartist Madame de Coigny sneered, in a letter to Lady Holland, that Louis XVIII had surpassed Molière. The latter had created only one *bourgeois gentilhomme*; the King had created twelve. He also created non-noble Chevaliers du Saint-Esprit, such as the royalist politicians Joachim Lainé and Simon Ravez. During the sixteen years of the Restoration, the Dauphine gave one ball. It was on 18 December 1828, to honour the marriage of the non-noble banker James Hainguerlot to Stéphanie Oudinot de Reggio, daughter of Maréchal Oudinot. Two weeks later Hainguerlot was ennobled and made a Baron. This may have been the government's riposte to the lavish, implicitly anti-Bourbon marriage on 30 January 1828 of Laffitte's daughter Albine-Etiennette-Marguerite to Joseph-Napoléon, Prince de La Moskowa, eldest son of Maréchal Ney. The wedding had been celebrated with what royalists considered scandalous magnificence: a distribution of 30,000 francs to the poor and a concert for 1,500 guests with a cantata in honour of Maréchal Ney. The new Princesse de La Moskowa later became so proud that she would not return other people's bows.[41]

In this fluid society, current political beliefs and connections were as decisive in defining status and party as social and political antecedents. Many liberals, including Orléans, La Fayette, Chauvelin and Courcelles, had been émigré nobles (indeed La Fayette and Orléans, in August 1792 and March 1793 respectively, had deserted the French revolutionary army while on active service). Other liberals like Pasquier, Molé, Guizot and Broglie had fathers who had been guillotined during the reign of terror. Some ultras, including Ravez, ten times President of the Chamber of Deputies, and Pierre-Nicolas Berryer, leader of the legitimists after 1830, were non-nobles who had not emigrated. Nobles were accepted by non-nobles as leaders during the Restoration if they so desired. As Pozzo wrote, having seen many nobles elected to departmental councils:

> These examples disprove those who accuse the mass of the nation of opinions hostile to the upper classes; the animadversion which they encounter is always provoked by the violence of their pretensions and the petulance of their prejudices; the moment they show themselves tractable, people hasten to welcome them and, I would even say, are even flattered to have them at their head.[42]

Thus the numerical predominance of nobles in the Chambers and ministries aroused little hostility. One of the most popular novels of the age, *Cinq-Mars* (1826) by Comte Alfred de Vigny, was specifically intended to defend the political role of the French nobility. Inspired by the historical novels of Walter Scott, it criticised the Cardinal de Richelieu for 'decimating' the influence of the nobility, *les bras du trône*, and turning them into courtiers.[43] Indeed, it was the growing prominence of nobles in public life that gave rise to Benjamin Constant's celebrated remark, on hearing of the appointment of the Duc de Doudeauville as Directeur-Général des Postes in 1822: 'Who has been appointed Duc de Doudeauville?'[44] The Paris National Guard was not less Parisian because colonels of four of the twelve legions into which it was divided were nobles (the Marquis de Fraguier, the Vicomte Sosthènes de La Rochefoucauld, the Comte de Quélen, the Marquis de Marmier) – as was a much larger proportion of the officers of the Garde Nationale à Cheval.[45] On 30 March 1827 the funeral of Doudeauville's cousin, a popular *grand seigneur* the Duc de Liancourt, president of the Vaccine Committee of the Ecole des Arts et Métiers of Chalons, and of the committee running the hospices of Paris, became an occasion for anti-government demonstrations by students of the schools he had patronised.[46] It was the view of a Swiss visitor to Paris in 1830, a friend of de Vigny called Juste Olivier, that 'nobles are richer and more fortunate than before the revolution.'[47]

The revival of the nobility received a boost from the money which many of them began to receive, after 1826, from the *milliard des émigrés*. In 1822 Princess Clary, daughter of the Prince de Ligne, on her first visit to Paris since her education in a convent there in the 1770s, had been astonished by the mean *entresols* in which her French friends now lived, with little room to move and few servants: 'the luxury of households and above all the quantity of servants who devour and ruin us in Vienna are unknown in Paris.' The ravages of the revolution precluded French nobles from living in the style of the foreign nobility.[48] However, at the same time that Paris was 'reroyalised' under Louis XVIII and Charles X, it was undergoing a process of 'rearistocratisation', as noble families recovered their family *hôtels* or purchased *hôtels* from Napoleonic nobles. Across the city there was a transfer of property almost as drastic as the 'property revolution' which had deprived so many French nobles of their Paris properties between 1792 and 1800.

In the transfer many foreign embassies were also rehoused. If the British and Prussian embassies occupied the former residences of Princess Pauline and Prince Eugène, the Austrian embassy rented the *hôtel* of Maréchal Davout – 'the finest in all Paris', in the words of an attaché Count Rodolphe Apponyi; 'we have no idea at home of such magnificence combined with such a refinement of luxury and conveniences.'[49] Like many other such *hôtels* in the Faubourg Saint-Germain, its grandeur came from the combination of suites of spacious, elegantly proportioned, richly decorated rooms, designed for entertaining, with the peace and quiet provided by a large walled garden.[50]

Many noble families recovered their *hôtels* as 'unsold sequestrated property' after 1814: between 1814 and 1820 in the rue de l'Université alone, the Prince de Poix recovered the Hôtel de Noailles at number 71; Comte de Maupeou the Hôtel de Maupeou at number 13; the Mailly family the Hôtel de Mailly at number 53; the Harcourt family the Hôtel d'Harcourt at number 106–8; the Chabrillan family number 73 (valued in 1820 at 200,000 francs). Similar transactions took place elsewhere in Paris.[51] Some *hôtels*, moreover, had remained in the hands of the same owners throughout the upheavals of the revolution and Empire: for example the Hôtels de Béthune and de la Briffe at numbers 80 and 2 rue de Lille (rue de Bourbon under the Restoration); and the Hôtel de Soyecourt, residence of Decazes' parents-in-law, at number 51 rue de l'Université.[52] These reversions reinforced the role of the Faubourg Saint-Germain as a noble stronghold in the heart of Paris. With streets which even today remain more 'sombre, sober and tranquil' than those of other *quartiers*, served by a large population of servants and shopkeepers, and often called *le noble faubourg*, *le saint faubourg* or simply *le faubourg*, it was unlike any other *quartier*.[53] An instantly recognised synonym for a class – the high nobility – and a cause – royalism – it would be described by many French writers in the next hundred years: Balzac, de Musset, Barbey d'Aurevilly, Paul Bourget, and finally Proust.

Nobles advertised their power and wealth not only by the size and splendour of their houses – which often displayed the owner's name and coat of arms above the entrance on the street – but also by the way they moved around Paris. If there had been anti-noble feeling in Paris, nobles would not have allowed the 'prodigious luxury' of their horses, carriages – all similarly decorated with their coats of arms – and liveried footmen to be seen in the streets of Paris. The carriages were larger, and more eye-catching, than even the most luxurious car today. The traditional carriage procession, dating from before the revolution, along the Champs Elysées to the site of the convent of Longchamp (founded in 1260, demolished in 1795) beside the Bois de Boulogne, during the three last days of Lent, had been revived under the Empire. It was watched by crowds of Parisians from the footpath on either side of the road, who commented aloud on the passing equipages and the elegant horsemen riding beside them. In 1819 the *Journal des débats* claimed that 'the pomp with which the rich and the grandees like to surround themselves, far from exciting the jealousy of the lower classes, inspires in them, under the rule of law, only a feeling of gratitude and emulation.'[54] In different years the carriages of the Duke of Wellington (1818), the Spanish and Danish ambassadors (1819), the Duchesse de Raguse (1824) and Princess Bagration (1829) were judged the finest in the procession. Unkind visitors, however, like Miss Berry and Lady Blessington, claimed that the carriages displayed once a year at the procession to Longchamp could not compare, in number and splendour, with those visible on 'the worst Sunday that ever shone on Hyde Park', or on the daily promenade along the Chiaia in Naples.[55]

At the same time, with similar determination and royal support, the Catholic Church was also re-establishing itself in Paris. Since the 1760s Paris, previously ultra-Catholic, had been the advance bastion of dechristianisation, and one of the most irreligious cities in France:[56] this process had accelerated under the Republic and the Empire. Between 1789 and 1814, through physical destruction or adaptation to other uses, the number of functioning churches in Paris had declined from 290 to 39, and of functioning priests from 6,000 to 689.[57] In 1814 Louis XVIII was told by the Director-General of Police Count Beugnot of 'the repugnance of a large part of the public for every sign of a return to the most respectable religious customs'. Referring to Christianity, a chambermaid told John Cam Hobhouse in 1815: 'we are too enlightened for all that.'[58] Police reports spoke of 'a profound and total ignorance of religious duties' among workers, who successfully resisted official efforts to have Sunday observed as a day of rest.[59]

King and Country

This ignorance was not limited to the poor. A survey of bourgeois wills reveals that few Parisian houses contained missals, altars or pious objects.[60] The only sign of Christianity in the family of the liberal deputy General Foy was the habit of eating fish on Friday: his children learnt nothing else about it.[61] According to Charles de Rémusat, two-thirds of the new deputies in 1819 believed only in Voltaire, the great enemy of the Catholic Church. Indeed over 56,000 copies of the complete editions of the works of Voltaire and Rousseau were printed between 1817 and 1824, amounting to a total of two million volumes.[62]

Alarmed by the appointment of Monseigneur Frayssinous Bishop of Hermopolis as Grand Master of the University, the Duchesse de Duras had warned Chateaubriand in 1822 that favours to the Church would destroy the ultra government: 'nothing is less popular in France than *les dévotions de métier.*'[63] In these years, when about a third of professors of higher education were priests, students frequently launched anticlerical demonstrations. When in November 1822 the Recteur of the Académie de Paris, the Abbé Nicolle – an émigré who owed his position to his friendship with the Duc de Richelieu in Odessa – arrived for a prizegiving, he was greeted with cries of 'Down with the extinguishers! Down with the *calotte!*' Anticlerical demonstrations led to the closure of the Ecole de Médecine for five months in 1822–3, and of the Ecole Normale Supérieure for four years between 1822 and 1826. Some students were encouraged to go and study in Strasbourg or Montpellier – far from 'the dangers of Paris'.[64] The Archbishop of Paris himself, Monseigneur de Quélen, had been jeered by students during a 'mission' in 1821, conducted by special preachers trying to win Parisians back to the Church.[65]

Such missions made little lasting impact. In 1826 the Papal Nuncio estimated that barely an eighth of the population of Paris were practising Christians, and nearly all of those were women – although grandiose religious processions and ceremonies attracted crowds.[66] Throughout this period just over a third of children born in Paris were illegitimate.[67] Figures for the proportion of children born in Paris who were not baptised rose from 33 per cent in 1817–19 to 46 per cent in 1833–5 – human proof of their parents' increasing indifference to Christianity.[68]

However, in some circles and among some individuals in Paris, Christianity was becoming fashionable again. From 1816 the Société des Missions de France, encouraged by the government, was in possession of a famous pilgrimage church on Mont Valérien, overlooking Paris from the west. When three gigantic crosses were inaugurated on

211

top of the hill before a huge crowd on 14 September 1816 – the Feast of the Exaltation of the Holy Cross – the Abbé Rauzan, one of the King's *aumôniers*, turned towards Paris and implored the Lord 'to draw to him this guilty city, the centre and source of so many iniquities'.[69]

Although, under accusation of political ambitions, Jesuits had been banned from France since 1761, they were allowed to open a number of schools under Louis XVIII. In the church of Saint-Sulpice in 1822 the sermons of Monseigneur Frayssinous, a less tactless preacher than the Abbé Rauzan, drew almost as many listeners as the Italian opera.[70] New churches begun by the government in the newly developed areas north of the boulevards included Notre Dame de Lorette in 1823 (finished in 1836), Notre Dame de Bonne Nouvelle in 1823 (finished in 1830), Saint-Vincent de Paul in 1824 (finished in 1844). The seminary of Saint-Sulpice, on the left bank, was built from 1820 to 1830.[71] In addition numerous pictures and statues with religious themes were commissioned by the Prefecture of the Seine for the churches of the department which had been emptied by the revolution.[72]

At the instigation of Madame Récamier, whose life-long *coquetterie* had not prevented her becoming a fervent Catholic, Baron Gérard painted a masterpiece of religious art, a portrait of St Teresa which still hangs above the altar of the chapel of the Infirmerie Marie Thérèse, at 86 rue d'Enfer (now 92 Avenue Denfert-Rochereau). The Infirmerie had been founded in 1815 by Madame de Chateaubriand, as a thank-offering for the Second Restoration of the Bourbons. The King of Prussia had made the first financial contribution and the institution, which opened in 1819, was named after, and placed under the protection of, the Duchesse d'Angoulême. Its purpose was to house infirm and indigent priests and gentlewomen ruined by the revolution, in a comfortable asylum far from the dirt and noise of central Paris.[73] Chateaubriand and his wife, who both devoted many hours to the Infirmerie, were only two of the most prominent Parisians who made Catholicism the basis of their lives. In Chateaubriand's view, as expressed in the final words of his *Congrès de Vérone* (1838): 'It is better to depend on heaven than on men: religion is the only power before which one can prostrate oneself without degradation.' Catholic Christianity, he reaffirmed in the conclusion to *Mémoires d'outre-tombe*, written in 1841, represented the future of the world, the only basis for the liberation of society from servitude.[74]

A former revolutionary turned ultra-royalist, the Governor of the Duc de Bordeaux, Duc Mathieu de Montmorency, was regarded as a model for young Parisians, not only in the simplicity of his clothes and manners, but also in the fervour and charity of his Catholicism.[75] His death from a heart attack at 3 p.m. on Good Friday 24 March 1826, while praying at the foot of the cross in the great Baroque church of Saint-Thomas-d'Acquin in the heart of the Faubourg Saint-Germain, aroused the admiration of his contemporaries.[76] In the salon of Baron Gérard a few days later, dressed in white for the occasion, a fashionable young poet Delphine Gay, who sometimes called herself *la muse de la patrie*, author of poems on Ourika, Jeanne d'Arc and the King himself, recited a poem on the death of Mathieu de Montmorency. Her mother, a former beauty of the Directoire reputed to have been *plus que galante* in her youth, who had taught her *l'art des salons, l'ode de circonstance, la strophe catholique et royaliste*, exclaimed: *ah! M. le duc de Montmorency mourant à la même heure que notre Sauveur, c'est une chose admirable, admirable!* The daughter went further: *c'est sublime, cela donne envie.* Her poem on the Duke's death ended with a line showing that even fashionable Catholicism could embrace the creed of nationalism:

> *son coeur toujours français prie encore pour la France.*[77]

Women were especially pious. When people noticed that the churches were 'not deserted' even on weekdays, and were crowded on Sundays, this was mainly due to the presence of women.[78] The Duc d'Orléans was a sceptic; his wife a model of 'fervent devotion'.[79] The Duchesse de Duras found Christianity a consolation for her sense of isolation, and for the creeping paralysis which deprived her of the ability to read, to write, and even speak, and finally led to her death in 1828 at the age of fifty. All the profits from her books went to charity. In her *Réflexions et prières inédites (publié au profit d'un établissement de charité pour de jeunes enfants)* (1839), she wrote:

> for man to find peace and happiness in this world God should be his unique goal. Passion has another goal and that is us creatures below. Hence the storms and misfortunes which come to besiege our heart when we allow passion to become its mistress. This is a deviation from the moral order which is bound to be punished. For if man found happiness in passion God would become useless.[80]

The Duchesse de Broglie was a devout Protestant who tried to present her mother Madame de Staël, in retrospect, as a pious Christian; she translated into French, in 1822 and 1826 respectively, two works by the Scottish evangelist Thomas Erskine: *Remarks on the internal evidence of the truth of revealed religion* and *Essay on Faith*.[81] Having encouraged her husband and her brother to found the Société de Morale Chrétienne in 1824, by the end of her life her religious preoccupations had begun to isolate her in her own family. From the Dauphine down, many women from the élite spent much of their time visiting and helping the poor. Some employed priests to distribute their charities, others themselves climbed staircases to the worst attics in the poorest districts.[82] Mesdames de Castellane and de Pastoret helped organise the first crèches and asylums for poor and orphaned children.[83] Madame de Montcalm raised money from the visitors to her salon for a school for young deaf girls.[84]

If noble power was displayed at the procession to Longchamp, royal power at the Fête de Saint-Louis or Saint-Charles and the state opening of parliament, clerical power was also displayed in processions: the annual procession of the Fête-Dieu in June; the Mass of the Holy Spirit at Notre Dame every year before the opening of parliament; the procession every 15 August commemorating the vow of Louis XIII dedicating France to the Virgin. On such occasions the King and the royal family in full dress, surrounded by what to many seemed like 'armies of priests', appeared to prostrate themselves almost to the ground at the moment of benediction.[85]

The most famous religious procession of Restoration Paris took place on 3 May 1826, five weeks after Montmorency's death. The King, the court, the Archbishop of Paris, peers, deputies and marshals of France in full costume, holding lighted candles in their hands, surrounded by priests escorting the relics of the crown of thorns and holy nails from the Sainte-Chapelle, proceeded on foot from Notre Dame through the streets of Paris to the recently renamed Place Louis XVI (the present Place de la Concorde),* stopping at churches on the way. The purpose was to mark the end of a Jubilee year proclaimed by the Pope and – on the anniversary of the entry of Louis XVIII to Paris in 1814, at the express wish of the Dauphine, who had shed tears in order to get her way – to lay the foundation stone of a colossal statue of Louis XVI, to be surrounded by figures of Justice, Piety, Good Works and Moderation, on the spot where he had been guillotined in 1793.[86] (The

---

* However, such was Parisian conservatism that twenty-five years later it was still being called by its traditional name, Place Louis XV.

Chapelle Expiatoire near the rue d'Anjou, where the Dauphine spent the day in prayer, was no longer considered enough.) Crowds covered the Place Louis XVI and the adjacent rooftops, and stretched far up the Champs Elysées; national guards surrounded a temporary altar, opposite which was a throne draped in black. The Archbishop blessed the King, who knelt on a *prie-dieu* and seemed 'deeply moved', held out the holy relics to be kissed by him, the Dauphin and the Duchesse de Berri, recited prayers, then blessed the foundation stone of the statue. The King, the Dauphin and the Duchesse de Berri each gave the stone three hammer blows, as artillery fired ceremonial salutes.[87]

After the ceremony the King, who had been concerned about Parisians' reaction, told Villèle that he was content with 'the ceremony and the appearance of the people'. But, whatever the feelings of the moment, the sight of Charles X in purple – the colour of royal mourning, but also a colour for bishop's vestments – openly deferring to priests had, in the long term, 'an extremely bad effect on public opinion in Paris'. In the summer of 1826 he also followed three other religious processions through the streets of Paris which, according to the leading historian of Restoration Paris, G. de Bertier de Sauvigny, seemed to have been transformed into a parade ground for priests. *Dans le bas peuple de Paris* many came to believe, as the King was later informed by Sosthènes de La Rochefoucauld, that he was a priest, even a Jesuit, and that he said mass in private every day:[88] 'People fear the influence of the clergy above all and it is believed to be absolute.' Priests began to appear at ministerial receptions: two cardinals were appointed to the Conseil d'Etat.[89] After conversing with Paris friends about 'the Jesuits and the abuse of religion', an English resident in Paris Anne Lister wrote in her diary: 'Everybody expects a revolution – a quiet setting aside of the Bourbons for the Orléans branch, perhaps, for the people will not suffer the Jesuit control.'[90]

Grandiose funerals – of Louis XVI and Marie Antoinette in 1815, the Prince de Condé in 1818, the Duc de Berri in 1820, Louis XVIII in 1824 – were one of the distinguishing characteristics of Paris in this period. Funeral processions afforded greater numbers of Parisians an opportunity to express their political opinions than elections or debates in the Chamber of Deputies. On 30 November 1825, despite rain, the funeral procession of the liberal speaker General Foy, *le Démosthène de notre époque*, from his house to Père Lachaise, had attracted a crowd of 50,000 drawn from every class. Orléans sent his carriage. Guizot, Casimir Périer, Benjamin Constant made graveside speeches. Laffitte (95,000 francs), Périer (20,000), Rothschild and Orléans (10,000 each) sub-scribed to a fund to benefit Foy's children.[91]

In 1826 the existence of a rival, anti-Catholic and potentially anti-Bourbon Paris was again advertised by the funeral of the actor Talma. When he lay dying in his neoclassical mansion at 9 rue de la Tour des Dames, beside the house of Mlle Mars in the Nouvelle Athènes, in part because actors were still considered excommunicate, Talma had refused to see the Archbishop of Paris. (The actor's last word on his deathbed on 19 October was said to be *Voltaire*.) He had also insisted on a non-Christian burial. On 21 October a funeral procession representing all professions – soldiers, writers, artists, workers, as well as actors – fol-lowed the coffin along the boulevards to the cemetery of Père Lachaise, watched by silent and respectful crowds. The coffin was borne first by actors of the Comédie Française, then by Talma's students at the Conservatoire. Rossini, Meyerbeer, Cherubini, Delacroix, Baron Gros, Béranger, Laffitte, Mlle Mars, officials of the Ministry of Fine Arts and a secretary of the Duc d'Orléans were among the mourners. A.V. Arnault, the author of *Germanicus*, who had returned from exile in 1820, pronounced a funeral oration, in which he claimed Talma for Paris: 'In the capital of Art the death of a great artist is a public calamity.'[92]

In the cemetery itself General Foy had been given a grand tomb in the shape of a temple, sheltering a statue of himself dressed as a Roman orator, friezes of his parliamentary and his military triumphs and the inscription: *Au Général Foy ses concitoyens*. Talma received a small classical-style altar tomb, inscribed with the word *Talma*. Neither made any refer-ence to Christianity. The occurrence of Talma's grandiose secular funeral in the Paris of Charles X shows – like the impossibility of enforcing Sunday closing in 1814, and the figures for illegitimacy – the degree to which the daily life of the capital eluded the control of the Catholic government. The Duchesse de Dino and the great liberal pol-itician Royer-Collard judged Talma's funeral the biggest blow to the Catholic Church since the Reformation.[93]

Parisian attitudes to the King and the government were revealed not only in elections, processions and funerals, but also through the medium of the Paris National Guard. Since the crisis of 1815 its effi-ciency and zeal had diminished. From 29,000 in 1817, numbers had declined to 16,000 in 1821: many performed their duties in civilian clothes,[94] for Parisians were increasingly unwilling to devote time to guard duty or money to buying a uniform.[95] On 4 March 1823 some national guards had refused to obey orders to expel the liberal deputy Manuel, after an incendiary speech in the Chamber of Deputies which had been construed as an apology for regicide. In the end gendarmes under the orders of the Vicomte de Foucauld led Manuel away: Sergeant Mercier, who had led the national guards' refusal, was dismissed by his superiors but rewarded by liberal supporters with a set of silver and a banquet at the Cadran Bleu. The toasts were: *Au roi et à la Charte! Au maintien de la paix et à la prospérité du commerce! A l'union de la garde nationale!*[96]

Military reviews in Paris could be like circus games in imperial Rome – both an entertainment for the people and its opportunity to make its views known to the monarch. As Colonel-General, Charles X had been popular in the National Guard and had personally intervened to prevent its suppression as an economy measure by the Conseil Municipal of Paris.[97] Every 12 April, anniversary of his entry into Paris in 1814 with an escort of national guards, he made a habit of reviewing the force. Accompanying the procession in 1826, as was customary on these occasions for women of the reigning family, was the Duchesse d'Orléans, driving in the same carriage as the Dauphine, while the King and their husbands proceeded ahead on horseback. 'All Paris', she noted, 'was in the streets, on the balconies, in doorways.' There were cries of *Vive la Charte! A bas les ministres! A bas les Jésuites! Vive la liberté de la presse!* But cries of *Vive le roi!* predominated and there was no disorder.[98]

By 1827 – following the great Catholic procession of 3 May 1826, further unpopular measures by the Villèle administration, and the publication of more books demonising the Jesuits – Parisians were more politicised. At a review of the Paris garrison and the Garde Royale in the Champ de Mars on 16 April, Charles X had been greeted with total silence, both on the way from the Tuileries and by the spectators placed on tiered seating around the parade ground. Many spectators refused to obey police injunctions to remove their hats when the King rode past, although *he* saluted *them*, constantly raising his hand to his *bicorne* hat. He later told Orléans that, although most people present were not too hostile, some looked at him with terrible expressions.[99]

On the following days, however, many Parisians had illuminated their houses as a sign of rejoicing at the government decision, in the face of opposition in the Chamber of Peers, to withdraw a law strengthening press censorship, introduced owing to relentless criticism of the government and the Church. Printing was one of the largest industries in the city.

Several thousand printing workers paraded through the streets of Paris, lighting fireworks and crackers, frightening passers-by and shouting: *Vive le roi! Vive la liberté de la presse! Vive la chambre des pairs!* To the Austrian diplomat Count Rodolphe Apponyi, Paris seemed like a city under siege.[100]

On 29 April the King again went to the Champ de Mars, to review the National Guard. The press law having been dropped, the King was cheered with enthusiasm on his way from the Tuileries and at the review. However, public opinion was convinced that the presence of Jesuits in France was both dangerous and illegal. Among loud and repeated cheers of *Vive le roi!* and *Vive la Charte!* from soldiers and an 'immense concourse' of spectators, there were other cries of *A bas les Jésuites! Vive la liberté de la presse! A bas les ministres!* One soldier shouted *A bas les Jésuites!* in front of the King. Red with anger, the King addressed the Major-General of the National Guard, Marshal Oudinot: 'Marshal, Marshal, have that man arrested!' Then, in a loud voice to the national guards around him: 'I have come here to receive the homage of my people and not insults.' After some hesitation the soldier was led away, protesting: 'All I ask is the execution of the laws of my country.'[101]

Once the review was over, the King professed himself pleased by his display of authority, and satisfied that cries of *Vive le roi!* had predominated. But his ministers, and above all the Dauphine and the Duchesse de Berri – who may have been subjected to insults by national guards as their carriage left the Champ de Mars – were not to be contained. 'I am sure that those who shout *A bas les Jésuites!* do not even know what the Jesuits are,' the Dauphine maintained.[102] And at the princesses' insistence, abetted by Villèle, on 30 April the King dissolved the National Guard, on the grounds of its offensive behaviour towards the crown. A government of provincial nobles had severed a crucial link between the Bourbon monarchy and the Paris bourgeoisie. Moreover the national guards were permitted to keep the weapons and uniforms for which they had paid. Like many other Parisians, Anne Lister could not at first believe the news: 'individually the people are well pleased to get rid of the trouble,' she wrote, 'but collectively they had been insulted.' The Duc de Dalberg commented that he would rather have had his head cut off than have counselled such an act: the only further measure needed to cause a revolution was the reintroduction of censorship.[103]

That summer censorship was reintroduced; relations between the royal government and the city of Paris deteriorated further. On 4 November, at the celebrations of the feast day of Saint-Charles in honour of the King, few spectators bothered to remove their hats when

Charles X appeared on the balcony of the Tuileries, where Louis XVIII had so often been cheered by the crowds. In the silence cries of *A bas Villèle!* could be heard from the garden below.[104] On 6 November the nomination of seventy-six new peers was seen as Villèle's vengeance against this popular institution. Many, including Chateaubriand, regarded it as a blow to the monarchy as well as the peerage.[105]

In the elections held later that month the liberal opposition received 84 per cent of the Paris vote; Casimir Périer, Benjamin Constant and Laffitte were among the deputies elected. Possibly intending to provoke an armèd confrontation, some radical Parisians erected barricades at night in the rues Saint-Denis and Saint-Martin: as the police and royal guard attempted to demolish them five died. If the National Guard had been there, Laffitte told Villèle, the deaths would have been avoided.[106] 'Oh no,' commented the Duchesse d'Escars, alluding to Benjamin Constant's celebrated remark, 'the people has not handed in its resignation – a fine phrase which used to be endlessly repeated at the *château* [of the Tuileries].'[107]

If many Parisians remained hostile, or at least indifferent, towards the King, he could take comfort from two factors. First, despite the riots of 1820 and 1827, and the apprehensions of the Duchesse d'Escars, Paris remained for the most part a tranquil city. 'This state of calm, of respect, of order and good manners has become a habit among all classes of the capital,' the Préfet de Police reported. The government only had to show a minimum of tact for people to cry *Vive le roi!*[108]

A moderate ministry led by the Vicomte Jean-Baptiste de Martignac (who, for his brilliance in parliamentary debate, was often called *la Pasta*, or *la Malibran parlementaire*, from the names of popular opera singers of the day), took office in January 1828, with the support of the Dauphin. The atmosphere lightened. To the delight of public opinion, censorship was relaxed, some Jesuit schools were closed. Liberals such as Ternaux and Sébastiani, an ex-Napoleonic general from Corsica, began to desert the Palais Royal for the Tuileries.[109] In 1828 and 1829 France seemed at rest. 'Provided it is not insulted,' Talleyrand wrote, 'it takes very little to satisfy it; a tired child does not sleep more sweetly.'[110] A former minister of Napoleon Comte Duchâtel wrote to Guizot, after a summer in the country, that he feared that France would die of languor. La Fayette himself, the particular enemy of the Bourbons, wrote to Lord Holland: 'Almost all France is perfectly happy within the constraints – in my opinion quite narrow – which the Charte has placed upon public freedoms.'[111]

The leading spirit of the Société des Amis de la Liberté de la Presse, Chateaubriand had waged unrelenting war against Villèle's ministry and against censorship. This one-time ultra even began to express admiration for the 1789 revolution.[112] His former patron Charles X came to find Chateaubriand as repugnant as Louis XV had found Voltaire: he personally helped to keep *l'ignoble ami*, as he called Chateaubriand, out of the ministry. And for himself Chateaubriand acknowledged: 'never would I have returned to the council without being master.' However, believing that the Charte would save both liberty and the Bourbons, in 1828 Chateaubriand ceased his opposition and, in June of that year, obtained the dignified and lucrative position of ambassador to Rome.[113] To Madame Récamier, who feared the influence on the King of his old friend and fellow ultra-royalist Jules de Polignac, he maintained: 'The entry of M. de Polignac in the council, in present circumstances, would be nothing less than a sort of revolution. The Chamber of Deputies would have to be dissolved etc. That is not even worth the bother of talking about nor for me to waste paper in proving to you the absurdity of such a rumour.'[114]

A monument to this interlude of calm is a sculpture, designed by the Premier Sculpteur du Roi Baron Bosio, representing the Restoration, escorted by two figures of victory and driving a four-horse carriage, 'holding in one hand the sceptre of the old monarchy and the laurels of new France, and in the other an olive branch'. Modelled on the Horses of St Mark whose removal from the Arc de Triomphe du Carrousel had aroused the fury of Parisians in 1815, it was erected in the same position on 26 April 1828, where it can still be admired today.[115] Under the Martignac ministry Paris experienced other improvements reflecting the growing orderliness of French society. Pavements were finally introduced in those streets large enough to contain them. In 1828–30 what was called 'the ancient domination of public women' – prostitutes – was removed by the police from the Palais Royal: mothers no longer felt frightened to take their daughters to its shops. Already, perhaps as a result of the religious revival that accompanied the Restoration, their tone had become less 'insolent' and *agaçant*: in May 1830 they were finally, at least in theory, forbidden to solicit on the streets of Paris.[116] The wooden galleries which had crossed the southern end of the Palais Royal courtyard were pulled down and replaced by elegant stone colonnades – the Péristyles de Montpensier and de Valois and the Galeries de Nemours and d'Orléans, named after the Duc d'Orléans and three of his sons.

From April 1828 a form of omnibus, drawn by three or four horses and containing up to thirty people, was introduced; there were ten omnibus lines, with names like *Carolines*, *Dames-Blanches*, *Ecossaises*, of which five went from one end of Paris to the other: tickets were relatively cheap. Soon omnibuses could be seen crossing the boulevards incessantly. Although the horses often stumbled on the cobbled streets, the omnibuses were considered so safe and efficient that even the Duchesse de Berri tried them.[117] In 1829 gas lighting, too, began to appear in the streets of Paris, first in the Cour du Carrousel, then in the rue de Rivoli, later in the rue de la Paix and the Palais Royal.[118]

Another factor which could reassure the King was the common belief that, although the attractive power of Paris was greater than ever, the real France lay in the provinces.[119] Some Frenchmen were almost as vehement in denouncing Paris as were the foreign artists in Rome demanding the return of works of art from the Louvre in 1815, or the Abbé Rauzan denouncing the 'guilty city' in 1816; for them it was a 'pit of centralisation' which corrupted its inhabitants and its artists. Stendhal deplored 'the fatal influence of egoistical Paris'. One provincial so resented its powers of attraction that he expressed regret that, during the occupation, the allied troops had not burnt it down.[120] Hostility to Paris was not restricted to words. In 1814 and 1815 provincial cities such as Bordeaux and Marseille, for the King, Grenoble and Lyon for the Emperor, had taken the political initiative against the government in Paris. Part of the passion in ultra-royalism had derived from the provincial royalists' hatred of Paris. The Marquis de La Maisonfort, for example, called the capital a 'pernicious foyer more fatal to France than Pandora's box'.[121] This dislike of Paris contributed to a growing taste for country life.

Before 1789 many members of the élite had spent most of the year in Paris.[122] After 1814, being poorer, they often spent six months a year away from the capital. This period saw the golden age of *la vie de château* – 'the constantly growing taste of high and good society for living in the country', as Délécluze described it – and the beginning of a fashion for spending some of the winter on the Côte d'Azur. By 1843 a Russian diplomat could write, as early as the middle of May, that Paris was at its last breath, like a dying gladiator. In the same year, according to Mérimée, 'Not to be in the country in October is a crime of *lèse-fashion* which people can expiate only with difficulty.' During the summer in Paris every day was as quiet as a London Sunday; in the evening not a carriage could be heard in the street.[123] Talleyrand spent long periods in his château of Valençay, south of Tours, not only because he was in political disgrace in Paris but also because he liked living in the country. In a letter to his mistress the Duchesse de Courlande, he defined happiness in these terms: *Valençay! Valençay! et vous! et vous!* He even became mayor of the town. The moment he was out of Paris, he no longer loved it. He would return there, after a summer spent in the country, only in time for the King's fête on St Charles's day, 4 November.[124]

Not only did Parisians spend time in the provinces, they now spent more time in the countryside around Paris. Indeed easy access to the forests, parks and villages of the Ile de France was one of the attractions of Paris. A British general Cavalié Mercer wrote in 1815:

> The country immediately around and the slopes of the hill itself [of Montmartre] on which we stood had the appearance of one vast and productive garden being divided into rectangular patches planted with rose-bushes, cherry-trees, vines, fig-trees, artichokes and several other sorts of culinary vegetables all growing in the greatest luxuriance and presenting a most extraordinary mass of verdure.

In London, the fogs, smog and coal-smoke often placed the city under what Madame de Boigne, whose father was French ambassador there in 1816–19, called 'an orange cloud streaked with black, grey and brown and saturated with soot'. Buildings – and white clothes – rapidly turned grey. At times it was difficult to see from one side of the Thames to the other.[125]

In Paris, however, as British visitors constantly remarked, 'the transparency of the air' ensured that the buildings remained the colour of the pale yellow stone in which they were constructed. From surrounding hills like Montmartre or Montparnasse, it was possible to see right across the city. Many contemporary landscape pictures show, below blue skies, the light green of the fields and gardens around the city, the white walls and red-tiled roofs of the surrounding villages, and the silver Seine shining in the sun, standing out against the dark green of the great royal forests of Vincennes, Saint-Germain, Marly and Meudon.[126]

Already Parisians had the habit of spending Sunday in the country, often going by carriage or omnibus. The valley of Montmorency north of Paris, 'the prettiest countryside in the world . . . as varied as possible', in the words of Count François Esterhazy, who visited it in 1827, was a favoured destination.[127] Often they chose a village outside Paris which was celebrating the annual feast day of its patron saint – the Fête de

Saint-Cloud for example was held every September. Some members of the élite owned or rented houses in the vicinity of Paris, for use during the summer, in addition to their châteaux in the provinces: the Duchesse de Duras built a small house for herself at Andilly in the Vallée de Montmorency; Baron Gérard lived at Auteuil; the Princesse de Vaudémont at Suresnes; Madame de La Briche at Le Marais; James de Rothschild at Boulogne; Talma at Brunoy. Even the humblest civil servant wanted to be able to refer to 'my house in the country'. Thus the servants may not have been lying when they informed the young Wagner, searching for patrons in Paris at the beginning of his career, *Monsieur est à la campagne.*[128]

Madame de Souza, however, had no house in the country, and never left Paris. Hence Flahaut's eagerness to assure his wife, in July 1820: 'you have no idea of the profusion of flowers one sees about Paris at this moment, a house in the country is quite superfluous.' Prince Clary agreed: 'No one in Austria knows what flowers are. You must come to see the gardens of Paris . . . every room is a garden.'[129] Summer evenings in Paris gardens, with the sight and smells of flowers, and the Judas trees in bloom, could be magical.[130]

No one enjoyed life in the Ile de France more than the Bourbons. The Duc d'Orléans frequently entertained at Neuilly in the summer, leaving guests with the impression of 'an opulent bourgeois family much more than a princely household' – a reflection of the obsequious-ness of the Duke's manner rather than the simplicity of his house-hold.[131] The Duchesse d'Angoulême bought a small house and park at Villeneuve l'Etang, near Saint-Cloud, from Marshal Soult in 1822 for 800,000 francs.[132] She hung one room with views of Vienna, another with pictures of the triumphs of the Duc d'Angoulême in Spain in 1823, and occupied herself with beautifying the property: 'that is all she loves, she devotes all her energy to it,' wrote Count François Esterhazy, the son of a close friend from her years as an émigrée princess in Vienna in 1795–9.[133]

Like her father, the Dauphine was an accomplished rider who knew the royal forests of the Ile de France as well as the streets of Paris. Count François Esterhazy and his family were taken by her from Maisons north-west of Paris to Saint-Cloud in 1827. He wrote:

it was she who guided the grooms and the postilions, she knows the distribu-tion of all the forests in her head and knows the names of all the routes, every crossroads, every junction and can often prove the forest guards wrong. She found a way of crossing this enormous forest [of Maisons] from one end to the other by the most beautiful drives and alleys. She is proud of all that and delighted to be able to show it off . . .

Prouder, perhaps, of the royal parks and forests than of the royal palaces.[134] When they visited Marly she sadly showed them the site of the old royal palace – demolished in 1816 by building speculators (like Bellevue, Sceaux and many other châteaux throughout France). If the palace had gone, however, the forest had been restocked after the depredations of the revolution. Despite the proximity to Paris, so many deer and other game were moving down the avenues in the forest that the royal party had to move aside to let them pass.[135]

The court itself spent more time outside Paris. Whereas Louis XVIII had loved Paris, and had only spent four to eight weeks a year at Saint-Cloud, in order to give the Tuileries the opportunity to have a thorough cleaning, Charles X spent six months every year at Saint-Cloud. Set on a hill with a magnificent view of Paris, Saint-Cloud had a celebrated cascade and fountains, French and English gardens, a park with 'noble chestnut trees', and easy access to the royal hunting forests. In the summer it seemed to float above the city on vaults of greenery – *voûtes de verdure*.[136] His fellow monarchs Nicholas I of Russia and Frederick William III of Prussia enjoyed nothing more than drilling or reviewing their troops. Charles X, however (who as a young prince had once pursued a stag into the heart of Paris), preferred more traditional pursuits, and still hunted every day in the hunting season. His hunts were so elaborate that, despite the presence of more than a hundred men in the Service du Grand Veneur, soldiers of the Garde Royale stationed at Versailles were also employed as beaters, *marchant en bataille*. On one hunt, Talleyrand noted, as a sign of the progress of civilisation, Charles X killed 1,793 pieces of game, a figure attained by no previous King of France.[137]

In the spring and autumn Charles X also often went for two weeks' hunting to the royal châteaux of Compiègne and Fontainebleau, north and south of Paris respectively. On such occasions, in contrast to Napoleon I, Charles X, absorbed by pleasure rather than politics, was accompanied by courtiers rather than ministers – a sign that the Restoration was, at this stage, a parliamentary rather than an autocratic regime.[138] So closely was Charles X identified with hunting that, as he was informed, many Parisians called him *Robin des bois*, or Robin Hood, after a popular opera of that name.[139]

After 1820, as the regime became more confident, members of the royal family began to venture out of the Ile de France. The Duchesse d'Angoulême regularly summered at the spa of Vichy; her sister-in-law the Duchesse de Berri in Dieppe and at her estate at Rosny on the Seine, where she built a hospice in memory of her husband and a chapel to contain his heart; the Orléans family in their château at Eu near the Normandy coast. Far from Paris, with its harrowing memories of the revolution, the Duchesse d'Angoulême was a different person: relaxed, friendly, even popular.[140] Even the King went to visit the provinces, and attend army manoeuvres, at Saint-Omer in northern France in September 1827, and at Lunéville in Lorraine, followed by a journey to Strasbourg, in September 1828. As the Duchesse de Berri had also found on her extensive provincial tours in 1828 and 1829, the King was better received in the provinces, even in the liberal redoubt of Strasbourg, than in Paris. In the opinion of the King – and of his ministers – reassured by the power of the government, the nobility and the Church, France appeared to desire only tranquillity.[141] Like many of his predecessors, Charles X complained of the inconstancy and ingratitude of Paris.[142] But, his ministers assured him, his army could control Paris.

8

The New Jerusalem

August 1829–December 1830

Le peuple a tout fait. Courage, intelligence, désintéressement, clémence envers les vaincus, tout a été fabuleux de beauté. Quelle différence même avec les premiers moments de 1789!

La Fayette, 12 August 1830

Monsieur, ce qui manque à tout ceci c'est un peu de conquête.

Talleyrand, August 1830

EMPIRES WERE AT the heart of the dreams and aspirations of the capitals of Europe in the nineteenth century, as well as the reason for much of their prosperity. London controlled the empire of the seas, and India. Berlin aspired to be capital of a great German empire. Vienna dreamt, while remaining the sole German *Kaiserstadt*, of new empires in Italy and the Balkans. In St Petersburg Russians hoped to 'hang up their shields in Tsarigrad' – Constantinople was to be a second Russian capital.

Parisians dreamt of recovering the French empire in Europe lost in 1813–15. Loss of empire affected Parisians more than memories of the revolution, and was more often lamented in songs, poems and speeches. Young men had been brought up, as de Vigny wrote in 1828, 'to the sound of the cannons and Te Deums of Bonaparte'. One reason for their discontent, later called the *mal du siècle*, was their bitterness at France's defeat and relative decline, compared to the increase in the power and territory of the other great powers.[1]

Until 1870 most Frenchmen, including Decazes, Balzac and Victor Hugo, considered the left bank of the Rhine to be France's 'natural frontier'. All territory on the left bank, Belgium included, should be French: as visiting Belgians noted, the wishes of the inhabitants themselves were not consulted.[2] Victor Hugo's father, a former aide-de-camp and Mayordomo of the palace of King Joseph-Napoleon, had been the last French general to leave Madrid in 1813. His son, admitting his *côté bonapartiste bête et patriote*, dreamt of French reconquest of the left bank of the Rhine, and refused to visit Waterloo, site of 'the victory of Europe over France', until it was French again.[3]

This feeling of nationalist indignation, in 1829 as in 1814, was one of the strongest political forces in Paris. The popular liberal orator General Foy, himself wounded at Waterloo, defended the 'glorious tricolour cockade' in speeches in the Chamber, and wrote in his diary: 'I shudder as a Frenchman at the insulting superiority which the English and Europe have granted themselves over us.'[4] For him and many others, military victory conferred legitimacy. If the Bourbons were to fight for the Rhine frontier, he believed, 'there will be a truly national restoration of their race' – although he also admitted of Waterloo, in a moment of lucidity: 'In reality Europe and even France benefited from it.'[5] In 1814 Chateaubriand had written that France should stop where the French language was no longer spoken. After 1820 he expressed horror at the treaties of Vienna, and hoped to create Bourbon monarchies in the New World and to give France what he called 'a just growth of our frontiers', in other words the left bank of the Rhine as far as Cologne – where the extent of discontent had been revealed by the conflicts between the Catholic archbishop and the Protestant Prussian authorities; in return Prussia would obtain Saxony.[6] In 1828, like many French statesmen, he believed that a Franco-Russian entente directed against their 'natural enemies' Austria and Britain could re-establish the French frontier on the Rhine, and European equilibrium.[7]

In 1828 and 1829, such dreams of empire were a staple of conversation in Paris – nowhere more so than in the Hôtel de Flahaut. Flahaut and his wife had returned from England and Scotland to live in Paris in the rue du Faubourg Saint-Honoré in 1827, moving in 1830 to an *hôtel* on the corner of the rue d'Angoulême and the Champs Elysées (a former residence of a mistress of the Comte d'Artois and a minister of Napoleon).[8] Their household was described by the diarist of English Paris, Thomas Raikes, as 'a happy combination of French and English habits'. The house itself was one of the most luxurious in Paris, containing magnificent furniture, wall hangings and porcelain in the eighteenth-century style which, partly owing to Madame de Flahaut's example, was beginning to return to fashion in Paris.[9]

Madame de Flahaut, who received on Sundays and Thursdays, was at first, according to Lady Granville, treated in her own house, by Frenchwomen still half in love with her husband, 'with a neglect which makes my blood boil'. Parisians were shocked by her brusque, even disagreeable manners, her *politicomanie* and habit of saying what she thought.* Nevertheless the Flahauts' house soon became a place 'to see the world and hear politics' – and, on Thursdays, music. It became 'the resort of all the liberal party', including Talleyrand and two of the most fashionable men about town, the illegitimate son of Napoleon I by Marie Walewska, Count Walewski, and Flahaut's own illegitimate son by Queen Hortense, Auguste Demorny (Flahaut's wife gave him only daughters).[10] Raised by Madame de Souza – although the money she had been given for his education had often been spent on her passion the lottery – Demorny now lived in Flahaut's house. When not roaming Paris in search of adventure, he was a pupil at the Ecole Polytechnique. Another visitor was a journalist of thirty-two called Adolphe Thiers, who since arriving in Paris from Marseille in 1821 had made his name as an ultra-liberal polemicist.[11] At dinner in 1829, Palmerston, who in Paris was considered *fort spirituel et fort aimable*, heard 'the ultra-liberals say they would support any minister who would recover this territory for France . . . every Frenchman raves about *nos frontières*.' General Sébastiani, a former Napoleonic general transformed into a liberal deputy, said to him: 'It is essential and indispensable to France to get back to the Rhine as a frontier.'[12] On 21 January 1830, when most Paris houses were shut out of respect for the anniversary of the death of Louis XVI, the Flahauts, for the same reason, gave a small ball. Disgust with Charles X, the possibility of substituting the Orléans for the reigning branch and the desirability of the Rhine frontier were frequent subjects of conversation in their house.[13]

The King himself felt the lure of the Rhine frontier. In 1788, in accordance with French policy since 1748, the young Comte d'Artois had asserted, in the salon of Madame de Polignac, that the annexation of Belgium would weaken France. In 1828, according to Pozzo, the aged Charles X told his lifelong friend, her son Prince Jules de Polignac, then French ambassador in London, 'perhaps a war against the court of Vienna would be useful to me because it would put an end to internal dissension and occupy the nation *en grand* as it desires.'[14]

---

* In 1831, when discussing the possibility of being appointed ambassador to Russia, Flahaut told his wife: 'your liberty of speech must be confined to bedroom conversation.'

Like Napoleon I, who believed that the internal authority of the monarchy was strengthened by external expansion, Charles X made the same calculation when on 8 August 1829 he chose a provocatively ultra-royalist ministry, while at the same time planning to redraw the map of Europe. Since April he had been preparing the new ministry in secret with *mon cher Jules* (de Polignac) and Ferdinand de Bertier. With the extremism and 'victim mentality' of the emigration, seeing anyone who disagreed as an irreconcilable enemy, the King suspected moderate politicians and deputies of opposing a strong Bourbon monarchy. The more he conceded, the more was demanded, so he believed; it was not his choice of ministers and alleged alliance with foreign invaders that had destroyed Louis XVI but his policy of concessions.

In reality in the last Chambers of the Restoration liberal deputies included a higher proportion of nobles and fewer former revolutionaries than the Chambers before 1820.[15] Most liberals accepted the Bourbon monarchy as the best guarantee against war, anarchy and a republic.[16] It was not the liberals but the King himself who destabilised the social order. The wealthy banker and liberal deputy Casimir Périer, for example, who lived in a luxurious *hôtel* in the rue Neuve du Luxembourg (present rue Cambon) near the rue de Rivoli, was in reality a conservative monarchist, owning extensive properties in Paris and the Dauphiné: charmed by Charles X's visit to his mines at Anzin in 1827, he sent the King a long *mémoire* warning him against Polignac.[17] The King would not listen. Moreover his son the Dauphin had renounced his previous moderation and turned ultra: his advisers were reported to say that 'the only good way of governing France is that of Bonaparte.' In private conversation in the Tuileries, the King also called Bonaparte *le maître*.[18]

The new ministry included some fatally unpopular names. The Minister of Foreign Affairs was Prince Jules de Polignac, whom the Duchesse de Maillé called more dangerous than if he had been as unintelligent as his enemies proclaimed.[19] General de Bourmont, who had deserted from the French army before Waterloo and been a crucial hostile witness in the trial of Marshal Ney, was Minister of War. La Bourdonnaye, an extreme ultra deputy known as *le jacobin blanc*, was Minister of the Interior. The ministry was more right-wing than the King had originally intended, owing to the refusal of moderate politicians to serve with such names; it had no chance of winning a majority in the Chamber of Deputies. According to the *Journal des débats*, Chateaubriand's newspaper, the ministry symbolised Coblenz,

Waterloo and the White Terror: 'So yet again the bond of love and confidence which united the people to the monarch is broken . . . unhappy
France! Unhappy King!' No one could believe the news, Castellane
wrote. Government stocks fell four francs in one day.[20] Ministerial
receptions had never been so deserted: the few guests attending felt
obliged to make excuses for their presence.[21]

Villèle wrote to his wife that, instead of destroying the revolution, the
ministers were destroying what remained of royalism. To the British
ambassador Lord Stuart de Rothesay the Ministry of Foreign Affairs
under Polignac resembled Milton's Paradise of Madmen.[22] Pozzo had
enjoyed particularly good relations with Charles X owing to Franco-
Russian cooperation over Greek independence in 1826–9: in 1829 he
had been allowed to add a golden fleur-de-lys to his coat of arms.[23]
However he commented that the King now had more difficulty in persuading politicians to become ministers than politicians had formerly
experienced in their efforts to become ministers. He feared the worst,
but could not believe that, at the age of seventy-three, the King would
risk disaster by ruling through *ordonnances*, as Article 14 of the Charte
gave him the power to do, without the prior approval of the Chambers.
Pozzo placed the blame for the crisis on Charles X alone. On 20
February 1830 he wrote to Tsar Nicholas I: 'the position in which the
King has placed himself is not the result of one error but of the error of
his entire life.'[24]

According to the liberal journal *Le Globe*, the gospel of the younger
intellectuals, the ministry had separated France into two: the court on
one side, the nation on the other. In reality most senior court officials –
the Ducs de Duras, Mouchy, Gramont, Guiche, Fitzjames, even
Polignac's own brother the Duc de Polignac – content with the existing
order, derided the government as incapable and unconstitutional. The
ministry represented ultras from a variety of backgrounds and, above
all, the King himself. No previous government had inspired him with so
much confidence.[25]

The government relied on two weapons: the loyalty of the army and
the passivity of the people. A magnificent review of the army and the
Garde Royale that October in Paris left such a shrewd observer as
Prince Leopold of Saxe-Coburg with a lasting impression of their
prowess and loyalty, and of the solidity of Charles X's throne.[26] Despite
the demonstrations of April 1826 and April 1827 the ministry believed
that, as the new Prefect of Police wrote in a report of 20 August
1829, 'the working class remains remote from all political discussion.'

Polignac repeated to the Piedmontese ambassador the right-wing catch-phrase: 'the French people was entirely remote from and indifferent to all these disorders . . . this people had handed in its resignation and would not take part in future disorders.'[27]

In addition to the choice of ministers, the ministry's allegedly pro-British complexion increased its unpopularity. Polignac had been French ambassador in London since 1823 and had married two Scottish heiresses in succession. He was not only an expert on the composition, powers and privileges of the House of Commons, but also a friend and admirer of Wellington: some called his government *le cabinet Wellington–Polignac*.[28] Such was the lure of Paris that, in addition to foreign ministers like Metternich and Canning, in 1825 the kings of both Prussia* and Württemberg had visited it for their own pleasure. However, despite his taste for French art and society, in 1829 George IV had to renounce his plans to visit Paris for fear of what he called 'false rumours and infamous lies' – namely the popular delusion that the Polignac ministry was subservient to Britain.[29]

In reality Charles X, who gave a personal direction to foreign policy, hoped to popularise the Polignac ministry by transforming the balance of power in Europe. The plan devised by Charles X and Polignac, and sent from Paris to St Petersburg on 4 September 1829, was for Russia, then at war with the Ottoman Empire, to take Romania and a third of Anatolia; Austria would obtain Bosnia and Serbia; Prussia Saxony and the Netherlands; the King of Saxony the Rhineland; the King of the Netherlands Constantinople; Britain the Dutch colonies; France Belgium. In fact this imperialist fantasy was turned down by Prussia, although Russia had shown some sympathy, particularly for the alternative French plan – to attack Algeria.[30]

The Algerian presence in Paris today, noticeable in streets and Métro stations, dominant in Belleville and Saint-Denis, owes its origin to the decision by Charles X and his ministers, made in Paris in January 1830, to attack Algiers. An invasion had already been discussed in 1827. Piracy, the refusal of Marseille merchants to pay their debts to the Dey of Algiers, and the Dey's insulting behaviour to the French consul, were the points of contention. The real motive, however, was the King's

---

* On visits to Paris in 1817 and 1818, the King of Prussia had not only questioned soldiers of the Garde Royale, in private, about their feelings towards the royal family, but had also walked around the city like a private person, enjoying frequent *excursions galantes*, and visits to the theatres and the Louvre.

hope to distract and satisfy hostile French opinion by creating a new empire in Africa as a substitute for the lost empire in Europe.[31]

In March 1830 there was a last confrontation between king and deputies over rival interpretations of the Charte. A hostile if respectful address had been voted on 16 March by a majority of 221 against 181 in the Chamber of Deputies. On 18 March, before Charles X and his court *en grand costume* in the throne room of the Tuileries, it was read out by an old royalist liberal Royer-Collard, once a supporter of the royal prerogative against *la chambre introuvable*. 'Sire,' it stated,

> the Charter which we owe to the wisdom of your august predecessor, and whose benefits Your Majesty has the firm intention to consolidate, consecrates as a right the participation of the country in deliberations of public interest . . . it makes the permanent agreement of the political views of your government with the wishes of your people the indispensable condition of the regular workings of public affairs. Our devotion condemns us to tell you that this agreement does not exist.

Furious but dignified, the King replied:

> Monsieur, I have heard the address that you present me in the name of the Chamber of Deputies. I had the right to count on the agreement of the two Chambers to accomplish all the good I was meditating; my heart is afflicted to see the deputies of the departments declare for their part that this agreement does not exist. Messieurs, I have announced my resolutions in my speech opening the session. These resolutions are invariable; the interest of my people forbids me to change them. My ministers will inform you of my intentions.[32]

Both in February 1820 and December 1821, when obliged to choose between his ministers and the majority of the Chamber of Deputies, Louis XVIII had chosen the latter, even in December 1821 when personally insulted by its address. Charles X, convinced that the deputies wanted to select his ministers, chose to confront the Chamber. On 16 May it was dissolved. New elections were called for June.

The government believed that foreign conquest and French honours were enough to win France. As Chateaubriand wrote: 'whatever a Frenchman does he will never be anything but a courtier, of no matter whom so long as it is the power of the moment.'[33] The novelist Stendhal, himself until 1814 an inspector of the palace furniture, thinking of the innumerable former revolutionaries who became servants of

Napoleon, believed 'a court was necessary to seduce this feeble nation of the French over whom the word court is all-powerful'.[34] In 1829–30, however, most Frenchmen refused to be seduced by the court system. Individual ambitions for money and place were not as important as the general desire for a liberal constitution. Public principles took precedence over private ambitions. On 28 August 1829 Chateaubriand himself, despite his calamitous financial situation, resigned his post as ambassador to the Pope and refused the ministry's advances and offers to pay his debts.[35]

Talleyrand, as Grand Chamberlain with a salary of 100,000 francs a year, was assumed to have been won to the Bourbons. It was said that his court duties were the only ones he considered sacred: they helped shield him from royalist attacks for the roles he had played under the Republic and the Empire.[36] However, possessing what one of his female admirers Madame de Rémusat called *un tact assez juste en révolutions*, he sensed impending disaster.[37] By 1829, or before, he had returned to the camp of revolution. The apartment of his niece the Duchesse de Dino in his *hôtel* on the rue Saint-Florentin, became, with the house of Madame de Flahaut, 'the centre of the liberal and even ... antidynastic opposition'.[38] Although he had lost two and a half million francs in a bank crash in 1828,[39] he helped Thiers to found a newspaper *Le National* on 3 January 1830 which galvanised the opposition to the ministry. Comparisons of the Bourbons and the Stuarts in its columns were frequent. On 15 January 1830, for example, it claimed: 'England was only truly free after having completed in 1688 its revolution of 1640.' The Orléans were the only solution.[40] That winter the Seine froze from bank to bank near the Louvre. While wealthy Parisians enjoyed the novelty of sleigh rides through the Bois de Boulogne, the poor suffered atrociously. At the charity fêtes held for their benefit during the carnival season, the Orléans were conspicuous, and applauded; the royal family, although generous with its contributions, rarely attended.[41]

Even more than Talleyrand and Chateaubriand, the younger generation of Frenchmen preferred public careers in the Chambers and journalism to personal service in the court. As Stendhal wrote in 1826: 'our Chamber of Deputies is acquiring more importance every day and most of our educated young people are beginning to consider it as the great instrument destined to effect changes in France.'[42] Charles de Rémusat, showing only contempt for the court office of Secrétaire du Roi à la conduite des Ambassadeurs which his parents had obtained for him in 1814, resigned it as soon as he could and refused to be presented at court. He preferred his career as a journalist, writing liberal articles for *Le Globe*.[43] Lamartine refused the office of Sous-Secrétaire d'Etat aux Affaires Etrangères offered by the Polignac ministry in 1829. Victor Hugo refused an increase in his pension and a post of Conseiller d'Etat.[44]

For Victor Hugo had also abandoned royalism for liberalism, as was evident in his poems and his play *Hernani*, a romantic drama set at the court of Charles V in sixteenth-century Spain. Its performance at the Comédie Française had given Charles X occasion for a last display of that simplicity and modesty which had won him the love of his family and his party. The old men in the Académie Française, committed to the unities of time, place and character traditional in the French theatre, were horrified by the defiance of these rules in *Hernani*. A deputation from the Académie, led by the Bonapartist author of *Germanicus*, A.V. Arnault, came to court asking the King to ban the play. The old King, who in his liberal moments had opposed censorship, replied: 'what can I do, Messieurs? Like you I only have a place in the *parterre*.'[45] On 25 February 1830 the Comédie Française was full of Hugo's supporters and a paid claque – some of whom, taking their cue from the play, were dressed like Spaniards in Velázquez portraits – as well as regular theatre-goers like the Duchesse de Maillé and Madame de Flahaut. Mlle Mars was superb as Dona Sol; that night changed the face of French theatre, marking a decisive step in the replacement of the rules and traditions of classical French drama. The salons talked of little else.[46]

Three months later the last great fête of the Restoration epitomised the dual role, both dynastic and revolutionary, of the Palais Royal. It took place on 31 May in honour of Francis I King of the Two Sicilies, father of the Duchesse de Berri and brother of the Duchesse d'Orléans. After taking his younger daughter Maria Cristina to Madrid to marry King Ferdinand VII, Francis was returning to Naples via Paris. The Duc d'Orléans wanted to show himself the most magnificent prince in Europe, in order to prove to his brother-in-law that Marie Amélie had not married beneath her. (A similar desire, to show that *cousins* of the King of France were equal in rank to other kings' *sons*, as well as the desire to bind the House of Orléans as closely as possible to the royal family, had led Charles X, on his accession, to elevate all the Orléans and the Duc de Bourbon to the rank of Royal Highness.)[47] Moreover, by the presence in the Palais Royal of Charles X himself, who never visited private houses, Orléans hoped to encourage a marriage between one of his daughters and the son of the King of the Two Sicilies.[48]

Four hundred workmen had been employed for weeks in the palace. The entire façade was illuminated. The weather was magnificent. The terraces were covered with plants and orange trees, hiding several orchestras; all the apartments were open; garlands of coloured vases illuminated by candles swung between the urns on the roof and the trees in the garden. Three thousand people – 'all Paris' – had been invited. At 8 p.m. they began to arrive, watched by spectators crowded into the windows of the houses opposite the palace, who were so well dressed that they too seemed like guests at the party. There were so many carriages arriving that it took one and a half hours to cover the distance from the Place du Carrousel to the Place du Palais Royal, which takes five minutes on foot.

From early morning the garden of the Palais Royal had been filling up with members of the public eager to watch the spectacle. As the guests, covered in jewels and orders, danced in the state apartments on the first floor, down in the garden, until the gendarmes arrived, some of the crowd – perhaps to avoid paying for their chairs – began to throw them in the air or burn them, and to cry *A bas les habits galonnés! A bas les aristocrates!*

When he appeared on the balcony the King was greeted with silence. An English officer leaning out of a window, recognisable by his red uniform, received cries of *A bas l'Anglais! A bas l'Anglais!* Another guest, the writer Narcisse de Salvandy, made a celebrated comment to Orléans: 'it is a truly Neapolitan *fête*, Monseigneur; we are dancing on a volcano.'[49] As he left, Charles X told Orléans that it was the finest ball he had seen, and that the wind would favour his fleet on its way to Algiers. Guests smiled at the depth of Orléans' bows as he escorted the King down the grandiose staircase of the Palais Royal, built by Boffrand in 1750. He bowed so low that his spine seemed bent in two.[50] Thereafter supper was served first to ladies, then to men, then to servants. Dancing lasted until 6 a.m.[51]

In June and July, as they left Paris to spend summer in the country, most members of the élite were like Lamartine *pénétrés d'inquiétudes* over the confrontation between the ministers and the majority in the Chamber of Deputies, but were convinced that in the end the King would retreat.[52] On 14 June, in a private conversation during a hunt at Rosny in honour of the King of the Two Sicilies, Charles X repeated to Orléans – according to the latter's account – 'Outside the Charte there is only abyss and perdition . . . I, you know, who are older than you and have known the old regime better than you, I tell you that if it [the return of the old regime] was possible it would not be desirable.'[53] To

Sémonville, Grand Référendaire de la Chambre des Pairs, he promised: 'For good or ill I am in the Charte. I will stay there.'[54]

On 19 June the French army landed on the coast of Algeria. The elections held at the end of June and the beginning of July, however, registered a humiliating defeat for the government. The opposition won 270 seats, the ministry 145, fewer than before. The King remained convinced that it was better to attack than to retreat, that he held his throne by right of birth rather than a constitutional contract, that the royal prerogative was the guarantee of order and happiness in France and that the opposition was his irreconcilable enemy.[55] As a result, on 9 July he decided, in accordance with his interpretation of Article 14 of the Charte, to govern by *ordonnances*. He did not consider the possibility of revolution or, indeed, the possibilities for manoeuvre and manipulation available to the crown within the framework of the Charte. At a last audience with the King on 13 July Pozzo, personally favourable to the Algerian expedition, begged him to do nothing rash and to temporise. However Metternich, who had long considered the Charte, and Paris liberals, a source of evil in Europe, and the Austrian ambassador Count Apponyi, advised strong measures.[56] French government stock fell on the news of the capture of Algiers on 14 July, since speculators feared that the government would thereby be encouraged to carry out schemes hostile to the Charte.[57]

The King's coup of 26 July 1830 was a combination of overconfidence, incapacity and *imprévoyance* – lack of foresight. To ensure an element of surprise, no precautions were taken; not even the Prefect of Police of Paris was warned.[58] Instead of the normal force of about 15,000 troops on duty in the capital, there were only about 11,000: approximately 4,600 soldiers of the Garde Royale; 5,000 troops of the line; 1,500 gendarmes.[59] About 1,500 gardes du corps, gardes à pied and gendarmes d'élite were guarding the King at Saint-Cloud. In contrast to the situation in 1820, there had been no effort to summon the regiments stationed around Paris at Caen, Rouen, Versailles, Saint-Denis, Orléans, Compiègne, Meaux, Melun, Fontainebleau and Corbeil, or from the military camps at Saint-Omer and Lunéville, which contained 40,000 men.[60]

Indeed there were fewer soldiers than normal, since two regiments of the Garde Royale were fighting rural fires in Normandy, while others were fighting in Algeria. The commander of the French army in Algeria was Bourmont, the Minister of War. Back in Paris Polignac was interim Minister of War. He had no military experience. Nevertheless he assured the Austrian ambassador: 'as Minister of War I have taken all measures and I promise you that they are well taken.'[61] Thus the war in Algeria, far from strengthening the position of the monarchy, by removing some of its best troops and officers, facilitated its overthrow. (The absence of crack troops at the front had also weakened Napoleon's control of Paris in March 1814 and June 1815, and would weaken Nicholas II's control of St Petersburg in February 1917 and Wilhelm II's control of Berlin in November 1918.) The Major-General of the Garde Royale on duty from May to September 1830 was Maréchal Marmont, whose reputation for 'betraying' Napoleon in 1814 had made him unpopular.[62] The economy, too, was weaker than in 1820: wages were falling, prices and unemployment rising. A third of the population was receiving bread cards to enable it to obtain free bread. The great banker Laffitte himself was on the verge of bankruptcy.[63]

On Monday 26 July *ordonnances* signed the previous day by the King at Saint-Cloud were published in the *Moniteur*. In violation of Articles 8, 35 and 50 of the Charte, the *ordonnances* suspended the liberty of the press; dissolved the newly elected Chamber of Deputies; reduced the number of deputies in future Chambers; withdrew their right of amendment; excluded the commercial bourgeoisie from future elections by dropping the *patente* as a voting qualification; appointed new and reactionary Conseillers d'Etat; and summoned new electoral colleges for September.[64] The King had declared war not only on the political élite, but also on the Paris publishing trade.

Astonishment was universal. Government stock fell three francs. The coup was not only badly prepared; it was undertaken, at least by some ministers, in a half-hearted fashion. Again the defeatism of some émigrés and ultras, courting disaster and sabotaging compromise, manifested itself. In a letter of 26 July to his patron Villèle, Minister of the Interior, a provincial noble the Comte de Montbel made it clear that he anticipated violence: 'God will save the King and France. The King displays an imperturbable courage. M. le Dauphin is determined to undertake anything. I am convinced that *la bonne cause* will triumph. *In any case the defence will be honourable*' (author's italics). Charles X's grandson the Comte de Chambord would also appeal to 'honour' in 1873, when he refused the throne of France because he would not accept the tricolour and renounce the white flag of Henri IV.[65]

Monday 26 July
Paris was experiencing a heatwave. Under a burning sun, clouds a lurid red, the temperature rose to over 30 degrees. Opposition deputies

present in Paris, including Generals Gérard, Sébastiani and Baron Louis, met at the house of Casimir Périer, but refused to sign a collective protest and failed to decide on collective action. Businessmen meeting at the Bourse were more hostile; bankers refused to discount bills. Most factory owners, including Baron Ternaux, closed their factories in protest at the *ordonnances* which had deprived some of them of the chance of being deputies – a measure which they had not taken in June 1820. Large numbers of factory workers therefore had nothing to do except protest; thus Sémonville, in his account of the revolution, could talk of 'the insurrectionary policy of the factory owners'.[66]

It was a sign of the importance of the press and the written word in this period that the revolution was launched in newspaper offices. Well-established newspapers like the *Journal des débats* and *Le Constitutionnel* obeyed the *ordonnances* and did not appear. As publishers agreed to cancel their orders to printers in conformity with the *ordonnances*, so many print-workers were thrown out of work the next day. In the offices of the *National* in the rue Saint-Marc between the Bourse and the Palais Royal, forty-three journalists, representing eleven newspapers, signed a collective protest. The most audacious of them, Thiers, his close friend Mignet and a semi-republican former Napoleonic soldier Armand Carrel, in an article published on 27 July, claimed that it was a public duty to refuse taxes.

> France . . . falls back into revolution by the act of the government itself . . . the legal regime is now interrupted, that of force has begun . . . in the situation in which we are placed obedience has ceased to be a duty . . . It is for France to judge how far its own resistance ought to extend.[67]

Popular opposition soon began to show itself. In the Palais Royal groups gathered around newspaper stands and cafés. When a police commissioner confiscated a newspaper press, a crowd shouted *A bas les Bourbons! Vive la Charte! Vivent les 221!* The carriage of Polignac was stoned on the Boulevard des Capucines as it turned into the Ministry of Foreign Affairs, bystanders crying *A bas Polignac! A bas les ministres!* Otherwise there was little further unrest: it was a Monday and most of the poorer population were eating and drinking in *guinguettes* outside the *barrières*. That evening the garden of the Palais Royal was closed.[68] The Préfet de Police, who was living in a dream, wrote in his daily *bulletin de Paris*: 'the most perfect tranquillity continues to reign in all parts of the capital. No event worthy of attention is recorded in the reports that have come through to me.'[69] However a Swiss visitor, Juste Olivier, recorded the fury of his printing-manager, expressed in the language of his profession: 'If they want a second edition of the revolution of the Stuarts, we will make one, corrected, revised and expanded.'[70]

Tuesday 27 July
Le Temps, Le National, Le Globe and *Le Journal du commerce* appeared despite the interdiction. *Le Temps* declared that the 'social pact' was dissolved. The presses of *Le Temps* and *Le National* were seized. Journalists continued to meet at the offices of *Le National*. Alarmed by the unprecedented number of people on the streets of Paris and the noise they made, Polignac requested the military commander in Paris, the Comte de Wall, to send extra troops to protect the ministries. The garden of the Palais Royal was closed at midday. At the same time Maréchal Marmont was given command of the troops stationed in and around Paris in the first military division, in addition to that of the Garde Royale.[71]

In the centre of Paris shopkeepers began to shut their shops for fear of riots and looting. Military posts were manned as normal throughout the city until, at 4.30 in the afternoon, officers received orders to concentrate their troops, guns at the ready, on the Place du Carrousel, the Places Louis XVI, Vendôme and de la Bastille, and the boulevards. The troops could be seen massed in long, dark, silent lines on the Place du Carrousel facing the Tuileries palace and Marmont's headquarters, in the offices of the Major-Général de la Garde Royale in the wing of the Tuileries looking on to the rue de Rivoli.

Patrols were sent to the boulevards, the Palais Royal, the rues de Richelieu and Saint-Honoré to maintain order and to protect gun-shops from attacks by crowds. At first, since it was a fine evening, the streets were full of carriages and strollers. About 7 p.m., however, fighting began. Since the Palais Royal was shut, the centre of action moved to the rue Saint-Honoré – running parallel to the rue de Rivoli between the Palais Royal and the Tuileries garden – and the Place du Palais Royal, so recently packed with crowds admiring the guests arriving for the Duc d'Orléans' ball. Parisians, rather than soldiers, were the aggressors. Paving stones, roof tiles and flowerpots from the upper windows, especially in the rue de Rohan, began to rain down on soldiers in the streets. At first the soldiers tried to avoid casualties and to fire in the air. Soon, however, Parisians could hear the rapid discharge of rifle-fire, followed by a moment of silence; then cries of pain from the wounded or *Vive le roi!* from the troops.[72] It was the first real fighting in the streets of Paris since Bonaparte's suppression of a royalist rising, in much the same area, in 1795.

One of the first victims of the 1830 revolution in Paris was an Englishman, Mr Foulkes. The soldiers in the street believed that he had thrown stones, or fired, from the balcony of Lawson's Hotel in 193 rue Saint-Honoré, and as a result shot him dead; waiters and an Englishwoman sitting at a window, with open shutters, received near misses. Having greater experience in such matters, for the duration of the revolution Parisians kept their shutters closed.[73] The guards managed to clear the first barricade in the rue Saint-Honoré, constructed around an overturned omnibus. In all, about twenty-one individuals were killed, including a woman.[74] In order to excite the crowd, one corpse was paraded through the city that night, to cries of *Mort aux ministres!*[75] Finally free movement was restored and military patrols were able to proceed throughout the city. However, most of the thousands of lamps which stretched on ropes from one side of the street to the other, and which cast a shadow like a giant spider's web, had been broken in order to spread confusion.[76] No special measures had been taken to guard arms depots or gunpowder factories.

Observers of the July revolution, as it was later called, rarely tell who composed the crowds or why they were there. An officer in the Garde Royale called them 'the lowest class of the people'.[77] However it has been shown that of the 211 dead and the 1,327 wounded who received compensation from the official commission set up after the revolution, fewer than 300 were labourers and servants. About 1,000 were skilled artisans, of whom 128 were carpenters and only 28 print-workers. Half were aged between twenty and thirty-five. Many students, armed with pistols, took part, including sixty *polytechniciens*, one of whom was Auguste Demorny, the illegitimate son of Flahaut and Queen Hortense.[78]

One motive for the Paris crowd's attacks was nationalism rather than economic distress or political liberalism. It was nationalism which inspired Parisians' fury at the appointment of the 'traitor' Marmont, and their joy at the sight of the tricolour flag hoisted, probably by a band of law students, in place of the white flag on the towers of Notre Dame, on 27 July. The growing cult of Napoleon since his death in 1821, as well as the Catholic and autocratic policies of Charles X, had made the Bourbons more hated in 1830 than in 1820. Memories of the detested despotism of Napoleon I had been effaced by nostalgia for the glory of his reign, expressed in the nationalistic poems of Béranger praising the Emperor, and the brilliant work of propaganda by one of Napoleon's chamberlains the Comte de Las Cases, *Mémorial de Sainte-Hélène*. Presenting the Emperor as an idealistic liberal, it had made so much money for its author that he was able to build the houses in the present rue Las Cases in the Faubourg Saint-Germain out of the proceeds. Peasants said that Napoleon was alive and would soon return. Visiting Malmaison in 1827, the Dauphine had seen scrawled on a vase in the garden the words *Vive le grand conquérant des sceptres du monde! Vive Napoléon II!*[79] A coachman on the Calais–Paris route was heard to regret that Napoleon had not conquered the whole world: if only he had not trusted his marshals, who were too rich and too frightened of their wives.[80]

One revolutionary proclamation would denounce the Restoration as 'the government of foreign origin and influence which has just ceased'.[81] Indeed, from the organisation and aggression of the crowds during *les journées de juillet*, it would appear that many of their leaders were former soldiers of the Napoleonic army. A former *officier d'ordonnance* of Napoleon I General Dumoulin led successful attacks on the Banque de France on 28 July and on the Hôtel de Ville on 29 July. A former soldier at Waterloo, Dubourg, advised insurgents on how and where to attack royal troops in the Faubourg Saint-Martin.[82] Just as important were former soldiers of the Garde Nationale, rapidly reorganised in their old formations by district, who used the arms, and in many cases wore the uniforms, which they had retained since its dissolution in 1827.[83] Some printed appeals for resistance, with instructions to citizens on how to use paving stones and to help *nos tirailleurs*, were phrased as if issued from a military headquarters.[84]

In the evening of 27 July, from his window on quai Malaquais, Juste Olivier saw

> a crowd of agitated people pass by and disappear, then a troop of cavalry succeed them. In every direction and at intervals cries are heard of *Vive la Charte! A bas les ministres!* Indistinct noises, gunshots, then all is silent again so that for a time one could believe that everything in the city was normal. But all the shops are shut; the Pont Neuf is almost completely dark, the stupefaction visible on every face reminds us all too much of the crisis in which we find ourselves . . . Credit is extinct.[85]

By 10 p.m. the crowds had dispersed: that evening Marmont sent Charles X a reassuring report. The Premier Gentilhomme in waiting, however, the Duc de Duras, who had seen revolutionary violence before, while on duty beside Louis XVI in Paris in April 1791, was more alarmed.[86]

Wednesday 28 July

This day was the turning-point. Juste Olivier wrote: 'it is hardly a quarter past eight and already shouts and gunshots can be heard. Business is at a standstill. On the first day government stock fell by four francs, on the second, yesterday, by eight.'[87] Paris began to hear the noise, familiar to survivors of an earlier revolution, of the 'maddening knell' of church bells and the pealing of the great bell – *le bourdon* – of Notre Dame, probably started by students from the Ecoles de Droit and de Médecine. The sound was all the louder as the ordinary sounds of the city – carriage wheels on cobbles, street-sellers hawking their wares – were stilled.[88] Marmont's plan was to guard the west of the city and the boulevards, the barracks, the Palais Royal, the Palais de Justice and the Hôtel de Ville and at the same time to keep open the most important lines of communication in the city: the rue de Richelieu and the rue Saint-Denis running north–south, and the rue Saint-Honoré running east–west. Three columns advanced through the city, under Colonels de Quinsonnas, de Saint-Chamans and Talon (the brother of Madame du Cayla).

This over-ambitious plan, much criticised both at the time and subsequently, led to suspicions that he had betrayed Charles X as, in popular mythology, he had 'betrayed' Napoleon I. For the strategy was almost doomed to fail. There were not enough troops for such a big city. The troops of the line, who made up half of those in Paris, were of doubtful loyalty. The provision of cartridges (eleven per man), as well as of food and drink for the troops, was inadequate: requests for more cartridges were intercepted by revolutionaries. The barricades which went up behind the troops as they advanced made movement difficult – although it was easier to operate on the left than the right bank.[89] The Faubourg Saint-Germain was relatively tranquil: the Lock family from Norbury, who were renting the Hôtel de Castries at 72 rue de Varenne, thought the hiss of a cannon ball landing in their garden was the sound of cats fighting, and that the firing in the centre of the city was the noise from a military review.[90]

Under any circumstances, the centre of Paris was difficult to control. In addition to the lack of troops, as Fouché and other Bonapartists had found when hiding from the royal police in March 1815, the buildings of Paris themselves acted against the government. What an officer of the Garde Royale called 'the very narrow and tortuous streets' of the city provided cover for attacks on troops. It was safe for Parisians, invisible behind shuttered windows, to fire on troops from the fifth or sixth floor of houses difficult for soldiers to identify or storm.[91] The problems facing the troops in the populous central streets of the city were expressed by one officer of the Lancers of the Garde Royale. He told Edmond Marc, a Huissier de la Chambre du Roi:

> when we meet a crowd they run as fast as their legs can carry them. Every door opens; in an instant everyone disappears; impossible to deal a single blow of a lance. Meanwhile gunshots, bricks, paving stones fall like hail from every window, without us even being able to see who is throwing them; and the moment we pass on, the doors open again and vomit forth all those wretches who fire bullets in our backs.[92]

In some cases the royal troops were less well armed than the civilians attacking them: throughout the city the gendarmes and police began to abandon their posts. In general, according to a report sent to the British ambassador Lord Stuart de Rothesay, they let the Parisians fight without showing any resistance.[93] Some Parisians on the ground floor, however – generally richer than those living on upper floors – willingly gave troops food, drink and shelter.[94]

Throughout the day the crowds, both on the streets and firing from the windows, became thicker and better armed as they pillaged the arms stores of the Ministry of War, or were given arms by troops of the line or the owners of arms-shops. Nevertheless the troops of the Garde Royale continued to perform their duty loyally and, eager to take on civilians, overturned barricades and recaptured the Hôtel de Ville.[95]

From his window on the quai Malaquais, Juste Olivier could see crowds rushing through the street, and hear the sound of cannon and gunfire and the tocsin ringing. Despite the fighting, carriages continued to drive through some streets. At 1 p.m. he noted that 'the firing is becoming ever louder.' Cries of *A bas le roi! A la guillotine!* began to be heard.[96] Government coachmen and postmen tore off their *plaques fleurdelisées*.[97] Either as a precaution to deflect popular fury or from political outrage, court tradesmen, *notaires* and *huissiers* erased their royal *brevets* with mastic, and took down shop signs that bore the Bourbon coats of arms.[98]*

---

* The sole surviving Bourbon coat of arms on a Paris shopfront today can be seen on the chocolate shop of Delbaume et Gallais, 30 rue des Saints-Pères, *fournisseurs des anciens rois de France*, built in 1819.

Edmond Marc watched in disgust as a crowd applauded and whistled at a locksmith who was removing the royal coat of arms from the shopfront on the rue de Richelieu of Evrard *tailleur du roi*.[99] At the same time the white flag disappeared from public buildings.[100]

However the crowd was volatile. On the Place de l'Eléphant (present-day Place de la Bastille) – thanks to the words and money of General de Saint-Chamans at the head of a detachment of the Garde Royale – the crowd, *dans une vive agitation*, was persuaded to shout *Vive le roi!*, to which, however, it later added: *Vive la Charte! A bas les ministres!* Told by Saint-Chamans that they would not gain by creating disorder, they replied that they had no bread and no work.[101] He later said that a van of gold coins from the Treasury, rather than a battery of artillery, would have calmed the Faubourg Saint-Antoine without a shot.[102]

Another observer of this revolution was a widow with a scandalous past who, as a young girl, had danced naked before a table of potential clients. The Countess of Blessington now lived with a former officer of the Garde Royale, the Comte d'Orsay, who was also her stepson-in-law. She was famous for her wit and beauty; he for his elegance, his insolence, and his debts. Byron called him 'a *cupidon déchaîné*'.[103] In the summer of 1830, temporarily jaded with London and Naples, they had rented the former *hôtel* of Maréchal Ney in the rue de Bourbon in the Faubourg Saint-Germain. Throughout 28 July, Lady Blessington, despite the fighting and the heat, continued to receive gentlemen visitors, including the Duc de Guiche and Count Walewski, while Lord Stuart de Rothesay, the British ambassador, continued to walk around the streets. They told her news of the fighting in the city and criticised Marmont's military measures. She interrupted her *déjeuner à la fourchette* to observe the action from her drawing room. 'Sitting in darkness with the sound of firing and the shouts of the people continually in our ears I can hardly bring myself to think that all that is now passing is not a dream . . . never did so great a change take place in the aspect of a city in so few hours.'[104] From her window she could watch troops of boys marching through the streets, crying *Vive la Charte! Vive la liberté!*[105]

Despite the firing she was determined to visit Orsay's grandmother, old Madame Craufurd, in the rue d'Anjou.* Walking with a *valet de pied*

---

* Born Anna Franchi in Lucca, a former mistress of, among others, Marie Antoinette's admirer Axel Fersen, she had finally married the collector Quentin Craufurd. In old age she looked, according to one of their guests, 'as if she had walked Bond Street'.

from the rue de Bourbon in the Faubourg Saint-Germain across the Seine to the rue d'Anjou beside the Madeleine, she noticed that the dogs in the streets were so terrified that they scuttled past with drooping tails. Despite the difficulty of climbing over barricades, she finally reached her destination. The porter unlocked and unbolted the porte cochère – normally left open in the daytime – muttering *les dames anglaises n'ont peur de rien, positivement rien*, and closed the door so rapidly, as she left, as 'almost to have endangered my heels'.[106]

Throughout the day the King listened to the recommendation of Polignac and his ministers to *tenir bon* – although in the morning, as they had walked from the Ministry of Foreign Affairs on the Boulevard des Capucines to take refuge in Marmont's headquarters in the Tuileries, the ministers had been able to see for themselves troops of the line on the Place Vendôme beginning to fraternise with members of the crowd offering them brandy.[107] In the opinion of the ministers the insurrection would end once the Parisians ran out of ammunition.

The opposition deputies who happened to be in Paris had formed a committee consisting of Laffitte, General Mouton Comte de Lobau, General Gérard, Casimir Périer and one of their leading writers and deputies, the brilliant historian François Guizot. At about midday they drew up a protest, drafted by Guizot, criticising not the King but his ministers – thereby disproving Charles X's conviction that his liberal opponents were enemies of his dynasty. In 1830, as in 1820, the banker Jacques Laffitte was one of the kingmakers. 'His vast wealth,' Lady Blessington wrote, 'and the frequent and extensive aid it has afforded to the working classes, have rendered him one of, if not the most popular man in Paris.'[108] In the afternoon Laffitte, Périer, Gérard, Lobau and Mauguin went to Marmont to appeal for a suspension of bloodshed. They asked for the marshal to act as a mediator between the army and the people and as a messenger from Paris to the King.

In the pandemonium of Marmont's headquarters, excited officers were all talking at the same time: many had come in civilian clothes to offer their services. Marmont explained to Laffitte that, much as he sympathised with their views, submission was the first condition of negotiation; he urged them to persuade Parisians to return to their houses and their duties. However he knew that the King regarded the *ordonnances* as necessary to the safety and dignity of the throne.[109] Polignac, who seemed as calm as if he was at a ceremony of the Order of the Holy Spirit, refused to meet Laffitte.[110] Colonel Komierowski, one of Marmont's aides, reached Saint-Cloud at about 4 p.m. with a message from the marshal for the King:

> Sire, it is no longer a riot, it is a revolution. It is urgent for Your Majesty to take measures of pacification. The honour of the crown can still be saved. Tomorrow, perhaps, there will be no more time . . . I await with impatience Your Majesty's orders.

A simultaneous message from Polignac, however, advised resistance.[111] A Napoleonic marshal tried to save the Bourbon monarchy; a royalist helped it commit suicide.

Charles X wrote to Marmont to hold fast, to group his troops around the Place des Victoires, the Place Vendôme and the Tuileries, protect the ministries, await further orders, and not to make new attacks against the *révoltés*.[112] Marmont did not have the initiative to summon troops from Vincennes or Saint-Denis, let alone from the military camps of Lunéville and Saint-Omer. All he did, at 4 p.m., was order his troops to fall back on the Louvre and the Tuileries. When they reached the Tuileries the troops expressed disgust that no member of the royal family had come to be with its defenders.[113] Like the print-worker earlier, Alfred de Vigny, who had his uniform ready in case the King summoned all officers to defend the throne, expressed his rage by invoking British history. He wrote in his diary: 'They do not come to Paris, people are dying for them. Race of Stuarts! Not one prince has appeared. The poor brave men of the Guard abandoned without orders, without bread for two days, hunted everywhere and fighting.'[114] At dinner that evening at Saint-Cloud, Charles X, the Dauphin and the Duchesse de Berri could hear the sound of cannon fire in Paris. The meal was frequently interrupted by aides-de-camp bringing news from the city. Courtiers expressed consternation and despair. Through telescopes they could see *une fumée rougeâtre* over the towers of Notre Dame. For a few hours in the night the cannon fire stopped. Then it started again, with, in the background, the maddening knell of the bells of Notre Dame.[115]

That evening a group of liberals meeting in the house of Guizot mentioned the Duc d'Orléans for the first time. Young men gathered outside the house, and other houses where politicians were meeting, urged action and taunted the politicians for their cowardice. Once more the deputies refused to sign a protest and, fearing a royal victory, simply permitted their names to be placed on a list of those present.[116]

Thursday 29 July

Royalists had disappeared from the streets of Paris – either because they had no arms or leaders, or because few supported the *ordonnances*.[117] Marmont did everything to fortify the area around the Louvre and the Tuileries and to ensure that no one could fire on his troops from houses nearby. Some observers, including General Exelmans, who offered his services to Marmont that morning, considered the military position, now concentrated in one area, more defensible than on the previous day.[118] Parisians however had acquired more arms, from museums as well as barracks, and by that morning, by a miracle of energy and organisation, 4,000 barricades had been constructed – of stones, furniture, carts – in almost every street in Paris. In some areas the streets were completely unpaved, the paving stones having been either thrown at soldiers or used to construct barricades. Trees too had been cut down in the night and stretched across the boulevards to strengthen the defences, some of which resembled large forts.[119]

Line regiments in Paris began to desert to the revolutionaries. Perhaps persuaded by Casimir Périer, the fifth and fifty-third line regiments marched in support of the revolution from Place Vendôme to Laffitte's house in the rue de Provence near the Boulevard des Italiens. In July 1830 it was the power centre of Paris, as Talleyrand's house on the rue Saint-Florentin had been in April 1814, although the politicians filling its sumptuous, gilded rooms were considerably less aristocratic. Camping in the courtyard, the soldiers placed themselves under the command of the liberal general Gérard, who ordered them back to barracks. Their attitude was decisive. No royal guard could resist, at the same time, the population of a city and troops of the line.[120]

In the morning Sémonville, the one royal official who showed initiative and intelligence in this revolution, in his capacity as representative of the Chambre des Pairs – 'addressing itself to authority so that it reflected on its acts', as the Parlement de Paris, of which he had been an officer, had often done before 1789 when persuading earlier monarchs to accept limits on their power – urged Marmont to arrest the ministers. Marmont, however, did not have a spirit of initiative.[121] His principal political act was to refuse Polignac's orders to arrest La Fayette, Gérard and Laffitte, as he had Sémonville's suggestion that he arrest Polignac and his colleagues.[122] Sémonville and the ministers then raced as fast as their carriages could take them to Saint-Cloud, to be the first to advise the King on what measures to take. Shaken, Charles X promised to discuss the situation with them after mass at 11 that morning. While some ministers continued to urge resistance from a base in the provinces, a dishevelled general was shown in to the King's *cabinet* with the news that the Louvre had been taken.[123]

The Louvre had been lost in part because of panic by its Swiss guards. Badly fed and led, they feared a repetition of the massacre on 10 August 1792, when 700 Swiss soldiers had been killed defending the Tuileries palace. Marmont moreover had ordered them not to start firing. Parisians, many of them students, had found a way in to the Louvre and begun to fire at the troops below from the windows of the Grande Galerie. At the sight of the Swiss troops in flight, a similar panic inspired the royal troops in the Tuileries and the Place du Carrousel, who retreated as far as the Champs Elysées.[124] The people of Paris had defeated the royal guard.

By 1.30 p.m. the tricolour flag flew from the Tuileries. The cries in the streets of *Vive la Charte!* were now joined by those of *Vive la liberté! Vive la nation!* and, particularly among *le bas peuple, Vive Napoléon II!*[125] Parisians again showed their rejection of the role of Bourbon court city. In the throne room of the Tuileries a corpse was draped over the throne of Charles X. Apartments were pillaged, furniture and pictures destroyed. The *Journal des chasses du roi*, in which every piece of game hunted or shot by Charles X was recorded, aroused especial derision. A man wearing a ball dress belonging to the Duchesse de Berri, with feathers and flowers in his hair, screamed from a palace window: *je reçois, je reçois!* Others drank wine from the palace cellars.[126]

The Palais de Justice and the Archbishop's palace on the Ile de la Cité were among other buildings sacked by Parisians on 29 July. Books, parchments, legal robes, ecclesiastical vestments and furniture floated down the Seine (beside which two fishermen tranquilly extended their lines). In contrast to *l'autre révolution*, of which survivors in 1830 still talked with terror, there was little robbery. If people tried to fish objects out of the river, bystanders yelled *A l'eau! A l'eau!* and threatened to drown the thieves.[127] The collections in the Louvre were protected by the crowd.

Meanwhile the royal troops had retreated through the Champs Elysées and the Bois de Boulogne to Saint-Cloud. Many cried that Marmont was a traitor. During their retreat they were attacked not only by the inhabitants of Chaillot and Passy, but also by 'intrepid' boys who fired on royal soldiers in the knowledge that they were less likely to risk retaliation.[128] Saint-Cloud now resembled a fortified castle rather than a rural retreat. Royal servants could see through their telescopes a red

The New Jerusalem

flag – the people's flag – flying from the Tuileries, and a black and red flag on the column in the Place Vendôme. The sole remaining white Bourbon flag in Paris flew above the Invalides.[129] At Saint-Cloud the King held the crown jewels, brought by faithful officials, and a supply of artillery which arrived from the fort at Vincennes, as well as loyal troops. The Dauphin had taken over command of the army from Marmont and was determined to die at its head.[130]

In the course of 29 July, however, power had shifted from the court to the city, from the palaces of Saint-Cloud and the Tuileries to the Hôtel de Ville of Paris. Begun under François Ier and finished under Henri IV, the Hôtel de Ville was an imposing mixture of Gothic and Renaissance architecture. A focus of power and bloodshed during the revolution as seat of the Commune, the Hôtel de Ville had subsequently become the seat of the administration of the department of the Seine. The building had been reroyalised during the Restoration and filled with pictures of Henri IV, Louis XIV and Louis XVIII.[131] Now it resumed its role as a power centre of revolution.

In the morning of 29 July revolutionaries, many of them former national guards, invaded the Hôtel de Ville, abandoned by royal troops for lack of supplies, and began to prepare tables for a provisional government. After eighteen years as Prefect of the Seine, under nineteen Ministers of the Interior, the Comte de Chabrol left on foot with his wife. People in the crowds commented: *voilà le préfet qui s'en va*.[132] Finally taking the initiative, the thirty deputies assembled in Laffitte's house in Paris chose a Commission Municipale of five non-nobles (Casimir Périer, Mouton Comte de Lobau, the radical deputy for the Seine Auguste-Jean-Marie Baron de Schonen, an even more militant deputy Audry de Puyraveau, Laffitte himself), and appointed Gérard to command the troops and La Fayette as head of the Garde Nationale, which had already spontaneously re-formed – forty-one years since its creation in July 1789 and for much the same reason: to protect the social order in the vacuum created by the defeat of royal troops by revolutionary crowds in Paris.[133]

At about 4 p.m. in the afternoon of 29 July, La Fayette and the Commission Municipale installed themselves in the Hôtel de Ville. Such was the power of Paris and the fame of La Fayette that they immediately began to act as the government of France.[134] A special edition of *Le Globe* which appeared at 4 p.m. proclaimed: 'Paris has delivered France: our enemies are in full retreat.'[135] The fighting on the three days of 27, 28 and 29 July, soon celebrated by French writers as *les journées de juillet*, *les trois journées* or *les trois glorieuses*, had cost about 150 killed and 600 wounded among royal troops, 600 dead and 2,000 wounded among civilians.[136]

Back at Saint-Cloud, a senior court official provided the last hope of a compromise between the King and the revolution. The Duc de Mortemart, an ambassador and general – still at forty-three relatively young – who had served in the Napoleonic army and enjoyed a reputation for liberalism, had come to Saint-Cloud on the evening of 28 July to perform his court office as Capitaine Colonel des Gardes à Pied and check on the state of his company: he had been amazed to find, despite the sound of cannon fire and the sight of flames in the sky above Paris, the court still in its 'accustomed order'. Not one extra soldier had been posted in the courtyard.[137] Entering the King's bedroom by right of his court office at 7 a.m. on the morning of 29 July, Mortemart had been heard by the King, and his liberal arguments resisted. Convinced that France needed firm government, Charles X was determined to make no concessions. In the course of the day Mortemart was appalled at the signs of disorder, disloyalty and confusion at Saint-Cloud: despite the catastrophe, Polignac – *Jeanne d'Arc en culottes* – maintained an air of superiority and self-satisfaction.[138]

Charles X continued to deny to Sémonville the truth of the reports from Paris as they arrived; Sémonville, increasingly agitated, was forced to protest: 'Tomorrow there will be no King, no Dauphin and no Duc de Bordeaux in France.' He even threatened the King that the Dauphine, then returning from a cure at Vichy, would suffer 'the fate of the daughters of Priam' (imprisonment and humiliation by their father's enemies). Finally at about 4 p.m. the King, whom Sémonville compared to Christ in agony on the cross, yielded to his pleas.[139] The *ordonnances* of 25 July were revoked. Mortemart was appointed Président du Conseil and Minister of Foreign Affairs – Charles X, in despair, was said to have forced the *ordonnance* of nomination into the folds of his sash, pleading that it was his last hope – and instructed to proceed to Paris. In another gesture of conciliation, Casimir Périer and Gérard were appointed Ministers of the Interior and War.

Mortemart however, who describes himself as having 'hell in his heart', hesitated. Instead of proceeding at once to the new focuses of power, Laffitte's house in Paris or the Hôtel de Ville, he slept at Saint-Cloud, justifying his delay by claiming that his powers were not sufficiently extensive and Charles X needed to make further concessions.[140] Moreover, although Polignac and the other ministers were dismissed, they continued, partly for their own safety, to live in Saint-Cloud. They wore black *fracs* instead of ministerial uniforms, but their presence at court provided liberals, including Orléans, with an excuse for believing, or claiming, that the King had not altered his policy.[141]

The deputies, even Laffitte, still wanted to remain within the bounds of legality and treat with the King at Saint-Cloud.[142] At 8.30 on the evening of 29 July Sémonville arrived at the Hôtel de Ville by cabriolet from Saint-Cloud, with the Comte d'Argout and the Baron de Vitrolles, bringing news of Charles X's revocation of the *ordonnances* and appointment of Mortemart. Their haste to save the monarchy was such that their carriage had sometimes to be physically lifted over the barricades. However, in their haste they had failed to obtain written credentials or copies of the new royal *ordonnances*. The atmosphere, both in the Hôtel de Ville and outside in the streets, reminded Sémonville of 1789. The tricolour was everywhere. That evening, all awaited the Duc de Mortemart – the Commission Municipale in the Hôtel de Ville, Laffitte in his house on the rue de Provence (present-day rue Laffitte). Mortemart, however, stayed on at Saint-Cloud.[143] The feebleness of the court nobles, compared to the spirit of initiative among Parisians, both bourgeoisie and people, helped destroy the monarchy.

Friday 30 July
At about 5 a.m. on 30 July Mortemart and Vitrolles had the King woken up and obliged him to grant more extensive powers, to sign an order reconstituting the National Guard, and to give an undertaking not to continue fighting.[144] Claiming that he would not be able to get past the Garde Royale's positions in the Bois de Boulogne – though this senior court general was well known to the guards – Mortemart left for Paris on foot. Owing to the fighting, carriage traffic was banned. (Sémonville however had managed to get through.) Covered in mud and dust Mortemart entered the city at 8 a.m. *en chemise*, through a gap in the wall near the Barrière de Vaugirard. Ignoring the realities of the situation, he went not to Laffitte's house, nor to the Hôtel de Ville, nor to the Chamber of Deputies in the Palais Bourbon, but to the Chamber of Peers in the Palais du Luxembourg. Defending his decision he later called it a natural 'central meeting-point', which in addition provided him with 'the excellent advice of M. de Sémonville and the entire staff of the Chamber perfectly organised'.

By 30 July, however, he was too late. His agents failed to find any newspaper willing to print the new *ordonnances*. In the Hôtel de Ville deputies shouted to Mortemart's agent, the Comte de Sussy, that the Bourbons were nothing any more. Casimir Périer and Gérard could not assist: they would lose all popularity if they were known to be serving Charles X.[145] To the speech to the deputies by Mortemart's envoy, Benjamin Constant delivered a crushing reply. He refused to pronounce, even at that stage, on the dynasty, but he pointed out that 'it would be too convenient for a King to order his people to be fired on and then be excused by saying that nothing had happened.'[146] When the same envoy finally met Laffitte and La Fayette at the Hôtel de Ville, he received the answer, so familiar in other revolutions: *il est trop tard*. Disgust and hate were now the dominant feelings of most Parisians for the royal family. According to an agent of the British ambassador: 'Nothing can equal the horror which the People has shown against the King and the Bourbons, conciliators will have a difficult role to play.'[147] Fearing to have their presses broken by revolutionaries, neither the *Moniteur* nor other newspapers would obey Mortemart's orders to publish Charles X's new *ordonnances*.[148]

It seemed to all observers, as a deputation of Guizot, Delessert, Augustin Périer and Sébastiani to the Chamber of Peers announced, that Charles X had lost his purpose. He was now seen as a threat, rather than a support, to the social order. Throughout 30 July, seeing a stream of politicians, Mortemart acquired the conviction that only the arrival of the Duc de Bordeaux, alone, could save the Bourbons. None of Mortemart's messengers reached Saint-Cloud, however, as the barriers were closed and could not be opened without an express order from La Fayette. At Saint-Cloud the King's inaction may have been due to his expectation of the arrival of loyal troops from the camps of Lunéville and Saint-Omer.[149]

While thousands of Parisians were fighting during the *journées de juillet*, some also preferred to do nothing. Stendhal sat in a hotel in 71 rue de Richelieu reading the *Mémorial de Sainte-Hélène* and correcting the proofs of his novel *Le Rouge et le noir*. Hitherto disgusted by the selfishness and vanity of Parisians, he now began to respect them for their coolness under fire. At 5 p.m. on 28 July, when the tocsin announced the taking of the Hôtel de Ville, Talleyrand looked at the clock on his mantelpiece and remarked: 'a few more minutes and Charles X will no longer be King of France.' As a precaution he had the words *Hôtel Talleyrand* removed from the arch over his porte cochère on the rue Saint-Florentin.[150] Like the Bonapartists in March 1815, many people fled or hid for fear of a royalist or a popular reaction: Thiers and Mignet went to the Vallée de Montmorency, Rémusat to the Hôtel de Broglie in the rue de Bourbon.[151] Victor Hugo sent his wife and children to Montfort l'Amaury outside Paris.[152]

Chateaubriand, however, returned to Paris in haste from a holiday in Dieppe. He wrote to Madame Récamier on 29 July: 'I entered Paris in the middle of cannon fire, shooting and the tocsin.' He blamed the ministers and Charles X. 'On what are kingdoms based! One *ordonnance* and six ministers without genius or virtue are enough to turn the most tranquil and flourishing country into the most troubled and unfortunate.' He was determined to remain loyal to the white flag and the King, to whom he wrote on the morning of 30 July.[153] His opinion, from which he never wavered and which most of the political élite shared, was that, *de gaieté de coeur*, the individual not the institution destroyed the Restoration. If Charles X had chosen different ministers, the regime would have survived.[154] His wife and others who had lived through the massacres of 10 August and September 1792, like Sémonville, were terrified. Yet he was struck by the relative order and silence in the streets of Paris compared to his memories of 1789 – a result of the increase in prosperity and in the forces of law and order, as well as the general disillusionment with violence.[155]

Walking on the quai de l'Ecole he was recognised by a group of students. Crying *Vive le défenseur de la liberté de la presse! Où allons-nous vous porter?* they carried him on their shoulders, dying of heat, to refresh himself in a café in the Palais Royal. They then returned past the Louvre, near which he saw trenches being dug to bury the dead, across the Pont des Arts, up the rue de Seine to the Luxembourg. To their cries of *Vive la Charte!* he replied *Oui, messieurs, vive la Charte! Mais vive le roi!*[156] In the Luxembourg he found twenty or thirty peers gathered, including Mortemart and Sémonville. In Chateaubriand's view nothing was lost; they should give an example to France and remain loyal to the King. However most peers were frightened: for a time Mortemart hid in an attic while Sémonville persuaded the crowd outside to disperse. If Charles X was so much as mentioned, Broglie claimed, the Luxembourg would be demolished like the Bastille.[157]

Despite the overthrow of Charles X, the dynastic factor was still fundamental. On 30 July the most important man in France was not Laffitte, Sémonville or Charles X, but the Duc d'Orléans. His liberalism did not stop him being considered as, primarily, a Bourbon: his son the Duc de

Chartres, a serving officer, was arrested by a crowd that day and threatened with death. Contrary to what Orleanists later claimed, the Duc and Duchesse d'Orléans' coats of arms were removed from shopfronts like those of other Bourbons.[158] Under Charles X Orléans had been more contented and – thanks to the *milliard des émigrés* and the Civil List law – richer than under Louis XVIII. Since 1823 he had refused suggestions from Talleyrand, Laffitte and his own son that he conspire against the King.[159] As his ball of 31 May had shown, his ambitions had been directed towards advancing the Orléans family within the Bourbon dynastic system.

Even in such a tense summer as 1830 his most trusted aides-de-camp, like other members of the élite, were away in the country with their families – proof that he was not contemplating political action. The Orléans themselves were at Neuilly. On 25 July the Duke and his son (but not the Duchess) dined with the Duc de Bourbon and the Baronne de Feuchères at Saint-Leu.[160] On the morning of 26 July, he entered his wife's boudoir as she was combing her hair, put the *Moniteur* on her dressing-table and cried: *Eh bien ma chère, c'est fait. Voilà le coup d'état!*[161] On 26 July Molé and the Comte d'Houdetot came to dinner and told of the consternation in Paris. On 27 July the park gates at Neuilly were closed. On the nights of 27, 28 and 29 July, Orléans slept in different pavilions in the park or on the other side of Paris at the château of Le Raincy which he had repurchased in 1819 – abandoning his family out of fear for his own safety and of an attempt by royal troops to take him to Saint-Cloud.[162] On the 28th Orléans thought the King would win.[163] On 29 and 30 July messengers started arriving at Neuilly with news of the Parisians' victory.

Their number and variety reveals the diversity of Orléans' political and social networks. They included the Duke's children's drawing-master, Ary Scheffer, a Dutch artist with revolutionary sympathies; the Duke's librarian, a revolutionary liberal Jean Vatout; his Secrétaire des Commandements Jean Oudard, and other household officials, including the Comtes de Chabot and Jules de La Rochefoucauld, whose names indicated that Orléans was not as anti-noble as he pretended; the architect Fontaine, reporting on the physical condition of the Palais Royal as well as informing them that 'the royal party is defeated and all is over'; Anatole de Montesquiou, a former Napoleonic officer, now Chevalier d'Honneur of the Duchesse d'Orléans; Madame de Bondy; Monsieur Uginet, Contrôleur de la Maison of the Duke, a former servant of Madame de Staël; M. de Lasteyrie, son-in-law of La Fayette; the great liberal lawyer Dupin; the poet Casimir Delavigne. In conversation with these visitors the Duc, the Duchesse and Mademoiselle d'Orléans decided the future of France, to the distant sound of cannon and rifle fire, drumbeats and 'the majestic tolling of the great bell of Notre Dame'.[164]

At times the Duchesse d'Orléans said that she would prefer to save the family honour through a regency by her husband in favour of Bordeaux. 'Madame, it is too late,' Vatout replied, in the phrase of 1830.[165] On 30 July Captain Gérard, a nephew of the liberal deputy Général Comte Gérard, arrived by horse 'to say that there was no time to lose, that the assembled commission was going to proclaim my husband King, that the decision was ours to save France from anarchy, that the King could not return any more and that if he did not accept probably the Republic would be proclaimed'. The Orléans faced eternal proscription and contempt if they did not agree. The Duchess's reply suggested her ambitions. Orléans could not accept while Charles X was still at Saint-Cloud. His usurpation would bring foreigners back to France.[166]

That same day Thiers arrived, on a horse lent by a son of Maréchal Ney, with a note from Laffitte for the Duke: 'I beg M. le duc d'Orléans to hear in all confidence M. Thiers and what he is charged to say on my behalf.' Trembling with emotion, Thiers said that, to calm popular agitation, it was essential that Orléans accept the deputies' offer of the Lieutenant-Generalcy of the Kingdom. The exchange between Thiers and the Duke's sister Mademoiselle, who had always regarded the Restoration like a hunting-dog about to pounce on its prey, is famous. 'We want a new dynasty which owes its crown to us,' Thiers announced. 'My brother is not here but if Paris needs someone as a guarantee here I am. I will go to the Palais Royal,' Mademoiselle replied. Using the language of dynasticism rather than revolution, Thiers responded: 'Today you place the crown in your House.'[167]

If Laffitte was the kingmaker, Orléans was thought to be the last rallying-point able to save society from dissolution. On 30 July, Laffitte had plastered all over Paris, and printed in newspapers, the following proclamation, written by Thiers and Mignet:

> Charles X can no longer re-enter Paris: he has shed the blood of the people.
> The Republic would expose us to terrible divisions; it would cause us to quarrel with Europe.
> The Duc d'Orléans has never fought against us.
> The Duc d'Orléans was at Jemappes.
> The Duc d'Orléans has borne the tricolour colours under fire. The Duc d'Orléans alone can still wear them; we do not want any others.

The Duc d'Orléans has declared himself; he accepts the Charte as we have always desired and understood it.

It is from the French people that he will hold his crown.[168]

At the same time the deputies and journalists meeting in the Palais Bourbon and at Laffitte's house also concluded that the Duc d'Orléans was the only alternative to a republic or a second empire. Already there were cries in the streets of Paris of *Vive Napoléon!* and *Vive la République!*[169]

Much of the proclamation was untrue – Orléans had deserted the French army in 1793, and between 1800 and 1814 had begged foreign governments to employ him against it. It was a deliberate attempt by Laffitte and Thiers to compromise the Duke's relations with Charles X. They wanted him to be king more than he wanted the crown they offered.[170] According to Vatout, Laffitte had said: 'Tell the Duc d'Orléans that we have just given him the crown but he should recognise that it is not by right of birth but by the will of the people. He has granted nothing, he has received everything from the nation.'

In this crisis Orléans neither consulted, nor was consulted by, Charles X. He later excused himself on the grounds that he had not been summoned to Saint-Cloud, although the duty of a prince in time of revolution was to offer his services to the King. His decisions were based, it later appeared, on the desire to save his family from exile and his country from anarchy.[171]

Meanwhile throughout that Friday despite pressing messages from his wife, Orléans remained at Le Raincy. Finally, on the suggestion of Laffitte and Gérard, he returned to Neuilly in a carriage with Oudard. Montesquiou rode ahead. As a measure of his hesitation, halfway through his journey Orléans attempted to turn his carriage round. Montesquiou rode back and told Orléans that his wife and sister needed him, that he was necessary to save France from anarchy and the threat of a republic, that he need only be head of the government.[172] At this stage, Orléans was as malleable as Napoleon in April 1814, when the Emperor had been forbidden by his courtiers to go to Paris or try to kill himself again. He was persuaded to continue to Neuilly.

Finally in the evening of 30 July – while the royal family was still at Saint-Cloud – Orléans left his Bourbon dynastic world for the world of nationalism and revolution which he had supported so ardently in 1789–93. In the park at Neuilly he told his wife that he was 'very sad but resigned to sacrifice himself for the good of France and to go quietly to the Palais Royal to receive there the deputation'. Madame Adélaïde gave him a tricolour ribbon which he placed in his buttonhole. At 9 p.m. he rode off with his aide-de-camp M. Berthois and Jean Oudard, slipping into the Palais Royal by a side entrance shortly before midnight.[173]

That same day Saint-Cloud received further reinforcements. The Garde Royale and Gardes du Corps continued loyal to Charles X. They were joined by 300 pupils of the famous military school at Saint-Cyr, come to help defend the King. Eager to fight, they clung to the railings of the courtyard in which they were camped, crying *Vive le roi!** The fiftieth line regiment, however, deserted and went to Paris. Compared to the crowds present at mass on the previous Sunday, the palace was silent and abandoned – the Duc de Duras and the Comte Alexandre de Girardin, Premier Veneur, were among the few court officials in attendance. Throughout the day servants were packing and leaving. In the evening the kitchen staff cooked the King's dinner but refused to wash up. The Dauphin had been placed in overall command. Seeking someone to blame instead of his father, he accused Marmont of being a 'double traitor' and, violet with rage, seized his sword and placed him briefly under arrest. That night, considering Saint-Cloud indefensible and badly provisioned, the Dauphin made the fatal error of ordering a retreat. Instead of remaining to influence the political situation in Paris, at 3 a.m. on 31 July the royal family, with their households and a long baggage train, set off west towards Versailles.[174] On the night that Orléans returned to Paris, the King abandoned it.

Saturday 31 July
That morning, at Orléans' suggestion, Mortemart came to the Palais Royal. In his account of his walk through the sombre and silent streets, Mortemart stood back to pay tribute to the city:

> it was no longer Paris the model of the arts and civilisation, the object of the envy of the people of the earth. It was no longer that city brilliant with luxury, overflowing with riches and palpitating with pleasure. It was no longer that terrible Paris, thunder of war, an object of fear after being one of admiration. It was a desert of houses and piles of paving stones.[175]

It was so hot that Mortemart found Orléans lying on a mattress on the floor, in an open shirt, sweating and in a 'terrifying state of exaltation'. Twisting a madras kerchief between his hands, Orléans reportedly said:

---

* Among them was the young Georges d'Anthès, later an émigré officer in the Russian Imperial Guard, and the man who shot Pushkin.

'Duc de Mortemart, I do not know if we will ever see the King again; but if you meet him before me, make sure to tell him that I will be cut into little pieces rather than let the crown be put on my head.' If Mortemart is to be believed, at this stage Orléans wanted, for the sake of the Bourbons, to be regent for the Duc de Bordeaux.[176] He also assured Mortemart that he had been taken to Paris by force.[177]

At 10 a.m. a deputation from the Chamber of Deputies arrived in the Palais Royal, with the offer, formally read out by their leader Laffitte, of the Lieutenant-Generalcy of the Kingdom. Orléans accepted. He claimed that he had not hesitated to share the dangers of the heroic population of Paris. True to the political message carried by the battle pictures in his gallery, he announced: 'In returning to the city of Paris I wear with pleasure these glorious colours that you have again adopted and that I myself have long worn . . . A charter will henceforth be a reality.'[178] Acknowledging where power lay, Orléans then set off to visit La Fayette in the Hôtel de Ville.

Among the deputies accompanying him were Benjamin Constant and Laffitte – both in sedan chairs since they were too ill to walk or ride, and carriages could not be driven over the barricades blocking the streets. Surrounding Orléans were officers of the Garde Nationale and ahead of him revolutionaries brandishing tricolour flags. The crowds were so dense, and the barricades so numerous, that Orléans' sleek brown horse had sometimes to be raised overhead. 'Poor Clio let herself be carried like a lamb,' his ADC the Comte de Rumigny reported, 'without giving one kick of the hoof.' Rumigny and Cuvillier-Fleury, the tutor of Orléans' younger son the Duc d'Aumale, also claimed to have heard cries of *Vive le duc d'Orléans! Vive la liberté! Vive la Charte!*[179] Most observers, however, state that the crowd did not at first know who Orléans was, and when they did, particularly in the Place de Grève in front of the Hôtel de Ville and inside the building, they revealed their hostility to him as a Bourbon with jeers and cries of *A bas les Bourbons! A bas le duc d'Orléans!*[180]

Known for his exploitation of his Paris properties, and his close relations with Charles X – epitomised in the ball of 31 May 1830 – Louis-Philippe had not enjoyed popularity in Paris before July 1830. Even among the élite, he had been despised. Talleyrand's epigram on him was well known: *Ce n'est pas assez d'être quelqu'un – il faut être quelque chose.* His architect Pierre Fontaine, while acknowledging his many amiable qualities, had written in 1825: 'immense in small matters, he is distracted, indecisive and almost always mediocre in important ones.'[181]

In the crisis of 31 July 1830, however, Orléans showed himself calm and decisive. In the Salle du Trône of the Hôtel de Ville, he listened as the deputy Jean-Pons-Guillaume Viennet read out his proclamation as Lieutenant-Général du Royaume and a declaration by the liberal deputies – thereby accepting a revolutionary investiture in a revolutionary setting. Some republicans in the room gave Orléans threatening looks. However, when La Fayette, radiant with joy in the uniform of the National Guard, appeared arm in arm with Orléans on a balcony of the Hôtel de Ville, both holding a massive tricolour flag, the crowd's mood changed.[182] The right imaginative gestures at the right moment stirred them anew. Cries of *Vive la République! Vive La Fayette!* were joined, when the two men embraced in public, by those of *Vive le duc d'Orléans!* In a famous exchange on the balcony, often recalled later by those who accused Louis-Philippe of 'betraying' the July revolution, La Fayette hailed the Duc d'Orléans as 'the best of republics'. In reply Orléans expressed his support for La Fayette's call for 'a popular throne surrounded by republican institutions'.[183] Returning to the Palais Royal surrounded by a cortège of semi-naked Parisians brandishing loaded rifles and crying *Prenons garde aux jésuites!*, Orléans was cheered by the crowds in the street and at the windows.[184]

Early that morning the King and the royal family, with about 4,000 troops, had arrived at the Grand Trianon.[185] Charles X had once again started consulting Polignac and his colleagues, thereby giving what Mortemart called 'the *coup de grâce* to the dynasty'.[186] Later that afternoon Charles X and his court, alarmed by shots fired at their cortège both by the townspeople of Versailles and by local peasants, moved on to Rambouillet, forty-eight kilometres south-west of Paris, where they arrived at about 9 p.m.[187]

August 1830 was the apotheosis of the Palais Royal. Despite his lack of political experience, Louis-Philippe coolly began to issue orders by telegraph to troops and prefects and to select ministers as if accustomed to his new role. He confirmed Charles X's summons of the Chambers for 3 August. When on 1 August the Commission Municipale arrived to resign its powers to Orléans, power returned from the east of the city to the west, from the Hôtel de Ville to the Palais Royal and the Palais Bourbon. Refusing to accept the nomination as Lieutenant-Général du Royaume despatched by Charles X from Rambouillet[188] – thus severing links with the elder branch of the family – the Duke formed a new ministry consisting of Guizot, Minister of the Interior; Broglie, Minister of

Public Instruction; Molé, Foreign Minister (partly to please Molé's friend Pozzo); Comte Gérard, Minister of War; Talleyrand's friend Baron Louis, Minister of Finance, and Sébastiani, Minister of Marine.

The Palais Royal continued its double role, as focus of monarchy and revolution. Once so clean and elegant, it was now filled with the sight, sound and suffocating smell of Paris workers. When the Duchesse d'Orléans, accompanied by her sister-in-law and children covered in tricolour ribbons and travelling together in one of the new omnibuses, had rejoined her husband on 31 July, she found her palace transformed: 'the two salons of his apartment were filled with all sorts of people, the tricolour flag was flying everywhere, the windows and walls were pierced with bullet marks, there were songs and dances on the square, everywhere an air of confusion and disorder which was distressing.'[189] Although no carriages could be seen in the streets, the shops and public services had reopened by 31 July. On Sunday 1 August Parisians paraded as usual in the Tuileries and Champs Elysées, as they had one week earlier on 25 July, when white flags not tricolours had flown from public buildings.[190] Prostitutes reappeared; paving workers and the unemployed were summoned to repave the streets and demolish the barricades.[191]

Though the King at Rambouillet was surrounded by sections of his guard and artillery and devoted officers, there was to be no Bourbon 'last stand' there or, as the Duchesse de Berri wanted, in the Vendée.[192] Eighteen years later another discredited monarch who had fled a rebellious capital, the Emperor Ferdinand I of Austria, abdicated to a young prince, the future Emperor Francis Joseph, at Olmütz, on the initiative of Princes Schwarzenberg and Windischgraetz. Under their command, the Austrian army reconquered Vienna for the monarchy. However Rambouillet was not Olmütz. There were no confident commanding figures in the royal army: the Vicomte de Foucauld, who brought his loyal Paris gendarmerie out to Versailles to give a last salute to Charles X, was too low in rank. Polignac and Mortemart were weak and indecisive. Marmont was discredited and thought Rambouillet indefensible. Charles X could not be manipulated as easily as Ferdinand I. Moreover Paris was more antimonarchical than Vienna; Swiss as well as French regiments of the Garde Royale were starting to disobey or desert.[193]

Above all, so pivotal was Paris to the government of the country that Charles X's vague plans to summon the Chambers and the Corps Diplomatique to a provincial town like Blois, Tours or Saumur – some royal troops were sent on from Rambouillet to Chartres – were soon abandoned. With the loss of Paris, he felt he had lost the throne. Even Napoleon I, who had had more, and more reliable, troops, had not dared make a stand at Fontainebleau in April 1814, once he had lost Paris.[194] On 2 August Charles X and the Dauphin abdicated in favour of the King's grandson the Duc de Bordeaux.

On the same day a crowd of about 14,000 Parisians, including 600 from each of the twelve legions of the Garde Nationale, was organised and paid by Guizot and Louis-Philippe to march on Rambouillet in order to intimidate Charles X: the French army was still too disorganised, some of its officers too royalist, to act. By then he had only about 1,350 infantry and 700 cavalry around him. In reality the crowd, transported in fiacres and omnibuses from which ordinary passengers had been expelled, was chaotic and disorganised, with fewer cannon than the King's forces. However, Charles X had lost heart. At 11 p.m. on the evening of 3 August, having been assured by the government's commissioners that the crowd numbered 60,000, Charles X left Rambouillet. Hoping that the new Lieutenant-General would ensure the survival of the monarchy in the person of Henri V – the Duc de Bordeaux – the King had sent back the crown jewels and most of the court officials to Paris. Thenceforth the funeral procession of the Bourbon monarchy proceeded by slow stages towards the port of Cherbourg in Normandy.[195]

Europe still played an important part in French internal affairs, and fear of its hostility had contributed to the rejection of a republic in the 30 July proclamation. As in 1815, Russia and Britain, in the persons of Stuart and Pozzo, played the most important role. On 30 July, while ignoring the King of France, Orléans had sought the advice of the British ambassador on whether it would be prudent to go to Paris. Considering Orléans' appointment as Lieutenant-General the only way of preserving the legitimate monarchy, Stuart also told Orléans that his elevation to the throne could not be countenanced by 'any among the Powers which are parties to the treaties placing the Bourbons on the Throne'.[196] Stuart feared that the fall of the Bourbons would lead, within a few months, to war with Europe for 'the recovery of the Frontier of the Rhine'.[197] On 31 July the ambassadors met as a body in Paris, as they had in 1815–20, to consult on French internal affairs. Sources disagree as to which of them wanted to join Charles X at Trianon.[198]

In 1824 'the assembled ministers of Europe', by their presence in the royal palace, had saved the throne of King João of Portugal, who was under attack by his own son.[199] In Paris in 1830, however, perhaps due to the influence of Pozzo, some ambassadors preferred Louis-Philippe to the King. On 1 August the Duchesse d'Orléans wrote in her diary:

> After lunch on 1 August I saw Madame de Boigne who was very agitated but who assured us that Pozzo was very well disposed for my husband, that it would be urgent that he talked to him but that in his position he could not do so openly. The foreign powers would see his acceptance of the throne as a guarantee of stability.[200]

In memoirs written many years later, Madame de Boigne claims that Pozzo decided to support the Orléans only when assured that his detested fellow Corsican Sébastiani would not become Minister of Foreign Affairs. On 2 August she arranged a secret meeting in her house between Pozzo and Mademoiselle.[201]

Pozzo was frightened by the revolution. 'Our work of fifteen years', he lamented, 'has been destroyed in three days!' Indeed some Parisians saw July 1830 as a blow against Europe and as wiping out the shame of the capitulation of 31 March 1814.[202] Pozzo, however, believed that Louis-Philippe provided the best protection for Europe in this crisis, and favoured speedy recognition of the new king by other monarchs. Nicholas I had wanted Europe to unite in refusing recognition to Louis-Philippe, *l'infâme usurpateur*, and ordered all Russian subjects, and Pozzo himself, to leave Paris.[203] But Pozzo, still an independent force, refused to obey his master. Like most other ambassadors, he considered the Bourbons a lost cause. A war on their behalf would foment Jacobinism. All Pozzo could do for Charles X was to ensure his safety and that of his family. Absolute neutrality was the best policy.[204]

The Chambers had reopened on 3 August and debated changes to the Charte and the offer of the crown, on the grounds that the throne was 'vacant', to Orléans. Deputies wore plain dark tailcoats, not, as hitherto, uniforms embroidered with silver fleurs-de-lys. Tricolour flags were everywhere; at the same time Sémonville, *ce vieux pilote de révolutions*, had draped the president's desk in the Chamber of Peers with the captured Austrian flags, which since the fall of the Empire he had hidden in the attics of the Luxembourg Palace (where, no doubt, trophies of the Restoration now replaced them).[205] The deputies passed reforms which included the abolition of the peerages created by Charles X and of the law of the double vote, and, by lowering the property qualification, the extension of the franchise from 200,000 to about 300,000 men. Censorship was never to be restored. The two Chambers would henceforth share the legislative initiative with the crown. The age of eligibility was lowered to thirty.

On 7 August, having made over his entire private fortune to his children (so that it would not revert to the crown), Louis-Philippe accepted the French throne from a group of deputies headed by Laffitte, in the Galerie des Batailles in the Palais Royal.[206] The new monarchy was to be a conditional monarchy, as had existed in 1791–2 and as Talleyrand had desired in April 1814. The King was not King of France and Navarre, ruling by divine right, but King 'of the French', freely called to the throne on condition that he swore to the Charte. To emphasise the break with the past, he took the title of Louis-Philippe I rather than Philippe VII.[207]

Meanwhile the British ambassador had been making a last attempt to save the Bourbons. He later tried to justify his interference, on his own initiative, in French internal affairs by writing to his Foreign Secretary that, 'having been accredited to the last Princes of the Royal Family, I had not been at liberty to abandon their interests and those of their descendants.'[208] On 1 August, when Charles X asked for advice, Stuart told him to put his own personal safety and that of the royal family first, and tried to help him obtain money from James de Rothschild.[209] Thereafter Stuart remained in secret communication with Charles X via a confidential agent called Mr Ivers and the Premier Veneur, the Comte de Girardin, and with Louis-Philippe via, among others, the Princesse de Vaudémont.[210] He admitted that Charles X was so unpopular in Paris that the proclamation of his confirmation of Orléans as Lieutenant-General would be 'fatal to monarchy in France'.[211] However, on his own initiative, but with the knowledge of Louis-Philippe, who also used Stuart as a channel of communication with Charles X, on 6 August Stuart sent an attaché Colonel John Caradoc, lover of the Princess Bagration, known as *le beau Caradoc*, to Charles X. Caradoc's message was that the King was on no account to 'carry the Duc de Bordeaux out of the country'; Stuart referred to the necessity of 'placing his life in danger for the sake of preserving his right to the crown'. Stuart hoped that Bordeaux could remain at Rambouillet or Rosny under his mother's care. The British ambassador tried harder than Charles X to maintain legitimacy in France.[212]

Between 7 and 9 August Charles X hesitated. There was no one, he feared, to whom he could entrust Bordeaux. The boy's mother the Duchesse de Berri would never consent to abandon her child, and Louis-Philippe would never have accepted her presence beside him.[213] Moreover Louis-Philippe may not have been serious about preserving the throne for Bordeaux. Already on 2 August he and his wife had discussed the matter with Chateaubriand, whom they found 'very dry and very recalcitrant; he speaks and dreams only of the Duc de Bordeaux. We replied that it was the dearest wish of our hearts but we very much feared that at this moment it would be very difficult to realise.'[214] Charles X, grateful for Stuart's interest, still in a state of shock at the revolution he had provoked, unburdened himself to Caradoc more than to most of his French advisers. Like some émigrés in the 1790s, he found comfort in conspiracy theories. In tears at his cold reception in the royalist west of France, he said that he had 'certain proofs of the long previous organisation of all that had happened and that the same events would have taken place a short time later had his *ordonnances* never appeared'.[215] On the morning of 16 August, with a last salute from faithful gardes du corps, the entire royal family, with Bordeaux, embarked from Cherbourg for exile in England.

On 7 August in the Chamber of Peers, determined to give unity to his life, Chateaubriand had made one of his great speeches:

> *Inutile Cassandre, j'ai assez fatigué le trône et la patrie de mes avertissements dédaignés; il ne me reste qu'à m'asseoir sur les débris que j'ai tant de fois prédit. Je reconnais au malheur toutes sortes de puissance, excepté celle de me délier de mes serments de fidélité.*

Thenceforth, despite Charles X's dislike, Chateaubriand would be the most celebrated leader of the legitimist opposition to Louis-Philippe. Even among the 250 deputies who attended the meetings of the Chamber – most royalists stayed away – many were secretly horrified and regretted Louis-Philippe's usurpation.[216]

At the time some republicans and liberals, including La Fayette, were dismayed that there was not a new revolutionary constitution like that of 1791, based on the extension of the elective principle to most institutions in France.[217] Students demonstrated outside the Chamber of Deputies with cries of *Vive la République!* until they were dispersed by the people and the National Guard.[218] Some thought of killing Louis-Philippe. On 7 August 1830 Godefroy Cavaignac, who had taken part in the attack on the Louvre and was son of a Republican *conventionnel*, had said to the Orleanist deputy Viennet: '*Eh bien!* . . . So you are going to give us a king! What infamy! You are betraying the people of whom you are the representatives, you are stealing the revolution from us.'[219] In reality at this stage most French people still wanted a monarchy.

On 9 August Louis-Philippe and his two eldest sons, the Ducs d'Orléans (as Chartres had become) and de Nemours, arrived at the Palais Bourbon to cries of *Vive le duc d'Orléans!* Tricolour flags were draped from columns beside the throne; as at the Restoration, red velvet and green baize hangings masked the wall paintings of the fallen regime.[220] It was a non-Catholic and non-military inauguration. The King, his sons, their aides-de-camp and four marshals were the only men in uniform. In a black tailcoat Casimir Périer, President of the Chamber, read the declaration calling the Duc d'Orléans to the throne. After accepting the title of King and swearing to observe the Charte of 1830, Louis-Philippe received the sceptre from Marshal Oudinot, the hand of justice from Marshal Molitor, the crown from Marshal Macdonald and the sword from Marshal Mortier. The Marseillaise was played outside. The royal party then returned to the Palais Royal.[221]

If there was no radical change to the constitution, the July revolution was accompanied, to a greater extent than the two restorations, by a transformation of government personnel. Throughout France, in contrast to 1815, the royal administration collapsed with little resistance: many officials and officers resigned rather than dishonour themselves by serving the usurper. The field for place-seekers was wide open. As Viennet wrote at the time: 'The hunt for jobs has begun. The quarry is in sight.' In one week that August, so Benjamin Constant complained, 7,000 people came to ask him for a job.[222] He himself, as the patron of French liberalism, was rewarded with the newly invented post of President of the Conseil d'Etat. Stendhal, a Bonapartist who had neither been to court nor held an official position since 1814, received, with the support of the Foreign Minister Molé and of his mistress Madame de Castellane, the post of Consul-General in Trieste. Throughout France royalist mayors, generals and magistrates were dismissed and replaced by liberals. Eighty-two out of eighty-six prefects, and 244 out of 277 sous-préfets were replaced.[223]

Among the many former Bonapartists who flocked to the Palais Royal in search of a job was the Comte de Flahaut. His letters of 9 and 14 August to his wife, who was spending the summer with their daughters in England, describe 'the extraordinary scenes' he saw there:

> The beautiful Hall and stairs of the Palais Royal full of a motley assembly of National Guards from all parts of France dressed in all sorts of ways and all colours and recalling the scenes of the Revolution one has heard of . . . you can have no conception what horrid bad company one meets at the Palais Royal. All the intrigants of all regimes flock there. They are so bad that La

Grange and Forbin Janson might be reckoned pure and immaculate. It has so disgusted me that I have only been there once. There have been some dinners but I have not been asked. The King lowers himself a great deal by his shaking of hands with every one and his *embrassades*: it does not add to his popularity and takes away from the respect so necessary to a crowned head and even to a President of a Republic. He must not forget that he does not owe his throne to popular enthusiasm and has not the qualities that can excite it – there are 100 times more people who would have been for Napoleon II but all reasonable men have given up their sentiment and affections to secure this country a wise and liberal government under a tried Prince. He is a King crowned by reason and should act the part.

When he pressed La Fayette to his heart on the palace balcony, as he often did, 'even the common people laugh at it. The fact is adhesion to his Government is general. Bonapartists, republicans, moderate Royalists and in short the whole of France except a few Ultras and Courtiers support cordially his Government and therefore he has advances to make to no one.'[224]

Two or three evenings a week that summer the Palais Royal was open to visitors. While bands in the courtyard played the Marseillaise, to shouts of *Vive le roi! Vive la reine! Vive l'Egalité!*, Louis-Philippe and Marie Amélie would appear on the balconies of their palace, the cheering on both the courtyard and the garden sides obliging them to go from balcony to balcony throughout the evening.[225] At each appearance they would be greeted by thunderous applause and the sound of the Marseillaise – or 1830's answer to it, *La Parisienne*. Written during the revolution by Casimir Delavigne, the friend of Louis-Philippe, set to music by Auber, it was sung at the reopening of the Opera on 4 August by the actor Adolphe Nourrit, dressed as a national guard and brandishing a tricolour flag:

Soudain Paris dans sa mémoire
A retrouvé son cri de gloire:
'En avant marchons,
Contre leurs canons,
A travers le fer,
Le feu des bataillons,
Courons à la victoire!'[226]

Sometimes Louis-Philippe sang the Marseillaise with the crowds below so heartily that his voice gave out and all he could do was beat time to the music. Eager to be all things to all men, above all to be different from Charles X, the new King allowed journalists and deputies to take him by the buttonhole and lead him to a window for a private talk. He shook men by the hand without distinction, held open house twice a week with sixty to eighty people to dinner and more coming in afterwards, called national guards his *camarades*, and to the despair of his wife and sister, walked through the streets of Paris with only one attendant.[227] Many more Parisians, Madame de Flahaut pointed out, showed their respect by raising their hats to him than they had to Charles X.[228] However, like her husband, many Frenchmen found the new King's lack of dignity and distance more distasteful even than his usurpation.[229] According to Victor Cousin, the King was desolated that he could not be *tutoyé*. Alfred de Vigny wrote that he had the features of Louis XIV and the manners of a *paysan parvenu*.[230]

On 1 August Louis-Philippe had abolished all departments of the enormous 3,000-strong Maison du Roi, discharging 300 Gentilshommes de la Chambre, the Bouche du Roi and so on. On 11 August, after the Maison Civile and the Maison Militaire, even the Garde Royale was disbanded: Louis-Philippe would be guarded solely by the National Guard and troops of the line. On 29 August 1830 he received 'the loudest cheers' at a great review, and distribution of tricolour flags to 50,000 national guards, on the Champ de Mars. In the following year he was still being cheered on the streets, on the way to the opera, even in the Faubourg Saint-Antoine.[231] The National Guard, of whom 3,500 were now on duty every day, was the main armed force in the city and the pillar of the July monarchy. Balzac, about to make his name as a novelist, wrote: 'for the present there is only one living thing in Paris. It is the National Guard! Everywhere blue, red uniforms, *pompons*, *aigrettes*, shackos, spurs, sabres.'[232]

Finally in February 1831, at the proposal of Laffitte – the enemy of the Bourbons since 1815, who had been appointed Président du Conseil the previous November – even the fleurs-de-lys themselves were removed from the King's and the government's coat of arms (although they remain to this day in the arms of the city of Paris). To his disgust the architect Fontaine had to organise their removal from all government buildings and churches in Paris, including the Tuileries, the Louvre and the Palais Royal. They were even excised from the interior of the Chapelle Expiatoire.[233] For a time the smell from the fresh plaster covering the old fleurs-de-lys on the staircase of the Palais Royal was strong enough to make guests feel ill.[234]

*

In 1789, from the day the Bastille was stormed and royal officials and officers were murdered, most foreigners and many Frenchmen had regarded that revolution with horror. The sight and sound of crowds of hitherto good-natured men and women laughing and applauding as heads were paraded through the streets on pikes, had outraged the German Parisian, Baron von Wolzogen. He denounced 'the ferocious and pitiless nature of this people, its vile sentiments and devastating fury'.[235] Partly for this reason the 1789 revolution had little immediate effect outside France, or territories conquered by the French army, except to strengthen both government and popular conservatism.

After the July revolution, however, despite or perhaps because of the number of people killed in the fighting, there was little pointless bloodshed. The defusion of class tension and anti-noble feeling was apparent. When stopped by a crowd as she was leaving Paris in a carriage from which she had refused to efface the royal coat of arms, the Duchesse de Guiche, a classical beauty married to the Premier Ecuyer of the Dauphin, 'courageously, and with a calm dignity, addressed the angry crowd, explained her sentiments and feelings to them in a few brief words, and they, won by her beauty and noble bearing, even perhaps still more by her courage . . . cheered her and suffered the carriage to proceed unmolested'.[236] Contemporaries did not know which to admire more in the July revolution, its speed, its heroism or its moderation. Flahaut praised 'the admirable behaviour of the Parisians'.[237] The Comte d'Orsay, brother of the Duchesse de Guiche, wrote: 'here everything is *digne et noble*, the great people feels its power. Every man feels himself raised in his own eyes.'[238] The young composer Berlioz, although he was too busy finishing a cantata on the death of Sardanapalus to join in the fighting, thought the people of Paris 'sublime'. Even Chateaubriand, in his speech of 7 August in the Chamber of Peers, said that no 'defence' had been more heroic or 'legitimate' than that of the people of Paris.[239]

In a move of great importance for the acceptance of the regime in Europe, James de Rothschild, who had trusted Polignac's assurances that there would be no *coup d'état*, rallied to Louis-Philippe, offering a loan of 60 million as early as 2 August, although he also provided Charles X with 600,000 francs in gold.[240] His nephew Lionel found the streets of Paris

> crowded with persons, all laughing and as gay as if they had come from some dance, in the squares and open places all the Garde Nationale and Royal Troops who had given up their arms marching and being cheered by people,

in every corner the three-coloured flags and every person with a red, blue and white cockade . . . Never was there a more glorious week for France, this people have behaved in a way that will be admired by every person and will make them be reckoned now among the first of nations.[241]

Paris in 1830, like St Petersburg in 1917, was a city acting on its own, independent of its state. Indeed in 1830 it functioned as the motor and magnet of Europe to a greater degree than in 1789. La Fayette did not exaggerate when he declared in the Chamber of Deputies: 'the electric commotion of the July revolution has been felt throughout the whole world.' He hoped that it would achieve the liberation of Europe.[242]

It was indeed an event in which many foreigners took part. Mr Donaldson of the London Dispensary, Place Vendôme, for example, helped storm both the barracks of the Swiss Guard in the rue de Babylone and the Tuileries palace.[243] Sir John Bowring brought to Paris the congratulations of radical societies of London and Manchester.[244] At meetings in Glasgow and London, the tricolour was displayed, and messages of support and congratulation sent to Parisians. By encouraging both radical hopes and conservative fears, the July revolution in Paris had a certain influence on the passage of the Reform Bill of 1832 in London.[245] Even Palmerston admired the Parisians. He wrote to Flahaut:

> it is the triumph of the Liberal over the despotic principle and Spain, Portugal and even Germany must sooner or later feel the effects of the Crisis. In the Mean time the French people have really done themselves immortal Honour and have acted not only like heroes but like Philosophers. Their Moderation and Sobriety in Success is still more striking . . . There cannot be more striking Proof of the good consequences of general Instruction and a Diffusion of political Information by means of a free Press and a popular and Representative system, than the contrast between the events of the present day and those of the Revolution of Louis 16.[246]

Until 1834, like Casimir Périer, Talleyrand, Flahaut and the King, Palmerston would pursue that policy of *entente cordiale* – a phrase first used in these years – between the two strongest nations in Europe, which they considered the best guarantee both of their own interests and of the peace of Europe. Flahaut wrote to his wife: 'let France and England go finally hand in hand.'[247] More pro-British than either Louis XVIII or Charles X, Louis-Philippe called the British alliance 'the foundation', 'the arch of the vault'.[248] A monument to this state of union was the decision taken in 1832 for each country's national library to receive a copy of the books printed in the other. Talleyrand wrote to his friend Lord Holland: '*c'est du petit bien* but after all it is something which contributes to unite us further.'[249]

With his desire 'to be employed in anything that can contribute to good intelligence, peace and harmony between this country and England', Flahaut hoped to be ambassador in London. However he faced the problem of what he called 'my peculiar situation', the clash between his rank as a French lieutenant-general and his nationality as a denizen of Scotland. That talent-pool of European officers and courtiers, who had previously switched services as they wished, now found their movements hampered by increasing nationalism. William IV objected that 'Flahaut has become a British subject and cannot therefore represent a foreign Sovereign at the Court of St James's.'[250] Though Flahaut was employed on a temporary mission in November 1830 on the grounds of his 'intimacy with the principal members of the new Cabinet', the permanent embassy was given to Talleyrand, at the personal insistence of Louis-Philippe who considered him indispensable for convincing Europe that the July monarchy wanted peace. Talleyrand's carriage was greeted in the streets of London with cries of 'Louis-Philippe for ever! No Charles Xth!'[251]

Talleyrand, who had quarrelled with Flahaut over the appointment, later said that, knowing the country so well, Flahaut would have been the perfect French ambassador to Great Britain, above all because he could equally well have been the perfect British ambassador to France. Their quarrel was inflamed by their women. The Comtesse de Flahaut wrote that the Duchesse de Dino smiled at her 'in a way that shows she would like to kill me on the spot. I despise her from the bottom of my heart.' For Flahaut she was 'a lying little devil'.[252] Talleyrand wrote to Madame de Vaudémont that Madame de Flahaut was detested in London and that her husband was not considered sufficiently important to be an ambassador.[253]

After brief missions to Berlin and London, Flahaut resumed his military career, attached to the staff of the new Duc d'Orléans.[254] When she returned to Paris, Madame de Flahaut became one of the most elegant hostesses of the new regime, receiving 'few but the violent Orleanists, the ministers and some of Flahaut's greatest friends from all parties'. She was particularly kind to her husband's young illegitimate son Auguste Demorny, whose recent admission into the French army had been helped by his record as an *héros de juillet*.[255] Guests admired the skill with which, at her soirees, 'certain ladies' manoeuvred for the attention of the handsome, charming heir to the throne, the Duc d'Orléans.[256]

When news of the July revolution reached Russia, Pushkin remarked that Russia needed one too: in their exile in Siberia Decembrist conspirators sang the Marseillaise 'full of hope for a better future for Europe'.[257] Even the fishermen on Heligoland shouted for joy, feeling that the July revolution was a victory for the poor. The ladies of Hamburg wore tricolour cockades to the opera. The Marseillaise was sung 'everywhere'.[258] Riots or insurrections inspired by the revolution in Paris broke out in Leipzig, much of the Rhineland, and Brunswick.* Because of the fears and hopes inspired by the revolution in Paris, new liberal constitutions were granted by the King of Saxony in 1831, by the Duke of Brunswick in 1832 and by the King of Hanover in 1833. The Italian peninsula was also affected: in February 1831 the duchies of Modena and Parma, and the city of Bologna in the Papal States, temporarily expelled their legitimate rulers.[259]

The most important mimic revolutions, however, occurred in Brussels and Warsaw. Like Charles X, King William I of the Netherlands believed that his royal authority preceded and was independent of the constitution; he too had been trying to restrict the power and freedom of the parliament and the press – already much inferior to what was allowed in France.[260] Moreover, for reasons both religious and economic, the Belgian half of the Netherlands had long been discontented with Dutch predominance. In 1787 revolution in Brussels had preceded that in Paris; in 1830 Brussels followed Paris. On 25 August at the Théâtre de la Monnaie, the audience was electrified by a song from *La Muette de Portici*, an opera by Auber, with words by Germain Delavigne and Eugène Scribe, which had been put on in honour of King William I's fifty-ninth birthday. The opera had taken Paris by storm when it opened on 29 February 1828: Mlle Noblet had been the mute heroine Fenella, who finally throws herself into a stream of molten lava. Rossini's *Il Viaggio a Reims*, written to celebrate Charles X's coronation in 1825, had been specifically European and royalist in intention, and ended with five different national anthems.[261]† In

---

* The Duke of Brunswick went into exile in Paris, where he became an aficionado of public executions.

† Concerning a party of foreigners hoping to see the coronation in Reims, it featured a Polish marquise, a French countess, a Tyrolean innkeeper, an Italian poetess, an English lord, a German baron, a Russian general, a Spanish grandee and a Greek orphan.

contrast, *La Muette de Portici*, about Masaniello's revolt against foreign
domination in Naples in 1647, though critical of revolutionaries, contained a paean to nationalism whose music had some of the rhythm of the
Marseillaise:

> *Amour sacré de la patrie!*
> *Rends-nous l'audace et la fierté!*
> *A mon pays je dois la vie,*
> *Elle me devra la liberté.*

Having reopened the Paris opera house after the July revolution,[262] it
now became the first opera to start a revolution. The performance over,
the audience, which may have included some Parisians and have been
organised, burst into shouts of *Vive le duc d'Orléans! Vive la France! Vive
Napoléon!* Riots broke out in the streets of Brussels. The weakness and
incompetence of Dutch reaction led to an armed uprising, soon joined
by volunteers from Paris in units bearing the names the Légion Belge de
Paris, the Légion Gallo-Belge and the Légion Belge-parisienne. On 4
October 1830 Belgian independence was declared.[263]

Many French politicians, including Talleyrand, the Foreign Minister
Sébastiani, Laffitte and for a time Flahaut, hoped for the 'reunion' of all
or part of Belgium to France.[264] Indeed Belgium was then so Francophile
that on 4 February 1831 the second son of Louis-Philippe, the Duc de
Nemours, was elected King by the Belgian National Congress. However,
in a famous statement, the conference of ambassadors meeting in
London declared that, in deciding Belgium's future, the tranquillity and
security of the European community limited the rights of individual
states.[265] Putting the peace of Europe before French nationalism and his
own dynasty, Louis-Philippe refused the offer: in June 1831 the Belgian
throne went, by agreement with the great powers of Europe, to Prince
Leopold of Saxe-Coburg. (Regarded by Louis-Philippe as the best way of
avoiding the Prince of Orange, he later married the King's eldest daughter Louise-Marie.) French troops under Orléans, advised by Flahaut,
besieged Dutch forces in Antwerp on behalf of Belgium from 19
November 1832 until it capitulated on 23 December. In 1839 the principle of permanent Belgian neutrality, already affirmed in 1831, was again
guaranteed by the great powers of Europe.[266]

Belgian neutrality gave France a friendly instead of a hostile neighbour on its northern frontier. Flahaut considered that it 'is as good if
not better than the reunion for it guarantees our North Eastern frontier
and gives us a defence . . . on which at so much cost the Duke of

Wellington had built a ring of hostile fortresses'.[267] Belgium had become part of France's defences. Already in 1830 France was prepared to go to war, as France and Britain eventually would in 1914, if the Prussian army entered Belgium.[268]

On 29 November 1830, three months after the rising in Brussels, an insurrection against Russia – originally a military coup – broke out in Warsaw. More than any other event in Polish history, it was inspired by events in Paris – as well as by Polish soldiers' fears that they would be sent to suppress the Belgian revolution. On 25 January 1831 Nicholas I was dethroned as King of Poland. Russian troops invaded. In the eighteenth and twentieth centuries, even in 1814, the fate of Poland had been regarded in Paris with the same relative indifference that prevailed in other European capitals. In 1830, however, just as many Poles looked to Paris, so many Parisians cried *A Varsovie!* Poland had a magic which even the liberation of Greece or Italy lacked. Not only did it profit from the general nineteenth-century symbiosis that existed between Paris and Europe, not only was its timing – four months after, and partly inspired by, the July revolution – opportune; Poland also appealed to France because of a shared Catholicism, liberal culture and hostility to tsarist autocracy. Alive, too, in people's memories was a sense of the humiliation that France had suffered by the partition of Poland in 1772 and, above all, the bravery of the thousands of Polish soldiers serving in the French army since 1795, many of whom had settled in Paris.[269]

Horace Vernet painted a picture of *Le Prométhée polonais*, a dying Polish soldier devoured by a Russian imperial eagle. Béranger, Musset, Lamartine and Hugo, among many others, wrote poems in honour of the Polish uprising. Casimir Delavigne composed *La Varsovienne* as a sister song to *La Parisienne*. (It has been the official march of the Polish army since 1918.) The fashionable Catholic priest and writer Lamennais wrote an *Hymne à la Pologne*. *Le National* urged a war on the Holy Alliance by France for the sake of Poland. La Fayette, who had resigned as commander of the National Guard in December 1830 and gone into opposition in order to favour a more radical constitution, made speeches in the Chamber of Deputies in favour of helping Poland. In January 1831 he helped form a Comité Polonais with Alexandre de Laborde, Odilon Barrot and other prominent liberals and Bonapartists, to raise funds and publicise the cause.[270] Chateaubriand praised 'this heroic Poland, advance guard of France'.[271] However, Warsaw was stormed by Russian troops on 8 September 1831: the separate Polish parliament and army were abolished.

After the fall of Warsaw, so Louis-Philippe complained, Poles fell on France like hailstones.[272] France was more hospitable than any other European country to Polish refugees – as it was to all refugees and exiles, except the Bonapartes. Every year in its address to the throne, the Chamber of Deputies inserted a phrase about the rights of Poland, guaranteed at the Congress of Vienna. Despite police efforts to refuse Poles *permis de séjour* in Paris, and to keep them in the provinces, Paris received about 4,000 Polish refugees, and acquired a new role, as capital of Poland in exile.[273] Too few Poles spoke English for London, Europe's other liberal metropolis, to be a viable alternative. The Poles soon had their own newspapers,* library,† schools, charities, church (Saint-Roch, succeeded in 1844 by the Eglise de l'Assomption) and cemetery (at Montmorency). Left-wing Poles in the Polish Democratic Society established an organisation known as *Centralizacja* at Versailles. However the focus of Polish diplomacy and society, the seat of the Association of National Unity and of the Institut de Demoiselles Polonaises, would be the residence of Prince Adam Czartoryski, a former foreign minister of Alexander I and president of the Polish 'national government' in 1831: the Hôtel Lambert at the eastern end of the Ile Saint-Louis.

Prince Czartoryski knew Paris from many visits since 1814, and his wife preferred it to London. Supported by the income of the remaining Czartoryski estates, and by donations from French and British sympathisers, the Polish government in exile in the Hôtel Lambert was able, for a time, to play a part in European diplomacy. It maintained its own agencies in London, Rome, Belgrade, Constantinople and the Caucasus.[274] From their constant references to the resurrection of the fatherland, its members were called 'the resurrected'.

One Polish Parisian, and protégé of the Czartoryski family, was Chopin. Born in Warsaw in 1810, of a French father who had left for Poland in 1787, he had disliked Vienna when he lived there in 1829–31: most Viennese preferred waltzes to his own music. Paris, however, where he arrived at the age of twenty-one in 1831 and lived until his death in 1849, not only had 'the best musicians and the best opera in the world', but was also a paradise of freedom: 'nobody cares what anyone else does.' Soon he was one of the most admired musicians in the city.[275]

---

* For example *Le Polonais. Journal des intérêts de la Pologne*, founded in Paris in 1833.

† Founded by Count Ladislaus Zamoyski it has been situated, since 1856, at his former house, 6 quai d'Orléans on the Ile Saint-Louis.

1. Horace Vernet. *Défense de la Barrière de Clichy, 30 mars 1814* (1822). Sword in hand, Maréchal Moncey is directing the defence of Paris by troops and national guards, including a Polish lancer serving in the French army (*left*). In reality the National Guard was unenthusiastic, if not disloyal. Commissioned by the famous goldsmith J.B.C. Odiot, who is shown in the centre talking to the marshal, as an example of Napoleonic propaganda, this picture was refused by the salon of 1822.

2. Jean Zippel. *The entry of the allied troops into Paris, 31 March 1814* (1815). On the Boulevard Saint-Denis, by an arch erected in honour of Louis XIV, Parisians are greeting Tsar Alexander I, flanked by the Austrian commander Prince Schwarzenberg (in white) and King Frederick William III of Prussia, with cries of *Vive Alexandre! Vivent les Bourbons! A bas le Corse!* As many witnesses noticed, women, hostile to the Emperor whose wars had deprived them of their men, were particularly enthusiastic in cheering his conquerors.

3. A. T. Vergnaux. *The entry of the Comte d'Artois into Paris, 12 April 1814.* The prince, who had not seen Paris since 1789, is crossing the Pont au Change to hear a Te Deum in Notre Dame. In the background is the Louvre. Artois wears the uniform of the Paris National Guard, by which he was escorted on this occasion, and which he subsequently reviewed every 12 April until its dissolution, on his orders, in 1827. To make the day appear entirely French, the foreign soldiers occupying Paris, without whom the prince would not have been there, were kept well away.

4. *The despair of the maker of wooden legs.* This royalist cartoon emphasises that there would be no more mutilated soldiers in need of wooden legs, after the fall of Napoleon I and the return of Louis XVIII.

5. Baron Gérard. *Pozzo di Borgo.* The earliest and most implacable enemy of Napoleon, since their childhood on Corsica, Pozzo was a force in European politics in his own right. While he was serving as Russian ambassador in Paris after Napoleon's fall, from 1814 to 1833, it was said that France had exchanged the government of one Corsican for that of another.

6. Henri-Joseph Fradelle. *Comte de Flahaut.* Flahaut, a favourite ADC of Napoleon I, and adviser to Napoleon III, is painted in Holland House in Kensington, home of the Emperor's Whig admirers Lord and Lady Holland, where Flahaut stayed after Waterloo. A living link between France and Britain, he married a Scottish heiress and in 1860–2 served as French ambassador in London. He was nevertheless an embodiment of French nationalism, as his enemy Pozzo was of European union.

7. Martinet. *Louis XVIII in the Tuileries gardens, 8 July 1815*. Louis XVIII mingles with crowds in front of his palace on the day of his return to Paris after the Hundred Days. Again, to emphasise their royalism, women are represented with unusual prominence.

8. Georges-Jacques Gatine. *Le premier pas d'un jeune Officier Cosaque au Palais Royal* (1814). Russian officers are ogling Paris prostitutes in their principal hunting-ground. A sequel to this print shows the officers visiting a pharmacy to buy a cure for venereal disease.

9. William Wyld. *The Palais Royal* (c. 1835). The Palais Royal was known as the Paris of Paris. From the 1780s to the 1830s its cafés, shops and brothels were the most famous in Europe. They had the reputation of supplying all the necessities and all the luxuries of life, as well as every sensual gratification.

10. *Les Habits retournés* (1814). Disloyal Napoleonic officials, including the former Archi-Chancelier de l'Empire Cambacérès on the far right, are shown literally turning their coats, in order to display the blue and silver colours of the King's livery instead of the green and gold of the Emperor's.

11. Martinet. *Véry Frères* (1815). During the allied occupation, three British visitors leave the most fashionable restaurant in Paris, in the Palais Royal, praising the fare in drunken tones, watched by an elegant and scornful French waiter.

12. Carle Vernet. *The English in Paris in 1815*. Parisian distaste for English faces, fashions and manners is reflected in this cartoon of English visitors to the Louvre.

13. Anon. *Scene in the Café des Mille Colonnes*. The cashier, known as *la belle limonadière*, presides over this famous café in the Palais Royal, seated on the former throne of King Jerome-Napoleon of Westphalia.

14. Eugène Isabey. *Princess Bagration*. This beautiful, witty widow of a Russian general, and great-niece of Prince Potemkin, had a soft grace of manner which few men could resist. She resided principally in Paris from 1815 until her death in 1857, married John Caradoc, a British Parisian fifteen years younger than herself, in 1830 and was said never to miss a session of the Chamber of Deputies.

15. René Berthon. *Lady Morgan* (1819). One of many portraits commissioned to commemorate the sitter's stay in Paris: the Irish writer is painted sitting in a fashionable neo-Gothic library in Paris, dressed in Paris fashion, one arm resting on the manuscript of her book on France, published in 1818.

16. Louise Cochelet. *View of the house of Queen Hortense* (1811). In this house near the Boulevard des Italiens, in 1814–15, the Queen and her friends discussed Napoleon's return from Elba. The house was later bought by Salomon de Rothschild.

17. H. Thierry. *Madame d'Osmond in her* hôtel (*c.* 1820). One of the richest heiresses in France, Mlle Destillière had married the impoverished Marquis d'Osmond in 1818. Her house, near the present-day Opera, was one of many buildings demolished during the remodelling of Paris by Napoleon III in the 1850s.

18. Robert Batty. *The King passing in front of the Chamber of Deputies* (1819). Louis XVIII's afternoon drives in or around Paris, with a heavy military escort, enabled him to test Parisians' feelings and to show them that he was well enough to leave his palace. Louis XVIII, in contrast to his brother Charles X, always selected ministers who commanded a majority in the Chamber of Deputies.

19. Achille Deverria. *Chateaubriand* (1831). Both a literary genius and a successful politician and diplomat, Chateaubriand was the principal model for younger writers of the Romantic generations.

20. Anon. *The Château de Saint-Ouen* (*c.* 1823). Saint-Ouen, at the gates of Paris, was built in 1820–2 by Louis XVIII to commemorate the Declaration promising a liberal constitution, which he had issued from the previous house on its site on 2 May 1814, the day before he entered the capital. He presented the château, with a commemorative picture and inscription, to his last attachment Madame du Cayla. The King is probably in the carriage driving in front of the château.

21. N.-L.-F. Gosse. *Tu revis en lui* (1820). The Duchesse de Berri is leaning on a bust of her assassinated husband the Duc de Berri, and pointing to the cradle offered by the city of Paris, containing her son the Duc de Bordeaux, *l'enfant du miracle*, born on 29 September 1820, seven months after his father's assassination.

22. Alphonse-Jacques Testard. *The Château de Saint-Cloud* (1838). With lodgings for 45 courtiers and 600 staff, stabling for 237 horses and an enormous park overlooking Paris, Saint-Cloud was the principal country residence of French monarchs between 1802 and its destruction in 1870 during the Franco-Prussian war. Its ruins were demolished in 1891.

23. Baron Lejeune. *Entry of Charles X into Paris at the Barrière du Trône, 6 June 1825*. On his return to Paris after his coronation at Reims, the King is greeted by the Corps Municipal. Despite the splendour of the procession, there was silence in the streets, owing to his government's unpopularity.

24. François-Joseph Heim. *Charles X distributing prizes to artists in the Louvre, 3 January 1825.* On the left of the King are two of the principal agents of the monarchy's artistic policy, his aide-de-camp the Directeur-Général des Beaux-Arts Vicomte Sosthènes de La Rochefoucauld, and the Comte de Forbin Directeur of the Louvre. Among the artists shown are, behind La Rochefoucauld, his protégé Rossini; Isabey is on the left wearing glasses; the miniature painter and favourite of Louis XVIII, Madame de Mirbel, is in the foreground, next to the sculptor Bosio. The pictures hanging in the salon show scenes from French royal history. Many hoped that under Charles X the monarchy would resume the role, as principal patron of the arts, which it had played under Louis XIV.

25. Jean-Louis Bézard. *The Fall of the Louvre, 29 July 1830* (1832). Fearing a repetition of the massacre of Swiss guards defending the Tuileries on 10 August 1792, many Swiss soldiers of the Garde Royale fled from the Louvre during the attack on the afternoon of 29 July.

26. Eugène Lami. *A Barricade on 28–29 July*. Over 4,000 such barricades were constructed during the July revolution, to prevent the movement of royal troops. The horse on the right can only pass with difficulty. Despite a heatwave, some bourgeois fighters kept on their tailcoats and top hats.

27. E. F. Féron. *Louis-Philippe arriving at the Hôtel de Ville, 31 July 1830* (1837). The ambiguity of Orléans' position during the July revolution, both cheered and jeered by Paris crowds, is revealed in this picture.

28. Baron Gérard. *The reading of the deputies' proclamation of the Duc d'Orléans as Lieutenant-General of the Kingdom* (1837). Orléans accepts the mandate from a revolutionary minority of deputies. Many people at this scene were revolutionaries favouring a republic. La Fayette stands behind Orléans, Casimir Périer to the right.

29. Philippe-Auguste Jeanron. *Scène de Paris* (1833). Not only were there many hungry people on the streets of Paris; despite official food subsidies, many died of hunger.

30. G.F. Ronmy. *Louis-Philippe and his family at Neuilly* (1822). Neuilly was the favourite country residence of the Orléans from 1818 until it was burnt by revolutionaries in 1848.

31. Eugène Guérard. *The Bal de l'Opéra.* The public balls in the opera house during the carnival season, started in 1716, lost all restraint after the price of admission was lowered from ten to five francs in 1833.

32. Baron Gérard. *Mademoiselle Mars.* Considered the finest actress in Europe, Mademoiselle Mars, a fervent Bonapartist, reigned over the Comédie Française from 1800 until her retirement, at the age of sixty-four, in 1843. In 1815 the discovery of her love letters to Flahaut caused Queen Hortense to end her own affair with him.

33. Mlle Le Mire. *Armandine de Richelieu Marquise de Montcalm*. Some salons were compared to a republic; the salon of Madame de Montcalm, sister of the Prime Minister, the Duc de Richelieu, at 37 rue de l'Université, was a despotic monarchy: chairs were arranged around her chaise longue as if it was a throne. Despite her difficult character, and her brother's loss of office in 1821, her guests remained loyal until her death from cholera in 1832.

34. Jean-Baptiste Isabey. *Madame de Boigne*. Madame de Boigne held one of the most brilliant salons, and wrote some of the most entertaining memoirs, of this period.

35. François-Joseph Heim. *Louis-Philippe greeting diplomats in the Galerie des Batailles in Versailles, 10 June 1837*. The King is shown in the gallery he had created to commemorate French victories, during the festivities in honour of the marriage of his eldest son the Duc d'Orléans to Princess Hélène of Mecklenburg-Schwerin.

36. Victor Jean Adam. *The funeral cortège of Napoleon descends the Champs Elysées, 15 December 1840.* The *retour des cendres,* as this occasion was called, symbolised the triumph of the Napoleonic legend and French nationalism over their opponents.

37. Achille Deverria. *Harriet Smithson* (1829). Smithson's Irish accent, while limiting her success on the London stage, was less of an obstacle in Paris. Berlioz wrote that he had seen 'the whole heaven of art' in her performance as Desdemona in *Othello* in 1827, and married her five years later at the British embassy. However she never learnt good French and grew fat and jealous. She died an alcoholic, separated from her husband, in 1854.

38. Henri Lehmann. *Franz Liszt.* A pupil of Gérard and Ingres, a German who lived in Paris from 1840 until his death there in 1882, Lehmann painted this portrait of his Hungarian-born friend Liszt, who also lived for many years in Paris, in 1839.

39. Ernst Benedikt Kietz. *Heinrich Heine and his wife Mathilde* (1851). Heine married his Parisian mistress in 1841. Attractive but capricious, she was said never to have read a word he wrote.

40. Ernest Seigneurges. *Carnival on the Place de la Concorde*. In the early nineteenth century Paris replaced Venice as a synonym of pleasure, and host to Europe's most famous carnival.

41. F. Grenier. *The last moments of the Duc d'Orléans, 13 July 1842*. Surrounded by the royal family and ministers, the heir to the throne lies dying in a cottage between Paris and Neuilly, where he had been brought after a carriage accident.

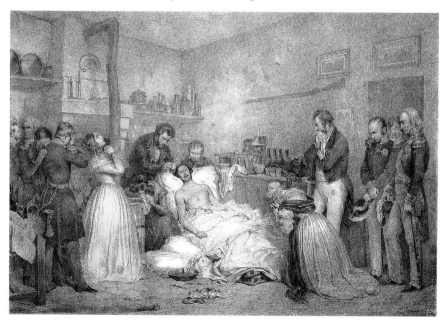

42. Horace Vernet. *Gabriel Delessert* (1821). Delessert came from a family of prominent Protestant bankers. Préfet de Police of Paris from 1836 to 1848, he underestimated the gravity of the situation in the months before the revolution of February 1848, just as a predecessor Jean-Claude-Henri Mangin had before the revolution of 1830.

43. Théodore Chasseriau *Alphonse de Lamartine* (1844). Lamartine had already helped destroy the July monarchy through his speeches and books, before he delivered the *coup de grâce* in a pro-republican speech on 24 February 1848 in the Chamber of Deputies. In the next four months, he exercised greater political power in France than any other nineteenth-century writer.

44. E.H.A. Hagenauer. *The burning of the Château d'Eau on the Place du Palais Royal, 24 February 1848.* On this occasion revolutionaries burnt alive several hundred soldiers guarding a water tower.

45. Lordereau. *The throne being burnt on the Place de la Bastille, 24 February 1848.* On the day that Louis-Philippe fled from the Tuileries, his throne was carried in procession from the palace, along the boulevards to the base of the column which he had erected to commemorate the July revolution, and there burnt.

46. Alexandre Josquin. *Troops camping on the Boulevard du Temple during the June days*. During the fight between the 'forces of order' and the Parisian poor, parts of the city looked as if they were occupied by an enemy army.

47. Théodore Iung. *Entry of Napoleon III into Paris, 2 December 1852*. Napoleon III is coming from Saint-Cloud, where he has just been proclaimed Emperor: he avoided the popular districts in the east of the city, where opposition to his coup had been fiercest, and proceeded straight to a banquet in the Tuileries palace.

48. Fritz von Dardel. *Baron James de Rothschild and Napoleon III at a Court Ball* (1859). The Adonis of his family, James de Rothschild is wearing the red and gold uniform of Austrian consul-general in Paris. Despite their intimacy – Rothschild later entertained the Emperor at his country house in Ferrières – Napoleon III often failed to follow the banker's advice, for example over war with Austria in 1859, the year this drawing was made by the Swedish military attaché.

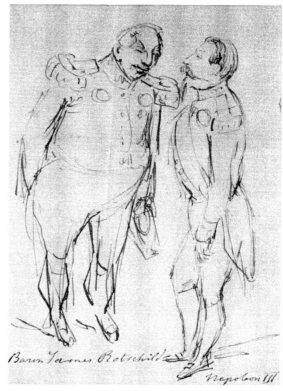

Baron James Rothschild

Napoleon III

49. Adolphe Yvon. *Napoleon III presents Baron Haussmann with the decree of annexation of the outlying communes, 16 February 1859* (1865). By this decree Paris doubled in size.

50. Jules Didier. *The Corps Législatif after the proclamation of the fall of the Second Empire, 4 September 1870.* The day after news reached Paris of the surrender of Napoleon III at Sedan, a crowd stormed into the Corps Législatif, which pronounced his overthrow. However, as in 1848, the new Republic was proclaimed at the Hôtel de Ville.

51. C. Lifflart. *Paris burning, 23–25 May 1871*. Facing defeat, the *communards* finally decided to realise the dreams of many foreigners and Frenchmen and burn Paris. For days afterwards the city was covered with a red cloud like a volcanic eruption. The blackened ruins of the Tuileries were demolished and sold by the Third Republic in 1882. To celebrate the Bonapartes' downfall, the Pozzo di Borgo family bought columns from the palace and re-erected them in their house in Corsica.

52. Ruins of the Hôtel de Ville, May 1871. Unlike the palaces of Saint-Cloud and the Tuileries, symbols of the French monarchy, the Hôtel de Ville, symbol of the city of Paris, was rapidly rebuilt.

53. *Demolition of the column in the Place Vendôme.* After the defeats in 1814 and 1815, the column in the Place Vendôme, honouring French victories in 1805, became a nationalist totem, and the site of frequent demonstrations. As a sign of their loathing of the Second Empire, the *communards* demolished it on 16 May 1871. It was re-erected in 1875.

If Chopin's *études*, *nocturnes* and *mazurkas* are a musical monument to Polish Paris, *La Pologne historique, littéraire, monumentale et pittoresque* (1839–42) edited by Leonard Chodzko, *dédiée à la France* and published for the benefit of Polish refugees, is a literary monument – as well as an encyclopedia, unsurpassed in French, of Polish history, literature, architecture and popular traditions. Its cover illustration shows French and Polish soldiers shaking hands above the inscription: *Français et Polonais de tous temps amis.*[276] However, Sébastiani, Minister of Foreign Affairs, had expressed the cynicism, or realism, of the French government in relation to Polish affairs in a famous remark made in the Chamber of Deputies on 16 September 1831, shortly after the fall of Warsaw to Russian troops: *L'ordre règne à Varsovie.*

This refusal to intervene abroad expressed the wishes of the King. By his letters to European monarchs pledging to respect the treaties of 1815, renouncing territorial expansion and condemning the July revolution as a catastrophe (as it was in the minds of European monarchs and even, at moments, in his own), Louis-Philippe had ensured his rapid recognition as King of the French by all rulers except the Duke of Modena, and had protected France from invasion by a European coalition like that of 1792. Nevertheless in the new world of revolutionary nationalism after 1830, the reign of European ambassadors in Paris was coming to an end. Once Pozzo had been the embodiment of European power in Paris. In March and September 1831, as Russia crushed the Polish insurrection, Pozzo (who felt that his opposition to Polish independence at the Congress of Vienna in 1814 had been justified by the rising of 1830) was 'pelted' and subjected to hostile student demonstrations outside his own windows, encouraged by the residence in the same street of his pro-Polish enemy La Fayette. Outside the embassy demonstrators shouted: *Vive la Pologne! Vengeance! Vivent les Polonais! Mort aux Autrichiens! Guerre aux Russes!*[277] The street and the embassy courtyard were packed with soldiers. Pozzo was advised not to leave his house; Lady Granville wrote that 'his nerves are at all times terribly shattered'.[278] There were pro-Polish demonstrations on the boulevards and the Place Vendôme. Ministers were forced by crowds to descend from their carriages; the King's popularity began to wane. In the courtyard of the Palais Royal, there were cries of *A bas Louis-Philippe! Vive Napoléon II! Vivent les Polonais! A bas les ministres!*[279] The government and the Chamber of Deputies, however, continued their policy of nonintervention.

*

Before 1830 Paris had been compared to a courtesan, a modern Babylon, *la guinguette de l'Europe*.[280] The 'miracle' of the July revolution, however, gave it a new image. It was 'the new Jerusalem', the holy city of liberty, the wonder of the world, *la ville grande comme Dieu*.[281] In addition to Casimir Delavigne's *La Parisienne*, poems were written to Paris and the Parisians, with titles like *Trois jours du peuple*, *Le Peuple*, *Le Triomphe national*, by Hugo, de Nerval and many others.[282] Hugo would hail Paris as the mother city, the spider in whose immense web nations were caught.[283] For J. P. Veyrat:

> *Coeur du monde, ô cité des révolutions!*
> *Tu pèses les destins du globe en ta balance,*
> *Et les peuples gravitent vers toi en silence,*
> *Paris! soleil des nations!*[284]

Indeed the city inspired such fervour that journalists joked as to whether, in the next work, the people of Paris would be compared to an ocean, an eagle or a volcano.[285] For the great historian Jules Michelet, a former history teacher of the daughter of the Duchesse de Berri, born and bred in Paris, revolution was a new religion. Paris had become 'the conscience of the world'.[286] Its cult was international. Ludwig Börne, a republican who saw himself as an intermediary between France and Germany, called the arrival of the news of 1830 in Germany 'like sunbeams packed in printed paper . . . Bold hopes rise up impassioned like trees with golden fruit . . . The great deeds of the French speak plainly to all nations and all intelligences, the highest and the lowest.' When he arrived in 'the capital of Europe' in September 1830, every tree in the Jardin des Tuileries seemed to him 'a blooming tree of liberty'; the paving stones in the streets were 'sacred'.[287]

   The greatest poem of the new cult of Paris, however, was written by a sceptical royalist. Like Lamartine, de Vigny rallied to Louis-Philippe out of necessity, as a way to prevent anarchy. A professional soldier, he had been disgusted by the feebleness of the royal family in 1830. In his poem *Paris*, dated 16 January 1831, he compared the city to a series of interlocking wheels, turned by the hand of God, going towards an unknown end. It was also a furnace forging a new world:

> *On la nomme Paris, le pivot de la France,*
> *Paris l'axe universel, Paris l'axe du monde,*
> *Puise ses mouvements dans sa vigueur profonde,*
> *Les communique à tous, les imprime à chacun . . .*

Paris! principe et fin! Paris arc et flambeau!
On sent jusqu'au fond de son âme
Qu'un monde tout nouveau se forge à cette flamme.
Que fais-tu donc Paris dans ton ardent foyer? [288]

If most writers celebrated Paris with wonder, others, however, regarded it with horror. Metternich had once praised Paris's 'singular effect of luxury and grandeur'.[289] Now, like many others in central Europe, he considered the city a new Sodom leading Europe to destruction. 'When Paris sneezes', ran his celebrated complaint, 'Europe catches cold.'[290]

His old enemy Pozzo felt similar revulsion. In the Palais Royal, where Pozzo often visited the King at night, in secret in a hired carriage – to avoid Parisians catching sight of his official carriage with its ambassadorial coat of arms and liveried footmen – he had at first been trusted as in the Tuileries under Louis XVIII. He considered Louis-Philippe the best hope for the two causes to which he had devoted his career, the French monarchy and European peace.[291] However, in the next two years, like James de Rothschild, Castellane and many others, he lost confidence in Louis-Philippe.[292] The new King was weak and dominated by avarice; the abolition of the heredity of the peerage in 1832 (all peers were henceforth life peers) removed 'the last feeble bulwark of the French aristocracy'. Society itself was under attack: 'the spirit of equality and levelling' would make any kind of government impossible. In a remark which would take eighty years to make sense, he wrote that the unity of Russia, Prussia and Austria against revolution was henceforth a condition of their existence.[293]

By 1832, full of 'the most sinister sentiments', he feared a deluge of blood. He felt proud that in Paris he had helped to keep the Corps Diplomatique united and to 'contain the revolutionary movement which regards Germany and Italy as its prey'. By preventing a European war against France, he had helped Russia reconquer Poland. Nevertheless his Paris had gone. Moreover the Tsar may have felt that he was too sympathetic to Louis-Philippe. In 1832 Pozzo paid a last visit to St Petersburg to see Nicholas I, followed by a last tour of the German courts. In January 1833 he left to be ambassador in London.[294]

Pozzo was not the only man disillusioned by the July monarchy. A poem by Auguste Barbier, published on 22 September 1830, also expressed a mood of disillusion. The people had been magnificent, rising like the sea, in

Paris, cette cité de lauriers toute ceinte
Dont le monde entier est jaloux;
Que les peuples émus appellent tous la sainte,
Et qu'ils ne nomment qu'à genoux,
Paris n'est maintenant qu'une sentine impure,
Un égout sordide et boueux
Où mille noirs courants de limon et d'ordure
Viennent traîner leurs flots honteux,
Un taudis regorgeant de faquins sans courage,
D'effrontés coureurs de salons,
Une halle cynique aux clameurs insolentes.

Moreover much of the army was bitter. Under difficult conditions the Garde Royale, both officers and men, had fought with 'sublime heroism', better than royal troops had done in 1789, 1792 or 1815. Their main grievance was the lack of opportunities, under inadequate leaders, to kill more Parisians.[295] If better led, by a better strategist, they might have won by evacuating the city and then surrounding and starving it into submission, as Russian troops did in Warsaw in 1831, and as Austrian and Prussian troops would do in Vienna and Berlin in 1848. The military lessons of the failed *coup d'état* of Charles X and of the fighting in the streets of Paris would not be lost on French officers, nor on an Austrian witness of the July revolution, the future victor over the Vienna revolution of 1848, Prince Schwarzenberg.

The chorus of praise after the July revolution also led many to forget that most French politicians had taken the side of the people of Paris only with reluctance, and only after its victory on 29 July. In their hearts many regretted that, as a former regicide and *conventionnel* Merlin de Thionville said on 3 August, the tiger had been unleashed.[296] This sense of fear and regret affected the highest in the land.

In private, the King called the French crown a crown of thorns, 29 July 1830 a 'forever fatal day'.[297] As early as November 1830 he had lost much of his popularity by his refusal to support revolution in Europe and his insistence on sparing the lives of Charles X's ministers. To cheat the crowds baying for their blood, Louis-Philippe removed them from the place of their trial, the Chamber of Peers in the Palais du Luxembourg, to the safety of the fortress of Vincennes (they were subsequently tried, condemned to prison and released after a few years). The fury of the people of Paris when it was proposed to abolish the death penalty for political offences was hard to imagine. Louis-Philippe's refusal to intervene against Austria to support revolutions in

Italy led to the resignation on 12 March 1831 of Laffitte, who believed in 'war rather than the abandonment of our principles'. Once open to all comers, from 1831 the Palais Royal was guarded by triple rows of national guards.[298]

The King's Catholic and conservative wife Marie Amélie, grand-daughter of the Empress Maria Theresa, sister of the King of Naples and the Queen of Sardinia, was horrified by the break with the elder branch of the Bourbons. She did not criticise the July revolution openly. However in her diary she called the monument her sister-in-law Madame Adélaïde erected in the garden of Neuilly, to mark the spot whence Louis-Philippe had left for Paris on 30 July – a bench decorated with bas-reliefs of figures of Vanity and Foolishness (Charles X, with his sceptre and the *ordonnances de juillet*) vanquished by Liberty, Wisdom and Justice – *le tombeau de mon bonheur*.[299]

After 30 July 1830 her lifeless eyes and heaving bosom betrayed her horror and distress. She wept for her cousin the Duc de Bourbon, who had been found hanging in the château of Saint-Leu in mysterious circumstances on 27 August 1830. She had fallen ill with distress follow-ing riots in February 1831, provoked by a royalist service in memory of the Duc de Berri at Saint-Germain-l'Auxerrois. Thiers had ordered the National Guard, which was already unenthusiastic, not to intervene. The Archbishopric of Paris had been sacked and burnt. In the middle of carnival, a crowd, dressed in stolen ecclesiastical vestments, had mim-icked a religious procession, scattering urine like holy water; crosses had been removed from the top of churches and priests attacked in the street.[300] As Queen of the French Marie Amélie could hardly be recog-nised as 'the same being who only a very few months ago looked the personification of happiness'.[301]

9

Blood on the Boulevards

1831–1838

Nous avons fait la guerre pendant vingt ans et nous ne sommes que des lâches auprès de cet homme-là.

General Pajol, military commander of Paris, on Louis-Philippe, 28 July 1835

THE JULY REVOLUTION gave Paris new martyrs as well as a new mon-archy. The royalist victims of one revolution were replaced by the revolutionary victims of another. An elaborate system of medals, scholarships, pensions, indemnities and hospital care was set up by the government, and private admirers, to reward over 1,000 *victimes de juillet*, killed or wounded in the July revolution, and their families.[1] The streets of Paris reflected the change in commemoration. The rue Charles X, a long street heading north-east from the heart of the city, was renamed rue La Fayette; the rue du duc de Bordeaux off the rue de Rivoli became the rue du 29 juillet; the rue d'Angoulême, where the Flahaut lived, the rue de la Charte (now the rue La Boétie); the rue d'Artois the rue Laffitte after the banker who lived at number 27. The rue Vaneau near the Faubourg Saint-Germain was named after a pupil of the Ecole Polytechnique who died there fighting royal troops; the Pont de Grève was renamed the Pont d'Arcole, after a young Parisian called Fournier who had helped seize it from royal troops and pro-nounced that he felt like the young Bonaparte at the Battle of Arcole (1796).[2]

Every 27, 28, and 29 July, the *fêtes de juillet* commemorating the 1830 revolution were the equivalent, for the July monarchy, of the *fête-Dieu* and the *fête du roi* under the Restoration. They provided opportunities for the King and the government to reaffirm the regime's ideological basis, for

Parisians to display their feelings of loyalty or discontent. All Bourbon ceremonies, including, by a unanimous vote of the Chamber of Deputies, official mourning for Louis XVI on 21 January, were terminated after the 1830 revolution, as were public religious processions in Paris (although not in provincial cities).[3] In 1832, in reprisal for the Duchesse de Berri's attempted insurrection in the Vendée (in which the Duchess was helped by, among others, Mme de La Rochejaquelein, daughter of the Duchesse de Duras), the Chapelle Expiatoire which was slowly being erected, in the form of a Doric temple, on the site of the Duc de Berri's murder in the rue Rameau, was demolished. It was replaced by the fountain which can still be seen today in the square Louvois.[4]

On the first annual commemoration of the revolution, on 27 July 1831, surrounded by *héros de juillet* singing the Marseillaise and the *Parisienne*, Louis-Philippe laid the foundation stone of a Corinthian column honouring the *combattants de juillet* – the July revolution's answer to the Colonne de la Grande Armée in the Place Vendôme.[5] In order to connect the 1830 revolution to the 1789 revolution, the column was built on the site of the Bastille, in the middle of the Place de la Bastille, previously adorned with a giant plaster statue of an elephant. The column is built of solid bronze and dedicated

A la gloire des citoyens français qui s'armèrent et combattirent pour la défense des libertés publiques dans les mémorables journées des 27, 28, 29 juillet 1830.

It is crowned by a statue of the genius of Liberty, bearing a torch and breaking the chains of tyranny.[6] The column was finally inaugurated by the King on 28 July 1840, the tenth anniversary of the revolution. The corpses of the 504 *combattants* to be buried beneath the column were exhumed from different cemeteries, taken to the church of Saint-Germain-l'Auxerrois and then transported on a massive ceremonial catafalque, drawn by twenty-four horses draped in black, along the *quais* to the Place de la Concorde, then along the boulevards to the foot of the column. The names of the *combattants* are inscribed in letters of gilded bronze running up the sides of the column. During the four-hour procession the *Grande Symphonie funèbre et triomphale* of Berlioz, specially composed for the occasion, was played by a marching orchestra of 200 dressed in National Guard uniform, conducted by the composer himself, also in the same uniform – although the spectators could hardly hear a note owing to the noise of the crowd, and of genuine national guards beating their drums. Also in the procession, the Opera choir sang words by Victor Hugo:

Gloire à notre France éternelle!
Gloire à ceux qui sont morts pour elle![7]

Celebrations on 28 July 1831 also included free performances in the-atres and music halls; 'aquatic jousts' or naval combats on the Seine; horse races on the Champ de Mars; balloons floating above the city; fairs and orchestras along the Champs Elysées. In the evening, accord-ing to Castellane, 'the dancing, the illumination of the boutiques and of the different dance halls which had been erected, the crowd of people enjoying themselves, all gave the Champs Elysées the appearance of a fairy palace.'[8] Families made special journeys from the provinces to enjoy the 'magic effect' of Paris *en fête*, especially at night when there were firework displays and thousands of lamps lit up the *quais*, the monuments and the boats on the Seine.[9]

Until the fall of the regime, such annual celebrations were the high-light of the year. They always included the sacred numbers *27 28 29*, dis-played in honour of *les journées de juillet* on tricolour flags, on balloons, on posts lining the Champs Elysées, on massive tricolour columns erected on the *quais* and, picked out in oil lamps, on the façades of official build-ings.[10] The grandest monuments in Paris were inaugurated during the *fêtes de juillet*: the Arc de Triomphe in 1836; statues of the towns of France and rostral columns on the Place de la Concorde in 1838.[11]

As these commemorations affirmed, Paris had changed roles; for-merly a court city it was now a revolutionary capital. In 1820 Pozzo had claimed that the only republicans were a few ageing veterans of 1789 and 1793. As early as 2 August 1830, however, he had noticed 'symptoms of republicanism which make one shudder'. By late 1831, most of the youth of Paris was thought to be republican. At carnival balls in 1832 students mingled 'the sanguinary refrains of 1793' with their indecent dances.[12]

Since the dismissal of Laffitte and the advent in March 1831 of the conservative ministry of Casimir Périer, compounded by the failure to help Poland in September 1831, the popularity of Louis-Philippe and his family had continued to plunge. Attacks in a rash of articles and books were, he complained, of unparalleled venom.[13] The King was denounced as a miser, a thief, a jailer, a Judas who had betrayed liberty – although Paris was so free that it was full of revolutionaries openly plotting to over-throw him. The column of the Place Vendôme was said to be the only thing in France resting on solid foundations.[14] By late 1831, in fear of his life, the King had less freedom to walk through the streets of his capital than the King of Prussia in Berlin or the Emperor of Austria in Vienna.[15]

In his articles for the *Augsburger Allgemeine Zeitung*, which he called the universal gazette of Europe, Heine provides an incomparable picture of life after the July revolution. Already a famous poet in Germany thanks to the *Buch der Lieder* (1827), he had arrived in Paris from Hamburg on 19 May 1831, aged thirty-four, to breathe the air of freedom. For him Paris was 'the beautiful city of marvels, which smiles with such grace on a young man', the capital not only of France but of the entire civilised world, where he could witness universal history taking place under his own eyes.[16]

No other city satisfied him. Germany was too repressive (his works would be banned there in 1836). He swore never to return to England, 'that abominable country where men function like machines and machines like men': Londoners looked to him like people in agony. In contrast he loved the gaiety and urbanity of the Parisians, the beauty of their language and the ease with which he could go from a meeting of the Society of the Friends of the People to a soirée in the Faubourg Saint-Germain.[17] Parisians liked him as much as he liked them. Within three days of arrival he had been hailed in *Le Globe* on 22 May 1831 as a young and courageous poet 'who defends the cause of progress' and 'the people's interests in Germany, without nevertheless shutting himself up in a narrow nationality'. Balzac would call him the representative in Paris of the spirit and poetry of Germany as, in Germany, he was of French critical intelligence.[18] Sainte-Beuve wrote that he was 'one of us'. While continuing to compose poems in German, mainly about Paris girls, he also wrote articles describing Paris during the outbreak of cholera in April and May 1832.[19]

At the news of the first deaths in April the balls and parties for carnival, which fell late that year, had continued. Soon, however, Heine wrote that it was as if a masked executioner was stalking through the city with an invisible guillotine. Dancers who suddenly felt ill were taken straight from carnival balls to cholera hospitals: it was said that some were buried in the fancy dress in which they had been dancing.[20] As the death toll mounted, the disease became the sole topic of conversation in the Tuileries garden. The rich (with exceptions such as the royal family and the Rothschilds) and the foreigners left.[21] So many deputies fled from Paris that not enough remained in the Chamber to take a vote. The city began to smell of the chlorine with which houses were painted as a disinfectant. The Pont Neuf was covered with patients on stretchers, lying beside the corpses of those already dead. Corpses were removed at night by torchlight from stricken houses, to be carried on hearses straight to Père Lachaise. The number of funerals led to some churches being permanently draped in black.[22] In an unprecedented measure to improve public hygiene the police began to remove rubbish from the streets to the countryside. In protest, the *chiffonniers* (ragmen, ragpickers) and *revendeuses* of Paris, who earned their livelihoods by picking through piles of rubbish, held demonstrations at the Porte Saint-Denis and Place du Châtelet, burning rubbish carts or throwing them in the Seine. Cavalry charges were needed to disperse the protestors.[23]

The epidemic revealed the ferocity of popular hatred of the regime. Many Parisians claimed that the government, even the King in person (in reality devoting all their energy and considerable sums to halting the epidemic), were poisoning the wells and fountains of the city, as well as fruit and vegetables in the marketplace. Cholera was an invention of the government intended to starve the people. The old revolutionary cry *A la lanterne!* was heard in the streets. Even Heine, who believed in 'the holy alliance of nations', compared 'the people' in Paris to a wild beast. Five Parisians were lynched, including a Jew found holding a box of camphor to his nose. A young man was torn to shreds on the quai Voltaire.[24] Women often delivered the first blows.[25] After a last kick to the corpse of a murdered man, a beautiful woman with blood on her hands asked Heine for money to buy mourning clothes to wear for her mother, whose death from cholera she blamed on poison.[26]

By May the total number of dead amounted to 18,402. Prominent victims included Baron Cuvier, the former prime minister Martignac, Madame de Montcalm and the favourite daughter of Comte Molé, dead at the age of twenty within eight hours of displaying the first symptoms.[27] The prime minister himself, Casimir Périer, who had visited hospitals with the Duc d'Orléans, died on 16 May 1832. The grandest monument in Père Lachaise was erected in his memory – a Roman mausoleum, isolated from others, surmounted by a life-size statue of Casimir Périer, draped in a Roman toga, above a figure of Eloquence and the inscription:

Sept fois élu député, Président du Conseil des Ministres sous le règne de Louis-Philippe I, il défendit avec éloquence et courage l'ordre et la liberté dans l'intérieur, la paix et la dignité nationale à l'extérieur. La ville de Paris pour consacrer la mémoire d'un deuil général a donné à perpétuité la terre où repose un grand citoyen.

There are many references on the monument to Casimir Périer, France and Paris, none to Christianity.

The last famous cholera victim was the liberal orator General

Lamarque. His funeral procession on 5 June 1832 almost provoked a revolution. As the coffin, having paused in homage at the foot of the column on the Place Vendôme, was escorted along the boulevards, there were cries in the crowd of *A bas Louis-Philippe! A bas la poire molle! Vive la République!* A red flag was brandished with the inscription *La liberté ou la mort!* A speech by La Fayette at the Place du Pont d'Austerlitz was greeted with rapture. To cries of *Aux armes! Aux barricades!*, a shot rang out and fighting began. At the beginning the revolutionaries were better organised than on 27 July 1830. Within a few hours, about 3,000 insurgents had seized a section of central Paris between the Châtelet and the arsenal, and the Faubourg Saint-Antoine. Men boasted that they would sup that night in the Tuileries palace. Fighting was so fierce, particularly around the rues Saint-Merri and Saint-Martin, that some Parisians felt that the revolutionaries might win.[28]

However some 40,000 soldiers and 20,000 national guards were patrolling the city's streets. Their commander the Maréchal de Lobau was abler than Marmont and had invented a technique for dispersing demonstrators by drenching them with water from fire-hoses. In addition, as in June 1820, the government was helped by a downpour of rain. Moreover, the National Guard, after a moment of indecision, was, as Heine wrote, 'totally against the republicans'. Knowing where power lay, he added: 'the matter is closed.'[29]

At this stage of his reign, moreover, Louis-Philippe was braver and more intelligent than Charles X. Instead of staying in Saint-Cloud far from the scene of action, the King returned to the Tuileries with his wife, sister and the Duc de Nemours. He held a council and then left the palace on horseback, accompanied by Nemours, to encourage and thank the troops, whom he called *mes chers camarades*. He was greeted by cheers of *Vive le roi!* and cries for justice to be executed against the revolutionaries. Paris was placed under a state of siege and *conseils de guerre* were established to judge insurgents taken with arms in their hands. By 6 p.m. on the evening of 6 June fighting was over. Casualties on both sides amounted to about 150 dead and 500 wounded, half of whom were soldiers.[30]

The King had been unmoved by a deputation headed by Laffitte, who with the scientist François Arago and the left-wing deputy Odilon Barrot pleaded for an end to the bloodshed and a more liberal and nationalistic policy in accordance with the promises of July 1830. Justifying himself by the fact that order had been maintained, the King promised to stick to the Charter of 1830:[31] he saw the July monarchy as the amelioration, not the destruction, of the Restoration. At this stage, indeed, armed revolution was unpopular with most Parisians. Distraught at the loss of business that resulted from disorder, some workers had attacked revolutionaries *à coups de batons*.[32] At a review on the boulevards on 11 June the King was met with cheers of *Vive le roi!*, above all from women (who, as under the Restoration, preferred governments which opposed violence). Most monarchs contented themselves with greeting their troops with a military salute: the right hand raised briskly to the side of the head. After the review, however, in his eagerness for popularity Louis-Philippe leant down from his horse for the entire length of the boulevards, with what Heine called 'unimaginable patience', to shake hands with national guards.[33]

The King, the government and bourgeois society, nevertheless, continued to be treated with derision by journalists – the 'Attilas of the pen' – and by such caricaturists as Honoré Daumier, Henri Monnier and Charles Philippon. Philippon founded a famous satirical review *Le Charivari* in December 1832, the model nine years later for the London review *Punch* (originally *Punch or the London Charivari*).[34] No king has been more vilified in his own capital. One caricature showed Liberty chained in prison, with the caption *Le cachot sera désormais une vérité* – parodying Louis-Philippe's remark *La Charte sera désormais une vérité*. Frequently, given the similarity in shape to his head, the King was represented as a pear, *la poire molle*. Another caricature combined blasphemy and *lèse-majesté* by portraying the ceremony of the elevation of the pear, in the manner of the elevation of the host during mass: Talleyrand, Lobau, and the royal family were among the people depicted.[35] Intimidated by republican threats, jurors frequently acquitted even the most extremist journalists prosecuted by the government.[36] Such was the rancour of revolutionaries that George Sand's lover, the militant Saint-Simonian journalist and teacher Michel Chevalier, walking with her along the *quais* one night and hearing the sound of violins coming from a ball in the Tuileries palace, declared that civilisation would not be regenerated until the river was red with blood, the Tuileries palace reduced to a pile of ashes, and Paris was a ploughed field.[37] Others compared the palace to a voracious vulture, perched with outstretched wings in the centre of the city.[38]

The republican leader Godefroy Cavaignac, whose father had been a regicide and whose mother, with a face like an old guillotine, was known as *la mère rouge*, was repeatedly arrested for his part in insurrections between 1830 and 1834. An admirer of Robespierre, he was the animator of the Société des Amis du Peuple and other revolutionary groups founded in the early 1830s.[39] Showing the anti-feminism of most French revolutionaries, he wrote that the symbol of Paris, traditionally a woman crowned with towers, should be replaced by a man with a tri-colour sash, holding in one hand 'the torch which enlightens and enflames Europe', in another a pike surmounted by a bonnet of liberty. At his feet should be the debris of the throne, and paving stones torn from the pavement in preparation for use by rioters.[40]

The growing unpopularity of the government and the King was revealed at another commemoration of the July revolution, the unveil-ing on 28 July 1833 of the statue of Napoleon – replaced, after an absence of nineteen years, on top of the column of the Grande Armée in the Place Vendôme. Every window in the square was packed. There were cries of *Vive l'Empereur!*, but for the King 'little enthusiasm'.[41] The July monarchy was proving the truth of Louis-Philippe's prophetic remark, made as a royalist émigré in London to Louis XVIII in 1804, that '*la force des choses* renders unstable every political institution whose base is revolutionary.'[42] If the Restoration had been, for much of its duration, a regime with a revolution foretold, the July monarchy appeared to be a regime in permanent revolution.

In April 1834, after a massive uprising by silk-workers in Lyon, there was another attempt at insurrection in Paris by a well-organised group of about 1,500 republicans, including Godefroy Cavaignac. Over thirty bar-ricades appeared in the area between the rues Saint-Martin, du Temple, de Beaubourg and Saint-Denis. Thiers, the energetic Minister of the Interior, while patrolling the streets on horseback in his minister's embroidered uniform, saw a young Auditeur au Conseil d'Etat killed beside him.[43] However, the Paris National Guard, hailed as *la grande armée de l'ordre public*, showed 'an extraordinary energy' and enthusiasm.[44] On 13 April the Tuileries was surrounded by a protective screen of troops and artillery. There were said to be 60,000 soldiers on the streets and they rapidly stormed the barricades and houses from which firing came, killing women and children in the process.[45] Passing the rue Saint-Martin the next morning, the King's eldest son the Duc d'Orléans saw pools of blood in the street, coming from the corpses on the barricades, and a housefront streaked with blood running down from an upper floor.[46] 'Is this the justice of the Citizen King?' passers-by asked.[47] In total, however, only twenty-five were killed and about thirty wounded. At a review the following day at the Tuileries the King was acclaimed with enthusiasm by the national guards of Paris and the suburbs.[48]

Insurrection having failed, republicans turned to assassination. Between autumn 1834 and summer 1835 seven attempts against the life of Louis-Philippe were discovered.[49] It was said that an assassination attempt had become part of the ceremonial of the state opening of parliament. The Citizen King had become a hunted animal – the only species, as he often remarked, for which there was no closed season.[50] However, despite many warnings of further assassination attempts, Louis-Philippe refused to cancel the annual review of the National Guard on 28 July 1835, commemorating the July revolution. The government prepared for it as for a battle.

Accompanied by his sons, his ministers and a brilliant staff, including Maréchal Mortier Duc de Trévise, the Maréchal de Lobau and Flahaut, that morning the King began the review on the boulevards. Soon after midday, as he was inspecting the first battalion of the eighth legion of the National Guard on the Boulevard du Temple, a thick cloud of smoke and the sound of an explosion came from a shuttered window on the third floor at 50 Boulevard du Temple, beside the Jardin Turc. Bullets had been fired from an 'infernal machine', a battery of twenty-five linked rifle barrels. The machine was the contrivance of a nomadic Corsican thief of fluctuating beliefs, called Joseph Fieschi. An ardent nationalist, like Louvel the assassin of the Duc de Berri, he had the arms of Murat King of Naples tattooed on his chest. He had been planning the assassination since January and had as accessories not only others from his milieu but even Godefroy Cavaignac: Stendhal also later expressed admiration for Fieschi's 'energy'. House to house searches by the police before the review had failed to locate the assassin or his machine.[51]

In the mayhem of smoke, dust, wounded men and horses, falling chairs and fleeing spectators, the King's Premier Ecuyer Baron Strada found himself wading up to his ankles in blood, as he went to see how his master was. Crying *Ceci me regarde*, the King rode on without dismounting, unhurt except for a bruise on his forehead and a graze to his horse. Many regarded the King's escape as a miracle: all admired his calm courage.[52] By prior arrangement the King's sons steered their horses as closely as possible beside him – Joinville seized his horse's bridle – in order to receive further bullets if there was a second attempt. At the head of a group of national guards Flahaut and an aide of the King stormed into the house from which the bullets had come, and seized the assassin to cries of *Vive le roi! Vengeance!*[53] In all there were twenty-two wounded and eighteen dead, including a girl of twelve and Maréchal Mortier. The soldier who had survived so many battlefields across Europe (and the defence of Paris in March 1814) died on a Paris boulevard.[54]

The King continued along the boulevards reviewing the National Guard, until he reached the Place Vendôme, where he was greeted by cheering spectators. The reunion in the Ministry of Justice on the Place Vendôme of the King and his sons with the Queen, Madame Adélaïde and their sisters, drew tears from all eyes. Normally the Queen's manner was, in contrast to her husband's obsequiousness, 'the perfection of royal dignity and benevolence combined'. The British ambassadress Lady Granville wrote: 'she has more dignity and calmness of manner than anybody and I never saw anyone who brought such conviction to one's mind that "her help is from above".'[55] Before her husband arrived, however, her mask fell to reveal the state of terror and suspicion in which she now lived. Red with rage and despair, refusing to believe the reassurances of those around her until she had seen her family with her own eyes, like her niece the Duchesse de Berri at Berri's deathbed in 1820, she is reported to have exclaimed: 'what a terrible people, what a dreadful country! Villains, monsters, they have killed my husband, my children.'[56]

Seven days later, on 5 August, there was yet another grandiose Parisian funeral, for the victims of the infernal machine. All Paris watched in stupefied silence as fourteen coffins, followed by the victims' relations and deputations from every state institution, were escorted in suffocating heat by 45,000 soldiers and national guards from the church of Saint-Paul in the Marais along the entire length of the boulevards (rather than the shorter route along the *quais*) over the Seine to the Invalides. The procession took five hours; the first coffin was surmounted by the crown of a virgin, the last by that of a duke (for the Duc de Trévise). For the first time since the July revolution the Paris clergy (under the legitimist Archbishop Monseigneur de Quélen) and Louis-Philippe attended the same public ceremony. As each coffin arrived in the courtyard of the Invalides, the King came out to sprinkle holy water on it. He almost fainted when he saw that of the twelve-year-old girl.[57]

In their horror and disgust many Parisians blamed the murders on press incitement: *Le Charivari* had indeed predicted, and encouraged, such an attempt, describing the King as an assassin covered with crimes. About thirty republican newspapers and magazines closed down.[58] Laws passed in September punished with deportation insults to the person of the King and attacks on the principle of government (in 1829

Béranger had received only a few months' prison for calling Charles X a dangerous idiot); censorship of prints and plays was re-established, and the repressive powers of the law courts were strengthened. To shield them from threats jurors' names were no longer published. Censorship became so strict that in 1840 the appearance, in a scene in Balzac's play *Vautrin*, of a character wearing a toupee like that of Louis-Philippe would suffice to get it banned. As Paris became more repressive, so London – Metternich considered – became the breeding-ground of revolution. Godefroy Cavaignac took refuge there in 1835. Two years later, obliged to leave Switzerland, the famous Italian nation-alist Mazzini – although he spoke better French than English – also chose to endure 'the hell of exile' in London rather than Paris.[59]

Assassination attempts on the King, however, continued. Louis Alibaud, a twenty-six-year-old revolutionary who had taken part in the insurrection of June 1832, fired on Louis-Philippe near the Tuileries in the evening of 25 June 1836, as the King was leaving for Neuilly. Although the shot was almost at point-blank range, the King was un-hurt. The King himself began to believe that he was doomed: students placed bets on when, not whether, he would be killed. The government obliged him, to his consternation, to cancel a review planned for the 1836 commemorations of the July revolution. The Duchesse de Dino caught the mood of despair in Louis-Philippe's family: 'poor people! . . . Nothing so sad as the Tuileries. I stayed there for two hours with an inexpressible heartbreak, an oppression and a desire to cry which I could hardly control, especially when I saw the King.'[60]

However, the laws of September 1835 made apparent what had been less so before: after the July revolution, France had an active monarch, with powers closer to those of an *ancien régime*, rather than a modern constitutional king. At first the King had been relatively unassertive. He had wanted to remain in the Palais Royal, the Orléans family home, rather than move into the Tuileries, preferring what he called the *petites commodités intérieures* of the former to the *tristes appartements* of the latter.[61] In October 1831 however, Casimir Périer, the most forceful Président du Conseil of the reign, obliged the King and his family to move out of the Palais Royal into the Tuileries. The Palais Royal had remained the focus of riots and demonstrations;[62] the Tuileries was easier to guard and had become the symbol of the French monarchy in the nineteenth century, as Versailles had been before 1789.[63] Louis-Philippe, despite his respect and admiration for Casimir Périer, regarded the minister as assertive and inconvenient. Castellane, by now a senior officer in the army, wrote that the King 'will always try to recover *le petit tripotage des affaires*'.

Périer had insisted that the King no longer attend the council of ministers.[64] After his death, however, the King not only attended but often acted as Président du Conseil himself. He attended council meetings and made daily interventions in politics, particularly foreign policy, on a scale matched only by Charles X in 1829–30 or Napoleon I before 1814. If the monarchy had lost prestige, it had kept most of its power. The King's sister Madame Adélaïde and even his aides-de-camp wielded political influence; one aide-de-camp General Bernard was twice Minister of War between 1836 and 1839.[65] Whereas Thiers proclaimed that 'the King reigns but does not govern', and another liberal deputy Duvergier de Hauranne that 'We want a parliamentary ministry!', a pamphlet by an aged ex-revolutionary Comte Roederer asserted that the King himself should choose ministers and run the government, and add to the force of the laws 'the model of public and private virtues'.[66] This view was reasserted in many later works inspired by the King. Moreover the letter of the Charte allowed deputies to discuss, but not to control, the government.[67]

The King would write to his ministers, whom he himself often selected, two or three letters a day containing instructions and advice on politics, and summon them at any time which suited him, even when he was dressing in his bedroom – they noticed that he had white skin 'like a woman'.[68] He frequently changed the texts of speeches prepared by his ministers or secretaries, to add the pronoun *je* and the adjective *mon*, and to substitute the word king for government.[69]

Like most Bourbons, Louis-Philippe was more interested in foreign than internal affairs. The Duc de Broglie, Minister of Foreign Affairs in the Soult–Guizot–Thiers ministry which dominated politics between 1832 and 1836, tried to act alone without consulting the King or the cabinet. In conversation with foreign ambassadors, Louis-Philippe called this most arrogant of foreign ministers, who detested Pozzo and 'the diplomatic world of 1815', *Sa Majesté Broglie Ier*.[70] Guizot was *Son Altesse Royale M. Guizot*.[71] The King also interfered in the conduct of internal policy. At a court ball in February 1835, Thiers as Minister of the Interior complained openly to Cuvillier-Fleury, tutor to the King's younger son the Duc d'Aumale: 'the King wants to do everything, he speaks and never listens, he wants to be in sole charge of foreign affairs.'

Cuvillier-Fleury, however, and many peers and deputies, regarded the

King with admiration. One entry in his diary reads: 'the ministers at Neuilly. Council in the *salon bleu*. The King speaks out loud. With what facility, what honesty and what *savoir faire* he treats political business! The ministers listen to him speaking and say little. They are right.'[72] The King's political dominance was demonstrated in 1836 when Thiers left office not over a vote in the Chamber or an election in the country, but over a disagreement with the King about policy in Spain. He was replaced by a ministry led by the King's favourite politician, the pliable Comte Molé. Parliament seemed impotent against the King.[73]

Another sign of the King's power was the reappearance, despite the regime's revolutionary origins, of the shadow of a court. In 1830 the King had sworn he would never have a court and tried to ban the use of the word.[74] Showing more hatred of his cousins than knowledge of how to establish a monarchy, on 1 August Louis-Philippe had even abolished departments of the Maison du Roi like the Musique-Chapelle, whose music had been one of the glories of Paris – and the asylum of impoverished musicians.

Under Charles X the Tuileries chapel had been so crowded that men almost sat on each other's knees; after 1829 tickets had been introduced for the Salle des Maréchaux in order to cope with the crowds attending court every Sunday.[75] Louis-Philippe, however, was the first French monarch not to attend mass in public on Sunday.[76] Hunting rights in the royal forests of the Ile de France were leased to private hunts. The Académie Royale de Musique and the Paris opera house were leased to private entrepreneurs.[77] On 14 August Flahaut had noted, with the *schadenfreude* of an ADC of Napoleon I who had lost his own court post in 1814:

> You have no conception of the pitiful faces of the courtiers, Maillé, Rougé, Cossé, Brézé, Claparède etc. The worst is that they have no chance for there is to be no Court. I tell them that I feel for them having known the same misfortune in 1814. Madame Juste [de Noailles, former Dame d'atours of the Duchesse de Berri] told me this morning that it was the duty of every good Frenchman to support the present government.[78]

The age of the court painter was also over. Baron Gérard resigned his appointment as Premier Peintre du Roi on the grounds that it was not in harmony with the new political order, in reality because he remained at heart legitimist.[79] Yet his legitimism did not stop him painting, with the same glacial lucidity with which he had depicted Louis XVIII and Charles X in coronation robes, hands holding a royal sceptre, many pictures glorifying the July revolution, including a state portrait of Louis-

Philippe Ier (1833), in the uniform of a lieutenant-general, one hand on the *Charte de 1830*.[80]

In keeping with the abolition of the Maison du Roi, Louis-Philippe had been voted a *liste civile* of only twelve million francs a year (compared to thirty million for his predecessors). There was no Maison Civile or Maison Militaire except for the King's eighteen ADCs. Diplomats complained that, compared to the deferential crowds under the Restoration, the Tuileries under Louis-Philippe resembled a desert. It was deprived not only of its court officials but also of many of its splendid fleurs-de-lys hangings.[81] Crimson velvet replaced gold brocade on the walls of the Salle du Trône.[82] Men were received on Sunday evenings, in uniforms or *fracs*, without order or distinctions of rank. 'This court does not shine by its dignity,' Castellane commented.[83] Since the King did not dare to put his *huissiers* in uniform, as they had been in the Palais Royal, they wore the same black *fracs* as most of his male guests. The King once asked a man which department of France he represented: *Sire, je suis huissier de Votre Majesté*.[84]

The King's social life resembled that of no other French monarch. He dined at 6, always *en famille*, with the addition, when in Paris, of the officers of the National Guard on duty at the Tuileries.[85] After 8 in the evening a 'privileged list' of ministers, marshals, generals, ambassadors and, after the riots of October 1831, deputies could drop in to visit the King and Queen in their salons on the first floor in the Tuileries, without needing special invitations. Some did not bother to stay more than a few minutes.[86] Guests could depart without taking formal leave.[87] Regular visitors included Molé, Flahaut, Decazes, Lord Granville, Pozzo, Alexander von Humboldt, many foreigners. The first evening Disraeli spent 'in the domesticity of a court' was at the Tuileries under Louis-Philippe.[88] The King would first read the English newspapers, generally including *The Times*, and a German newspaper (never a French newspaper), sitting on a bench in a small billiard room, sometimes falling asleep. Then he would emerge to talk or joke with male guests, particularly the diplomats. At about 10 p.m., when most guests had left, he would approach the round table in the *salon de famille* where the Queen, her daughters and ladies endured long sessions of sewing and embroidery (their work was later sold for the benefit of the poor) and launch into conversation. After putting in brief appearances, his sons would leave in search of more exciting company.[89]*

---

* Such as the great actress Mlle Rachel, of whom the Prince de Joinville remarked, when told that she would welcome a visit: 'Where? When? How much?'

The King talked for hours at a time. Pozzo said that he loved talking so much that, if he were condemned to speak nothing but Syriac, he would still manage.[90] In the opinion of the Duchesse de Dino, however, and many others, 'there is no more interesting conversation than that of the King.' She knew Talleyrand and Thiers intimately, but called Louis-Philippe the cleverest man in France.[91] Indeed, his conversation so charmed Victor Hugo that the great Romantic became an Orleanist courtier. He once stayed so late listening to the King that the servants, thinking they had retired, put out the candles and went to bed. The King himself took a lamp and showed Hugo out. Gay and affable, far from being ashamed of his past, the King liked to reminisce – about Versailles, the revolution and the emigration: he remembered that Robespierre had looked like a cat drinking vinegar. With an 'inexpressible smile' he recalled a moment during the siege of Cadiz in 1810, when Maréchal Soult had hoped to capture him and have him shot; Soult, who was also present, replied with another 'inexpressible smile' that he had merely wanted to 'compromise' the Duc d'Orléans. After the marshal had left, the King commented: 'Compromise! Compromise! Today it is called compromise! In reality he would have had me shot!'[92]

If Louis-Philippe was one of the most criticised rulers of his time, he could also criticise back. The stupidity and idleness of his ministers, treating the most important matters in haste, particularly exercised him: 'little grandeur, no consistency in their projects, no persistence in their plans.'[93] He quoted to Hugo the judgement of Talleyrand that Thiers was so ambitious that he could only be satisfied by a Cardinal's hat. 'Sire, you are clever but I am cleverer than you are,' Thiers once remarked to him. 'Proof to the contrary is that you are telling me so,' Louis-Philippe replied.[94]

England and the English were another favourite topic: the advantage of the Chamber of Deputies, where the tribune isolated the speaker, over the House of Commons where speakers, by speaking from their benches, were encouraged to adopt the opinion of others by 'a magnetic communication'; the silence of people walking in the streets of London compared to the noise made by the French. 'One always begins by detesting the English,' he said, but nonetheless he esteemed them. He feared the effect in France if he was either too well, or too ill, received on a forthcoming visit to Windsor: 'Oh it is not easy to travel when one is Louis-Philippe, is that not so, Monsieur Hugo?'[95]

Despite the casual nature of these evenings, less formal than many private salons, splendour returned to the Tuileries. On New Year's day 1833 over a thousand people filed past the King and Queen to pay their respects; by 1835, the number had increased to nearly 1,300 – the same number, despite a very different composition, as used to come to the Palais Royal on New Year's day before 1830.[96] Groups of foreigners were presented at court, 'arranged in the throne room by nations, the English first', the diarist Charles Greville noted with satisfaction. All stood in a straight line, down which walked the King and Queen, who 'by some strange stretch of invention find something to say'.[97]

The King improved access to the state apartments by building a new staircase, and, partly in order to encourage trade, from 1832 gave balls for up to 4,000 in the carnival season. Guests ranged from ambassadors to shopkeepers. English visitors found the palace of the Citizen King more impressive than Buckingham Palace. Describing one ball in which the entire first floor of the Tuileries was used, Charles Greville wrote:

> the long line of lights gleaming through the whole length of the Palace is striking as it is approached and the interior with the whole suite of apartments brilliantly illuminated and glittering from one end to the other with diamonds and feathers and uniforms and dancing in all the several rooms made a magnificent display. The supper in the theatre was the finest thing I ever saw . . . the whole thing as beautiful and magnificent as possible and making all our fetes look pitiful and mean after it.[98]

Americans agreed. George Ticknor wrote of a ball for 4,000 in 1838: 'there was no crowd, so vast was the space, and so well was the multitude attracted and distributed through the different rooms. Nothing could well be more brilliant than the lighting, nothing more tasteful than the dresses.'[99]

One element in the propaganda of the House of Orléans, since the eighteenth century, had been its love of Paris, in contrast to the alleged detachment of the royal family. Philippe Egalité, as his descendants remembered, had been called the King of Paris; Louis-Philippe owed his throne to the people of Paris. Indeed, since he did not hunt, he had no special reason to love the country. However, once in power, the Orléans felt the attractions of the Ile de France, and the disadvantages of Paris, even more than their cousins. For most of his reign Louis-Philippe spent only five months a year in the Tuileries, during the winter – less time than most French nobles spent in Paris.[100] For Louis-Philippe and his family the royal residences in the Ile de France represented freedom; Paris, in some years, was a death trap.[101] Inheriting the properties of all three branches of the Bourbons, Louis-Philippe and his family had even more residences from which to choose than their cousins. Neuilly was his favourite; Saint-Cloud had the charm of childhood memories. But the Orléans appeared happiest, and most at their ease, at the château of Eu near the Normandy coast, which Louis-Philippe had inherited from his mother. There – a sign of the power of the July monarchy – Louis-Philippe added a special wing to accommodate his ministers when they came to stay.[102] Louis-Philippe's sons used Chantilly, north of Paris, inherited by the Duc d'Aumale from the Duc de Bourbon in 1830, for hunting and horse racing: the first of the horse races still run today at Chantilly began in 1834.[103]

Charles X had used the old royal palace of Compiègne, north of Paris, for brief hunting-trips (Louis XVIII never used it except on his way to Paris in 1814). Louis-Philippe and his sons, however, used Compiègne, in the summer and autumn, for longer visits.[104] On the site of an old tennis court a small pink and gold court theatre was built by Louis-Philippe for the festivities in honour of the marriage, on 9 August 1832, of his eldest daughter Louise-Marie to Leopold I of the Belgians. The theatre was also used when Compiègne served as the royal family's base during the *camps de manoeuvre* held nearby – for the instruction and inspection of troops – for the first time since the last *camp de Compiègne* of Louis XV in 1769. There were six camps between 1833 and 1847: during the *camp de Compiègne* of 1837, nearly 700 people (including servants) were lodged in the palace.[105]

Even though Louis-Philippe did not hunt, he also revived the tradition of the French court's annual autumn visit to Fontainebleau, south-east of Paris, during the hunting season. Discontinued in 1787, it had been revived by Napoleon in 1807–11, and, although on a far more modest scale, by Charles X. Louis-Philippe's visits were grander than his cousin's. About ninety guests, including ambassadors, ministers and marshals, were invited to stay in the palace for three days at a time. Entertainments included hunts, drives in the forest, military reviews, balls, and performances of a different play in the court theatre every night. There, and elsewhere outside Paris, Louis-Philippe maintained a way of life which he considered unwise in the capital. Crowds of servants in red and silver Orléans livery waited on his guests: 'there is a luxury of details, an effort at attention which you would not find in the richest private person,' wrote the Orleanist deputy Viennet.[106] No guest failed to admire both the palace and the host: Louis-Philippe, with his *manie de la pierre*, particularly enjoyed showing guests the restoration work he was carrying out.[107]

In the autumn of 1834 one guest, Madame de Boigne, noticed with joy *'un certain parfum de trône* . . . it was the first time since the revolution that I saw the King dare to remember that he was a descendant of Henri IV.'[108] Recording the same occasion, Lady Granville wrote: 'The theatre is pretty and all the women being very smart it made altogether a beautiful coup d'oeil . . . the whole thing grandiose, magnificent and luxurious and I liked it of all things.' Count Rodolphe Apponyi, who followed in the next *fournée* of guests, noting the government's recent successes in elections and in the suppression of insurrections, had precisely the reaction the King wanted: 'never since King Louis-Philippe came to the throne have I seen the court more brilliant, more assured, more solidly established than at Fontainebleau; the ministers [Thiers, Montalivet, Duchâtel] had a triumphant air.'[109]

The marriage of the Duc d'Orléans in 1837 was the apogee of the July monarchy. Brave and intelligent, handsome and charming – 'I must say I never saw a more agreeable prince,' the English diplomat Henry Greville wrote[110] – the Duke was the idol of the army and of much of the people. In April 1837 Flahaut, long a military adviser and intimate of the prince, was appointed his Premier Ecuyer and Directeur de la Maison Civile. Back at the centre of a court for the first time since 1815, he wrote to his wife: 'if God preserve him for us you may depend he will be a good and great Prince. He is perfectly adored by all the troops here.'[111] Calling himself 'a revolutionary prince', Orléans professed to hate Bourbons, nobles and Christianity.[112]

The prince had many mistresses. Louis-Philippe became so worried for his son's health that he insisted that Orléans married. In the quest for a bride, the Orléans dynasty suffered many humiliations. No Bourbon, Habsburg or even Württemberg would marry a prince from a dynasty which was both insecure and illegitimate. In the end (with the help of the German Parisian Alexander von Humboldt) a Protestant from the small, if respected, House of Mecklenburg-Schwerin was selected.[113] None of Louis-Philippe's children was married in Paris. The marriage of Louise-Marie took place at Compiègne, while that of Orléans was celebrated, on 30 May 1837, in the chapel of Fontainebleau. In August 1830 at a reception in the Palais Royal Baron Gérard had been one of the few people who wore his official costume (as a member of the Institut) – thereby winning a smile of gratitude from the Queen. In 1835 at the New Year's reception at the Tuileries men in *fracs* were 'isolated among the great majority of uniforms'. By 1837 at Fontainebleau Laffitte, the kingmaker of 1830, was the only guest in a *frac* and not in uniform.[114]

Intelligent, well-read and dignified the new Duchesse d'Orléans, although no beauty, made a favourable impression. The sense of unease the Orléans brought to the throne of France is suggested by the praise bestowed on this German Protestant. Her manner was described as 'more natural than that of any of the rest of the family . . . always more attentive, more gracious and more perfectly up to it all than any of those around her'.[115] When she made her state entry down the Champs Elysées through the Place de la Concorde to the Tuileries, although she saluted with grace and dignity, and it was a summer day scented with lilac and chestnut, there was more curiosity than enthusiasm, and no cheers. However in the evening there were enough cries from the crowd in the Jardin des Tuileries for the King and his family to leave the dinner in the Salle des Maréchaux and come to the palace balcony. There, like Louis XVIII before him, he addressed words of thanks to the crowd. According to the Duchesse de Dino, his words were received with 'infinite transports'.[116] Unlike Louis XVIII on 8 July 1815, however, Louis-Philippe did not descend to mingle with the crowd.

After Fontainebleau and the Tuileries, Versailles. Before 1815 both Napoleon I and Louis XVIII had hoped to reside in this embodiment of the French monarchy. After 1830, however, the splendour of Versailles was acceptable only if devoted to public instruction rather than royal pleasure. Louis-Philippe decided to transform Versailles into a museum. Between 1833 and 1847, according to his architect Fontaine, he paid 398 visits to Versailles, often staying nearby in the Grand Trianon and being carried by sedan chair to the palace. He discussed and decided everything himself. The apartments of Louis XIV in the central block were restored. Those of princes and court officials in the two wings to the right and left of the central block, and in the attic floor, were destroyed. They were replaced by the Musée de l'Histoire de France, dedicated *à toutes les gloires de la France*, royal, revolutionary and imperial.

In the apotheosis of the Orléans' love of pictures, Louis-Philippe filled the new museum with 4,000 historical portraits and narrative pictures and 1,000 sculptures, many especially commissioned by himself, in order to teach the history of France to visitors. Thus there are three Versailles today: the state apartments of Louis XIV; the private apartments of Louis XV, his children and grandchildren; and the historical museum of Louis-Philippe. The most remarkable ensemble, in the Aile du Midi, consisted of three halls: first, the Salle de 1792, decorated with pictures of the campaign in which the young Louis-Philippe had served in the republican army against the invading émigrés, Austrians and Prussians. It was followed by the massive Galerie des Batailles, 120 metres long and 13 metres wide, lined with 33 pictures of French victories, from Clovis at the Battle of Tolbiac in 496 to Napoleon at Wagram in 1809.[117] After the Galerie des Batailles, the Salle de 1830 at the end of the Aile du Midi contains narrative pictures of Louis-Philippe riding to and being greeted in the Hôtel de Ville; receiving the offer of the crown in the Palais Royal; swearing to the Charte in the Chamber of Deputies; presenting tricolour flags to the Garde Nationale in front of the Ecole Militaire. Allegorical scenes on the ceiling show *France defending the Charter* and Truth, accompanied by Justice and Wisdom, protecting France (represented as half the globe) against Hypocrisy, Fanaticism and Discord.[118] If the Salle de 1792 shows Louis-Philippe serving the nation, the Salle de 1830, although commemorating the revolution of July 1830, is in the tradition of royal self-glorification. It exaggerates the King's popularity, and denies discord. In his embroidered Lieutenant-General's uniform, wearing the grand cordon of the Légion d'Honneur, Louis-Philippe is the centre of every picture.[119]

Beneath the obvious desire to reconcile different parties in the common glory of French history, the King had two other motives: first, the desire to make a battle gallery glorifying French victories, like the battle galleries being created, at the same period, in the Winter Palace in St Petersburg and the Residenz in Munich; second, the desire for revenge on his cousins of the elder branch of his family. The three halls created by Louis-Philippe, the Salle de 1792, the Galerie des Batailles and the Salle de 1830, were the equivalent, both in sequence and theme, of the Salon de la Guerre, Galerie des Glaces and Salon de la Paix created by Louis XIV in the central block of the palace. They were moreover in the wing where before 1789 the Orléans had an apartment as *princes du sang*, and had suffered, in their own imaginations, so many humiliations in ceremonial from their cousins of the elder branch.

On 10 June 1837 the new museum was formally opened in honour of the royal marriage. At 3 p.m., 1,500 guests were entertained to dinner, by tables of twenty, in the Galerie des Glaces and adjoining salons. Contrary to etiquette most guests finished their meal in three-quarters of an hour, and placed their napkins on the table before the King had finished his. He then led them to the red and gold palace theatre for the first entertainment held there since the banquet of the Gardes du Corps on 3 October 1789: Molière's *Le Misanthrope* was performed, with Mlle Mars, followed by extracts from *Robert le Diable*.

Guests were then entertained with a torchlight promenade through the garden and park. Male guests wore uniform or a form of embroidered eighteenth-century court dress, *habit habillé* (even Delacroix wore the latter). A hundred deputies in *fracs* were the sole, deliberately disrespectful, exceptions. To Madame de Boigne it seemed as if the bourgeoisie had taken the palace of Louis XIV by storm.[120] The new museum proved popular both with French and foreign visitors. Delphine de Girardin, the former *muse de la patrie* Delphine Gay, who had married Emile de Girardin and become a journalist and hostess whom Balzac called 'the queen of conversation', hailed it as one of the wonders of the world; it would be an inspiration behind the creation of the National Portrait Gallery in London.[121] Most newspapers praised the ideas of national reconciliation and glory which presided over the museum. However, *Le Siècle* commented that the government of the July monarchy had forgotten to invite to the fêtes of Versailles 'the people to whom it owes its existence and its fortune'.[122]

When on 24 August 1838 the Duchesse d'Orléans gave birth to a son, the future of the July monarchy seemed secure. His title emphasised the importance of the capital to the regime. Napoleon I had revealed his European ambitions by calling his son the King of Rome. Louis XVIII had recognised his debt to the provinces by naming the Duc de Berri's son the Duc de Bordeaux. Louis-Philippe paid tribute to Paris by calling his grandson the Comte de Paris. Amid similar pomp, similar protestations of loyalty and optimism, and similar arrays of representatives of the principal institutions of France, all three princes were baptised in Notre Dame, the cathedral of Paris.

If Paris was the scene of violent conflicts between Orleanists and republicans, it was also the focus of another war which, in words if not deeds, was no less ferocious: between Orleanists and legitimists. After their disarray in August 1830, the latter had regrouped around Charles X's Premier Aide-de-camp the Duc de Fitzjames, Chateaubriand, and their leading deputy, the great orator and advocate Pierre-Antoine Berryer. They were driven as much by loathing for the July monarchy as by loyalty to the Bourbons. Some peers had based their resignations from the Chamber of Peers in 1830 on dynastic loyalty, referring to 'questions which are not questions for me'; more resigned in 1832 when their Chamber, rather than the throne of France, ceased to be hereditary. The Duc de Duras, for example, the former Premier Gentilhomme, resigned his peerage in 1832, deploring 'the most fatal access of all doctrines subversive of property and even inheritance'.[123] Property was more important to him than dynastic loyalty.

Unable or unwilling to provide court offices, hereditary peerages, pensions or military glory, Louis-Philippe had little with which to tempt French royalists to rally to his monarchy. Nobles who had been proud to serve Napoleon I disdained to rally to the Citizen King. Their hatred led them to exaggerate the bourgeois nature of the regime. Ignoring the many bourgeois legitimists (Berryer, Bellart, Lainé) and Orleanist nobles (the Broglie, Talleyrand, Ségur, Castellane and Molé families), and the fact that half the ministers of Louis-Philippe were nobles, the Duchesse de Maillé wrote: 'the House of Orléans is in place but not established. It is a means not an end. It has served as an instrument for the middle class to come to power.'[124]

Many legitimists, even the former Prefect of the Seine the Comte de Chabrol, abandoned Paris, city of riots and treason, and emigrated to their estates, partly in a conscious attempt to build up their influence, and royalist votes, in the countryside.[125] A former Ecuyer Cavalcadour du Roi, the Comte de Neuilly, left Paris in 1830 for his Château de Rigny in Poitou, and, although he lived another thirty-three years, never revisited the capital.[126] After the July revolution, so the young British diplomat Henry Lytton Bulwer noted, his friend the Marquis de Fitzjames, son of the Duc de Fitzjames, spent eight months a year on his estates, and devoted himself to politics: 'He has dismissed even the appearances of pleasure. In Paris he goes nowhere but to the club in the Rue de Grammont' (the Cercle de l'Union, aristocratic, royalist and fashionable). Such was the family abhorrence of Louis-Philippe that the King's name was used as a bogey-man to scare his children. In this milieu Henri V was seen more as 'a guarantee of stability and durability', 'as a link between the past and the present', than as the embodiment of divine right.[127]

Chateaubriand, who lived at the Infirmerie Marie Thérèse until he moved to 112 rue du Bac in 1838, continued to be at the centre of royalist plans and conspiracies: he was briefly imprisoned in July 1832 when the Duchesse de Berri, his favourite member of the royal family since her encouragement of his book on the Duc de Berri in 1820,[128] disembarked in France and tried, without success, to start a royalist insurrection in the Vendée. After she was captured in January 1833, his pamphlet *Mémoire sur la captivité de Madame la duchesse de Berri*, with its cry *Madame, votre fils est mon roi!*, sold thousands of copies. Thereafter he journeyed to Prague (1833 and 1835), London (1843) and Venice (1845), often as representative of the Duchesse de Berri, to offer homage and advice to the exiled Bourbons. He had doubts about the future of monarchy in general and the Bourbon monarchy in particular:[129] 'the old European order is expiring,' he wrote in *Mémoires d'outre-tombe*; the present distribution of property and disproportion of fortunes and conditions were too unjust to last.[130] However he was one of the few writers prescient enough to query whether nations would do better than monarchs. He also affirmed that, apart from a sense of honour, and his horror of the July monarchy, reason made him legitimist: 'legitimate constitutional monarchy has always seemed to me the gentlest and most secure route to entire liberty.'[131]

The geographical centre of the legitimists in Paris was the Faubourg Saint-Germain, which, as the centre of plots and discontent, played the role, under the July monarchy, of the Palais Royal under the Restoration. The nobility was again able to indulge its taste for insult and opposition, which had inspired many to hope for the death of the *gros cochon* Louis XVIII in 1816–21.[132] Insults could turn to physical assault. On 17 February 1831, driving a cabriolet very fast, Comte Albert de Bertier tried to run down the King, the Queen and Madame Adélaïde as they were walking from the Tuileries to the Palais Royal. He later said that he had been unable to hold his horses and, since the King was wearing a *frac* and a large tricolour cockade, and carrying an umbrella, nothing had distinguished him and his wife from any other bourgeois couple.[133] Such was the social power of the legitimists in Paris that few private balls were held there during the carnivals of 1833 and 1837, while they mourned the imprisonment of the Duchesse de Berri and the death of Charles X respectively.[134] The annual charity ball started in 1832 to benefit former pensioners of the *liste civile* of Charles X received every superlative known to Delphine de Girardin: some considered it too sumptuous for a charity ball.[135] In 1843, as an aide-de-camp of Louis-Philippe, the Comte de Chabannes was defeated in his candidacy for the Jockey Club, although it had been founded ten years earlier under the auspices of the Ducs d'Orléans and de Nemours: the Cercles de l'Union and Agricole were also bastions of legitimism.[136]

Far from being weak and pitiful, as Talleyrand claimed,[137] the Faubourg Saint-Germain attracted some of the most original talents, and largest fortunes, in France. Indeed, as contemporaries realised, it consciously set out to recruit talent.[138] Royalism could appear intellectually and emotionally more satisfying than the complacent liberalism of the July monarchy. Like the radical republicans, royalists had the attraction of contesting fundamental principles of society. The young Balzac, for example, was converted from liberalism to royalism in 1831, partly through conversations with the Duchesse d'Abrantès, and through the efforts of two admirers, the Marquise de Castries and her uncle the Duc de Fitzjames: the former had begun their friendship by writing Balzac an anonymous fan-letter; the latter, former Premier Aide-de-camp of Charles X, signed a letter to the novelist *A vous du fond du coeur*.[139] Although admiring Napoleon, Balzac soon considered himself a faithful subject of Henri V, said that he wrote in the light of the two 'eternal truths' of monarchy and religion, and had little but contempt for the July monarchy. 'What a dismal contrast with the court of Charles X is the present court, if indeed it is a court!' he wrote in 1840.[140]

Another recruit was one of the most brilliant French writers of the century, Jules Barbey d'Aurevilly, later known as *le connétable des lettres*. Born in Normandy in 1808 of a family ennobled in the eighteenth century, he first came to Paris in 1827 to study at the Collège Stanislas. A writer and journalist, he published a defence of dandyism, *Du dandysme et de George Brummel*, in 1845. Preferring the devil himself to solitude and death by isolation, he 'conquered' salons in the Faubourg Saint-Germain, especially that of the legitimist Madame de Maistre. Believing in *le sublime de l'idée monarchique*, he marked the *fêtes de juillet* of 1838 by walking on the boulevards wearing green and white carnations – the colours of royalism. Through the influence of Madame de Maistre, he became a practising, as well as an intellectual, Catholic.[141]

One of the most cultivated women in the Faubourg Saint-Germain, among 'all these cats who scratch and bite each other',[142] was the Duchesse de Rauzan, daughter of the Duchesse de Duras. Mortified by her father's remarriage, within a year of her mother's death, to the Swiss widow of a Portuguese Jewish banker, she continued her mother's tradition of mixing intelligent men, irrespective of background or belief (but generally unaccompanied by their wives), with women of her own milieu. In the evening her salon could be 'full of women all screaming at the top of their shrill voices'.[143] In the morning she might receive writers such as Salvandy, Sainte-Beuve and Villemain.[144] Her salon also became famous for concerts and readings. The critic Ernest Legouvé was impressed:

No woman ever fulfilled better the idea one has of a *grande dame* . . . With her fine figure, her smiling dignity, her nuanced politeness, she knew how to mix ranks while keeping distances. When there was a marriage in society (for the Faubourg Saint-Germain, society is its society), the new husband had no duty more pressing than to take his young wife to the Duchesse de Rauzan's; it was like a presentation at court . . . her salon was her life, her pride, her passion; until the last days of her life, afflicted with an incurable disease, she had herself got up in the middle of the day, dressed herself, adorned herself, disputed with the ravages of the disease what remained of her attractions and then at four in the afternoon she appeared gracious, amiable and attentive and there, gathering all the strength which she had been given by a day of rest, she expended it in two hours of smiles, often paid for later by cruel sufferings. She raised the role of a society lady to the level of heroism. Her salon was her battlefield, she left it only to die.[145]

If Chateaubriand reigned in the salon of Madame Récamier, Eugène Sue, the king of the popular novel, was the idol of the Duchess's salon, and her lover. A dandy, author of *Mathilde*, a novel about legitimists, he was renowned for always wearing, according to Captain Gronow, 'a very broad-brimmed hat, of glossy newness, and remarkably tight, light-coloured trousers'. The first copy of his latest novel was usually visible on the Duchesse de Rauzan's table, magnificently bound and engraved with her coat of arms.[146]

The Faubourg Saint-Germain's main activity, after the pursuit of pleasure, was pursuit of the Orléans. Embassies became battlefields. When Casimir Périer asked ambassadors not to invite people who did not go to the Tuileries, they refused: those who did go were people they did not know. At the Tuileries they were likely to see – but would refuse to acknowledge – their shoemaker, their ribbon merchant, or one of the most despised women in Paris, the Duc de Bourbon's former mistress Madame de Feuchères.[147] In 1829 she had persuaded the Duke to leave his fortune to Orléans' younger son the Duc d'Aumale, in return for the Duc and Duchesse d'Orléans' request to Charles X to receive her at court: the *sexual* relationship of the Duc de Bourbon and the Baronne de Feuchères received the *social* sanction of the King and his court on condition that it led to the *financial* advantage of the House of Orléans. Madame de Feuchères, who had been left four large estates, two million francs, and a house in Paris by the Duc de Bourbon, was suspected of a role in his mysterious death by hanging on 27 August 1830.* Nevertheless she was invited to court balls by Louis-Philippe.[148]

Such was legitimist hostility to the Orléans that at a ball at James de

---

* He may have died as the result of an accident in the course of *pratiques strangulatoires efficaces mais dangereuses . . . nécessaires pour ranimer sa virilité chancelante*, in which he was assisted by the Baronne de Feuchères. It is significant that, at the time of his death, he may have been planning to follow his cousin Charles X into exile.

Rothschild's the Prince de Léon shouted *Voilà le gros poulot!* when he saw the Duc d'Orléans. In the end he was persuaded to sign an attestation, in the presence of Flahaut acting as the prince's representative, that his remark had not been intended for the prince.[149] Soon however the princes no longer visited private salons, where they were obliged to face so many disagreeable encounters.[150] The women, in particular, were like furies. At the sight of legitimists at a ball in Baron Delmar's gilded salons, Madame de Flahaut was described as looking like an 'an enraged she-wolf'.[151] Some called her, not Madame de Flahaut, but *Madame Fléau* – the scourge.[152]

While Orleanists, legitimists and republicans were fighting for control of France, the Catholic Church was fighting for its soul. Heine claimed that the Church was a corpse. 'All the facts of public and private life' showed that France was the land of materialism. The mass believed only in money: there had been a monetisation of God and a deification of money.[153] He was misled by his own atheism. Strengthened by its dissociation from government since 1830, Catholicism was in reality becoming fashionable again. At Lent sermons in Notre Dame in 1834 there were 1,300 in the congregation; in 1836, 5,000 when Abbé Lacordaire was preaching – 'almost all young students from the faculties', in contrast to fifteen years earlier, when students had led anticlerical demonstrations.[154] His successor the Abbé de Ravignan preached at 6 a.m. for workers, 2 p.m. for women and 8 p.m. for men from 'the superior classes of society. All the seats in the cathedral were packed over an hour before the preaching started': the space in front was crowded with carriages and footmen. The congregation included Guizot, Thiers, Lamartine and Victor Hugo. Over 1,500 men communicated after his Easter retreat and sermons. 'The clergy has a future here,' recorded a young Russian diplomat, Victor Balabine, in the diary he kept from the time of his arrival at the embassy in 1842.[155]

By the 1840s Mérimée claimed that there was not a single lady of fashion who was not writing a mystical treatise: two volumes on dogma by Madame du Ludre in 1842; four volumes by Princess Belgiojoso, *Essai sur la formation du dogme catholique* in 1842–3.[156] In the opinion of a visiting Piedmontese nobleman, Count Camille de Cavour: 'There is a very marked return to religious and Catholic ideas. The professors who are the most markedly Catholic are the most popular.' The courses of the Abbé Coeur, a Catholic democrat and professor of sacred eloquence in the Sorbonne, filled lecture halls.

In his first lecture he spoke magnificently of the mission of the nineteenth century . . . in making the intellect an active political power and in developing more and more in the social world the great principles of brotherhood and human dignity which Christianity has already made dominant in the religious world. The Abbé declared strongly amid the applause of the élite of the youth of Paris the alliance of Catholic doctrines with those of social progress.[157]

The inspiration for the first factory legislation in France, banning labour for children under eight, limiting children below twelve years to eight hours and below sixteen years to twelve hours a day, came from Catholic royalists such as the Comte de Villeneuve-Bargement. The law, however, governed only enterprises employing more than twenty workers and even then was rarely applied. More concerned about the poor than republicans or Orleanists, some royalists asked why slavery should be abolished in the colonies, when many French workers were treated worse than slaves.[158]

So fashionable had Catholicism become that even a sinner like the debauched dandy Casimir de Montrond died a good Catholic.[159] At the end of his life, Talleyrand himself, 'the apostate bishop', under the influence of his niece the Duchesse de Dino and their daughter Pauline de Périgord, developed a special devotion for the Virgin; the *Imitation of Christ* became his favourite reading. On the morning of the day he died, 17 May 1838, through the intermediary of the fashionable priest the Abbé Dupanloup, in front of seven witnesses, he signed a profession of faith and submission, a retraction of past errors and scandals, and a letter to the Pope requesting absolution. The reason for signing at the last possible moment a document written on 10 March may have been the desire to escape the comments of his friends. Before he died he had time to receive a visit from Louis-Philippe and Madame Adélaïde, and, after making his confession, the last sacraments of the Catholic Church.[160] Princess Lieven remarked, with the cynicism of a woman of the world, and a rival's envy for the Duchesse de Dino's coup:

> But what humbug the whole deathbed scene was, that recantantion dragged from him when all his strength had left him. Indeed how can one believe that he signed it when he had not even the strength to move his fingers? Nevertheless Madame de Dino used all her powers and cleverness for that purpose and she has assured herself a good position with the Faubourg Saint-Germain.[161]

Talleyrand's death inspired a last bon mot from his old enemy Pozzo. Talleyrand, he said, had been very well received in Hell. The Devil had only one complaint: 'but you exceeded my instructions.'[162]

IO

City of Ink

1830–1848

Le cri de Paris, c'est la plume qui gratte le papier!

Marquis de Custine, *Ethel* (1839)

LITERATURE AND POLITICS in France were so intertwined that the July revolution had been, in part, both provoked and won by writers. One cause of the *ordonnances* of 25 July had been government determination to censor the press, denounced in the preamble as 'an instrument of disorder and sedition, an active agent of dissolution'.[1] For their part journalists like Rémusat and Thiers had been bolder than most deputies or businessmen in directing revolutionary action – leading Chateaubriand to prophesy that a monarchy which had risen by the press would fall by the press.[2] After the revolution, writers rose in status. As an aide-de-camp of Louis-Philippe noted with regret, journalists regarded themselves as more important than deputies. Novelists like Balzac and Eugène Sue were worshipped by some readers as gods.[3]

The importance of the publishing industry in Paris was one reason for the prominence of journalists at the time of the July revolution. After 1800 dramatic improvements in techniques of producing paper had made books cheaper and easier to publish.[4] By 1834 a mass edition of the *Chansons* of the famous liberal poet Béranger, the principal propagandist of the Napoleonic legend, could be sold for as little as 50 centimes (about sixpence).[5] In *Fragmens des silhouettes de Paris* (1837) a German writer Adalbert von Bornstedt expressed astonishment at the multitude of translators, poets, journalists and 'writers of every sort in Paris', in addition to printers, booksellers, bookbinders, stenographers and compilers: 'Millions of people live off the theatre, the book trade and newspapers.'[6]

Paris was a city of readers as well as writers. Of 1,000 Parisians only 193 were illiterate in the early 1830s, compared to an average of 496 per 1,000 in the rest of France (a figure nonetheless higher than in the United States, Prussia, England and Austria).[7] In a manner unimaginable today books filled daily life. 'The war of life', Delacroix considered, was only made tolerable to people with the help of the books they read. Madame du Cayla's ability to quote Racine is said to have secured her the favour of Louis XVIII. Madame Récamier spent much of the day reading the classics of French literature, before her guests arrived in her salon – where the conversation was principally about books.[8]

Every social class could enjoy reading. Flower sellers or street porters could be seen reading books on the pavements of Paris. The astonishment of British observers suggests the rarity of such sights in London. 'In every hand there is now to be found a book! Enter into the rudest porter's lodge of the simplest hotel, in the remotest quarter and you will find cheap editions of the best authors, which are beyond the means only of the very lowest indigence,' wrote Lady Morgan. Captain Gronow agreed:

> The French read with avidity whenever they can snatch the opportunity. They read standing in the open air, into which they are driven by the want of air at home. They read in garrets and cellars. They read at one end of a counter when a person is hammering a lock or a piece of cabinet work at the other without taking their eye from the book or picking quarrel with the person who is making the noise.[9]

Thomas Raikes once saw a public coachman reading the poems of Horace in Latin.[10] The illiterate could also enjoy books. A popular triumph like *Les Mystères de Paris* by Eugène Sue would be read aloud to illiterate people gathered around a doorway.[11]

Reading aloud was also a pastime in salons. It served to publicise, and test reactions to, new works. Queen Hortense received the news of Waterloo while weeping with Benjamin Constant over his novel *Adolphe*, which he had just read to her. Lamartine read his *Méditations* in the salon of Madame de Sainte-Aulaire; another handsome young poet Alfred de Vigny *La Frégate* at Madame d'Agoult's; Charles de Rémusat read his play *L'Insurrection de Saint-Domingue* at the Duchesse de Broglie's. To read a five-act play in an evening was quite common. Balzac wrote that no man or woman *de bonne compagnie* could escape *une lecture de salon*, and the subsequent cries of applause: *Miraculeux! Immense! Prodigieux! C'est tout l'Orient! C'est le passé qui se lève! . . . C'est l'univers! C'est Dieu!*[12]

From 1834 extracts from the memoirs which Chateaubriand was engaged in writing – and scenes from his plays – were read out to a carefully chosen group of critics in the salon of Madame Récamier, who in 1826 had moved to a larger apartment on the first floor of the Abbaye aux Bois. The adulatory atmosphere nauseated Lamartine and Legouvé. With wrinkles sunk deep into his face and features grown hard, Chateaubriand was worshipped in her salon as if he were the holy sacrament, though rarely deigning to utter a word.[13] Custine, who had read an earlier version and revered Chateaubriand as his master, claimed that entire chapters had been rewritten from a new and narrow point of view. There was a complete absence of sincerity and simplicity (criticism of Louis XVIII and Charles X, for example, had been softened). Son of one of Chateaubriand's abandoned mistresses, he blamed the *minauderies* of Madame Récamier: 'I see there the man confiscated for the benefit of the salon.'[14]* Most, however, considered Chateaubriand's *Mémoires d'outre-tombe* a masterpiece, a brilliant interweaving of the private life of a French royalist with the public drama of the fall of the French monarchy.

So vital was the publishing trade in Paris after 1814 that it provided much of the patronage and stimulus once obtained at court. In 1813 3,749 books had been published in the whole French Empire; in 1825 7,605 were published in France alone.[15] In 1828 there were 580 *libraires brevetés*† in Paris.[16] Book sales could be large enough to enable writers to live from their earnings. After the revolution of 1830 Lamartine and Chateaubriand could afford to resign from their positions as diplomat and peer of France respectively: by reducing writers' dependence on official positions, literacy stimulated legitimism. In 1826 Chateaubriand had received 350,000 francs‡ for a complete edition of his works (which helped ruin its publisher Ladvocat).[17] In 1836 he obtained a further capital sum of 156,000 francs and income of 12,000 a year for the rest of his life, in return for ceding the property of his memoirs and unpub-

---

* Mérimée likewise considered that his friend Ampère, who was in love with Madame Récamier and saw her every day, was a once original philosopher who had been castrated by an old coquette. When she died, he seemed relieved.
† Licensed booksellers, as opposed to those selling books and pamphlets in the street.
‡ The price of a large *hôtel* in the Faubourg Saint-Germain, about £20,000 in pounds sterling of the day.

lished works to the publisher Delloye.[18] Balzac obtained a similar deal at the same time. Victor Hugo, when a young poet, could sell twelve years' property of one work, his odes, to the publisher Ladvocat for 2,000 francs.[19] By a contract with the bookseller Paulin in 1839, Thiers was guaranteed 500,000 francs on delivery of the manuscript of his history of the Consulate and the Empire. Paulin had made an excellent bargain. Six years later 10,000 copies of Thiers' book were sold on the day of publication.[20]

The most popular playwright of the age, for thirty years the delight of France and Europe, was Eugène Scribe. Hardly living away from his desk, he managed to write 48 plays, as well as 28 opera librettos, 95 *opéra-comique* librettos, 242 *vaudevilles* and eight *arguments de ballet*. His use of co-authors to help increase production prompted the remark that the Académie Française should have given him a bench rather than a seat.[21] His witty, perceptive plays such as *Le Mariage de raison* (1826) and *Le Verre d'eau* (1840) opposed all forms of enthusiasm and romanticism. According to the English writer and diplomat Henry Lytton Bulwer, he had one of those faces which 'one sees everywhere, with a quick eye – small sharp and regular features, with nothing either to strike or astonish'.[22] Gautier attributed his success to the fact that he had not a spark of poetry in him. Victor Hugo compared him to Thiers in politics and Horace Vernet in painting, all three facile, rapid talents, living for the moment and destined to 'an immense celebrity and an immense oblivion'.[23] In *La Camaraderie* (1839) Scribe revealed one route to literary success. Edmond is a writer with a *modestie de dupe*. He gets nowhere. Oscar belongs to 'a mutual admiration society' of writers and journalists who praise his wit and talent: 'you arrive when you have comrades.' As a description of the Romantics' methods of self-advancement, this is no exaggeration. Scribe sometimes obtained 50,000 francs for one play, and enjoyed an annual income of between 100,000 and 180,000 francs in the years 1830–50. Soon this son of a shopkeeper in the rue Saint-Denis, where he was born in 1791, lived *en grand seigneur*, with a house in Paris, a villa in Meudon and a château in Seine et Marne, where he kept open house. Every year he was able to invest money from his literary earnings in property and government stock.[24]

Publishers and booksellers had power. At a party in the apartment of the Duchesse d'Abrantès in the Abbaye aux Bois, Bulwer saw the bookseller Fournier distributing looks and glances among the guests as if he was the Duc de Choiseul at the height of his power. He was 'the life and

soul and bread and soup and fame and glory' of the party. Bulwer concluded: '*la librairie est une des aristocraties de l'époque* and a bookseller of
talent and reputation is in point of honour and consequence far above
a peer of France.'[25]

Despite the rise of the public market, however, writing and politics
remained closely connected. Many writers continued to rely on the
French court and government for financial support. In addition to such
rising stars as Lamartine and Hugo, writers now forgotten such as
Louise Swanton Belloc (translator of Byron, Thomas Moore and Mrs
Gaskell, and grandmother of Hilaire Belloc), Alissan de Chazet, Elzéar
de Sabran and Charles Nodier also received government pensions of
over 1,000 francs a year – as would, from 1836 to 1848, despite advocating the lordship of the proletariat, the greatest of German Parisians,
Henri Heine.[26] After 1830 Chateaubriand lived not only from his earnings as a writer but also from the pension of 12,000 francs a year which
he received from the King in exile.[27] The July monarchy used the post
of librarian in a royal château or a ministry as a means of providing
sinecures for, and winning the support of, writers such as Casimir
Delavigne, Sainte-Beuve, Alexandre Dumas. Alfred de Musset,
appointed keeper of the library of the Ministry of the Interior in 1837,
with the help of his old schoolfriend the Duc d'Orléans, wrote sonnets
to Louis-Philippe on his escape from an assassination attempt and on
the birth of his grandson the Comte de Paris.[28]

Thus even, or especially, in the nineteenth century, inside many
French writers there was a courtier struggling to get out – as Victor
Hugo's frequent attendance on Louis-Philippe at the Tuileries confirms. When the young poet Antoine-Etienne Fontaney's verses were
shown to Queen Marie Amélie in 1831, he wondered: 'will this lead me
to harbour?' Indeed he briefly became an Attaché d'Ambassade in
Spain. However, having failed to transform this promising start into an
enduring career, he died in poverty in 1837 at the age of thirty-four,
soon after his mistress – and like her, probably of tuberculosis.[29] After
1830 the radical historian Jules Michelet taught history to Princess
Clémentine, daughter of Louis-Philippe, as he had, before 1830, to the
daughter of the Duchesse de Berri. While glorifying the French revolution, he was sometimes lent a room in the palace of Saint-Cloud so that
he could change clothes after lessons, before dining with the royal
family.[30]

Another sign of the link between politics and literature was the
number of professional writers in Paris who became leading politicians –

among others, Constant, Chateaubriand and Lamartine – and of politicians, including Talleyrand, Molé, Pasquier, Thiers and Guizot, who devoted much of their time to writing, especially their own memoirs. Talleyrand for example, after his fall from power in 1815, wrote to the Duchesse de Courlande that it would be 'curious' to recount when he wrote about it.[31] Like the fashion for commemorative buildings and ceremonies, the torrent of memoirs written in this period was a sign of the intensity of the dramas through which their writers had recently lived and which they felt the need to record. Political instability was a spur to creativity. Mme de Genlis claimed that almost all her contemporaries had written memoirs.[32]

In Twickenham in 1816, in order to justify his own conduct and attack the King's, Louis-Philippe published his diary of the beginning of the Hundred Days. In 1822 Louis XVIII himself published an account of his flight from Paris in 1791. When convalescing in Meudon in 1833, the Duc d'Orléans, son of Louis-Philippe, wrote biting memoirs of the Restoration. The cult of memoirs led to the publication of many which were apocryphal or fictitious.[33] 'Ghosting' the memoirs of a chamberlain of Napoleon, a Paris executioner and the Duchesse d'Abrantès was one of the first literary activities to earn the young Balzac large sums.[34] In Molé's opinion memoirs were 'the mania of our epoch'. Following his own principle that they should be as individual, rather than as impartial as possible, this glacial politician, frustrated in his marriage to a daughter of Madame de La Briche, living in an emotional desert, wrote of love like a prophet: 'Love is the happiness of angels, it is Plato's concert of the spheres, it is what is most ideal and most real, highest and most useful, most serious and most delicious.' In 1827 he recovered the favours of Madame de Castellane, a blonde beauty *d'un esprit vif et original*, of whom it was said that she could not give a *sou* to a beggar without trying to make him fall in love. Molé regarded her as a goddess: 'all her charm came from her soul and yet nothing equalled the purity of her features.'[35] In the freedom of Paris he saw her two or three times a day, and every evening: he often made the tea in her salon as if he was in his own house.[36] The life of his life, as he was of hers, she read, reread, dictated and copied out in her own hand (so that no secretary learnt his secrets) his memoirs. Molé remembered that she wanted them to be a monument erected to 'our common memory and to our mutual and incomparable devotion'.[37]* Her

---

* Nonetheless his descendants published an expurgated edition from which her name was omitted.

husband, described as the ugliest and most disgusting of men, was an army officer usually stationed in the provinces; when in Paris, he would appear in his wife's salon at the beginning of the evening, discuss the day's news for half an hour, then leave. His diary is an invaluable source for this period, except for the fact that it never mentions Molé's affair with his wife.[38]

His portraits of Talleyrand and Fouché, among others, make Molé's memoirs a masterpiece of ferocity. Talleyrand, 'half man, half serpent', had a mouth which expressed at once debauch, satiety and disdain. His morning ablutions of nose, mouth and the 'paws which were his equivalent of feet' are described with a novelist's eye for physical detail. Of Fouché Duc d'Otrante, *le plus comme il faut des révolutionnaires*, who combined the ease and arrogance of a *grand seigneur* with 'bourgeois habits' (unspecified), Molé wrote:

> All his person bears witness to the passions which have agitated his life; he is tall, with thin limbs, a dry voice, rapid movements, a fiery expression, fine features, piercing bloodshot eyes, the dry hair of an albino; something at once ferocious, elegant and agile makes him resemble a panther.[39]

History was another fashionable form of writing. One sign of the fashion for history was the foundation, in 1822, of the Ecole des Chartes, to train historians and archivists. Many liberals reacted to the ultra-royalist triumph of those years by retreating into the past – as royalists had under the Empire. Rémusat wrote: 'political means being exhausted or adjourned, we must act on minds; it is through philosophy, the arts, history, criticism and if possible literary creation that they should be attacked.'[40] According to the Duc de Broglie: 'our salons are losing interest in politics. We are beaten, so beaten that we are no longer worth the effort of persecuting. Everyone is turning towards literature, political economy and philosophy.'[41] The liberal politician Barante wrote a twelve-volume *Histoire des ducs de Bourgogne de la maison de Valois 1364–1477* (1824–6), the Comte de Sainte-Aulaire a three-volume *Histoire de la Fronde* (1827). In addition to his translations of English seventeenth-century memoirs, Guizot edited an extensive *Collection des mémoires rélatifs à l'histoire de France depuis le règne de Philippe Auguste au commencement du siècle* (1823–35), running to thirty volumes in all. Augustin Thierry, a protégé of La Fayette and Broglie, wrote an *Histoire de la conquête d'Angleterre par les Normands* (1825) and *Lettres sur l'histoire de France* (1827). Comte Daru, a former senior official of Napoleon I who wrote a six-volume history of Venice, estimated that in 1825 alone forty million pages of history were printed.[42] In 1834 Guizot also founded the Société de l'Histoire de France, in order to publish historical documents.[43]

Love of the past also revealed itself in a new attitude to interior decoration. One of the most fashionable beauties in Paris in the 1830s was the Comtesse Le Hon, wife of the first Belgian ambassador to France, known as *l'ambassadrice aux cheveux d'or.* Heine compared her to a ravishing Flemish beauty escaped out of a Rubens picture; the Duc d'Orléans made her his principal mistress.[44] With another friend of the prince, Madame de Flahaut, Madame Le Hon helped introduce a revolution in interior decoration. Instead of fitting out all rooms in the latest fashion, she was the first person to fill them with furniture and objects from the past, in particular from the reigns of Louis XV and XVI, bought at Parisian antique dealers. Her lover the Duc d'Orléans, who also enjoyed visiting antique shops, adopted this fashion, ordering old pieces from the royal *garde-meuble* for his apartment in the Tuileries.[45]

By 1841 the reigning fashion for furniture, decoration and sculpture was the period of François Ier (1515–47). Parisians were so subjugated by the Renaissance that Heine compared its 'almost frightening' appeal to 'the memory of a secret life that we might have traversed in a dream'.[46] Many houses reflected this unprecedented love of the past. The house of the Marquis de Fitzjames, according to Bulwer, was

> furnished with that nice tact, almost exclusively aristocratic, which escapes being ostentatious without falling into the still more vulgar [fault] of simplicity. One of the salons below is in chintz, the other in the old damask silk of Louis XIV and the antique pieces of precious porcelain and the rich chairs of silver brocade have each a kind of family history attached to them.[47]

Balzac furnished his house with pictures, furniture and objets d'art from every century and country, especially if they had a royal provenance.[48] A house in François Ier style, still standing, was built by the architect Renaud on the Place Saint-Georges, opposite Thiers' house, in 1840.[49] The reign of neoclassicism, the tyranny of the contemporary, were over.

It was commonplace to say that women had been dethroned by the French revolution. Before it they were goddesses; afterwards slaves. Indeed under the Code Napoléon a married woman's legal status was that of a minor owing obedience to her husband, who administered and enjoyed the profits of her property. Even if a woman had been authorised by her husband to exercise a trade, she was never placed on lists of businessmen as it was not 'in the spirit of our institutions'.[50] At court a few months before the July revolution, the Duchesse de Berri told the Duc de Chartres that women were important only in times of agitation: otherwise 'no one even looks at us'.[51]

In practice women of the élite, such as the Duchesse de Duras and Madame de Flahaut, could exercise, through their husbands, their lovers or their salons, at least as much influence as their grandmothers in the eighteenth century, and often more. The Duchesse de Berri was sufficiently independent to try to start a rising against Louis-Philippe in Marseille and the Vendée in 1832. The Duchesse de Dino was said to seethe with rage that she was not a minister. Yet she was regarded as his best adviser by her uncle and lover Talleyrand, whom she accompanied both to the Congress of Vienna in 1814 and the French embassy in London in 1830. Her passion for politics was such that, when Molé visited her after a setback to Talleyrand's ambitions, she seemed ready to eat him alive: 'I have never seen a woman so angry, even in the street.' Normally dark as an Italian, she had gone green with fury, and was weeping and shaking from head to toe.[52] In 1836 Sémonville remarked that an ideal ministry would consist of Madame Adélaïde as Président du Conseil; the Duchesse de Broglie at Justice et Cultes; the Duchesse de Dino at Foreign Affairs; Madame de Boigne at the Interior; and Madame de Flahaut as Minister of War.[53]

Writing, as well as salon management or the exercise of political influence, could be a means for women to pursue careers of their own. One of the most famous women of the period, George Sand, having reached an agreement with her husband, came to Paris, like so many others, in the magic year 1831. Assuming not only a man's name but often men's clothes, she wrote a novel, or more, a year in order to achieve financial independence. Many deal with the injustice and horror of marriage.[54]

Memoirs also gave women an activity in which they could equal men and express their own political views. The memoirs of Mesdames de Rémusat, de Boigne, de La Tour du Pin, d'Agoult, de Chastenay and many others, are masterpieces in the great tradition of French memoir-writing. Until the 1850s Madame de Boigne had what the Duchesse de Dino called 'the important salon of the moment': many of her guests were inherited from the salon of her friend Madame de Montcalm, who had died from cholera in 1832. Among the politicians who attended were Broglie, Guizot and Thiers, but the idol of her salon was her lover Baron Pasquier, soon to be President of the Chambre des Pairs and Chancellor of France. Politics was the principal subject of conversation.[55] Her political role in 1830 as representative of Pozzo in his first contacts with Louis-Philippe after the July revolution has already been described. Thereafter the King himself would often come to talk to her, when she was visiting Madame Adélaïde; Chateaubriand also used her as a channel of communication with the French government.[56] Pretty, intelligent, glacial, Madame de Boigne never had a hair or a pleat out of place. Apponyi wrote that she appeared never to have experienced an emotion and would have frozen desire before it could express itself.[57] One day the young Albert de Broglie saw that a ribbon on her bonnet was out of place. He was not surprised to learn two days later that she was dead.[58]

Her memoirs are her masterpiece. Madame de Boigne describes the court of Versailles; the emigration in London; Parisians' detestation of Napoleon I; the salons and quarrels of the Restoration; and such friends as Maréchal Marmont and Pozzo. Pozzo, she wrote, would have descended into hell to find adversaries for Napoleon; in her view his *langage un peu étrange et rempli d'images avait quelque chose de pittoresque et d'inattendu qui saisissait l'imagination.*[59] With an affectation of simplicity typical of the Faubourg Saint-Germain, Madame de Boigne called her memoirs *une causerie de vieille femme, un ravaudage de salon, un ouvrage de tapisserie, un vieux fauteuil de plus.** In reality they were the political and social testament of an ardent Orleanist. Marie Amélie, a friend since the emigration, is presented as a model of virtue. Accounts of the marriage and death of the Duc d'Orléans, and the death of Princess Marie d'Orléans, are semi-hagiographical. The Bourbons are denigrated, the rumour that Charles X said mass is repeated.[60] In her accounts of other people (as opposed to her own experiences), inaccuracies and distortions are so frequent as to make Madame de Boigne's memoirs unreliable.[61] On some matters, however, her judgements are irrefutable. On the revolution of 1830: 'Never has a catastrophe been more foretold than that towards which the doomed party was working with so much zeal.'[62] On the fall of nineteenth-century French monarchies:

---

* Her rival Madame de La Tour du Pin called her own memoirs *Journal d'une femme de cinquante ans.*

Since my arrival at the age of reason, I have seen three powerful governments collapse, all three by suicide and abuse of the principle which had created them: the Empire by perseverance in despotism and in war, the Restoration by an unintelligent and inopportune recrudescence of legitimist pretensions, the July monarchy by the fear, pushed to the point of pusillanimity, of breaking the bounds of legality and of failing in respect for the bourgeoisie of Paris.[63]

If power was the main subject of memoirs, in other works it was Paris itself. Especially after the city's apotheosis in 1830, it was said that the appearance of the word Paris in the title of a play or book guaranteed its success: Parisians found nothing more interesting than Paris.[64] Among the books devoted to 'the queen of cities', 'the city of prodigies, the city of illusions, the wonder of the world', was *Paris ou le livre des cent-et-un* (1831–4). Its fifteen volumes contained articles and poems about most aspects of the new tricolour Paris, its history, monuments, dynasties, street life, inhabitants, pleasures, manners and customs, by 101 writers, including Chateaubriand, Lamartine, Balzac, Custine, Eugène Sue and George Sand.[65] *Notre Dame de Paris* (1831), a historical novel by Victor Hugo, celebrated Paris under Louis XI. Other books on the city included *Muséum parisien. Histoire physiologique, pittoresque, philosophique et grotesque de toutes les bêtes de Paris et de la banlieue* (1841), by Louis Huart; *La Grande Ville. Nouveau Tableau de Paris comique, critique et philosophique*, edited by the popular novelist Paul de Kock (1844); and *Les Rues de Paris* (1844), with 300 illustrations, edited by Louis Lurine. *Le Diable à Paris. Paris à la plume et au crayon* (1845–6) is a monument to most aspects of life in the Paris of Louis-Philippe, with brilliant illustrations by Gavarni and Grandville, including a representation of the five floors of a Paris house, occupied by people from five different economic categories. *Les Français peints par eux-mêmes* (1840–2), with brilliant illustrations by Gavarni and H. Monnier set in the text as well as on separate pages, is a masterpiece of book design as well as a satirical portrait of Parisians by a variety of authors. It begins with *L'Epicier par M. de Balzac*, and includes such Paris types as *la cantatrice de salon, la mère d'actrice, la maîtresse de table d'hôte, le gamin de Paris*.

Under Louis-Philippe, individual novels and plays established some of the basic Paris myths. Henry Murger's *Scènes de la vie de bohème* (1851, published in a satirical review *Le Corsaire-Satan* in 1845–9) established the standard images of students and their *grisettes*, living in attics in the Latin Quarter in Paris. Alexandre Dumas *fils* fixed the image of Paris courtesans in *La Dame aux caméllias* (1852), based on his 1844 affair with

Marie Duplessis, who had died of consumption in 1847 and rapidly inspired a posthumous cult: the camellia had been the fashionable flower in Paris in 1844.[66]

Balzac, the greatest French novelist of the day, was obsessed with the city. Since his family's arrival in Paris from Tours in 1814, when Honoré was fifteen, he had become intimately acquainted with the life of its streets, boulevards and faubourgs. One month after the publication of his first great success, *La Peau de chagrin*, on 7 September 1831 Fontaney saw him in the salon of Baron Gérard:

> I see him at last, this new star. Literary glory born from the *Physiology of Marriage*. A fat man. Lively eyes, a white waistcoat, the manner of a botanist, the clothes of a butcher, the air of a gilder, impressive ensemble. He is the man of literary commerce *par excellence*.[67]

Soon Balzac was a star in other, grander salons and in the Austrian embassy, the most elegant of the day.[68]

Balzac was familiar with almost every aspect of the city, from embassies to prisons. He considered Paris the capital of pleasure, vanity, ideas, thought and chance:[69] a monster with a thousand paws, 'an astonishing assembly of movements, machines and thoughts, the city of a hundred thousand novels . . . the head of the world, a brain exploding with genius, the leader of civilisation . . . the most adorable of all *patries*'.[70] He also called it a torrent, an ocean, a Vesuvius in perpetual eruption, and a hell where *tout fume, tout brûle, tout brille, tout bouillonne, tout flambe, s'évapore, s'éteint, se rallume, étincelle, pétille et se consume*.[71]

Like many other writers – Custine has a character say 'What can we do, my dear? Society is no longer possible; money dethrones us, money will replace and destroy everything' – Balzac saw the city as dominated by two passions: gold and pleasure.[72] In *Le Cabinet des antiques*, for example, the Marquis d'Esgrignon, a provincial noble, says to his son Victurnien: 'today the only thing that matters any more is to have money: it is the only reality I see among the benefits of the Restoration.'[73] The passions for liberty, nationalism and European hegemony which dominated the political life of Paris in this period, and had led to the July revolution, are ignored – as are most of the political events, even the revolutions, through which Balzac's characters live.[74]

Some of Balzac's novels concentrate on certain sections of Paris and its population: *La Peau de chagrin* begins with the hero losing a fortune in a gambling den in 'the El Dorado of love', the Palais Royal. It also contains famous descriptions of 'the roofs of Paris, the

undulations of those pressed roofs, an ocean of immobile waves'.[75]
La Duchesse de Langeais (1834) describes the Faubourg Saint-Germain;
details of social life had been checked by Balzac's *illustre élégante* the
Marquise de Castries.[76] *La Fille aux yeux d'or* describes the Sunday
promenade in the Tuileries gardens, *Illusions perdues* (1837–43) the
Quartier Latin and the publishing trade, *Cousine Bette* (1846) the
sordid streets opposite the Tuileries palace. *Le Père Goriot* (1835)
begins in a boarding house in the Quartier Latin and ends with the
young hero Eugène de Rastignac, looking down from the cemetery
of Père Lachaise at the city 'tortuously lying along the two banks of
the Seine'. Staring greedily at the focus of the *beau monde* between the
column of the Place Vendôme and the dome of the Invalides, he
utters his grandiose cry: *A nous deux maintenant!*[77] He then goes to
dine with Madame de Nucingen, the banker's wife.

Paris was a city of newspapers as well as books. The number of subscribers to Paris newspapers rose from about 60,000 in 1830 to 200,000
by 1848.[78] *Le Constitutionnel* had 23,333 subscribers, and many more
readers, in 1831. *La Presse* – founded by Emile de Girardin, illegitimate
son of the Premier Veneur of Charles X, who had started his career in
the Ministère de la Maison du Roi – had 10,000 subscribers in 1836;
22,409 in 1845. Its success was due to its low price (only forty francs a
year, half the normal charges) and copious advertisements – it was the
first newspaper to have them. By 1847 there were twenty-six daily newspapers with 180,000 subscribers.[79] Newspapers, and journalists, became
so important that Henry Reeve, an English Parisian, translator of
Tocqueville and friend of Thiers, could write: 'they [the ministers] do
not rule the papers but the papers them.'[80]

Hitherto courts and courtiers had been the standard targets of
writers' indignation; now newspapers and journalists began to replace
them. The flattery and baseness once symbolised, so Custine said, by the
oeil de boeuf (the celebrated Versailles antechamber preceding the King's
bedroom) were now to be found in newspaper offices.[81] The wife of
Emile de Girardin agreed: journalism was king and everyone flattered
him.[82] Alfred de Musset considered the liberty of the press 'one of the
blackest sewers of our civilisation'; journalists, in his opinion, dined in
the evening off the filth they had vomited in the day.[83] Balzac, as usual,
touched the nerve: journalism, he said, killed, or stole, 'the richest hopes
of literature'. More hypocritical than Jesuits, journalists used 'liberty of
the press' only to oppress the weak and the isolated.[84] Marshal Bugeaud,

the commander of the French army in Algeria in 1836–47, also denounced journalists as hypocrites who 'were themselves generally the most corrupt people in the world, who pretend to be dragons of virtue when attacking the government'.[85]

Nevertheless, just as the most hostile critics of courts had often been courtiers, or aspiring courtiers, so many critics of journalism practised it for their livelihood. The great novelist Barbey d'Aurevilly denounced 'those masked prostitutions called articles', but wrote as many of them as he could.[86] Balzac wrote for innumerable newspapers, and founded two ephemeral newspapers of his own: *La Chronique de Paris* in 1836, *La Revue parisienne* in 1840. The first novel to be serialised in France was Balzac's *La Vieille Fille*, which appeared in *La Presse* in 1836. He received 48 centimes a line for serialisation of another novel in *La Presse*. In April 1847 Balzac had three novels under serialisation in three different newspapers. The demands and financial rewards of newspaper serialisation dictated the structure of many of his novels.[87]

In addition to reading and writing books and newspapers, Parisians also wrote thousands of letters. In 1826, 36,000 letters and 60,000 newspapers left Paris every day.[88] Over the year 1829, 9,212,802 letters were delivered in Paris. With only 3.2 per cent of the population of France, the city received 27 per cent of its letters.[89] Letters formed a paper universe parallel to – and for some Parisians more real than – the physical world, like e-mail and the Internet today. By the system local to Paris known as the *petite poste*, much used in love affairs, you could receive letters on the same day, only a few hours after they had been posted. There were 200 postboxes throughout the city and seven distributions a day.[90] The Marquis de Custine, then beginning his literary career, claimed that fashionable or ambitious people wrote twenty letters or notes every hour.[91] Women in particular made letter writing a vocation: the letters of Madame de Souza, the Duchesse de Duras, the Duchesse de Dino and Lady Granville, among many others, justify Balzac's comment that Paris contained a thousand women who 'certainly' wrote better letters than Madame de Sévigné.[92]

Correspondence could be so revealing that the French police kept agents in London, Brussels and elsewhere, as well as a special office known as *le cabinet noir* in Paris, to intercept letters of prominent politicians. Servants were suborned to rifle through their employers' desks and copy letters. Thus some of the letters of Chateaubriand and Madame Récamier, Flahaut and Madame de Souza, quoted in this book were read at the time by Louis XVIII. Since this was known, many people, as Princess Lieven complained to Guizot, never wrote all they thought.[93] Many Parisians, including Madame Récamier, kept the letters they received, and copies of those they had written – or stolen from their friends – with a view to publication or blackmail.[94] An English Parisian, Mary Clarke, forbade the destruction of her correspondence with the scholar of Greek and Provençal literature Claude Fauriel, author of a three-volume *Histoire de la poésie provençale* (1847), so that it could be printed after her death.[95]

As well as helping Molé write his memoirs, the Comtesse de Castellane kept her letters from Chateaubriand. Thanks to her foresight posterity can read such declarations as: 'it is you whom I have long loved without knowing you, my angel, my life, I know not what else, I love you with all the folly of my first years . . .'; 'Come back to intoxicate me with your love, to render me the proudest and happiest of men.'[96] Since Madame de Castellane pencilled in the dates on the letters and envelopes she received from Chateaubriand, we know that he often wrote to her and to the Duchesse de Duras on the same day.[97] Through his surviving letters, Chateaubriand's many different lives, amorous, social, political, financial, medical and marital, are recorded with a precision which would have dismayed him. He himself often destroyed letters, and urged correspondents to follow his example. On 23 December 1820 a police agent observed Chateaubriand burn letters the moment he read them: as a result only his own selection of the letters he received has survived.[98] Talleyrand also, while keeping official correspondence (some of which he tried to sell to Metternich, who merely had it copied and returned), told the Duchesse de Courlande to burn his private letters: *en général, chère amie, ne gardez point de lettres.*[99]

The explosion of creativity in Paris in this period was due to several factors: the dynamism of the city and its publishing trade; the stimulus of the Chambers, salons and cafés; the multiplication of European influences in the long peace after 1815; and the return of freedom and debate after the long revolutionary and Napoleonic dictatorships. Censorship of books in this allegedly repressive period was so light that defences of the revolution and the terror could be published under Louis XVIII, best-selling denunciations of the Jesuits under Charles X.[100] Thinking of the isolation of German writers in Jena, Königsberg, Berlin, Vienna, or, in his case, the small court city of Weimar, Goethe analysed the magnetism of Paris. He told his companion and literary executor the poet Eckermann:

we all lead a very isolated miserable sort of life! From the people properly so called we derive very little culture . . . one day with Alexander von Humboldt [the German Parisian and friend of the Duchesse de Duras] . . . leads me nearer to what I am seeking and what I require to know than I should have done for years in my own solitary way . . . But now conceive a city like Paris where the highest talents of a great kingdom are all assembled in a single spot, and daily intercourse, strife and emulation mutually instruct and advance each other; where the best works both of nature and art, from all the kingdoms of the earth, are open to daily inspection: conceive their metamorphosis of the world, I say, where every walker over a bridge or across a square recalls some mighty past and where some historical event is connected with every corner of a street. In addition to all this, conceive not the Paris of a dull spotless time but the Paris of the nineteenth century in which, during three generations, such men as Molière, Voltaire, Diderot and the like have kept up such a current of intellect as cannot be found twice in a single spot on the whole world, and you will comprehend that a man like Ampère who has grown up amid such abundance can easily be something in his twentieth year.[101]

Paris was the intellectual and scientific, as well as literary, capital of Europe. Many people, French and foreign, came to live in Paris not for pleasure but to educate their children. Paris was the seat not only of the Sorbonne but also of the *collèges* and *grandes écoles*: the Ecoles Polytechnique, des Ponts et Chaussées, des Arts et Métiers, des Chartes and so on. In 1819–22, for example, one of the great engineers of the century, Isambard Kingdom Brunel, was sent to the Collège Henri IV (where Louis-Philippe's eldest son also went), as the mathematics instruction was so good, although his French émigré father and English mother remained in London.[102] Lady Morgan did not exaggerate when she wrote: 'The schoolmaster is everywhere in France . . . Busy, preoccupied money-making London offers nothing approaching to it . . . Paris has become one great university and every quarter has its classes.'[103] The number of pupils attending primary schools in the capital went up by 60 per cent between 1830 and 1848.[104] In addition Parisians could attend free public lectures at the Jardin des Plantes on mineralogy, entomology and natural history, by the great zoologist and geologist Georges Cuvier, founder of comparative anatomy and author of a 22-volume *Histoire naturelle des poissons* (1828–49); and in the Sorbonne by Guizot on history, Villemain on literature, Victor Cousin on philosophy and Charles Dupin on economics. The great amphitheatre of the Sorbonne would be filled two hours before lectures began.[105]

On a trip to Paris in 1829, Lord Palmerston himself attended these lectures, as well as clubs, salons and the court. The Villèle ministry had suspended them between 1822 and 1828, but, in an effort to demonstrate its liberalism, Polignac permitted them to continue.[106] In addition the Bibliothèque Royale on the rue de Richelieu, and the Archives Royales in the former Hôtel de Soubise in the Marais, famous for their helpfulness to foreigners, drew many visitors: Heine consulted the former within two days of arriving in Paris.[107]

One author of a book on Paris, the journalist Alphonse Esquiros, claimed that Paris contained within its walls 'all human knowledge . . . all useful discoveries'.[108] In addition to Baron Cuvier, scientists of European reputation teaching and writing in Paris included Joseph-Louis Gay-Lussac, professor of physics at the Sorbonne, author of 111 scientific works, an expert on prussic acid and the first man who, in order to measure atmospheric conditions, ascended as high as 7,000 metres in a balloon. François Arago, the great astronomer and radical politician, demonstrated one of the most important inventions of the century, photography, to the public for the first time at a session of the Académie des Sciences in Paris on 7 January 1839, a few months after Louis-Jacques Daguerre had executed the first photograph on the Boulevard du Temple. André-Marie Ampère the mathematician and theoretician of electro-dynamics, known as 'the Newton of electricity', was famous for his absent-mindedness, frequently using his blackboard cloth as a handkerchief during lectures. Geoffroy Saint-Hilaire, a former priest turned zoologist, was author of *Principes de philosophie zoologique* (1830) and first professor of zoology in the University of Paris.

Paris was also the medical capital of the world. An Academy of Medicine was founded in 1820 and no other capital contained so many government-controlled hospitals. They received over 50,000 patients a year; corpses were available for dissection and analysis on a scale unknown in other cities. The great doctor Guillaume Dupuytren, a surgeon at the Hôtel-Dieu hospital who had attended the Duc de Berri's deathbed, was the founder of the French clinical tradition and had few rivals in Europe in the treatment of venereal disease. Students came from America as well as England and Ireland to enrol in the Ecole de Médecine, and established their own Paris Medical Society.[109]

Paris also became the musical capital of Europe, with higher levels of performance, and financial reward, than other capitals – although Berlioz frequently complained that there was no decent concert hall.[110]

Paris experienced its musical revolution, like its literary revolution, under Charles X, in the years 1827 to 1829. The Société des Concerts du Conservatoire, founded in 1828 with government subsidies, rapidly became one of the best in Europe. The music of Beethoven was introduced to the city at its concerts – in part at the suggestion of the Duchesse de Berri, as adventurous in her cultural patronage as she was reactionary in her political views.*

Jean-François Le Sueur, composer of now forgotten operas such as *Les Bardes* (1804) and *Le Triomphe de Trajan* (1807), and Surintendant de la Musique du Roi, said such music as Beethoven's ought not to be written. However, Berlioz, soon to be the most famous French composer of his day, left a Beethoven concert as transfixed as he had been a few months earlier by listening to Shakespeare. He no longer believed in God or Bach.[112] He commented: 'in comparison Le Sueur did not stand up and all knew it.'[113]

At the same time as Beethoven revolutionised music, Rossini, who lived in Paris from 1824 to 1836, and was director of the second opera house, the Théâtre Italien, from 1824 to 1826, helped revolutionise Paris opera. In the eighteenth century the opera had been a place for the élite to meet, to display and observe rank and riches, as well as to hear music. It had sometimes been considered bourgeois to listen attentively; singers and dancers had been the sexual fodder of the rich.[114] The opera's social and sexual functions continued in the nineteenth century. Courtiers like the Ducs de Gramont, de Maillé, de Fitzjames came either to meet their friends or to hunt actresses. In 1821 the *foyer de l'opéra* was described as 'the rendezvous of the Corps Diplomatique'.[115] With the court and the Bourse, it was one of the main centres of news and gossip in the capital.[116] In 1822, according to Prince Clary, the Théâtre Italien was like a *spectacle de société*: 'the boxes are open, the ladies well dressed and displayed as in a salon, which accounts for half the vogue of this theatre.'[117]

Many men only arrived at the opera after dinner, in time for the ballet in the second act, when dancers could be examined at leisure through *lorgnettes-monocles*. The *foyer de la danse*, where dancers met admirers before and after the performance, was like a stud farm where men could choose

---

* The animator of court life before 1830, organising balls on 'Turkish' and sixteenth-century themes, she was also the patron of the Théâtre du Gymnase where many of Scribe's early plays were performed, and of Emile de Girardin's fashion magazine *La Mode*, which helped launch Gavarni, Balzac and George Sand.[111]

remounts. Prince Tufiakin, former Director of Theatres in St Petersburg, had lived in Paris since 1815. A man with a brown wig, a grotesque face, a crooked neck and a sideways walk, he loved Paris actresses 'by whom he was duped and laughed at'. The dying words of this Russian Parisian were said to have been: *qu'est-ce qu'on donne ce soir à l'opéra?*[118]

However, since the 1780s, and especially since Rossini's arrival in Paris in 1824, more serious attention had begun to be paid to music. Paris audiences became quieter, performers and management more professional. Singers shouted less and sang better.[119] In 1829 the German traveller and writer Prince Pückler-Muskau noted that he had left the Paris opera in 1822

> a kind of bedlam where a few maniacs screamed with agony as if on the rack . . . [in its place] I now found sweet singing in the best Italian style united to very good acting. Rossini who, like a second Orpheus, has tamed even this savage opera is a real musical benefactor and natives as well as foreigners have reason to bless him for the salvation of their ears.[120]

The character of Paris in this period is suggested by the changes Rossini made to those of his operas which had been originally performed in Italy. In order to increase their appeal for Parisians the Italian text was rewritten in French; regular arias were removed and replaced by extended ensemble scenes; ballets were added. Paris needed more drama, more female flesh and larger choruses. Thus Rossini's *Maometto II* (1820) became *Le Siège de Corinthe* (1826) (heavily rewritten), whose story of Greeks battling for freedom from the Turkish Empire suited the current Philhellene mood, and whose première was described as the dawn of a new era in Paris opera. *Mosè in Egitto* (1818) was transformed into *Moïse et Pharaon* (1827).[121] The Paris versions of Rossini operas, retranslated into Italian, were sometimes played in Italy in preference to the Italian originals.[122]

A revolution in ballet took place at the same time as the revolutions in music and the opera. The great dancer Marie Taglioni, from a Milanese family but herself brought up in Paris, made her debut there on 23 July 1827 in *Le Sicilien*, by the inescapable Scribe. She danced on her *pointes* with an ease, grace and purity, an absence of violent effort, which seemed revolutionary. Lady Blessington wrote: 'Here is a totally new style of dancing . . . she seems to float and bound like a sylph across the stage.' Hailed by the *Figaro* as the spirit of Romanticism applied to dance, she was also the first dancer to have flowers thrown at her on the stage of the opera.[123]

After 1831 the royal opera house, no longer part of the Maison du Roi, was run as a commercial enterprise. The director was Dr Véron who enjoyed the financial backing of the Spanish banker Alexandre Aguado, Rossini's best friend, and a large but diminishing government subsidy. After lavish redecoration and regilding, the opera house, Véron maintained, had become the Versailles of the bourgeoisie. The public was certainly less aristocratic than before 1830.[124] *Robert le Diable* by Meyerbeer,* with a libretto by Scribe and Marie Taglioni dancing as the Abbess, although composed before 1830 at the instigation of the Directeur-Général des Beaux-Arts Sosthènes de La Rochefoucauld, was first performed on 22 November 1831. It was received in reverential silence, by an audience drunk with enthusiasm. The opera became the talk of Paris, from salons to shops – particularly the scene when, in order to seduce the hero Robert, a chorus of ghosts of lapsed nuns, who had been unfaithful to their vows, danced in nightdresses in a moonlit ruined cloister.[125] The aged Spontini, whose *La Vestale* had been performed before Alexander I on 1 April 1814, the day after the allied entry into Paris, expressed the disgust of an older generation: 'Oh this man is capable of anything! Unhappy time! Unhappy world!'[126]

Spectacular scenery, as well as crowd scenes, ballets and female flesh, were another distinguishing feature of the Paris opera. In 1814 Prince Wilhelm of Prussia had written that 'the *Triumph of Trajan* [by Le Sueur] alone is worth a journey to Paris' – for the ballet and the processions more than the opera itself. The great set-designer Pierre-Luc-Charles Ciceri had been sent to Switzerland by Sosthènes de La Rochefoucauld to study mountains, before painting backdrops of Vesuvius for *La Muette de Portici* and of the Alps for *Guillaume Tell*.[127] Like Prince Wilhelm of Prussia, Lady Granville wrote that it was worth crossing the Channel just to experience the beauty of the singing and admire the scenery and decor of these operas.[128] After 1830 there were even larger crowd scenes: a bazaar in Cherubini's *Ali Baba* (1833); a magnificent ball in Auber and Scribe's *Gustave III ou le bal masqué* (1833), which aroused such enthusiasm that some of the audience rose from their seats and joined in the dancing; the Emperor's and Cardinals' processions in Halévy's *La Juive* (1835) featured real horses.[129]

By then Paris had replaced Vienna as the capital of music in Europe.

---

* From 1825 Meyerbeer divided his time between Paris, where he became Directeur de la Musique in the Académie Royale de Musique, and Berlin, where he held the court offices of Kapellmeister and Generalmusikdirektor at the opera.

Referring to the Paris opera, the Austrian diplomat Comte Rodolphe Apponyi commended it as 'all that is magnificent: no one has any idea of it *chez nous*.'[130] On a visit to Paris in 1836, another Austrian, the great dramatist Grillparzer, also considered the magnificence of the Paris opera unimaginable in Vienna. He praised the ease of the acting – and the freedom of Paris compared to 'the shameful oppression of minds and the humiliation of my fellow men' in Vienna. Vienna was a 'Capua of the mind', where intellectual effort was impossible.[131]

The greatest composers in Europe came to work in Paris: Liszt, whom the Duchesse d'Orléans called 'a real little prodigy', arrived from Budapest in 1823, at the age of eleven.[132] Chopin came from Vienna, and Paganini from Parma, in 1831; Offenbach from Cologne in 1833 (his first waltzes were played in the Café Turc on the Boulevard du Temple);[133] Bellini from Milan in 1833, Donizetti from Naples in 1835. As well as being the best place to perform operas, Paris also supplied plots for many of their librettos. Bellini found his idea for *I Puritani* (1835), Donizetti the story of *L'Elisir d'amore*, in French plays. Verdi (who lived in Paris from 1847 to 1849) derived the stories of *Nabucco* (1842), *Ernani* (1844), *Rigoletto* (1851), *La Traviata* (1853), *Un ballo in maschera* (1859), from contemporary Parisian plays. Equally at ease in French and Italian cultures, Verdi considered Paris the capital of the modern world.[134]

Another sign of the primacy of Paris was the foundation in 1834 of the *Revue et gazette musicale de Paris*, soon to be the main musical magazine in Europe, by Maurice Schlesinger, a German who had come to Paris with the Prussian army in 1815, at the age of eighteen, and never left. A friend of Laffitte, he worked in the publishing firm of Bossange and then established a firm of his own, publishing music from 97 rue de Richelieu. The success of *Robert le Diable* made his name: until his ruin in 1846, this editor of genius published the works of Wagner, Meyerbeer, Chopin, Liszt, Berlioz, Mendelssohn.[135]

Nevertheless, even in this golden age, many writers and musicians, far from finding Paris a magnet or stimulus, shunned the city. Some called it a *cloaque infecte*, a cauldron of the damned beside which Dante's inferno was a paradise.[136] Neither Byron, Goethe nor Pushkin visited Paris. Stendhal preferred Milan, Walter Scott Edinburgh; English writers such as Coleridge, Carlyle and George Eliot increasingly turned for inspiration to Germany. Old, deaf, forgotten, Goya came to Paris for three months in 1824, visiting the Louvre and the public monuments; he preferred to live in Bordeaux.[137] Many other artists, as the 1815 petition supporting the removal of works of art from the Louvre had revealed, preferred Rome to Paris. Although Donizetti appreciated the respect and financial rewards which artists obtained in Paris – Scribe, Rossini and Auber, for example, could live *en grands seigneurs* off their work – in 1839 he wrote: 'I do not like it here. I burn with a desire to return to Naples, there where I have my home . . . Paris is not my city.'[138]

The king of the opera and the Opéra Comique, as well as the Gymnase and the Comédie Française, was Scribe. He wrote the librettos for some of the most popular operas of the day, *La Muette de Portici, Comte Ory, Robert le Diable*, and many others.[139] In 1839, spurred by a letter from Scribe to whom he had sent an early opera, as well as by the presence of his brother-in-law Brockhaus who ran a bookshop in the rue de Richelieu – and by the need to flee debts in Germany – Wagner arrived in Paris. At the age of twenty-six, he was happy to feel, at last, in communication with Paris. In his Parisian phase, he wrote 'little French compositions', including settings of the Marseillaise and of Heine's poem *Les Deux Grenadiers* – hymns to French not German nationalism. At this stage he believed that 'intimate union' between the two nations would produce a 'magnificent fecundity' in art.[140]

In time, however, failing to secure appreciation for his music in Paris, he found the city, its people, its music and the 'wretched little alley' where he lived antipathetic. He went to the opera only four times; none of his own works was accepted for performance there. On 7 April 1842 'the day arrived on which, as I devoutly hoped, I would be turning my back on Paris for ever.' On 20 October 1842 his first success, *Rienzi*, rejected in Paris (it is his dullest opera), was acclaimed in Dresden, where he later became Hofkapellmeister. Paris had proved less receptive than a German court city to the man who would be the most original composer of the age.[141]

II

Nationalists and Europeans

1838–1840

Paris représente le monde. L'influence que Paris a exercée sur nos provinces, il
l'exerce aujourd'hui sur l'Europe . . . C'est le grand carrefour où viennent aboutir
les routes des nations . . . Paris est le congrès permanent des âges et des peuples.
Jules Michelet, inaugural lecture at the Collège de France, 23 April 1838

Two women symbolised the clash between nationalists and
Europeans which, like those between legitimists and Orleanists,
Catholics and sceptics, soldiers and civilians, marked Paris in this
period. Both were foreign princesses: Princess Belgiojoso came from
Milan, Princess Lieven from St Petersburg.

Before 1830 most Italians had been attracted to Paris to serve its role
as a capital of pleasure: La Pasta had come to sing, Rossini to direct
operas, Tortoni to sell ice-creams. The lack of an international metropolis in Italy made Paris particularly attractive. After 1830 there were
additional, political reasons for Italians to move there. Italy was divided
into seven states: the Kingdom of Sardinia (which included Piedmont
and Savoy); the Kingdom of the Two Sicilies, whose King Ferdinand II
was a nephew of Queen Marie Amélie; Lombardy-Venetia, which
formed part of the Austrian Empire; the Grand Duchy of Tuscany
under a Habsburg Grand Duke; the Duchies of Parma and Modena,
both also ruled by Habsburgs; and, in the middle, the States of the
Church under the Pope. All these states were opposed to Italian nationalism and, with the exception of Tuscany, heavily policed. In these
circumstances Italian nationalists found Paris irresistible. Italians
fought on the barricades during the July days; among them was the
appropriately named Count Libri, later a celebrated professor and book

thief. The revolutionary projects of Italian refugees in Paris had induced the Austrian ambassador to maintain an agent among them (as Metternich maintained an agent in La Fayette's entourage).[1] Soon they had their own newspaper, *L'Italiano*. One Italian refugee in Paris Count Charles Pepoli wrote the libretto for Bellini's *I Puritani*.[2] Another, Count Rossi, a former official of Murat King of Naples (whose army had, in 1815, been the first to fight for Italian unity), came to Paris, switched nationality, became a professor of political economy in the Collège de France (1833), dean in the law faculty, and peer of France (1839), before returning to Italy, as French ambassador to the Holy See, in 1847.[3]

After Rossini, Princess Belgiojoso was the most famous Italian in Paris. Born Cristina Trivulzio in Milan in 1808, heiress of an ancient and wealthy family, in 1826 she had married a frivolous voluptuary called Prince Emilio Belgiojoso. She already suffered from epilepsy; he may have infected her with syphilis; they separated after two years.[4] Italian nationalism became her passion. In early 1831, she helped fund an unsuccessful invasion of Piedmont by Italian exiles from Marseille. In March 1831, the same year as Heine and Chopin, she arrived in Paris. At first, she had to live without a servant, doing her own cleaning on the fifth floor of 7 rue Neuve-Saint-Honoré.[5] Soon however, despite her loathing of Austrian rule in Lombardy, whose legality she denied, she recovered her income from her estates and was able to entertain.

To intelligence, charm and rank, Princess Belgiojoso added the attractions of black hair, a transparent 'marble pallor' (possibly accentuated by her diseases), and 'the great wide apart eyes of an ancient statue'. She became as much a cult as Mlle Mars.[6] Lady Granville met her for the first time in September 1831. She wrote to her sister: 'Yesterday I saw at Mme Bourke's Princess Belgiojoso, slim, *distinguée*, pale eyes big as saucers, very slender hands, grand and gracious manners, extremely intelligent, *de l'esprit comme un démon*.' Although irritated by the ceremony and flattery which surrounded Chateaubriand, the princess became a regular guest of Madame Récamier. She was also La Fayette's last love. In 1834, the year of his death, he climbed five flights of stairs every day to see her.[7] For twenty-five years the blind historian Augustin Thierry loved her as a sister.[8] Another historian François Mignet enjoyed an agitated *amitié amoureuse* with her for even longer, and may have been the father of her daughter Marie, born in Versailles in 1838.[9] Liszt, who dedicated his piano variations *Hexameron* to her, became another intimate, perhaps a lover. When asked to compare him to a rival, the Austrian court pianist Sigismund Thalberg, with whom he had had a 'trial of strength' at a concert in aid of Italian refugees in her salon, she said: 'there is only one Thalberg in Paris and there is only one Liszt in the world.'[10]

Balzac, who met her at Baron Gérard's, called her *la princesse bellejoyeuse* and may have modelled Fédora in *La Peau de chagrin* on her. Her salon in 23 rue d'Anjou Saint-Honoré attracted, among many others, Bellini, Thiers and Baron d'Eckstein.[11] At a court ball in 1838, wrote George Ticknor, 'after the King and Queen, nobody attracted so much attention as the very picturesque Princess Belgiojoso'.[12]

An intellectual, frank and unconventional, the princess encouraged writers to speak their minds. Musset wrote to her in 1839 that Parisian literature was 'the most disgusting market imaginable'.[13] For five years he was obsessed with her. Finally, when she continued to refuse to be his mistress, he took revenge in a famous hate-poem *Sur une morte* (1842). After denouncing her for sterility, cruelty, pride, he concluded:

> Elle est morte et n'a point vécu:
> Elle faisait semblant de vivre.
> De ses mains est tombé le livre
> Dans lequel elle n'a rien lu.[14]

For Heine, however, Princess Belgiojoso was 'the most complete person I know'. Having little in common with his mistress Créscence Eugénie Mirat, a shoe-shop assistant who hardly knew what a poet was, he loved Princess Belgiojoso and was haunted by her face. He told her that he maintained a religious cult of *everything* pertaining to her and that her smile came from heaven.[15] 'I have never yet seen anything so poetic, so magic as that black hair falling in rebellious curls on the diaphanous pallor of your face. That face you have stolen from a picture of the sixteenth century, an old fresco of the Lombard school.'[16] Less captivated Parisians said that she looked as if she had forgotten to bury herself; she would have been beautiful – if she were alive.[17]

As Heine's passion cooled into friendship – in 1841 he married his mistress – Princess Belgiojoso became one of his most determined patrons. They were both radicals. Princess Belgiojoso learnt German to read him in the original, introduced him to her friends and obtained for this German revolutionary, with the help of Thiers, a pension of 4,800 francs a year, on the grounds that he was a political exile who had always shared France's ideas and had suffered for her cause. With another pension from his own family, this gave him financial security in Paris for the rest of his life.[18]

Fascinated by politics, Princess Belgiojoso regularly attended the Chamber of Deputies and wrote articles for *Le Constitutionnel*.[19] However, it was the fate of Italy, and the principle of nationality, which dominated both the conversation and the decoration in her salon. It was filled not only with Italian Renaissance furniture and paintings (at the same time that Paris was rediscovering its own Renaissance), but with Italian refugees. Believing that a monarchy was more likely to unify Italy than a republic, the princess wanted Italy organised in a federated monarchy under the House of Savoy.[20] In Paris she gave concerts,* held auctions of pictures by friends like Delacroix and Henri Lehmann, in aid of Polish and Italian refugees, and edited the nationalist *Gazzetta italiana*. In 1846 she published a call for action: *Etude sur l'histoire de la Lombardie dans les trente dernières années, ou des causes du défaut d'énergie chez les Lombards*. The weakness of the Lombards was blamed on the omnipotence of the Austrian police: but if the Lombards tried to resist, she predicted, the fragile structure of Austrian power would disappear for ever.[21]

One of her guests – who on his visits to Paris also acccompanied Prince Belgiojoso to the Café de Paris, the Jockey Club and other haunts – was a young Piedmontese noble who would become the first Prime Minister of Italy, Count Camille Cavour. Considering Paris from the Tuileries to the Arc de Triomphe 'the finest city in the world', he visited it frequently between 1835 and 1843. Although he lost money on the Bourse, he enjoyed the opera, the Chambers and the salons – although sometimes, in Princess Belgiojoso's salon, so little notice was taken of him that he resolved not to return.[22]

In May 1838, however, in a celebrated letter to a Parisian mistress the writer Mélanie Waldor, Cavour rejected both the idea and the reality of Paris as capital of Europe. Despite his cosmopolitan background and education – he had studied in Geneva as well as Turin – the voice of a new era can be heard: the era of exclusive nationalism, putting birth before choice, countries before cities. Cavour not only links human qualities to geographical locations, but overlooks the fact that, in the development of civilisation, cities have been as important as nations. Rejecting Mélanie Waldor's suggestion that he remain in Paris and become a writer or scientist, he declares that not only would he not 'plunge a dagger in the breasts of my parents', but Paris in his view was bad for Italians:

---

* A typical invitation of 7 February 1839 reads: *La Princesse de Belgiojoso prie Madame la Princesse Czartoriska de vouloir bien lui faire l'honneur de venir passer la soirée chez elle le lundi 11 février 1839 à 8 heures 1/2. On fera de la musique.*

And why, Madame, abandon my country? . . . What does all this crowd of strangers whom choice or misfortune have thrown far from their homeland do in Paris? Who amongst them has rendered himself truly useful to his fellows; which of them has carved out a great career for himself or won an influence over society? Not one.* Those that would have been great upon the soil that bore them vegetate obscure in the whirl of Parisian life . . . the genius which would have soared beneath its native sky droops in a foreign land. Not a single one has fulfilled the brilliant promise of his earlier years . . . No, no, it is not in flying from one's country because it is unfortunate that one can attain a glorious end. Unhappy is he who abandons with scorn the land that gave him birth, who disowns his brothers as unworthy of him! As for me I am decided: never will I separate my lot from that of Piedmont.

Not even French talent flourished in Paris, according to Cavour: 'This artificial society is an atmosphere little suitable to one who wishes to study the laws of humanity.' Philosophers like Victor Cousin had not fulfilled 'the brilliant hopes of their debut in the world of science'; no French philosopher could rival Kant.[23] Cavour may, however, have been spurning not Paris but his mistress. He later confessed:

For real pleasure there is nothing to my mind comparable with the salons of Paris. It is the only place where statesmen, men of science and literature and men of good society can meet together regularly to exchange ideas and opinions. Paris is undoubtedly the intellectual capital of the world.[24]

Moreover, as he knew when he became Prime Minister of Piedmont, Paris was the key to Italy's political future. He was able to help achieve Italian unity, only after a coup in Paris, and with the support of a French monarch and army.

If Princess Belgiojoso was a nationalist who considered herself an exile from her motherland, Princess Lieven was a European who felt more at home in Paris than in her own country. Born Dorothea von Benckendorff in Riga in 1785, this clever, attractive woman, hungry for power, had won a position of influence for herself in London, where her husband was Russian ambassador from 1812 to 1834. Possessing an imperious, epigrammatic style of conversation, a forceful personality and striking angular features (although Chateaubriand complained of

---

* Cavour thus dismisses, among others, Cherubini, Rossini, Bellini, Donizetti, Paganini and Princess Belgiojoso herself.

her *visage aigu et mésavenant* and Mérimée of her red nose), she had become an intimate of George IV, Wellington, Lord Grey, Lord Aberdeen and Canning. In 1818, during the Congress of Aix-la-Chapelle, she became a mistress of Metternich: hence Chateaubriand's epithet for her, *la douairière des congrès*, and the nickname *l'enfant du congrès* given to a son born in 1819.[25]

Princess Lieven had once called Russia her pride and her love, and had regarded with pity all dynasties other than the Romanovs.[26] After her husband's recall in 1834 to become Governor to the Tsarevich, however, Princess Lieven missed the freedom of London. At the court of St Petersburg, she claimed, conversation was restricted to the rise and fall of the thermometer. Two of her sons died at the ages of nine and fifteen, from scarlet fever. Bored, sad, far from Europe, she fell ill, left for a season in Baden-Baden, and arrived in Paris in September 1835.[27]

Rapidly recovering her spirits, she began to see diplomats 'all and every day', old friends such as Talleyrand, the Duchesse de Dino, new ones such as Flahaut, Broglie, Molé, Guizot, Thiers and Madame de Boigne.[28] Despite her adulation of rank and royalty, and her intimacy with the imperial family, she came to prefer revolutionary Paris to St Petersburg, feeling so happy there that she refused the Tsar's orders to rejoin her husband in Russia. Paris, she claimed, was necessary for her health. In comparison her former hunting-ground seemed grey: 'Paris is beautiful, animated, what a difference to London!'[29]

Politics was the attraction, she admitted: 'I think a bit more than usual of Paris today, now that you are in a ministerial crisis.' Paris was, for her, 'a comedy on which the curtain never falls', a city of constant movement and excitement where 'everything is known an hour after it has happened'. It also became a city of happiness.[30] At dinner with the Duc de Broglie on 15 June 1836, she sat beside Guizot, a politician with a brilliant future. Their conversation became intimate.[31] Both were Lutheran, both had lost children: both were intelligent, apparently austere figures of the same age who loved power. Nine days earlier Guizot had written to Madame de Gasparin of his 'ardent desire of complete abandon, such a vivid pleasure in the absence of all reticence, of all constraint'. Like his political enemy Count Molé, he considered love 'the union of body and soul . . . a true fusion of the two natures . . . the great mystery of humanity'.[32] The French bourgeois and the Russian princess fell in love. On 24 June 1837, during a walk in the park at Châtenay outside Paris, after dinner with Madame de Boigne, they promised themselves to each other for eternity. Soon she would write to him: *je vous aime, je vous aime, je vous attends . . . si je ne vous avais pas, je n'aurais plus rien.*[33]

Thanks to her incomparable network of connections, her salon became a bastion of Europe in the heart of Paris. Its influence, and that of the salon of Madame de Flahaut, were discussed by Madame de Girardin in *La Presse* on 15 December 1836. Madame de Flahaut was described as intelligent, determined and capable: her influence was visible and vivacious. Princess Lieven, on the other hand, was compared to a planet with many satellites. She had the calm of power, the patience of a will which knows its own strength. No one knew better how to 'sew' conversation. 'Madame de Lieven has chosen the only political role which suits a woman: she does not act, she inspires those who act.'[34] After several changes of address, in 1838 she moved into the former Hôtel de Talleyrand, now de Rothschild, with a view across the Place de la Concorde to the Chamber of Deputies. To the fury of the Duchesse de Dino, she occupied the *entresol* where Talleyrand had lived and the Provisional Government had met in April 1814.

The physical setting of her salon is described by the young Russian diplomat Victor Balabine who, like all Russian diplomats, was expected by the princess to be a constant visitor. Guests would come between 9 and 10.30 in the evening. 'Princess Lieven seated on her sofa and surrounded by her society forms the core, the great hearth of her salon. Opposite in front of the fireplace stands a group of five or six people, diplomats, deputies and others: that is the little circle; M. Guizot circulates and goes from one to the other.' Guizot arrived first and left last. Mérimée joked that Guizot's late-night conversations with Princess Lieven appeared to wear him out.[35]

Lady Granville, one of her closest friends, admired her technique of salon management: 'she can keep off bores because she has the courage to *écraser* them . . . It would kill me to have Berryer and Molé *tête à trois*, looking daggers at each other, *mais elle sait nager* and gets out of every difficulty . . . Here [the British embassy] fools rush in, there angels fear to tread.'[36] Her treatment of unwanted guests, who lacked the magic of office, is illustrated in the following incident. An acquaintance from a summer at Bad Ems, a good-looking smart young man, was shown into her salon one evening.

– *Monsieur, je ne vous connais pas.*
– *Comment, Madame! Ne vous rappelez-vous pas, à Ems?*

– *Non, Monsieur*, and she bowed him out. I never saw anything so cool; but it was very clear to the company, who could not conceal their smiles, that a gentleman who may be useful at Ems may be *de trop* at Paris.[37]

So free of nationalistic feeling was Princess Lieven that she regarded diplomats, 'a race apart formed out of all nations', as her true compatriots. To her old friend Lord Grey she wrote, with joy: 'I live in Paris exactly as I used to do. I receive every evening and the diplomats form the main source of my society, with such birds of passage as will come to call on me.'[38] She would interrogate diplomats stationed in or passing through Paris for the latest news. If they did not come for a few days, she would complain in a pitiful voice that no one cared to devote even a few moments to her, that she felt abandoned, then launch into tirades against other people's egoism.[39]

Diplomacy was her world. It was inconceivable to her to behave like Madame de Castellane, who paid more attention to Eugène Sue than to the Russian ambassador.[40] Indeed at one time 'my ambassador', Pozzo's replacement Count Pahlen, 'never missed an evening with me'.[41] In contrast Princess Lieven claimed to have few French friends: 'The fact is that I do not know a single Frenchwoman; I dislike them all. As for men the Duc de Noailles is the only one with whom I am on fairly intimate terms.'[42] On the other hand her salon always contained large numbers of *mes chers anglais* – friends from her years in London. One of them, the diarist Charles Greville, wrote: 'Madame de Lieven seems to have a very agreeable position at Paris. She receives every night and opens her house to all comers. Being neutral ground, men of all parties meet there and some of the most violent antagonists have occasionally joined in amicable and curious discussion.'[43] She could be a force for peace, often more effective than diplomats in strengthening friendship and eliminating misunderstandings between the British and French governments: her friendships with Lord Aberdeen and Guizot made her useful as a channel of communication. When hoping to change English electoral law, Aberdeen asked her to consult Guizot for information about French parliamentary procedure – a tribute to the impact, even in Westminster, of the French Chamber of Deputies.[44]

Princess Lieven also acted as a Russian agent, serving as an intermediary between French and Russian ministers. Aggrieved at first by her wilful refusal to leave the evil city of Paris the Tsar, according to the French ambassador in Berlin Comte Bresson, finally accepted her presence there in exchange for a journal which she sent to her brother

Count Benckendorff, head of his secret chancery, detailing 'all political affairs, all anecdotes,' and relaying in particular Guizot's and Thiers' conversations with her. She was also believed to write to the Empress everything which was said in her salon. In the crisis of 1840, she was publicly accused by Thiers of being a Russian spy.[45] By then some Russians were allowed by the Tsar to visit Paris, provided they were not presented at the court of Louis-Philippe, whom the Tsar still despised as a usurper. Princess Lieven's house was described as their headquarters; they flocked to it like crows around the towers of Notre Dame.[46]

Her attitude to class was more Russian than French. If they were successful and amusing, and occupied elevated official positions, even men from humble backgrounds were welcome in the princess's salon. Thiers, more talkative even than Louis-Philippe, she described as 'a perpetual firework display; he is the most abundant mind I have encountered', although at heart a revolutionary, with the pride of Satan. She praised Guizot for having an elevation, and Molé an elegance, of mind and manners rare at that time. Berryer was a magnificent orator. Louis-Philippe, however, was 'the most sensible, sound and well-judging man of them all', 'more able than any other sovereign or minister in Europe'.[47] Thiers, for his part, called Princess Lieven's salon 'the observatory of Europe'. Although he complained of her, he consulted her and used her as an intermediary with other politicians during negotiations for the formation of a ministry in April 1837.[48]

Cosmopolitanism was not restricted to the salon of Princess Lieven. Paris was considered to belong to Europe as well as France. Attracting 'people of all nations and languages' was one of its functions and a condition of its brilliance.[49] In a work of 1842 Paris was celebrated as 'the city of foreigners par excellence': the real foreigner there was the Parisian.[50] A later book called it 'the great European and cosmopolitan city *par excellence*, receiving men and ideas from all the countries in the world and sending them back after having struck them with her impress'.[51]

It was the beginning of the golden age of Americans in Paris. Some of the most magnificent houses belonged to rich Americans such as Messrs Gould, Thorn, Moulton, retired businessmen who, if they provided lavish entertainments, could attain, in Paris, the social position denied them in the city of their birth. James Fenimore Cooper, whose novels inspired Balzac and Mérimée, had lived there in 1826–8. Mr Thorn, a New Jersey banker, lived in what is now the official residence of the Prime Minister, the Hôtel Matignon, 54 rue de Varenne, which he refurnished in Renaissance style. His wealth was such that he could put on an entire performance of Bellini's *I Puritani* – the sensation of 1835 – in his own salons.[52] William Williams Hope (a relation of the Anglo-Dutch banking family) bought, and then demolished, the house of Maréchal Davout at 131–3 (present 57) rue Saint-Dominique. On the curtains in his previous residence, there was said to have been enough gold braid to provide epaulettes for all the senior officers in the French army. His new residence, built and decorated in the fashionable neo-eighteenth-century and neo-François Ier styles and finished in 1841, was known as a little Versailles. It was said to have cost seven and a half million francs. There were three dining rooms – to seat six, twenty-five, and two hundred respectively.[53]

Foreign hosts gave the most lavish parties in Paris, often – like Rothschild and Hope – asking Comtesse Juste de Noailles to draw up the guest list. 'It is foreigners who do the honours of Paris,' Castellane commented. When Mr Thorn started to entertain, his French friends agreed to compose his guest list on condition that it contained not one American. He agreed and his house became the rendezvous of the most elegant women in Paris.[54] After a splendid *bal à l'américaine* given by Gerald Gould, it was said that he only needed a napkin on his arm to look like his own maître d'hôtel.[55] In 1837 another diarist wrote: 'a magnificent ball at the Comte de Stackelberg's, former minister of Russia in Naples . . . everywhere one heard foreign languages, above all English, German and Italian. The best society in France was there.'[56] On occasions, so Lady Morgan boasted, there were 'twelve nations in my salon'.[57] Custine praised to Princess Czartoryska 'the crowd of nations and men from every class' whom he met in her house.[58]

These private salons were more successful than the nebulous plans for European cultural institutions in Paris being prepared at the same time: Prince Elim Mestcherski's project for 'an ideal literary city [or debating club] where all nations would be represented'; Alexandre Vallemor's for 'a general system of scientific and literary exchange between every corner of the globe, Paris becoming the centre of these well-intentioned communications'; Humboldt and Sainte-Beuve's plan for a German Institute or Academy in Paris, with a reading room, lectures and a journal, to 'link in friendship, in the domain of their respective literatures, the two most cultivated nations of the continent'. All failed, as had their equivalent in the field of international relations, Pozzo's plan for a European 'association' after 1815.[59] Apart from the salons, the only functioning European institution in Paris was a school, the European Academic Institution, 852 avenue de Saint-Cloud, Versailles.[60]

The publishing industry, as well as the social life, of Paris reflected its European vocation. Its dominion over European literature stretched further than the Napoleonic Empire. In addition to Galignani's Franco-British bookshop in the rue Vivienne, there were Franco-German and international bookshops and publishers in Paris such as Nicolle; Treuttel et Würtz (publishers of Madame de Staël and her family); its successor Klingsieck (which, founded in 1842, survives to this day), and the Spanish bookseller and publisher the Librairie Hispano-Américaine. Brockhaus and Avenarius, who bought the business and vast premises of Bossange at 60 rue de Richelieu near Galignani in 1836, had the specific mission, as its prospectus stated, 'to facilitate the literary relations between France, Germany, the North and East of Europe': it had different rooms for Spanish, Italian, German and English books, and branches in London and Leipzig.[61] Another bookshop, Baudry, 3 quai Malaquais, produced 'Baudry's European Library' of books in English (such as *The Idler in France* by the Countess of Blessington), published in Paris and sold there and 'by all the principal booksellers on the Continent'.

Paris magazines also reflected the city's European vocation. *Le Censeur européen*, edited between 1817 and 1825 by the liberals Charles Comte and Charles Dunoyer, was so anti-Bourbon that they were often obliged by government lawsuits to leave Paris, until the review's forced closure in 1825. The *Revue européenne ou l'esprit et ses productions en France, en Angleterre, en Italie, en Allemagne* etc. was launched in 1824, with a mission to inform each national public of the literature of others. Its prospectus stated that 'Europe is no longer anything but one great nation, divided in interests but united by culture', but the review closed in 1826.[62]

The *Revue européenne*, with contributions from Guizot, Berlioz and Béranger among others, was liberal. *Le Panorama littéraire de l'Europe ou choix des articles les plus remarquables sur la littérature, les sciences et les arts, extraits des publications périodiques de l'Europe par une société des gens de lettres*, which appeared between July 1833 and September 1834, was royalist. It was run by the coterie of the old Société des Bonnes Lettres, under the editorship of Edouard Mennechet, a former Secrétaire de la Chambre and Lecteur du Roi. Believing in the future of 'a vast republic of European intelligence' in which 'Europe will soon have no more than one thinking and directing soul', this luxurious review was proud of its European mission. It planned to compare the different characters of

European literatures, to end the French preoccupation with French literature* and make known those of other countries.[63] It published among others Heine, Grimm, Pushkin, Berlioz and Victor Hugo as well as literary bulletins from England, Germany, Spain, Italy. Another review with a similar mission, and articles, appeared at the same time: *L'Europe littéraire*. Balzac first published the *Vie de Napoléon* and the opening chapters of *Eugénie Grandet* in this review, at one time signing a contract to write articles only for it.[64] Other reviews bringing Europe to Paris, and vice versa, were the *Revue des deux mondes*, founded in 1829 (and still in existence today), which absorbed the *Revue des voyages* and specialised in long articles on the politics and literature of foreign countries;[65] and the *Revue du Nord, ou choix d'articles traduites des nouvelles publications de l'Allemagne, la Suisse, la Belgique, la Suède, le Danemarck, la Pologne, la Russie etc*, founded in 1836.

Thus, far from devoting themselves to the service of a fatherland, like Wagner and Cavour, many Parisians propounded ideologies of cosmopolitanism. In one article in the *Revue du Nord* Philarète Chasles, a professional Anglophile journalist and critic, claimed: 'we are heading, no one can doubt it, towards a universal republic of minds.' Like many other Parisian writers in this period, including Victor Cousin, Custine and Augustin Thierry, Philarète Chasles believed that the nations of Europe would soon learn to settle their general problems together without considering national interests. Expressions of hope by these writers were many and various: *les nationalités se confondent*; *les nations vont s'entendre*; *il n'existe plus de nations en Europe*.[66] Heine also had an ideology of cosmopolitanism: Jesus, he believed, was the saviour who had delivered his fellow Jews from their nationality, and sooner or later cosmopolitanism would triumph. Although he refused to be naturalised French, Heine asserted in his will of 7 March 1843 that, after his family and his wife, 'I have loved nothing so much on this earth as the French people, the dear land of France', and that he had dedicated his life to bringing France and Germany together.[67]

The greatest novelist of Paris was also European in his sympathies. After about 1835 Balzac tired of his 'perpetual combat without break' in 'this monstrous Paris'.[68] Moreover, he resented the hours of service which, like all Parisian men of a certain income after the revolution of 1830, he was obliged to perform as a national guard. Like Musset,

---

* In reality already ending, thanks to the popularity of Walter Scott, Byron and Shakespeare.

Gautier, Eugène Sue, Berlioz and many other writers and artists (only Alfred de Vigny, a former army officer, became a conscientious officer in the National Guard, helping to suppress the rising of 1834), he suffered imprisonment for failure to perform these duties, serving a term in a prison on the quai d'Austerlitz known as *l'hôtel des haricots*.[69] Thenceforth, he lived for much of the time in relative solitude in the suburbs at Sèvres or on a hill above the Seine at Passy (the present Maison de Balzac, 47 rue Raynouard, in the sixteenth arrondissement). The house there had a magnificent view over Paris and the advantage of several entrances, so that Balzac could escape if creditors appeared. He compared his life to that of a hunted hare. Like Mérimée, Gautier, Hugo and Custine, Balzac regularly left Paris to travel the continent. This quintessential Parisian knew, loved and dreamed of Geneva, Dresden, Vienna, Venice, Turin, Milan and Rome. In 1835 he wrote that he preferred the banks of the Danube to those of the Seine,[70] and while in Milan in 1837–8 he planned one of his most Parisian works: *Splendeurs et misères des courtisanes*, dedicated to his Milanese host, the Austrian chamberlain Prince Porcia.[71]

If Balzac loved Europe, Europe loved Balzac. His glory, visiting Germans told him in the salon of Baron Gérard, started on the other side of the French frontier.[72] As early as 1832 he claimed that he was receiving two or three letters a day from female readers abroad: the first letter from his future wife, Eve Hanska – *l'étrangère*, as she signed herself – was sent from Odessa on 28 February 1832. (They met eighteen months later when she was visiting Switzerland with her husband, and became lovers the following year, meeting and corresponding frequently thereafter.)[73] Balzac's works were generally published in French in St Petersburg soon after (in the case of *Le Lys dans la vallée* before) they appeared in Paris; they were also translated into Russian. Dostoyevsky's translation of *Eugénie Grandet* was published in 1846.[74] In 1841 a Russian wrote that 'In Russia, Balzac, thanks to the universality of the [French] language, is almost one of our own.'[75] During the carnival of 1834 Venetians dressed up as characters in his novels. In Naples ladies admired him as *le grand Magnétiseur des coeurs et des imaginations malades*.[76]

In part because Madame Hanska needed the support of the Tsar in property disputes with relations, Balzac advocated a Franco-Russian alliance and developed a passion for Russian absolutism: in 1833 he thought of entering Russian service 'like Pozzo di Borgo'. To Madame Hanska he wrote of his 'profound indifference for all that I would leave in France . . . without you France bores me and I have had it up to the eyes.' In order to be with her, he spent the summer of 1843 in St Petersburg, the winter of 1847–8 and October 1848–March 1850 on her estate at Wierzchownia, an island of Francophone culture in the steppes of the Ukraine. They married in Kiev on 14 March 1850. However, perhaps because he was ill and needed French doctors, he returned to Paris to die.[77]

Another manifestation of the symbiosis between Paris and Europe was the fashion for travel books. According to a former Napoleonic censor turned liberal Etienne de Jouy, Parisians traditionally feared foreign travel as much as famine. 'Abroad', he wrote in 1815, 'begins for them at a few miles beyond the barriers and a sort of anxiety seizes them from the moment they can no longer see the paternal towers of Notre Dame.'[78] After 1815, however, Parisians began to discover Europe through books not battles, as if writing about Europe was compensation for, or a means of reconquering, the empire lost in it. Although Balzac (with de Vigny) was one of the few major French writers in this period not to write a travel book,[79] he acknowledged the connection between conquest and creativity. Following Victor Hugo, he called the leading French writers 'literary Marshals of France', and believed: 'if France enjoys a preponderance in Europe she owes it to her men of intelligence. Today the pen has replaced the sword . . . the *Book* is more influential than the *Battle*.' He himself hoped to accomplish with the pen what Napoleon had been unable to finish with the sword – the conquest of Europe – much as Berlioz compared his musical tours in Europe to the campaigns of the Grande Armée. The literary careers of Hugo, Eugène Sue, de Musset were, in some ways, attempts to compete with the military or political careers of their fathers – officers or officials of the Napoleonic Empire in Europe. The sons did not forget the gold embroidery gleaming on their fathers' chests.[80]

Instead of withdrawing into relative isolation, like Vienna and Constantinople after their loss of empire in 1918, after 1814 Paris expanded its cultural horizons. Even its wallpaper confirms this wandering spirit: views of Rome, Venice, the Bosphorus, India, China, Peru, Brazil, El Dorado, began to enliven French interiors, in addition to the traditional subjects, *Les Monuments de Paris* and *Les Amours de Psyché*. Panoramas of London, Venice, Rome, Naples, Jerusalem attracted crowds to the Passage des Panoramas, built in Paris in 1799, and known from the elegance and licence of its public as *le petit Palais Royal*: it was there, one evening in October 1834, that Heine had first met Créscence Eugénie Mirat, the passion and torment of his life.[81]

Travel was on Parisians' minds. Chateaubriand told Ticknor in 1817 that in fifty years there would not be a legitimate sovereign from Russia to Sicily: 'I foresee nothing but military despotisms.' 'In high spirits, excited and even exalted', he said that he yearned to see Spain and Russia, 'the power that threatens to overwhelm the world', to fix his last home in Rome (he had been painted against a Roman landscape in a celebrated portrait by Narcisse Guérin in 1811), 'and there amid the ruins of three empires and three thousand years I would give myself wholly to my God'.[82]

Chateaubriand was not the only French politician who liked to travel. After his loss of office in 1819, the Duc de Richelieu travelled in the provinces, in Holland, Germany, Switzerland and Italy, always followed by *ma folle de reine*. Italy was then as much the fashion among the French as among the British and Irish, as is shown by Stendhal's *Rome, Naples et Florence* (1817) and *Promenades dans Rome* (1829); Chateaubriand's *Voyage en Italie* (1827); and many other works. Lamartine travelled there as a young man in 1811, and between 1820 and 1829, thanks in part to the influence of Madame de Montcalm, served in Naples and Florence as a diplomat. The beginning of the French cult of Venice is evident in the *Lettres d'un voyageur* (1833) of George Sand, who enjoyed a much publicised romance there with Alfred de Musset in 1833–4.[83]

At the same time Paris was reinforcing the traditional French connection with the Ottoman Empire, which since the sixteenth century had been one of the few fixed points in European diplomacy. The first half of the nineteenth century was the golden age of travel in the Ottoman Empire. Since steamboat services started before the creation of a European railway network, it was easier to travel from Paris to Constantinople than to much of Europe, as is revealed by M. Marchebeus's account of the first organised steam cruise there, in 1833, *Voyage de Paris à Constantinople*. By 1838, according to Léon de Laborde, who published books about his travels in Arabia, Syria and Asia Minor, journeys to the Orient had become commonplace. Many erudite travel books on the Ottoman Empire were published in Paris, generally handsomely illustrated and often subsidised, like their authors' travels, by the French government. They included Antoine Ignace Melling's *Voyage pittoresque de Constantinople et des rives du Bosphore*, published for the Fête de Saint-Louis in 1819; *Voyage dans le Levant* (1820) by the Comte de Forbin, Director of the Musées Royaux of France, who had been sent to the Levant to acquire antiquities to fill the gaps left in the Louvre after Waterloo; and Charles Félix Marie Texier's *Description de l'Asie Mineure faite par ordre du Gouvernement français de 1833 à 1837* (1839–49).[84]

However, the most popular book published in Paris on the Orient was Lamartine's four-volume *Voyage en Orient. Souvenirs, impressions, pensées et paysages* (1835) (notable also for its definition of museums as 'the cemeteries of the arts'). Like Tocqueville, in 1830 Lamartine had resigned his official position out of a sense of honour. Although from a legitimist family, he considered France lost without Louis-Philippe.[85] Freed, as he had long hoped to be, from the constraints of his diplomatic career, he travelled with his family to Syria and Palestine in 1832, in order to 'nourish the mind and the soul', and to visit the holy places.[86] Welcomed like an old friend, finding the area remarkably safe, he wrote, like many travellers before and since: 'to understand Europe well, you must be in Asia! All these rumours, all these [political and intellectual] systems of Paris are pitiful when one sees them from the mountains of Lebanon or the middle of the desert!' Such sentiments, however, did not stop Lamartine, after a few months, from returning to pursue his literary and political careers in Paris.[87]

Lamartine was not the only Parisian fascinated by the Orient. When the young Théophile Gautier first saw a view of a square in Cairo by Prosper Marilhat at the Salon of 1833, he at once felt a nostalgia for the Orient where he had never been: this was his true *patrie*.[88] He retained a taste for Islamic art. After visiting Spain in 1840, he wrote that the most delicious moments of his life had been spent in the Alhambra. Its beauty had been captured in a work which was the origin of the countless 'Alhambras' later built in the West: Joseph Girault de Prangey's *Souvenirs de Grenade et de l'Alhambra* (1837), a handsome volume which employed the new process of colour lithography (black and white lithography had already been introduced in Paris, partly by German print-workers, after 1815).[89]

After the Napoleonic wars Paris painters and architects set off for the Ottoman Empire with the same eagerness with which previous generations had left for Italy. Protected by France's ally Mohammed Ali Pasha, the modernising governor of the Ottoman province of Egypt, the architect Pascal-Xavier Coste worked in Cairo between 1818 and 1828, later publishing *Architecture arabe ou monuments du Kaire* (1837–9) whose seventy hand-coloured illustrations helped introduce Islamic architecture to Europe. Delacroix, who had hitherto left France only for a short visit to England in 1825, accompanied the Comte de Mornay on an embassy to the Sultan of Morocco in 1832, sent to forestall Moroccan opposition to the French conquest of Algeria. He was enchanted by Morocco's beauty and the 'naturalness which is always disguised in our lands', and returned with sketches which were later used as the base of celebrated paintings – of Jewish women of Algiers, the Sultan of Morocco and his guard – which laid the foundations of the French orientalist tradition.[90]

Paris was also a magnet for the study of the Orient. In 1822 the first Société Asiatique in Europe was founded in Paris. Early members included Orléans (Président d'honneur), Talleyrand, Chateaubriand, Pozzo and the Duchesse de Duras. In 1826 the French government began to commission the Collection Orientale, modern editions of oriental classics. Julius Mohl, who had come to Paris from Württemberg in 1823 at the age of twenty-three to study oriental languages, published the first modern edition of the national epic of Persia, Firdausi's *Shahnameh*, in six bilingual volumes in 1833–68. He became French in 1843, professor of Persian literature in the Collège de France, long a centre for the study of oriental languages, in 1847, and after twenty years as one of its secretaries President of the Société Asiatique in 1867.[91]

Paris attracted students from, as well as of, the Orient. Mohammed Ali sent the first educational mission of fifty students from Egypt to Paris in 1826. At a prizegiving on 4 July 1828 they were told by a French professor that their mission was to regenerate their country. France, by giving them a modern education, was only beginning to repay the debt owed by all Europe to the peoples of the Orient. By 1833 there were 115 pupils living in the Egyptian school at 33 rue de Clichy. One pupil, Rifa'a Bey al-Tahtawi, a future Minister of Education in Egypt, wrote the first Arabic book on Paris, *The Gold of Paris*, after his return to Cairo.[92] He admired the city and the revolution of 1830, but was shocked both by men's role as the 'slaves' of women – shown by the fact that women were seated and saluted before men – and by Parisians' 'curiosity, passion for novelties and love of change'.[93] A Moroccan visitor in 1845 was also shocked: 'The people of Paris are tireless in their pursuit of wealth. They are never idle or lazy. The women are like the men in that regard or perhaps even more so.'[94] The grandson of Mohammed Ali, Ismail Pasha, who would redesign sections of Cairo in the 1860s on the model of Paris, was also educated with other Egyptians, in an Egyptian military school in Paris in the years 1845–8.[95] The Egyptian students were followed by others sent from

Constantinople by the Ottoman government, as well as by many private Armenian students of medicine and architecture. (For a century or more, encouraged by French and Italian missionaries, ambitious Armenians had begun to turn to the West.)[96] The great Ottoman reformers of the mid-nineteenth century Mustafa Reshid Pasha, Aali Pasha and Ahmed Vefyk Pasha had served or been educated in Paris. The city had become a metaphor for the modern world. At a time when Disraeli was telling Englishmen 'Go east, young man!', Ottomans were urged:

> Go to Paris, young sir, if you have any desire;
> If you have not been to Paris, you have not come into the world.

Reflecting its reputation as the universal language of science and progress, between 1820 and 1840 French replaced 'Levant Italian' as the Ottoman Empire's language of communication with Europe. (French had already become the first language of many educated Italians, including the patriotic novelist Alessandro Manzoni, who wrote his famous novel *I Promessi Sposi* in Italian, but spoke French at home in Milan.)[97] By 1840 French was the language of the recently founded Constantinople military academy and school for military and naval surgeons, as well as of despatches from Ottoman diplomats abroad to the Foreign Ministry in Constantinople, and of educated Armenians.[98]

While some Parisians were fascinated by the Ottoman Empire, others preferred Greece. The sympathy, on both right and left, for the war of independence being waged there against Ottoman forces had led to the foundation of a Comité Philhellénique in Paris in 1824. It included Chateaubriand and the Duc de Fitzjames among royalists, Laffitte, Alexandre de Laborde and Ternaux among liberals.[99] In 1825, two enemies published pamphlets in favour of the same cause: Benjamin Constant the *Appel aux nations chrétiennes en faveur des Grecs*, Chateaubriand his no less passionate *Note sur la Grèce*. French soldiers who volunteered to fight for Greece included F.-R. Schack, *étudiant en droit à Paris, ancien palicare du Général en Chef Coloctroni*, whose book predicted for the Ottoman Empire an end as sudden and unexpected as Waterloo had been for the Napoleonic Empire.[100] Greek freedom songs were translated into French by the classical scholar Claude Fauriel and the popular playwright Népomucène Lemercier. Greek subjects, including Delacroix's celebrated pictures of the *Massacre of Chios* and *Greece expiring on the ruins of Missolonghi*, dominated the salons of 1824 and 1826. The French expedition of 14,000 soldiers, sent to the Morea in 1828 to deliver it from Ottoman forces, was accompanied by a staff with separate scientific, archaeological and architectural sections which produced, in imitation of Denon's *Description de l'Egypte*, another monument of Parisian erudition, describing some of the most famous sites of the region, Blouet's *Expédition scientifique de Morée* (1832–8).[101]

Travel writing received a further boost from the revolution of 1830, since many legitimists, like the Bourbons themselves, settled or travelled abroad (as Bonapartists had done after 1815). For many legitimists, the residence of their rightful King – whether it be Edinburgh (1830–2), Prague (1832–6) or Gorizia (1836–44) – was henceforth the capital of France.[102] It was partly disgust with the reign of the middle classes under Louis-Philippe, as well as desire to see how a republic functioned, which, in 1831–2, led the political philosopher Alexis de Tocqueville, son of a prefect of Charles X, to travel to the United States. It inspired his four-volume masterpiece of political analysis *De la démocratie en Amérique* (1835–40). Tocqueville's vision of the future was aristocratic and prophetic. He foresaw a society of equals existing only for themselves and their family, and dedicated to 'small and vulgar pleasures with which they fill their souls'. The state would control and regulate their actions and pleasures, fixing them 'irrevocably' in a state of childhood. Every day the action of free will would be consigned to a smaller space. In the end every nation would consist of 'a herd of timid and industrious animals, of which the government is shepherd'.[103]

Another semi-legitimist noble, Tocqueville's friend the Marquis de Custine was, in Balzac's opinion, *le voyageur par excellence*.[104] Like Tocqueville and Chateaubriand, Custine was an aristocrat in search of a solution. He described himself as 'an aristocrat by character as much as by conviction', who believed that 'without aristocracy there is only tyranny, in monarchies as in democracies'. Feeling little attachment for the dynasties competing for the throne of France, he held aristocracy to be the best barrier against 'the most redoubtable of tyrants' – revolution.[105] A man who claimed that 'the struggle between love and virtue is only a question of time',[106] Custine had special motives to travel. On 28 October 1824, having gone to Saint-Denis on the pretext of viewing the decorations for the funeral of Louis XVIII, he had been assaulted by soldiers of the Garde Royale with whom he had fixed a rendezvous. Thereafter, Custine had been subject to the rage of the 'holy Faubourg' – although able, owing to the decriminalisation of homosexuality in France since 1790, to continue to live with *mon ami anglais*, Edward Sainte-Barbe, and to be received by such hostesses as his 'second mother' the Princesse de Vaudémont, the Duchesse d'Abrantès and Sophie Gay – but not the Duchesse de Duras.[107]

Already in 1818 he had referred to Paris as a 'prison', an 'abyss', an 'extinguisher'. Anticipating many later writers, he wrote: 'I am only truly myself when enjoying the independence of the traveller';[108] 'I am a born traveller as others are born statesmen'.[109] Fluent in English, German and Italian, an enemy of 'narrow patriotism', he was as European as Pozzo. France and Germany were *mes deux patries*; Italy was *une patrie adoptive*, where he often spent half the year. His conversation at dinner reminded Barbey d'Aurevilly of a conjuror pulling all Europe, person by person, out of his pocket. Indeed at one of the parties he gave in his château of Saint-Gratien north of Paris, 'a Florentine villa arranged in the English manner' filled with statues and pictures from every country in Europe, where guests ranged from Marie Antoinette's favourite portraitist, Madame Vigée-Lebrun, to Victor Hugo, an Italian exclaimed: 'Paris is now Rome, it is the whole world.'[110]

Custine's first travel book was on Spain. After the successful campaign of 1823 to restore Ferdinand VII, a cult of Spain had swept Paris, evident in plays (*Rita l'Espagnole*, *L'Andalouse de Paris*, *La Fille du Cid*, Mérimée's *Le Théâtre de Clara Gazul*), poems, and dances such as *la cachucha*, later parodied as *la caoutchoucha* which, according to Théophile Gautier, made the epileptic somersaults of the Aissaoua in Algeria seem tame.[111] De Musset, Dumas and Gautier, among many others, wrote books on Spain. Custine's account of a visit in 1831, *L'Espagne sous Ferdinand VII*, was published in 1838.[112] At this time he regarded the Charte as 'a constitutional formality as laughable as court etiquette', and wanted a 'pure monarchy mitigated by the *douceur* of European customs'.[113] He appreciated the contrast between Spain, land of monarchy, tranquillity, faith and enthusiasm, and France, land of revolution, agitation, incredulity and sarcasm. French poets might be better than Spanish, but in Spain poetry was everywhere. In the absolute monarchy of Spain, in Custine's opinion, individuals were more free and independent in their behaviour towards the rich and powerful than in France or America: 'Everything which is real in society is independent of political forces . . . What an admirable religion, what a noble people, what a terrible government!'[114] Unlike Tocqueville he did not believe that democracy was the future of the world: indeed he predicted that it would soon lose its last partisans in America.[115]

After the death of Ferdinand VII and the accession of his daughter Isabella II in 1834, Louis-Philippe – unlike Napoleon and Louis XVIII –

refused all suggestions from both French and Spanish governments to send French troops to Spain to fight the ultra-royalist forces of her uncle Don Carlos (although units of the Légion Etrangère were lent to the Spanish government). More aware than most Frenchmen of the extent of Spanish Francophobia, in August 1836, while the Chambers were on vacation, he dismissed Thiers as Président du Conseil. Thiers, as eager to reassert French (and his own) prestige in Europe as Chateaubriand had been in 1823, had refused to give a formal guarantee not to intervene against the Carlists in Spain: Thiers retired for a year to Italy.[116] Instead of sending soldiers, in 1835–7 the King sent Baron Taylor, Inspecteur-Général des Beaux-Arts and a key figure in official cultural patronage, and an artist-traveller Adrien Dauzats. Their mission was not to make war but to buy pictures – readily available owing to the secularisation of Spanish monasteries by the government of Isabella II after 1836. Thanks to Louis-Philippe, from 1838 a Musée Espagnol in a wing of the Louvre, with 450 works by Zurbarán, El Greco, Velázquez, Goya and others, began to introduce Parisians – including the young Manet – to Spanish painting.[117]

Another admirer of Spain was the writer Prosper Mérimée. He led a quadruple life in Paris: writer, lover and man of the world, he was also Inspecteur-Général des Monuments Historiques and a member of, among other similar bodies, the Commission des Arts et Monuments. Nonetheless, since his first visit in 1830, he also maintained a Spanish life, both in Paris and Madrid. Many of his stories, such as *Carmen*, were set in Spain.[118] His most amusing letters, composing a brilliant fresco of life in Paris, were written to a mistress in Madrid, the Comtesse de Teba (who had told him the story on which *Carmen* is based). Between 1834 and 1837 she educated her daughters in Paris: hence the fluent French, and familiarity with Paris, of her younger daughter Eugénie de Montijo* when she married Napoleon III in 1853.

At the same time as more Frenchmen were travelling to Madrid, owing to frequent political upheavals more Spaniards were moving to Paris. In 1814 a hero of the Peninsular War, General Francisco Mina, fled there from the repressive regime of Ferdinand VII, the king he had helped to restore. The former liberal prime minister Martinez de la

---

*She had been educated with her sister at the Convent of the Sacré Coeur, rue de Varenne (1835–6), and the Gymnase Normal, Civil et Orthosomatique of Colonel Amoros (1836–7). An *afrancesado* refugee, Colonel Amoros had introduced gymnastics to the French army after 1821.

Rosa, who later applied notions acquired in Paris to drafting the Spanish *Statuto*, or constitution, of 1836, lived in Paris from 1824 to 1831. One of the richest men in Paris was a Spaniard. Alexandre Aguado, who like Montijo and Amoros had fought on the French side in the Peninsular War, settled in Paris after 1814. At first a wine merchant, he later became banker to Ferdinand VII, who created him Marquis de las Marismas del Guadalquivir. He made a fortune, and was naturalised French in 1828. He also became the mayor of Ivry, and one of the financial patrons of the Paris Opéra after its privatisation in 1831. Rossini wrote *Guillaume Tell* in his château of Petit-Bourg outside Paris.[119]

After 1840 the widow of Ferdinand VII, the former Queen Regent Maria Cristina, also preferred living in freedom in Paris (she had bought the château of Malmaison and a house in the rue de Courcelles), with her handsome second husband Fernando Muñoz, to ruling Spain: her presence, and that of her sister the Infanta Luisa Carlota and her children, meant that more Spanish Bourbons lived in Paris than in Madrid.[120] Another exile from Spain living in Paris was the former royal favourite and Generalissimo Manuel Godoy, who had governed Spain between 1791 and 1808. He moved from Rome to Paris in 1832, and lived in an attic at 20 rue de la Michodière near the Opéra. With more creditors than friends, he had little to do except write his memoirs (published in Paris in French translation in 1836–7) and stroll in the gardens of the Palais Royal and the Tuileries: children called him *Monsieur Manuel*. Abandoned by his wife, forgotten by the world, he died in 1851 and is buried in Père Lachaise.[121] So many Spaniards lived in Paris, and so many Parisians were interested in Spain, that a section of the Spanish Academy of Archaeology and Geography was founded in Paris: Mérimée and Victor Hugo, whose plays *Hernani* (1830) and *Ruy Blas* (1838) were inspired by Spanish history, were among its members.[122]

The most famous French travel book of the period, however, was about Russia. Based on a journey made there in the summer months of 1839, Custine's *La Russie en 1839*, published in May 1843, was an international intellectual and popular success, as influential in its day as Solzhenitsyn's *Gulag Archipelago* in 1973. It has been cited ever since in the West, particularly during the Cold War, as an analysis of Russia.[123] In contrast to the admiration for Alexander I and Russia prevalent in Paris in 1814, disdain is the predominant attitude expressed by Custine. 'I went to Russia to look for arguments against representative government,' he wrote; 'I return a partisan of constitutions . . . When your son is discontented in France, follow my advice, tell him: "go to Russia".'[124] Beneath polite portraits of the Tsar and Tsarina, it is an attack on the policy of rapid modernisation through autocracy, what he called the *fausse méthode de perfectionnement*, practised by Peter the Great and his successors.[125]

'The Russian government', Custine stated, 'is the discipline of the camp substituted for the order of civilisation, a state of siege become the normal state of society . . . a society where no happiness is possible.' Six thousand 'obscure martyrs' had died in order to rebuild the Winter Palace, after the fire of 1838, in record time to please the Tsar.[126] 'Russia is an invalid being treated with poison': the capital should return to Moscow.[127] Custine shows no awareness of the lack of support for constitutional monarchy in Russia, or Nicholas I's relative mercy to political conspirators. No practical alternative to Romanov autocracy is suggested. Forgetting the cruelty of French soldiers in Russia in 1812, and the forbearance of Russian soldiers in Paris in 1814 and 1815, he wrote: 'the Russians are not yet civilised. They are regimented Tartars:* nothing more . . . Russians superficial in everything are profound only in the art of pretence.'[128] Ignoring the moderation of Russia's territorial demands after its victory over the Ottoman Empire in 1829, he warned that Russia dreamt of the domination of the world: Europe would suffer the fate of Poland.[129] This elegant Parisian appreciated the *profils grecs* and *taille élégante et souple* of Russian men, including the Tsar himself. However, he considered most of the women hideous and repulsively dirty: even at a distance, the poor had a *parfum redoutable* of onions and cabbage.[130]

Custine's hostility was sharpened by his love for a young Polish refugee from Russian rule in Poland, Count Ignace Gurowski. From 1835 Gurowski had lived with Custine and Edward Sainte-Barbe in *notre trio*, until abducting the Infanta Isabella-Ferdinanda of Spain from a convent in Paris in May 1841, and eloping with her to Brussels.[131] With such loyalties, Custine had a hidden agenda. At the time of publication, he wrote to the leader of Polish Paris, Prince Czartoryski, that his book advocated the Polish interest 'hotly and in a fashion all the more effective for being indirect'. Moreover, 'one of the articles of my catechism' was gratitude for Poles' hospitality to his mother and grandmother during the emigration.[132] His account is an attack on the Russian court as well as Russia. He had detested the court of the Comte d'Artois,

---

* Similarly he had said of Spain: *tout y rappelle la race arabe.*

whom he had followed from Basle to Paris in 1814 and whom he later called *le pauvre lâche*.[133] But the court of Russia he loathed even more. 'In Russia', Custine stated, 'one breathes the air of the court from one end of the empire to the other . . . the Emperor and the court are made manifest to Russians wherever there is a man obeying a man who commands.'[134] Russia was 'a land where the court is everything . . . the court of Russia is still a power; the court of all other countries, even the most brilliant, is just a spectacle.'[135] Disagreeing with Balzac's and Chateaubriand's advocacy of a Franco-Russian alliance, Custine believed that the salvation of Europe and the future of the world lay in a solid alliance between France and Germany.[136]

Germany was, however, one European country little visited or studied by Parisians. Only Madame de Staël, in *De l'Allemagne*, had attempted to provide a complete account of German life in French. It had been published first in London in 1813, having been forbidden by the Napoleonic police on the grounds that, with its enthusiastic account of German literature, philosophy, religion and art, its praise of German poets and thinkers such as Goethe, Schiller, Wieland and Herder, it was 'not French'.[137] In the eighteenth century the rising power of Prussia had attracted the attention of a stream of French visitors, including Voltaire and Mirabeau, and admiring young officers like La Fayette and Berthier. In the nineteenth French visitors to Germany included writers like Victor Cousin (later known as 'the tutelary deity of all the Germans of Paris'), Edgar Quinet and Jules Michelet. They studied philosophy rather than power, Hegel not the Prussian army. *La savante Allemagne* was believed to be *la patrie de l'âme, cette noble et sainte patrie de tous les penseurs*.[138]

The growing power of Prussia and of German nationalism remained underestimated.[139] It needed a German, Heinrich Heine, to denounce the *brutale ardeur batailleuse* of the Germans and, writing in the *Revue des deux mondes* of 15 December 1834, to prophesy that one day, when Germany had found the man for which it was waiting, the world would hear a *craquement* such as it had never heard before: 'In Germany a drama will be performed, beside which the French revolution will be nothing but an innocent idyll.' The French would have more to fear from a liberated Germany than from the entire Holy Alliance.[140]

Another barrier to German power disappeared after 1830. Democratic and revolutionary France having shown itself unstable, it lost the little influence it had retained with the smaller German monarchies such as Bavaria, Saxony, Baden. Some German princes may have wanted to maintain their alliances with France. France had been their traditional defender against the ambitions of Austria and, recently, Prussia; it had helped prevent the annexation of Saxony by Prussia in 1814. However, monarchical solidarity, German nationalism, above all the restrictions imposed by membership of the German Confederation, made alliances between German princes and revolutionary France impossible. Another barrier to Austrian and Prussian power, and eventual German unification, had disappeared.[141]

As can be seen from the number and quality of books analysing foreign countries, of which only a small selection have been cited here, the French élite was never so well informed about other European countries, nor French writers so outward-looking, as in the years between 1814 and 1848. No longer could they believe 'that everything is always and everywhere French' or that Paris and France were 'the whole world'. The number of travel books, in particular those on Britain, as well as Tocqueville's on the United States and Custine's on Spain and Russia, also suggests the intensity of French writers' anxiety about the future of France during the unstable reign of Louis-Philippe.[142]

In addition to people like Heine, Balzac and Princess Lieven, financiers and politicians defended European interests in Paris. The Rothschild brothers, the richest bankers in Paris and Europe, were enemies of nationalism. After 1830, they were described by journalists as greater than emperors. Although at first contemptuous of the July monarchy, the Rothschilds frequently intervened in its early years to help avert war between France and Austria. In Vienna Salomon von Rothschild refused to give Metternich money for war. In Paris James de Rothschild encouraged Louis-Philippe, to whom he had constant access, to dismiss the bellicose government of Laffitte, on the grounds that wealthy people disliked his aggressive foreign policy.[143] Rothschild couriers and carrier pigeons gave favoured governments news quicker than their own diplomats; Rothschild loans helped underwrite European peace.[144]

The Rothschilds showed sympathy with the European court system in the decoration of their houses as well as the choice of their clients. The Salon François Ier of James de Rothschild's triple *hôtel* on the rue Laffitte (incorporating the *hôtels* of Queen Hortense and Fouché) was redecorated in Renaissance style in 1836, adopting a consciously European theme: its pictures show five different events of sixteenth-century European history, with Charles V, François Ier, Henry VIII, Leo X and Luther as their subjects. The juxtaposition of the Medici and

Rothschild coats of arms on the walls revealed the Rothschilds' image of themselves as successors to the Medici in Florence three hundred years earlier – as bankers, art patrons and sovereigns (of the Jews of Europe, rather than the Grand Duchy of Tuscany). Many aristocratic *hôtels* were decorated relatively simply. Rothschild's Paris *hôtel*, and his country houses outside Paris at Suresnes, Boulogne and Ferrières, however, displayed a profusion of gilt and gilding on curtains, walls, picture-frames, furniture, vases: 'a luxury which surpasses all imagination' according to Rodolphe Apponyi.[145] The royal pretensions of the Rothschilds were affirmed by the acquisition of large numbers of pictures and works of art with French royal provenances: many were bought at the first sale of the collections of the Duchesse de Berri in 1836.[146]

The most important European Parisian, however, was on the throne of France. Although Louis-Philippe often boasted of having served in the armies of the Republic, he had also been an émigré between 1793 and 1814, living in, among other places, Switzerland, Havana, London and Palermo and learning German, Spanish, English and Italian. In 1816 he had written: 'I am a cosmopolitan who takes root nowhere and the place I inhabit is indifferent to me . . . Palermo, Paris, Twick, the Seine, the Thames are all one to me.'[147] *Notre polyglotte couronné*, as Viennet called Louis-Philippe, boasted that he could speak to every ambassador accredited to Paris in their native tongue – except the Russian. However, Pozzo himself had never bothered to learn Russian.[148] Louis-Philippe may indeed have been a prisoner of his émigré past. He may have been influenced – or blackmailed – by the knowledge that Metternich possessed letters written by him as an émigré prince asking to serve against France in the Austrian army. Their publication in a Paris newspaper could have led to a crisis – as did the publication in the legitimist *Gazette de France*, in 1841, of three of Orléans' *émigré* letters, applying for British money and protection, and swearing eternal loyalty to his Bourbon cousins.[149]

Married to a Bourbon of Naples, whose mother was a Habsburg, Louis-Philippe had close relations on the thrones of Austria, Spain, Naples and Sardinia. In 1830 his public commitment to peace and private reassurances to European sovereigns had helped prevent a war between revolutionary France and monarchical Europe (the Austrian government's lack of men and money, and the Polish uprising, were other factors).[150] The presence of a peace-loving monarch on the throne of France prevented the Bourbons in exile from being able to present their restoration as a necessity, as they had done during the wars of 1792–1814. Louis-Philippe thus gave the July revolution of 1830 a better chance of survival than the revolution of 1789.

After 1830, both in word and deed, Louis-Philippe remained a king of peace. After dinner at Saint-Cloud in September 1833, he told Lord Granville that he wanted to efface the spirit of military glory and conquest, so long dominant in France, and replace it by the spirit of commercial and industrial enterprise.[151] Two prime ministers, Laffitte and Thiers, resigned over his refusal to intervene abroad, in Italy in 1831 and Spain in 1836 respectively. He wrote to Lord Holland, whom he had known since his *émigré* days in London, letters in English of remarkable prescience:

> it is difficult after so great a convulsion to subdue the irritation [of public opinion] and to re-establish public confidence. I am striving incessantly to maintain the peace within and the peace without. War, bad as it is at all times, would be in the present state of Nations attended with miseries and misfortunes unparalleled in any former wars. Therefore more now than ever no effort shall be wanting on my part to preserve my country and nation from that terrible scourge and I do not despair of ultimate success.

In 1837 he reiterated the same ideas:

> peace is the necessary guardian of freedom and real liberty . . . The law must end where war begins. [The desire to avoid military rule was] the guide and polar star of my political conduct . . . the union of our countries and the close and intimate connection of our Governments has always appeared to me the most efficacious measure to prevent war.

He advocated 'the maintenance of the present Status Quo without losses or conquests for anyone and the independence and security of every State. I know of no clashing interests between us.'[152] The wars which, under his sons Orléans, Nemours and Aumale, were then extending French territory in Algeria, often employing a third of the army, ought to be enough, so he thought, to satisfy French desire for expansion. In his view the conquest of Algeria, which he commemorated in vast battle frescoes by Horace Vernet for the Salle de Constantine in Versailles, made France the only country in Europe with a battle-trained army.[153] Perhaps he did not realise the extent to which the Algerian war was brutalising that army. One soldier, the actor Edmond Got, wrote in his diary: 'Oh the man-hunt! Strange intoxication! It is astonishing how infectious cruelty is and how quickly the savage in every man resurfaces.'[154] For most French opinion, however, fixed on Belgium and the Rhine, Algeria remained a sideshow. It never acquired the prestige of the empire then being established by Britain in India – although regiments formed in Algeria, the *zouaves*, the *spahis* and the *tirailleurs d'Afrique*, won many hearts when they paraded through the streets of Paris.

The clash between Europeanism and nationalism was also a clash between generations. Louis-Philippe's son, the Duc d'Orléans, like many younger Parisians, was a nationalist who wanted war. One reason for his hatred of the Restoration had been what he termed 'the anti-national disposition of the King', and the government's predilection for foreigners 'to the disadvantage of the sympathies and interests of France'.[155] To his sister in Brussels he wrote this *cri de coeur*: 'I plunge deeper and deeper into my passionate and exclusive cult of France, around which, in my imagination, I am erecting a great wall of China.'[156] This was no passing mood: in 1839 he praised the *culte exigeant de la nationalité* in preference to the *faciles vertus du cosmopolitisme*. In 1840 he recommended his son to be the 'passionate, exclusive servant of France and the revolution'.[157] Believing in the 'necessity' of reconstructing Europe on bases less 'hostile' to France and to other peoples, feeling personally humiliated by the monarchs of Europe in his search for a bride, he wrote that, if necessary, he would sign a rupture of the treaties of 1815 in his own blood. He wanted to reconstruct the German Confederation under French influence and prepared, in writing, a military strategy for the defence of France in a war against Europe.[158]

This was the spirit of the age: Alfred de Vigny wrote that war seemed 'the natural state of our country' to his generation of Frenchmen, born to the beat of the drum.[159] The pacific outlook of Louis-Philippe was regarded with contempt. Chateaubriand called him Europe's gendarme in Paris. In 1814 Chateaubriand had defended France's loss of its conquests; in the 1830s he denounced 'the revolting treaties of Vienna' and believed that, as long as France did not occupy 'our natural frontiers', there would be war in Europe.[160] By then many royalists felt shame and horror at the joy with which they had reacted, in 1814, to the restoration of the Bourbons through the agency of a European coalition.[161]

The new nationalism had turned increasingly strident after 1830. From being an instinct, nationalism was becoming a religion. For many it was taking the place of Christianity. *Le Globe* began to refer to France as the 'Christ among nations', a 'nation-religion'.[162] For the inauguration of the Musée de l'Histoire de France in 1837, itself in part a celebration of French victories over foreigners, no ambassadors were invited: as they had the right to the first places, the King would have been surrounded by foreigners, which would have been unpopular with the French. He was already reproached for his love of foreigners. It was said that a foreign accent, especially an English one, opened all doors at the Tuileries.[163] By 1839 most of the European literary reviews had closed for lack of readers or in the case of *L'Europe littéraire*, because the editor had spent too much money on balls and dinners: Parisian readers had become more interested in French subjects. From 1837 the *Revue britannique* became less English and more French. A *Chronique parisienne*, by a Frenchman rather than a foreigner, was introduced.[164] On his return from London in 1843, Chateaubriand felt – as he had not when returning in 1800 or 1822 – that 'Paris and London are two foreign worlds which do not know each other.'[165] A few years later, in his lectures at the Collège de France on *notre nationalité*, Michelet taught that it was *peu associable à l'anglaise*: England 'knows only hatred'.[166] At the same time the figure of a nationalistic ex-Napoleonic soldier called Nicolas Chauvin, who detests foreigners and Algerians, having made a first appearance in popular songs of the 1820s, became a stock character in plays and poems.[167] The words chauvinism and chauvinist were born in Paris under Louis-Philippe.

In 1840, a clash between the Europeanism of Louis-Philippe and the nationalism of the younger generation almost led to war. The occasion was the destiny of the Ottoman Empire. As it grew weaker, Princess Lieven wrote to Lord Aberdeen that the empire's future had become 'the great affair of all Europe'.[168] Heine called it *la grande question sanglante du monde, cette question fatale et inévitable que nous appelons la question d'Orient*, a secret disease fermenting in the European body politic.[169]

Clever, daring and pro-French, the Ottoman governor of Egypt Mohammed Ali had begun to modernise Egypt, its army and navy, with greater success than the Sultan was able to achieve in the rest of the empire. Having seized Syria from the Sultan in 1830, he easily defeated Ottoman attempts to reconquer it in 1833 and 1839. In 1840 Mohammed Ali was hoping to obtain from the Ottoman government the hereditary governorship of Egypt for his family, and confirmation of his control of Syria, at least for his own lifetime. At moments, to the horror of the European powers, he wanted complete independence from the Ottoman Empire.[170]

Mohammed Ali became a French cause, praised in the Paris press as the successor and avenger of Bonaparte. French officers served in his army; French merchants and travellers admired his transformation of Egypt.[171] In *Voyage en Orient* the poet Gérard de Nerval blamed the Ottoman Empire for the 'obscurantism' of the Middle East in the last three centuries. In Cairo, on the other hand, he found a city already being modernised, with English tourists, French merchants and European palaces.[172] Paris still contains a celebrated symbol of the friendship between France and Egypt, an obelisk from Luxor originally given by Mohammed Ali to Charles X. Louis-Philippe chose to place it in the middle of the Place de la Concorde, where Charles X had laid the foundations of a monument to Louis XVI: not having a political message, the obelisk would be in no danger of demolition. On 25 October 1836 it had finally been erected in the presence of 200,000 spectators, including the King, the royal family and the Corps Diplomatique, while an orchestra played tunes from *I Puritani*. Sitting by a window overlooking the *place*, the King had hidden from the crowds until the operation was successfully completed. He then appeared at the window to receive their applause.[173]

A ministry under Marshal Soult having lost a vote in the Chamber over a proposed endowment on his marriage for the King's second son the Duc de Nemours, the King had been obliged with reluctance, on 1 March 1840, to accept Thiers, who was then forty-two, as Président du Conseil.[174] Thiers was, as Heine wrote, 'the man of nationality', who knew that whoever understood the national idea in France exercised an irresistible charm over the masses and could lead them where he wished.[175] Indeed he told Princess Lieven that he had little to do with foreigners: 'we have nothing to say to each other.'[176] In another salon he once called the Germans 'nothing but a herd of wild animals'.[177] Determined to restore 'the enthusiasm of 1830' by left-wing and nationalistic measures, such as granting an amnesty to radicals and more support to Mohammed Ali, he was also resolved to reduce the power of the King and make the July monarchy a truly parliamentary regime.[178]

Thiers claimed to pursue the traditional French policy of commitment to the Ottoman Empire. He regarded Mohammed Ali as the man who, by modernising Egypt, had 'reawoken the pride of the Ottoman people' and so become an 'essential and necessary part of the Ottoman Empire'.[179] Thiers wanted to impose a settlement between the Ottoman government and Mohammed Ali, giving the latter and his descendants hereditary possession of Syria. The British Foreign

Secretary Palmerston, however, regarded Mohammed Ali as an 'ignorant barbarian . . . as great a tyrant and oppressor as ever made a people wretched'.[180] The Ottoman Empire followed the advice of the British government.

As the confrontation between Mohammed Ali and the Ottoman government reached its climax, France's diplomatic isolation became evident. Its only allies were the Two Sicilies and Greece.[181] Thiers had refused an international conference on the *question d'Orient* on 20 April. By a treaty signed in London on 15 July 1840, Russia, Britain, Austria and Prussia, rather than work with Thiers, decided to impose their own settlement between the Sultan and the Pasha, if necessary by force. In order to save the Ottoman Empire, Palmerston was prepared to ally with Russia and fight France.[182] As in the search for a bride for the Duc d'Orléans, and the 'mendicant marriages' of his brothers and sisters, France was humiliated by Europe – although in reality Thiers and Guizot, then French ambassador in London, had known that such a treaty was in preparation.[183] It is possible that news of the treaty first reached the French government by means of a letter from Madame de Lieven to Madame de Flahaut.[184]

Nationalism in France was so sensitive that the exclusion of France from a diplomatic concert over the Ottoman Empire, and the threat to Mohammed Ali's power in Egypt and Syria, aroused popular outrage in Paris. On all sides people talked of war.[185] The *Revue des deux mondes*, normally so pro-European, thundered: 'France should remember that even alone she has resisted Europe.' *Le Temps* wrote: 'Europe is very weak against us. She can try to play against us the terrible game of war, we can play with her the terrible game of revolution.'[186] The *Journal des débats* summoned France to prepare for war.[187] Theatre audiences called for the music of the Marseillaise and sometimes sang the words, still considered dangerously inflammatory (although, according to Heine, they were sung so badly that they seemed to have been forgotten).[188] The Anglomania of the 1820s and 1830s had turned to hate. British servants were 'maltreated' in the Champs Elysées, while the British ambassador's carriage was attacked on the rue du Faubourg Saint-Honoré by a mob crying *A bas les Anglais!*[189]

Conscripts were called up, the army placed on a war footing, an armaments programme launched. A new protective wall around Paris (on the site of the present *boulevards périphériques*), protected by a system of outlying forts, was voted – a project cherished by Louis-Philippe in the interests of both his own and his capital's security. Thiers, who was writing a history of the Napoleonic Empire and saw himself as a war leader, was convinced that the forts would help France win a future war.[190] He wrote to his personal agent in Alexandria, Comte Walewski, the illegitimate son of Napoleon by Marie Walewska who had fought both in Poland and Algeria, that France was preparing for war in the spring of 1841, possibly in order to gain territory in Europe.[191]

The main force for peace in Europe remained Louis-Philippe, although even he, at times, made threatening remarks to ambassadors, in his wife's presence, about unleashing the tiger of revolution, and proving to Europe that he was King of the French.[192] To keep the peace and undermine his own ministers Louis-Philippe used the diplomatic system. His main British interlocutor in Paris that summer, in the absence of the ambassador Lord Granville, was a cosmopolitan young diplomat and writer, and protégé of Palmerston, Henry Lytton Bulwer. He had already written a substantial book, with maps and statistics, on *France Social, Literary and Political. The Monarchy of the Middle Classes* (1836) in which he indicated, as one of the great differences with England, the existence of five million landed proprietors.[193] He had many admirers. A former mistress of Chateaubriand, Hortense Allart, told him that he had become Parisian in manners, language and clothes: there was nothing English left in *mon petit secrétaire d'ambassade*. Madame de Castellane begged Bulwer to remember that she was at home to her friends every evening after 7.30.[194] Princess Lieven wrote that he had 'a thousand times more intelligence than the whole Diplomatic Corps in Paris put together'.[195] Indeed Bulwer had already negotiated the Treaty of Balta Liman in Constantinople in 1838, which had opened the Ottoman Empire to British commerce – and damaged the economic policies of Mohammed Ali.[196] His judgement of Louis-Philippe was to the point: 'Remarkably shrewd in dealing with present difficulties, H.M. Louis-Philippe is not a person of considerable foresight and is rather distinguished by the skill with which he extricates himself from difficulties than for the judgement with which he avoids them.'[197] Yet below the diplomatic façade, as his subsequent career in Madrid and Constantinople would confirm, and his debts in England already showed, Bulwer was ruthless, dishonest and corrupt. Mérimée described him as 'very false, very crooked and very witty when he is not on his deathbed, which happens four times a week'.[198]

On 27 July Louis-Philippe remarked to Bulwer: 'Ah Mr Bulwer, you have wished to give me a lesson . . . you think, I know you do, that

France may be bullied into anything.' He admitted that he had to follow Thiers' policy for the moment, as Thiers was talking of 'the dishonour of France'.[199] At the same time he told his ambassador in Vienna that he would not be led too far by 'my little minister. At heart he wants war and I do not want it . . . I will crush him rather than break with all Europe.'[200] On 11 September, to try to force Mohammed Ali to evacuate Syria, British and Austrian forces bombarded Beirut.[201] On 14 September, Thiers wrote to King Leopold of the Belgians, often an intermediary between the French and British governments: 'if Europe wants to tackle us, she only has to try. I guarantee that the map of the world will be changed. Paris will become an immense fortress that not all the coalitions in the world will ever be able to force.'[202] However, on the same day Louis-Philippe promised Bulwer that, unless the expression of public opinion was irresistible, he would never be the attacking party in a war. Palmerston's knowledge of the King's commitment to peace encouraged him to take a more aggressive attitude to France.[203] Thiers told Bulwer that he was prepared to set fire to the four corners of the world; in response Bulwer showed Thiers despatches in which he informed Palmerston of the King's doubts about Thiers' policy.[204] On the same day the Porte deposed Mohammed Ali.

Paris might be at the height of its importance as capital of Europe. The number of foreigners living in the department of the Seine had risen from 47,000 in 1830 to 104,000 in 1840 (and 174,000 in 1847), increasing from 5 to 10 per cent of the population.[205] Already in the revolution of July 1830 the flight of foreigners had, rightly, been expected to lead to the disappearance of the splendour of the city, 'in which they have a large share'.[206] If there was war in 1840, the Prefect of the Seine reminded the King, 50,000 foreign visitors would leave Paris: the effect on trade and employment would be catastrophic, and potentially revolutionary.[207] Yet the weight of diplomatic, commercial, cultural and personal connections between Paris and Europe could not supersede its role as capital of France. Most Parisians wanted war – even over an issue so remote from French national interests. The sense of humiliation since Waterloo was so fierce that peace seemed ignoble, war both honourable and inevitable. The crisis sprang from the Nile to the Rhine. Reflecting the Parisian urge to travel, Nerval, Hugo, Dumas had already written about this castle-lined river flowing between France and Germany. In his history and travel book *Le Rhin* Victor Hugo had written: 'France and Germany are the essence of Europe: Germany is the heart; France is the head.' *Le Rhin* contains an eloquent description of the mysterious equilibrium in the political system of pre-revolutionary Europe, which had functioned like a piece of *orfèvrerie* to protect the small states of the Holy Roman Empire and Italy. Nevertheless it is a nationalist call 'to give back to France what God has given her': the left bank of the Rhine. Thereafter the union of the two brother nations of France and Germany, against Britain and Russia, would be the salvation of Europe.[208] Like Hugo, the Duc d'Orléans and others nourished the illusion – encouraged by the popularity of the 1830 revolution in parts of Germany – that in the Rhineland the people, if not the princes, were waiting to unite under 'the finest, the most noble, the most popular flag in the world' – the tricolour.[209]

However, the German reaction to the European crisis led the French, for the first time, to understand that they would not be greeted with joy on the other side of the Rhine. A wave of Francophobe fury, almost as ferocious as that of 1813–15, swept Germany, including the Rhineland. Michelet talked of a 'fatal divorce' between France and Germany. French diplomats agreed.[210] According to Heine, Thiers had reawoken Germany from its lethargic sleep, and brought it into the political arena of Europe. Thiers was like the fisherman in the Arabian nights: he had let the demon of war out of the bottle and was struggling to put it back.[211] On 18 September Nickolaus Becker, a Cologne lawyer and poet much rewarded at the time by German rulers, wrote in *Der deutsche Rhein*, 'They will not have it, the free German Rhine.' His theme was taken up by other poets. 'Courage brothers, strike hard, our old father the Rhine, the Rhine will stay German,' wrote the revolutionary George Herwegh. Another, Max Scheckenbruger, wrote a famous nationalistic song *Die Wacht am Rhein*; Hoffman von Falkersleben *Deutschland, Deutschland über alles* – above all *über* France.[212] Musset, who believed that the youth of France were thirsting to take up the sword, replied in an angry poem evoking past French victories, mocking *vos vertus germaines* and bearing the refrain: *Nous l'avons eu, votre Rhin allemand*. The last, mocking question, referring back to the unforgotten humiliations of 1814, was:

> *Combien, au jour de la curée,*
> *Etiez-vous de corbeaux contre l'aigle expirant?*[213]

Edgar Quinet, formerly a Germanophile who considered Germany 'land of the soul and of hope' and had resided there for long periods between 1826 and 1834, had become fervently anti-German and wrote a pamphlet, *1815 et 1840*, advocating French recovery of the Rhine frontier.[214]

On 2 October news that Beirut had fallen reached Paris: Mohammed Ali, more realistic than Thiers, would already have yielded to the great powers and withdrawn from Syria but for French pressure.[215] In 1814 a force for peace, in 1840 Paris pushed for war. *Guerre aux Anglais*, Paris mobs cried, *ils ont pris notre Beyrout!* English students were driven from lectures at the Sorbonne; outside the Théâtre des Variétés an Englishman was assassinated by a *gamin* of sixteen. On 3 October Heine wrote of 'an agitation which defies all belief. The thunder from the cannon of Beyrouth finds an echo in all French hearts.' Queues in front of army recruitment offices were as long as for a fashionable play. The gardens and arcades of the Palais Royal were packed with men with serious faces reading newspapers. The storm was approaching.[216] The cry went up in *Le National*: 'O France, draw your sword; the time has come . . . Think of your supreme mission and the grandeur of your destiny!'[217]

Even Queen Marie Amélie caught the fever and asked to have the swords of her five sons blessed by the Archbishop of Paris. The Duc d'Orléans, well aware of the link between French nationalism and the French monarchy, and believing that the more hostile Europe was to Louis-Philippe the more popular he would be in France, remarked: 'I would rather be killed on the Rhine than in the Paris gutter.'[218] At 6 p.m. on 15 October, indeed, a shot was fired at Louis-Philippe, at the junction between the quai des Tuileries and the Place de la Concorde, by a street cleaner called Darmès. Partly inspired by the fall of Beirut, calling Louis-Philippe the greatest tyrant of modern and ancient times, he claimed to have the support of thirty thousand republicans. At the same time Princess Lieven told Thomas Raikes that her apprehensions of eventual war were as strong as his own.[219] She considered war an absurdity: France had no reason to provoke it and, as in 1815, Europe was bound to win.[220] Hitherto Louis-Philippe had aroused feelings of almost universal disrespect. The Darmès attempt, however, produced a reaction in his favour. Before it theatre audiences had called for the Marseillaise every evening; afterwards none did.[221]

With constant access to the King, the ministers and European ambassadors, James de Rothschild was another force for peace. In these years 'the Louis XIV of the counting-house' was at the height of his power.[222] Heine, a friend of the Baronne, alleged that he had seen a stock-market speculator take off his hat to James de Rothschild's chamber pot, as it was being removed in the morning by a liveried footman, adding that the man was bound to become a millionaire:

'everyone pays homage to M. de Rothschild in the hope of being warmed by his golden rays.'[223] In addition to his love of peace, James de Rothschild had personal reasons for supporting Louis-Philippe and opposing Thiers. In April 1840 he had given Louis-Philippe a rare personal loan of two million francs. On 2 June, over a 'ritual murder' accusation against Damascus Jews which had been supported by the French consul, Thiers had made remarks in the Chamber of Deputies deploring the alleged power and disloyalty of Jews. The Rothschilds' dislike of Thiers' nationalism and arrogance increased and they cleared out of French government stock. The 3 per cent stock fell from 87 in July, to 79 on 6 August and 73.5 in early October, lower than at any time since 1831, thereby increasing the French government's difficulties in its search for funds to finance army expansion.[224] The financial background to the political crisis was well known. On 12 October *Le Constitutionnel*, which favoured Thiers, denounced Rothschild as an Austrian agent with little concern for the honour and interests of France. That day a crowd outside the Ministry of War had to be dispersed by force.[225]

If most Parisians were belligerent, many others in the élite, in addition to Rothschild, favoured peace. Once so bellicose, from September the *Journal des débats* began to denounce as unpatriotic the caprices of Thiers and the threats addressed by French radicals to Europe. A war between France and Germany would be tantamount to civil war; the slightest failure abroad would lead to revolution at home.[226] By mid-October, even Thiers, knowing that France had only 489,000 men in the army, was unwilling to go to war against the rest of Europe. He and Louis-Philippe were both manoeuvring to ensure that the other took the blame for the impending French climbdown.[227] On 21 October, at a council meeting at Saint-Cloud which lasted until midnight, Louis-Philippe refused to accept the warlike text of a speech from the throne prepared for him by Thiers: it talked of 'new measures' in armaments, the call-up of an additional 150,000 men, the need for sacrifices for France to keep her rank among nations, and 'this sacred store of independence and national honour which the French Revolution has placed in his hands'. The King said that he refused to provoke the powers of Europe or to bind the fate of France to that of the Pasha of Egypt. Although partly or secretly agreeing with the King, Thiers and his colleagues resigned.[228]

Congratulating himself on having saved France from a war with no reason and no aims, the King summoned Guizot, then serving as

French ambassador in London, to Paris. A new administration was formed under Guizot, with Maréchal Soult as nominal Président du Conseil. On 5 November when Louis-Philippe opened the Chambers, he was escorted from the Tuileries to the Palais Bourbon by an army of soldiers and police; the populace was kept at a distance; inside the Chamber the deputies of the *côté gauche* refused to cheer.[229] That autumn peace, based on the *status quo ante* of 1832, with the difference of the Ottoman government's guarantee of hereditary possession of Egypt for the descendants of Mohammed Ali, returned to the Ottoman Empire.[230] Lamartine, by now the most popular speaker in the Chamber of Deputies, called it the Waterloo of French diplomacy.[231]

Such weeks of tension in Paris, with war in sight, were, however, unusual. Most of the time the daily life of Paris was dominated not by the clashes of the great powers but, as Balzac claimed, by the pursuit of gold and pleasure. Paris was still considered by foreigners the Jerusalem of pleasure, the Mecca of the West.[232] Its carnival had become a European event, far surpassing in popularity the carnivals of Rome and Venice. There were so many balls, Mérimée wrote, that 'carnival makes every woman in Paris lose at least three kilogrammes of flesh and ages her by two years'.[233] Madame de Girardin compared the carnival to an avalanche of pleasure, during which the streets of Paris appeared to be filled with devils on holiday from hell.[234] Eight thousand people danced the polka, the *galop* and the can-can at the opera balls: their disguises enabled them to indulge in a 'cynicism' of gestures, and a freedom of language, which would have made the gods and goddesses on the pillars blush. Since men as well as women were allowed to attend masked, and courtesans were now admitted, the balls had become wilder than ever. Women hunted for partners as eagerly as men. Everything was permitted.[235]

In the carnival of 1839 the Préfet de Police Gabriel Delessert, a rich banker, who had helped lead the National Guard during the riots of 1830–3 (and whose wife Valentine was Mérimée's principal mistress), had written, rather optimistically: 'never has the taste for pleasure and diversion manifested itself to such an extent, among the multitude above all . . . everywhere high spirits, propriety, gaiety and obedience.'[236] However, the most popular public dance in Paris, the Bal Musard, held in a former riding school in the Faubourg Saint-Honoré with room for 1,200 couples and women 'raving with delight, panting with fatigue', reminded Thomas Raikes of 'the mysteries of a pagan deity, performed by satyrs and bacchantes'.[237]

Lined with fashionable shops, cafés and theatres, the boulevards were at the height of their glory. After the Palais Royal had been cleaned up and deprived of its brothels in 1829–31 and its gambling clubs in 1836 (gambling was forbidden in Paris from 31 December of that year), it lost much of its animation. Soon there were signs advertising shops for rent. It was said that Paris had emigrated to the boulevards. In 1837 they were paved in asphalt and given gas lamps: the mud of Paris was becoming a thing of the past.[238]

The most elegant restaurant in Paris, with the finest service and cellar, was no longer Véry (which the English had killed) or the Grand Véfour in the Palais Royal, but the Café de Paris. It had opened in 1822 on the Boulevard des Italiens, on the ground floor of the house occupied by Lady Hertford. A dandy, Roger de Beauvoir, later wrote: 'if you have not seen the Café de Paris . . . in 1840, you have seen nothing.' De Musset was said to eat *veau à la casserole* there three times a week.[239]

For de Musset the boulevards were 'one of the points of the earth where the pleasure of the world is concentrated'.[240] Balzac called them 'the poem of Paris', what the Grand Canal was to Venice. Although he complained of Paris, he admitted that whoever stepped on to the boulevards was lost: *on ne peut que s'amuser . . . on y boit des idées.*[241] The German writer Friedrich Hebbel wrote: 'The magnificence of the boulevards, the life quivering there in a perpetual flux and reflux, can never be sufficiently praised.'[242] They gave strollers that sense of freedom, of the possibility of anything happening, which was one of the attractions of Paris. This was the golden age of the Parisian *flâneur*, or stroller, passing the day between cafés, *cabinets de lecture*, and theatres, the boulevards, the Palais Royal, the Jardin des Tuileries and the *quais*. In *Le Flâneur* in *Les Français peints par eux-mêmes*, Auguste de Lacroix proclaimed: 'Paris belongs to the *flâneur* by right of conquest and by right of birth. He sees everything for himself and he walks ceaselessly through Paris with his hare's ears and lynx's eyes.'[243] Then as now, people often met on the boulevards acquaintances they thought in the antipodes.[244] In one stroll along the boulevards in October 1840, Liszt ran into, among other friends, Heine, Balzac, Chopin and Berlioz.[245]

The Champs Elysées were, however, beginning to rival the boulevards. From 1834 to 1848 theatres, restaurants, cafés and fountains were built there under the supervision of the Cologne-born architect Jacques-Ignace Hittorff, who had been working for the department of Fêtes et Cérémonies since 1818.[246] 'All Paris is coming to the Champs Elysées,' Balzac remarked, and forsaking the Tuileries gardens.[247] Some of the most fashionable women in Paris, mesdames de Flahaut, de Girardin and Le Hon, lived on the Champs Elysées.[248] On a fine Sunday three to four thousand carriages could be seen there, displaying the servants, coats of arms, elegance and wealth of their owners. The Champs Elysées also served other functions. On summer evenings it was a fashionable promenade, lined with cafés, orchestras, street vendors, 'for the *beau monde* and the *monde* that is not *beau* who prefer the open air and the moonlight to the spectacle and the salons'.[249] In the winter, Balzac wrote:

> despite the cold I still meet fiacres in the Champs Elysées going at walking pace, with lowered blinds, which shows that Parisians still make love, furiously, despite everything and those fiacres seem to me even more magnificent with passion than the two lovers whom Diderot surprised, at midnight, in the pouring rain saying goodnight in the street under a gutter.[250]

The carriage procession down the Champs Elysées to Longchamp at Easter, in eclipse in the early years of the July monarchy, had never been more brilliant than in 1840, according to Madame de Girardin. She noted the contrast between the pre-eminence of Paris and the humiliation of France. Referring to the foreigners who continued to flood in 'torrents' to the city, despite the crisis of 1840, she wrote: 'if France is not called to be part of the great European concert (parliamentary jargon), in compensation Europeans of every kind are generously called to contribute to the immense and eternal concert of Paris.'[251] A symbol of Parisian confidence was the reconstruction in 1837–41 of the Hôtel de Ville, executed in Renaissance style to rival the Tuileries. The Galerie des Fêtes was especially elaborate.[252]

A Dutchman called J. Kneppelhout made a journey to Paris at this time. His motives were to buy a new coat and to see the sensational new actress, Mlle Rachel. However the street life of Paris fascinated him even more than its shops or theatres:

> my God, what a happy people the people of Paris are, how alert and cheerful! Anything amuses them . . . What facility, what vivacity, what warmth, what a frank and correct way of speaking, which always conveys its meaning directly and without hesitation . . . of all peoples Parisians speak best. I think it comes from the sound made by the cobbles. Speech is a battle for them. What noise in the streets! Thousands of carriages, salesmen shouting, a population buzzing, an immense murmur coming from every window, exuded from the pores of every house, the air heavy with uproar and *brouhaha* . . . In Paris one lives in the street.[253]

After 1840, as passions cooled and the fashion for riot and assassination waned, few people lived in the streets of Paris more than the King
himself. Mrs Gore wrote: 'At all hours, from daybreak till sunset, Louis
Philippe may be met, sometimes on horseback, sometimes in a private
equipage, accompanied by his architect or a single aide de camp or even
alone, nimbly inspecting the progress of the public works in the most
remote quarters of the town.' Inspecting building works was his favourite form of relaxation and of forgetting the constant attacks on his
person and his policies.[254] The new fortified walls built round the city in
1840–3, with bastions on the top for cannon, surrounded by wide
ditches and protected by sixteen individual forts, each a cannon shot
away, gave him confidence. They made him, he told the Austrian
ambassador, master of both Paris and France. Having survived assassination attempts, insurrections and war fever, he believed he could
henceforth reign in peace.[255]

12

Funerals

1840–1844

Chez nous la fascination de la guerre et de la conquête dure toujours.

Marquis de Custine
La Russie (1839)

I<small>F PEACE HAD</small> triumphed in the chancelleries of Europe in October 1840, war triumphed on the streets of Paris, on 14 December 1840. Slowly through the morning mist the Emperor's funeral catafalque advanced down the Champs Elysées. Shrouded in purple velvet, supported by columns, caryatids and gilded figures of victory, draped in conquered enemy flags, the coffin towered above the sixteen horses, caparisoned in cloth of gold, which pulled the funeral chariot. The moving mountain of purple and gold was escorted by gendarmes of the department of the Seine; soldiers; pupils of military schools; cavalry of the National Guard, bearing the flags of every department of France; sailors from the *Belle Poule*, the ship which had sailed to St Helena to bring back the body; veterans of the Garde Impériale in Napoleonic uniforms. Marshals and generals of the Empire, led by Marshal Oudinot, Marshal Molitor, Admiral Roussin and General Bertrand, acted as pall-bearers. Nearest of all to the funeral chariot were the King's handsome, sun-tanned son the Prince de Joinville, who had commanded the *Belle Poule*; Generals Gourgaud and Bertrand, who had accompanied Napoleon to St Helena; and a diplomat, Comte Philippe de Rohan-Chabot. They were followed by a horse covered by the saddle used by Bonaparte at the Battle of Marengo in 1800; 200 former servants of the Emperor wearing his green and gold livery; more courtiers, generals and marshals of the Empire on foot.[1] 'The whole apparition was so fabulous,' Heine wrote, 'so magical that one could hardly believe one's eyes, it seemed as if one were dreaming.'[2]

At the beginning of the processional route, in the centre of the Place de l'Etoile, was a recently finished monument to the Napoleonic legend, the Arc de Triomphe. Conceived by Napoleon I in 1805, interrupted from 1814 to 1823, the Arc de Triomphe had been completed in time for the *fêtes de juillet* of 1836. It was covered in sculptures and inscriptions commemorating the battles and generals of the Republic and the Empire. Friezes showed, among other scenes, 'liberty guiding the people in 1792', the triumph of Napoleon in 1810, the resistance of 1814, the peace of 1815. The name *Arc de Triomphe* was in reality inappropriate, since the wars it celebrated had twice ended in debacle. Nevertheless it is by far the largest of the many triumphal arches erected since the Renaissance, in honour of monarchs and generals, from Lisbon to St Petersburg – far larger than the arches in honour of Louis XIV on the rues Saint-Denis and Saint-Martin.

For the *retour des cendres* the Arc de Triomphe was temporarily crowned with a massive plaster statue of Napoleon I, standing in coronation robes in front of his throne, flanked by statues of war and peace, grandeur and glory.[3] From the Arc de Triomphe, down the Champs Elysées to the Place de la Concorde, over the Seine to the Invalides, the route was lined with other colossal plaster statues, of kings and military heroes of France; pyramids draped in tricolours and surmounted by gilded Napoleonic eagles; military trophies, flags and boards inscribed with the names and dates of Napoleon's victories; pillars bearing funerary urns belching flames and smoke.[4]

The temperature was fourteen degrees below zero, the gutters in the streets were frozen and there had been snow early in the morning.[5] The cold was so bitter that boys who had climbed trees to gain a better view lost their grip and fell off.[6] A few waiting soldiers and veterans died of cold – prompting the comment that, not content with the numbers he had killed while he was alive, Napoleon even killed people when he was dead.[7] Nevertheless, even well-dressed Parisian women had left their houses at 2 in the morning in order to secure good places along the processional route.[8] Balconies along the route were said to have been hired for 3,000 francs.[9] There was no one in the streets of Paris, away from the path of the procession, except the occasional old woman. In Victor Hugo's words: 'it felt as if the whole of Paris had been poured to one side of the city, like liquid in a vase which has been tilted.'[10] In all about 600,000 people were thought to be watching along the Champs Elysées and in the wide open space in front of the Invalides.

People in the crowd from every class, party and generation were moved, so Custine noted, watching from near the Arc de Triomphe, though he himself detested Napoleon and his cult. But 'nothing', he also noted, 'serves as a clearer measure of the progress of disbelief in France than the degree to which this ceremony was not religious.'[11] As one of the Emperor's few surviving ADCs, Flahaut followed the procession on foot. Madame de Flahaut had invited several Empire widows, including Maréchales Ney and Suchet, and the Duchesse de Rovigo, to watch the procession from her *hôtel* on the Champs Elysées. Dressed in deep mourning, they were saddened by the lack of outward respect and piety, the absence of raised hats, in the crowd.[12] When the boat carrying the Emperor's body had gone up the Seine, the banks had been lined with country people kneeling out of respect. Parisians remained standing, shuffling, shouting and singing. However, a sudden silence occurred when the procession went by.[13]

After the humiliation suffered by France in the diplomatic crisis over Mohammed Ali, French nationalism and Anglophobia were particularly strong. Even Tocqueville, a liberal Anglophile with an English wife, dreamt of a French army landing on the south coast of England; troops were stationed in the courtyard of the British embassy in case of riots. As the procession went past, amid cheers of *Vive le roi!* and *Vive le prince de Joinville!* cries were heard – even, contrary to military discipline, from units of the National Guard – of *A bas Guizot! A bas les traîtres! Vive l'Empereur! A bas les Anglais!*[14]

Victor Hugo – since the *Ode à la Colonne de la Place Vendôme* of 1827, transformed from court poet of the House of Bourbon into court poet of the cult of Napoleon – was stationed on one of the stands erected in front of the Invalides.[15] In the freezing weather, he noted, women were almost invisible under their furs and coats, while men wore 'extravagant nose-shields'. The noise of feet being stamped to keep out the cold was interrupted every quarter of an hour by the sound of the cannon of the Invalides; once used to announce the Emperor's victories to Parisians, they were again being fired in his honour. At 12.30, as the first men in the cortège reached the esplanade of the Invalides, the sun came out. 'An immense murmur enveloped this apparition,' reported Victor Hugo, when the catafalque itself, glinting in the winter sun, appeared: 'it seemed as if the chariot were trailing the acclamation of an entire city, as a torch trails its smoke.'[16] Another Bonapartist poet Auguste Barthélemy wrote:

Tout Paris dans Paris ruisselle,
Paris dans Paris s'amoncelle
Pour voir passer le char du dieu.[17]

The Emperor's coffin was then carried by the sailors of the *Belle Poule* into the church of Saint-Louis in the Invalides, where a memorial service took place in the presence of the King, the royal family, the peers and the deputies.

Napoleon I's was the most grandiose of the many grandiose funeral processions through the streets of Paris since 1814: the royalist funerals of Louis XVI and Marie Antoinette in 1815, the Duc de Berri in 1820, and Louis XVIII in 1824; the liberal and revolutionary funerals of General Foy in 1825, Talma in 1826, General Lamarque in 1832, the victims of the *machine infernale* in 1835, the *victimes de juillet* in July 1840. The decision to bring back the Emperor had been one of the nationalistic measures taken by Thiers at the beginning of his ministry. Queen Marie Amélie, no doubt reflecting her husband's views, attributed the move to Thiers' desire for popularity.[18] Her own view was that, whatever people said in Napoleon's favour, no man had caused more tears to be shed.

But the King also hoped to appropriate the glory of the Napoleonic Empire to the July monarchy, as the Musée de l'Histoire de France in Versailles had that of the monarchy of Louis XIV. The Minister of the Interior Rémusat wrote that only liberty had nothing to fear from the comparison with glory.[19] In the press the funeral was hailed as a 'noble project which since 1830 has become the desire of the nation'.[20] Most Parisians considered the splendour of the ceremony and the orderliness of the crowd yet another cause for self-congratulation: 'What an admirable people are the people of France,' wrote Madame de Girardin,[21] a legitimist who had succumbed to sentimental nationalism.

In effect the funeral acknowledged the victory of the Napoleonic cult. For many Frenchmen Napoleon was no longer a dead Emperor but a god, *Lui*, the mystical personification of the past and future glory of the country, like King Sebastian for the Portuguese after his defeat and death in Morocco in 1578.[22] Bonapartism, like nationalism, was becoming a religion. The rival Bourbon cult of Henri IV began to fade. Under the Restoration, although Béranger and many other popular poets had been able to publish Bonapartist poems, the slightest reference to Napoleon on the stage had been censored. Between August and December 1830 fourteen plays glorifying Napoleon and the Empire were performed in Paris.[23] Workers became increasingly Bonapartist: above all, according to police reports, they hoped for a war of revenge for the national humiliation at Waterloo.[24] The pacifism of Louis-Philippe strengthened the cult of Napoleon. In 1831 Sémonville, *le vieux renard du Luxembourg*, prophesied that *tout cela* (the July monarchy) would not last and that *le petit aiglon*, 'Napoleon II', would return.[25] Heine too thought that Napoleon II would only have to show himself to over-throw the King.[26] Chateaubriand noted that Napoleon was more power-ful dead than alive: 'the young today adore the memory of Bonaparte, humiliated as they are by the role which the present government obliges France to play in Europe.'[27] He knew of what he wrote: in his memoirs, he himself exalts as a giant the man whom, in 1814, he had called *un faux grand homme*.[28]

History was being rewritten by nostalgia and nationalism. The horrors of the Napoleonic wars, the contempt and 'general malediction' felt for Napoleon in April 1814 and on his return from Waterloo in June 1815 – when he had been labelled Nero, Attila, and Genghis Khan – were, the Duchesse de Dino noted, obliterated from the national memory.[29] Indeed after the funeral there was a continuous pilgrimage to the Emperor's tomb. An 'interminable queue' waited for hours outside the Invalides despite the cold: it remains today one of the most visited monuments in Paris.[30]

Within the élite, however, the cult of Napoleon had many enemies. The deputies in the church of the Invalides were less respectful than the people outside. Princess Lieven considered the ceremony an act of madness or treason which could only cause trouble among the French.[31] Underestimating the force of masochism in mass politics, the legitimist newspaper *La Mode* asked: 'but what madness drives men to make heroes in this world of those who seem rather to have been sent by God to punish them?'[32]

The most celebrated anti-Bonapartist was Lamartine, now consid-ered the greatest orator in the Chamber of Deputies as well as the most popular politician in the country.[33] Even more women than usual attended debates in the Chamber when he was speaking. Madame de Girardin, not easily moved, wrote after one of his speeches: '[it] made on us an impression so profound that we can no longer think of anything else. Never has the poet shown himself more of an orator; never has his voice seemed more sonorous, his attitude more proud, his regard more noble, his tone more passionate.'[34] Increasingly revolutionary in outlook, he regarded the Faubourg Saint-Germain, and by implication his former friends the royalists, as 'ferociously stupid [and] in the *crapule* of morality as in the time of the *régence*'.[35] After his celebrated speech on 10 January 1839, proclaiming that 'France is a nation which is bored', he had refused several offers of ministries.[36] On 26 May 1840, when the government had announced its decision to bring back the Emperor's body, Lamartine's speech had created a sensation and reduced even Thiers to silence:

> I am not of this Napoleonic religion, of this cult of force, which one has noticed for some time substituting itself in the spirit of the nation for the serious religion of liberty. I do not think it right thus unceasingly to deify war . . . as if peace which is the happiness and glory of the world could be the disgrace of nations . . . let us not seduce to such an extent the opinion of a people which understands far better what dazzles it than what serves it (*Très bien!*) . . . let us not efface, lessen, diminish to such an extent our monarchy of reason, our new representative pacific monarchy. It would end by disappearing in the eyes of the people.

He went on to denounce the adoration of success, and the Bonaparte dynasty, to considerable applause on the left, and later refused to attend the funeral. His words were echoed by the extreme left deputy for Loudéac in Brittany, Alexandre-Louis Glais-Bizoin, who called the fall of the Empire the greatest benefit Providence had conferred on France and Europe.[37]

In response to the eruption of nationalism during the 1840 crisis, Lamartine had written a poem he entitled *La Marseillaise de la paix*:

> *Le monde en s'éclairant s'élève à l'unité . . .*
> *Chacun est du climat de son intelligence:*
> *Je suis concitoyen de tout homme qui pense,*
> *La vérité, c'est mon pays!*[38]

However the *retour des cendres* was the funeral not only of Napoleon I but also of the cosmopolitan Paris which had flourished since 1814. The sense of nationalistic outrage in the streets at French 'humiliation' and loss of hegemony was palpable. Thenceforth it was less easy to resist the cults of war and nationalism. Heine claimed that in France it would be easier to install a Bonaparte than a republic.

The Bonaparte dynasty – the only lasting political, as opposed to administrative, legal or military legacy of Napoleon – although excluded from the funeral ceremony, profited from it, as many Parisians had anticipated. In Baron Thénard's words, the reburial was 'more than the glorification of a great man, one might call it the restoration of his dynasty'; another politician, Dufay de l'Yonne, told Comte Rodolphe Apponyi that Louis-Philippe was tying his own noose.[39] The principal Bonaparte representative in 1840 was the eldest surviving son of Queen Hortense, Prince Louis-Napoleon.

In a small house at Arenenberg on a mountain above Lake Constance, surrounded by Napoleonic relics and portraits, Queen Hortense had kept alive the memory and prospects of the Bonaparte dynasty as a nationalistic, military alternative to the July monarchy. One of her many visitors from Paris, the Duchesse de Dino,* found her more dignified in exile than when she had been a *reine de théâtre* under the Empire.[40] Educated by Queen Hortense in Germany and Italy, having fought in the Italian nationalist rising in the Romagna in 1831, and served in the Swiss army,† Louis-Napoleon spent much of the 1830s studying military science. During a brief visit to Paris in 1831 he had asked Louis-Philippe for permission to serve in the French army; he refused when told that he could do so only if he took the title given to his mother by Louis XVIII in 1814, of Duc de Saint-Leu. In 1836 a *coup d'état* he attempted in Strasbourg – with the help of his cousin Stéphanie de Beauharnais, Grand Duchess of Baden – was a fiasco. Few officers joined his side. Instead of marching on Paris like his uncle in 1815, he was arrested and sent into exile in the United States.[41] He was able to return to Arenenberg in order to be present at his mother's sick-bed on 5 October 1837. At her funeral at Rueil, near Malmaison, on 8 January 1838 her former lover Flahaut showed as little emotion, in the eyes of critical female observers, as he had over the death of his mother, the aged Madame de Souza, a year earlier: Queen Hortense's attendant Valérie Masuyer called him *une vitrine à vanité*.[42] Thereafter Louis-Napoleon set up court in London, the natural alternative to Paris for French pretenders (the Comte de Chambord would hold court there in 1843).

On 6 August 1840, coming from London, Louis-Napoleon had made

---

* Others included Chateaubriand and Madame Récamier, Prince Belgiojoso, Maréchale Ney and Comtesse Le Hon, lover of her illegitimate son Morny.
† Hence the comment, on his arrival in Paris in 1848: *rien n'est changé, il n'y a qu'un Suisse de plus.*

a pitiful second attempt to stage a coup, in Boulogne-sur-mer where he landed with a few companions and a caged vulture (impersonating an eagle). Wishing to neutralise him before the *retour des cendres*, the French government may have provoked the coup through its agent in his entourage, the former chamberlain of Napoleon I the Comte de Montholon. Easily captured, since no troops joined his side, Louis-Napoleon was tried for high treason in the Chamber of Peers, like Ney, Louvel and the ex-ministers of Charles X before him. With a weak face – *une mine assez chétive* – speaking in a low, unclear voice, Louis-Napoleon did not impress. His trial, which lasted from 28 September to 6 October 1840, aroused less interest than that of Madame Lafarge, accused of poisoning her husband.[43]

Meanwhile Flahaut was in Paris looking for a job, having lost his post in Orléans' household two years earlier after a quarrel over precedence with General Baudrand, head of the prince's Military Household. Although efficient and polite, Flahaut had offended other courtiers by the 'little air of disdain and condescension which he adopted towards them'.[44] He commented to his wife:

> What do you say of that mad attempt of Prince Louis? Was there ever anything so absurd? I suppose he must have been reduced to the last extremity which I told you must soon be the case *au train dont il y allait* . . . he can only be considered as a madman but who would have guessed that I should sit as judge at the trial of the nephew of Napoleon?[45]

In fact, out of respect for the memory of the Emperor and Queen Hortense, Flahaut abstained from sitting with other peers in judgement on her son. In 1842 Louis-Philippe appointed him French ambassador to Austria.

Nevertheless Louis-Napoleon was more than a mere individual. He represented a dynasty and a cause: that of French nationalism and popular sovereignty – or, more precisely, the use of plebiscites by adult manhood suffrage to ratify changes proposed by the government. As he said at the trial – in words written by his celebrated lawyer the great legitimist Berryer: 'I represent before you a principle, a cause and a defeat. The principle is the sovereignty of the people; the cause that of the Empire; the defeat Waterloo. The principle you have recognised, the cause you have served, the defeat you want to avenge.'[46] Still basing his political position on the plebiscites of 1804 and 1815, he regarded the changes of regime since 1815 – as Louis XVIII had those since 1789 – as illegitimate.[47] He was imprisoned in the castle of Ham north-east of

Paris, like Polignac and the ministers of Charles X, and given a clean local girl as a mistress.

There, visited by admirers such as Princess Belgiojoso, he perfected his doctrines. He claimed to be both European and nationalist. He advocated European institutions, uniformity of measures and laws, a European code and central scientific Institute, *une association européenne solide*. Indeed he protested against his imprisonment to ambassadors of sovereigns to whom the Bonapartes were related – thereby inviting European interference in French affairs. Germany, Poland and Italy should become nation states, he asserted; however, it was also incumbent on France to recover the Rhine frontier and 'the rank due to it' in Europe, in order to prevent another humiliation like that of October 1840.[48]

The funeral of Napoleon's earliest enemy, as well as that of Napoleon himself, also symbolised the end of an era. As Russian ambassador to Britain after 1833, Pozzo had hated not only Palmerston but also the boredom and solitude of London. He lamented 'this purgatory made up of a climate that depresses me, anxieties, deprivations, regrets that devour me to the marrow of my bones'. By spending two winters in London, he wrote, he had given the Tsar ten years of his life.[49] In 1836 he bought the former Hôtel de Soyecourt, 51 rue de l'Université, from the Duc de Blacas. He had become fond of his nephew and heir Charles-Jérôme, whose marriage with Valentine de Crillon, one of the beauties of her generation, he had helped arrange. In order to enjoy their domestic happiness, he began to take several months' leave in Paris every year.[50]

The last act of his diplomatic career was intended to confirm the peace of Europe. In London in 1839 he signed the final treaty establishing European guarantees for Belgian neutrality – which would be the occasion of British intervention at the beginning of the First World War. Then he fled to Paris, a physical and mental wreck. His successor as the personification of Europe in Paris, Princess Lieven, saw the former ambassador one evening at Madame de Boigne's, appearing 'terribly thin, shrunken, stooping, his eyes enclosed in a circle of coal, words hesitant, round-shouldered, bent legs, clothes too large, his mind as stumbling as his words'. Confusing people and places, hardly able to hear or see a thing, he was a man reduced to the state of a machine.[51] He died on 15 February 1842 and is buried in Père Lachaise in a simple grave with little decoration except his bust and the inscription *Pozzo di*

Borgo. In a letter to Lady Palmerston, Princess Lieven judged Pozzo's conversation as a connoisseur judges vintages:

> Pozzo was foolish enough to die two years before his funeral service. Very few people went to it and he has passed out of everybody's thoughts. I, however, think constantly about him. He was one of the great historical figures of our century, and his presence lent great distinction to Russian politics! The variety and fertility of his intelligence will be difficult to replace. I personally can find no substitute for the charm of his conversation in his best period.[52]

The defeated Emperor was buried under the dome of the Invalides, the victorious ambassador in an alley of Père Lachaise: from beyond the grave Napoleon I had won the war for hearts and minds. However, Pozzo was the better businessman. He was said to have left eight million francs – more than Napoleon I. The Bonapartes have no house in Paris today; the Pozzo di Borgo descendants still own the *hôtel* on the rue de l'Université.[53]

The Bonapartist triumph was assisted by the death of the most popular member of the royal family, the King's eldest son, the Duc d'Orléans. Heine wrote in 1840: 'he has won all hearts and his death would be more than pernicious for the present dynasty. The popularity of the prince is perhaps the sole guarantee of its survival.'[54] Orléans was moreover the July monarchy's personal link to the French army, in which he had served in Belgium and Algeria. The French army meant more to him than the pleasures of Paris: 'it is only by being everywhere and always with the army', he wrote in 1837, 'that I will honour my name, which I respect and which I do not want to drag through the salons and the boulevards.'[55]

Orléans was also the adored favourite child of Queen Marie Amélie; even in her own opinion, she loved him too much.[56] On 13 July 1842, at his mother's special request, he drove in a small *calèche* from the Tuileries to Neuilly, to lunch with his parents. The horses bolted. As he jumped or fell from the carriage, the prince hit his forehead on the paving-stones with fatal effect. He was taken to a small two-storey house in the rue de la Révolte, within sight of the Arc de Triomphe. It had a shop on the ground floor, with the words *Commerce d'Epicerie* painted on the outside.[57] There, six hours later, lying on a filthy mattress, beside a wall decorated with prints of the wandering Jew, Napoleon, the *Attentat de Fieschi*, and the prince's own father, surrounded by relations, marshals and ministers, his mother kneeling and holding his hand as his pulse faded, he died from a fractured skull.[58] His body was then taken on a stretcher to the chapel at Neuilly. It was followed by his parents, supporting each other, while his aunt and sisters, incapable of walking, left in a carriage. Onlookers cried *Vive le roi!*

In the château of Neuilly the only sounds were weeping and the chanting of priests.[59] The King was devastated, but could still give orders; the Queen was supported by her faith and her husband. The King and Queen reluctantly agreed to Guizot's desire for a grand royal funeral – although, always eager to dissociate the Orléans from the elder branch, they insisted their son be buried in the Orléans mauso-leum at Dreux rather than in the royal mausoleum of Saint-Denis. A credit of 400,000 francs – compared to 500,000 for the funeral of Napoleon I – was opened.

That year there were no *fêtes de juillet*. On 29 July the prince's body was taken from Neuilly down the Champs Elysées and along the *quais* to lie in state in Notre Dame, in another grandiose funeral procession through the streets of Paris. The procession included all the regiments in which the prince had served (which were about to participate in the strategic manoeuvres the prince had planned for that summer); the firemen and national guards of Paris; courtiers, ministers, and for the first time since 1830, several hundred priests.[60] The procession set off an hour late as, in their agony, the King and Queen would not permit the funeral casket containing their son's remains to leave Neuilly: in the end the Archbishop of Paris and other priests took it out of their hands by force.[61]

The 'incalculable immensity' of the crowds lining the funeral route, the side streets and the roofs indicated the depth of the nation's grief, among the people as well as the bourgeoisie. Although there was some irreverence, as there had been during the funeral procession of Napoleon, most onlookers were sad and respectful. Many wept. There was silence but for the sound of the cannon of the Invalides firing and the pealing of church bells. The prince had been popular. Everyone replied to the questions of the Russian diplomat Victor Balabine in the same words: *ah monsieur, c'est un affreux malheur pour la France.*[62] Comte Duchâtel, the Minister of the Interior, wrote to Louis-Philippe: 'if something can lessen the sorrow of the King it is the feeling shown today by the population of Paris . . . sorrow was visible on all faces . . . the appearance of Paris should be a consolation for the King.' For the next three days people queued for up to six hours to file past the prince's body in Notre Dame.[63] The funeral service on 3 August was attended by all deputies and peers, even legitimists. During the service holy water was sprinkled on the corpse first by the Archbishop and his clergy; then by Soult representing the Council of Ministers; by Pasquier and Laffitte representing the Chambers of Peers and Deputies respectively; finally by Comte Apponyi, the Austrian ambassador, for the Corps Diplomatique.

The feelings of horror and grief evident on the streets of Paris were represented by government newspapers as a sign of the bond of love uniting the capital and the dynasty.[64] Victor Hugo, speaking in the name of the Institut, told Louis-Philippe that France and the dynasty had the same heart and the same blood.[65] Heine, however, with his usual prescience, thought that the emotion was addressed to the person of the prince rather than the institution of the monarchy; 'but how long', he asked, 'will this sombre honeymoon last?'[66] Others wondered if God had damned France.[67] Balzac called the prince's funeral procession the funeral convoy of a monarchy; Lamartine thought that, with this handsome young man, the little that remained of monarchy in France had also died. In the words of the prince's younger brother the Duc d'Aumale, then proving himself a brilliant general in Algeria, the dynasty had been decapitated.[68]

The shadow cast by the death of the Duc d'Orléans on the future of the July monarchy was evidence of the determining role that dynasties played in the political future of France. France was no less affected by the biology and personalities of the Bourbon, Bonaparte and Orléans dynasties than by the mass movements of nationalism, revolution, liberalism, imperialism and, in the future, socialism. The dynasties' prospects depended on a constantly changing interaction of events and personalities. The death of one prince – Berri in 1820, Orléans in 1842 – the personality of one monarch – Charles X or Louis-Philippe – could change the destiny of France and Europe.

The new religion of nationalism, cultivated so fervently by the Duc d'Orléans and by Louis-Napoleon Bonaparte, received its intellectual consecration in the lectures at the Collège de France of one of the most famous of French historians, Jules Michelet, and the most famous Polish poet and philosopher, Adam Mickiewicz. Already in 1840 the republican intellectual Alphonse Esquiros in *L'Evangile du peuple* had talked of France as the new Messiah, which had suffered its passion at Waterloo.[69] Michelet now called for schoolchildren to be taught to worship France as a religion. France was like Jesus Christ. The salvation and pilot of humanity, it had given its life for the world, and had been redeemed by Joan of Arc and the miracles of the revolution.[70]

The shared religion of messianic nationalism reinforced the importance of Polish Parisians. In *Le Livre des pèlerins polonais* (1832), translated from Polish by the Comte de Montalembert, Mickiewicz had written that Poland, after a period of prayer and pilgrimage, having expiated the sins of other nations, as Christ on the cross expiated the sins of humanity, would rise from the dead like Christ, to 'liberate all the peoples of Europe from slavery'.[71] Since the crushing of the Polish insurrection in 1831 Mickiewicz had lived in Paris, Rome, Dresden and Lausanne. In 1840, during the Thiers ministry, partly owing to the influence of Prince Czartoryski, he had been appointed to a chair of Slav languages and literatures especially created for him at the Collège de France. Most lectures at the college attracted few listeners but Mickiewicz's became immensely popular, revealing to Parisians unknown treasures of Polish, Russian and Czech literature. But, despite official warnings to avoid politics and concentrate on literature, Mickiewicz soon began to preach nationalism and Panslavism. Looking like a visionary prophet with luxuriant grey hair and sad eyes, speaking French with a vibrant Polish accent, he announced his lectures as a call of the Polish nation to the spirit of the French nation. Ignoring Pushkin, the greatest Russian poet of the day, he described Russian as the language of command, while Polish was the language of conversation. All Russian poems were poems to the sovereign and the power of the country.[72] George Sand, one of his many admirers, claimed: 'Since the tears and imprecations of the prophets of Sion, no voice had risen with such force to lament a subject as vast as the fall of a nation.'[73]

A fervent if unorthodox Catholic, Mickiewicz was also a follower of a fraudulent faith-healer, André Towianski, whose spiritual practices among Polish émigrés in Paris, he believed, could of themselves generate sufficient force to liberate Poland. Towianski staged seances in Mickiewicz's apartment at which both the Virgin Mary and Napoleon I spoke. After Towianski had been expelled by the French government, Mickiewicz, on his knees, read out messages from 'the Master' to his followers in Paris.[74] In March 1844, describing himself as a spark fallen from the torch, Mickiewicz electrified his audience in the Sorbonne by asking those in it, both Poles and French, who knew of a new revelation of the Word incarnate (Towianski) to say so. Many replied in the affirmative 'with an indescribable exaltation: among the women, above all, one remarked stifled shouts, sighs, tears, all the symptoms of mystical enthusiasm bordering on ecstasy.' One lady kissed Mickiewicz's feet.

After a lecture on 28 May that year, he distributed among his listeners a lithograph which united Bonapartism, Catholicism and his desire to redraw the map of Europe. It showed Napoleon, wearing boots, uniform and a white veil like a girl at her first communion, looking towards heaven, with his hand on the map of Europe. The drawing was based on a vision of a new Europe experienced by Towianski on the field of Waterloo. The authorities finally lost patience. Mickiewicz was put on half pay and suspended from lecturing.[75]

The message of the new nationalism, however, was increasingly popular. On 28 May 1846 moreover, a prince determined to redraw the map of Europe, Louis-Napoleon Bonaparte, escaped from the prison of Ham disguised as a labourer. Settled in London, he awaited the fall of Louis-Philippe.

13

The People

1844–1852

IN *La Confession d'un enfant du siècle* (1836), Alfred de Musset described the *haine de tigre* glinting in the wine-reddened eyes of the people of Paris, as they threw flour, mud and insults at the carriages of the rich during the carnival: 'I began to understand the century and to realise in what times we lived.'[1] Even when there was no revolution or insurrection in progress, flour and mud were often replaced by sharper instruments. In 1844 Madame de Girardin described the atmosphere of terror and the frequency of nocturnal ambushes and robberies in Paris. Pistols, daggers and swordsticks were kept on the same table as sewing-kits, for guests to take with them as they departed into the night.[2]

Such warfare between poor and rich had long been feared in Paris – as the allied armies had approached in March 1814 men had threatened to pillage the houses of the bourgeoisie. After 1830, even more after 1840, not only was the warfare discussed more openly, and brutally, but there were frequent outbursts on the streets. Paris became the arena for struggles between classes as well as causes.

Like other great capitals, Paris presented what the *Journal des débats* called 'the shocking contrast of abject misery in the middle of riches and abundance, of idleness and vagabondage in the middle of the most active industry and the most perfect civilisation'.[3] Behind the city of palaces and museums, chambers and salons, was a second, far more densely populated, city. In what the radical novelist and journalist Jules

Janin called *recoins affreux*, rented rooms and cellars, lived a 'seething, sweating population unlike anything else'.[4] Their living conditions were degrading. Since the population of the city had increased more rapidly than the available accommodation, poor Parisians often had only five to ten square metres a head living space. In streets such as the rue La Mortellerie in the heart of the city, where in 1832 the cholera count had been especially high, some inhabitants had only three square metres a head.[5]

Distinguished by their 'pale and livid complexion', filthy, ragged clothes and high mortality rates, the poor in Paris seemed older than their years. They looked like a different race from the nobles and bourgeois, who indeed often referred to them as 'savages', 'nomads', 'barbarians'.[6] In an article in the *Journal des débats* on 8 December 1831, one of the most respected journalists of the day Saint-Marc Girardin wrote: 'the barbarians who menace our society are neither in the Caucasus nor on the steppes of Tartary; they are in the *faubourgs* of our manufacturing cities.'[7]

Barbarism, however, was conspicuous on both sides of the class barrier. Until 1831 (when public executions were removed to the Barrière Saint-Jacques), in order to overawe the people the government had criminals, including the Duc de Berri's assassin Louvel, pilloried, branded or executed in public on the Place de Grève or the Place du Palais de Justice. Such occasions were watched by thousands of Parisians, from the square or from rented places in the surrounding windows. At the critical moment they showed 'ferocious joy', uttering screams, cheers and 'indecent cries'.[8] Another popular spectacle was the annual departure from Paris, for prisons in the provinces, of the chain gang of criminals, each wearing a *cravate* or iron triangle round their neck, linking them to the chain.[9]

Politics was increasingly seen in class terms, even by the royal family,[10] and classes were increasingly defined by money. As early as 1798 a royalist had denounced 'the bourgeoisie, this truly ruling class'.[11] Historians like Thierry, Sismondi, Guizot, and the school of radical economic thinkers founded by the Comte de Saint-Simon, thought of historical events as determined by continuous conflict between economic classes. In the opinion of Saint-Simonians, society, scientifically reorganised, should be governed by its natural leaders – financiers, industrialists, scientists and engineers – rather than by nobles, priests and rentiers.[12] In one of his most celebrated speeches in the Chamber, on 3 May 1837, Guizot declared: 'I desire, I strive for, I serve with all my might, the political preponderance of the middle classes in France.' In reality this preponderance was restricted to a small section of the propertied class, while one of Guizot's political bases was the aristocratic salon of Princess Lieven. In 1846 aristocratic Britain had a million voters; with a much larger population, revolutionary France had approximately 240,000.[13] Money was the openly proclaimed basis of society – as it was of many politicians' loyalties. To those who wanted the franchise widened, Guizot advised: *enrichissez-vous!* Chateaubriand wrote a paean to money, source of liberty: 'with you one is young, handsome, adored.'[14] 'Money', Heine believed, 'is the god of our period and Mohammed is his prophet.'[15] Madame d'Agoult defined the contemporary view of marriage as 'two fortunes which join each other to make a larger fortune'.[16] She herself, however, left her husband in order to live with Liszt. Indeed, the cult of the Romantic artist struggling against materialistic society – epitomised in, for example, de Vigny's play *Chatterton* (1835) – was a sign of contemporary disgust with money worship.[17]

The class struggle in France was embittered by the industrialisation which, after the long hiatus caused by the military and trade wars of the Republic and the Empire, finally occurred under the July monarchy. Between 1840 and 1848 the number of steam engines in operation doubled, from 2,592 to 5,212.[18] The supreme symbol of the early industrial revolution, the railway, reflected French backwardness in comparison with its British neighbour. By 1836, although Britain had 2,000 miles of railways, France, in a much larger area, had only 150 miles.[19] The sight of a model railway on the Champs Elysées had aroused feelings of bewildered apprehension in Michelet: 'who can judge, for each of these brilliant *bagatelles*, how many drops of sweat and sighs have been expended?'[20] Thiers, an embodiment of 'liberal' bourgeois values, and the great chemist François Arago, were equally suspicious.[21]

Slowly France moved into the nineteenth century. On 25 August 1837 Marie Amélie opened the country's first railway, from Paris west to the old court suburb of Saint Germain-en-Laye, in the presence of two of the railway's principal financiers, Rothschild and Péreire. Eighteen and a half kilometres were covered in twenty-eight minutes. Soon it was taking 20,000 passengers a day.[22] In 1842 a national network was approved in the Chamber of Deputies, prompting railway fever on the Bourse as frenzied as the property fever of the early 1820s.[23] On some lines British capital took over: by 1847 half the capital invested in French railways was British.[24] The English Parisian Edward Blount, a partner with Laffitte's nephew Charles in the banking house Charles Laffitte, Blount et cie, laid the foundation stone of the first railway bridge over the Seine at Maisons. In the construction of the Paris–Rouen line, which opened in 1843, 'English and French workmen were found to work fairly well together': many of the early locomotives and drivers were British – hence the fact that French trains, unlike French road vehicles, drive on the left.[25] Given the opportunity, however, French workmen would try to expel their better-paid English colleagues.[26]

On 14 June 1846, to celebrate the inauguration of the Chemins de Fer du Nord, James de Rothschild took 1,700 male guests – women were excluded – from Paris to lunch in Lille and dine in Brussels: Berlioz composed a *Chant des Chemins de Fer* to mark the occasion.[27] The great railway stations of central Paris provided a more modern set of gates into the city than the old Portes de Saint-Denis or de Saint-Martin. The Gare Saint-Lazare was built in 1840–3; the Gare de l'Est in 1844–9; the Gare du Nord (with statues of Frankfurt and Amsterdam on either side of the main entrance, to mark its function linking Paris to Europe) in 1845–6; the Gare de Lyon in 1847–52.[28]

Another sign that Paris was entering the industrial age was its rapid development as a centre of manufacture. *Articles de Paris*, luxury goods such as carriages, dresses, gloves and jewellery, were exported throughout Europe. The value of exports going through the *octroi*, the customs barriers of Paris, trebled between 1828 and 1845, rising from 11 per cent to 23 per cent of French exports.[29] By 1847 there were 330,000 industrial workers in Paris, although 89 per cent of firms employed less than ten workers.[30] By 1847, helped by a network of recently constructed canals (the canals Saint-Denis, de l'Ourcq and Saint-Martin were opened between 1821 and 1825), Paris was the largest port in France, handling over 21,000 boats a year.[31] Its proportion of the French urban population rose from 15 per cent in 1811 to 19.5 per cent in 1851. At the same time, between 1811 and 1850 the population of Paris grew by 86 per cent, from 550,000 to 1,053,000.*

Despite a doubling of the wealth of Paris between 1820 and 1847, there was a growing contrast between rich and poor and a deterioration in living standards for all but a minority of workers.[32] For most Parisians the figure of Abundance carved on the pediment of the Chamber of

---

* The population was 622,000 in 1817; 714,000 in 1831; 866,000 in 1836; 936,000 in 1841; 1,055,000 in 1846.

Deputies had no meaning. In the 1820s three out of every four inhabitants of Paris were buried in a pauper's grave – the *fossé commune* – as they could not afford to pay for their own funerals.[33] About one in twelve of the population – 84,461 in 1818, 65,292 in 1825, 68,896 in 1832, 73,901 in 1847 – were officially classified by the municipal authorities as indigent.[34] The real figure, however, was higher: at least two-thirds of households throughout this period lived in a state of indigence or near-indigence.[35] Paris contained twenty-four workhouses for the poor, while 69,000 people received relief at home administered by the *bureau de charité* of their arrondissement.[36] In addition there was a system of *bons de pain* and *soupes économiques* by which, from lists drawn up by the *bureau de charité* in each arrondissement, the department of the Seine and the *mairies* of Paris supplied the poor with tickets which entitled them to receive soup or one free *livre* of bread a day. Many refused to fill in the necessary forms, as they judged them humiliating.[37] According to the Prefect of the Seine before 1830, the Comte de Chabrol, a total of ten million *bons de pain* were being delivered by sixty-six offices throughout the city. In July 1828 and July 1830, 227,399 individuals or almost a third of the population were being helped. If the rich came to Paris for pleasure or instruction, many poor foreigners came for cheap bread.[38]

Despite this safety net, many Parisians did not have enough to eat – as their fellow citizens could see for themselves on the streets. On the Place de Grève in the heart of the city, the men who gathered to look for work every morning were often trembling with hunger and, in winter, cold.[39] The Paris police did not doubt the truth of the pleas of 'the torments of hunger' made as an excuse for begging – in the street, at the doors of churches and museums, inside private houses, even to Louis-Philippe himself. In certain years Parisians died of hunger. A poem published in 1844, *Le Cadavre* by Charles Lassailly, ended with the following verses, printed in capitals:

> AU BOULEVARD DE GAND, LE CORPS D'UN PROLÉTAIRE,
> MORT DE FAIM ET DE FROID, EST ÉTENDU PAR TERRE.[40]

After 1830, in response to economic changes as well as to the July revolution, new ideas about the distribution of power and property led to attacks on both the reality and the theory of bourgeois society and the state. Balzac, no radical, described workers as reduced by industrialisation to the state of social zeros.[41] Hitherto a rarity, in theory illegal, after 1830 strikes – by butchers, cab drivers or carpenters – became frequent. Wages were indeed lower after the July revolution than they had been under Louis XVIII. The strikers demanded four francs for a day's work. Sometimes strikes were specifically directed against foreign workers or machines. During peaks in 1830 and 1833, thousands of troops were brought to Paris to contain them.[42] On 4–9 September 1840, in protest against working hours and the role of labour contractors in forcing down wages, there was a general strike by almost the entire working population of Paris. Paris was filled with troops, who easily destroyed the one barricade erected.[43]

In a letter of 1815 to Madame de Staël, with characteristic condescension, the Duchesse de Duras had expressed pity for 'the poor people who are always considered of secondary importance'.[44] After 1830, from being secondary players, the people took centre stage. Students and workers formed societies whose purpose was to enjoy carnival and swear hatred of the bourgeoisie.[45] In 1833, in a pamphlet *Boutade d'un riche aux sentiments populaires*, an aged revolutionary the Comte d'Argenson, demanded of the poor why they did not rise against their oppressors.[46] Speaking in the Chamber of Deputies on 3 March 1835, Lamartine predicted that 'the question of the proletarians' would cause 'the most terrible explosion'.[47] Studies of pauperism emphasised the misery in which 'the poor and vicious classes' lived and the dangers in the great cities from bands of criminals, who had their own private language, *l'argot des voleurs*.[48] The leaders of the extreme left, Armand Barbès and Auguste Blanqui, who advocated the abolition of private property, led an attempted revolution on 12 May 1839. They briefly took the Hôtel de Ville, and issued proclamations denouncing 'the tyrant of the Tuileries'; but the people did not rise.[49]

The year 1839 also saw the publication of *L'Organisation du travail* by Louis Blanc, a prominent socialist and, through his mother, a relation of Pozzo di Borgo. Advocating workers' cooperatives and social workshops – he invented the phrase 'from each according to their capacities, to each according to their needs' – it sold 6,000 copies in a few weeks. Books on workers' rights, newspapers bearing the title *La Fraternité* or *Le Populaire*, founded by Etienne Cabet, reflected the spirit of the age. Cabet invented the word 'communist', Pierre Leroux, a former printworker and friend of George Sand, 'socialism'. Believing in institutionalised sexual liberation, and wanting to create *phalanges* in which 2,000 people would lead a communal existence, the philosopher Charles Fourier attacked marriage as well as property; the early feminist Flora Tristan favoured equal wages and legal status for women.[50] Custine

The People

noted how rapidly property had passed from being sacred to being regarded as an abuse: he feared the reign of brigands.[51] To the question in the title of his pamphlet *Qu'est-ce que la propriété?* (1840), the great anarchist and socialist Proudhon provided a celebrated answer: 'property is theft.'[52]

George Sand thought a communist revolution inevitable and began to publish socialist novels such as *Le Compagnon de la tour de France*. Eugène Sue became a socialist in 1841. The people were the heroes, the rich the villains, of his novel *Les Mystères de Paris*. Published in instalments in the *Journal des débats* from June 1842 to October 1843, set partly in the impoverished streets and taverns of the Ile de la Cité, it bewitched Parisians – and readers throughout Europe – as much as the most popular television serial today. Such was its authenticity that some poor Parisians looked to its hero, the kind German prince Rodolphe, to help them in real life, as he helped characters in the novel.[53] There were no kind princes in the Tuileries, however: neither Louis-Philippe nor Guizot paid attention to economic or social problems.[54]

In this class-conscious capital, at an economic and ideological turning-point, Karl Marx arrived at the end of October 1843. Like Heine, and unlike Wagner, he found freedom and stimulation in Paris.[55] His stay provides one of the most convincing instances of the city functioning as a factory and crossroads of ideas – and capital of Europe. He had come in order to work with another German revolutionary, Arnold Ruge, on the recently established *Deutsch-Französische Jahrbücher*. Ruge, who lived in Paris from 1843 to 1845, claimed that in Europe France alone represented the pure and unalterable principle of human liberty: 'the nation fulfils a mission of cosmopolitanism.' Paris was 'the cradle of the new Europe, the great laboratory where world history is formed and has its ever fresh source. It is in Paris that we should live our victories and our defeats.'[56]

Paris was at this time a centre of German, as well as British, Italian and Polish life. The number of Germans increased from about 7,000 in 1831 to 23,000 in 1839 and, despite the war crisis of 1840, 59,000 in 1846: one in twenty Parisians was German.[57] Novels describing their presence in Paris include *Le Cousin Pons* by Balzac and *Le Fils du Diable* by Paul Feval. German Parisians replaced Bonapartists as the principal patrons of the Café Lemblin. *Vorwärts*, the most radical German paper in Europe, was their newspaper, the *League of the Just* their secret society.[58] Some Germans were artists: Ignace Hittorff, who came from

Cologne in 1810, Architecte du Roi pour les Fêtes et Cérémonies, designed, among many other buildings, the church of Saint-Vincent de Paul and the Gare du Nord. Henri Lehmann came from Berlin in 1831, Winterhalter from Munich in 1834, both to paint portraits. Börne, Heine, Herwegh were among the many Germans who came to Paris to write, often about Paris itself.[59] A large proportion of German Parisians were print-workers.[60] Others were tailors or bootmakers. The bourgeoisie of Paris were dismayed by their habit of returning from the taverns beyond the barriers late on Sunday evenings, loudly singing German drinking-songs.[61]

At first Marx lived in the rue Vaneau, in the same street as the offices of the *Deutsch-Französische Jahrbücher*. He studied the history of the French revolution and read Proudhon. After the collapse of Ruge's journal, he wrote in *Vorwärts*, on the Jewish question and Hegel. Hitherto exposed mainly to university towns (Bonn and Jena) and the university district in Berlin, in Paris he saw for himself the misery and degradation of a large urban proletariat and learnt of the possibility of 'the brotherhood of man'.[62] As a modern biographer writes: 'Marx's sudden espousal of the proletarian cause can be directly attributed (as can that of other early German communists such as Weitling* and Hess) to his first hand contacts with socialist intellectuals [and books] in France.' He met, among others, early Russian revolutionaries like Bakunin and Annenkove, debated all night with Proudhon, saw Heine almost every day. Despite his government pension, Heine already saw the future of France in terms of a class struggle between communism and the bourgeoisie, and hoped for 'the reign of the proletariat'.[63] For Marx the July monarchy was nothing but a joint stock company for the exploitation of French national wealth.[64]

At the Café de la Régence on the Place du Palais Royal† on 28 August 1844 Marx started the most important friendship of his life. Engels, then working on his masterpiece *The Condition of the Working Classes in England*, had come to Paris to discuss with Marx the publication of articles criticising liberal economists. Engels wrote: 'our complete agreement in all theoretical fields became obvious and our joint work dates from that time.'[65] In his articles Marx analysed the credit system and

---

* Author of the first book on communism in German, *Humanity as it is and as it should be*, published in Paris in 1838.
† Founded in 1718, this café had been frequented by, among others, Diderot and the young Bonaparte.

classical economics, attacking 'the vicious struggle of the capitalist and the worker', inevitably terminated by the triumph of the former. He believed that private property rendered us 'stupid and limited'. The abolition of this horror would lead to the total emancipation of the senses and of all human qualities, and prevent men from being reduced to machines. In a famous phrase he dismissed religion as 'the opium of the people'.[66] Perhaps because of Proudhon's dislike of coercion and organisation, he attacked Proudhon with vindictive spite, accusing him of wishing only to remedy the wrongs of the system rather than to destroy it.[67]

In January 1845, after *Vorwärts* had expressed pleasure at an assassination attempt on the King of Prussia, Guizot ordered Marx's expulsion, partly at the suggestion of Alexander von Humboldt. Louis-Philippe is said to have exclaimed: 'We must purge Paris of German philosophers!' Heine, the only person whom Marx was sorry to leave behind, was not expelled, since he could claim his rights as a French citizen, born in Düsseldorf in 1805, in what was then the French Empire.[68]

Insular and puritanical, London could induce a sharper sense of exile and alienation in resident foreigners than Paris. However, English laws gave greater protection from police interference. Like Mazzini, Kossuth, Herzen – and subsequently many Frenchmen – Marx eventually found London, whatever its disadvantages, a safer haven than Paris from which to work for, and write about, revolution. Thus even in the role of lighthouse of liberty, as well as in that of industrial metropolis, nineteenth-century London could eclipse Paris.

The birth of modern anti-Semitism was another sign of the rise of socialism in Paris. A book published in 1847 attacked Jews, Calvinists, above all the Rothschilds, and 'any unproductive parasite living off the substance of others' work'.[69] As socialism became more fashionable, so did nationalism. It was aggravated by the French humiliation of 1840 and the accompanying sense that France was too indulgent to foreigners. As Tocqueville had said in a celebrated speech in the Chamber, if France no longer made the affairs of the world its own, the monarchy would soon be buried under the ruins of national honour.[70] Whenever anti-British sentiments were expressed in the theatre or the Académie Française, people rose from their seats waving handkerchiefs, or singing – from Halévy's *Charles VI* – *Guerre aux tyrans, jamais en France l'Anglais ne règnera!*[71] Even the Guizot ministry – hitherto so pro-British that Guizot ('Lord Guizot') had arranged three meetings between Queen

Victoria and Louis-Philippe in 1843 (at Eu), 1844 (at Windsor) and 1845 (Eu again) – now changed tack after a crisis over the 'Spanish marriages' in 1846.

The Queen Mother Maria Cristina, who had returned to Spain from Paris in 1845, had been intriguing both with Bulwer, British minister in Madrid since 1843, and the French ambassador Comte Charles-Joseph Bresson, over whether to marry her daughter Queen Isabella II to either a Coburg or a Bourbon prince. Despite or because of his years in Paris, Bulwer was as anti-French as his patron Palmerston and urged Maria Cristina to betroth Isabella II to a Coburg. This gave the Guizot ministry the excuse to support Isabella II's marriage to a Spanish Bourbon cousin, the Duke of Cadiz. Though suspected of impotence, he married her on 10 October 1846, the same day that the Duc de Montpensier, the youngest and favourite son of Louis-Philippe, married her sister and heir, the Infanta Luisa Ferdinanda.[72] A Bourbon operating on the assumptions behind the Bourbon 'family compact' of 1761, when the Kings of France and Spain had transformed the dynastic links between their two branches of the House of Bourbon into a political alliance, Louis-Philippe cherished the hope that the Montpensiers might succeed to the Spanish throne.[73]

The British government was enraged. The Foreign Office released for publication some of Louis-Philippe's legitimist and anti-Napoleonic letters written during his emigration before 1814.[74] The new British ambassador in Paris was Lord Normanby, a tall, blond writer, former Lord Lieutenant of Ireland and admirer of, among many others, Princess Belgiojoso. He was praised in Paris for his 'English air . . . elegant, gracious, *grand seigneur, bon garçon et dandy*'. In January 1847 he was forbidden by Palmerston to attend the first *cercle diplomatique* held at the Tuileries in honour of the new Duchesse de Montpensier. Social warfare broke out. A few weeks later Normanby not only withdrew the invitation he had sent Guizot to a ball at the British embassy, but advertised the fact in *Galignani's Paris Messenger*.[75] In retaliation most French ministers, officials, peers, deputies and foreign diplomats refused to attend the ball, and preferred to go to a concert at Guizot's, held on the same night: only the left, the legitimists and the British Parisians were seen at the embassy.[76] For a few days, until Guizot and Normanby shook hands again at a reception at the Austrian embassy, salons talked of little else. The language used by the British embassy staff about Guizot was described as 'of extreme indecency'. The Normanbys ostentatiously made friends with the Thiers and other politicians opposed to Guizot: Thiers signed his letters to *mon cher ambassadeur, tout à vous de coeur.*[77] British investments in France diminished.[78]

Class hatred increased with the slump and a rapid decline in living standards, consequent on catastrophic potato and wheat harvests in 1845 and 1846.[79] In 1847 the Tribunal de Commerce of the Département de la Seine heard 1,326 bankruptcy cases. According to the Prefect of the Seine the Comte de Rambuteau, in conversation with Victor Hugo, in the winter of 1846–7 450,000 people, far more than usual, had been supplied with *bons de pain.*[80] In the course of a campaign of 'reform banquets', speakers claimed that the July revolution had been betrayed and demanded universal male suffrage and other reforms.[81] Speaking in the Chamber in March 1847, however, Guizot had called universal male suffrage an absurdity whose day would never dawn.[82] By July 1847, according to an article in *La Presse* by Madame de Girardin, all Paris was talking of imminent revolution:

> – The sky is darkening!
> – Danger is imminent!
> – A crisis cannot be avoided!
> – A *fête* on a volcano!
> – We are on the eve of great events!
> – All this can end only in a revolution!
> – We are in 1830 – 92 – 89.[83]

On 5 July a party given by the Duc de Montpensier in the forest of Vincennes served the same function as his father's ball for the Kings of France and the Two Sicilies in the Palais Royal in May 1830. Bringing together different classes in the same arena, it provided a foretaste of revolution. Parisians watching carriages arrive at the palace on 31 May 1830 had been so well dressed that they seemed like guests at the party. As guests drove in stifling heat along the *quais* and the rue Saint-Antoine to Vincennes, a triple row of spectators, standing behind the police, booed, spat, threw mud and dust and yelled *Bon appétit! Le pain ne vous manque pas!* Victor Hugo, whose attendance at court had been rewarded with the rank of Peer of France, wrote: 'at every moment this crowd hurled at these embroidered and glittering passers-by in their carriages sombre and malignant words. It was like a cloud of hate around the splendour of the occasion.'

When they arrived at Vincennes, the guests were at first pensive and subdued. They soon recovered their spirits. If the Duc d'Orléans in 1830 had given a Neapolitan *fête*, the Duc de Montpensier's *fête* in 1847 was oriental: the captured state tents of the Sultan of Morocco and of the leader of the Algerian resistance Abd el-Kader, which had been displayed in the Tuileries gardens as trophies of conquest, had been re-erected in the forest of Vincennes. Splendid as they were, they were outshone by a tent given by the Ottoman sultan Selim III to Napoleon I in 1806, which from the inside gave visitors the impression of being in a chest of gold brocade. Coloured lights draped from branch to branch of the trees resembled necklaces of emeralds and rubies. Military trophies, knights in armour and ancient cannons were placed between the trees in the forest. Guests included Queen Maria Cristina of Spain (who had settled in Paris again, after marrying her daughters in Madrid), Guizot, James de Rothschild, Alexandre Dumas, Lord Normanby and the Algerian chief Bou Maza – *beau comme un tigre*, in Théophile Gautier's words.[84]

Six weeks later the murder of a Duchess heightened hatred of the monarchy. The Duc de Praslin was having an affair with his children's attractive, if domineering, governess Mlle Deluzy; the Duchess, by whom he had had eleven children, became frustrated and aggressive. Maddened by his wife's physical demands, on 18 August 1847 the Duc de Praslin murdered her by cutting her to pieces with a knife. The marks of the Duchess's bloodstained hands could be seen on the silk hangings and gold-embroidered curtains of her bedroom as, like a wild animal caught in a trap, she had darted round the room looking for a way out. An official of the Paris Sûreté commented: 'it is badly done; professional murderers work better; it is *un homme du monde* who has done it.'

The Duc de Praslin was not only rich and noble but also a Chevalier d'Honneur of the Duchesse d'Orléans. *Quel chevalier! Quel honneur!*, Mérimée commented. The public invented a new verb, *prasliner* – as in *prasliner sa femme* – and was disgusted to be cheated of the Duke's trial and execution when he poisoned himself in prison. Further blows to the reputation of the regime were the condemnation to three years' hard labour for corruption of a peer of France and former minister of public works, M. Teste, and a former minister of war General Cubières; the suicides of two overworked French ambassadors, Comtes Mortier and Bresson; and the arrest of the unstable Prince d'Eckmühl for stabbing his mistress.[85] With characteristic inhumanity, Thiers remarked that the corruption of Teste and General Cubières was more degrading and unfortunate than the loss of life at one of the most sanguinary of Napoleon's battles, Eylau. All knew that the government, including Guizot's chef de cabinet M. Génie, a synonym for venality, bought newspapers and deputies with money, jobs and favours. The Chamber of Deputies of 1846 contained 185 government officials. Guizot was compared to an honest woman running a brothel.[86]

Not even in 1789, despite the affair of the Diamond Necklace and the pornographic pamphlets vilifying the King and Queen, had the French monarchy been surrounded by such an aura of doom and discredit. The great radical journal *La Réforme* noted the contrast between the scandals of the regime, whose sudden accumulation could not be pure chance, and the horror of workers' lives: after a fifteen-hour day, many could still not pay for their own food and had to queue for *bons de pain*.[87] Comte Molé, an opponent of Guizot, sensed that the July monarchy was afflicted with *cet esprit de vertige et d'erreur, de la chute des rois funeste avant-coureur*. In July 1847, in conversation with his friend Lord Normanby who shared his hatred of Guizot, he agreed that in France there was 'neither attachment to any individual nor respect for any institution'.[88]

The rehabilitation of the revolutions of 1792–4 was another nail in the coffin of monarchy. In 1840 the sight of a black banner on the boulevards, inscribed with the date 1793, had been enough to make 100,000 strollers flee 'as one woman', according to Madame de Girardin.[89] However, one of the most popular books of the century, Lamartine's *Histoire des Girondins*, published in March–June 1847 in eight volumes, glorified the 1789–94 revolution as a necessity: in a speech made in July that year Lamartine also predicted that the July monarchy would face a revolution of contempt. Chateaubriand said of the *Histoire* that he would never have believed that M. de Lamartine would have wanted to gild the guillotine.[90] The French revolution had replaced seventeenth-century Britain as the model for French politics. That autumn a play by Alexandre Dumas, *Le Chevalier de Maison-Rouge*, featured a 'song of the Girondins' which, like *La Muette de Portici* nineteen years earlier, expressed the cult of martyr-hungry nationalism: *Mourir pour la patrie, c'est le sort le plus beau, le plus digne d'envie!* Such was the political influence of the Paris theatres that it became the song of the February revolution.[91] In the same year both Michelet and Louis Blanc published adulatory histories of the revolution: Michelet, who also gave lectures on the revolution in the Collège de France, claimed that 1789 was not the revolution but the foundation of modern France, the moment when the people entered into possession of its house, which the monarchy had left empty.[92]

Forgetting 'the parliament of the streets', the government restricted its horizons to the Chamber of Deputies. When the ministry won elections in 1846, Guizot wrote to Princess Lieven: 'they are the first truly governmental elections since 1814: that is the universal comment.'[93] During his oratorical duels in the Chamber with Thiers, Lamartine or the leader of the left in the Chamber, the lawyer Odilon Barrot, Guizot, in the words of Captain Gronow, 'seemed, with his proud head thrown proudly back, his eagle glance, his hard flashing eye, his biting sarcasm and disdainful eloquence, to hurl defiance at his adversaries and to dare them to the combat; just as a matador tries to irritate the bull he is going to fight by dashing a scarlet flag in his face'.[94]

Outside the Chamber, Guizot spent much of his time with Princess Lieven. Despite women's exclusion from a public role, the reality of their participation in politics is suggested by the following description of Guizot and Princess Lieven in April 1844, by Comte Rodolphe Apponyi (although the envious Austrian diplomat may exaggerate the role of the Russian princess):

> he goes to see her three or four times a day, she herself spends hours in his office and, for this purpose, he has had an armchair made especially for her; then from the moment she leaves him it is an interminable exchange of notes from morning to night . . . M. Guizot abandons the most pressing business to serve Princess Lieven.[95]

Tout Paris believed that they were married, and complimented the princess on the progress Guizot had made *sous le rapport des usages du monde*.[96]

There had been fifteen different ministries in the ten years before 1840; by 1848, however, Guizot had been in power for eight years. Like Charles X with Polignac, Louis-Philippe was determined to keep Guizot. Moreover, at the age of seventy-four, having reigned for eighteen years, Louis-Philippe was convinced of his own infallibility. With his industry and readiness to risk unpopularity, Guizot was one of the few ministers whom the King did not consider a coward. The King had no wish to replace him by the popular alternative, Thiers, whose policies he feared would lead to war between France and Europe – as well as to a diminution of royal power.[97]

Love of hunting had been the principal reason for the Bourbons' preference for the châteaux of the Ile de France; for Louis-Philippe it was fear of Paris. By the end of his reign he was spending less time in his capital than Charles X. In 1842 he had returned from Saint-Cloud for the winter season at the Tuileries on 5 December; in 1847 he returned as late as he decently could, on 21 December. *Le roi citoyen* had abandoned his city. Such prolonged absences, and the resulting loss of trade for Paris shopkeepers, increased his unpopularity. Moreover his failure to complete the ancient project to join the Louvre to the Tuileries caused, according to Chancellor Pasquier, 'continual murmurs' in Paris. In reality, by giving him a Civil List of only twelve million francs a year, the deputies themselves had deprived him of the means of linking the palaces.[98]

In the opinion of Lord Normanby, and others, by 1847 Louis-Philippe was a changed man, his intellect less subtle, his conversation less coherent and more voluble, than in the past. On occasions he repeated himself 'over and over again', and was 'almost unintelligible with excitement'.[99] So unpopular were the King and his minister that Normanby foresaw the fall of Guizot, even of the monarchy itself.[100] To members of his own family, and the Prefect of the Seine the Comte de Rambuteau, who warned him of impending revolution, Louis-Philippe replied: 'I have a firm seat on my horse.'[101] But King Leopold of the Belgians predicted that his father-in-law would soon be chased from the throne like Charles X. Joinville wrote to Nemours: 'there are no more ministers, their responsibility is null, everything goes to the King.'* He liked to govern and to show that it was he who governed. The Queen was more 'shut in and unapproachable' than ever; his sons still hoped that the King's eyes would open. But the King was preoccupied with the will of his beloved sister Madame Adélaïde, who had left him the usufruct of all her properties.[102] Her death on 31 December 1847 deprived him of an adviser from whom he had no secrets, and who was clearer-sighted than himself. It also put the court into mourning, thus cancelling the winter balls at the Tuileries and withdrawing an important source of income from the shopkeepers of Paris.[103] On 29 January 1848, in another famous speech in the Chamber, Tocqueville proclaimed that the workers' passions were no longer political but social, tending to challenge the distribution of property. He prophesied 'the most redoubtable revolutions . . . at the present time we are sleeping on a volcano'.[104]

In the end not Paris but the equally inflammable city of Palermo gave the starting signal for Europe's year of revolutions. Discontent with the Bourbon government in Naples, and desire for the separatist Sicilian constitution of 1812, caused a rising in Palermo on 12 January 1848. The occasion was local. However Paris was still a factory of ideas: the

---

* Joinville was said to have been sent to Algeria, at the end of 1847, in punishment for having thrown his cigar in Guizot's face during a political argument.

new constitution of the Kingdom of the Two Sicilies, proclaimed on 29 January, was largely based on the Charte of 1830, with amendments derived from the Belgian constitution of 1831.[105] On 11 February growing hostility to Austrian rule led to the proclamation of a state of siege in Milan. According to Comte Rodolphe Apponyi: 'Europe appears to be on the eve of a general combustion. It can only end in disorder and pillage, it is the war of those who have nothing against those who have something.'[106] On 12 February, for the first time, an audience in a Paris theatre was heard to sing republican songs from the first revolution, *Ça ira* and the *Carmagnole*.[107]

On 20 February a long anticipated 'reform banquet' in Paris was cancelled, for fear – so the deputies organising it maintained – of causing a revolution. One of the negotiators of the agreement between the deputies and the government was M. de Morny (as Auguste Demorny was now called), by then a promising young deputy, financed by his mistress the Belgian ambassadress Madame Le Hon (they lived in adjoining houses on the Rond-point des Champs Elysées).* Radicals were furious at the climbdown: Lamartine announced his readiness to go to the banquet even if accompanied by no more than his own shadow.[108]

To oppose revolution Louis-Philippe's government depended on the army: the number of uniforms in the streets of Paris still startled British visitors.[109] There were 37,000 troops in Paris – three times more than in 1830 – a plan for occupying key positions in the event of emergency, and tools for demolishing barricades in the barracks. However, neither General Sébastiani, the commander of the Paris garrison, nor General Jacqueminot, commander of the National Guard and father-in-law of the Minister of the Interior, were effective commanders.[110] The Préfet de Police Gabriel Delessert, a friend of Flahaut who had fought in the defence of Paris on 30 March 1814, was misled by his informers, some of whom were working for the republicans, into believing that radicals had abandoned plans for demonstrations. Revolutionaries were not arrested; troops were not put on the streets.[111]

On 21 February the last ball of the July monarchy took place at the Hôtel de Flahaut on the Champs Elysées. While Flahaut was serving as

---

* Hence the rhyme about her daughter:

> *Quel est donc ce visage blond,*
> *Qui ressemble à la reine Hortense?*
> *C'est la fille de M. Le Hon.*
> *Morny soit qui mal y pense.*

French ambassador to Austria, his *hôtel* was rented by the Prince de Ligne, the Belgian ambassador to France. The heat was stifling as the servants kept the windows closed, to prevent guests hearing the sound of demonstrations outside. Guests spoke of little but politics. With characteristic ignorance the Minister of the Interior, the Comte Duchâtel, in his note of excuse to his hosts, said that he anticipated 'perhaps' a light cloud, but no storm.[112]

On 22 February, despite rain, demonstrations began in and around the Place de la Concorde and the Champs Elysées. Students and workers sang the Marseillaise and the song of the Girondins, *Mourir pour la patrie, c'est le sort le plus beau, le plus digne d'envie!* and cried *A bas Guizot! Vive la réforme!* Barricades began to be constructed out of trees and carriages. In the evening soldiers and gardes municipaux – the most reliable, and therefore hated, of all forces in the capital, successors of the gendarmes of the Restoration – occupied public places and dispersed demonstrators. They showed extraordinary patience under showers of paving-stones.[113] People who remembered the earlier event said that it was very like the first day of the July revolution.[114] On 23 February the chiefs of secret societies and clubs ordered their members on to the streets. All observed that repression was neither 'energetic' nor 'serious'. By relying on national guards rather than soldiers, the government hoped to avoid bloodshed and the mistakes of Marshal Marmont in July 1830.[115] At 2 in the afternoon, although requests for invitations were still pouring in, the Austrian ambassador decided to cancel a ball for 900 and to distribute the food already ordered to the poor. Later that day his cousin Comte Rodolphe Apponyi could see youths cutting down trees and destroying street lamps on the Champs Elysées 'to the acclamations of the populace'. More barricades were erected in the small streets in the centre of the city. Instead of merely teasing or annoying soldiers, organised bands of demonstrators began to attack them. Fighting broke out around the Porte Saint-Martin.[116] Delirious crowds shouted *A bas Guizot!* and sang the Marseillaise.[117] As in 1830 and 1832 *gamins* – boys of twelve to sixteen, often beggars sleeping rough – were especially bold in singing revolutionary songs, destroying street lamps, digging up paving-stones, building barricades and firing at troops.[118]

The National Guard remained the key. Their commander General Jacqueminot, a feebler figure than his predecessor the Maréchal de Lobau, thought, incorrectly, that only six or seven of 384 companies of the National Guard were unreliable.[119] In reality, by 1848 the National

Guard was hostile to the government and even the monarchy, which in the 1830s it had done so much to sustain. They were tired of risking their lives in defence of a regime which refused to give most of them the vote.[120] Since 1840 the King had not reviewed the National Guard, his ministers fearing the clamour for reform, and against themselves, that he would hear: the Citizen King had become more unpopular in Paris than Charles X before 1829.[121] In all but the First Legion, which represented the richest quarter around the Champs Elysées, officers and junior officers began to feel that they could no longer count on their men: at critical moments on 23 February national guards would cry out to the soldiers *Vive la réforme!*, giving them drink and urging them not to shoot. By interposing their bodies, some prevented soldiers firing on crowds. As the vote rejecting a *dotation* for Nemours in 1840 had shown, there was little affection for the Orléans dynasty among the Paris bourgeoisie. When finally convinced of the National Guard's unreliability, the King was shattered.[122]

Pressed by his family, in particular the Queen and his beloved youngest son Montpensier, at 2.30 on the afternoon of 23 February he reluctantly dismissed Guizot and Duchâtel, although they were still convinced that they could control the situation. At 4 p.m. they were replaced by Count Molé, the former minister of Napoleon I and Louis XVIII – a choice almost as aristocratic and unimaginative as that of the Duc de Mortemart by Charles X on 29 July 1830. When Balzac heard that the King had yielded and sacked Guizot, he commented, like many Parisians, that it was the first step on the King's road to exile or the scaffold: like praetorian guards, 'the 60,000 national guards of Paris have become sovereigns'. Moreover, Molé did not formally accept the King's commission. As casual and dilatory as Mortemart on 30 July, Molé wrote to his ally the British ambassador that evening, as Paris raged: 'My dear Marquis, you have shown me too much friendship for me to let you learn from any but me that the King has summoned me – I have asked him for time to reflect and I do not yet know what my reply will be. *Tout à vous Molé.*' He finally consulted Thiers at 9 p.m. that evening. Thiers insisted on electoral reform and the dissolution of the Chamber.[123]

By the evening hundreds of barricades had sprung up. The troops showed 'sublime' patience as they demolished them with pikes and axes.[124] Discontent had been calmed by news of the fall of Guizot: the boulevards acquired a magical appearance as the houses along them, often at the insistence of revolutionaries, hung lamps in their windows to show their support.[125] However, the revolution needed martyrs. At

10 p.m., bearing torches, a crowd reached the Ministry of Foreign Affairs on the Boulevard des Capucines, where Guizot had been living (and where Polignac had been jeered on 26 July 1830). They hoped to enter. After fifteen minutes of discussion and provocation – demonstrators tried to grab the guns of the soldiers on duty – a shot rang out, probably fired by a revolutionary. Fighting started, followed by a fusillade from the soldiers. Again there was blood on the boulevards. About fifty died. The organisers of the demonstration seized sixteen corpses, placed them on chariots and paraded them through the city, as similar corpses had been paraded on 27 July 1830. This time the cry was: *A bas Louis-Philippe! Vengeance! On assassine nos frères! Aux armes!*[126]

That night left-wing newspapers called on the National Guard to give 'a great example' to Paris. Pasted around the city walls were posters drawn up by the staff of *Le National* and *La Réforme* stating *Citoyens, Louis-Philippe nous fait assassiner comme Charles X! Qu'il aille rejoindre Charles X!* Chateaubriand's prophecy that a monarchy created by the press would be destroyed by the press was coming to pass.[127] In increasing panic, the royal family spent part of the night leaning out of the windows of the Tuileries, listening to church bells being rung across the city.[128] The Duc de Nemours had been placed in supreme command of the troops; wine was distributed among those stationed around the Tuileries. No one of the royal family, however, came down to visit them.[129] Early in the morning, having been told that without a left-wing ministry he would not sleep the following night in the Tuileries, the King replaced Molé with Thiers and the even more radical, and to him repugnant, figure of Odilon Barrot.[130] Like Charles X with Polignac, however, he continued to consult his old minister Guizot, who came to the Tuileries on the morning of 24 February.[131]

At first the King had not wanted to call on Marshal Bugeaud, the ruthless commander of the repression of 1834 and subsequently of the French army in Algeria, who was alleged to have said that he could save the monarchy by shooting ten thousand *canaille*.[132] But at 1.30 on the morning of 24 February Bugeaud was named commander of the army and the National Guard. At 6 a.m. he sent three columns of troops through Paris, to the Panthéon, the Hôtel de Ville and along the boulevards to the Bastille. They accomplished their missions. At 8.30 a.m. however, on the command of the King's new ministers Thiers and Barrot, Bugeaud ordered troops to cease fire. Badly led and demoralised, lacking ammunition, soldiers began to fraternise with the crowds. Some gave weapons to demonstrators and marched back to barracks;

others were ordered out of Paris, possibly in an effort to maintain what was left of their discipline – events which led to this revolution being summarised as 'order – counter-order – disorder'.[133]

Signs of revolution were everywhere in Paris: empty streets; shut shops; no carriages or passers-by; no street cries; groups of neighbours talking in doorways with scared faces and lowered voices.[134] Pupils of the Ecole Polytechnique began to call for the King's abdication. In the face of overwhelming numbers, as if a human ocean had risen, Rambuteau hurried away from the Hôtel de Ville as quickly as Chabrol had done in 1830: other *mairies* also fell to the insurgents.[135] By the end of the morning of 24 February, according to later official counts by the municipal authorities, 4,013 trees had been cut down, and 1,512 barricades built, in the streets of Paris.[136] The barricades were generally constructed by a small number of men watched by a placid public. A gap was left at the side to allow walkers to pass by. Women spread broken bottles and china on the streets, to hinder cavalry charges.[137]

News that a riot had broken out on the Place de la Concorde reached the Tuileries at 10.30, in the middle of *déjeuner*. At about 11, encouraged by the Queen and accompanied by Nemours, Montpensier, Bugeaud and Thiers, the King set off to review troops and national guards on the Cour du Carrousel, as Louis XVI had done, in the same place and under similar circumstances, on the morning of 10 August 1792.[138]

Reactions were similar. Cries of *Vive le roi!* were drowned by those of *Vive la réforme! A bas les ministres!* Guards left the ranks and threatened the King. Without having reached the troops of the line, he turned round and retreated to the palace. Back in his study, he sat sunk in what the Intendant of his Civil List, and confidential adviser, the Comte de Montalivet, called 'the last degree of discouragement'.[139] Eighteen years on the French throne, above all the death of his eldest son, had sapped the energy and confidence so evident in the 1830s.

The revolutionaries had a monopoly of resolution. On the side of the government, in contrast to 1832, 1834 and 1839, ministers and generals were resolved only to avoid bloodshed. News arrived at the Tuileries of desertions and assassinations. While on duty at the Château d'Eau outside the Palais Royal, a post of troops was burnt alive by revolutionaries. Thiers proposed withdrawing to Saint-Cloud with the two Chambers and there rallying the troops. Most people, however, including the King, considered that to leave Paris was to lose everything.[140] From about midday the crowd in the King's study (which included Thiers, Soult, Sébastiani, Rémusat and Bugeaud), led by Emile de

Girardin, urged him to abdicate as quickly as possible in order to prevent further bloodshed. It was the same situation as at Neuilly on 30 July 1830, but in reverse: a crowd of advisers pleaded with Louis-Philippe to abandon, rather than to assume, power. 'Sire, you will destroy us all,' said one. Many looked green with fear: outside they could hear pealing church bells, drums beating the call to arms and guns firing.[141] Girardin, and possibly others such as Montpensier and Odilon Barrot, hoped for a regency by the Duchesse d'Orléans, whom they believed malleable; but the King insisted on Nemours.[142] Montpensier, his favourite son, continued to hurry him: 'The abdication, the abdication, there is no more time, they are coming, they are coming!' Writing out his abdication in favour of his grandson the Comte de Paris, the King replied: 'I cannot go faster.'[143] Marie Amélie was appalled. In 1848 as in 1835, she spoke her mind. 'You are ungrateful, you did not deserve such a good king,' she said to Thiers. And as people snatched the act of abdication from the King's hands: 'You have it, you will repent of it.' The royal family, courtiers and officials then fled from the Tuileries.[144]

At about 12.30 the Comte de Montalivet, with a few loyal troops and officials, escorted the King, the Queen and some of their children and grandchildren on foot, out of the palace, through the Jardin des Tuileries to the Place de la Concorde, which was still protected by a cordon of troops. Near the obelisk they got into three carriages – a few onlookers crying *Vive le roi!* – and were escorted to Saint-Cloud.[145] Charles X had remained at Rambouillet from 31 July to 3 August 1830, in an attempt to save something from the wreckage. However, the panic of the moment and the influence of Paris were so overwhelming that once outside the city Louis-Philippe did not choose to make a stand, either at the forts he had built at such cost on its perimeter or at Saint-Cloud, or at Rouen, where both city and troops, under the command of the Comte de Castellane, were loyal.[146] He headed for Eu. He had left in such haste that he had forgotten to take money or papers with him. Finally, unshaven, wigless, wearing a black silk handkerchief round his head and calling himself Mr William Smith, the former King found a boat at Dieppe and landed, with his wife, at Newhaven on 2 March.[147]

In England they were reunited with most of their family: in the panic of the royal flight many people had been abandoned in the Tuileries, even the young and pregnant Duchesse de Montpensier, for whose hand in marriage Louis-Philippe had striven so hard, and for whom he had created a particularly magnificent apartment in the palace.[148] It is said that when she did finally escape, disguised and travelling in a hired carriage on a British passport, the Duchess exclaimed that even this ordeal was preferable to another evening spent sewing at her mother-in-law's table in the Tuileries.[149] Mérimée delivered a damning, but widely shared, verdict on the Orléans: 'the King and the princes have been much inferior to their cousins of the elder branch in all this. They have destroyed themselves and have destroyed royalty in France.' The King himself is said to have muttered, as he fled from Paris: 'Worse than Charles X! A hundred times worse than Charles X!'[150] Called by Parisians *Louis Filevite*, or 'Louis the runaway',[151] he died in England in 1850, as forgotten as if he had been a Merovingian. By then he was again, at heart, a legitimist, hoping for a reconciliation with the elder branch which would enable the Comte de Paris to succeed the Comte de Chambord as King of France.[152]

It had taken a week to overthrow the Restoration; only twenty-four hours were needed to eject the July monarchy. Indeed, as Tocqueville noted, it was not overthrown; it was allowed to fall.[153] The Duchesse d'Orléans was the only member of the royal family to show powers of leadership. While Louis-Philippe fled with the Queen, at about 1.30 p.m. the Duchesse d'Orléans with her two sons, escorted by the Duc de Nemours and a few politicians and courtiers, had arrived at the Chamber of Deputies, seen as the seat of sovereignty, to secure the accession of her son the Comte de Paris. A forlorn figure in her widow's dress, she sat at the foot of the tribune. The Chamber at first applauded her with cries of *Vive la duchesse d'Orléans! Vive le comte de Paris! Vive le roi! Vive la régente!* However, the Chamber was divided between defeatist Orleanists and republicans. Suggestions to move to Saint-Cloud – where the Chamber had been transferred in order to facilitate Bonaparte's coup of November 1799 – were rejected. Outside a crowd yelled: 'We do not want the regency or the little one! No Bourbons! No more Bourbons! Down with Guizot!'[154] On the Place de la Bastille another crowd protested: 'No! No! No regency! Down with the Bourbons! Neither king nor queen! No masters!' Nemours, who had done nothing with the troops under his command on the night of 23/24 February, had none of the glamour or popularity of his elder brother: Victor Hugo called him both embarrassed and embarrassing.[155] In a state of fright the President of the Chamber, Sauzet, failed to request troops stationed nearby on the Place de la Concorde to come to the defence of the deputies. An armed and well-organised republican mob was allowed to invade the Chamber.[156]

Few spoke in favour of the regency of the Duchesse d'Orléans. She was asked to go and sit in a less prominent position at the top of the hemicycle. Almost as much as Talleyrand in April 1814 and Orléans on 30 and 31 July 1830, Lamartine held the fate of Paris in his hands. In a decisive speech he advocated a 'rational government' – a republic – and warned against the dangers of 'false pity' for the Duchesse d'Orléans and her sons. Convinced of their own nullity, deputies allowed the Republic to be proclaimed.[157] Those like Barrot and Duvergier de Hauranne who had wanted the regency stayed silent.[158] 'All our heroes of the tribune have been careless or foolish when they have not been traitors . . . no one did their duty and now we are at the mercy of the populace,' commented the arch-Orleanist Viennet.

The Comte de Paris was rejected in the city from which he took his title, more decisively than his cousins the King of Rome and the Duc de Bordeaux had been. Indeed, in the crowd, he was only saved from death by suffocation by three Orleanist officers of the National Guard, Comte Oudinot, the Prince de Chalais and M. de Périgord.[159] His mother took him from the Chamber to the *hôtel* of Maréchal Soult. There she was reunited with her second son the Duc de Chartres, who had also been saved from possible murder only by being disguised as a labourer's child.[160]

The Duchesse d'Orléans and her sons left for Eisenach in Germany where she was sheltered by a relation, the Grand Duke of Weimar. Terrified and tearful, moaning to Victor Hugo 'the sea is rising, rising, rising', Thiers fled to the villa of an Italian friend.[161] Cursing the cowardice of the royal family, Princess Lieven, her jewellery sewn into her skirts, was escorted by a painter called James Roberts to London.[162] Guizot hid in the houses of friends for a week, reading Walter Scott, until able on 1 March to take a train for Brussels, disguised as a servant of the ambassador of Württemberg. James de Rothschild sent his women and children to London but, warned by Lord Normanby that his flight would cause a financial panic that would ruin his bank, he himself remained in Paris.[163] Berlioz, who had claimed to find nothing but imbecility, indifference, ingratitude and threats in Paris, remained in London, where he had been touring: music, he believed, was dead in Paris.[164] Madame de Boigne and Pasquier, stupefied by the speed of the revolution, retired to Tours.

The level of destruction in Paris in 1848 was greater than in 1830. Neuilly was burnt down with all its contents, possibly at the instigation of its staff, towards whom the King had not been generous. Nothing remains today of the favourite home of the Orléans.[165] The Palais Royal was invaded and numerous pictures destroyed.[166] The Tuileries was pillaged. The princesses' clothes, jewellery and perfumes soon adorned favoured revolutionaries. Surrounded by broken glass and china and scattered papers, wearing the caps and bonnets of the princesses, men with blood-caked arms brandished red flags in the royal apartments, shouting *Mort à Louis-Philippe!* The Queen's cat writhed in agony on the point of a spear held by a *bonnet rouge*.[167] In 1830 revolutionaries had done no more than sit on the throne in the Tuileries. In 1848 four strong workers carried it out of the palace. It was then taken in procession along the boulevards by a crowd draped in stolen royal liveries, and burnt on the Place de la Bastille, at the foot of the Colonne de Juillet.[168] With the crowd in the Tuileries had been Balzac, who had not only seen 'everything' but, with his instinct for royal *provenances*, had taken ornaments and draperies of the throne for himself. *Ah! quel spectacle!* he wrote to Madame Hanska.[169] The revolution made him want a despotic government in France, of any kind, he did not mind which: loathing and despising the Republic, he did not want to be a French citizen.[170] Eight months later he fled to Madame Hanska's estate in the Ukraine.

The private apartments of every member of the royal family were defiled, according to the account of the revolution later published by the British ambassador Lord Normanby, by 'crimes of every description'. Only that of the late Duc d'Orléans, kept 'perfectly untouched' since 13 July 1842, the day of his death, and still containing that day's newspapers, had been respected.[171] Many revolutionaries stayed in the palace for ten days. Drunk with joy and wine, still wearing the royal family's clothes, they treated the royal cooks as their servants, and were able to offer guests a choice of *gigot aux truffes* or *gigot aux petits pois*.[172]

As on 29 July–1 August 1830, the Hôtel de Ville became the seat of power in Paris. The Republic was proclaimed there, with a provisional government of, among others, Lamartine, Arago, Hippolyte Carnot, son of Napoleon's Minister of the Interior in 1815, and Louis Blanc. By its first proclamation a 'retrograde and oligarchical government' was pronounced to have been overthrown 'by the heroism of the people of Paris'.[173] A symbol of the interaction between politics and literature, nobles and public life then prevalent, for the next three months Lamartine ruled Paris. 'All now depends on [his] life and health,' Lord Normanby wrote to Palmerston.[174] Lamartine was determined to avoid bloodshed in Paris and Europe. In a celebrated outburst defending the tricolour, which had carried the name, the glory and the liberty of the fatherland around the world, he defied a group of workers come to impose the red flag of socialism as the flag of France.[175] In a manifesto of 2 March he claimed that the new republic was intent on entering the family of nations as a state like any other, not a disruptive element. Although the hated treaties of 1815 were no longer considered valid, the Republic wanted peace not war. France would intervene abroad only in Italy or Switzerland, whose nationalist movements were threatened by Austria.[176]

Thanks to Lamartine, a degree of confidence began to return to Paris. Emile de Girardin wrote articles urging people to rally to the Republic. On 27 February *L'Univers* proclaimed: 'Who in France today thinks of defending the monarchy? France still thought it was monarchical and it was already republican.' By 28 February traffic was circulating in the streets again.[177] Work began on demolishing the barricades; street lamps were repaired; shops, although not factories or workshops, reopened. The streets seemed strangely calm. Baudelaire wrote in praise of the 'unique moment in history' when one immense hope had replaced the feelings of innumerable individuals. From the quantities of 'trees of liberty', generally poplars, planted in squares, crossroads and courtyards, Paris began to resemble a wood.[178]

Throughout the city, observed Tocqueville, the forces of law and order had disappeared. Not a soldier, a gendarme or a policeman was in sight: 'The people alone bore arms, guarded public places, watched, gave orders, punished; it was something extraordinary and terrible to see in the hands of those who possessed nothing this immense city, full of so many riches, or rather this great nation; for thanks to centralisation, he who reigns in Paris commands France.'[179] Soon however, in order to defend their properties, nobles and bourgeois began to undertake patrol duty in the National Guard, more eagerly than under the July monarchy. Looters could be shot on sight.[180]

If palaces suffered greater damage than in 1830, churches were better treated. In 1830 crosses had been ripped off the summits of churches and Parisian crowds had been aggressively anti-Catholic.[181] In 1848, however, a cross was ceremonially escorted from the Tuileries to Saint-Roch by a crowd of revolutionaries. The liberal Catholic Père Henri Lacordaire preached in Notre Dame on the indissoluble alliance of France and Religion. The Archbishop blessed a tree of liberty in front of Notre Dame, celebrated an episcopal mass in the throne room of the Tuileries, transformed into a hospital, and presented his formal respects to the provisional government.[182] So sympathetic to Christianity was the revolution of 1848 that one song claimed that Paris had risen from the grave radiant as a new Christ.[183]

More than in 1830, Paris was transformed into a revolutionary city. Humanitarian reforms included the abolition of slavery, of public exposure of criminals, and of the death penalty for political offences.[184] Noble titles were abolished; for a time official letters were addressed to *Citoyen* rather than *Monsieur*, and ended with the formula *Salut et Fraternité*.[185] Indifferent to the lives of most Parisians, Mérimée complained: 'there is no more Paris' – that is to say, his friends in the *beau monde* no longer entertained.[186] The Tuileries and the Champs Elysées lost their air of luxury and elegance: the brilliant carriages of the wealthy in *habits* were replaced by workers in *blouses*, smoking pipes.[187] Salons and theatres closed. Parisians found alternative occupation in over 200 newly opened revolutionary clubs, representing every variety of opinion. A Club de la Révolution was presided over in the Palais Royal by Barbès, who wanted to tax the rich and remove soldiers from Paris;[188] the Société Républicaine Centrale in the Conservatoire de Musique was under the other leader of the rising of 1839, Auguste Blanqui; while legitimist clubs, feminist clubs, a Club Fraternel des Lingères, even a Club de l'Intelligence were all to be found.[189] To occupy Parisian workers, the government, which had guaranteed the *droit au travail*, opened workshops known as *ateliers nationaux*: since the *ateliers* produced little, employers dubbed them state-subsidised strikes. By June they employed 110,000 workers and cost the state 170,000 francs a day.[190] Thousands more, however, remained out of work, banks closed, bankruptcies were frequent, including those of respectable firms such as the Franco-British bankers Laffitte et Blount et cie.[191] Money fled abroad. Rents were unpaid.[192]

Despite the lack of armed French intervention abroad, Paris became a metropolis of revolution. On 7 March the Lord Lieutenant of Ireland reported sourly to Palmerston that the success of the revolution had 'put the Irish in ecstasies': they hoped for 'French assistance to redress Irish wrongs' – although Lamartine later received an Irish deputation very coolly.[193] On 13 March, stimulated by the news from Paris, another revolution broke out in Vienna: Metternich fled to London and the Emperor promised a constitution. Insurrections also started in Rome on 15 March, Berlin on 17 March, and Milan on 18 March. Having left Paris for Florence in November 1847, in 1848 Princess Belgiojoso became the heroine of the revolution in Naples. Hailed as the paragon of Italian women, she founded and edited a newspaper, *Le National*. She wrote to the historian Thierry: 'I do not think anyone has enjoyed *so suddenly* a popularity as great as mine . . . now that we have freedom of the press, it is in Italy that Italian problems must be solved.'[194] On 6 April she entered Milan in an open carriage, wearing a plumed Calabrian hat, greeted by crowds crying *Viva l'Italia! Viva Pio Nono!*, bringing with her the first Neapolitan volunteers, to fight in a crusade to drive the Austrian forces out of Italy.[195] For her Paris had been a means not an end, a city in which to work for the 'liberation' of Italy. Later, when, despite Louis-Napoleon's promises, French troops in Italy opposed the policy she advocated, she came to regard France as a tormentor.[196]

Although Paris helped galvanise the 'springtime of nations' – and many Poles, Germans, Armenians and Hungarians had fought on the barricades in February – its European role was less significant than its role as capital of France.[197] There were no separate European institutions to counterbalance the weight of the French state. Paris was dominated, not by the European struggle for liberty but by a denouement in the long-expected war between rich and poor. As early as 24 February, on the very first day of the Republic, the British ambassador had written: 'there must be a reaction. One cannot believe that a great nation like this can really permanently submit to the dictation of a few low demagogues . . . hoisted into power by the base desertion of their duty of all the armed forces and the pleasure of the lowest scum of the earth.'[198]

In April France held its first national elections under universal male suffrage – before the United States or the United Kingdom. Eighty-four per cent of voters – 7,385,327 of 9,395,035 persons entitled – went to the polls. They returned a conservative assembly dominated by provincial notables; it included many landowners, three bishops and three nephews of Napoleon I. Few workers or *clubistes* were elected. Lamartine, idolised as a saviour, was elected in Paris and eleven departments; Thiers was defeated.[199] The opposition between Paris and France was now obvious. The Minister of the Marine, Jules Bastide, told Lord Normanby that France was unfit for universal suffrage.[200] Civil war seemed inevitable.[201]

Meanwhile, as Germans, Hungarians and Italians sought to create their own democratic states, foreign residents in Paris were meeting at the Hôtel de Ville to demonstrate their support for revolution in Europe.[202] In March, 500 Belgian democrats planned an attack on their embassy; in

April the Société Démocratique Allemande formed the German Legion of Paris which crossed the Rhine into Swabia in support of revolution in Germany.[203] In May Paris rediscovered its Polish soul. Already in 1847 a Comité Central pour la Cause Polonaise had been refounded in Paris with Georges La Fayette, Berryer, Chopin, Victor Hugo and thirty deputies, eager to proclaim France's 'unalterable' attachment to the Polish cause and to assert that 'Polish nationality will not perish.'[204] A Polish Legion under the auspices of the French War Ministry had been created in March 1848.[205]

On 13 May 1848 radicals demonstrated on the Place de la Bastille in favour of what Blanqui called the 'magic name' of Poland; on 15 May 100,000 Parisians, organised by revolutionary clubs, took to the streets, again ostensibly for the sake of Poland. Although soldiers had returned to Paris, some revolutionaries were able to invade the National Assembly, 'screaming and shouting and tumbling over each other', demanding an immediate proclamation of war on Russia and Prussia for the sake of Poland. In keeping with the theatrical nature of the 1848 revolution, some were dressed like characters in Dumas' popular play *Le Chevalier de Maison-Rouge*. To cries of *Vive la Pologne!*, they dissolved the Assembly and proclaimed an insurrectionary government under Barbès, Blanqui and Louis Blanc.[206] When Lamartine tried to calm the crowd, a voice rang out: *Assez de lyre!* The laughs with which the remark was received forced Lamartine to retire to an office in the same building. However, soldiers and national guards were able to arrest the three ringleaders in the Hôtel de Ville. The ease with which demonstrators had at first reached the Assembly suggests that the entire *journée* may have been a trap, organised by government-paid *agents provocateurs*, to encourage the radical left to insult and attack the Assembly, and thus to give the government an excuse to begin the movement of reaction.[207] The hopes of the spring of 1848 were vanishing.

In Tocqueville's opinion the Paris workers had been persuaded, by the pamphlets and speeches of the day, that the rich had stolen their property from the poor, and that inequality of wealth was contrary to society, morality and nature. Provoked by the closure of the *ateliers nationaux*, and the invitation to their workers to join the army or work in the provinces, on 22 June about 15,000 insurgents started an uprising in the east of the city, crying 'Liberty or Death!', 'Bread or Lead!'[208]

The poor were convinced that their moment had come. As the insurrection started, a young servant boy in the household of the revolutionary leader Blanqui said, while serving dinner: 'Next Sunday it will be us who eat the chicken wings.' A servant girl added: 'And it will be us who wear the beautiful silk dresses.' Only after the insurrection had been defeated did Blanqui dare to send them back to their parents' hovel.[209]

The Republic proved more ruthless in its repression of insurrection than either Louis-Philippe or Charles X had dared to be. On 23 June the Minister of War General Cavaignac, to whom the executive commission had resigned its powers, abandoned the eastern half of the city to about 400 barricades. Building workers and furniture-makers formed the backbone of insurrection. Many Poles also joined in: Polish was spoken on every barricade, so Mérimée later recalled.[210] Victor Hugo's house was sacked and burned, three days after he had made a speech comparing the temporary glory of London, gained at the cost of the economic distress in Paris, with the permanent hegemony of Paris:

> Paris is the present capital of the civilised world. What Rome once was Paris is today: Paris has a dominating function among the nations: it is the privilege of Paris, at certain periods, to accomplish imperiously, perhaps brusquely, great things. It is the thinkers of Paris who prepare the way for them and for the workers of Paris who execute them.[211]

On 24 June in the Chamber of Representatives Hugo was told by a fellow representative: 'The insurrection is mistress of Paris at this moment. We are lost.' Lamartine, whose weakness in these days Normanby attributed to blackmail by the new republican Minister of the Interior, Auguste Ledru-Rollin, who had evidence of his financial dealings with Louis-Philippe's last Minister of the Interior, gave up hope.[212] However Cavaignac, at first strangely passive, led his troops from the west for what was called *nettoyage systématique*, 'systematic cleansing'. For the first time troops and national guards, as well as bread to feed them, could be rapidly brought by railway from the provinces to suppress the people of Paris. Artillery and engineers used to street fighting arrived from the provinces on 25 June. Thus, although nineteenth-century French governments would complain of the difficulty of controlling Paris, the railway and the ballot box were in reality making it easier. An insurrection in Paris was henceforth less likely to be successful than in February 1848, July 1830 or July 1789. The introduction of universal male suffrage proved that the workers of Paris did not, as they had once believed, represent the French people.[213]

As troops conducted house to house searches, there was said to be more blood on the streets of Paris than during the siege of Saragossa in the Peninsular War. The young gardes mobiles, raised from the *gamins de Paris* and only trained for four months, fought with fury on the government side, often better than regular soldiers and national guards – in part from hatred of the older generation of workers serving on the other side.[214] Fighting around the Porte Saint-Denis and the Quartier Latin was ferocious; many national guards supported the insurgents. Victor Hugo called it the greatest street battle in history. However, on the early afternoon of 26 June, Cavaignac could send telegrams to prefectures in the provinces: *L'ordre a triomphé de l'anarchie. Vive la République!*[215]

In the course of the fighting 1,600 soldiers and perhaps 3,000 civilians were killed; afterwards over 11,000 people were arrested, 4,000 transported to Algeria without judgement. For having protested against the closure of eleven newspapers, Emile de Girardin himself was held in solitary confinement in a subterranean prison cell for eleven days. With bloodstains and bullet-holes scarring innumerable houses, and troops at every street corner, Paris looked like a city taken by assault. It remained under a state of siege until October.[216] On 6 July there was another grand political funeral on the Place de la Concorde, for the *victimes de juin*, presided over by General Cavaignac acting as temporary President of the Republic.[217]

The viciousness of the repression, worse than in any previous insurrection, horrified contemporaries: the young Ernest Renan lamented that there was no attempt to rethink a brutal system which forced men to behave as the insurrectionaries had, although he admitted that their triumph would have been even worse. George Sand felt ashamed of being French and of a republic which began by killing its workers; the liberal Catholic politician the Comte de Montalembert condemned the insurrection as the long-feared invasion of barbarians. When Proudhon tried to speak in the Assembly in favour of a reduction of rents, he was greeted with cries of *A Charenton! A la ménagerie!*[218]

Mérimée, who at the age of forty-five had fought in the National Guard for four days without stopping, wrote to Madame de Boigne that the insurrectionaries had, in his experience, fought better than the forces of law and order; but they had cut off prisoners' hands, feet and heads, assassinated peace envoys (on 27 June the Archbishop of Paris died from a stray bullet after trying to mediate on the barricades) and fired cartridges designed to inflict as much pain as possible. In 1814–15 foreigners had admired the gentleness of the Parisians, their 'amenity of manners' and 'absence of all disgusting excesses'.[219] In 1830 the lack of gratuitous violence in the revolution had again won Parisians the admiration of Europe. In June 1848, however, in the opinion of Mérimée and others, the people of Paris showed all the instincts of 'wild animals'. Mérimée wondered if it would ever be possible to wean the French nation from the stupidity and savagery in which it liked to wallow.[220] He himself, however, was just as savage as those he denounced. On 28 June he expressed the views of many members of his class when he wrote to Théodore de Lagrenée words which early editors of his letters did not dare to print: 'as for me I do not think that, unless Paris is destroyed from top to bottom, order can ever be reestablished in France.'[221]

Once the most admired of cities, by 1848 Paris was regarded by some Frenchmen as a disease. Henri Lecouturier, author of *Paris incompatible avec la République. Plan d'un nouveau Paris où les révolutions seront impossibles* (1848), denounced it as the most revolutionary city in the world, the metropolis of vice, where debauch could be seen at every street corner and in every public garden. While half the population was dying of hunger, the other half ate enough for two.[222] Even Proudhon, in 1839, had condemned this 'land . . . of thieves and prostitutes': 'one day the funeral lament will resound over Paris and it will come from the provinces.'[223] Much as he loved Paris, in one of his novels Balzac had Marshal Blücher describe it as a cancer which would kill France.[224] Tocqueville found, among voters in Normandy, that Paris inspired hatred and terror.[225] Some Frenchmen thought the capital should be moved to Bourges.[226]

In this city of fear and hate, which many of its inhabitants compared to a volcano in constant eruption, the death of Chateaubriand on 4 July marked the end of an era. He had continued his daily visits to Madame Récamier even when she was blind and he was paralysed, and partly dumb. His loud laughter coming home from his wife's funeral in 1847 had been taken by some as a sign of senility, by others as proof of lucidity. His sole comment on the fall of Louis-Philippe had been: *C'est bien fait!* On the proclamation of the Republic: *Cela vous fera-t'il plus heureux?*[227]

Despite the deaths and bloodshed, however, the life of the city soon resumed. When the Théâtre Français reopened in July with as large a government subsidy as ever – thereby permitting the élite to enjoy itself at government expense – the journalist Alphonse Karr was inspired to coin the phrase: *Plus ça change, plus c'est la même chose.*[228]

Soon after Chateaubriand's death the name of Bonaparte began to be mentioned in Paris, not as a dream of glory but as a possible President. A brief visit from London to Paris by Louis-Napoleon Bonaparte, in June, when he had been voted one of the representatives for Paris, had led to some demonstrations and cries of *Vive Napoléon!* on the Place de la Concorde. At the Porte Saint-Denis cries were heard of *Nous l'aurons, nous l'aurons! Louis-Napoléon!*[229] A regiment of dragoons marching through Versailles and passing a tree of liberty had shouted *A bas la liberté! Vive l'Empereur!*[230] However, for fear of the anger of the republican Chamber of Representatives, the prince went back to London.

On 24 September 1848, having been elected representative for five departments, he returned to Paris. Almost all other politicians were discredited by the recent bloodshed. Associated with disorder and poverty, the Republic had become unpopular in the countryside. Thanks to his name – the only name in France with electoral magic – Louis-Napoleon represented at once glory, monarchy and revolution. In contrast Henri V was considered to represent the nobility, Louis-Philippe the bourgeoisie. A popular song in Paris ran:

> *Veux-tu un coquin?*
> *Prends Ledru-Rollin.*
> *Veux-tu du mic-mac?*
> *Vot' pour Cavaignac.*
> *Mais veux-tu le bon?*
> *Prends Napoléon!*[231]

On 10 December 1848, in the elections for President of the Republic he won 5,587,759 votes, compared to only 1,474,687 for Cavaignac (despite the backing of the government), and smaller numbers for Ledru-Rollin and Raspail. Lamartine, a messiah nine months earlier, received 17,000 votes. In Paris Louis-Napoleon received 58 per cent of the votes, compared to 74 per cent in France as a whole.[232] The people had spoken. In one of the most decisive votes in French history, the people had voted against the advice of the government and the great majority of the élite. Montalembert called the result the defeat of democratic rationalism by a name. *Honte à nous! honte à la France! honte à la République! honte à la démocratie! honte au peuple!*, wrote Madame d'Agoult. 'No one believes that the presidency of Louis Bonaparte will last,' commented Rodolphe Apponyi.[233]

In the next three years, however, Louis-Napoleon Bonaparte

strengthened his power base and increased his popularity. Soon he was greeted by ordinary Parisians in the street, and by soldiers at military reviews, with cries of *Vive l'Empire! Vive le prince Napoléon! Vive l'Empereur!*[234] Having few acquaintances in Paris, a city he knew less well than London, he at first followed the advice of politicians like Molé, Thiers and Odilon Barrot. At the same time he was advised by his mother's former lover Flahaut, and their son, his illegitimate half-brother Auguste de Morny. Flahaut had once called the prince a 'madman'; now he was fascinated, as many others would be including Queen Victoria, by his distant, royal manner, his mystical confidence in his 'star', and his simplicity – although Flahaut so hated the Republic that he refused to serve under it.[235] Like many others, he believed that France, weak and demoralised, needed regeneration by strong government.

Morny first met his brother the President in January 1849, in the house of Madame Le Hon. Soon they were meeting every day. Himself a former deputy and friend of the Orléans princes, he became the President's intermediary with Orleanist politicians. He tried to wean his half-brother from what he called 'sentimental liberalism': 'the President had great ignorance of men and many illusions about things.'[236]

His fundamental traits, according to Tocqueville, were contempt for parliamentary assemblies and a belief in his dynastic right equal to Charles X's. A court began to form around him, including a military cabinet through which he increased his control of the army. By February 1849 he was giving balls for 1,200 in the Elysée Palace, where guests were announced by their titles, although titles had been abolished by the constitution. By April 1849 etiquette at his Monday evening receptions was described as more formal than in the Tuileries under Louis-Philippe.[237] On 30 November 1849 Castellane wrote in his diary: 'People are beginning to talk of the Empire again.' In January 1850 those trees of liberty which had not already died were cut down.

In the years 1849–51 the President had to submit to the control of ministries dominated by former Orleanists like Thiers and Odilon Barrot.[238] He was attacked by the Assembly over his income as well as his policies: in February 1851 it rejected his demand for an increased *dotation*.[239] From July 1851, despite their terror at the idea of violating the constitution which the President had sworn to protect, he and his advisers were contemplating a coup. It was planned at Saint-Cloud, as Charles X's had been, by Morny (who had fought in July 1830 against Charles X's coup), General Saint-Arnaud, M. de Maupas, Préfet de

Police de Paris, and the President's chief political advisers the conservative politicians Eugène Rouher and Jules Baroche, and his companion
in exile Auguste Fialin de Persigny.[240]

The coup was in part financed, like Morny's own career, by his mistress Madame Le Hon. When they separated six and a half years later –
prompting his celebrated remark, 'When I took her I was a second lieutenant, when I left her I was an ambassador' – they signed an agreement
by which he recognised that he owed her three and a half million
francs.[241] The prince's English mistress the courtesan Elizabeth Ann
Howard, who had moved with him from London, also contributed
funds, as did another friend of English origin the Marquise Campana
and Marshal Narvaez Duke of Valencia, Prime Minister of Spain in
1848–50, 'the very incarnation of the militaristic spirit of nineteenth-
century Spain', who had settled in Paris and was probably acting, in this
matter, on behalf of Queen Maria Cristina.[242] This decisive event in the
history of Paris was financed by four foreigners, for the benefit of a
prince who had spent his life abroad.

The prince's power base was the army. Its sense of isolation from the
rest of the nation and hostility to civilians, already apparent in 1814–15,
had been analysed in a prophetic paragraph by Heine in 1841: 'it is not
impossible that one fine day the army will overthrow the present reign
of the bourgeoisie, this second Directory, and make another dix-huit
Brumaire. The government of the sabre would then be the end of the
story.'[243] Some of the coup's organisers saw it as retribution for the
humiliations of the monarchy and the army in the revolutions of 1830
and 1848.[244] By 1851 army officers and soldiers were showing open
antipathy to the deputies, denouncing them as *bavards* who should be
thrown into the Seine.[245] Fifty thousand soldiers were stationed in Paris
in December 1851. At the same time the Assembly was attempting to
secure for the President of the Assembly the legal right to request soldiers to come to its protection if it was attacked.[246] Two visions of
France, military and parliamentary, were at odds.

Fear of socialism was another of the President's weapons. Despite
the bloodbath of June 1848 there had been renewed demonstrations in
May 1849. Workers on the Place de la Concorde had cried: *Vive la
République démocratique et sociale! Unité des peuples! Unité de l'Allemagne! Mort
aux rois!*[247] Some sections of Paris continued to elect socialists in 1850
and 1851. *Le spectre rouge* haunted the bourgeoisie.

The progress of the coup, and the mentality of its organisers, can be
followed in the letters of Flahaut and Morny – two of the President's

most trusted advisers – and also of Morny's private secretary, his mistress's son Léopold Le Hon. (Morny's letters to Madame Le Hon, which would have been the most revealing of all, have been burnt.)

Flahaut to Madame de Flahaut, 24 November: Things are getting too hot not to catch fire soon. The assembly is a disgusting set of *intrigants*.

Flahaut to Madame de Flahaut, 30 November: The army requires much more to be calmed than excited . . . The assembly is every day falling more into discredit. It is in short in a state of dissolution. Adieu my dearest Margaret. I embrace you with all my heart.[248]

On 1 December Morny was appointed Minister of the Interior: poacher turned gamekeeper, he would succeed where Charles X, against whom he had fought during the July revolution, had failed.[249] On the morning of 2 December the *coup d'état* began with the military occupation of the National Assembly. Proclamations were pasted on the walls of the city dissolving the Assembly, re-establishing universal suffrage, calling for a constitution resembling that of 1800, which had led to the First Empire. The coup was so well planned that special agents had been selected to protect the men pasting the proclamations on walls, and thereafter to stop the proclamations being torn down. The ropes attached to church bells were cut, so that they could not be used to summon revolutionaries to action.[250]

Flahaut to Madame de Flahaut, 2 December, 7 a.m.: I am just returned from the other side of the Pont de la Concorde where I accompanied Auguste on his way to the Ministère de l'Intérieur of which he is gone to take possession. The Chamber is occupied and surrounded with troops and having passed before General Changarnier's house I saw it full of sergents de ville and gendarmes mobiles who were arresting him. There are a good many besides who are to be arrested. The troops hate the Assembly and are well disposed to the President. There may be partial struggle but I believe there can be no doubt of the success at Paris. The President has asked me to accompany him on horseback and has sent me a horse.[251]

Indeed later that morning Flahaut accompanied the President through the streets of Paris on horseback, with a party which included Napoleon I's surviving brother the former King Jerome-Napoleon of Westphalia, General Exelmans and the President's dedicated aides, Colonels Fleury and Edgar Ney.

On 2 and 3 December some Parisians took to the boulevards,

hooting the troops, singing the Marseillaise and crying *Vive la République! A bas les prétoriens! Vive la constitution!* About seventy barricades were built; yet again there was fighting on the rue Saint-Denis and a torchlight parade of corpses on the boulevards.[252] In contrast to 1830 and 1848, and to the violent reactions in certain rural areas, however, most Parisians, disillusioned by the Second Republic and the June Days, were indifferent. They felt little enthusiasm for fighting for a republic which had made little, if any, improvement to their living conditions. Above all, this time soldiers, with their *air farouche*, were well led and eager to kill in revenge for Parisians' humiliation of the army in 1830 and 1848. Between 300 and 1,000 civilians were to perish: among them a representative of the people Jean-Baptiste Baudin, who was haranguing troops from a barricade, and unarmed men and women strolling on the boulevards or sitting in the Café Tortoni. In Paris terror and stupefaction reigned.[253]

Léopold Le Hon, from the Cabinet du Ministre de l'Intérieur, to Madame Le Hon, 2 December: Reports from the prefecture are still reassuring. The representatives are hunted down in all directions. The Assembly will be destroyed. There are almost 100 representatives arrested. They leave at 7 o'clock for Ham.
Later the same day: Force is always force and victory will rest assured to us.
Still later: (very confidential) My agents are not enough. The crowds are preparing for battle. *De l'audace, de l'audace et toujours de l'audace.*
Thursday: All is calm now; the rising is tamed. There are a lot of dead on their side. The news from the departments is excellent. Lyon is completely quiet.[254]

Flahaut to Madame de Flahaut, 3 December: Never was secret better kept and plan better executed. Auguste has been heroic.

Magnan (commander of the army in Paris) to Morny, 3 December, 6 p.m.: The barricades of the rue de Rambuteau and the adjacent streets have been captured without striking a blow by a battalion of chasseurs à pied and a battalion of the Republican Guard. I had assembled 5 battalions and 6 cannons at the Pointe Saint-Eustache to attack these barricades face on, 6 battalions and 6 cannons to attack them from the side by the adjacent streets which also had barricades. You see that I like mass movements and know the dangers of small *piquets* [military posts]; one is nowhere when one is everywhere.

Léopold Le Hon to Madame de Flahaut, 4 December: The troubles of yesterday have been quickly and energetically repressed. The Minister of War has published a proclamation declaring that all individuals taken at barricades or with arms in their hands would be immediately shot.

Morny to Madame de Flahaut, 5 December: All is over. We are victorious all along the line and all France approves. How glorious it would be to see society preserved for a long period.[255]

Flahaut to Madame de Flahaut, 5 December: Everything is going on well in Paris and better in the provinces where the enthusiasm is immense and most of the people cry *Vive Napoléon* . . . The soldiers are admirable . . . the *blouses* [workers] this morning were replacing the *pavés* and the women applauding the soldiers as they passed. Auguste is heroic and I wish all his colleagues were like him.[256]

On 11 January Flahaut sent a letter to Queen Marie Amélie, still living at Claremont in England. The former Premier Ecuyer of her beloved eldest son, her husband's ambassador to Austria, was temporarily acting as what Normanby called 'the real Agent for the Foreign Policy of the Elysée'.[257] He claimed to have been motivated in his support of the Bonapartist coup by patriotism, necessity and hatred of the authors of the revolution of 1848.

I can say with a perfect security of conscience that as in 1830 my determination has been motivated by love of my country, the desire to save it from the immense danger which threatened it and that my conduct has been directed by no sentiment of ambition or personal interest. I believe that I have done nothing contrary to the sentiments which I have vowed to Your Majesty.[258]

This letter drew down on Flahaut the odium of the Orleanists, as had the similar letters of self-justification, including offers of financial compensation, written by Marie Amélie herself to the Dauphine and the Duchesse de Berri during their journey from Rambouillet to Cherbourg in August 1830. Like Marie Amélie also, Flahaut received no reply.[259]

In their eagerness for victory, and determination not to fail like Marmont in 1830 or Bugeaud in 1848, Morny and the army had over-reacted. Among the 220 *représentants du peuple* arrested and briefly imprisoned were some of the great names of France: the Ducs de Broglie and de Montebello, Thiers (taken, terrified, straight from his bed), Molé, Tocqueville, Eugène Sue, Cavaignac, Falloux, Berryer, Barrot and Changarnier. In all France 26,000 people were arrested, 9,530 deported to Algeria, 2,804 interned, 1,545 sent into exile. Among the eighty-eight deputies expelled from French territory were Thiers, Victor Hugo, Rémusat, Emile de Girardin. The most popular writer in

Paris, Eugène Sue, would die six years later in exile in Savoy. Victor Hugo lived on Guernsey until the fall of Louis-Napoleon.[260]

The coup permanently alienated many members of the political élite. The army, so Tocqueville said, had seized France, bound and gagged her, and laid her at the feet of her ruler.[261] Orleanists and legitimists, loyal to the parliamentary system practised since 1814, sounded like Jacobins in their *atroces propos* against the President.[262] So often regarded as synonyms of frivolity, the salons remained loyal to the Chambers whose debates they had done so much to animate; they were the last strongholds of free speech and criticism in Paris (clubs, even the Cercle de l'Union, had notices on their walls forbidding political discussion), and were for that reason attacked in government newspapers. Persigny denounced their influence in the salon of Princess Lieven herself. As late as 1862, Mérimée was writing that 'the salons are as hostile as can be.' However, under the Second Empire they had been deprived of their political role.[263]

As Charles X and Polignac had found in 1829–30, much of France refused to support the court, if the court defied the constitution. The act of violation of the Assembly was often regretted more than the Assembly itself. Princess Bagration, who was still entertaining in her salon in the rue du Faubourg Saint-Honoré, wearing gauze dresses, although she now resembled an Egyptian mummy, called the President 'an executioner'.[264] The Maréchale de Lobau, a former Dame d'Honneur of the Duchesse d'Orléans, screamed from her window on the Place du Palais-Bourbon, when she saw troops arresting deputies: *C'est une infamie! C'est une horreur!* She told Flahaut that she felt humiliated to see France sunk so low. If the President had not crushed the socialists, he replied, they would have burnt her house down.[265] The British ambassador Lord Normanby was also disgusted by the President's violation of his oaths to maintain the constitution, the destruction of parliamentary government and the loss of life. 'My humanity', he wrote, 'is not local in its Character and what happens at Paris I judge the same as if it was at Perth or at Naples.'[266] Palmerston, on the other hand, having immediately approved the coup without consulting the Cabinet or the Queen, was obliged to resign.

Princess Lieven had returned to Paris in September 1849 and, while continuing her intimacy with Guizot, had become *une fervente elyséenne*, heart and soul for the President. During the coup, her salon had resembled a military headquarters: Guizot and the Austrian ambassador came there to learn or impart the latest news.[267] She herself believed that the end justified the means and that the President had saved society from imminent shipwreck.[268] After the crisis, however, opinions were so divided that the Princess sometimes found herself alone in the evening; her guests did not want to risk finding themselves in the same room as their political enemies.[269]

Flahaut had once been considered one of the most agreeable men in Paris. After the coup he found, for the first time, that his arrival would often drive people out of a salon, since anti-Bonapartist guests preferred to leave. Partly to help look after his dying daughter Louisa, he sold his *hôtel* on the Champs Elysées and moved to England. There he continued to be used as an intermediary between the French and British governments, explaining the policy of one to the other, assuring the French government of British goodwill, the British government that Louis-Napoleon had no desire for war or expansion.[270] In 1860–2 he served as French ambassador to Britain; when he came across the Orléans princes in London, he pretended not to see them.[271]

If the salons were hostile, many Parisians were overjoyed by the end of 'the reign of chatterers' and journalists.[272] The Bourse approved: after the coup of December 1851, 3 per cent government stock had risen from 56 to 64 francs.[273] In effect France had reverted to the style of military monarchy practised by Napoleon I, which Charles X had hoped to reimpose in 1830 and which was being reimposed by force in most of Europe at the same time. Prince Schwarzenberg, who had witnessed the July revolution in Paris, was now principal minister of Austria, leading his government's return to autocracy with the support of a loyal army. As he had told Joinville, 'you can do anything with bayonets except sit on them.'[274] Paris switched roles, from beacon of revolution to model of authoritarianism. Schwarzenberg was inspired by the coup of 2 December in Paris to suspend the constitution in Austria on 31 December 1851.

The Empire swiftly appeared as the end of the story, as Heine had prophesied. On 20 December 1851, voted under strong government pressure, a plebiscite approved the President's coup by 72 per cent of those inscribed on electoral lists: 7,471,431 votes against 641,351. (Paris remained more republican than the rest of France with 133,000 voting for the plebiscite, compared with 80,000 against.) The people had spoken. George Sand said that it would have voted for Napoleon *envers et contre tout*, even without government pressure and fear of socialism.[275] The remonarchisation of Paris continued. In January 1852 the words *Liberté, Egalité, Fraternité* were removed from the façades of public buildings.[276] On 29 March 1852 the first session of the new subservient Senate and Corps Législatif was opened by the Prince President – not in the Palais Bourbon but in the Salle des Maréchaux of the Tuileries.[277] On 10 April, after a Sunday review at the Tuileries at which soldiers had greeted the President with cries of *Vive Napoléon*, Vielcastel wrote: 'everything is being prepared for the Empire.'[278]

On 16 October 1852, after a triumphant provincial tour, the Prince President received an even more triumphant welcome back to Paris, from the authorities and the people alike. Banners proclaimed *Vive Napoléon III!* On 7 November, in the Galerie d'Apollon at Saint-Cloud, the same room where his uncle had received a similar deputation in 1804, the Prince President received a deputation from the Senate re-establishing the dignity of Emperor in his person. On 21 November the decision was ratified by a plebiscite giving 7,824,189 yes votes to 253,000 noes, with two million abstentions.[279] On 1 December a deputation from the Corps Législatif saluted the new Emperor at Saint-Cloud: 'Sire, take from the hand of France this glorious crown which it offers you. No royal forehead will ever have worn a more legitimate or more popular crown.'

The next day – anniversary of his coup and the Battle of Austerlitz – the new Emperor made a state entry into Paris, preceded by the carriage of the Duke and Duchess of Hamilton (she was one of his Beauharnais cousins). His route, from the Arc de Triomphe, down the Champs Elysées, lined with troops, to the Tuileries palace, excluded the radical centre and east of the city. His reception, especially by soldiers, was 'really enthusiastic'. In a deliberate monarchical retort to the Hôtel de Ville's role in the revolutions of 1830 and 1848, Napoleon III was proclaimed Emperor in front of the building by the Prefect of the Seine. The façade was draped with tricolours, eagles, the imperial coat of arms, a banner inscribed *VIVE L'EMPEREUR*, the initials LN and – *ultima ratio imperatoris* – a banner inscribed with the magic number of affirmative votes in the plebiscite: 7,824,189.[280] By the will of the people, and the bullets of the army, Paris was again the capital of an empire.

Conclusion

Birth of an Empire

Versailles, 18 January 1871

NAPOLEON III TRANSFORMED the face of Paris. One wall of his study in the Tuileries was dominated by a map of the city, on which, in his own hands, he drew plans for new streets. From 1852 the Boulevards Malesherbes, de Sébastopol, de Magenta, Richard-Lenoir, Saint-Germain, the rues des Ecoles and de Rennes and the Avenue de l'Opéra, were driven through the medieval heart of Paris, which had been strangled by its narrow streets.[1] In accordance with an older plan, the rue de Rivoli was extended east to the rue Saint-Antoine.

For twenty years Paris was a city of scaffolding and construction sites, traversed by bands of demolition men, stonemasons and carpenters. Some districts changed overnight. Between 1852 and 1869, 20,000 houses (including many historic *hôtels* and churches) were demolished, and 43,000 new ones constructed. The filthy old quarters around the Hôtel de Ville and the Halles disappeared. On the Ile de la Cité, one of the worst slums in Paris, a centre of crime and debauch described in Sue's *Les Mystères de Paris* was replaced by law courts, hospitals and government buildings. Modern aqueducts, canals, drains and reservoirs, as well as schools, hospitals and barracks, were built. By 1857 the second wing linking the Louvre and the Tuileries, along the rue de Rivoli, balancing the wing built 230 years earlier along the Seine, had been finished. A special Salle des Etats was built in the new wing, in which the Emperor could open the annual legislative session of the two Chambers.[2]

In addition the city was extended in the west. The Bois de Boulogne was remodelled and enlarged, partly on the lines of Hyde Park. In 1860

423

the outlying suburbs were annexed, doubling the size of the city, although, in a strange survival of the *ancien régime*, the *octroi* at the *barrières* continued until 1943. Napoleon III was responsible for the largest, and quickest, peacetime transformation of a capital in the history of Europe. In its execution the Emperor was seconded by the Prefect of the Seine Baron Haussmann. This 'Attila of expropriation', who had the right to communicate directly with the Emperor, saw Paris as the metropolis of the civilised world.[3]

Formerly a semi-medieval city, Paris had become one of the most modern in Europe. The eclectic neoclassical architecture and decoration of the large new grey-brown buildings was, and is, so uniform that it is often difficult to tell one district or street from another. In 1870 Théophile Gautier called the Paris of before 1848 as remote from the present as Pompeii:

> sometimes we ask ourselves, looking at these wide streets, these grand boulevards, these vast squares, these interminable lines of monumental houses, these splendid districts which have replaced the fields of market gardens, if it really is the city where we passed our childhood.[4]

One motive for this urban revolution was to facilitate traffic; the new streets, unlike the old, were devoted to the circulation of vehicles rather than the interaction of people.[5] Other motives were to bring people back to the centre of the city by giving them hygiene, air and light; and to reinforce government control. Down the broad new streets of Paris troops could march without difficulty, and without fear of showers of projectiles from attic windows. Providing clear lines of fire for artillery, the streets often ran directly from barracks into such 'citadels of insurrection' as the Faubourg Saint-Antoine.[6] One barracks, the Caserne Napoléon, was situated behind the Hôtel de Ville.[7] Revolutions like those of 1830 and 1848, insurrections like those of 1832, 1834 and 1839, were, it was hoped, henceforth impossible.

Queen Victoria noticed on her state visit in August 1855 that many streets were macadamised, 'to prevent the people taking up the pavement [during revolutions] as hitherto'. She was impressed by the Tuileries and the centre of Paris: 'Everything is so truly regal, so large, so grand, so comprehensive it makes me jealous that our great country and particularly our great metropolis should have nothing of the same kind to show!'[8] She was also impressed by the silence and 'excellent order' at Napoleon III's court, compared to the 'noise, confusion and bustle' of 'the poor King's time', when there was 'no court'.[9]

As President of the Republic, Louis-Napoleon had maintained that his true friends were to be found in cottages, not in gilded salons. But as Emperor he made use of the gilded palaces in and around Paris, creating a lavish imperial household staffed by descendants of the great names of the First Empire: Edgar Ney (one of the founders of the Jockey Club) was Premier Veneur; the Duc de Bassano Grand Chambellan; Duc Cambacérès Grand Maître des Cérémonies. There was an imperial guard, hunt and chapel, and court balls in the winter. More than in any other reign in the nineteenth century, the Tuileries, Saint-Cloud, Fontainebleau and Compiègne became centres of entertainment as well as power. Since Louis-Philippe's theatre inside the palace of Compiègne was no longer big enough for the numbers the Emperor wished to entertain, a second was built beside the palace to accommodate the hundreds of guests invited during the court's autumn visits.[10] The director of the Compiègne theatre, and an actor in some of its performances, was Mérimée, an intimate friend of the Empress Eugénie and her mother and the last French writer to be a professional courtier; he also corrected proofs of the works of Napoleon III and the correspondence of Napoleon I.[11]

Many of the new Paris street names – Sébastopol, Magenta – commemorated Napoleon III's victories. He could never have been reproached with the 'fault' of which Louis-Philippe was accused, of having been 'modest in the name of France', or with forgetting that France was by nature, according to Victor Hugo, *une nation conquérante*.[12] The cry with which Louis-Napoleon had seduced French voters in 1852, *L'Empire c'est la paix*, was a lie. In the pursuit of glory, and a vain attempt to create a new empire under the Archduke Maximilian, Napoleon III sent French troops as far as Mexico. As he intended, his war against Russia in 1854–6 over the future of the Ottoman Empire destroyed one of the foundations of peace in Europe, the friendship between Austria and Russia. Since Austria failed to support Russia in the Balkans, Russia would fail to support Austria in Italy.

Nationalism, the religion preached with such success in Paris since 1830, was the foundation of Napoleon III's policy in Europe. The Second Republic had opposed German and Italian national unity; the Second Empire supported them.[13] Napoleon III wanted to impose a new pattern on the states of Europe as he had on the streets of Paris. In 1859, despite the efforts of Thiers and James de Rothschild, France and Piedmont declared war against Austria in order to expel it from Italy.[14] The war for Italy delighted the people – but dismayed the *cercles* and salons – of Paris. Soldiers left as if for a ball. In the streets Parisians covered them with flowers and kisses, and told them to kill as many Austrians as possible.[15] When Napoleon III himself left for Italy on 10 May, Parisians gave him the ovation of his life. The further he moved from the Tuileries and the nearer to the Faubourg Saint-Antoine, the louder grew the cheers of *Vive l'Empereur! Vive l'Italie!* 'It was a poignant emotion, a *furia* which those who have not witnessed it will never be able to understand,' wrote an eye-witness, one of the Louvre's curators, Horace de Vielcastel. At the end delirious workers unhorsed the Emperor's carriage and pulled it into the Gare de Lyon.[16] The war resulted in a centralised Kingdom of Italy, covering most of the peninsula (although Napoleon III had hoped for an Italian confederation under the Pope), and the French annexation of Savoy and Nice.

Nationalism was, however, bound to work against French interests. First, by substituting the new and powerful states of Germany and Italy for the small German and Italian states that had hitherto bordered France, it diminished both French national security and French diplomatic weight in the European power balance. Second, Germany's rate of population growth (in 1816–1900 its population rose by 250 per cent, compared to France's 45 per cent over the period 1800–1900),[17] as well as its superior levels of education and military organisation, were bound to result in a united Germany replacing France as the leading nation of the continent. In one of his great speeches in the Corps Législatif, on 3 May 1866, in the last weeks before the war for domination of Germany between Austria and Prussia, Thiers proclaimed, with the lucidity of his generation, his fear of a new German Empire, for the sake not only of the smaller states of Germany but also of the equilibrium of Europe. The unification of Italy under Piedmont, of Germany under Prussia, was an 'irreparable misfortune'. Guizot wrote to his old enemy to congratulate him on having saved the honour of political intelligence in France. On 6 May, however, Napoleon III replied in an equally celebrated speech proclaiming, yet again, his detestation of the treaties of 1815.[18] He regarded Prussia as liberal, progressive, enlightened – a better ally for France than Austria.

After the Prussian victory over Austria and Saxony at Sadowa on 3 July 1866, Prussia annexed Hanover and Hesse-Cassel, formed the North German Confederation and signed military treaties with Baden, Württemberg and Bavaria in south Germany. In 1867–9 attempts by Napoleon III to gain France 'compensation' in Belgium, Luxembourg or the Rhineland, for Prussian expansion in Germany, won him nothing but contempt and suspicion. Bismarck refused to cede one German village. In foreign policy, Thiers remarked, not one mistake remained to be made.[19]

Paris's last moment of imperial glory occurred during the universal exhibition of 1867. Napoleon III welcomed the Emperor of Russia (whom some Parisians greeted with cries of *Vive la Pologne! A bas les Cosaques!*), the Emperor of Austria, the King of Prussia (who asked for a map of the Emperor's new boulevards in Paris, for use in Berlin) and the Ottoman Sultan, among other sovereigns. Years later the eldest daughter of Queen Victoria, who had visited Paris as Prussian Crown Princess, remembered that the Empress Eugénie had been 'the perfection of a hostess . . . No one ever came up to that.' However, the magnificence of their reception in Paris could not hide the fact that the French Empire was no longer, as it had been in 1856–66, the arbiter of Europe. Numerous demonstrations and election results showed that, dismayed by the rise of Prussia, emboldened by the liberalisation of the regime, and embittered by memories of the coup of 2 December 1851, Parisians themselves were turning against the Empire. When the Emperor took an afternoon drive on the boulevards, he received no signs of sympathy, respect or even curiosity, from passers-by.[20] Pessimistic and unpopular, he no longer had the authority to impose on France the large, well-equipped conscript army which he knew it needed.[21]

Napoleon III was both creator and destroyer of the new imperial Paris. Since his urban revolution, Paris had regarded itself, more than ever, as the capital of the world: indeed the number of foreigners living there had reached a peak of 120,000.[22] In reality, as in 1840, this role was overshadowed by its role as capital of France. The clash between France and the North German Confederation came over a question of pride. France had secured a diplomatic triumph in obtaining the renunciation, by a cousin of the King of Prussia, Prince Leopold of Hohenzollern, of his candidature to the throne of Spain. The danger of Prussian influence in Madrid was avoided. However, much of France felt humiliated by what the Foreign Minister the Duc de Gramont, as futile and thoughtless in 1870 as his great-uncle Jules de Polignac in 1830, called the Prussian government's 'haughtiness and discourtesy' in refusing a formal guarantee that the prince would never renew his candidature.[23]

In 1840 Louis-Philippe had refused to start a war, so he told the British ambassador Lord Granville, because he refused 'to be intimidated or deterred from doing what he thought to be His duty by the abuse of the Press or by public clamour'.[24] In 1870 Napoleon III was pushed into war by Paris journalism and Paris opinion, as well as by the desire of the Empress and himself for a dynastic triumph (although the regime had just been strengthened by a massive vote of confidence in a plebiscite over its liberal reforms). The rest of France was relatively pacific; however, in July 1870 as in October 1840, the 'capital of the world' was swept by a delirium of nationalism. *La Liberté*, edited by Emile de Girardin, advocated a return to the 'natural frontiers' and the annexation of all territory on the left bank of the Rhine. The boulevards echoed with cries of *A bas Bismarck! Au Rhin! A Berlin!* The war declared by Napoleon III against Prussia and the other German states on 17 July was more popular, Mérimée wrote, even with the bourgeoisie, than all Napoleon III's previous wars.[25] Gautier witnessed in Paris 'a delirious enthusiasm, a universal joy . . . Everyone wants to eat the Prussians. The old rancour of 1814 is not extinguished.' Napoleon III's cousin the Duchesse de Mouchy led the audience at the opera, after a performance of *La Muette de Portici*, in singing the Marseillaise. Anyone advocating peace would have been murdered on the spot. Thiers, who had warned the Chamber of the dangers of war, suffered hostile demonstrations outside his house on the Place Saint-Georges.[26]

The Minister of War is said to have remarked that the army was ready down to the last gaiter-button.[27] However the war was soon lost: the German armies were better educated and better led, by their princely and noble officers, than the French army by an officer corps 92 per cent non-noble. Moreover German armies were larger, and more easily mobilised.[28] Flahaut died in the Hôtel de Salm, where he had resided since 1864 as Grand Chancelier de la Légion d'Honneur, on 1 September 1870, just before the fall of the Second Empire, and the third debacle provoked by the policies of the Emperors he had served so well. On 2 September, after his defeat at Sedan, Napoleon III surrendered his sword and person to Wilhelm I. As Napoleon I had learnt in 1814 and 1815, defeat in battle meant deposition in Paris. In 1851 the power base of his regime, in 1870 the French army was not prepared to defend a defeated Emperor. On 4 September, after crowds had invaded the Palais Bourbon shouting *Déchéance! A bas l'Empire! Vive la République!*, the Republic was proclaimed at the traditional site, the Hôtel de Ville. Like Louis-Philippe and Marie Amélie before her, the Empress Eugénie fled from the Tuileries to exile in England. Foreign Parisians, in this case the Austrian and Sardinian ambassadors and an American dentist Dr Evans, were as critical in helping her escape, as others had been in financing her husband's *coup d'état* nineteen years earlier.[29]

The government of the Republic fought on. From October 1870 to March 1871, despite pleas from Victor Hugo to spare 'the city of cities . . . the city of nations', Paris was besieged by German armies. Parisians suffered near famine – dogs, cats, finally rats and the elephant at the zoo, were eaten in the capital of cooking. The palace of Saint-Cloud, a symbol of French monarchies in the nineteenth century (the Empire had been proclaimed there in 1804 and 1852, Napoleon I married Marie Louise there in 1810, Charles X and Louis-Napoleon planned their coups there in 1830 and 1851), caught fire on 13 October and burnt down: whether French or German bombs were responsible is uncertain.[30]

The Franco-Prussian war helped kill the cosmopolitan Europe of which Paris had been capital. To make your life's work the promotion of an 'entente cordiale between France and Germany',[31] as Heine had boasted in his will, was henceforth impossible. Heine's worst fears about the brutal drama being prepared in Germany would be fulfilled: Franco-German enmity would help cause two more wars in Europe. German Parisians such as the painter Henri Lehmann and Madame d'Agoult (whose mother was a Bethmann of Frankfurt) renounced contacts with Germany: the former, naturalised French in 1847, refused after 1871 to write any letters in German except to his old mother.[32] The world of nationalist Paris-haters like Cavour and Wagner (who in 1870 hoped that Paris would be burnt down) had replaced that of European Parisians like Pozzo and Rossini. Pozzo had believed that 'the union of Europe is a truth which is beginning to establish here [in Paris] all its authority.' The leading statesman of Europe was now Bismarck, who called Europe a fiction.[33] Mérimée had once lamented the follies committed in the name of nationality.[34] In September 1870, ten days before he died, he signalled the surrender to nationality:

> all my life I have tried to be free of prejudices, to be a citizen of the world before being French, but all these philosophical covers serve nothing. I bleed today from the wounds of these imbecile Frenchmen, I weep for their humiliations and however unpleasant and absurd they are, I still love them.[35]

A decisive step in the nationalisation of Europe took place in the palace of Versailles. During the siege of Paris, from 5 October 1870 until 7 March 1871, Versailles acquired a new role, as headquarters of the King of Prussia and his allies. Prussian officers enjoyed their new billet, although some thought the gardens at Potsdam 'far superior to those at Versailles'.[36] The palace dedicated by Louis-Philippe *à toutes les gloires de la France* became a German hospital. The Iron Cross was distributed in the *cour d'honneur*. Lutheran hymns were sung in the chapel of Louis XIV.[37] One of the troops' favourite tunes was the *Wacht am Rhein*, first heard during the war crisis of 1840 – although some German poets were beginning to fear that the enemy was not on the Rhine but on the Spree.[38] The fever of war and the exaltation of victory consolidated German unity. One militaristic empire bred another: the Hohenzollern empire in Germany was in part the product of the Bonaparte empire in France.[39]

On 18 January 1871, anniversary of the proclamation of the Elector of Brandenburg as King of Prussia in 1701, came the fulfilment of what his great-great-great-great-grandson the Crown Prince of Prussia called 'the long cherished hopes of our ancestors, the dreams of German poets'.[40] The proclamation of *German* unity in a *French* palace at once reflected, and ended, the hegemony of Paris in Europe. Proof that military monarchy, rather than socialism or liberalism, had won the battle for the nineteenth century, the proclamation was a military and royal, rather than a constitutional and popular, ceremony. The palace courtyards and Louis XIV's state apartments on the first floor (temporarily cleared of hospital beds) were full of German soldiers 'all spurred, sabred, strapped and polished in metal and leather'.[41] Through lanes of soldiers arrived the German princes serving in the war against France: the Crown Princes of Prussia and Saxony, the Grand Dukes of Baden, Weimar, Oldenburg, the Dukes of Saxe-Coburg, Saxe-Meiningen and Saxe-Altenburg, three Bavarian and two Prussian princes, generals, courtiers, officers. Soon the entire Galerie des Glaces was full, and officers spilled out into the Salon de la Paix. Finally, at midday, to a roll of drums, while soldiers sang regimental hymns, the conqueror stalked into the Galerie des Glaces: Wilhelm I King of Prussia, wearing the uniform of his First Guards Regiment. As a young prince of sixteen he had had the 'indescribable joy' of entering Paris in the triumphant allied procession of 31 March 1814.[42] That had been the *fête de l'Europe*. This was the baptism of Germany.

Surrounded by regimental flags and German princes, Wilhelm I placed himself below the inscription in honour of Louis XIV, painted on the ceiling by Lebrun, *le roy gouverne par lui-même*. A black-robed Lutheran priest preached on the text 'God hath done wonders in this land and we have done them for him'.[43] After prayers and hymns, the King was proclaimed German Emperor. He thanked the German princes for their part in the war and read a short address. Bismarck, wearing the uniform of a reserve Cuirassier although he had never served in the Prussian army, read an address to the German people. Then, in the words of the Crown Prince of Prussia, writing in his diary:

> The Grand Duke of Baden came forward with the unaffected quiet dignity that is so peculiarly his, and with uplifted right hand cried in a loud voice: 'Long live his Imperial Majesty Emperor Wilhelm!' A thundering hurrah at least six times repeated, shook the room, while the flags and standards waved above the head of the new Emperor of Germany and *Heil dir im Siegerkranz* rang out. The moment was extraordinarily affecting, indeed overwhelming and in every way wonderfully fine.

The princes filed past to offer their congratulations. The Crown Prince later wrote: 'I have witnessed coronations, oaths of allegiance and many unusual ceremonies but I have known none either so august or so well contrived and so incomparable in external significance . . . Germany had her Emperor again!' In the eyes of the Goncourt brothers the ceremony was the end of the greatness of France.[44] It was also, for the next eighty years, the end of Europe.

If the proclamation of the German Empire was the end of one world, the war against the Paris Commune was the end of another. Paris capitulated to German forces on 27 January 1871. A right-wing and monarchist National Assembly, which radicals considered the shame of France, was elected in February 1871. Owing to the war and the siege of Paris it sat in Versailles. The head of the executive power, the man chosen to negotiate peace, was the indestructible Adolphe Thiers. On 28 February the Assembly ratified the treaty he had negotiated: the new German Empire realised the dreams of 1815 and obtained Alsace and part of Lorraine. It also secured a massive indemnity and, on 1 March, the joy of a victory parade down the Champs Elysées. In 1871, however, in contrast to 1814–15, foreign leaders and armies remained spectators of, rather than participants in, French politics.

Wounded patriotism, as well as desire for a better life – what one revolutionary called the opportunity to enjoy the shining new cafés and operas from which their poverty debarred them – turned many Parisians into enemies of the National Assembly and the government. Such was the magnetism of the city that, unlike the rest of Europe, there was also a desire for municipal autonomy – even, among some Parisians, for semi-independence, with Paris controlling its own destiny and, in order to increase the city's freedom, the removal of the central government to another city. Violent incidents took place in Paris. On 18 March Thiers and the government withdrew to Versailles. On 28 March a new radical Commune installed itself in the Hôtel de Ville.[45] One of its chief supports was the National Guard, whose numbers had been raised to 300,000 armed men.[46]

L'année terrible, 1871, saw the long-awaited denouement between revolutionary Paris and the 'forces of order'. From Versailles in 1871 Thiers was able to do what he had failed to do in 1848: crush the capital from a base in the Ile de France.[47] Fighting between the Paris Commune and the rest of France lasted from 11 April to 21 May. It affected the buildings as well as the inhabitants of the city. On 16 May the column of the Grande Armée on the Place Vendôme was demolished as a symbol of militarism and imperialism, falling with a crash to the sound of the Marseillaise and cries of *Vive la Commune!* Only the end of fighting prevented the Chapelle Expiatoire of Louis XVI suffering a similar fate.[48]

Finally on 21 May the forces of order – *les Versaillais* – entered Paris, easily bypassing the few barricades erected by the *communards*. Most of the population remained spectators or supporters of the *Versaillais*. In a week known as *la semaine sanglante*, symbols of nineteenth-century French monarchy like the Tuileries palace, the Palais de Justice and the Palais Royal were deliberately set alight on the orders of the Commune. Clouds of smoke hung above the burning city. Paris seemed like a vision of hell. On both sides men and women turned into savages.[49]

The hatred of Paris which had been festering since 1830, or earlier, exploded in an orgy of killing. It was a prolonged and deliberate settling of accounts for Paris's years of riot, revolution and domination. As *communards* were hunted down, the streets were covered in blood and rubble. On 24 May the Archbishop of Paris was shot on the orders of the Commune – the second Archbishop of Paris to die in civil fighting that century.[50] Thiers abandoned Parisians to the mercy of the generals. In the Jardin du Luxembourg, and the cemetery of Père Lachaise, prisoners were shot systematically and without quarter. Up to 25,000 died. There was yet another wave of emigration from Paris to England.[51] On 25 August 1871 the Paris National Guard was abolished. Freed from the constraints of monarchy, the conservative Republic had accomplished what other nineteenth-century French regimes had been unable to achieve: the extinction of Paris as a political force. The Franco-Prussian war had ended the hegemony of Paris in Europe: the war against the Commune ended the hegemony of Paris in France.

Appendix I

The Royal Family of France

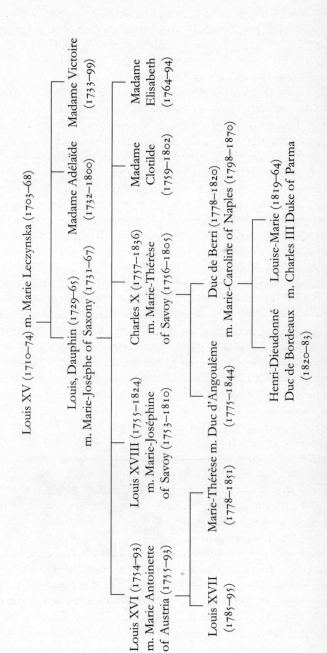

Louis XV (1710–74) m. Marie Leczynska (1703–68)

Louis, Dauphin (1729–65)
m. Marie-Josèphe of Saxony (1731–67)

Madame Adélaïde (1732–1800)

Madame Victoire (1733–99)

Madame Clotilde (1759–1802)

Madame Elisabeth (1764–94)

Louis XVI (1754–93)
m. Marie Antoinette of Austria (1755–93)

Louis XVIII (1755–1824)
m. Marie-Joséphine of Savoy (1753–1810)

Charles X (1757–1836)
m. Marie-Thérèse of Savoy (1756–1805)

Louis XVII (1785–95)

Marie-Thérèse m. Duc d'Angoulême (1778–1851)   (1775–1844)

Duc de Berri (1778–1820)
m. Marie-Caroline of Naples (1798–1870)

Henri-Dieudonné Duc de Bordeaux (1820–83)

Louise-Marie (1819–64)
m. Charles III Duke of Parma

Appendix II

The Three Cousins

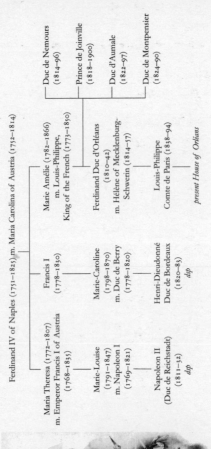

Ferdinand IV of Naples (1751–1825) m. Maria Carolina of Austria (1752–1814)

Maria Theresa (1772–1807)
m. Emperor Francis I of Austria
(1768–1835)

Francis I
(1778–1830)

Marie Amélie (1782–1866)
m. Louis-Philippe,
King of the French (1773–1850)

Marie-Louise
(1791–1847)
m. Napoleon I
(1769–1821)

Marie-Caroline
(1798–1870)
m. Duc de Berry
(1778–1820)

Ferdinand Duc d'Orléans
(1810–42)
m. Hélène of Mecklenburg-
Schwerin (1814–57)

Duc de Nemours
(1814–96)

Prince de Joinville
(1818–1900)

Duc d'Aumale
(1822–97)

Duc de Montpensier
(1824–90)

Napoleon II
(Duc de Reichstadt)
(1811–32)
dsp

Henri-Dieudonné
Duc de Bordeaux
(1820–83)
dsp

Louis-Philippe
Comte de Paris (1838–94)

present House of Orléans

Les Trois Cousins (c. 1831). The Ducs de Reichstadt (left), d'Orléans (top) and de Bordeaux (right) were heirs of the three dynasties competing for the French throne, the Bonapartes, the Orléans and the Bourbons respectively. Through their mothers – daughters or granddaughters of Ferdinand IV of Naples – all three princes were first or second cousins

Appendix III

Foreign Writers, Painters and Musicians Resident in Paris

Alexander von Humboldt 1806–27
Jacques-Ignace Hittorff 1811–d. 25 March 1867
Alessandro Manzoni 1819–20
Thomas Moore 1820–2
Frances Trollope 1823, 1827, 1835, 1839–40
Franz Liszt 1823–39 intermittently
Gioachino Rossini 1824–36, 1855–d. 13 November 1868*
Jakob Meyerbeer 1825–42 intermittently; d. Paris, 2 May 1864
J. Fenimore Cooper 1826–8
Frédéric Chopin 1831–d. 17 October 1849*
Henri Lehmann 1831–d. 30 March 1882 (French nationality 1847)
Heinrich Heine 19 May 1831–d. 17 February 1856
Felix Mendelssohn-Bartholdy November 1831–April 1832
Jacques Offenbach 1833–d. 5 October 1880 (French nationality 1860)
Vincenzo Bellini August 1833–d. 23 September 1835*
William Makepeace Thackeray 1834–9
Gaetano Donizetti 1835–46 intermittently
Richard Wagner 17 September 1839–7 April 1842
Adam Mickiewicz 1840–8
Karl Marx October 1843–2 February 1845
Mikhail Bakunin 1844–7
Alexander Herzen March–October 1847

---

* = buried in the cemetery of Père Lachaise

Charles Dickens 1847–8
Giuseppe Verdi July 1847–July 1849, October 1853–November 1855,
  June 1866–March 1867

Appendix IV

Franco-British and Franco-Irish Marriages

Comte d'Arblay m. Fanny Burney 31 July 1793

Hyacinthe Gabrielle Roland m. Lord Mornington (later Marquess Wellesley) 29 November 1794

Charlotte Charpentier m. Walter Scott 24 December 1797

Duc de Castries m. Eliza McCoghlan 1803

Corisande de Gramont m. Lord Ossulston 28 July 1806

Comte de Montalembert m. Elisa Rose Forbes 25 May 1809

Vicomte de Rohan-Chabot m. Lady Isabella Fitzgerald 1 June 1809

Louis-Jacques Daguerre m. Georgina Arrowsmith 10 November 1810

Comte Jules de Polignac m. Barbara Campbell 6 July 1816

Comte de Flahaut m. the Honourable Margaret Mercer Nairne 20 June 1817

Baron de Feuchères m. Sophie Dawes 6 August 1818

Comte Alphonse de Lamartine m. Eliza Birch 6 June 1820

Marquis de Chévigné m. Lady Frances Seymour Conway 1 February 1822

Duc de Coigny m. Miss Dalrymple Hamilton, 15 June 1822

Prince Jules de Polignac m. Marquise de Choiseul, née Marie Charlotte Parkyns daughter of Lord Rancliffe 8 June 1824

Comte Alfred de Vigny m. Lydia Bunbury 8 February 1825

Frédéric de Chabannes-La Palice m. Mathilde Dawes 16 August 1827

Comte Alfred d'Orsay m. Lady Harriet Gardiner 1 December 1827

Duc de Montebello m. Eleanor Marie Jenkinson 10 July 1830

Comte Walewski m. Lady Caroline Montagu 1 December 1831

Marie de Dalberg m. Sir Ferdinand Richard Acton 6 June 1832

Hortense Claire de Bassano m. Francis Baring, MP January 1833
Hector Berlioz m. Harriet Smithson 9 October 1833
Mathilde Rapp m. Adrian James Hope January 1835
Comte de Tocqueville m. Mary Motteley 26 October 1836
Emily de Flahaut m. Lord Shelburne 8 November 1843
Angélique Léontine Sabine de Noailles m. Lionel Widdrington Standish
    10 October 1846
John Bowes* m. Benoite Josephine Chevallier 23 August 1852
Maréchal Canrobert m. Flora Macdonald 20 January 1863

---

* Founder of the Bowes Museum, Durham.

Notes

1 Death of an Empire: Europe takes Paris *March–June 1814*

1. T. R. Underwood, *A Narrative of Memorable Events in Paris, preceding the capitulation, and during the occupancy of that city by the Allied Armies in 1814* (1828), 73; Madame de Marigny, *Journal inédit* (1907), 52 (31 March 1814).

2. Revd John Chetwode Eustace, *A Letter from Paris, to George Petre Esq.* (1814), 48; Cecil Gould, *Trophy of Conquest* (1967), 35.

3. *Marianne et Germania 1789–1889. Un siècle de passions franco-allemandes* (Petit Palais, 1997), 152, 160.

4. Jean Cassaigneau et Jean Rilliet, *Marc-Auguste Pictet ou le rendez-vous de l'Europe universelle* (Geneva, 1995), 431 (letter of Charles Pictet to his brother, 28 January 1814).

5. Madame Reinhard, *Lettres . . . à sa Mère* (1901), 392, 396 (letters of 22, 27 March 1814); Marigny, 48 (28 March 1814); Underwood, 48 (29 March 1814).

6. Underwood, 24, 37–8 (entry for 23 March 1814).

7. G. Lacour-Gayet, *Talleyrand* (4 vols, 1928–34), II, 349; Underwood, 129 (1 April 1814); Marigny, 41, 43 (17, 20 March 1814).

8. Underwood, 53 (29 March 1814); Reinhard, 394 (letter of 30 March 1814); cf. Mgr de Pradt, *Récit historique sur la Restauration de la royauté en France le 31 mars 1814* (1816), 33.

9. P. Mansel, *Louis XVIII* (1981), 161.

10. Archives Nationales, Paris (hereafter AN) F7 3783 (police report of 7 November 1814).

11. Julien Antoine Rodriguez, *Relation historique de ce qui s'est passé à Paris, à la mémorable époque de la déchéance de Napoléon Buonaparte* (1814), 90–1; *Talleyrand intime d'après sa correspondance avec la duchesse de Courlande* (1894), 189 (letter of 27 March).

12. Maréchal de Castellane, *Journal* (5 vols, 1896–7), I, 246 (24 January 1814); Louis Girard, *La Garde nationale 1814–1871* (1964), 14; Jean Tulard, *Paris et son administration (1800–1830)* (1976), 358 (Pasquier to Minister of Interior, 16 March 1814).

13. John Scott, *Paris Revisited in 1815, by Way of Brussels* (2nd ed., 1816), 289; André Rostopchine, *Matériaux en grande partie inédits pour la biographie future du comte Théodore Rostopchine* (Brussels, 1871), 358 (letter of 1817); Lady Morgan, *France in 1829–30* (2 vols, 1830), II, 274; cf. Balzac, *Illusions perdues* (Booking International, 1993), 144.

Notes

14. W. D. Fellowes, *Paris during the interesting month of July 1815* (1815), 21 (11 July 1815).

15. Underwood, 49–50 (29 March 1814); Stendhal, *Oeuvres intimes* (1955), 1409 (*Journal*, 29 March 1814).

16. Lt Francis Hall, *Travels in France in 1818* (1819), 61; General Cavalié Mercer, *Journal of the Waterloo Campaign* (2 vols, 1870), II, 263 (9 August 1815); Alfred Fierro, *Histoire et Dictionnaire de Paris* (1996), 276, 705.

17. Edward Stanley, *Before and After Waterloo* (1907), 118 (8 July 1814); Pierre Saint-Marc, *Le Maréchal Marmont duc de Raguse* (1957), 137.

18. *L'Attaque de Paris par les troupes alliées le 18[30] mars 1814* (1814) (an official Russian campaign journal), 1, 5, 8.

19. Mercer, II, 200; Hermann Granier (ed.), *Hohenzollernbriefe aus den Freiheitskriegen 1813–1815* (Leipzig, 1913), 228 (Prince Wilhelm to Princess Charlotte of Prussia, 30 March 1814); A. Mikhailofsky-Danilefsky, *History of the Campaign in France in the Year 1814* (1839), 371; P.-F.-F.-J. Giraud, *Campagne de Paris, en 1814, précédée d'un coup d'oeil sur celle de 1813* (3rd ed., 1814), 86, 91.

20. Chateaubriand, *Mémoires d'outre-tombe* (3 vols, 1951), II, 205; Lucien Pérey, *Histoire d'une grande dame. La comtesse Hélène Potocka* (n.d.), 432 (Countess to Count Vincent Potocki, 4 April 1814).

21. Louis Chevalier, *Classes laborieuses et classes dangereuses à Paris pendant la première moitié du dix-neuvième siècle* (1984 ed.), 273.

22. Chevalier, 274n–275n.

23. Underwood, 90 (30 March 1814).

24. Lacour-Gayet, II, 359–60.

25. A. Smirnov et al., *Les Russes découvrent la France au XVIIIe et au XIXe siècle* (Moscow, 1990), 114, 119–20, 123–5 (account of Michael Orlov); Saint-Marc, 147, 151; Maréchal Marmont, *Mémoires* (9 vols, 1857), VI, 249–50; Mikhailofsky-Danilefsky, 378.

26. Comte de Caulaincourt, *Mémoires* (3 vols, 1933), 56–7, 60; Comte Belliard, *Mémoires* (3 vols, 1842), I, 173.

27. Marquis de Noailles, *Le Comte Molé 1781–1855. Sa vie, ses mémoires* (hereafter *Molé*) (6 vols, 1922–30), II, 94–9; Marquise de Montcalm, *Mon journal pendant le premier ministère de mon frère* (1934), 106 (23 October 1815).

28. Archives Rohan-Chabot, unpublished memoirs of Comte de Chabrol, Prefect of the Seine (hereafter Chabrol), I f10v0.

29. Lacour-Gayet, II, 366; Chateaubriand, *Mémoires d'outre-tombe*, II, 209.

30. Reinhard, 395 (letter of 1 April 1814); Smirnov, 134–5 (memoirs of Ivan Jirkevich); *Feuilles d'histoire* (1908) 166 (letter of Bulgakov, 19/31 March 1814); Underwood, 105–6 (31 March 1814).

31. Giraud, 94–5; Janet Hartley, *Alexander I* (1994), 135; Rodriguez, 100–1 (proclamation of Marshal Prince Schwarzenberg, 31 March 1814).

32. Comte de Sémallé, *Souvenirs* (1898), 165.

33. Smirnov, 134 (memoir of Ivan Jirkevich); Granier, 231–2 (Prince Wilhelm to Princess Charlotte of Prussia, 6 April 1814).

34. Mikhailofksy-Danilefsky, 385–6; Général de Langeron, *Mémoires* (1902), 478.

35. *Feuilles d'histoire*, 361 (letter of Bulgakov, 19/31 March 1814); Général de Langeron, 478; Baron de Löwenstern, *Mémoires* (2 vols, 1903), II, 373, 381; cf., for similar sentiments, Granier, 237 (Prince Wilhelm to Princess Charlotte of Prussia, 11 April 1814).

36. Caulaincourt, III, 91n (account of General Fabvier); Général de Langeron, 478; Löwenstern, II, 388.

37. Underwood, 105 (31 March 1814); Viscount Castlereagh, *Correspondence, Despatches and*

other papers (12 vols, 1848–53), IX, 419–20 (Charles Stewart to Lord Castlereagh, 1 April 1814); cf. Pradt, 60.

38. Caulaincourt, III, 88, 102n (Caulaincourt to Napoleon, 31 March 1814); ibid., 90n–91n (account by General Fabvier).

39. William Roots, *Paris in 1814: or a Tour in France after the First Fall of Napoleon* (Newcastle, 1909), 51 (5 September 1814); Revd William Shepherd, *Paris in 1802 and 1814* (1814), 175; Henry Wansey, *A Visit to Paris in June 1814* (1814), 73 (letter of 12 June 1814).

40. Anon., *The Englishman's Mentor. The Picture of the Palais Royal; describing its Spectacles, Gaming Rooms, Coffee Houses, Restaurateurs, Tabagies, Reading Rooms, Milliners' Shops, Gamesters . . . and That High Change of Fashionable Dissipation and Vice of Paris* (1819), 58.

41. Shepherd, 233 (diary for 9 July 1814); Baronne du Montet, *Souvenirs* (1914), 123 (letter of M. de Lort, April 1814); Duchesse de Maillé, *Souvenirs des deux restaurations* (1984), 184; Marigny, 53–6 (31 March 1814); Arthur Chuquet, *L'Année 1814* (1914), 134–7; cf. for confirmation of the fervour of female royalism, Lord Granville Leveson Gower, *Private Correspondence 1781 to 1821* (2 vols, 1916), II, 512 (letter of Lady Bessborough, 29 November 1814).

42. Reinhard, 396 (letter of 1 April 1814); Stanley, 119 (8 July 1814).

43. Girard, *La Garde nationale*, 21, 27.

44. Général de Langeron, 480; Duc de Pasquier, *Histoire de mon temps* (6 vols, 1893–5), II, 264; Mikhailofksy-Danilefsky, 390.

45. BL (British Library, London) Add. MSS 43085 [Aberdeen papers] f186vo (Madame de Beker to Lord Aberdeen, 6 September 1830); Lacour-Gayet, III, 322 (letter of Barante, 30 September 1826).

46. Edouard Gachot, *Marie Louise intime* (2 vols, 1911), II, 15.

47. Lady Morgan, *France in 1829–30*, II, 59.

48. Underwood, 101–4, 113–14, 130–2; Emmanuel de Waresquiel et Benoit Yvert, *Histoire de la Restauration 1814–1830. Naissance de la France moderne* (1996), 38; Sémallé, 398.

49. Stanley, 287 (Edward to Bella Stanley, 9 July 1816).

50. Smirnov, 136–40 (memoirs of Ivan Jirkevich); *Feuilles d'histoire* (1908), 362 (letter of Bulgakov, 21 March/2 April 1814); Underwood, 137 (1 April 1814). I am grateful for information about Paris theatres to M. Bruno Villien.

51. Michel Roussier, 'Le Conseil Municipal de Paris et le retour des Bourbons (1814–1815)', *Bulletin de la Société de l'Histoire de Paris* (1962), 92, 93, 97; Underwood, 147–8 (2 April 1814).

52. *De Buonaparte et des Bourbons et de la nécessité de se rallier à nos princes légitimes pour le bonheur de la France et celui de l'Europe* (1814), 13, 14, 56, 79, 84, 87; Underwood, 157 (3 April 1814).

53. Comte Beugnot, *Mémoires* (2 vols, 1866), II, 88; Reinhard, 401 (letter of 7 April 1814); Pasquier, II, 269.

54. Marigny, 67 (5 April 1814); Pierre-François-Léonard Fontaine, *Journal* (2 vols, 1987), I, 393 (4 April 1814); Caulaincourt, III, 75.

55. Caulaincourt, III, 126, 230n (Caulaincourt to Napoleon I, 5 April 1814).

56. Ibid., III, 178n, 182.

57. Lacour-Gayet, II, 386–8.

58. Chateaubriand, *Mémoires d'outre-tombe*, II, 247; Bodleian Library Oxford, MSS diary of Edward Mangin f117 (30 August 1815).

59. Mikhailofksy-Danilefsky, 404; Underwood, 171 (10 April 1814); Fontaine, I, 404 (10 April 1814); Pasquier, II, 339; Granier, 237 (Prince Wilhelm to Princess Charlotte of Prussia, 11 April 1814).

60. Underwood, 165 (7 April 1814); Dorothy Gies McGuigan, *Metternich and the Duchess* (1975), 269; Marie-Louise Biver, *Le Paris de Napoléon* (1963), 163–74; cf. Peter W. Graham (ed.), *Byron's Bulldog. The Letters of John Cam Hobhouse to Lord Byron* (Columbus, Ohio, 1989), 122, 125 (letters of 20, 27 April 1814).

61. Guillaume de Bertier de Sauvigny, *Metternich* (1986), 199 (Metternich to Eleonore de Metternich, 23 April 1814); Maria Ullrichova (ed.), *Clemens Metternich–Wilhelmine von Sagan. Ein Briefwechsel, 1813–1815* (Graz, 1966), 243–4, 253 (Metternich to Duchesse de Sagan, 13, 23 April 1814).

62. Ullrichova, 248 (Metternich to Duchesse de Sagan, 19 April 1814); Georges Kastner, *Les Voix de Paris. Essai d'une histoire littéraire et musicale des cris populaires de la capitale* (1857), 64n, 79, 80, 85, 87. Many prints also celebrated *les cris de Paris*, for example the series by Adrien-Jean-Baptiste Muffat, *Arts, métiers et cris de Paris (c.* 1815).

63. Béranger, *Chansons* (Garnier Frères, n.d.), 86–9; Reinhard, 412 (letter of 2 July 1814); Françoise de Bernardy, *Charles de Flahaut* (1954), 13n.

64. Comte Lefebvre de Behaine, *Le Comte d'Artois sur la route de Paris en 1814* (1921), *passim*; Charles Dupuis, *Le Ministère de Talleyrand en 1814* (2 vols, 1919), I, 221n.

65. Michel Poniatowski, *Louis-Philippe et Louis XVIII* (1982), 182; Lacour-Gayet, II, 383, 394–6.

66. Underwood, 175–6 (12 April 1814); Lady Burghersh, *Letters . . . from Germany and France during the Campaign of 1813–14* (1893), 228 (letter of 13 April 1814); Reinhard, 402 (letter of 12 April 1814) gives a less enthusiastic account.

67. Caulaincourt, III, 303n, 360–6.

68. AN 359 AP 99 (Marquis to Marquise de Clermont-Tonnerre, 16 April 1814); Pictet de Richemont et François d'Invernois, *Correspondance diplomatique* (2 vols, 1914), I, 24 (relation of J.-G. Eynard, 22 April); Major W.E. Frye, *After Waterloo. Reminiscences of European Travel 1815–1819* (1908), 92; James Simpson, *Paris after Waterloo* (1853), 158.

69. Marigny, 59, 69 (2, 6 April 1814).

70. National Library of Scotland (NLS) MSS 6399 (diary of Hon. W.F. Mackenzie MP, 26 April 1814); AN 395 AP [Saint-Priest archives] 1 (Auguste de Staël to Comte de Saint-Priest, 5 May 1814); cf. BL Add. MSS 52441 f14 (letter of James Mackintosh, 30 August 1814): 'The army and the populace of the towns are Napoleonists.'

71. Underwood, 187, 191, 192 (29 April, 1, 9, 10 May 1814); Tom Taylor (ed.), *The Life of Benjamin Robert Haydon* (hereafter *Haydon*) (2nd ed., 3 vols, 1853), I, 256, 258.

72. AN 349 AP [Montesquiou papers] 23 (*ordre du jour* of Dessoles, 19 May 1814, letter of Dessoles, 9 May 1814).

73. Caulaincourt, III, 387.

74. Comtesse Potocka, *Mémoires* (1897), 101; Baron de Maricourt, *Madame de Souza et sa famille* (1907), 64, 126, 254.

75. General Foy, *Notes autobiographiques* (3 vols, 1926), I, 291 (11 November 1821), II, 311 (21 June 1823); Leveson Gower, II, 536 (Lady Bessborough to Lord Granville Leveson Gower, 11 October 1815).

76. Fontaine, I, 393 (4 April 1814).

77. Captain Gronow, *Reminiscences and Recollections* (2 vols, 1892 ed.), II, 253.

78. AN 565 AP [Flahaut papers] FL5. The translations in *The First Napoleon. Some unpublished documents from the Bowood Papers*, ed. Earl of Kerry (1925) are unreliable.

79. AN 565 AP FL5 (Flahaut to Souza, 7, 18 April 1814); Mlle Cochelet, *Mémoires sur la reine*

Hortense et la famille impériale (2 vols, 1836), I, 288 (Mlle Cochelet to Hortense, 14 April 1814).

80. AN 565 AP FL5 (letter of 18 April 1814).

81. Wansey, 71 (letter of 12 June 1814); Prince de Metternich, *Mémoires, documents et écrits divers* (8 vols, 1880–4), I, 196; New York Public Library (hereafter NYPL), Berg Collection (Hobhouse diary, 3 May 1814); Chateaubriand, *Mémoires d'outre-tombe*, II, 244.

82. Baron Hennet de Goutel, 'Les derniers jours de l'Empire racontés par un Cent-suisse, d'après le journal inédit de M. de Marsilly (1811–1816)', *Revue des études napoléoniennes* (January 1918), XIII, 189; Chuquet, 150 (Schaffer to Duke of Nassau, n.d.); Underwood, 190 (3 May 1814).

83. Granier, 251 (Prince Wilhelm to Princess Charlotte of Prussia, 5 May 1814); NLS MSS 6399 f47 (journal of a visit to France by Hon. W. F. Mackenzie of Seaforth).

84. Granier, 252 (Prince Wilhelm to Princess Charlotte of Prussia, 5 May 1814); Pictet de Richemont, I, 32 (Pictet de Richemont to Turrettini, 4 May 1814).

85. Perey, 448–9 (account of Comtesse Hélène Potocka, May 1814); Pasquier, II, 410; Etienne de Jouy, *Guillaume le franc-parleur* (2 vols, 1816), I, 33–4 (14 May 1814).

86. Underwood, 191 (6 May 1814).

87. Caulaincourt, II, 339, recording Napoleon's comment that the *anciennes limites* were inseparable *du rétablissement des Bourbons*; Gaston Zeller, 'Les frontières naturelles. Histoire d'une idée fausse', in *Aspects de la politique française sous l'ancien régime* (1964), 107; AN 37 AP [Bonnay papers] 1 (Blacas to Bonnay, 7 April 1813); A. Polovtsov (ed.), *Correspondance diplomatique des ambassadeurs et ministres de Russie en France et de France en Russie avec leurs gouvernements de 1814 à 1830* (3 vols, St Petersburg, 1902–7), I, 51 (Pozzo to Nesselrode, 13 July 1814).

88. Lacour-Gayet, II, 407; McGuigan, 286 (Metternich to Laure Metternich, 23 May 1814); Underwood, 195 (2 June 1814).

89. *Journal des débats*, 5 June 1814; *Moniteur*, 5 June 1814, 617.

90. *Marianne et Germania*, 160; Dupuis, I, 369–71, II, 188n.

91. Beugnot, II, 147–234; Polovtsov, I, 87 (Pozzo to Nesselrode, 14 September 1814).

92. Reinhard, 406 (letter of 20 May 1814); Charles-Emmanuel de Rivaz, *Mes souvenirs de Paris 1810–1814* (Martigny, 1967), 237, 241–3, 248.

93. Jouy, *Guillaume le franc-parleur*, I, 92 (25 June 1814).

94. See for examples of this attitude Castellane, I, 258n (July 1814).

95. Hennet de Goutel, 189, 192.

96. Pierre Kohler, *Madame de Staël et la Suisse. Etude biographique et littéraire* (Lausanne, 1916), 630.

97. Stanley, 111 (30 June 1814); Charles de Rémusat, *Mémoires de ma vie* (5 vols, 1958–67), I, 357.

98. Polovtsov, I, 5 (letter of 1/30 May 1814); *Journal of a Trip to Paris by the Duke and Duchess of Rutland, July 1814*, 14 (26 July).

99. Polovtsov, II, 546 (Pozzo to Nesselrode, 26 December 1817, 7 January 1818).

100. Karl Hammer, *Hôtel Beauharnais, Paris* (Munich–Zurich, 1983), 130–1; Mary Beal and John Cornforth, *British Embassy, Paris* (1992), 1.

101. Polovtsov, I, 25, 39 (Pozzo to Nesselrode, 10/24 June 1814, 9/21 July 1814).

102. Lacour-Gayet, II, 399.

103. AN 03 [papers of the Maison du Roi 1814–1830] 244 (*Etat nominatif des artistes, des entrepreneurs, des marchands, des fournisseurs, attachés par brevets à l'administration des menus-plaisirs du roi* (1816).

104. AN 03 566 (*administration 1816, rapport au Ministre*, 13 February 1816).

105. Duke of Wellington, *Supplementary Despatches* (hereafter *SD*) (15 vols, 1858–72), IX, 315 (Wellington to Castlereagh, 4 October 1814).

106. Vicomte de La Boulaye, *Mémoires* (1975), 265, 267, 270, 271.

107. Benjamin Constant, *Journaux intimes* (1952), 401, 402, 406 (16, 28 April, 29 July 1814).

108. Madame de Staël, *Dix années d'exil* (1996, ed. Simone Balayé), 106; Foster Dormer MSS, Journal of Elizabeth Duchess of Devonshire (13, 22 April 1814).

109. MSS Maison Charavay 38807, 39408 (Madame de Staël to Duc de Richelieu, 21 July 1815, to James Mackintosh, 24 May 1815); *Revue de Paris*, 1 January 1897, 7 (Madame de Staël to Alexander I, 8 June 1815).

110. Chateaubriand, *Correspondance générale* (hereafter *CG*) (in publication), II (1979), 208, 217 (to Madame de Montcalm, 5 May 1814; to Duchesse de Duras, 25 September 1814).

111. L. Babboneix, 'Lamartine garde du corps', *Revue d'histoire littéraire* (1925), XXXII, 346 (Lamartine to Virieu, 16 May 1814).

112. Jouy, *Guillaume le franc-parleur*, I, 64 (18 June 1814); Castellane, I, 259 (entry for 14 July 1814).

113. Stanley, 136 (11 July 1814); cf. Roots, 47 (5 September 1814); Seth William Stevenson, *Journal of a Tour through Part of France, Flanders and Holland, including a Visit to Paris . . . made in the Summer of 1816* (Norwich, 1817), 132–3 (27 May 1816); *Memorandums of a Residence in France* (1816), 63–4.

114. Stanley, 121 (8 July 1814).

115. AN 300 AP [Orléans papers] III 16 (Orléans to Madame de Saint-Laurent, 1 June 1814); Guy Antonetti, *Louis-Philippe* (1994), 436.

116. Albert Sorel, *L'Europe et la Révolution française* (8 vols, 1885–1904), VII, 335; Polovtsov, II, 830 (instructions to Richelieu, September 1818).

117. Antonetti, 480.

118. Lacour-Gayet, III, 345; cf. Prince de Talleyrand, *Mémoires* (5 vols, 1891), IV, 243.

119. Norman King, *Correspondances suédoises de Germaine de Staël 1812–1816* (1998), 32 (Madame de Staël to Etienne Dumont, 13 October 1812); Balayé, 7.

120. André Monchoux, *L'Allemagne devant les lettres françaises, de 1814 à 1835* (1953), 142–4; Constant, *Journaux intimes*, 406 (11, 29 July 1814); Benjamin et Rosalie de Constant, *Correspondance 1786–1830* (1955), 205 (Benjamin to Rosalie de Constant, 23 December 1814).

121. (1992 ed.), 45, 105.

122. *De Buonaparte et des Bourbons* (1814), 79.

123. Mikhailofsky-Danilefsky, 409; Underwood, 156 (3 April 1814).

124. Lady Charlotte Bury, *Diary Illustrative of the Times of George the Fourth* (3rd ed., 2 vols, 1838), II, 56 (26 July, 1814); Edmond Géraud, *Un homme de lettres sous l'Empire et la Restauration* (1893), 184 (July 1815).

125. Frédéric-César de La Harpe, *Correspondance de . . . et Alexandre Ier* (3 vols, Neuchâtel, 1978–80), II, 521–2 (2 June 1814).

126. Royal Archives Windsor Castle MSS 21534 (Père Elisée to Prince Regent, 12 November 1814); Comte de Saint-Simon et A. Thierry son élève, *De la réorganisation de la société européenne ou de la nécessité de rassembler les peuples de l'Europe en un seul corps politique en conservant à chacun son indépendance nationale* (October 1814), 41, 46, 92, 96–7.

2   Paris takes Europe *July 1814–March 1815*

1. See e.g. Georges Firmin-Didot, *Royauté ou empire. La France en 1814 d'après les rapports inédits du comte Anglès* (n.d.), 16 (report of 27–8 May 1814).

2. Jean Tulard, *Napoléon* (1977), 340.

3. F. Carracioli, *Paris, le modèle des nations étrangères, ou l'Europe française* (Vienna and Paris, 1777), 176, 293.

4. Smirnov, 37 (letter of Dennis Fonvizine, 14 June 1778).

5. Thomas Macgill, *Travels in Turkey, Italy and Russia during the Years 1803, 1804, 1805 and 1806* (1808), I, 2; Byron, *Letters and Journals* (12 vols, 1973–82), VI, 234, 17 (letters of 28 October 1819 to Richard Belgrave Hoppner and 3 March 1819 to James Wedderburn Webster).

6. Edgar Peters Bowron and Joseph J. Rishel (eds.), *Art in Rome in the Eighteenth Century* (Philadelphia, 2000), 37; Christopher M.S. Johns, *Antonio Canova and the Politics of Patronage in Revolutionary and Napoleonic Europe* (Berkeley, 1999), 76.

7. J.B.S. Morritt, *A Grand Tour* (1985 ed.), 26, 308 (letters of 22 May, 15 June 1796).

8. Peter Clark and Bernard Lepetit (eds.), *Capital Cities and their Hinterlands in Early Modern Europe* (1996), 1, 147.

9. Lucienne Netter, *Heine et la peinture de la vie parisienne* (Frankfurt, 1980), 58; Dominic Lieven, *The Aristocracy in Europe 1815–1914* (1992), 173; Charles Pertusier, *Promenades pittoresques dans Constantinople et sur les rives du Bosphore, suivies d'une notice sur la Dalmatie* (3 vols, 1815), III, 311.

10. Chateaubriand, *CG*, V, 74 (to Duchesse de Duras, 27 April 1822); Richard Rush, *A Residence at the Court of London* (1987 ed.), 34, 66 (20 January 1818, 1 March 1818).

11. BL Add. MSS [Lieven papers] 47245 f129 (Nesselrode to Lieven, 7 April 1814).

12. *Moniteur*, 22 April 1814, 414.

13. McGuigan, 283 (Metternich to Eleonore de Metternich, 2 May 1814); Reinhard, 405 (letter of 14 May 1814).

14. Guides to Paris published for English visitors in 1814 include: Louis Tronchet, *Picture of Paris; being a Complete Guide to all the Public buildings, Places of Amusement and Curiosities in that Metropolis* (May); Edward Planta, *A New Picture of Paris; or the Stranger's Guide to the French Metropolis; accurately describing the Public Establishments, Remarkable Edifices, Places of Amusement, and every other Object worthy of Attention* (July).

15. Field Marshal Sir William Maynard Gomm GCB, *Letters and Journals* (1881), 343 (Gomm to aunt, 5 August 1814); A Visitor, *A slight sketch of Paris; or some account of the French Capital in its improved state, since 1802* (1814), 6; *Haydon*, I, 239.

16. Wilhelm von Wolzogen, *Journal de voyage à Paris 1788–1791* (1998), 97 (25 June 1789); *Le Palais-Royal* (1988), *passim*, and 181–2.

17. *Galignani's New Paris Guide* (1842), 190; Castlereagh, X, 391 (bulletin of 22 May 1815); *The Englishman's Mentor*, iii; cf. Frye, 59 (letter of 7 August 1815: 'My first visit was, as you will no doubt have guessed, to the Palais Royal').

18. André Lechner, diary, 2 April 1814, in *1812–1814* (4 vols, Moscow, 1992), IV, 362.

19. Frye, 60 (letter of 7 August 1815); *Galignani's New Paris Guide*, 190.

20. [H. Deterville], *Le Palais Royal ou les filles en bonne fortune* (1815), ix, 15; *The Englishman's Mentor*, 19–21 ('this temple of merchandise and sin', this 'vortex of profligacy').

21. Gronow, I, 87–90; A.D. Certkov, *Quelques remarques sur Paris*, in *1812–1814*, IV, 422.

22. Thomas Jessop, *Journal d'un voyage à Paris en septembre–octobre 1820* (1928), 78; Löwenstern, II, 396; cf. Pavel Annenkov, 'Lettres de Paris' (1847–8), in Smirnov, 317–18.

23. Decin State Archives, Czech Republic, Prince Clary, unpublished diary, 12 May 1822.

24. McGuigan, 287. I am grateful for information about Bréguet to Mme la Baronne Elie de Rothschild.

25. BL Add. MSS [Holland House papers] 51638 f87vo (Madame de Coigny to Lady Holland, 20 May 1814).

26. Lady Charlotte Bury, II, 44 (22 July 1814); McGuigan, 486.

27. Gronow, II, 5.

28. Thomas Raikes, *A Portion of the Journal* (4 vols, 1857), III, 271 (25 June 1838).

29. *L'Art culinaire au XIXe siècle* (Orangerie de Bagatelle, 1984), 20, 26–7, 38; Cumbria County Record Office, Lowther papers, Lonsdale diary, 2 August 1817; Rebecca L. Spang, *The Invention of the Restaurant. Paris and Modern Gastronomic Culture* (Harvard, 2000), *passim* and 24, 83, 140–1.

30. *Le Palais Royal*, 288; H. Blanc, *Le Guide des dîneurs ou statistique des principaux restaurants de Paris* (1815), 13, 194, 196–7; Stevenson, 221.

31. Löwenstern, II, 390–1; *Le Guide des dîneurs*, 15, 97, 99; Jonathan Keates, *Stendhal* (1995 ed.), 162.

32. G. de Bertier de Sauvigny, *Nouvelle Histoire de Paris. La Restauration 1815–1830* (1977), 126.

33. Shepherd, 175; Wansey, 42 (8 June 1814); cf. Wolzogen, 29 (13 October 1788).

34. Jessop, 78.

35. Bodleian Library Oxford, Mangin diary f63 (18 August 1815).

36. Hon. Mrs N. Grosvenor (ed.), *The First Lady Wharncliffe and her Family* (2 vols, 1927), I, 210 (letter of 1 October 1814); Doris Gunnell, *Sutton Sharpe et ses amis français* (1925), 65 (letter of October 1819 to Catherine Sharpe).

37. W. Scott Haine, *The World of the Paris Café. Sociability among the French Working Class 1789–1814* (Baltimore, 1996), 3.

38. *Galignani's Paris Guide or Stranger's Guide through the French Metropolis* (10th ed., Paris–Calais–London, 1822), xciv.

39. Count André Rostopchine, *Matériaux en grande partie inédits pour la biographie future du comte Théodore Rastaptchine* (Brussels, 1864), 335 (letter of 1816 to Countess Rostopchine).

40. Balzac, *La Fille aux yeux d'or* (Presses Pocket, 1992), 342; cf. Comte Rodolphe Apponyi, *Journal* (4 vols, 1913–26), III, 42 (April 1835) for a description; François Gasnault, *Guinguettes et lorettes. Bals publics et danse sociale à Paris entre 1830 et 1870* (1986), 29, 39–42; Bertier de Sauvigny, *Nouvelle Histoire de Paris*, 386–9.

41. Scott Haine, 9, 60–1; Charles Ledré, *La Presse à l'assaut de la monarchie* (1960), 18.

42. 'An Englishman in Paris', *Notes and Recollections* (2 vols, 1892), I, 31.

43. *Oeuvres intimes* (1955), 1409 (*Journal*, 29 March 1814).

44. Mérimée, *Correspondance générale* (hereafter *CG*) (15 vols, 1941–61), II, 102 (Mérimée to Sutton Sharpe, 18 May 1837); J. Barbey d'Aurevilly, *Memoranda. Journal intime 1836–1864* (1993), 128; Henry-Melchior de Langle, *Le Petit Monde des cafés et débits parisiens au XIXe siècle. Evolution de la sociabilité citadine* (1990), 53.

45. Berlioz, *Memoirs from 1803 to 1865* (New York, 1966), 102n.

46. Eugène Delacroix, *Journal* (3 vols, 1893–5), I, 76, 122 (31 March 1824, 20 May 1824).

47. James Simpson, 153.

48. Gronow, II, 283–7; Lady Morgan, *France in 1829–30*, I, 402; Mérimée, 'Lettre d'Espagne', 15 November 1830, in *Carmen* (1965 ed.), 381; Jules Janin, *The American in Paris* (1843), 39–42.

49. Heine talks of *la bourse de nuit chez Tortoni* in 1840: *Lutèce* (Geneva, 1979), 130 (7 October 1840).

50. Etienne de Jouy, *L'Hermite de la Guiane* (3 vols, 1816–18), III, 126–30 (2 December 1816);

Notes

James Simpson, 114; Mercer, II, 265 (10 August 1815); Underwood, 285; Stanley, 142 (11 July 1814).

51. Bertier de Sauvigny, *Nouvelle Histoire de Paris*, 198–9; Jouy, *Guillaume le franc-parleur*, II, 103 (25 February 1815).

52. J.P.R. Cuisin, *Les Nymphes du Palais-Royal* (1815), *passim*; Théophile Gautier, *Paris et les Parisiens* (1996), 472.

53. *Le Palais-Royal ou les filles en bonne fortune* (1815), 15; cf. *The Englishman's Mentor*, 111; *La Grande Ville. Nouveau Tableau de Paris comique, critique et philosophique*, ed. Paul de Kock (2 vols, 1844), II, 339; Jill Harsin, *Policing Prostitution in Nineteenth-Century Paris* (Princeton, 1985), 119. To a connoisseur such as Mérimée, however, women in London were *fraîches comme pas une fille de Paris*: *CG*, I, 214 (to Hippolyte Royer-Collard, 17 December 1832).

54. Balzac, *Splendeurs et misères des courtisanes* (Booking International, 1993 ed.), 40.

55. Harsin, 15; Philippe Vigier, *Paris pendant la monarchie de juillet* (1991), 494; F.-F.-A. Béraud, *Les Filles publiques de Paris, et la police qui les régit* (2 vols, Paris and Leipzig, 1839), *passim*.

56. *The Englishman's Mentor*, 111; Cuisin, 103.

57. David Carey, *Life in Paris* (1822), 198, 335; *The Englishman's Mentor*, 63.

58. Harsin, 32, 39.

59. Brigitte de Montclos, *Les Russes à Paris au XIXe siècle* (1996), 16–17.

60. Bertier de Sauvigny, *Nouvelle Histoire de Paris*, 271.

61. David Magarshack (ed.), *Turgenev's Literary Reminiscences* (1958), 178; Boris Uxkull, *Arms and the Woman. The Intimate Journal of a Baltic Nobleman during the Napoleonic Wars* (1966), 181, 184, 189, 192 (1–25 March, 26 March, 19 April, 10 May); cf., for similar Parisian encounters, Löwenstern, II, 423, 438.

62. Egon Conte Corti, *Ludwig I of Bavaria* (1938), 127 (Crown Prince to Crown Princess of Bavaria, 2 May 1814); Jean Puraye et Hans-Otto Lang (eds.), *Lettres de Léopold Ier . . . 1804–1864* (Liège, 1973), 93 (Léopold to Sophie de Mensdorf-Pouilly, 25 April 1814); cf. Du Montet, 122: *60,000c***, sans compter les femmes honnêtes, sont en permanence de service, femmes d'employés, civils et militaires* (letter of M. de Lort, April 1814).

63. Wolzogen, 161 (27 November 1790); AN F7 (police reports) 3783 (report of 19 December 1814); E.J. Délécluze, *Journal 1824–1818* (1948), 343 (3 April 1826).

64. Pierre Citron, *La Poésie de Paris dans la littérature française de Rousseau à Baudelaire* (2 vols, 1961), I, 381n.

65. Biver, 338–9; Louis Bergeron, *Paris. Genèse d'un paysage* (1989), 198.

66. Burghersh, 229, 231 (letter of 13 April 1814). However, Boris Uxkull, 181, described the *quais* along the Seine as 'hardly anything at all compared with those of the Neva. Taste, luxury and elegance are found everywhere but nothing is very majestic' (1–25 March 1814).

67. Foster Dormer MSS, Journal of Elizabeth Duchess of Devonshire, 6 May 1814.

68. John Morley, *Regency Design 1790–1840* (1993), 151, 273; Richard S. Wortman, *Scenarios of Power. Myth and Ceremony in Russian Monarchy* (Princeton, 1995), I, 316–21.

69. William Hazlitt, *Notes of a Journey through France and Italy* (1826), 35; cf. Henry Milton, *Letters on the Fine Arts written from Paris in the Year 1815* (1816), 3: 'we entered Paris yesterday; and you will easily believe that very soon after our arrival we found ourselves at the door of the Louvre.'

70. Milton, 15n, 25n.

71. Stanley, 113 (30 June 1814); cf. Francis Horner MP, *Memoirs and Correspondence* (2 vols, 1843), II, 183–4 (Horner to Miss Horner, 30 August 1814): 'Our chief objects in coming to

447

Paris were the Louvre and the theatre . . . As to the Louvre I cannot attempt a description of it: the magnificence and the riches of the gallery quite confounded and overwhelmed me with astonishment . . . Paris surpasses London infinitely in the number and magnificence of the public buildings.'

72. Uxkull, 181 (1/25 March 1814); Stanley, 109 (30 June 1814); Roots, 70 (8 September 1814).

73. *Haydon*, I, 235–6.

74. Stanley, 198–9 (4 July 1814); Revd Thomas Frognall Dibdin, *A Bibliographical, Antiquarian and Picturesque Tour in France and Germany* (3 vols, 1821), II, 77–9 (18 June 1818); Gunnell, 44 (Sutton Sharpe to Catherine Sharpe, 11 September 1819); cf. Mercer, II, 137 (13 July 1815), 252–3 (12 August 1815).

75. Morgan, *France in 1829–30*, I, 399; Anon., *Impressions and Observations of a Young Person during a Residence in Paris* (3rd ed., 1845), 82.

76. Dibdin, II, 76–9.

77. Heine, *De la France* (1994), 89 (25 March 1832).

78. *Haydon*, I, 241; cf. C. Nowell Smith (ed.), *The Letters of Sydney Smith* (2 vols, Oxford, 1953), I, 429 (letter of 18 April 1826): 'such is the state of manners that you appear to have quitted a land of barbarians . . . I have not seen a cobbler who is not better bred than an English gentleman.'

79. [Mary Berry], *Social Life in England and France from the French Revolution of 1789 to that of July 1830* (1831), 149; Jane Vansittart (ed.), *Surgeon James's Journal 1815* (hereafter *James*) (1964), 73, 81; Bodleian Library Oxford, Mangin diary ff118, 130 (August, September 1815).

80. John Griscom, *A Year in Europe* (2 vols, New York, 1823), I, 271 (25 August 1818); Stanley, 141 (11 July 1814); cf. Jessop, 42, at the *fêtes* for the birth of the Duc de Bordeaux: 'little drunkenness was seen nor was there any of that riot which is seen in a London mob.'

81. Mercer, II, 123, 244, 276 (13 July, 7 August 1815); cf. *James*, 81: 'a Frenchman of any class but seldom departs from the rules of good breeding and manners'.

82. Granier, 240 (letter of Prince Wilhelm of Prussia, 20 April 1814); Bodleian Library Oxford, Mangin diary ff61, 102 (17, 26 August 1815).

83. Granier, 257 (Prince Wilhelm to Princess Charlotte of Prussia, 19 May 1814); Leveson Gower, II, 508 (letter of Lady Bessborough, 15 November 1814).

84. Miss Berry, *Extracts of the Journals and Correspondence* (3 vols, 1865), III, 17, 77 (J.W. Ward to Miss Berry, 11 May 1814; Mary to Agnes Berry,16 March 1816).

85. *Le Constitutionnel*, 10 April 1821: in Paris *Tous les rangs s'y confondent, toutes les distinctions y disparaissent . . . si un grand seigneur et un bourgeois se recontrent dans un salon de Paris on les y traite en égaux*; *James*, 73, 80–1; Comte François Esterhazy, *Journal* (Budapest, 1940), 32 (8 July 1827).

86. Castellane, I, 325 (November 1816).

87. Staël, *Dix années d'exil*, 94; AN 40 AP [Beugnot papers] 10 (report of 26 September 1814); *The Times*, 14 October 1814.

88. Cassaigneau et Rilliet, 443–4 (Eynard to Pictet, 26 May 1814).

89. Constant, *Journaux intimes*, 403 (25 May 1814).

90. A copy of Lady Dalrymple Hamilton's diary has been consulted thanks to Mrs Laing, Rulegas House, Ayrshire; Jouy, *Guillaume le franc-parleur*, II, 8 (7 January 1815).

91. Lady Dalrymple Hamilton's diary.

92. BL Add. MSS 41648 ff8–9 (22 April 1814, 'An Account of the Entrance of His Most Christian Majesty Louis XVIII King of France and Navarre into London by George Nayler, York Herald'; Dupuis, I, 309.

93. Castlereagh, X, 93 (Castlereagh to Wellington, 14 August 1814).

94. BL Add. MSS 38257 f237 (Louis XVIII to George IV, 12 May 1814); Foster Dormer MSS, Journal of Elizabeth Duchess of Devonshire, 6 May 1814; Roots, 47, 61–2, 102 (5, 7, 13 September).

95. AN 40 AP 9 f67 (Beugnot to Louis XVIII, 9 July 1814): and F7 3783 (police report of 8 July 1814, *re* Louis XVIII, exceptionally, wearing the Légion d'Honneur; Foster Dormer MSS, Journal of Elizabeth Duchess of Devonshire (12 October 1814): 'he wears the Garter constantly and showed it me round his knee.'

96. AN F7 3785 (police reports of 2, 3 March 1815).

97. Jean Chagniot, *Paris au XVIIIe siècle* (1988), 66.

98. For claims of betrayal, see, among others, Wansey, 31 (6 June 1814); Stanley, 106 (28 June 1814); *Haydon*, I, 254 (4 July 1814); John Mayne, *Journal . . . during a Tour on the Continent* (1909), 29, 40 (2, 7 September 1814).

99. *Haydon*, I, 239; Dupuis, I, 352; cf. Comte de Jaucourt, *Correspondance . . . avec le prince de Talleyrand* (1905), 157 (Jaucourt to Talleyrand, 20 January 1815): *La France veut la paix et l'armée la Belgique.*

100. *The Manuscripts of J.B. Fortescue esq. preserved at Dropmore* (10 vols, 1892–1927), X, 388 (Thomas Grenville to Lord Grenville, 2 August 1814); Jean Poirier, 'Lycéens impériaux 1814–1815', *Revue de Paris*, 15 May 1921, 381–2, 399; Jaucourt, 75 (Jaucourt to Talleyrand, 9 November 1814).

101. Jacques Godechot, 'Nation, patrie, nationalisme et patriotisme en France au XVIIIe siècle', *Annales historiques de la Révolution française* (1971), XLIIII, 489; cf. AN C 185 (draft letter of Louis XVI and Monsieur to Necker, 16 July 1789): *toutes les troupes sont pour la nation . . . la confiance que la Nation vous témoigne; Archives historiques du Poitou*, LII (1942), 78 (Marquis de Villermont to Comte François d'Escars, 26 November 1790): *la nation du Palais-Royal . . . est aujourd'hui la nation par excellence.*

102. Caulaincourt, II, 341, cf. 311, 366; AN 40 AP 9 f67vo (report of 9 July 1814).

103. Polovtsov, I, 27 (Pozzo to Nesselrode, 24 June/6 July 1814).

104. Bibliothèque Nationale Nouvelles Acquisitions Françaises (BN NAF) 24062 ff254, 270 (minutes for meeting of 20 June 1814).

105. BN NAF 24062 (Procès-Verbaux du Conseil, 1814–15), f91.

106. AN 40 AP 8 ff176, 203vo, 211 (police reports of 25, 29, 30 June 1814).

107. AN 40 AP 10 (report of 27 August 1814).

108. Castellane, I, 259, 261 (5 August, 8 September 1814).

109. Morgan, *France in 1829–30*, II, 501–4, 507n describes one such procession in 1829.

110. Firmin-Didot, 39 (report of 12 June 1814).

111. *Haydon*, I, 249; Castellane, I, 196, 257 (11 June, 6 July 1814).

112. AN 40 AP 9 f103vo (report of 14 July 1814); F7 3783 (report of 19 July 1814); Mansel, *Louis XVIII*, 215; Wansey, 64 (12 June 1814); cf. Fontaine, I, 423, 433 (12 July, 18 November 1814).

113. Mabell Countess of Airlie (ed.), *Lady Palmerston and her Times* (2 vols, 1922), I, 170 (Palmerston to Lady Cowper, 14 December 1829).

114. MM. Sewrin et Dumersan, *Les Anglaises pour rire ou la Table et le Logement* (1815), 12–14.

115. AN F7 3783 (reports of 9 September, 2, 10 November, 19 December 1814).

116. Castlereagh, X, 9 (Castlereagh to Liverpool, 5 May 1814); Emma Sophia Countess Brownlow, *The Eve of Victorianism* (1940), 45.

Notes

117. Donald Sultana, *From Abbotsford to Paris and Back. Sir Walter Scott's Journey of 1815* (Stroud, 1993), 69.

118. BL Add. MSS 52441 ff122, 158 (12, 25 November 1814); cf. AN F7 3783 (police report of 10 November 1814).

119. Foster Dormer MSS, Journal of Elizabeth Duchess of Devonshire, 3 November 1814.

120. Leveson Gower, II, 507 (letter of Lady Bessborough, 13 November 1814).

121. Castlereagh, X, 182 (Wellington to Castlereagh, 1 November 1814); Fanny Burney, *Journals and Letters* (13 vols, 1972–84), VII, 451 (D'Arblay to Madame d'Arblay, 30 August 1814).

122. Maurice Girod de l'Ain, *Vie militaire du Général Foy* (1900), 243, 251, 253–4, 258 (15 April, 22, 23, 26 October, 12 November 1814); Foy, I, 70 (22 September 1820, *re* Caulaincourt).

123. BL Add. MSS 52441 f165vo (28 November 1814); cf. AN F7 3785 (police report of 2 March 1815): *la haine contre cette nation est à son comble.*

124. S. de Saint-Exupéry and Chantal de Tourtier, *Les Archives du Maréchal Ney et de sa famille conservées aux Archives Nationales* (1962), 130–1.

125. Madame de Chastenay, *Mémoires* (2 vols, 1896–7), II, 361, 363, Natalie Petiteau, *Elites et mobilité. La Noblesse d'Empire au XIXe siècle (1808–1914)* (1997), 53, 114; *La Rue de Lille* (1983), 122; Lord Broughton, *Recollections of a Long Life* (6 vols, 1909), I, 114 (diary for 4 May 1814).

126. AN 40 AP 10 (report of 23 September 1814).

127. Eugène Welvert, *Napoléon et la police sous la première restauration* (n.d.), 267 (report of 13 November 1814).

128. Granier, 234 (Prince Wilhelm to Princess Charlotte of Prussia, 7 April 1814); Private collection, journal of Frances-Elizabeth Burgoyne, 14 December 1814.

129. Léon-G. Pélissier, *Le Portefeuille de la comtesse d'Albany 1806–1824* (1902), 193 (Madame de Souza to Albany, 2 May 1814); Bernardy, *Flahaut*, 102.

130. Frédéric Loliée, *Le Duc de Morny et la sociéte du Second Empire* (1909), 47n; AN F7 3783 (report of 20 November 1814); BL Add. MSS 52441 f196 (Mackintosh letter, 9 December 1814).

131. Leveson Gower, II, 509, 511 (letters of Lady Bessborough, 18, 24 November 1814).

132. Pélissier, 227 (Souza to Albany, late 1814); cf. AN F7 3784 (police report of 4 March 1815).

133. Reine Hortense, *Mémoires* (3 vols, 1927), II, 294n; cf. Jaucourt, 156 (Jaucourt to Talleyrand, 20 January 1815).

134. Hortense, II, 281; Reine Hortense, 'Lettres à Alexandre Ier', *Revue de Paris*, 15 October 1897, 681 (letter of 4 October 1814).

135. *Revue des deux mondes*, 15 August 1937, 580 (letter to Eugène de Beauharnais, 9 January 1815).

136. *La Reine Hortense. Une femme artiste* (Malmaison, 1993), 84–97; Cochelet, II, 264.

137. Hortense, II, 282, 290, 292n; Ian Bruce, *Lavallette Bruce* (1953), 77 (Michael Bruce to Mr Bruce, 9 December 1814); AN 565 AP FL5 (Flahaut to Madame de Souza, 9 April 1814).

138. Chancelier Comte de Nesselrode, *Lettres et papiers* (11 vols, 1904–11), V, 215–17 (Hortense to Alexander I, 15 July 1815); Hortense, II, 304.

139. Vicomtesse de Noailles, *Vie de la princesse de Poix née Beauvau* (1855), 96; Hortense, II, 295–6; Comtesse d'Armaillé, *Quand on savait vivre heureux (1830–1860). Souvenirs de jeunesse* (1934), 109.

140. Hortense, 'Lettres à Alexandre Ier', 690 (Hortense to Prince Eugène, 14 October 1814).

141. Cochelet, I, 421; NYPL Berg Collection, Hobhouse diary, 13 May 1814, recording Lord Kinnaird (thus the account in Broughton, I, 122, 13 May 1814, is bowdlerised); Général Baron de Dedem de Gelder, *Mémoires* (1900), 402.

142. AN F7 3783 (reports of 11, 18, 20 July 1814).

143. Ibid. (reports of 7, 19 October 1814).

144. Leveson Gower, II, 505, 509 (9, 15 November 1814); Pictet de Richemont, II, 442.

145. Private collection, Burgoyne diary, 13 December 1814.

146. AN F7 3783 (reports of 2, 5, 11 January 1815); F7 3784 (report of 25 January 1815).

147. Jaucourt, 103 (Jaucourt to Talleyrand, 30 November 1814); Welvert, 298 (report of 2 December 1814).

148. AN F7 3783 (report of 9 November 1814).

149. *Réflexions politiques sur quelques écrits du jour et sur les intérêts de tous les Français* (1814), 39, 44–5, 62–3, 122, 136, 140.

150. AN F7 3784 (report of 18 January 1815); Firmin-Didot, 210–21 (reports of 17–18 January 1815); Polovtsov, I, 139–40 (Boutiaguine to Nesselrode, 17 January 1815).

151. Jaucourt, 177, 210 (letters of 1, 25 February 1815).

152. Jaucourt, 135, 189–90 (letters of 31 December 1814, 11 February 1815); NLS MSS 6399 f41 (diary of W.F. Mackenzie MP, April 1814); cf. *Haydon*, I, 245.

153. Archives du Ministère des Affaires Etrangères, Paris (hereafter AAE) 681 ff84, 92 (reports of 10, 31 December 1814).

154. René Sédillot, *Le Coût de la Révolution française* (1987), 134.

155. Diary of Lady Isabella de Chabot, quoted in Renagh Holohan, *The Irish Chateaux* (Dublin, 1989), 177; Lamb papers (consulted by kind permission of Richard Lamb), John Bowes Wright to J. Lamb, 29 January 1815; Fontaine, I, 440 (21 January 1815).

156. Constant, *Journaux intimes*, 407 (16 August 1814).

157. AAE 681 f84 (letter of 10 December 1814); Hennet de Goutel, 200 (diary for 3 March 1815).

158. Sismondi, 'Lettres écrites pendant les Cent Jours', *Revue historique*, III (1877), 92, 100, 322 (letters of 8, 21 January, 9 February 1815).

159. Castellane, I, 263, 264, 266 (23 September, 16, 20 October 1814); Jaucourt, 138 (4 January 1815).

160. Perey, 452 (Hélène Potocka to Vincent Potocki, 22 May 1814); see Edmond Géraud, *Un témoin des deux Restaurations* (1893), 284 (September 1815) for a Bordelais' astonishment at Parisians' dislike of the Duchess; Roots, 47, 102 (5, 13 September 1814); cf. Frances Lady Shelley, *Diary* (2 vols, 1912–13), I, 108 (July 1815); Berry, III, 84 (letter of 31 March 1816): 'In short she is hated by the people.'

161. Polovtsov, II, 266 (Pozzo to Nesselrode, 12/24 June 1817).

162. BN NAF 11771 f19 (diary for 6 March 1815).

163. AN F7 3785 (police reports of 1, 2, 3 March 1815).

164. AAE 681 f138 (unsigned letter to Talleyrand, 14 February 1815).

3 War *March–December 1815*

1. Hennet de Goutel, 200 (3 March 1815).

2. Napoleon I, *Correspondance générale* (hereafter *CG*) (32 vols, 1858–70), XXVIII, 1–5 (proclamations of 1 March 1815).

3. Polovtsov, I, 155 (Boutiaguine to Nesselrode, 7 March 1815).

4. Sismondi, 333 (9 March 1815); Georges Solovieff (ed.), *Madame de Staël. Ses amis, ses correspondants. Choix de lettres* (1970), 492 (Madame de Staël to Princesse Louise de Prusse, 20 February 1815); Victor de Pange (ed.), *Le plus beau de toutes les fêtes. La correspondance inédite de Madame de*

Notes

Staël et d'Elizabeth Hervey duchesse de Devonshire (1980), 115 (Madame de Staël to Elizabeth Duchess of Devonshire, 18 February 1815). The *ordonnance* of payment is in AN 03 533 f218 (*rapport au Roi*, 19 September 1815).

5. Comtesse de Boigne, *Mémoires* (2 vols, 1979 ed.), I, 261–2; Ernest Daudet, *Louis XVIII et le duc Decazes* (1899), 333 (souvenirs of Duchesse Decazes).

6. J.C. Hobhouse, *The Substance of some Letters, written by an Englishman resident at Paris during the Last Reign of the Emperor Napoleon* (2 vols, 1816), II, 248.

7. Jean Tulard (ed.), *Napoléon à Sainte-Hélène* (1981), 589, quoting Montholon.

8. Lamb papers, John Bowes Wright (letters to J. Lamb of 10, 11 March 1815; in his letter of 22 March he refers to the 'hostile and evil spirit that unequivocally displayed itself against the English').

9. Emile Bary, *Les Cahiers d'un rhétoricien de 1815* (1890), 6 (11 March 1815).

10. Polovtsov, I, 157, 160, 161 (despatches of 8, 11, 12 March 1815); Bibliothèque Historique de la Ville de Paris (BHVP) MSS 1013 (unsigned letter of 13 March 1815).

11. Hennet de Goutel, 273, 274, 275, 276 (11, 13, 14, 17 March 1815).

12. Possibly via a young official called Fleury de Chaboulon: see Foy, II, 103 (30 June 1822); Général Baron Gourgaud, *Sainte-Hélène. Journal inédit de 1815 à 1822* (2 vols, 1899), I, 492 (22 February 1817).

13. Hortense, II, 304.

14. Foy, I, 70 (22 September 1820).

15. Hortense, II, 320.

16. Sismondi, 334 (11 March 1815); Constant, *Journaux intimes*, 435 (12 March 1815).

17. Hortense, II, 313–14.

18. Nesselrode, V, 217 (Hortense to Alexander I, 15 July 1815); cf. BN NAF (journal of Madame de Chastenay) 11771 f23 for the belief of Ney and others that Austria was behind Napoleon.

19. Hortense, II, 317–19, 321.

20. Jaucourt, 237 (letter of 14 March 1815); Hennet de Goutel, 275 (14 March 1815).

21. Castellane, I, 281–2 (17, 20 March 1815).

22. John Scott, *Paris Revisited*, 266.

23. Jaucourt, 225, 231 (letters of 8, 11 March 1815); Louis Philippe d'Orléans, *Extraits de mon journal du mois de mars 1815* (Twickenham, 1816), 51–2.

24. Hennet de Goutel, 276 (16 March 1815); Castellane, I, 281 (16 March 1815); *Moniteur*, 17 March 1815, 301; Reiset, III, 106 (16 March 1815).

25. Louis Philippe d'Orléans, 43 (15 March 1815).

26. Chateaubriand, *Mémoires d'outre-tombe*, II, 271.

27. Napoleon, *CG*, XXXI, 76.

28. Maréchal Macdonald, *Souvenirs* (1892), 364.

29. Hennet de Goutel, 277 (19 March 1815); Jaucourt, 255, 300 (letters of 2, 26 April 1815).

30. *L'Autographe*, 15 January 1865; Comte de Rochechouart, *Souvenirs sur la Révolution, l'Empire et la Restauration* (1933), 404; Hennet de Goutel, 278 (19 March 1815).

31. Burney, VIII, 58.

32. Un grenadier de la Garde Nationale [Alexandre de Laborde], *Quarante-huit heures de garde au château des Tuileries* (1816), 14–15.

33. Broughton, I, 247 (diary for 13 April 1815: eye-witness account of Lady Kinnaird); Hennet de Goutel, 278 (20 March 1815).

34. Sismondi, 343 (letter of 20 March 1815); Hennet de Goutel, 278 (20 March 1815); Hortense, II, 328; cf. Hobhouse, I, 179 for Parisian hostility.

35. Fontaine, I, 448 (20 March 1815); BHVP MSS 1013 (unsigned letter of 21 March 1815).

36. Laborde, 19–20; Pierre Pinon, *Paris, biographie d'une capitale* (1999), 121; Hortense, II, 329; Comte de Lavallette, *Memoirs* (2 vols, 1831), II, 190.

37. Lavallette, II, 187; Hortense, II, 333–5.

38. Sismondi, 344; Bary, 46 (26 March 1815).

39. Le Palais-Royal, 163; Hobhouse, I, 208–9 (19 May 1815); Gregor Dallas, *1815. The Roads to Waterloo* (1997), 418–19, 322.

40. Napoleon I, *CG*, XXVIII, 35, 103 (to Conseil Municipal, 26 March 1815; to Garde Nationale, 16 April 1815).

41. Hobhouse, I, 212 (19 May 1815).

42. Castlereagh, X, 320 (Pozzo to Castlereagh, 21 April 1815).

43. Antonetti, 462–7; Solovieff, 499 (Staël to Talleyrand, 25 April 1815).

44. Constant, *Journaux intimes*, 437–8 (4, 14 April 1815).

45. Ibid., 438–9 (19, 23, 26, 27 April 1815).

46. Sismondi, 146 (2 April 1815); Jaucourt, 274 (Talleyrand to Jaucourt, 18 April 1815); Earl of Kerry, *The First Napoleon* (1925), 109 (Napoleon to Flahaut, 18 April 1815).

47. Sismondi, 144 (31 March 1815); NYPL, Hobhouse diary, 13, 16, 27 April 1815.

48. Baron de Barante, *Souvenirs* (8 vols, 1892), II, 146 (Barante to Madame de Barante, 15 May 1815); Frédéric Bluche, *Le Plébiscite des Cent Jours* (Geneva, 1974), 109, 113.

49. Bary, 79–80 (9 April 1815).

50. Ibid., 26 (20 March 1815); *L'Autographe*, No. 11266, unsigned letter, 23 June 1815; Robert Chantemesse, *Le Roman inconnu de la duchesse d'Abrantès* (1927), 221.

51. Castellane, I, 285 (9 April 1815); cf. Sismondi, 356 (18 June 1815).

52. Castellane, I, 288 (15 May 1815); Emile le Gallo, *Les Cent Jours* (1924), 305–7.

53. Robert Alexander, *Bonapartism and Revolutionary Tradition in France. The Fédérés of 1815* (Cambridge, 1991), 201, 207.

54. Carlo Bronne, *Les Abeilles du manteau* (Brussels, 1944), 82; Helen Maria Williams, *A Narrative of the Events which have taken place in France from the landing of Napoleon Bonaparte on the 1st of March 1815, till the Restoration of Louis XVIII* (1815), 65 and n, 70; Hortense, III, 7; Chastenay, II, 483.

55. Montcalm, *Mon journal*, 42 (21 May 1815).

56. Williams, 69.

57. Le Gallo, 209.

58. NYPL Hobhouse (1 June 1815); Comte de La Gardie, 'Mémoires. Séjour en France', *Revue d'histoire diplomatique*, October, 1933, 503 (diary for 24 September 1815).

59. Hobhouse, I, 404, 406–7, 416, 440 (7 June 1815).

60. Fontaine, I, 454 (25 May 1815).

61. Ibid., I, 460 (21 June 1815).

62. Hobhouse, II, 13 (28 June 1815).

63. Montcalm, *Mon journal*, 83 (4 July 1815).

64. Comte Vigier, *Davout Maréchal d'Empire* (2 vols, 1898), II, 306; cf. for evidence of the popularity of Orléans, Harriet Countess Granville, *Letters* (2 vols, 1894), I, 69 (to Lady G. Morpeth, 4 August 1815).

65. *Molé*, I, 227.

66. *Moniteur*, 24 June 1815; NYPL Hobhouse (3 July 1815), recording Flahaut's denunciation of treachery.

67. Barante, II, 156n; *Molé*, I, 234.

68. Bary, 135 (23 June 1815).

69. Hortense, III, 26–49, 59.

70. Mansel, *Louis XVIII*, 250.

71. Talleyrand, *Mémoires*, III, 228 (Metternich to Talleyrand, 24 June 1815).

72. Lacour-Gayet, III, 16; Chateaubriand, *Mémoires d'outre-tombe*, II, 324.

73. PRO FO 27/117 (despatch of Stuart, 30 June 1815).

74. Mercer, II, 71–86 (July 1815); Gronow, I, 201.

75. Williams, 231–2; Hobhouse, II, 111, 119 (1, 2 July 1815).

76. Williams, 240.

77. Ibid., 241–2; Montcalm, *Mon journal*, 85–6 (5, 6 July); Hobhouse, II, 120 (3 July 1815); Lt-Col. William Tomkinson, *The Diary of a Cavalry Officer in the Peninsular and Waterloo Campaigns* (1894), 324 (6 July 1815).

78. Dallas, 423; Fontaine, I, 465 (3 July 1815).

79. Castlereagh, X, 413 (Convention for the evacuation of Paris, 3 July 1815).

80. AN 349 AP 23 (*ordre du jour* of 5 July 1815 by Maréchal Masséna); Williams, 251.

81. Alexander, 211; Colonel Sir Augustus Simon Frazer KCB, *Letters . . . written during the Peninsular and Waterloo Campaigns* (1859), 598 (letter of 8 July 1815); AN 359 AP 99 (Clermont-Tonnerre to Madame de Clermont-Tonnerre, 7 July 1815).

82. Sismondi, 107 (letter of 7 July 1815); AN 359 AP 99 (Clermont-Tonnerre to Madame de Clermont-Tonnerre, 7 July 1815); Granville, I, 69 (to Lady G. Morpeth, 4 August 1815); NYPL Hobhouse (12 July 1815).

83. Baron von Müffling, *Passages from my Life and Writings* (2nd ed. rev., 1858), 256, 260.

84. Williams, 267–8; *Molé*, I, 268.

85. Fontaine, I, 467 (7, 8 July 1815); Metternich, II, 525 (Metternich to Marie de Metternich, 13 July 1815). For Saint-Cloud see Shelley, I, 110; Simpson, 141. Blücher removed many Bonaparte portraits from Saint-Cloud to his family castle in Silesia.

86. Dallas, 428–9.

87. Mercer, II, 87, 89 (7 July 1815).

88. *Mémoires d'outre-tombe*, II, 335; cf. Marquis de La Maisonfort, *Mémoires d'un royaliste* (1999), 281.

89. Caulaincourt, III, 139; Hobhouse, II, 149 (7 July 1815); Williams, 263.

90. NYPL Hobhouse (6 July 1815); Williams, 261; Polovtsov, I, 286 (despatch of 8 July 1815); Marquis de Toustain, *Mémoires* (1933), 308.

91. *Moniteur*, 9 July 1815, 781.

92. AN 197 AP [La Châtre papers] (Louis XVIII to La Châtre, 20 July 1815); AN 359 AP 99 (Clermont-Tonnerre letter of 9 July 1815); cf. for similar royalist accounts, Toustain, 310; A.H. Heriot de Vroil, *Mémoires d'un officier de la Garde Royale* (1904), 115.

93. Lord Malmesbury, *Letters* (2 vols, 1870), II, 456 (Captain G. Bowles to Lord Fitzharris, 9 July 1815); *Molé*, I, 269.

94. Williams, 271; Mrs Charles Bagot, *Links with the Past* (1901), 122 (Charles to Susan Perry, 8 July 1815); John Colville, *The Portrait of a General* (1980), 211 (Charles to John Colville, 9 July 1815).

95. Williams, 274; Castlereagh, X, 420 (to Liverpool, 8 July 1815).

96. Shelley, I, 99 (July 1815); J.W. Croker, *Correspondence and Diaries* (3 vols, 1884), I, 61 (to Mrs

Notes

Croker, 12 July 1815); Comte d'Haussonville, *Ma jeunesse 1814–1830* (1883), 110; Hennet de Goutel, 284, 285 (31 July, 2 August 1815).

97. Mercer, II, 255 (8 August 1815); Bodleian Library Oxford, Mangin diary f21.

98. Fellowes, 122 (24 July 1815); Granville, I, 69 (to Lady G. Morpeth, 4 August 1815); [Walter Scott], *Paul's Letters to his Kinsfolk* (Edinburgh, 1816), 443; Corti, 146–7.

99. Broughton, I, 309 (9 July 1815); Metternich, *Mémoires, documents et écrits divers*, II, 524 (to Marie de Metternich, 13 July 1815).

100. Beugnot, II, 307.

101. Talleyrand, III, 236n (letter of Louis XVIII, 15 July 1815); Roger André, *L'Occupation de la France par les alliés, juillet–novembre 1815* (1924), 20, 49.

102. Castellane, I, 296 (12 July 1815).

103. Frazer, 606 (letter of 15 July).

104. Wellington, *SD*, XI, 73 (general order of 28 July 1815).

105. AN F7 3786 (reports of 8 August, 10 September 1815); E. Forgues, *Le Dossier secret de Fouché* (1908), 49 (note of 5 August 1815); Anthony Powell (ed.), *Barnard Letters 1778–1824* (1928), 246 (Müffling to Colonel Sir Andrew Barnard, 18 August 1815); John Scott, *Paris Revisited*, 28.

106. Tulard, *Paris*, 445.

107. V. Sackville-West, *Knole and the Sackvilles* (1958 ed.), 205 (Robert Peel to Lord Whitworth, 16 July 1815); Hortense, III, 58; Wellington, *SD*, XI, 44 (private intelligence from Paris, 18 July 1815); AN F7 3786 (police reports of 17, 18 July 1815); Forgues, 21 (19 July 1815); Hobhouse, II, 221 (22 July 1815): Hobhouse also refers to the hyacinth as Orléans' flower on 13 April (NYPL); Fellowes, 108 (20 July 1815).

108. Granville, I, 66–8 (to Lady G. Morpeth, 1 August 1815).

109. Hortense, III, 67n.

110. NYPL Hobhouse diary (28 June 1815).

111. Granville, I, 70 (to Lady G. Morpeth, 4 August 1815); Castlereagh, X, 452 (Castlereagh to Liverpool, 3 August 1815).

112. Benjamin et Rosalie de Constant, 209 (Benjamin to Rosalie de Constant, August 1815); Daudet, *Louis XVIII*, 69; Constant, *Journaux intimes*, 445, 446 (24 July, 3 August 1815); Boigne, I, 342.

113. *Procès de Charles de Labédoyère ex-colonel du 7e de ligne* (1815), 66, 68, 95.

114. *CG*, III, 50 (to Madame de Duras, 20 August 1815).

115. Alexandre Théodore Brongniart (Musée Carnavalet, 1986), 295–303; James Simpson, 241–3. In 1816 there were 2,000 *concessions perpetuelles* in the cemetery, in 1830 31,000.

116. F.M. Marchant de Beaumont, *Manuel et itinéraire du curieux dans le Cimetière de Père La Chaise* (1828), 24n.

117. Bibliothèque Thiers Fonds Frédéric Masson, MSS 1248 f92 (note by Madame de La Bédoyère, 2 September 1816), cf. Marie Amélie, *Journal* (1981 ed.), 249 (20 April 1818).

118. John Scott, *Paris Revisited*, 294, 297; John Scott, of Gala, *Journal of a Tour to Waterloo and Paris in company with Sir Walter Scott in 1815* (1842), 102; Bodleian Library Oxford, Mangin diary f140 (5 September 1815); cf. Catherine Clerc, *La Caricature contre Napoléon* (1985), 227–313.

119. Bodleian Library Oxford, Mangin diary f132 (4 September 1815); Dibdin, II, 510n.

120. Nina Athanassoglou-Kallmyer, *Eugène Delacroix. Print, Politics and Satire 1814–1822* (New Haven, 1991), 19.

121. John Scott, *Paris Revisited*, 277; Walter Scott, 416–17.

122. John Scott, *Paris Revisited*, 278–9; Tomkinson, 326 (July 1815); James, 60–2.

123. Adeline Daumard, *La Bourgeoisie parisienne de 1815 à 1848* (1996 ed.), 429 (all references to Daumard are to this work unless otherwise indicated); Athanassoglou-Kallmyer, 19.

124. John William Kaye, *The Life and Correspondence of Major-General Sir John Malcolm GCB* (2 vols, 1856), II, 111 (diary for 2 August 1815); Gronow, I, 129.

125. Broughton, I, 293 (28 June 1815); George Thomas Earl of Albemarle, *Fifty Years of My Life* (2 vols, 1876), II, 53–4; Colville, 212 (Charles to John Colville, 9 July 1815).

126. McGuigan, 492; Granville, I, 74 (to Lady G. Morpeth, August 1815).

127. Kaye, II, 111 (letter of 2 August 1815); Gronow, I, 209.

128. John Scott, *Paris Revisited*, 287; Perey, 475 (Hélène to Vincent Potocki, 18 September 1815); AN F7 3786 (report of 12 September 1815).

129. Williams, 258; James Simpson, 153; Frye, 75 (August 1815).

130. Granville, I, 70 (to Lady G. Morpeth, 4 August 1815).

131. Castlereagh, X, 429 (Liverpool to Castlereagh, 15 July 1815); Gould, 121.

132. Johns, 22, 171, 176; C.K. Webster, *The Foreign Policy of Castlereagh 1815–1822* (1925), 473; Fontaine, however, claims that the naked Napoleon was sold to Wellington for 80,000 francs: *Journal*, II, 1000 (1841).

133. Castlereagh, X, 462 (undated memorial of foreign artists).

134. Walter Scott, 381; Milton, 27; P.W. Clayden, *Rogers and his Contemporaries* (2 vols, 1889), I, 201 (Richard Sharp to Samuel Rogers, 23 August 1815).

135. *Marianne et Germania*, 162; John Scott, *Paris Revisited*, 316.

136. Gould, 117–19.

137. M. Mazier du Heaume, *Observations d'un Français sur l'enlèvement des chefs-d'oeuvre du Muséum de Paris en réponse à la lettre du duc de Wellington au Lord Castlereagh sous la date du 23 septembre 1815* (1815), 28–9.

138. F. von Gentz, *Tagebücher* (4 vols, Leipzig, 1873), I, 410 (19 September 1815).

139. John Scott, *Paris Revisited*, 327; Mercer, II, 145, 148.

140. John Scott, *Paris Revisited*, 329–30.

141. Castlereagh, XI, 39 (Castlereagh to Liverpool, 1 October 1815); *Briefe des Feldmarschalls Fürsten Schwarzenberg an seine Frau 1799–1816* (hereafter Schwarzenberg), ed. J.F. Nowak (Vienna, 1913), 422 (letter of 29 September 1815); Baron von Müffling, *Passages from my Life and Writings* (2nd rev. ed., 1858), 263–4.

142. John Scott, *Paris Revisited*, 350; Milton, 177–80.

143. Clayden, I, 204–5 (Samuel to Sarah Rogers, 14 October 1815); John Scott, *Paris Revisited*, 352.

144. Schwarzenberg, 423 (letter of 1 October 1815).

145. Paul d'Ariste and Maurice Arnety, *Les Champs Elysées. Etude topographique, historique et anecdotique* (1913), 153.

146. La Gardie, 511–12 (diary for 2 October 1815); cf. Perey, 479 (Hélène to Vincent Potocki, 5 October 1815).

147. Gould, 125–8; Johns, 186–90.

148. Francis Ley, *Madame de Kruedener 1764–1824. Romantisme et sainte alliance* (1994), 146 (letter to Madame de Staël, 29 July 1802).

149. Ibid., 291, 301–3; McGuigan, 488.

150. Ley, 300, 304–6.

151. Constant, *Journaux intimes*, 448, 450, 451 (6, 8, 26 September, 11 October 1815).

152. Castellane, I, 299 (10 August 1815).

153. Chateaubriand, *CG*, III, 41, 43 (letters of 12 and 16 August 1815).

154. Ibid., III, 55, 58 (to Madame de Kruedener, 27 August, 14 September 1815): Bibliothèque Municipale de Genève, diary of Juliana de Kruedener (hereafter Kruedener), 15, 23 September 1815; Montcalm, 93, 95 and n (28 September 1815).

155. Géraud, 292 (22 September 1815); Wellington, *SD*, XI, 167, 170 (Castlereagh to Liverpool, 21, 25 September 1815).

156. Montcalm, *Mon journal*, 93 (28 September 1815).

157. AN 565 AP FL6 (Madame de Souza to Flahaut, 25 November 1815, 3 January 1816).

158. Hobhouse, I, 283 (proclamation of Davout, 28 April 1815).

159. Sorel, VIII, 487, 488.

160. Walter Scott, 379, 383.

161. James Simpson, 259.

162. Sorel, VIII, 467. A protocol of one session is in NLS MSS Stuart de Rothesay 21264 f80 (*séance du 4 septembre 1815*).

163. Webster, 58–9; Dallas, 442–3.

164. Dallas, 449–53; G. de Bertier de Sauvigny, *Metternich et la France, après le Congrès de Vienne* (3 vols, 1968–72), II, 14n.

165. Polovtsov, II, 117, 517, 772 (Pozzo to Nesselrode, 1/13 December 1817; Capo d'Istria to Pozzo, 10/22 July 1818); cf. Chateaubriand, *Congrès de Vérone* (Geneva, 1979), 114.

166. Polovtsov, III, 143 (to Nesselrode, 14 July 1819).

167. C.L. Le Sur, *La France et les Français en 1817. Tableau moral et politique* (1817), 33.

168. Monchoux, 148; cf. for references to the European republic, Vicomte de Bonald, *Réflexions sur l'intérêt général de l'Europe, suivies de quelques considérations sur la noblesse* (1815); Walter Scott, 57; Abbé de Pradt, *L'Europe et l'Amérique en 1822 et 1823* (2 vols, 1824), I, 27.

169. Tulard, *Napoléon à Sainte-Hélène*, 409 (Las Cases, 11 November 1816); Polovtsov, III, 187 (despatch of 20 September 1819).

170. Mansel, *Louis XVIII*, 262; id., *Pillars of Monarchy. An Outline of the Political and Social History of Royal Guards 1400–1984* (1984), 46, 132–3; Pasquier, III, 409–10.

171. Polovtsov, I, 398 (Pozzo to Nesselrode, 25 January/6 February 1816).

172. See e.g. Montcalm, *Mon journal*, 85–6 (5, 6 July 1815).

173. AN 349 AP 23 (*ordres du jour* of 23 June, 14 July 1815). From 23 June, 200 were on guard at the Tuileries, 150 at the Hôtel de Ville, 150 at the Luxembourg, 200 at the Palais Royal, 150 at each *mairie*, 1,000 at the Palais Bourbon.

174. Fontaine, I, 469 (20 July 1815); AN 349 AP 23 (*ordre du jour* of 14 July 1815); *James*, 56; cf. for similar praise of the National Guard: Laborde, 7–8; Chastenay, II, 566; Daumard, 562–3.

175. Félix Pigeory, *Les Monuments de Paris. Histoire de l'architecture civile, politique et religieuse sous le règne de Louis-Philippe* (1847), 314–17.

176. David Pinkney, *The French Revolution of 1830* (Princeton, 1972), 102; Daumard, 553.

177. Gunnell, 61–2 (to Catherine Sharpe, October 1819).

178. Firmin-Didot, 141 (report of 6 October 1814).

179. Girod de l'Ain, 286 (29 June 1815); cf. Barante, II, 162, 164 (Barante to Madame de Barante, 29 June, 3 July 1815: *le peuple est gai, tranquille . . . Paris est toujours d'un calme parfait*).

4 Chambers and Salons *1815–1820*

1. Marquis Dugon, *Au service du roi en exil* (1968), 288 (diary for 12 November 1814); Maréchale Oudinot, *Récits de guerre et de foyer* (1894), 331.

2. Gautier, *Paris et les Parisiens*, 111; Françoise Magny (ed.), *Palais Bourbon. Sa place* (1987), 23, 59–60, 72, 75; Robert Batty, *French Scenery from Drawings made in 1819* (1822); Marchant, *Nouveau Conducteur de Paris* (1822), 132.

3. Frye, 74 (August 1815).

4. *Palais Bourbon*, 64; Shepherd, 261–3 (14 July 1814); Stevenson, 198–9 (3 June 1816); Batty.

5. Private collection, journal of Anne Lister, 14 March 1825.

6. Charles Abbot Lord Colchester, *Diary and Corrrespondence* (3 vols, 1861), II, 556 (diary for 7 October 1815); cf. Stanley, 129 (10 July 1814).

7. Wellington, *SD*, XI, 226 (Charles Arbuthnot to Liverpool, 30 October 1815); cf. Comte de Villèle, *Mémoires et correspondance* (5 vols, 1888–96), II, 137 (Villèle to Madame de Villèle, 13 December 1816); *Molé*, III, 149 (*re: la session absorbant tous les esprits*, in 1817).

8. Madame de Girardin, *Lettres parisiennes du Vicomte de Launay* (hereafter Girardin 1) (1986 ed.), 394 (19 January 1839); cf. Villèle, II, 148 (Villèle to Madame de Villèle, 24 December 1816).

9. Rémusat, *Mémoires*, I, 379–80.

10. NLS MSS 9236 f137vo (Mrs Allen to Miss Millars, April 1829). At first, however, British visitors had found speeches extremely dull: cf. Knight, II, 122; Berry, III, 81.

11. NLS MSS 9236 f135 (Mrs Allen to Miss Millars, 8 March 1829); cf. for the popularity of parliamentary debates among women: Anne Martin-Fugier, *La Vie élégante ou la formation de Tout-Paris 1815–1848* (1990), 215; Girardin 1, 637 (28 March 1840); Duc d'Aumale, *Correspondance du . . . et de Cuvillier-Fleury* (4 vols, 1910–14), I, 234 (Cuvillier-Fleury to Duc d'Aumale, 26 January 1844).

12. Duc Victor de Broglie, *Souvenirs 1785–1870* (4 vols, 1886), II, 121 (diary of 15 January 1820).

13. Nesselrode, V, 290, VIII, 77–8 (Comtesse to Comte Charles de Nesselrode, 27 January 1818, 26, 28 November 1840); cf. Duchesse de Dino, *Chronique de 1831 à 1862* (4 vols, 1909), II, 205 (13 January 1838), 422 (1 December 1840, quoting a letter of Princess Lieven); and Piotr Kozlowski, *Diorama social de Paris par un étranger qui y a séjourné l'hiver de l'année 1823 et une partie de l'année 1824* (1997), 87, who also compared the Chamber to the opera.

14. *Léopold avant Léopold Ier*, 96 (Léopold to Sophie, 8 November 1814); Ernest Daudet, *La Police politique. Chroniques des temps de la Restauration* (1912), 94–7; Gronow, II, 300; Castellane, II, 58 (26 January 1825), III, 18, 168, 217 (23 September 1832, 29 March 1838, 23 May 1840).

15. Foster Dormer MSS, Journal of Elizabeth Duchess of Devonshire, 20 January 1822.

16. Archives du Château de La Ferrière (Luxembourg to Madame de Podenas, 5 August 1824).

17. G. Pailhès, *La Duchesse de Duras et Chateaubriand* (1910), 460 (Duras to Rosalie de Constant, 15 May 1825); cf. Victor Broglie, II, 375: *La session terminée rien ne me retenait plus à Paris* (1823).

18. Benjamin et Rosalie de Constant, 235, 310 (letters of 7 November 1820, 7 October 1829).

19. Shepherd, 264–5 (14 July 1814); Berry, *Journals*, III, 88 (10 April 1816).

20. *Molé*, II, 37; *Mémoires d'outre-tombe*, II, 392.

21. *Molé*, II, 69; Castellane, I, 307 (21 November 1815); Frye, 140 (5 December 1815).

22. Pasquier, IV, 44; Bruce, 161; Castellane, I, 308 (7 December 1815).

23. Roger Langeron, *Decazes ministre du roi* (1960), 82; Polovtsov, I, 364 (Pozzo to Nesselrode, 18/30 December 1815).

24. Jean-Paul Clément, *Chateaubriand. Biographie morale et intellectuale* (1998), 285 (article of 5 December 1818); Ferdinand-Philippe Duc d'Orléans, *Souvenirs 1810–1830* (Geneva, 1993), 142, 143n.

25. Daudet, *Louis XVIII*, 115; Emmanuel de Waresquiel, *La Vie de de Richelieu* (1990), 260;

Notes

Pasquier, IV, 164; Wellington, *SD*, IX, 301 (Wellington to Bathurst, 13 February 1816); cf. Webster, 74–87. This conference was still meeting in 1820, two years after the departure of allied forces from France: NLS 6198 f369 (Stuart to Castlereagh, 27 January 1820).

26. Duc de Richelieu, *Lettres au marquis d'Osmond 1816–1818* (1939), 71, 111 (letters of 31 October 1816, 8 May 1817).

27. Granville, I, 96 (to Lady G. Morpeth, May 1817); Decin State Archives, Czech Republic, Prince Clary, unpublished diary, 27 April 1822. Some actresses' letters to Stuart are preserved in the National Library of Scotland: MSS 21328 f119 (letter of 29 August: Eugénie asks for a lock of his hair: *adieu amour, adieu toi qui me faisait rêver du charme de la vie, aime-moi un peu*); 21266 f20 (letter of 3 June 1816: 'Palmyre' asks, *vous m'aimez n'est-ce pas?*).

28. F. de Gentz, *Dépêches inédites aux hospodars de Valachie* (3 vols, 1876–7), I, 180–1 (despatch of 25 September 1815).

29. Villèle, III, 206 (Montmorency to Villèle, 12 November 1822); *Molé*, III, 93, 383–6, IV, 271; cf. Daudet, *Louis XVIII*, 53n (Louis XVIII to Decazes, 7 September 1818).

30. Chateaubriand, *CG*, III, 145 (to Duchesse de Duras, 18 September 1817).

31. *Molé*, II, 174, III, 27; Polovtsov, I, 560 (Pozzo to Nesselrode, 3/15 July 1816), II, 546 (26 December 1817/7 January 1818); cf. ibid., 180 (7/19 May 1817), *re: une audience particulière où il m'a permis de lui parler longuement de ses propres affaires et de celles de l'Europe qui s'y attachent essentiellement.*

32. Daudet, *Louis XVIII, passim.*

33. Bertier de Sauvigny, *Nouvelle Histoire de Paris*, 432.

34. Richelieu, 33, 39, 53 (letters to Osmond of 8 May, 13 June, 5 August 1816).

35. Daudet, *Louis XVIII*, 143; *Molé*, II, 247.

36. AN 565 AP FL6 (Madame de Souza to Flahaut, 14 October 1816).

37. Lady Morgan, *France* (3rd ed., 2 vols, 1818), I, 203.

38. Montcalm, 95 (28 September 1815).

39. Jaucourt, 310 (to Talleyrand, 28 April 1815).

40. Daudet, *Louis XVIII*, 159–61 (Goltz to Hardenberg, 22 September 1816); Montcalm, 192 (25 September 1816); Chateaubriand, *CG*, III, 365 (Decazes to Chateaubriand, 18 September 1816); Clément (1998), p. 272.

41. Charles de Rémusat, *Correspondance pendant les premières années de la Restauration* (6 vols, 1883–6), II, 243 (Charles to Madame de Rémusat, 17 November 1816).

42. Daumard, 300.

43. Général Lamarque, *Mémoires et souvenirs* (3 vols, 1835–6), I, 427 (diary for 20 May 1822); Montcalm, 299 (26 October 1817).

44. Castellane, I, 338 (May 1817); Pasquier, IV, 192.

45. Archives Rohan-Chabot, Chabrol memoirs ff26vo–27vo; cf. Roger Langeron, 93 (Louis XVIII to Decazes, 17 April, 3, 16 May, 5 September 1816).

46. Richelieu, 139 (to Osmond, 29 September 1817).

47. Montcalm, 227 (March 1817); Polovtsov, II, 123 (Pozzo to Nesselrode, 31 March/12 April 1817); J.P.F. Viennet, *Journal* (1955), 32–7 (23, 25 March 1817); Dalrymple Hamilton, diary, 8 October 1816, 23 March 1817; Castellane, I, 336 (diary for 22 March 1817).

48. Viennet, 37 (25 March 1817).

49. Waresquiel et Yvert, 185, 201, 204–5.

50. Daudet, *Louis XVIII*, 69; L.M. Lomuller, *Guillaume Ternaux 1763–1833* (1978), 364, 379, 405.

51. W.H. Zawadski, *A Man of Honour. Adam Czartoryski as a Statesman of Russia and Poland*

1795–1831 (Oxford, 1993), 261; Paul W. Schroeder, *The Transformation of European Politics 1763–1848* (1994), 597–8; Neill Macaulay, *Dom Pedro. The Struggle for Liberty in Brazil and Portugal 1798–1834* (Durham, NY, 1986), 162–4; B. Mirkine-Guetzevitch, '1830 dans l'évolution constitutionnelle de l'Europe', in *Etudes sur les mouvements libéraux et nationaux de l'Europe* (1930), 15–17.

52. *Krone und Verfassung. König Max I Joseph und der neue Staat* (2 vols, Munich, 1980), II, 304; *Baden und Württemberg im Zeitalter Napoleons* (2 vols, Stuttgart, 1987), I, i, 342.

53. Anton Chroust, *Die Berichte der Franszösichen Gesandten* (Munich, 1935), I, 106 (Lagarde to Dessolles, 11 June 1819).

54. Stendhal, *Rome, Naples et Florence en 1817* (1964 ed.), 29, 189 (17 November 1816, 18 July 1817).

55. G.R.V. Barratt, *Voices in Exile. The Decembrist Memoirs* (Montreal and London, 1974), 334 (Baron V.I. Shtyengel to Nicholas I, 11 January 1826); Polovtsov, III, 335 (La Ferronays to Pasquier, 16 March 1820); Chateaubriand, *CG*, IV, 114 (to Pasquier, 10 March 1821).

56. Brigitte de Montclos, *Les Russes à Paris au XIXe siècle* (1996), 15–18; *Historic Archive of Alexander Mavrocordato* (Athens, 1963), I, 22 (letter of 10 September 1820).

57. *Molé*, II, 412 (speech of 16 February 1816).

58. Morgan, *France*, II, 224; J. Fenimore Cooper, *Recollections of Europe* (Paris, 1837), 149.

59. Lacour-Gayet, III, 65–7; Pasquier, IV, 137; *Molé*, III, 291.

60. Pange, 202 (Madame de Staël to Duchess of Devonshire, 29 January 1817).

61. Morgan, *France*, I, 220n.

62. AN 565 AP FL6 (Madame de Souza to Flahaut, 18 February 1817).

63. BL Add. MSS 51638 f170vo (Madame de Coigny to Lady Holland, 23 March 1818).

64. Daudet, *La Police politique*, 167 (Louis XVIII to Decazes, n.d.); M.F.P.G. Maine de Biran, *Journal* (3 vols, Neuchâtel, 1954–7), II, 99 (1 January 1818).

65. Maine de Biran, II, 100 (3 January 1818).

66. AN 565 AP FL7 (Madame de Souza to Flahaut, 31 August 1818).

67. Maine de Biran, II, 59, 175 (31 July 1817, 11 November 1818).

68. Waresquiel, *Richelieu*, 363.

69. Montcalm, 344 (February 1819); *Molé*, IV, 267.

70. Polovtsov, III, 105 (Pozzo to Nesselrode, 23 May 1819).

71. Bodleian Library Oxford, Mangin diary f183 (20 May 1819); Victor Broglie, II, 119 (diary for 15 January 1820); *Journal and correspondence from 1808 to 1852 of Sir Francis Thornhill Baring afterwards Lord Northbrook* (2 vols, 1905), I, 16, 17 (9, 10 April 1818); cf. Apponyi, I, 22 (27 August 1826).

72. A. Bardoux, *La Duchesse de Duras* (1888), 274 (Duchesse de Duras to Chateaubriand, April 1821); Daudet, *Louis XVIII*, 374 (Louis XVIII to Decazes, 16 November 1819).

73. Comte de Serre, *Correspondance* (6 vols, 1876), III, 216 (La Boulaye to Serre, 20 March 1820); *Molé*, III, 206; cf. Stendhal, *Vie de Napoléon* (1929), 218, on the Comte de Ségur, who *n'ayant pas de place s'est fait libéral.*

74. Archives du Château de La Ferrière (Duchesse d'Escars to Madame de Podenas, 14 December 1818).

75. Victor Broglie, I, 142, 149.

76. *Considérations sur la Révolution française*, 459.

77. *Molé*, IV, 143.

78. Ibid., III, 371–2, IV, 239; H. de Schaller, *Souvenirs d'un officier fribourgeois 1798–1848* (Fribourg, 1890), 103–6; Emmanuel de Waresquiel et Benoit Yvert, 'Le duc de Richelieu et le comte

Notes

Decazes d'après leur correspondance inédite', in *Revue de la Société d'Histoire de la Restauration*, II (1988), 91 (Richelieu to Decazes, 7 October 1818).

79. Richelieu, 53 (Richelieu to Osmond, 5 August 1816); Henri Rossi, *Mémoires aristocratiques féminins 1789–1848* (1998), 303; Beugnot, II, 238; Morgan, *France in 1829–30*, I, 331.

80. Castellane, I, 400 (22 March 1820).

81. Polovtsov, II, 216 (Pozzo to Nesselrode, 2/14 June 1817).

82. Ibid., II, 181 (Pozzo to Nesselrode, 7/19 May 1817); Bibliothèque Administrative de la Ville de Paris, Lévis notes, April 1825, for Charles X's admiration for Napoleon I.

83. Granville, I, 97–8, 109 (Lady Granville to Lady G. Morpeth, May, June 1817); Boigne, I, 272; Baron de Frénilly, *Souvenirs* (1908), 440; Bertier, *Metternich et la France*, II, 108; Villèle, II, 272n (*carnet* for 14 and 16 November 1819).

84. Clément (1998), 388; Daudet, *La Police politique*, 274; Henri Guillemin, *L'Homme des Mémoires d'outre-tombe* (1964), 131; Chateaubriand, *CG*, III, 87, 102, 267, 268, 452 (Chateaubriand to Jules de Polignac, 27 September 1816; to Duc de Fitzjames, 12 April 1817; to Madame d'Orglandes, 20 October 1820; to Jules de Polignac, 28 October 1820). In 1820 Chateaubriand asked *notre excellent maître* Monsieur to reassure Madame de Chateaubriand in person about his future.

85. Chateaubriand, *CG*, III, 218 (Chateaubriand to Madame de Marigny, 2 October 1819).

86. Polovtsov, II, 585 (Pozzo to Nesselrode, 3/15 February 1818); Bertier de Sauvigny, *Metternich et la France*, I, 182–3.

87. Polovtsov, II, 120 (Pozzo to Nesselrode, 31 March/12 April 1817).

88. *Molé*, III, 101; Roger Langeron, 93 (Louis XVIII to Decazes, 16 May 1816: *j'irai aujourd'hui à Vincennes et chemin faisant et défaisant je verrai quelle mine on nous fera dans notre Faubourg*); Richelieu, 107 (to Osmond, 17 April 1817).

89. Daudet, *La Police politique*, 174 and n (letters to Duc de Bourbon, 6 November 1817; from Goltz to Hardenberg, 4 November 1816); Gunnell, 30 (Sutton Sharpe, letter of 3 September 1819).

90. Bertier de Sauvigny, *Nouvelle Histoire de Paris*, 435.

91. *Revue hebdomadaire*, July 1937, 494–5 (letter to Marquis d'Aragon, 26 September 1819).

92. Mansel, *Louis XVIII*, 387; Victor Broglie, II, 114 (diary, 3 December 1819).

93. Barante, II, 393 (Barante to Madame Anisson du Perrson, 6 December 1819).

94. Daudet, *Louis XVIII*, 386, 398.

95. Barante, II, 519 (Rémusat to Barante, 16 August 1821); cf. Maurice Levaillant (ed.), *Chateaubriand. Lettres à Madame Récamier* (1998 ed.), 297 (Chateaubriand to Madame Récamier, 17 March 1829).

96. Serre, II, 446 (Broglie to Serre, 16 November 1819), 464 (Louis XVIII to Decazes, 18 November 1819).

97. Polovtsov, I, 591 (Pozzo to Nesselrode, 4/16 August 1816); cf. Montcalm, 100 (11 October 1815); Maine de Biran, I, 98 (January 1816).

98. Montcalm, 88 (12 July 1815).

99. Archivio di Stato Turin (AST) Lettere Ministri Francia 1829 in 1830 35 f174 (despatch from Comte de Brignole, 16 September 1829).

100. Pasquier, IV, 12, 213; Chateaubriand, *Mémoires d'outre-tombe*, II, 397; Villèle, II, 416 (to Madame de Villèle, 1 December 1820: *J'ai diné chez Piet avec tous nos fous*), 422 (id. to id., 8 December 1820); Frénilly, 444; Rémusat, *Correspondance*, I, 212 (Charles to Madame de Rémusat, 10 January 1816).

101. Lomuller, 437; Ernest Daudet, *L'Ambassade du duc Decazes en Angleterre (1820–1821)* (1910), 306 (intercepted letter of 21 February 1820); cf. Serre, III, 53, 73 (La Boulaye to Serre, 20 February 1820; Comte Siméon to Serre, 21 February 1820).

102. Rémusat, *Mémoires*, II, 82–3; Villèle, II, 277 (to Madame de Villèle, 26 November 1819).

103. Noailles, 101; Boigne, II, 14.

104. George Ticknor, *Life, Letters and Journals* (3 vols, Boston, 1876), I, 131 (diary of 6 May 1817).

105. Montcalm, 131n (28 February 1816).

106. Duchesse de Broglie, *Lettres* (1896), 30 (to Madame Anisson du Perron, 13 December 1819).

107. Madame de Genlis, *Dernières Lettres d'amour. Correspondance inédite avec le comte Anatole de Montesquiou* (1954), 25 (June 1821); cf. Rémusat, *Correspondance*, I, 149 (Charles to Madame de Rémusat, 7 December 1815), about the salon of Madame de Catellan: *la politique y absorbe tout . . . les femmes se taisent, c'est aujourd'hui leur lot*; Comte L. de Carné, *Souvenirs de ma jeunesse au temps de la Restauration* (1872), 33.

108. Adeline Daumard, 'La vie de salon en France dans la première moitié du XIXe siècle', in Etienne François (ed.), *Sociabilité et société bourgeoise en France, en Allemagne et en Suisse (1750–1850)* (1986), 89; Boigne, II, 20.

109. Daudet, *Louis XVIII*, 290, 293n; Montcalm, 125, 175, 192 (7 February 1816, March 1816, 25 September 1816); cf. François Rousseau, 'Un observateur secret de M. de Chateaubriand (1820–1821). Documents inédits', *Le Correspondant*, 25 March 1912, 1182, 1184 (Madame de Montcalm to Chateaubriand, 21 July, 8 August 1821).

110. Haussonville, *Ma jeunesse*, 263; cf. Carné, 65–6.

111. Pailhès, 413 (Duchesse de Duras to Chateaubriand, 1822).

112. Lamartine, *Correspondance générale* (hereafter *CG*) (2 vols, 1943–8), I, 270, 273 (Lamartine to Virieu, 22 April 1832; to Edmond de Cazalès, 7 May 1832). Some of Lamartine's admiring letters to Madame de Montcalm are in Emmanuel de Lévis Mirepoix (ed.), *Correspondance de la marquise de Montcalm* (1949), 257–93.

113. *Journal des Maires*, 5986 (11 December 1820); cf. Daudet, *Louis XVIII*, 331 (souvenirs of Duchesse Decazes).

114. Kozlovski, 128; cf. Daudet, *Louis XVIII*, 338.

115. James Silk Buckingham, *France, Piedmont, Italy, Lombardy, the Tyrol and Bavaria. An Autumnal Tour* (2 vols, 1847), I, 35; cf. for the frequency of ministerial entertainments, Rémusat, *Mémoires*, III, 338.

116. *Molé*, II, 18, 45, III, 121; Villèle, II, 363 (Villèle to Madame de Villèle, 29 February 1820).

117. Leonore Davidoff, *The Best Circles* (1986 ed.), 99.

118. *Ferragus* (Presses Pocket, 1992), 51.

119. Archives privées, Duchesse de Luynes douairiaire to Duc de Luynes, 27 June 1819; cf. for the role of salons in the education of Guizot and Charles de Rémusat, Pierre Rosanvallon, *Le Moment Guizot* (1985), 148–9.

120. Carné, 67; cf. for these salons as information centres, Nesselrode, V, 290 (Comtesse to Comte Charles de Nesselrode, 27 January 1818).

121. Granville, I, 344 (to Lady G. Morpeth, 27 February 1825).

122. Cf. the diary entry of the Duchesse de Berri in her *Journal de mon voyage au Mont d'or*, 30 August 1821 (Archives of Schloss Brunnsee, Austria): *Aussitôt après mon arrivée j'ai reçu les autorités et les Dames.*

123. AN 03 90 (*distributions Soirées de la Duchesse d'Escars*). The Duchesse de Polignac had performed a similar role at Versailles, entertaining 'all Europe' on the orders and on behalf of the King and Queen: Comte de Vaudreuil, *Correspondance avec le comte d'Artois* (2 vols, 1890), I, 69 (Vaudreuil to Chevalier de Coigny, December 1789 [copy]).

124. Mrs Warenne Blake (ed.), *An Irish Beauty of the Regency, compiled from 'Mes Souvenirs', the unpublished Journals of the Hon. Mrs Calvert 1789–1822* (1911), 298, 300.

125. Archives du Château de La Ferrière (Duchesse d'Escars to Madame de Podenas, 28 June 1816, 11 November 1816).

126. Christina Colvin (ed.), *Maria Edgeworth in France and Switzerland* (Oxford, 1979), 122 (Maria Edgeworth to Mrs Edgeworth, 14 May 1820); Archives du Château de La Ferrière (Duchesse d'Escars to Madame de Podenas, 7 July 1816); AN 565 AP FL7 (Madame de Souza to Flahaut, 16 October 1823).

127. Polovtsov, III, 107 (to Nesselrode, 11/23 May 1819).

128. Rostopchine, 232, 241; Archives Woronzov, Moscow 1874, VIII (letters of Count Rostopchine) 367, 413, 417, 431.

129. Rostopchine, 232.

130. AN 03 199 (*registre des présentations*, number 135).

131. Rostopchine, 348 (letter to his wife, 1817).

132. Rémusat, *Correspondance*, IV, 308 (Madame to Charles de Rémusat, 14 June 1818); Ticknor, I, 132 (diary of 11 May 1817); *Molé*, III, 74.

133. *Molé*, II, 29; Dino, II, 208, 239 (letters of 28 January 1838, 10 May 1839).

134. Morgan, *France*, I, 407n.

135. *Revue de Paris*, 7 August 1925, 738: *je vis seul, absolument seul, le boulevard est ma promenade* (Chateaubriand to Comtesse de Castellane, 24 February 1826).

136. Ticknor, I, 253 (journal, 10 December 1818–12 January 1819); Comtesse d'Agoult, *Mémoires, souvenirs et portraits* (2 vols, 1990), I, 180. For London, see Alison Adburgham, *Silver Fork Society. Fashionable Life and Literature 1814–1840* (1983), 49.

137. Jouy, *Guillaume le franc-parleur*, II, 81 (18 February 1815).

138. Morgan, *France*, I, 407n, 408, 410; Granville, I, 342 (to Lady G. Morpeth, 7 February 1825).

139. Gunnell, 10, 29 (letter of 3 September 1819, 6 October 1819); cf. Boigne, II, 7.

140. E.g. Molé and Pasquier left the salon of Madame de Montcalm, after a discussion there with the Duc de Richelieu, on foot: *Molé*, IV, 363.

141. Morgan, *France*, I, 343–4 and 344n; Cooper, 99.

142. Countess of Blessington, *The Idler in France* (2 vols, 1841), I, 115–16; Madame de Girardin, *Correspondance parisienne* (1853), 349 (22 June 1844).

143. Morgan, *France*, I, 413; Rostopchine, 344.

144. Morgan, *France*, I, 238, 411; Henry Edward Fox, *Journal* (1923), 71 (8 June 1821).

145. Ticknor, I, 253 (10 December 1818–January 1819).

146. Colvin, 139 (Harriet Edgeworth to Louisa Beaufort, 21 May 1820).

147. Villèle, II, 96, 122 (Villèle to Madame de Villèle 19, 29 November 1816).

148. Lord Glenbervie, *Diaries* (2 vols, 1928), II, 267 (diary of 16 December 1817).

149. Martha Wilmot, *Impressions of Vienna 1816–1829* (1935), 45, 304 (to Alicia Wilmot, 21 December 1819, 10 October 1827); Gronow, I, 226.

150. Buckingham, I, 34.

151. Boigne, II, 10; Decin State Archives, Czech Republic, Prince Clary, unpublished diary (7 May 1822).

152. Comte Raczynski, 'Le dernier hiver d'un règne. Paris 1824', *Revue d'histoire diplomatique* (1903), 138, 140 (22 January, 6 February, 18 March 1824); cf. Kozlowski, 191–4.

153. Pailhès, 278, 424 (Duras to Rosalie de Constant, 28 October 1823; to Madame Swetchine, 19 November 1817).

154. Ibid., 406, 485; Antoine Fontaney, *Journal intime* (1925), 9 (24 August 1831).

155. Washington Irving, *Journals* (3 vols, Boston, 1919), II, 50 (31 October 1824); Gérard, 257 (Humboldt to Gérard, 1825).

156. Pailhès, 413; Bardoux, 198.

157. Ticknor, I, 254–5, 259, 261–3 (diary for 10 December 1818/12 January 1819); Bardoux, 302 (Duchesse de Duras to Chateaubriand, 1821).

158. Marquis de Custine, *Lettres inédites . . . au marquis de La Grange* (n.d.), 67 (4 October 1818); cf. Marquis de La Maisonfort, *Mémoires d'un royaliste* (1999), 277.

159. Pailhès, 412, 418, 440.

160. *Molé*, II, 219; Pailhès, 284 (to Rosalie de Constant, 6 April 1824); cf. Maillé, 103.

161. Boigne, I, 260; Apponyi, I, 5 (21 March 1826).

162. Maillé, 231 (January 1828); Madame de Duras, *Olivier ou le secret*, ed. Denise Virieux (1971), 142, 147.

163. Carné, 89; Pailhès, 344, 457 (to Rosalie de Constant, 29 December 1824).

164. Boigne, II, 10–11; Montcalm, 248 (30 April 1817); Pailhès, 261, 457 (to Rosalie de Constant, 29 December 1824); Duras, *Olivier*, 24 (Duras to Rosalie de Constant, 14 January 1825); Chateaubriand, *CG*, III, 133 (to Duras, 7–9 August 1817). For Félicie's inheritance, see J. Silvestre de Sacy, *Le Faubourg Saint-Germain* (1966), 239.

165. Bardoux, 316 (Duras to Chateaubriand, 14 May 1822); Madame Récamier, *Souvenirs et correspondance* (2nd ed., 1860), II, 298 (Chateaubriand to Madame Récamier, 3 January 1829).

166. Pailhès, 396.

167. Bardoux, 281, 284 (Duras to Chateaubriand, n.d.); Pailhès, 451, 458 (to Duras, 1 August 1824, 1 January 1825 or 6).

168. Pailhès, 156, 269 (2 February 1818, n.d., to Madame Swetchine); cf. Boigne, I, 348–9; Montcalm, 252 (15 May 1817); *Molé*, IV, 132, 266.

169. *CG*, IV, 36 (Chateaubriand to Duchesse de Duras, 16 January 1821); cf. for evidence of their friendship as a political partnership, ibid., 221–33 (daily notes during the change of government in December 1821).

170. *CG*, III, 104 (Chateaubriand to Duchesse de Duras, 23 April 1817).

171. Pailhès, 275 (to Madame Swetchine, 25 September 1823), 438.

172. Ibid., 306, 313, 448 (to Rosalie de Constant, 24 July 1824).

173. *Ourika* (Ladvocat ed. 1824), 123. Her former best friend Madame de La Tour du Pin, remembering the model on which the novel was based, commented in a letter to the Duchess's daughter Félicie, to whom she had transferred her friendship: *Ourika toute véritable était plus intéressante*: *Mémoires de la marquise de La Tour du Pin* (1989 ed.), 387 (letter of December 1823).

174. Pailhès, 527.

175. Granville, I, 320 (to Lady G. Morpeth, 9 December 1824); Apponyi, I, 14 (19 May 1826).

176. Rostopchine, 340 (letter of 1816).

177. Blessington, I, 187–8, 243.

178. *Molé*, III, 354, IV, 412.

179. Lavallette, II, 316–18, 377.

180. Barante, III, 397 (Sainte-Aulaire to Barante, 25 July 1827).

181. Erwin H. Ackerknecht, *Medicine at the Paris Hospital 1794–1848* (Baltimore, 1967), 18, 116, 153.

182. Amédée Fayol, *La Vie et l'oeuvre d'Orfila* (1930), 132 (1 May 1814 to father), 137; cf. for the same attitude expressed by a Prefect of the Seine, Comte de Rambuteau, *Mémoires* (1903), 271.

183. Stendhal, *Promenades dans Rome* (Gallimard, 1997), 33, 318.

184. Marie-Renée Morin (ed.), *Correspondance Lamartine–Virieu* (2 vols, 1987), II, 239, 248, 342 (Lamartine to Virieu, 16 March 1819, 4 April 1819, 17 January 1820).

185. Cf. Madame Swetchine, *Nouvelles Lettres* (1875), 43 (Madame Swetchine to Edouard de La Grange, 28 February 1823: *elle s'est occupée de tous vos intérêts avec M. de Chateaubriand*), 58 (id. to id., 16 December 1823).

186. Niall Fergusson, *The World's Banker. The Rise of the House of Rothschild* (1999), 214.

187. Rostopchine, 344.

188. Fayol, 137.

189. Pierre Moisy, *Les Séjours en France de Sulpice Boisserée (1820–1825)* (1956), 54–6; Foy, III, 163 (26 December 1824); Morgan, *France in 1829–30*, I, 469; Balzac, *Lettres à Madame Hanska* (4 vols, 1967–8), I, 480 (15 January 1837), II, 41 (10 January 1842); cf. for other praise of Gérard's salon, Fontaney, 36, 59 (14 September, 2 November 1831). Pozzo's pictures are described in Françoise Magny (ed.), *Rue de l'Université* (1987), 95.

190. Montcalm, 280 (9 July 1817).

191. Rémusat, *Correspondance*, III, 218 (Madame to Monsieur de Rémusat, 10 July 1817).

192. Comtesse de Bassanville, *Les Salons d'autrefois. Souvenirs intimes* (1862), 89.

193. BL Add. MSS 51717 f107 (Flahaut to Lady Holland, February 1822). A few years later he painted both the coronation of Charles X and the tomb of Napoleon I: Morgan, *France in 1829–30*, I, 465, 467.

194. Maricourt, 327–8; François Gérard, *Correspondance* (1867), 321 (Souza to Gérard, 25 November 1814); AN 565 AP FL7 (Madame de Souza to Flahaut, 2 February 1818).

195. Mme Ancelot, *Les Salons de Paris* (1858), 77; Gérard, 27; Balzac, *Lettres à Madame Hanska*, I, 480 (15 January 1837); id., *Correspondance* (5 vols, 1960–9), III, 222 (to Comtesse Sanseverino, 13 January 1837).

196. Foster Dormer MSS, Journal of Elizabeth Duchess of Devonshire, 28 July 1821.

197. AN 384 AP (Suchet papers) 207, 1 (*Listes pour les invitations au Bal du dimanche gras de 1819*).

198. AN 565 AP FL7 (Madame de Souza to Flahaut, 16 April 1818).

199. Barante, III, 18n; cf. Rambuteau, 204.

200. Foy, II, 9, 17 (13, 27 January 1822), I, 122 (4 February 1821).

201. Magny, *Rue de l'Université*, 106–9, 112, 118, including reproductions. Some of the Marshal's Zurbarans are now in the Louvre and the Wallace Collection. His bedroom furniture was sold by Sotheby's at the Château de Groussay sale, 3 June 1999, as lot 798.

202. Michel Bourjon et Bruno Pons, *Le Quai Voltaire* (1990), 86–9.

203. Comtesse de Sainte-Aulaire, *Souvenirs* (Périgueux, 1875), 119, 154.

204. Barante, II, 310–13; Rambuteau, 254.

205. Ticknor (diary for December 1818/12 January 1819); Castellane, I, 387, 388 (15 January 1820).

206. *La Rue de Lille*, 122; Rémusat, *Correspondance*, V, 139 (Madame to Monsieur de Rémusat, 4 December 1818); Leveson Gower, I, 548 (letter of Lady Bessborough, 17 June 1821). For a description of the *hôtel* a few years later see Blessington, I, 97–102.

207. AN 565 AP FL231/1 (Flahaut to Madame de Flahaut, 22 October 1832); cf., for similar attitudes, Gronow, I, 247 and Rambuteau, 209.

208. Barante, II, 523 (letter of Duchesse de Broglie, 16 August 1821).

209. Daumard, 'La vie de salon', in *Sociabilité et société bourgeoise*, 90; Archives privées, letter of 24 May 1819.

210. *Molé*, III, 291; Foy, I, 309 (8 December 1821); Glenbervie, II, 283 (diary for 2 January 1818).

211. Frénilly, 521; cf. Barante, II, 394 (Barante to Madame Anisson du Perron, 6 December 1819), calling the salon *l'institution la plus solide et la plus régulière de la monarchie.*

212. Viennet, 85–9 (1 July 1827); cf. for the aristocratic salons he frequented later in his life, ibid., 311–13. For a list of salons in 1861–3, see Xavier Marmier, *Journal 1848–1890* (2 vols, Geneva, 1968–), I, 188–96, 276.

213. Mérimee, *CG*, V, 205 (Mérimée to Madame de Montijo, 20 November 1847).

214. Lamb archives, John Bowes Wright to Joseph Lamb (6 January 1826, 29 January, 22 March 1815).

215. Benjamin et Rosalie de Constant, 259 (Rosalie to Benjamin de Constant, 1 December 1824).

216. Morgan, *France*, I, 224.

217. Blessington, I, 113, 274.

218. Anouar Louca (ed.), *L'Or de Paris* (1998), 125.

5 The British Parisians *1814–1830*

1. Dupuis, I, 315; cf. Talleyrand, IV, 458 (Talleyrand to Princesse de Vaudémont, 23 May 1832).

2. E.g. Maine de Biran, I, 108, 232 (16 February, 13 November 1816); Boigne, I, 220.

3. Roger Langeron, 50; Daudet, *Louis XVIII*, 374 (letter of 18 November 1819).

4. Vicomtesse de Noailles, 69, 100.

5. AN 565 AP FL6 (Souza to Flahaut, 1 November 1815), FL7 (Souza to Flahaut, 14 August 1820).

6. Orléans, *Souvenirs*, 118n, 121; Fontaine, II, 798 (6 June 1829); Talleyrand, V, 174 (Louis-Philippe to Talleyrand, 25 May 1833).

7. Byron, VII, 121 (Byron to Hobhouse, 22 June 1820); Paul Johnson, *The Birth of the Modern. World Society 1815–1830* (1996 ed.), 438, 441, 532–3.

8. Mansel, *Louis XVIII*, 270; Chateaubriand, *CG*, III, 95 (to Madame de Marigny, 9 December 1816); Louis Thomas (ed.), *Correspondance générale de Chateaubriand* (5 vols, 1912–24), V, 60 (Chateaubriand to La Ferronays, 1 November 1823); *Mémoires d'outre-tombe*, I, 502.

9. Antonetti, 467, 471; Richelieu, 59 (Richelieu to Osmond, 2 September 1816).

10. Pasquier, IV, 301; Waresquiel, *Richelieu*, 364n.

11. Ethel Jones, *Les Voyageurs français en Angleterre de 1815 à 1830* (1930), *passim*; Margaret I. Bain, *Les Voyageurs français en Ecosse 1770–1830 et leurs curiosités intellectuelles* (1931), *passim*; Foy, I, 188 (19 December 1822); cf. Charles Dupin, *Force commerciale de la Grande Bretagne* (2 vols, 1826). Rémusat, in his *Mémoires*, II, 160, wrote: *l'exemple de ce pays remplissait notre pensée, influait sur notre conduite.*

12. François Crouzet, *Britain Ascendant. Comparative Studies in Franco-British Economic History* (Cambridge–Paris, 1990), 349–50.

Notes

13. Alfred de Vigny, *Correspondance générale* (hereafter *CG*) (1989–), ed. Madeleine Ambrière, III (1994), 145 (to La Grange, 28 August 1836); Levaillant, 406, 503 (Chateaubriand to Madame Récamier, 5 August 1835, November 1843).

14. Bertrand Lemoine, *Les Passages couverts en France* (1990), 148. Winsor died in Paris in 1830 and is buried in Père Lachaise.

15. Jean Lambert-Dansette, *Genèse du patronat* (1991), 276–7; Bertier de Sauvigny, *Nouvelle Histoire de Paris*, 307–8.

16. Ibid., 247, 303.

17. Philip Ziegler, *The Sixth Great Power. Barings 1762–1929* (1988), 79–85; Leland Hamilton Jenks, *The Migration of British Capital to 1875* (New York, 1927), 41.

18. Archives Rohan-Chabot, Comte de Chabrol, unpublished memoirs, I ff45–6.

19. Athanassoglou-Kallmyer, *Eugène Delacroix*, 24; according to Bertier de Sauvigny, *Nouvelle Histoire de Paris*, 172, the numbers of British arrivals rose from 13,832 in 1815 to 20,184 in 1821.

20. Stanley, 291 (Edward to Bella Stanley, 9 July 1816).

21. 'The King was very gracious and spoke to me in English': Cornelia Knight, *Autobiography* (2 vols, 1861), II, 97 (27 May 1816); cf. II, 104 (14 June 1816): 'The King has given orders that all whose names are sent in by Sir Charles Stuart are to be accommodated' (with invitations to the festivities in honour of the wedding of the Duc de Berri). Lists of presentations in 1816–21 are in AN 03 199.

22. NLS MSS 21268 f137 (Oxford to Stuart, 19 September 1816).

23. AN 03 195 f8vo (La Châtre to Stuart, 23 June 1816): *désirant autant qu'il peut dépendre de lui complaire aux dames anglaises*; NLS MSS 15386 f26 (Stuart to La Châtre, 23 June 1816), regretting *le nombre exceptionel de dames anglaises à Paris*.

24. Castellane, I, 449 (19 December 1823).

25. *A Lounge in the Tuileries; or, Rhymes in the Gardens* (2nd ed., Paris, printed for the author by J. Smith, rue Montmorency), No. 16, 71; in 1830 there was a charity ball, attended mainly by British guests, for impoverished British residents of Paris: Christophe Léribault, *Les Anglais à Paris au XIXe siècle* (1994), 81.

26. Mercer, II, 210 (3 August); Jacques Boulenger, *Sous Louis-Philippe. Le Boulevard* (1933), 193; cf. Girardin 1, 557 (30 November 1839).

27. Boulenger, 196–7; James Simpson, 106; Bodleian Library Oxford, Mangin diary f195 (25 May 1819).

28. Boulenger, 196; Keates, 255, 297.

29. Mérimée, *CG (supplément)* (Toulouse, 1961), 35n; Kathleen Jones, *La Revue britannique. Son histoire et son action littéraire 1825–1840* (1939), 11–12. For a recent collection of these articles see Stendhal, *Paris–Londres*, ed. René Dimier (1997).

30. Stevenson, 213; cf. Fellowes, 18 (11 July 1815).

31. Byron, VI, 65 (Byron to James Wedderburn Webster, 8 September 1818), VII, 170, 180 (to Thomas Moore, 31 August 1820; to John Murray, 23 September 1820).

32. Gordon N. Ray, *Thackeray. The Uses of Adversity* (1955), I, 175; Private archive, Anne Lister journal, 4 February 1828; cf. Lady Morgan, *Passages from my Autobiography* (1859), 146 (letter of 8 October 1818).

33. Lady Morgan, *Passages from my Autobiography*, 292.

34. Bodleian Library Oxford, Mangin diary ff182, 192, 195, 202 (diary for May 1819).

35. When Picard's *Le Conteur*, parodying English manners, was performed in front of Wellington at Le Marais in 1818 the way he exclaimed 'Oh! Oh!' was so comic that the audience

had difficulty stifling its laughter: Barante, II, 331 (Barante to Madame de Barante, 20 July 1818); cf. MM. Théaulon et Saint-Laurent, *John Bull au Louvre, vaudeville en trois tableaux* (1827); Charles Marchal, *Physiologie de l'Anglais à Paris* (1844), 28, 31: *en général l'Anglais prête à rire par son costume, sa tournure guindée, ses gestes symmetriques quoique décents, ses manières brusques et vives . . . sa prononciation est bizarre, sauvage, risible.*

36. Granville, I, 220 (Lady Granville to Lady G. Morpeth, 9 December 1824); cf. Blessington, I, 331: *elle est très bien pour une Anglaise.*

37. Dalrymple Hamilton diary, 25 November 1816; Archives du Château de La Ferrière (Duchesse d'Escars to Madame de Podenas, 14 August 1816); Barante, III, 118 (Talleyrand to Barante, 11 August 1823); cf. Foy, III, 189 (24 January 1825): *je dîne chez le maréchal Soult avec toute l'Angleterre.*

38. Granville, I, 397 (to Lady Carlisle, 9 October 1826).

39. Françoise Waquet, *Les Fêtes royales sous la Restauration ou l'ancien régime retrouvé* (Geneva, 1981), 65–8.

40. Gronow, II, 285; Decin State Archives, Czech Republic, Prince Clary, unpublished diary, 25 April 1822; Malmesbury, I, 77 (27 April 1837).

41. *The Creevey Papers*, ed. Sir Herbert Maxwell (2 vols, 1903), II, 67 (Creevey to Miss Ord, 17 March 1823); A.M.W. Stirling, *The Letter-Bag of Lady Elizabeth Spencer-Stanhope* (2 vols, 1913), I, 329–30; Gronow, I, 120.

42. Gronow, I, 121; Morin, II, 183 (Lamartine to Virieu, 3 October 1818).

43. Viennet, 40 (8 November 1818). Coralie in *Illusions perdues*, however, was sold by her mother for 60,000 francs.

44. Gronow, I, 304; NLS MSS 21322 f152; Cumbria Record Office, Lonsdale diary, 2 December 1821.

45. Ivor Guest, *The Romantic Ballet in Paris* (1966), 58.

46. For example Lord Blessington returned in 1829, to vote for Catholic Emancipation: Blessington, II, 5. The ambassador himself returned in 1831: Granville, II, 113 (to Lady Carlisle, 3 October 1831); cf. Raikes, II, 250 (22 October 1835) *re* the arrival, to spend the winter, of the Duke of Sutherland and his family with thirty servants and six carriages.

47. See the relevant entry in G.E.C., *Complete Peerage* (12 vols, 1910–59).

48. For Lady Aldborough see Granville, II, 246 (15 May 1828); Apponyi, IV, 62 (diary for 1 February 1845); for Hamilton see Mérimée, *CG*, 2e série, V, 438 (Mérimée to Panizzi, 16 July 1863). Other peers and peeresses who died in or near Paris included the Countess of Lisburn (I) in 1822; the Earl of Thanet (E) in 1825; Lord Fitzwilliam (I) in 1830; the Earl of Barrymore (I) in 1823; the Countess of Barrymore (I) in 1833; Lady Lyndhurst (E) (wife of the chief Baron of the Exchequer) in 1834; the Earl of Granard (I) in 1837); the Countess of Ranfurly (I) in 1839; the Earls of Ranfurly (I) and Stair (S) in 1840; the Earl of Elgin (S) in 1841; Lord Cowley, a former ambassador in Paris, (E) in 1847); Lord Wallscourt (I) in 1849; Lady Rancliffe (S) in 1852; Lady Ashburton (E) in 1857; the Countesses of Donegall (I) and Elgin (S) in 1860. See the relevant entries in G.E.C., *The Complete Peerage*. (In this footnote, E, I and S stand for English, Irish and Scottish respectively.)

49. Claire Tomalin, *Mrs Jordan's Profession* (Penguin, 1995), 299; Gronow, I, 29. Mrs Clarke's daughter Ellen was mother of George Du Maurier, author of a novel of the British in Paris, *Peter Ibbetson* (1892).

50. Thomas Moore, *Journal* (6 vols, 1983), I, 301 (16 January 1820), 311 (11 April 1820), 316 (2 May 1820), 351 (11 October 1820); Castellane, I, 388 (15 January 1820); cf. Stirling, I, 334

(letter of 30 April 1818), for further complaints of the 'not very genteel' English and Irish living in Versailles.

51. Allen Burdett, *Thomas Moore en France. Contribution à l'histoire de la fortune des oeuvres de Thomas Moore dans la littérature française 1819–1830* (1911), 2–3, 16.

52. Gronow, II, 93–5.

53. Ibid., I, v, 2.

54. Carey, 74, 200, 478.

55. *The English in Paris. A Satirical Novel* (3 vols, 1819); Lesley Blanch (ed.), *The Game of Hearts. Harriet Wilson and her Memoirs* (1957), 384, 397.

56. Ibid., III, 202, 243, 262.

57. Ray, I, 124, 170, 174, 197–8.

58. Thackeray, *The Paris Sketch-book* (1868 ed.), 9, 155, 157.

59. Marquis de Luppé, *Astolphe de Custine* (Monaco, 1957), 207; Custine, *Mémoires et voyages* (2e ed., 2 vols, 1830), II, 102, 103; id., *Lettres à Varnhagen d'Ense et à Rahel Varnhagen d'Ense* (Brussels, 1870), 450–1 (letter of 5 April 1843).

60. Mrs Gore, *Greville; or, A season in Paris* (Galignani, 1841); id., *Paris in 1841* (1842), 71; Adburgham, 239.

61. *Hargrave* (1995 ed.), 1–2.

62. Roger Boutet de Monvel, *Les Anglais à Paris 1800–1850* (1911), 162.

63. Boigne, I, 262; Esterhazy, 18 (diary for 26 July 1827).

64. André Castelot, *Le Duc de Berri et son double mariage* (1951), 75.

65. Maison Charavay, *Autographes*, 39437 (Berry to Bourbon, 18 April 1816).

66. Pierre Cornut-Gentille, *La Baronne de Feuchères (1790–1840)* (2000), 56–62; Marie Amélie, *Journal*, ed. Suzanne d'Huart (1981 ed.), 357 (2 July 1827); Alfred Cuvillier-Fleury, *Journal intime* (2 vols, 1900–3), I, 180–1 (30 April 1830).

67. Montcalm, 171 (12 August 1816).

68. Vicomte A. Révérend, *Titres, anoblissements et pairies de la Restauration 1814–1830* (7 vols, 1901–8), II, 126, III, 91; Luppé, *Custine*, 91.

69. Alfred de Vigny, *CG*, I (1989), 252, 319 (letters to Comtesse de Clérembault, 5 February 1827; to Madame de La Grange, January 1829).

70. Bernardy, *Flahaut*, 98–9, 124, 125, 128–9.

71. Daudet, *La Police politique*, 203.

72. See her letters to *ma très chère Lady Holland* in BL Add. MSS 51718.

73. AN 565 AP KF68/1 (Lord and Lady Holland to Souza, 11 December 1815).

74. AN 565 AP FL6 (Flahaut to Souza, 18 September 1816; Souza to Flahaut, 9 June 1817).

75. AN 565 AP FL6 (Souza to Flahaut, 25 November 1815, 13 December 1815, 3 January 1816).

76. Marie Amélie, 236 (4 December 1816).

77. AN 565 AP FL6 (Souza to Flahaut, 22, 31 May 1817).

78. AN 565 AP FL6 (Souza to Flahaut, 8 May, 6 June 1817); cf. Richelieu, 103 (Richelieu to Osmond, 3 April 1817); Bernardy, *Flahaut*, 149.

79. AN 565 AP FL8/62 (Flahaut to Madame de Flahaut, June 1817).

80. BL Add. MSS 40349 f7 (Flahaut to Peel, 9 August 1822).

81. AN 565 AP FL7 (Souza to Flahaut, 24 May 1817, June 1819).

82. AN 565 AP FL6 (Souza to Flahaut, 3 August 1817).

83. AN 565 AP FL7 (Souza to Flahaut, 18 January 1821).

84. Jacques Charles (ed.), *De Versailles à Paris. Le destin des collections royales* (1989), 115.

85. Michel Beurdeley, *La France à l'encan. L'exode des objets d'art sous la Révolution 1789–1799* (1981), 124.

86. Morgan, *France*, II, 95.

87. Stendhal, *Promenades dans Rome*, 351.

88. Emile Dard, *Un rival de Fersen* (1947), 98–101, 112. For a description of Craufurd's gallery, see Dibdin, II, 469–80.

89. Rutland, 27 (6 August 1814).

90. AN 565 AP FL6 (Souza to Flahaut, 15 November 1817).

91. Granville, I, 73 (August 1815); Deborah Devonshire, *The House* (1982), 155, 187; the Haussonvilles recognised, at a party at Devonshire House in 1820, old chandeliers they had sold a few years previously (Haussonville, *Ma jeunesse*, 102).

92. Sarah Medlam, *The Bettine Lady Abingdon Collection* (1996), 24, 49.

93. Talk by Hugh Roberts, Royal Collection Studies, Windsor Castle, 20 September 1999; *Sèvres Porcelain from the Royal Collection* (1979), 23–4. Jacob Desmalter came to England in 1825 to redecorate Windsor Castle: Morley, 396.

94. Charles, 186–7; J.M. Robinson, *Buckingham Palace* (1995), 57; id., *Windsor Castle* (1997), 88, 105.

95. *Carlton House. The Past Glories of George IV's Palace* (1991), 100; Richelieu, 95 (Richelieu to Osmond, 10 February 1817).

96. *Anatole Demidoff Prince of San Donato*, exhibition catalogue, Wallace Collection (1994), 74.

97. Charles, 187–9; Boulenger, 76; Donald Mallet, *The Greatest Collector. Lord Hertford and the Founding of the Wallace Collection* (1979), 43; Granville, II, 121 (to Lady Carlisle, 20 January 1832).

98. AN 565 AP FL6 (Souza to Flahaut, 15 November 1817).

99. *Carlton House*, 37.

100. William Playfair, *France as it is, not Lady Morgan's France* (2 vols, 1818), I, 117.

101. NLS MSS 21267 (Lord Egerton to Louis XVIII, 15 January 1816); Boutet de Monvel, 233–4; Louis Lurine, *Les Rues de Paris* (2 vols, 1844), II, 319. The Hôtel Egerton was later demolished to form the present rue d'Alger. See *Plans et façade en six planches de l'Hôtel, rue Saint-Honoré appartenant au très honorable Francis Henry Egerton*, c. 1829.

102. Dibdin, II, 75, 86, 90, 442, 444n.

103. NLS MSS 21268 f109 (Woodthorpe to Stuart, 6 September 1816); cf. for a general survey, Maurice Agulhon, *Le Cercle dans la France bourgeoise 1810–1848. Etude d'une mutation de sociabilité* (1977), *passim*.

104. Alfred Marquiset, *Jeu et joueurs d'autrefois 1789–1837* (1917), 168.

105. Blessington, *The Idler in France*, I, 62; Gronow, II, 41; *Cercle de l'Union*, 1838, *passim*; Charles Yriarte, *Les Cercles de Paris 1828–1864* (1864), 9. See, for Flahaut's role in recruiting members from the Napoleonic nobility and the United Kingdom, the volumes of *Délibérations du Comité* and of lists of candidates, with seconders, in the archives of the Nouveau Cercle de l'Union, 33 rue du Faubourg Saint-Honoré, consulted with the help of Prince Gabriel de Broglie and Marie-Françoise Brizay.

106. Airlie, I, 167–8 (Palmerston to Lady Cowper, 14 December 1829).

107. Comte de Luppé, 'Plaisirs de cercle', *Le Correspondant*, 25 February 1929, 591.

108. Raikes, III, 95 (17 December 1836).

109. Gronow, I, 237; Apponyi, III, 46 (March 1835).

110. Hippolyte de Villemessant, *Mémoires d'un journaliste* (6 vols, 1872–8), I, 214; Comte

d'Alton Shee, *Mes mémoires (1826–1848)* (2 vols, 1869), I, 137; Jean Stern, *Lord Seymour dit Milord l'Arsouille* (1954), *passim*; Martin-Fugier, *La Vie élégante*, 334.

111. Gautier, *Paris et les Parisiens*, 392–3. In 1819 there were only 16,382 horses registered in this city of 700,000 inhabitants: Alain Fauré, *Paris Carême-prenant. Du carnaval à Paris au XIXe siècle 1800–1914* (1978), 31.

112. Marquis Philippe de Massa, *Souvenirs et impressions 1840–1871* (1897), 5.

113. Nicole de Blomac, *La Gloire et le jeu. Des hommes et des chevaux 1766–1866* (1991), 166; Stern, 88–9; James Grant, *Paris and its People* (2 vols, 1844), I, 37–8.

114. See Christophe Léribault, *Les Anglais à Paris au XIXe siècle* (1994), 34–5; A. Pugin, *Paris and its Environs displayed in a series of two hundred picturesque views* (2 vols, 1831). Other British artists painting Paris included William Batty (1819); Frederick Nash (1819–21); George Hayter (1829–30); William Callow (1829–30, 1831–41); John Frederick Lewis (1838).

115. Athanassoglou-Kallmyer, *Eugène Delacroix*, 11, 14, 15, 19, 20, 24–5.

116. Timothy Wilson-Smith, *Delacroix. A Life* (1992), 67; John Ingamells, *Richard Parkes Bonington* (1979), 7, 10; Carlos Peacock, *Bonington* (New York, 1980), 81; Paul Johnson, 615; E.J. Délécluze, *Journal 1824–1828* (1948), 482 (6 November 1827).

117. Byron, IV, 101, 132 (to Annabella Milbanke, 20 April 1814; to Augusta Leigh, 24 June 1814), VIII, 56, 91 (to Thomas Moore, 2 January 1821; to Douglas Kinnaird, 9 March 1821).

118. Ibid., V, 33 (contract of 20 April 1818); Edmond Estève, *Byron et le romantisme français* (1907), 59, 92–3, 95, 111, 208, 335.

119. Stendhal, *Paris–Londres*, 723.

120. Alfred de Vigny, *Journal d'un poète* (1928), 9–10 and n (6 November 1826).

121. James Smith Allen, *In the Public Eye. A History of Reading in Modern France 1800–1940* (Princeton, 1991), 45; Françoise Parent-Lardeur, *Les Cabinets de lecture. La lecture publique à Paris sous la Restauration* (1982), *passim*. Estimates for the number vary between 130 and 520: Bertier de Sauvigny, *Nouvelle Histoire de Paris*, 346.

122. Louis Maigron, *Le Roman historique à l'époque romantique. Essai sur l'influence de Walter Scott* (1896), 99–133; Marvin Lyons, 'The Audience for Romanticism. Walter Scott in France, 1815–51', *European History Quarterly*, 1984, XIV, 28–9, 32.

123. Amédée Pichot, *Voyage historique et littéraire en Angleterre et en Ecosse* (3 vols, 1825); Maigron, 114–17; Bain, 131, 137, 153, 164.

124. M.G. Devonshire, *The English Novel in France 1830–1870* (1929), 5.

125. Ibid., 272.

126. Ibid., 29, 41–2; Estève, 93n; Papers of Henry Lytton Bulwer, Heydon, Norfolk (hereafter Heydon MSS), Philarète Chasles to Henry Bulwer, 8 March 1842; Kathleen Jones, 31, 115, 159.

127. *Revue britannique*, 1825, iv.

128. Granville, I, 431 (Lady Granville to Lady Carlisle, 1 October 1827); NLS MSS 19424 f6vo (diary of Sir Thomas Frederick Elliott, September 1827).

129. David Cairns, *Berlioz* (2 vols, 1989–99), I, 229–30; Délécluze, 454 (16 September 1827); Eugène Delacroix, *Correspondance générale* (hereafter *CG*) (5 vols, 1935), I, 197 (Delacroix to Soulier, 28 September 1827).

130. Douglas Johnson, *Guizot* (1963), 114; J.-N. Luc, *L'Invention du jeune enfant au XIXe siècle, de la salle d'asile à l'école maternelle* (1997), 17–21.

131. Lawrence Bongie, *David Hume. Prophet of Counter-Revolution* (Oxford, 1965), vii, 1.

132. Philip Mansel, 'The Influence of the Later Stuarts and their Supporters on French

Royalism 1789–1840', *Royal Stuart Papers*, XXI, 1983, *passim*; Olivier Lutaud, *Des révolutions d'Angleterre à la Révolution Française. Le tyrannicide et Killing No Murder* (The Hague, 1973), *passim*.

133. *Considérations sur la Révolution française* (1983 ed.), 579.

134. Ibid., 447, 449, 479, 531, 553.

135. E.g. among many others: M. Nougarède, *Parallèle de la révolution d'Angleterre en 1642 et de celle de France*, 1797; Benjamin Constant, *Des suites de la Contre-Révolution de 1660 en Angleterre*, 1798; Charles de Lacretelle, *Parallèle entre César, Cromwell, Monk et Bonaparte*, 1802; Comte de Saint-Simon, *Des Bourbons et des Stuarts*, 1814; Louis-Ange Pitou, *L'Urne des Stuarts et des Bourbons*, 1815; Quentin Craufurd, *Notice sur Marie Stuart reine d'Ecosse et sur Marie Antoinette reine de France*, 1819; Armand Carrel, *Histoire de la Contre-Révolution en Angleterre sous Charles II et Jacques II*, 1827; Louis-Napoléon Bonaparte, *Fragments historiques. 1688 et 1830*, 1841; Maxime de Choiseul d'Aillecourt, *Parallèle historique des révolutions d'Angleterre et de France sous Jacques II et Charles X*, 1844. In the Chamber Camille Jordan talked of the Stuarts and the Bourbons on 30 May 1820, Manuel on 26 February 1823.

136. Douglas Johnson, 441; Rosanvallon, 274, 338n.

137. Clément, *Chateaubriand*, 181–3.

138. J.-L. Carr, *Le Collège des Ecossais à Paris (1662–1962)* (1962), 18: I am grateful for this reference to Dr Edward Corp; G. Daumet, *Notices sur les établissements religieux anglais, écossais et irlandais fondés à Paris avant la Révolution* (1910).

139. NLS MSS 6228 f37 (Stuart to Canning, 13 September 1824); *Moniteur*, 12 September 1824, 1241; Edward Corp and J. Sanson (eds.), *La Cour des Stuarts à Saint-Germain-en-Laye aux temps de Louis XIV* (1992), 224.

140. *Molé*, II, 388.

141. Montcalm, 264n (2 June 1817).

142. Ephraim Harpaz, *L'Ecole libérale sous la Restauration* (Geneva, 1968), 331.

143. Richelieu, 41 (Richelieu to Osmond, 17 June 1816).

144. Wellington, *SD*, XII, 213 (Wellington to J.C. Villiers, 11 January 1818); cf. Polovtsov, II, 546 (Pozzo to Nesselrode, 26 December 1817/7 January 1818), III, 379 (id. to id., 5 May 1820).

6 Murder at the Opera *1820–1824*

1. Byron, VI, 10 (Byron to Thomas Moore, 2 February 1818).

2. Swetchine, 65 (Madame Swetchine to Edouard de La Grange, 28 February 1824).

3. Jean-Paul Bled, *Histoire de Vienne* (1998), 355.

4. AN F7 3784 (police report of 8 February 1815).

5. Gasnault, 184–90; Ray, 124.

6. AN 104 AP 3, 3 (*cahiers de la Comtesse Amable d'Ecquevilly*); Serre, II, 553, 580 (Decazes to Serre, 9 February 1820; La Boulaye to Serre, 13 February 1820); Castellane, I, 389, 391 (29 January 1820).

7. Reiset, 54, 77.

8. Anselm Gerhard, *The Urbanisation of Opera. Music Theatre in Paris in the Nineteenth Century* (Chicago, 1998), 27; J.B.A. Hapdé, *Relation historique, heure par heure, des événemens funèbres de la nuit du 13 février 1820, d'après des témoins oculaires; quatrième édition augmentée de plusieurs traits inédits de feu S.A.R.* (1820), 5.

9. Hapdé, 7.

10. Perey, 445; Roger Langeron, 147 (Louis XVIII to Decazes, 5 March 1817); Castellane, III, 87 (11 September 1833).

Notes

11. Chateaubriand, *Mémoires . . . sur le duc de Berri* (hereafter *Mémoires*) (1820), 223–6, 238.
12. Ibid., 228–37.
13. Ibid., 232–3; Hapdé, 14n.
14. Maillé, 56; Hapdé, 10; Chateaubriand, *Mémoires*, 231–5, 241–5; id., *Mémoires d'outre-tombe*, II, 409, 411.
15. Polovtsov, III, 302 (Pozzo to Nesselrode, 22 February 1820); cf. for different versions of her words, Castellane, I, 397 (19 February 1820); Villèle, II, 351 (letter of 23 February 1820).
16. Chateaubriand, *Mémoires*, 241, 245–7, 249; Hapdé, 25, 27.
17. Marie Amélie, 275 (13 February 1820).
18. Chateaubriand, *Mémoires*, 252–3.
19. Ibid., 254, 259–60; Hapdé, 31–2.
20. J. Lucas-Dubreton, *Louvel le régicide* (1923), 81, 89, 225.
21. Polovtsov, III, 302, 307 (Pozzo to Nesselrode, 10/22 February 1820).
22. Wilson-Smith, 57; Michelet, *Mon journal* (1888), 39–40.
23. Serre, III, 161 (Gémeau to Serre, 6 March 1820).
24. Daudet, *L'Ambassade*, 285 (letter of Marquis de Sailly), 282 (letter of Madame de Nansouty), 291 (letter of Duchesse de Duras).
25. Daudet, *Louis XVIII*, 402.
26. Daudet, *L'Ambassade*, 281 (intercepted letter of Madame de Nansouty).
27. Ibid., 297, 301 (police reports 18, 19 February 1820); Pierre Chalmin, *L'Officier français de 1815 à 1870* (1957), 151.
28. Daudet, *Louis XVIII*, 415, 419.
29. Ibid., 418; id., *L'Ambassade*, 278 (Charles to Madame de Rémusat).
30. Duchesse de Broglie, 37 (Duchesse de Broglie to Madame Anisson du Perron, 22 February 1820).
31. Polovtsov, III, 302 (to Nesselrode, 10/22 February 1820).
32. Castellane, I, 396–7 (16, 19 February 1820); Daudet, *L'Ambassade*, 283 (letter of Marquis de Coislin, 19 February 1820); Daudet, *Louis XVIII*, 410, 418–19, 424–5.
33. Daudet, *L'Ambassade*, 303–4 (police report, 19 February 1820).
34. Polovtsov, III, 7 (Pozzo to Nesselrode, 20 December 1818/1 January 1819).
35. Serre, II, 12 (Broglie to Serre, 15 February 1820); Daudet, *Louis XVIII*, 422; id., *L'Ambassade*, 306 (note of 21 February 1820); cf. PRO FO 27/224 (Stuart to Castlereagh, 21 February 1820).
36. Polovtsov, III, 309 (Pozzo to Nesselrode, 10/22 February 1820).
37. Daudet, *Louis XVIII*, 427, 432.
38. Ibid., 434–6.
39. Castellane, I, 397 (20 February 1820).
40. Daudet, *L'Ambassade*, 288 (La Fayette to Madame de Lasteyrie); Fontaine, I, 589 (24 February 1820); Chateaubriand, *Mémoires*, 264–7; NLS MSS 21285 f38 (*Au souvenir immortel de S.A.R. Monseigneur le duc de Berry* by D. Cabello Félix, 22 February 1820).
41. Fontaine, I, 592 (24 July 1821).
42. Serre, II, 155 (La Boulaye to Serre, 5 March 1820).
43. Archives Woronzov, Moscow 1874, VIII, 367.
44. Victor Broglie, II, 147 (diary 27 April 1820).
45. Foy, I, 133 (21 February 1821); Prosper Duvergier de Hauranne, *Histoire du gouvernement parlementaire en France* (10 vols, 1857–72), V, 442; *Moniteur*, 1820, 336 (13 March 1820).

46. Pasquier, IV, 405–8; Duvergier de Hauranne, V, 532–3, 552.

47. Duvergier de Hauranne, V, 560.

48. Polovtsov, III, 328, 441 (La Ferronays to Pasquier, 23 February/8 March 1820, 1 September 1820); cf. Ley, 403 (Alexander I to Galitzine, 10 March 1821).

49. Serre, III, 295 (Pasquier to Serre, 7 April 1820); Pasquier, IV, 389; Foy, I, 130 (15 February 1821).

50. Laure Murat, *Paris des écrivains* (1996), 14.

51. Jean-Claude Caron, *Générations romantiques. Les étudiants de Paris et le Quartier Latin 1814–1851* (1991), 225, 227.

52. Ibid., 51.

53. Ibid., 113, 122.

54. Alan B. Spitzer, *The French Generation of 1820* (Princeton, 1987), 21, 32, 75, 92.

55. Caron, 183, 232–3.

56. Spitzer, 42, 51; Castellane, I, 365–6 (January 1819).

57. Spitzer, 17.

58. Duvergier de Hauranne, V, 522.

59. *Molé*, IV, 350.

60. Victor Broglie, II, 267 (diary for 24 February 1822).

61. Polovtsov, III, 389 (Pozzo to Nesselrode, 12/24 June 1820).

62. Pasquier, IV, 414, 416; Colvin, 157 (Harriet Edgeworth to Honora Edgeworth, June 1820).

63. M. Reymondin de Bex, *Histoire de la première quinzaine de juin 1820* (1820), 14; Villèle, II, 382, 391 (to Madame de Villèle, 4, 11 June 1820).

64. Serre, III, 447–52 (M. Jacquinot-Pampelune to Serre, 5 June 1820); Viennet, 48 (3 June 1820).

65. Most royal guards came from the countryside; all had to have a certificate of 'good conduct' and 'devotion to the King' signed by three notables: Mansel, *Pillars of Monarchy*, 46, 132–3; Pasquier, IV, 420.

66. Polovtsov, III, 390 (despatch of 24 June 1820).

67. Caron, 247; Pasquier, IV, 417. The soldier was later tried and acquitted.

68. Polovtsov, III, 391 (despatch of 24 June 1820).

69. NLS MSS 6200 ff111, 176 (Stuart to Castlereagh, 5, 12 June 1820).

70. Caron, 248–9; Spitzer, 55–60.

71. Reymondin de Bex, 96, 98.

72. Caron, 250–1; Pasquier, IV, 423–4; Rémi Gossez, *Un ouvrier en 1820. Manuscrit inédit de Jacques Etienne Bedé* (1984), 13.

73. Pasquier, IV, 393; Serre, III, 462, 476 (Eckstein to Serre, 5, 11 June 1820).

74. Reymondin de Bex, 137, 139, 148, 156.

75. Ibid., 167; Bertier de Sauvigny, *Nouvelle Histoire de Paris*, 438; Edgar Leon Newman, 'The Blouse and the Frock Coat. The Alliance of the Common People of Paris with the Liberal Leadership and Middle Class during the Last Years of the Bourbon Restoration', *Journal of Modern History*, XLVI, 3, 1974, 38–9; Villèle, II, 388 (to Madame de Villèle, 9 June 1820).

76. Reymondin de Bex, 167–8.

77. Colvin, 165 (to Mrs Edgeworth, 15 June 1820).

78. Roger Langeron, 93, 126; *Moniteur*, 19 June 1820, 855.

79. *Revue d'histoire diplomatique*, 1930, 320, 367–9 (Countess Tolstoy to Empress of Russia, 22 April, 12 May 1820).

80. NLS MSS 6201 f750 (Stuart to Castlereagh, 2 October 1820); *Moniteur,* 30 September 1820.

81. NLS MSS 6201 f763 (Stuart to Castlereagh, 2 October 1820, 'private'). Stuart was not present, but could have been informed by his friend the Vicomtesse de Gontaut, Gouvernante des Enfants de France.

82. Marie Amélie, 279 (29 September 1820).

83. Barante, II, 468; Boigne, II, 41.

84. Mansel, *Louis XVIII,* 378.

85. Comte de Moré, *Mémoires (1758–1837)* (1898), 252–3 (Moré to Pontgibaud, 26 May 1821).

86. Victor Broglie, II, 216 (27 September 1821).

87. Foy, I, 201 (24 June 1821).

88. Leveson-Gower, II, 548 (letter of 9 July 1821).

89. Foy, I, 209–10 (11 July 1821).

90. Ibid., I, 208–9 (6 July 1821).

91. Herbert F. Collins, *Talma. A Biography of an Actor* (1964), 273.

92. Barante, II, 508 (letter of Duchesse de Broglie, 21 July 1821).

93. General Bro, *Mémoires* (1914), 163; BL Add. MSS 51717 f103 (Flahaut to Lady Holland, 24 December 1821).

94. Waresquiel, 420–1; Mansel, *Louis XVIII,* 384.

95. Apponyi, I, 22 (27 August 1826).

96. Duc de Doudeauville, *Mémoires* (15 vols, 1861–4), VIII, 339 (La Rochefoucauld to Madame du Cayla, n.d.)

97. Bardoux, 238, 281 (Duras to Chateaubriand, 1 March 1821).

98. *CG,* IV, 33, 36 (to Madame Récamier, 13 January 1821; to Duchesse de Duras, 16 January 1821).

99. Bardoux, 355, 403 (Duras to Chateaubriand, 10 July 1822, 21 October 1822).

100. *CG,* V, 139 (to Duras, 6 June 1822).

101. *CG,* IV, 90 (to Pasquier, 20 February 1821).

102. Gérard, 242 (Humboldt to Gérard, 1822); Chateaubriand, *Congrès de Vérone,* 51–2.

103. Chateaubriand, *Congrès de Vérone,* 145, 370–6, p. 106 (Alexander I to Chateaubriand, 24 June 1824: *la bonne cause vous doit une juste reconnaissance*); Thomas (ed.), *Correspondance générale de Chateaubriand,* V, 23 (Chateaubriand to Prince Jules de Polignac, 2 October 1823).

104. Barante, III, 75; BL Add. MSS 51538 f12 (A. Bourke to Lord Holland, 19 June 1823); cf. for similar plots in 1822, *Molé,* V, 40 (note of Molé, 4 August 1822). Born Maria Assunta Leonida Butini, she erected a magnificent monument to herself and her husband in Père Lachaise. Her letters to Sir Charles Stuart can be found in NLS MSS 21319 ff57–68.

105. Pasquier, V, 528; Helen Maxwell King, *Les Doctrines littéraires de la Quotidienne 1814–1830* (1920), 24.

106. Bertier de Sauvigny, *Nouvelle Histoire de Paris,* 442–3.

107. Chateaubriand, *CG,* V, 40 (to Talaru, 15 October 1823); *Molé,* IV, 397, 421 (Pozzo to Molé, 3 December 1820, 2 March 1821); Barante, III, 306.

108. Polovtsov, III, 102 (despatch of 23 May 1819).

109. Barante, II, 371 (letter of Duchesse de Broglie, 13 June 1819).

110. Morin, II, 350 (Lamartine to Virieu, 23 March 1820); Anne Martin-Fugier, *Les Romantiques 1820–1848* (1998), 12, 27, 29, 50.

111. Victor Hugo, *Correspondance familiale et écrits intimes* (4 vols, 1988–), I, 104 (Victor Hugo to Adolphe Trébuchet, 20 April 1820).

112. Caron, 265; *Correspondance d'Alfred de Vigny*, I (1989), 153 (de Vigny to Aymon de Montépin, March 1824); Margaret H. Peoples, 'La Société des Bonnes Lettres (1821–1830)', *Smith College Studies in Modern Languages*, V, 1 October 1923, *passim*.

113. Doudeauville, VII, 125 (*résumé rétrospectif*), VIII, 511, IX, 15, 83 (Sosthènes de La Rochefoucauld to Charles X, 7 October 1824, 1 March 1825).

114. *Rossini à Paris* (Musée Carnavalet, 1992), 56–63; Albert Soubiès, *Le Théâtre Italien de 1801 à 1913* (1913), 31 (contract of 27 February 1824); Alan Kendall, *Gioacchino Rossini the Reluctant Hero* (1992), 137, 143, 147.

115. Hugo, *Correspondance familiale*, I, 858–65 gives full details.

116. Moré, 255 (to Comte de Pontgibaud, 7 January 1822).

117. Foy, III, 252 (4 July 1825).

118. Brongniart, 131, 140; Madame de Genlis, 128 (Anatole de Montesquiou to Madame de Genlis, 13 November 1826); Bertier de Sauvigny, *Nouvelle Histoire de Paris*, 320–1.

119. AN 03 566, 1820 (note by J. Antin, 25 June 1820).

120. *Molé*, IV, 376; Moré, 274 (letter to Comtesse de Pontgibaud, 20 May 1824); Metternich, IV, 150, 159 (notes of 30 January, 11 April 1825); Villèle, V, 170.

121. Villèle, V, 18, 57 (Rothschild to Villèle, 23 March 1824); *Mémoires d'outre-tombe*, II, 489–90; Géraud, 233 (12 June 1824); Récamier, II, 114, 117 (Doudeauville, Duc de Laval to Madame Récamier, 4, 5 July 1824).

122. Anka Muhlstein, *Baron James. The Rise of the French Rothschilds* (1984), 47; Fergusson, 94–6.

123. Georg Heuberger (ed.), *The Rothschilds. Essays on the History of a European Family* (Frankfurt, 1994), 82.

124. Richelieu, 205 (Richelieu to Osmond, 13 July 1818).

125. Daudet, *L'Ambassade*, 310.

126. Mansel, *Louis XVIII*, 306, 308.

127. Muhlstein, 59.

128. AN 565 AP FL8 (Flahaut to Madame de Flahaut, 27 June 1820).

129. AN 565 AP FL8 (Flahaut to Madame de Flahaut, 16 July 1820); Maillé, 50, 146.

130. Apponyi, I, 19 (23 July 1826); cf. for her elegance, popularity and kindness, Daudet, *Louis XVIII*, 409–10; Granville, I, 325, 339 (letters to Lady Carlisle, 14 December 1824, 26 January 1825).

131. Pauline Prévost-Marcilhacy, 'Un hôtel au goût du jour. L'hôtel de James de Rothschild', *Gazette des Beaux Arts*, July 1994, 36; Henri Bouchot, *Le Luxe français. La Restauration* (1894), 247–62.

132. Fergusson, 208.

133. Foy, I, 138 (3 March 1821).

134. AN 234 AP [papers of Baron Mounier] 2 (report of 3 March 1821).

135. Villèle, III, 454 (Angoulême to Villèle, 16 May 1823).

136. Raczynski, 134 (diary for 20 January 1824); Apponyi, I, 7 (19 April 1826); Castellane, II, 201 (10 November 1827); Morgan, *France in 1829–30*, II, 411.

137. Fergusson, 286.

138. *Moniteur*, 18 September 1824, 1264; Christine Piette, *Les Juifs de Paris (1808–1840). La marche vers l'assimilation* (Quebec, 1983), 35, 58, 79.

139. AN 565 AP FL8 (letter of 8 April 1825); cf. Foy, III, 140 (14 November 1824).

140. Bro, 159; Apponyi, I, 87–9 (6 December 1827); Blessington, I, 160–2.

141. Bardoux, 335–6 (Duchesse de Duras to Chateaubriand, 1822).

142. Decin State Archives, Czech Republic, Prince Clary, unpublished diary (23 April, 9 May 1822); cf. Fontaine, I, 628 (1 December 1822).

143. Moré, 280 (letter of 19 August 1824); Foy, III, 140 (14 November 1824); Bertier de Sauvigny, *Nouvelle Histoire de Paris*, 74.

144. AN 565 AP FL7 (Souza to Flahaut, 8 June 1823).

145. Bertier de Sauvigny, *Nouvelle Histoire de Paris*, 56, 317; Lemoine, *passim*.

146. Gilles Antoine Langlois, *Folies, tivolis et attractions. Les premiers parcs de loisir parisiens* (n.d.), 117; Pinon, 160–4.

147. AN NIV Seine 89 (map by M. de Moléon, 20 March 1825).

148. Cairns, I, 110.

149. Biver, 174; Bertier de Sauvigny, *Nouvelle Histoire de Paris*, 72.

150. Fontaine, I, 596–7 (20 October 1820, 13 November 1820).

151. Doudeauville, VII, 65, 427, 579 (du Cayla to La Rochefoucauld, 1820, 20 October 1827).

152. Edouard Perret, *Le Château de Saint-Ouen* (1940), 36.

153. Mansel, *Louis XVIII*, 382; Doudeauville, VII, 22.

154. Castellane, I, 413, 431 (March 1821, 27 December 1821); Cathérine Decours, *La Dernière Favorite* (1993), 175, 266.

155. Castellane, I, 460, 464 (16 June 1823, 2, 7 November 1823).

156. Délécluze, 25 (4 December 1824); Fontaine, I, 631 (20 December 1822); *Un âge d'or des arts décoratifs 1814–1848* (Grand Palais, 1991), 90; Daniel Alcouffe, 'Le goût de la comtesse du Cayla', *Dossier de l'Art*, no. 5, December 1991, 6–15.

157. Maillé, 83; Esterhazy, 17 (15 September 1827).

158. Doudeauville, VII, 580 (letter of Madame du Cayla, 20 October 1827); Viennet, 247 (7 March 1840). The desk is now in the stores of the Archives Nationales. The portrait hangs at the Château d'Haroué in Lorraine, property of Princess Minnie de Beauvau, descendant of Madame du Cayla.

159. Perret, 65; Doudeauville, VII, 579 (letter of Madame du Cayla, 27 October 1827).

160. Doudeauville, VII, 577–83 (letter of Madame du Cayla, 20 October 1827).

161. Fontaine, I, 492, 525, 646 (12 January 1816, 21 January 1816, 25 January 1824); John Elliot, *The Way of the Tumbrils* (1963), 99.

162. Marie-Claude Chaudonneret, *L'Etat et les artistes. De la Restauration à la monarchie de juillet (1815–1833)* (2000), 163, 165; George Lenôtre, *Le Jardin de Picpus* (1928), 165.

163. Marie Amélie, 243 (19 August 1818).

164. Alain Erlande-Brandebourg, *L'Eglise abbatiale de Saint-Denis* (2 vols, 1990), *passim*. Nevertheless, by a strange omission, no tombs or statues were erected at Saint-Denis for Louis XVII, the Prince de Condé, the Duc de Berri or Louis XVIII himself.

165. Barante, III, 334; Foy, I, 203 (28 June 1821).

166. Marie Amélie, 298n; Fontaine, I, 635 (3 June 1823).

167. Genlis, 45.

168. Antonetti, 490.

169. *Le Palais-Royal*, 99; Gérard, 333 (letter from Orléans, 1 October 1817).

170. Marie-Claude Chaudonneret et Alain Pougetoux, 'Les collections princières sous la Restauration', *Revue de la Société d'Histoire de la Restauration*, III, 1989, 46–9; Chaudonneret, 143. For a description of the Orléans gallery, see Lady Morgan, *France in 1829–30*, II, 20–39. Part of the Duchesse de Berri's collection of French royal portraits can be seen today in the château of Chambord.

171. Polovtsov, III, 308 (Pozzo to Nesselrode, 22 February 1820); Colvin, 166 (Fanny Edgeworth to Mrs Edgeworth, 19 June 1820).

172. Marie Amélie, 286 (6 May 1821).

173. Ibid., 309 (12 September 1823).

174. Mansel, *Louis XVIII*, 426–8; Marie Amélie, 316–17, 25 (31 August 1824).

175. Mathieu Couty, 'Les derniers jours de Louis XVIII', *Revue de la Société d'Histoire de la Restauration*, V, 1991, 11.

176. NLS MSS 6228 f2 (Stuart to Canning, 11 September 1824); Barante, III, 220 (Decazes to Barante, 15 September 1824).

177. Couty, 14–15; Mansel, *Louis XVIII*, 430.

178. Général Comte de Rumigny, *Souvenirs* (1921), 171 (22 September 1824).

179. Rumigny, 167 (18 September 1824); NLS MSS 6228 f210 (Stuart to Canning, 28 September 1824).

180. Sir Thomas Lawrence, *Letter-bag* (1906), 197 (Lawrence to Canning, 27 August 1825); Haussonville, 130.

181. Bertier de Sauvigny, *Nouvelle Histoire de Paris*, 445; Boigne, II, 95; Maillé, 131 (20 September 1824); NLS MSS 6228 f211 (Stuart to Canning, 28 September 1824).

7 King and Country *1824–1829*

1. Foy, III, 235–6 (6 June 1825); Béatrix Saule, *Visite du Musée des Carrosses* (Versailles, 1997), 34–6.

2. Waresquiel et Yvert, 378; Antonetti, 519; Délécluze, 80, 82, 89 (1, 3 January 1825).

3. Fontaine, I, 638 (25 June 1825).

4. Délécluze, 233 (6 June 1825); Foy, III, 235–6 (6 June 1825).

5. Castellane, II, 85 (31 July 1825); Maillé, 171.

6. Barante, VI, 231 (Guizot to Barante, 16 October 1824); Foy, III, 137, 141 (8, 16 November 1824).

7. Délécluze, 105–12 (14 January 1825).

8. Comte Joseph de Maistre, *Lettres et opuscules inédits* (2 vols, 1851), I, 513 (Maistre to Duchesse d'Escars, 28 May 1819).

9. Duchesse de Broglie, 88 (to Comtesse de Castellane, 15 February 1821).

10. Victor Broglie, III, 98.

11. Thomas (ed.), *CG*, III, 345.

12. Haussonville, *Ma jeunesse*, 226, 231–5; cf. Blessington, I, 139: the Marquis de Dreux-Brézé 'appears not to have studied either his toilette or his manners . . . [and] bestows more thought on the *Chambre des Pairs* than on the *salons à la mode*'.

13. Rambuteau, 243; BN NAF 11771 f48 (journal of Madame de Chastenay, 17 January 1825).

14. *Mémoires de deux jeunes mariées* (Garnier Flammarion, 1979), 116.

15. Bertier de Sauvigny, *Nouvelle Histoire de Paris*, 446; Waresquiel et Yvert, 381–2; Daumard, 242.

16. Ledré, 70.

17. Gunnell, 108 (A. Taillandier to Sutton Sharpe, 29 March 1826).

18. See for example Rémusat, *Correspondance*, V, 31 (Charles de Rémusat to Madame de Rémusat, 20 October 1818).

19. Henry Lytton Bulwer, *The Monarchy of the Middle Classes* (2 vols, 1836), I, 243; population figures from www.google.com.

20. Foy, I, 136 (27 February 1821); Barante, III, 174 (Sainte-Aulaire to Barante, 4 February 1824); Castellane, II, 162 (27 February 1827).

21. Castellane, II, 155, 157, 160 (28 January, 2, 7, 15 February 1827); Apponyi, I, 48 (6 February 1827).

22. Hugo, *Correspondance familiale*, I, 663, 696, 701 (Victor to General Hugo, 6, 18 July 1825).

23. Lamarque, I, 427 (20 May 1822).

24. Foy, I, 133 (21 February 1821); Rosanvallon, 179, 182–3, 197; cf. *Molé*, III, 266, reporting the voters of Seine et Oise who said to him, *vous êtes noble et nous ne le sommes pas, nous avons des biens nationaux et vous n'en avez pas.*

25. Lomuller, 388.

26. David Higgs, *Nobles in Nineteenth-century France* (1992), 14; Lomuller, 279, 390.

27. Lomuller, 237; Morgan, *France in 1829–30*, II, 480–90; Waresquiel et Yvert, 74.

28. MM. Picard et Mazères, *Les Trois Quartiers*, Comédie en Trois Actes et en Prose (3e ed., 1827), 59.

29. Chateaubriand, *Mémoires*, 289.

30. Picard et Mazères, 101, 104.

31. Pinkney, *The French Revolution of 1830*, 184.

32. Morgan, *France in 1829–30*, I, 326.

33. Ibid., I, 395; Balzac, *Correspondance*, I, 114n. For the marriage of their daughter Laurence, in 1821, to a poor noble, M. de Montzaigle, the Balzac family sent two *faires part*, one with the name Balzac, the other with the name *de Balzac*: *Balzac et la Révolution française* (1988), 18.

34. *Correspondance*, II, 710 (to Alcide de Beauchesne, July 1835), IV, 187 (to Roger de Beauvoir, 14 September 1840), V, 488 (to Laurent-Jan, 9 February 1849).

35. Ibid., V, 747 (to Dr Nacquart, 17 March 1850).

36. Hugo, *Correspondance familiale*, I, 734; Castellane, I, 407 (November 1820); later self-created nobles included two ministers and a marshal of Napoleon III, Fialin de Persigny, Drouyn de Lhuys and Le Roy de Saint-Arnaud.

37. Christophe Dipper, 'La noblesse allemande à l'époque de la bourgeoisie', in *Les Noblesses européennes au XIXe siècle* (Ecole Française de Rome, 1988), 182; cf. Michel Bruguière, 'L'aristocratique descendance des affairistes de la Révolution', in ibid., 105–20; Daumard, 303–4; Alexandre Pradère, 'Du style troubadour au style Boulle', *Connaissance des arts*, June 1991, 75.

38. AN 565 AP FL7 (letter to Comtesse de Flahaut, 10 May 1818); Révérend, III, 237; Glenbervie, II, 287 (8 January 1818); Berry, III, 75 (Mary to Agnes Berry, 14 March 1816).

39. Adeline Daumard, 'Noblesse et aristocratie en France au XIXe siècle', in *Les Noblesses européennes au XIXe siècle*, 91.

40. *Révue d'histoire diplomatique*, 1906, 41 (Montalembert to Baron Anckarsvard, 10 February 1830).

41. Petiteau, 271; Castellane, II, 223, 393 (26 January 1828, 21 November 1830); Révérend, V, 237, III, 285.

42. Polovtsov, I, 799 (despatch of 5/17 August 1818).

43. *Cinq-Mars* (Livre de Poche, 1970), 44, 469.

44. Moré, 255 (to Comte de Pontgibaud, 7 January 1822).

45. *Almanach royal* (1821), 766–72.

46. Doudeauville, IX, 297 (Sosthènes de La Rochefoucauld to Charles X, 31 March 1827).

47. Juste Olivier, *Paris en 1830. Journal* (1951), 128 (23 June 1830).

48. Decin State Archive, Czech Republic, Prince Clary, unpublished diary (26 April 1822).

49. Apponyi, I, 4 (21 March 1826).

50. Blessington, I, 98–105, 115.

51. Magny, *Rue de l'Université*, 40, 101, 124, 128, 222.

52. *La Rue de Lille. Hôtel de Salm* (1983), 57, 62, 78.

53. Morgan, *France in 1829–30*, I, 406.

54. Wolzogen, 84 (8 April 1789); Bertier de Sauvigny, *Nouvelle Histoire de Paris*, 379.

55. Henrietta Litchfield (ed.), *A Century of Family Letters* (2 vols, 1915), I, 114 (Charlotte Wedgwood to Henry Allen, 19 March 1818); Henrica Rees van Tets, *Voyage... en France en 1819* (1966), 15–16 (8 April 1819); Foy, III, 66–7 (16 April 1824); Willard Connelly, *Count D'Orsay* (1952), 149; Berry, III, 89 (13 April 1816); Blessington, II, 34–7; cf. Cooper, 251.

56. See Pierre Chaunu, *Le Basculement de Paris* (1997), *passim*.

57. Tapies, 435.

58. AN 40 AP 10 (report of 1 November 1814); Hobhouse, II, 231; cf. Stevenson, 239.

59. Bertier de Sauvigny, *Nouvelle Histoire de Paris*, 248 (bulletin of 17 May 1824).

60. Daumard, 349.

61. Caron, 273; Foy, II, 260 (28 March 1823).

62. Rémusat, *Correspondance*, V, 390 (Charles to Madame de Rémusat, 30 April 1819); Bertier de Sauvigny, *Nouvelle Histoire de Paris*, 344.

63. Bardoux, 327 (letter of 27 May 1822), 333.

64. Caron, 262, 267; Bertier de Sauvigny, *Nouvelle Histoire de Paris*, 441.

65. Bertier de Sauvigny, *Nouvelle Histoire de Paris*, 409.

66. Ibid., 417.

67. Chevalier, 514; Bertier de Sauvigny, *Nouvelle Histoire de Paris*, 203.

68. Bertier de Sauvigny, *Nouvelle Histoire de Paris*, 475: the proportion varied greatly from parish to parish. There was a decline in 1822–4 to 23 per cent.

69. Abbé Ernest Sevrin, *Les Missions religieuses en France sous la Restauration 1815–1830* (2 vols, Saint Mandé, 1948–57), 31; Waresquiel et Yvert, 225.

70. Adrien Garnier, *Frayssinous. Son rôle dans l'Université sous la Restauration* (1925), 6–7, 13.

71. Bertier de Sauvigny, *Nouvelle Histoire de Paris*, 50, 65, 403.

72. Chaudonneret, 171.

73. Pailhès, 201n; Jean-Paul Clément (ed.), *Madame de Chateaubriand* (1990), 56–7; Clément, *Chateaubriand*, 405–7.

74. *Mémoires d'outre-tombe*, III, 672–3.

75. Caron, 265; Baronne de Gérando, *Lettres . . .* (1880), 365 (letter of August 1822).

76. See e.g. Récamier, II, 200 (Duchesse de Broglie to Madame Récamier, 25 March 1826).

77. Agoult, I, 238–9; Délécluze, 330–7 (26, 29 March 1826).

78. Eustace, 72.

79. Orléans, *Souvenirs*, 103.

80. Pailhès, 325n, 327, 483, 495 (to Rosalie de Constant, 29 April, 6 September 1826).

81. Duchesse de Broglie, 278 (to Vicomtesse d'Haussonville, 1 August 1837).

82. Rémusat, *Mémoires*, III, 96; Edmond Marc, *Mes journées de juillet 1830* (1930), 2; Apponyi, II, 266 (13 October 1832).

83. Rambuteau, 345.

84. NLS MSS 21323 f48 (Montcalm to Stuart de Rothesay, n.d.)

85. Orléans, *Souvenirs*, 92.

Notes

86. Archives Rohan-Chabot, Chabrol memoirs, II f12; Chaudonneret, 164.

87. Apponyi, I, 11–13 (19 May 1826); Délécluze, 346–8 (4 May 1826).

88. Délécluze, 348 (4 May 1826); Villèle, V, 205 (Charles X to Villèle, 3 May 1826); Bertier de Sauvigny, *Nouvelle Histoire de Paris*, 412; Doudeauville, IX, 287 (La Rochefoucauld to Charles X, 6 February 1827); Castellane, II, 158 (8 February 1827); cf. Stendhal, *Paris–Londres*, 698–9.

89. Doudeauville, IX, 330 (La Rochefoucauld to Charles X, 19 August 1827).

90. Anne Lister, unpublished diary (1 February 1828); cf. for other prophecies, under Charles X, of an Orléans reign, Doudeauville, IX, 286 (La Rochefoucauld to Charles X, 6 February 1827); Henry Lytton Bulwer, *The Life of . . . Viscount Palmerston* (3 vols, 1870–4), I, 350 (Palmerston to William Temple, 4 December 1829).

91. Rumigny, 186 (1 December 1825).

92. Collins, 370–5; Bruno Villien, *Vie de Talma*, unpublished manuscript, 1999, 323–30.

93. Barante, III, 359 (Dino to Barante, 3 November 1826).

94. Bertier de Sauvigny, *Nouvelle Histoire de Paris*, 40.

95. Archives Rohan-Chabot, Chabrol memoirs II, f21.

96. Bertier de Sauvigny, *Nouvelle Histoire de Paris*, 40; Waresquiel and Yvert, 339, 354; Girard, *Garde Nationale*, 129–34.

97. Archives Rohan-Chabot, Chabrol memoirs, II f21.

98. Daumard, 564n; Marie Amélie, 345–6 (29 April 1826).

99. Marie Amélie, 356 (17 April 1827); Antonetti, 527.

100. Antonetti, 527; Apponyi, I, 58 (19 April 1827).

101. Anne Lister, unpublished diary (29 April 1827); Orléans, *Souvenirs*, 81–3; Antonetti, 527–8.

102. Apponyi, I, 63 (6 May 1827); Maillé, 212; Villèle, V, 266–7.

103. Waresquiel et Yvert, 392; Bertier de Sauvigny, *Nouvelle Histoire de Paris*, 255; Anne Lister, unpublished diary (30 April 1827); Castellane, II, 176 (letter of 30 April 1827).

104. Castellane, II, 197–8 (26 October, 1 November 1827); AN 03 138 (Brossard to La Bouillerie, 5 November 1827).

105. Castellane, II, 199, 203 (6, 12 November 1827).

106. Bertier de Sauvigny, *Nouvelle Histoire de Paris*, 449–50.

107. Archives du Château de La Ferrière (letter to Madame de Podenas, 27 November 1827).

108. Bertier de Sauvigny, *Nouvelle Histoire de Paris*, 446 (report of 20 August 1826).

109. Castellane, II, 214 (6 January 1828); Waresquiel et Yvert, 413; Orléans, *Souvenirs*, 102; cf. Viennet, 90 (23 February 1829).

110. AN 40 AP 17 (Talleyrand to Beugnot, 21 September ?1827); cf. Pailhès, 474 (Talleyrand to Duchesse de Duras, 23 November 1825).

111. Orléans, *Souvenirs*, 192n (Duchâtel to Guizot, 5 August 1829); Mansel, *Louis XVIII*, 402 (quoting letter of 14 April 1830).

112. Guillemin, 219.

113. Clément, *Chateaubriand*, 327; Ernest Daudet, *Le Ministère de M. de Martignac* (1875), 126; Villèle, V, 316 (Charles X to Villèle, 11 January 1828); *Mémoires d'outre-tombe*, II, 531, 536.

114. *Lettres à Madame Récamier*, 266 (letter of 3 February 1829), cf. 253 (letter of 15 January 1829).

115. Doudeauville, IX, 410 (letter of 26 April 1828); Bertier de Sauvigny, *Nouvelle Histoire de Paris*, 71.

116. Bertier de Sauvigny, *Nouvelle Histoire de Paris*, 283; Harsin, 43.

117. Fontaine, II, 815 (November 1829); Bertier de Sauvigny, *Nouvelle Histoire de Paris*, 105; Prince von Pueckler-Muskau, *Tour in England, Ireland and France, in the Years 1826, 1827, 1828 and 1829* (Zurich, 1940), 365 (14 January 1829).

118. Boulenger, 12.

119. Stendhal, *Paris–Londres*, 318; Doudeauville, IX, 88 (La Rochefoucauld to Charles X, 5 March 1825); cf. Lacour-Gayet, II, 422 (Talleyrand to Alexander I, 14 June 1814: *les provinces, voilà la vraie France*).

120. Géraud, *Un homme de lettres*, 236 (letter to Soulié, 17 September 1824); cf. Ernest Renan, *Cahiers de jeunesse 1845–6* (2 vols, 1906–7), I, 285; Stendhal, *Vie de Napoléon* (1929), 181; Michelet, *Journal*, I, 76 (28 April 1830).

121. La Maisonfort, 298; cf. Abbé Liautard, *Mémoires* (2 vols, 1844), ed. Abbé Denys, II, 241 (letter of 28 January 1828: *Paris absorbe tout pour tout corrompre*).

122. Frénilly, 24.

123. Délécluze, 437 (8 April 1827); Victor de Balabine, *Journal* (1914), 116 (19 May 1843); Mérimée, *CG*, III, 442 (to Madame de Montijo, 20 October 1843); 2e serie, I, 53, II, 114 (id. to id., 23 April 1853, 5 September 1854).

124. Lacour-Gayet, III, 72 (letter of 8 February 1817); Pailhès, 469 (Talleyrand to Duchesse de Duras, 9 October 1825); cf. Barante, III, 363 (Molé to Barante, 10 November 1826).

125. Mercer, II, 104, 110 (10 July 1815); Boigne, I, 374; Castellane, I, 348 (November 1817).

126. Stevenson, 157–8 (29 May 1816); Roots, 69.

127. Frédéric Soulié, 'Le bourgeois campagnard', in *Les Français peints par eux-mêmes* (4 vols, 1841), III, 25–32; Esterhazy, 35, 37 (19 July, 13 August 1827).

128. Daumard, 134–5; Wagner, *My Life* (1983), 182.

129. Maricourt, 354; AN 565 AP FL8 (letter of 5 July 1820); Decin State Archives, Czech Republic, Prince Clary, unpublished diary (23 April 1822).

130. Granville, I, 114 (to Lady G. Morpeth, June 1817).

131. Foy, I, 187 (29 May 1821).

132. Decin State Archives, Czech Republic, Prince Clary, unpublished diary (5 May 1822).

133. Esterhazy, 42 (11, 27 June 1827).

134. Ibid., 44 (2 August 1827).

135. Ibid., 36 (7 August 1827).

136. Philip Mansel, *The Court of France 1789–1830* (1989), 168; Stevenson, 189 (2 June 1816); Marc, 80 (28 July 1830).

137. Schaller, 130; Lacour-Gayet, III, 176.

138. Comte Alexandre de Puymaigre, *Souvenirs sur l'emigration, l'Empire et la Restauration* (1884), 271. Puymaigre was prefect of the department in which Compiègne is situated.

139. Doudeauville, IX, 27 (La Rochefoucauld to Charles X, 17 June 1825).

140. Castellane, I, 417, 426 (6 June, 26 September 1821); Esterhazy, 45 (8 August 1827); Boigne, II, 75; Apponyi, I, 182 (16 August 1829); cf. Fontaine, II, 716 (27 June 1826).

141. Cf. Archives of Schloss Brunnsee Austria, Album verde (Charles X to Duchesse de Berri, 27 August 1825, 24 June 1827).

142. Archives Rohan-Chabot, Chabrol memoirs, II f65.

8   The New Jerusalem *August 1829–December 1830*

1. De Vigny, *Correspondance*, I, 297 (letter to Paul Foucher, 20 April 1828); cf. for the same feelings Alfred de Musset, *La Confession d'un enfant du siècle* (1993 ed.), 26.

2. See e.g., among many others, de Pradt, *Du Congrès de Vienne* (London, 1816), 201; Cuvillier-Fleury, II, 12 (16 January 1832); Balzac, *Correspondance*, II, 128 (to Zulma Carraud, 23 September 1832); Comte de Mérode-Westerloo, *Souvenirs* (2 vols, 1864), II, 121.

3. Hugo, *Correspondance familiale*, I, 543 (*extrait de baptême de Léopold Victor Hugo*, 16 August 1823), II, 469 (to Madame Victor Hugo, 5–6 September 1837); id., *Le Rhin* (2 vols, 1912 ed.), I, 10, 12, 15; id., *Choses vues 1847–48* (1972), 41 (January 1847).

4. Foy, I, 210 (11 July 1821).

5. Ibid., I, 133, 327 (21 February 1821), III, 88 (20 June 1824).

6. Chateaubriand, *CG*, V, 61 (to La Ferronays, 1 November 1823); id., *Congrès de Vérone*, 145, 191 (mémoire of 1829).

7. *Mémoires d'outre-tombe*, II, 664 (mémoire to La Ferronays, December 1828).

8. Bernardy, *Charles de Flahaut*, 158, 172; Carlo Bronne, *La Comtesse Le Hon et la première ambassade de Belgique à Paris* (Bruxelles, 1952), 113.

9. Raikes, *Journal*, III, 182 (9 May 1837); Castellane, III, 64 (3 February 1833).

10. Granville, I, 431, 433, 435–6 (to Lady Carlisle, October 1827); Charles Greville, *Memoirs* (8 vols, 1938 ed.), I, 381–3 (8, 9 March 1830).

11. Haussonville, *Ma jeunesse*, 287–9; Françoise de Bernardy, *Flahaut fils de Talleyrand, père de Morny* (1974), 202–3; Duc de Morny, 'La genèse du coup d'état', *Revue des deux mondes*, 1 December 1925, 513; Joseph Tanski, *Souvenirs d'un soldat journaliste à Paris* (1869), 8.

12. Maillé, 292; Bulwer, *Palmerston*, I, 315, 322 (diary for 10, 23 January 1829).

13. A.E. Kozmian, 'Le carnet d'un mondain sous la Restauration', *Revue de Paris*, 15 January 1900, 339 (diary for 24 January 1830).

14. Marquis de Bombelles, *Journal* (Geneva, 1977–), II, 235 (15 September 1788); Bertier de Sauvigny, *Metternich et la France*, III, 1218.

15. Thomas D. Beck, *French Legislators 1800–1834. A Quantitative History* (1974), 97.

16. Cf. Viennet, 90 (23 February 1829) *re* the Bourbons: *ils ne peuvent être remplacés que par l'anarchie*.

17. Madeleine Bourset, *Casimir Périer. Un prince financier au temps du Romantisme* (1994), 47, 94, 120, 173, 181.

18. Castellane, II, 267, 275 (23 November 1828) 17, 21 January 1829); cf. Boigne, II, 136.

19. Maillé, 277.

20. Waresquiel et Yvert, 439; Castellane, II, 297 (10 August 1829).

21. Castellane, II, 329 (10 March 1830).

22. Villèle, V, 430, 456 (Villèle to Madame de Villèle, 4 May 1830; Genoude to Villèle, 2 July 1830).

23. Révérend, V, 425.

24. Vicomte de Guichen, *La Révolution de juillet 1830 et l'Europe* (1917), 8, 9, 31 (despatch of 1/13 February 1830); cf. PRO FO 27/411 f172 (Stuart to Aberdeen, 23 July 1830).

25. Archivio di Stato Turin, Lettere Ministri Francia 1829 in 1830 35 f150 (despatch of 30 August 1829); 37 f32 (despatch of 3 May 1830: *Le roi ne s'est jamais senti plus à l'aise avec ses ministres*); Archives du Château de La Ferrière (Marquise to Marquis de Podenas, 18 September, 18 November 1829).

26. *Léopold avant Léopold Ier*, 176–7 (Leopold to his mother, 1 November 1830).

27. Tulard, *Paris et son administration*, 501 (bulletin of 20 August 1829); Archivio di Stato Turin, Lettere Ministri Francia 1828 in 1835 36 f137 (despatch of 12 January 1830).

28. Doudeauville, IX, 505 (La Rochefoucauld to Charles X, 7 August 1829); Villèle, V, 269

(Polignac to Villèle, 2 May 1827). To Lady Blessington Polignac seemed formed to live in England: Blessington, II, 136.

29. AN 300 AP III 21 (George IV to Orléans, 16 October 1829). I am grateful for this reference to Sheila de Bellaigue. For the King of Prussia's visits, see Fontaine, I, 545 (30 August 1817); Montcalm, 291 (26 August 1817); Daudet, *La Police politique*, 63, 71 (notes of 23 August 1817, August 1818).

30. Georges Grosjean, *La Politique extérieure de la Restauration et l'Allemagne* (2e ed., 1930), 147–8, 167.

31. Prince Sixte de Bourbon-Parme, *La Dernière Conquête du roi. Alger 1830* (2 vols, 1930), I, 52.

32. Waresquiel et Yvert, 444–6; Victor Broglie, III, 234, 241.

33. *Mémoires d'outre-tombe*, II, 397.

34. Stendhal, *Vie de Napoléon*, 208.

35. *Mémoires d'outre-tombe*, III, 84–5 (Chateaubriand to Polignac, 28 August 1829).

36. Maillé, 139 (December 1824); cf. Comte de Neuilly, *Dix années d'émigration. Correspondance et souvenirs* (1865), 396.

37. Rémusat, *Correspondance*, V, 173 (Madame to Monsieur de Rémusat, December 1818).

38. Boigne, II, 358.

39. Genlis, 261 (Montesquiou to Madame de Genlis, 23 April 1828).

40. Lacour-Gayet, III, 216, 219; Antonetti, 561.

41. Maillé, 294, 297; Apponyi, I, 221–2 (diary of 3, 6 February 1830); Doudeauville, IX, 584, 592, 594 (La Rochefoucauld to Charles X, 21 January 1830, 6 February 1830, 19 February 1830).

42. *Paris–Londres*, 748.

43. Rémusat, *Correspondance*, I, 366n.

44. Marquis de Luppé, *Les Travaux et les jours d'Alphonse de Lamartine* (1942), 126; Graham Robb, *Victor Hugo* (1997), 144.

45. Vincent W. Beach, *Charles X of France* (Boulder, 1971), 280.

46. Graham Robb, *Victor Hugo* (1997), 147; Maillé, 307–9; Kozmian, 342 (25 February 1830); Martin-Fugier, *Les Romantiques*, 117, 128.

47. Apponyi, I, 244 (16 April 1830); Antonetti, 516; NLS MSS 6228 f162 (Stuart to Canning, 23 September 1824); Marquis de Villeneuve, *Charles X et Louis XIX en exil* (1889), 60.

48. Apponyi, I, 255 (22 May 1830); Maillé, 317–18.

49. Apponyi, I, 258, 260–2 (31 May, 2 June 1830); Cuvillier-Fleury, I, 186–9 (31 May 1830); Fontaine, II, 836 (31 May 1830); N.A. de Salvandy, 'Une fête au Palais-Royal', in *Paris ou le livre des cent et un* (15 vols, 1831–5), I, 398.

50. Antonetti, 556–7.

51. Cuvillier-Fleury, I, 188 (31 May 1830).

52. Lamartine, *CG*, I (1943), 35 (Lamartine to Virieu, 27 June 1830).

53. Antonetti, 559.

54. AN 115 AP (Mounier papers) dr 2 (account of 1830 by Sémonville written in 1830 for Baron Mounier),

55. NLS MSS 6241 f20 (Stuart to Aberdeen, 12 April 1830, describing the King's mentality).

56. Guichen, *La Révolution de 1830*, 97; Henri Contamine, *Diplomatie et diplomates sous la Restauration 1814–1830* (1970), 344; Alan Sked (ed.), *Europe's Balance of Power 1815–1848* (1979), 45.

57. NLS MSS 6242 f163 (Stuart to Aberdeen, 12 July 1830).

58. Marmont, *Mémoires*, VIII, 235; Antonetti, 562.

59. Pinkney, *The French Revolution of 1830*, 100 (references to Pinkney throughout these notes are to this work unless otherwise specified); *La Garde Royale pendant les événements du 26 juillet au 4 août 1830, par un officier employé à l'état major* (1830), 5, gives a lower estimate of the troops available.

60. Bertier de Sauvigny, *Nouvelle Histoire de Paris*, 44.

61. Guichen, *La Révolution de 1830*, 96 (Apponyi to Metternich, 26 July 1830).

62. *La Garde Royale*, 48.

63. Pinkney, 61, 62, 263.

64. Ibid., 81 and *passim*, for the following account of the revolution; Antonetti, 564.

65. Villèle, V, 464 (Montbel to Villèle, 26 July 1830).

66. D. Turnbull, *The French Revolution of 1830; the Events which produced it, and the scenes by which it was accompanied* (1830), 51; Sémonville f12; cf. for similar views, NLS MSS 6242 f333 (report of 28 July 1830); Newman, 'The Blouse and the Frock-coat', 37n.

67. Pinkney, 83–8; Rémusat, *Mémoires*, II, 313–14; Ledré, 107–8.

68. Antonetti, 566–7; Pinkney, 91; Bertier de Sauvigny, *Nouvelle Histoire de Paris*, 455.

69. Pinkney, 93.

70. Olivier, 235 (26 July 1830).

71. Ibid.; Pinkney, 92, 99; Marmont, *Mémoires*, VIII, 239.

72. Marmont, *Mémoires*, VIII, 240; *La Garde Royale*, 8–9, 12–13; Marc, 45–6, 48–50 (27 July).

73. Turnbull, vii.

74. *Juillet 1830* (Musée Carnavalet, 1980), 28; Marc, 51.

75. *La Garde Royale*, 12; Pinkney, 100.

76. Bertier de Sauvigny, *Nouvelle Histoire de Paris*, 97; Marc, 56 (27 July).

77. *La Garde Royale*, 13; cf. 46: *ce furent les classes les moins aisées de Paris qui prirent seules part aux combats de cette journée.*

78. Pinkney, 253, 256, 260, 269.

79. Ibid., 267; Turnbull, 128, 149; Ledré, 56; Comte Emmanuel de Las Cases, *Las Cases le mémorialiste de Napoléon* (1959), 384 (although the speculation went badly); Esterhazy, 38 (29 August 1827).

80. Pueckler-Muskau, 355 (2 January 1829).

81. General La Fayette, *Mémoires, correspondance et manuscrits* (6 vols, 1838), VI, 408.

82. Pinkney, 153–4; Turnbull, 99–100 (letter from Dubourg, 31 July 1830).

83. *La Garde Royale*, 15; Turnbull, 143; NLS MSS 6242 f334 (Stuart de Rothesay to Aberdeen, 28 July 1830).

84. Ledré, 111.

85. Olivier, 243 (27 July 1830).

86. Pinkney, 107–8.

87. Olivier, 245–6 (28 July 1830).

88. Turnbull, 149; Olivier, 258 (27 July 1830).

89. *La Garde Royale*, 17, 21, 25, 46–7; Pinkney, 118–22.

90. Duchess of Sermoneta (ed.), *The Locks of Norbury* (1940), 342, 346 (letters of 30 July 1830, 9 September 1830).

91. *La Garde Royale*, 24; Chateaubriand, *Mémoires d'outre-tombe*, III, 112–14.

92. Marc, 71 (28 July 1830).

93. NLS MSS 6242 f360 (report of 29 July 1830).

94. Pinkney, 122.

95. Marc, 87, 90 (28 July); *La Garde Royale*, 33, 36, 39, 40, 44n, 45.

96. Olivier, 249, 250–3 (28 July).

97. Chateaubriand, *Mémoires d'outre-tombe*, III, 110.

98. Marc, 59 (28 July); Olivier, 247 (28 July); *La Garde Royale*, 15.

99. Marc, 56.

100. NLS MSS 6242 f360 (report to British ambassador, 29 July 1830).

101. *La Garde Royale*, 27.

102. Pinkney, 263.

103. Connelly, 47, 54, 64.

104. Blessington, II, 150, 161, 164, 167, 187.

105. Ibid., II, 168.

106. Shelley, I, 100; Blessington, II, 171–3, 176.

107. Pinkney, 113.

108. Ibid., 123–4; Antonetti, 569; Blessington, II, 194.

109. NLS MSS 6242 f364 (report of 29 July to Stuart de Rothesay); Pinkney, 124–5.

110. Sémonville f22; Antonetti, 570.

111. Marmont, *Mémoires*, VIII, 243n, 249; Pinkney, 126.

112. Marmont, *Mémoires*, VIII, 252n–3n (letter of 28 July 1830).

113. *Mémoires d'outre-tombe*, III, 115.

114. De Vigny, *Journal d'un poête*, 33 (29 July 1830).

115. Marc, 77, 86.

116. Pinkney, 127; Caron, 307.

117. Alexandre Mazas, *Saint-Cloud, Paris et Cherbourg* (1832), 13.

118. Marmont, *Mémoires*, VIII, 258.

119. Pinkney, 129–30; Olivier, 262, 275 (29, 30 July 1830).

120. Marmont, *Mémoires*, VIII, 259; Jacques Lafitte, *Mémoires* (1932), 158.

121. Sémonville ff13–16, 21.

122. Marmont, *Mémoires*, VIII, 254–5.

123. Pinkney, 132–3.

124. *Mémoires d'outre-tombe*, III, 120–1; Caron, 309; Pinkney, 134–5.

125. Olivier, 268 (29 July); NLS MSS 6242 ff384–5 (report to Stuart de Rothesay, 30 July 1830: *le bas peuple crie Vive Napoléon II!*).

126. *Mémoires d'outre-tombe*, III, 120; Fontaine, II, 849 (letter of 9 August 1830); Blessington, II, 185; Mary Berry, 200n.

127. Olivier, 267 (29 July 1830); cf., for the fishermen, B. Durand, 'Le joueur de boules', in *Les Français peints par eux-mêmes*, II, 295.

128. Comte Fleury, *Le Palais de Saint-Cloud. Ses origines – ses hôtes – ses fastes – ses ruines* (1902), 207–8 (diary of Duc de Guiche, 29 July 1830); *Mémoires d'outre-tombe*, III, 139.

129. Marc, 126; Mazas, 312.

130. Comte de Caraman, *Notice sur la vie militaire et privée du Général Mis de Caraman* (1857), 100–1.

131. Morgan, *France in 1829–30*, I, 479–81.

132. Archives Rohan-Chabot, Chabrol memoirs, II ff71, 74.

133. La Fayette, VI, 390.

134. Pinkney, 139–45; Antonetti, 574–5.

Notes

135. Ledré, 112.
136. *Juillet 1830*, 39.
137. Duc de Mortemart, 'Trois journées, avant, pendant et après mon ministère', *Le Correspondant*, CCCXXI, 10 December 1930, 645.
138. Ibid., 647–52.
139. Sémonville ff27, 28, 30.
140. Mortemart, 653–8.
141. Antonetti, 573; Marc, 114 (29 July); cf. Mortemart, 815.
142. NLS MSS 6242 ff384–5 (report to Stuart de Rothesay, 30 July 1830).
143. Mazas, 46, 67.
144. Mortemart, 802–3.
145. Ibid., 803–7.
146. La Fayette, VI, 399.
147. Mortemart, 578; NLS MSS 6242 f386 (report of 30 July).
148. Chateaubriand, *Mémoires d'outre-tombe*, III, 127.
149. Mortemart, 809–12, 818.
150. Stendhal, 'Souvenirs d'égotisme', in *Oeuvres intimes*, II, 451, 473–4; Keates, 338; Lacour-Gayet, III, 227.
151. Antonetti, 570–1.
152. Robb, *Hugo*, 156.
153. Chateaubriand, *Lettres à Madame Récamier* (1988), 335–6 (to Madame Récamier, 29 July 1830).
154. *Mémoires d'outre-tombe*, III, 97–8; *Congrès de Vérone*, 137.
155. *Mémoires d'outre-tombe*, III, 130; *Lettres à Madame Récamier*, 335–6 (to Madame Récamier, 29 July 1830).
156. *Mémoires d'outre-tombe*, III, 132–3.
157. Ibid., III, 133, 134; Mazas, 107.
158. Cuvillier-Fleury, I, 209, 252; Hervé Robert, 'Louis-Philippe duc d'Orléans et la Révolution de 1830. Hasard et nécessité', *Revue de la Société de l'Histoire de la Restauration*, VI, 1992, 43, 47; La Fayette, VI, 387 (letter of 29 July 1830); Pinkney, 294.
159. Robert, 'Louis-Philippe', 38–9.
160. Ibid., 38; Baron de Vitrolles, *Mémoires* (2 vols, 1950–2), II, 372.
161. Marie Amélie, 394 (26 July 1830).
162. Ibid., 395–6.
163. Robert, 'Louis-Philippe', 40–1.
164. Ibid., 41–2, 47; Fontaine, II, 844 (letter of Fontaine, 9 August); Comte Anatole de Montesquiou, *Souvenirs sur la Révolution, l'Empire, la Restauration et le règne de Louis-Philippe* (1961), 455; Cuvillier-Fleury, I, 213–19 (29, 30 July 1830); *Mémoires d'outre-tombe*, III, 143, 144; Antonetti, 581. Other visitors to Neuilly included an aide-de-camp of the Duc de Bourbon, M. de Lambot, and a nephew of Baron Louis, Edouard de Rigny.
165. Cuvillier-Fleury, I, 220; Marie Amélie, 396–7 (29 July 1830).
166. Marie Amélie, 398 (30 July); Robert, 'Louis-Philippe', 48; Antonetti, 580.
167. Robert, 'Louis-Philippe', 45; J.P.T. Bury and R.R. Tombs, *Thiers 1797–1877. A Political Life* (1986), 35; Pinkney, 147; Antonetti, 581; Marie Amélie, 397–8 (30 July).
168. Robert, 'Louis-Philippe', 44.
169. Ibid., 44; Pinkney, 149; cf. Marie Amélie, 397 (30 July 1830).

170. Robert, 'Louis-Philippe', 44.

171. Marie Amélie, 396 (29 July 1830); *Molé*, V, 68.

172. Montesquiou, 466–7; cf. Montesquiou's account to de Vigny in de Vigny, *Journal d'un poète*, 54 (6 January 1831).

173. Robert, 'Louis-Philippe', 49; Marie Amélie, 398 (30 July).

174. Mazas, 31; Marc, 132, 134, 137–8, 142, 151–2, 156; *Mémoires d'outre-tombe*, III, 140.

175. Mortemart, 813.

176. Ibid., 814.

177. Mazas, 127.

178. Pinkney, 157–8, 160.

179. Rumigny, 237 (31 July 1830); Cuvillier-Fleury, I, 235–6.

180. Pinkney, 161; Mazas, 138; Laffitte, 204; Viennet, 102–3 (31 July 1830).

181. Cooper, 144; Fontaine, II, 691 (28 October 1825). Another version of Talleyrand's remark was: *Le duc d'Orléans? Ce n'est pas quelqu'un, mais c'est quelque-chose* (Laffitte, 222).

182. Viennet, 104 (31 July 1830); Laffitte, 204.

183. Pinkney, 162.

184. Rumigny, 238 (31 July 1830).

185. NLS MSS 6242 f419 (Stuart to Aberdeen, 31 July 1830).

186. Mortemart, 821; Pinkney, 165.

187. Mazas, 223–5.

188. Pinkney, 170–2.

189. Cuvillier-Fleury, I, 231, 240; Marie Amélie, 400 (31 July).

190. Cuvillier-Fleury, I, 242 (1 August); Marc, 183–4 (1 August).

191. Pinkney, 228–9.

192. Ibid., 155, 166–7.

193. Marmont, *Mémoires*, VIII, 315–16.

194. Pinkney, 167–9; Marmont, *Mémoires*, VIII, 314, 317.

195. Cairns, *Berlioz*, I, 363 (letter of 5 August 1830); Pinkney, 172–3, 175–6; Rumigny, 242 (5 August 1830).

196. NLS MSS 6442 ff425, 427 (Stuart to Aberdeen, 30, 31 July 1830).

197. NLS MSS 6442 f395 (Stuart to Aberdeen, 30 July 1830 [cypher]).

198. M. de Grovestins, *Le Baron Robert Fagel* (The Hague, 1857), 33.

199. Wendy Hinde, *Canning* (1989), 377.

200. Marie Amélie, 401 (1 August).

201. Boigne, II, 202, 231, 239; cf. Pierre Ordioni, *Pozzo di Borgo diplomate de l'Europe française* (1935), 235 (Boigne to Pozzo, n.d.: *J'ai vu la soeur ce matin, elle m'a dit qu'on désirait vous voir; je suppose que cela est pressé puisque je reçois ce billet. Bonjour, cher. A tantôt n'est-ce pas?*).

202. La Fayette, VI, 597 (speech of 15 August 1831); Boigne, I, 202; Olivier, 286 (2 August 1830).

203. *Molé*, V, 110; NLS MSS 6244 f549 (Stuart to Palmerston, 10 December 1830); Guichen, 120, 153; Ordioni, 233.

204. Guichen, 112, 130, 144–5, 152 (Pozzo to Nesselrode, 25 August 1830).

205. Fontaine, II, 762 (6 November 1826); Théodore Anne, *Mémoires, souvenirs et anecdotes sur l'intérieur du palais de Charles X, et les événements de 1815 à 1830* (3 vols, 1831), II, 159; Castellane, II, 437 (25 July 1831).

206. NLS MSS 6242 f585 (Stuart to Aberdeen, 7 August 1830).

207. Pinkney, 187, 192.

208. NLS MSS 6242 f677 (Stuart to Aberdeen, 10 August 1830 'private').

209. NLS MSS 6242 f459 (Stuart to Aberdeen, 2 August 1830).

210. NLS MSS 6242 f511 (Stuart to Aberdeen, 5 August 1830); MSS 21307 f119 (Stuart to Princesse de Vaudémont, 11 August 1830).

211. NLS MSS 6242 f467 (Stuart to Aberdeen, 2 August 1830).

212. MLS MSS 6242 ff434, 518, 640 (Stuart to Aberdeen, 3, 5, 9 August 1830).

213. NLS MSS 6242 f645 (report of Cradock to Stuart, 9 August 1830).

214. Marie Amélie, 401 (1 August); cf. Ordioni, 221.

215. NLS MSS 6242 ff643–9 (report of Cradock, 9 August 1830); cf. Marmont, VIII, 262.

216. Clément, *Chateaubriand*, 337.

217. Viennet, 106 (1 August 1830).

218. Fontaine, II, 852.

219. Viennet, 109 (7 August 1830); *Mémoires d'outre-tombe*, III, 146.

220. Viennet, 110–11, 113 (9 August); Cuvillier-Fleury, I, 265 (August 1830).

221. Bourset, 198; Pinkney, 194.

222. Viennet, 108 (5 August); Fontaine, II, 862 (1 September 1830).

223. Keates, 339; Pinkney, 284–91.

224. AN 565 AP FL7 116, 120/2 (letters of 9, 14 August 1830).

225. Cuvillier-Fleury, I, 262 (August 1830).

226. Ibid.; Casimir Delavigne, 'La Parisienne. Marche nationale', in *La Lyre nationale 1789, 1815, 1830* (1831), 112; Cairns, I, 363.

227. Laffitte, 229; Rumigny, 251 (20 August); Viennet, 115 (20 October); Blessington, II, 240; AN 565 AP FL7/129 (Flahaut to Madame de Flahaut, 28 August 1830); Cuvillier-Fleury, I, 264 (October 1830).

228. BL Add. MSS 47375 f139 (letter to Princess Lieven, 1830).

229. See e.g. Castellane, III, 390 (2 November 1830).

230. Hugo, *Choses vues 1847–48*, 248 (1848); Vigny, *Journal*, 41 (12 November 1830).

231. Cuvillier-Fleury, I, 272, 287, 330 (29 August 1830, 4 March, 6 August 1831); Fontaine, II, 862 (29 August 1830), 866 (20 October 1830).

232. 'Lettres sur Paris', 18 October 1830, in *Oeuvres diverses* (3 vols, 1935–40), II, 80.

233. Fontaine, II, 883 (13 March 1831).

234. Rémusat, *Mémoires*, II, 433.

235. Wolzogen, 106, 142 (14 July 1789, 20 February 1790).

236. Blessington, II, 212; cf. ibid., II, 224 for the crowd cheering the Comte d'Orsay.

237. AN 565 AP FL7/119 (Flahaut to Madame de Flahaut, 11 August 1830).

238. R.R. Madden, *The Literary Life and Correspondence of the Countess of Blessington* (2nd ed., 3 vols, 1855), I, 374 (Orsay to Walter Savage Landor, 22 August 1830).

239. Cairns, I, 362 (letter of 2 August); *Mémoires d'outre-tombe*, III, 179.

240. Fergusson, 229; Rumigny, 241 (2 August 1830); NLS MSS 6242 f523 (Stuart to Aberdeen, 5 August 1830).

241. Fergusson, 232.

242. La Fayette, VI, 597 (speech of 15 August 1831); Morgan, *France in 1829–30*, II, 557 (La Fayette to Sir Charles and Lady Morgan, 21 August 1830).

243. Turnbull, viii; cf. for another British participant, Dickens, *Pickwick Papers*, chapter 2, *re* 'that glorious scene . . . noble time, sir'. I am grateful for this reference to Roger Hudson.

244. Sir John Bowring, *Autobiographical Recollections* (1877), 137; NLS MSS 6242 f272 (Stuart to Aberdeen, 5 November 1830).

245. Clive H. Church, *Europe in 1830* (1983), 32; Roland Quataert, 'The French Revolution of 1830 and Parliamentary Reform', *History*, October 1994, 382, 390; cf. for evidence of British admiration of the July revolution, Lacour-Gayet, III, 247 (Duchesse de Dino to Madame Adélaïde, 2 November 1830).

246. AN 565 AP KF11/1 (Palmerston to Flahaut, 3 August 1830).

247. Raymond Guyot, *La Première Entente Cordiale* (1926), 77; Lacour-Gayet, III, 239, 253 (Talleyrand to Sébastiani, 27 November 1830); AN 565 AP FL7 218 (Flahaut to Madame de Flahaut, 29 September 1832).

248. AN 565 AP FL7 305/1 (Flahaut to Madame de Flahaut, 27 October 1830, quoting Louis-Philippe: *c'est là le fond, c'est la clef de la voûte; le reste n'est que des ennuis*).

249. BL Add. MSS 51635 f79 (Talleyrand to Lord Holland, 29 July 1832).

250. AN 565 AP FL7 120/2, 316 (Flahaut to Madame de Flahaut, 14 August 1830, 12 November 1834).

251. NLS MSS 6244 f357 (Stuart to Palmerston, 24 November 1830); Talleyrand, IV, 29 (Sébastiani to Talleyrand, 21 January 1831).

252. Castellane, III, 79 (21 May 1833); AN 565 AP FL7 222/1, 244 (Flahaut to Madame de Flahaut, 7 October, 27 November 1832).

253. Lacour-Gayet, III, 235; Mérimée, *CG*, I, 365 (Mérimée to Requien, 19 December 1834).

254. Bernardy, *Charles de Flahaut*, 174, 177.

255. Granville, II, 77 (Lady Granville to Lady Carlisle, 17 January 1831); Apponyi, II, 357 (4 March 1833).

256. Henry Greville, *Leaves from the Diary* (2 vols, 1883), I, 42 (2 December 1834).

257. G.R.V. Barratt, *Voices in Exile. The Decembrist Memoirs* (1974), 278.

258. Heine, *De l'Allemagne* (1998 ed.), 292, 295 (9, 10 August 1830).

259. James J. Sheehan, *German History 1770–1866* (Oxford, 1989), 604–7; C. Vidal, *Louis-Philippe, Metternich et la crise italienne de 1830–1831* (1931), 77–8; Church, 38, 130–1.

260. Henri Pirenne, *Histoire de Belgique* (7 vols, Brussels, 1900–32), VI, 252, 291, 334; Yves Schmitz, *Guillaume Ier et la Belgique* (1945), 298.

261. Gerhard, 127; *Rossini à Paris* (Musée Carnavalet, 1992), 69–73; Kendall, 129.

262. James H. Johnson, *Listening in Paris* (1995), 255; Cairns, I, 363.

263. Gerhard, 131; James H. Johnson, 252; Adam Zamoyski, *Holy Madness. Romantics, Patriots and Revolutionaries 1776–1871* (1999), 267; Georges-Henri Dumont, *Histoire de Bruxelles. Biographie d'une capitale* (Brussels, 1997), 282–4, 305.

264. Guyot, 66; Talleyrand, IV, 28 (Sébastiani to Talleyrand, 21 January 1831); cf. Fl. De Lannoy, 'L'idée favorite de Talleyrand', *Revue d'histoire moderne*, VI, 1931, 445–9.

265. Schroeder, 682; Talleyrand, IV, 84n (protocol of 19 February 1831).

266. Talleyrand, IV, 18n (protocol of 20 January 1831); Schroeder, 677–91.

267. AN 565 AP FL9 133/1 (Flahaut to Madame de Flahaut, n.d.).

268. Rémusat, *Mémoires*, II, 421n.

269. M. Kukiel, *Czartoryski and European Unity 1770–1861* (Princeton, 1955), 165–71.

270. La Fayette, VI, 524 (speech by La Fayette in the Chamber of Deputies, 15 January 1831); Guichen, *La Révolution de 1830*, 244–9, 388; Mark Brown, 'The Comité Franco-Polonais and the French reaction to the Polish uprising of November 1830', *English Historical Review*, XCIII, 1978, 780.

271. *Lettres à Madame Récamier*, 353 (letter of 27 May 1831).

272. Bourset, 253 (Louis-Philippe to Casimir Périer, n.d.).

273. Kukiel, 204; Cracow, Czartoryski Archive, MSS 6488 (Argout to Czartoryski, 27 February 1834).

274. Zamoyski, *Holy Madness*, 275, 283; Andrzej Nieuwazny, 'La Pologne', in *Dictionnaire du Second Empire*, 1025–7; Zawadski, 329–32. In 1876, after the loss of Polish hopes as a result of the Franco-Prussian war of 1870–1, the collections and archives of the Hôtel Lambert were moved to Cracow. For a list of Polish agencies abroad see Czartoryski Archive, MSS 6454 (*compte rendu politique*, August 1847).

275. Adam Zamoyski, *Chopin. A Biography* (1979), 72, 76, 87, 89.

276. Another literary monument to Polish Paris is *La Brise du Nord. Keepsake Polonais*, published in 1838 and 1839 by Karol Forster.

277. Cf. *Molé*, V, 93 (Louis-Philippe to Frederick Wiliam III, 19 August 1830); Castellane, II, 420 (8 March 1831); Ordioni, 237 (Pozzo to Nesselrode, November 1830); Guichen, *La Révolution de 1830*, 321, 385n, 437; Bourset, 236.

278. Granville, II, 92, 93 (to Lady Carlisle 11, 14 March 1831).

279. Castellane, II, 449, 451 (16, 17, 18 September 1831).

280. Citron, I, 118, 159, 383.

281. Olivier, 282 (1 August 1830); Citron, I, 150, 265, 296, 297n, II, 68, 142.

282. Citron, I, 220, 229n, 237.

283. Ibid., II, 109.

284. Ibid., II, 297 (*La Ville Sainte*, August 1834).

285. Gautier, *Paris et les Parisiens*, 462; Citron, II, 88, 150.

286. Citron, II, 248–51; Zamoyski, *Holy Madness*, 309–10.

287. Heinrich Heine, *Ludwig Boerne. Recollections of a Revolutionist* (1881), 75, 78 (6 August 1830); L. Boerne, *Lettres écrites de Paris pendant les années 1830 et 1831* (1832), 17 (17 September 1830); *Marianne et Germania*, 221–2.

288. Joseph Dresch, *Heine à Paris 1831–1856* (1956), 54.

289. McGuigan, 269 (to Laure de Metternich, 23 April 1814).

290. Nesselrode, VII, 148 (Metternich to Nesselrode, 1 September 1830); cf. Keith Hitchins, *The Romanian National Movement in Transylvania 1780–1849* (Cambridge, Mass., 1969), 162.

291. Guichen, *La Révolution de 1830*, 323, 384.

292. Castellane, II, 413 (14 February 1831); Fergusson, 234–6.

293. Guichen, *La Révolution de 1830*, 257, 261, 438, 456, 458 (despatches of 2, 7/19 December 1830, May 1831, 25 October/6 November 1831, 3/15 January 1832).

294. Ordioni, 229, 237, 251, 254–5.

295. *La Lyre nationale* (1831), 231; Marc, 112 (29 July); *La Garde Royale, passim*.

296. Viennet, 107 (3 August 1830).

297. Fontaine, II, 973 (19 May 1833).

298. Castellane, II, 386–7, 398, 15, 17, 20 October, 20 December 1830); Jacques Laffitte, *Mémoires* (1932), 241, 268.

299. Fontaine, II, 890–2 (29 April 1831); Marie Amélie, 416 (28 April 1831). The King also disliked the monument.

300. Viennet, 111 (7 August 1830); Rumigny, 256 (11 September 1830); Bury and Tombs, 44; Alain Fauré, *Paris Carême-prenant*, 112; Castellane, II, 411–17 (14–22 February 1831).

301. Blessington, II, 238 (7 August 1830).

9 Blood on the Boulevards *1831–1838*

1. Pinkney, *The French Revolution of 1830*, 245–50.

2. *Juillet 1830*, 77, 78, 232.

3. Cuvillier-Fleury, II, 41 (15 January 1833).

4. Pailhès, 268n; François Macé de Lépinay, 'Un monument parisien éphémère. La chapelle expiatoire du duc de Berry', *Bulletin de la Société de l'Histoire de l'Art Français*, 1973.

5. Apponyi, II, 40 (27 July 1831).

6. Caroline Mathieu et Sylvain Bellenger, *Paris 1837. Vues de quelques monuments de Paris achevés sous le règne de Louis-Philippe Ier. Aquarelles de Félix Duban* (1999), 92.

7. Pinkney, 251; Françoise Hamon et Charles Mac Cullum, *Louis Visconti 1791–1853* (1991), 142–53; Rémusat, *Mémoires*, III, 396–401; Berlioz, 234; Cairns, II, 208–9.

8. Apponyi, II, 43 (28 July 1831); Castellane, II, 439 (28 July 1831).

9. Girardin, I, 725–7 (31 July 1840).

10. Girardin, I, 208 (3 August 1837); *Lettres de François Guizot et de la princesse de Lieven* (3 vols, 1963–4), I, 175 (Lieven to Guizot, 26 July 1838); Hamon and Mac Cullum, 142–61; Sylvain Bellenger et Françoise Hamon, *Duban. Les couleurs de l'architecte* (1996), 191–8.

11. *Hittorff. Un architecte du XIXe siècle* (1986), 102–53.

12. Polovtsov, III, 393 (despatch to Nesselrode, 24 June 1820); Ordioni, 222 (Pozzo to Matuszewic, 2 August 1830); Gasnault, 60.

13. Castellane, III, 84 (28 July 1833); Cuvillier-Fleury, II, 131–2 (3 March 1835); Heine, *De la France*, 283 (salon de 1833); Antonetti, 743.

14. Ledré, 135–45; Heine, *De la France*, 100 (25 March 1832).

15. Hugh Collingham with R.S. Alexander, *The July Monarchy* (1987), 103.

16. Heine, *De la France*, 21; Joseph A. Kruse (ed.), *La Loreley et la liberté. Heinrich Heine (1797–1856). Un poète allemand de Paris* (1997), 114 (to Friedrich Merckel, 24 August 1832).

17. Heine, *De la France*, 65 (10 February 1832); Kruse, 113, 131; Heine, *De l'Allemagne*, 276 (1 July 1830), 437.

18. *Marianne et Germania*, 220, quoting *Le Globe*, 22 May 1831; Dresch, 51.

19. Heine, *De la France*, 10.

20. Ibid., 108, 110, 111 (19 April 1832); Philippe Vigier, *Paris pendant la monarchie de juillet* (1991), 78.

21. Heine, *De la France*, 115, 116; Castellane, II, 499, 502 (31 March, 8 April 1832).

22. Apponyi, II, 163, 178 (2, 18 April 1832); Castellane, II, 499–503 (28 March–13 April 1832).

23. Heine, *De la France*, 110–11 (19 April 1832); Castellane, II, 499 (2 April 1832).

24. Castellane, II, 499, 500 (1, 4 April 1832); Fontaine, II, 928 (13 April 1832); Heine, *De la France*, 22, 113; Vigier, 86.

25. Fontaine, II, 928 (5 April 1832).

26. Heine, *De la France*, 112–14 (19 April 1832).

27. Ackerknecht, 158; Castellane, II, 503 (14 April 1832).

28. J. Lucas-Dubreton, *Louis-Philippe et la Machine Infernale* (1951), 111; Heine, *De la France*, 186 (6 June 1832); Duchesse de Maillé, *Mémoires 1832–1851* (1989), 61, 64 (May–June 1832).

29. Heine, *De la France*, 186, 188 (6, 7 June 1832).

30. Lucas-Dubreton, *Machine Infernale*, 115–20; Talleyrand, IV, 475 (Madame Adélaïde to Talleyrand, 8 June 1832); cf. Bro, 208–9 (letter of General Gourgaud, 13 June 1832).

31. Antonetti, 694; Laffitte, 300.

32. Castellane, II, 435 (14 July 1831).

33. Heine, *De la France*, 195 (11 June 1832).

34. Richard D. Altick, *Punch. The Lively Youth of a British Institution 1841–1851* (Columbus, 1997), 6.

35. Antonetti, 736–42; Lucas-Dubreton, *Machine Infernale*, 166; *Caricatures politiques 1829–1848. De l'éteignoir à la poire* (Maison de Chateaubriand, 1994), *passim* and 88, 117; Ledré, 139, 142.

36. Collingham, 62.

37. Joseph Barry, *George Sand ou la scandale de la liberté* (1982), 205.

38. *Paris révolutionnaire* (4 vols, 1838), IV, 422, 427.

39. Collingham, 137; Castellane, IV, 175 (21 June 1849).

40. Citron, II, 10.

41. Castellane, III, 84–5 (28 July 1833), cf. Cuvillier-Fleury, II, 131–2 (3 March 1835).

42. Ernest Daudet, *Histoire de l'Emigration* (3 vols, 1905–7), III, 60 (letter of August 1804).

43. Lucas-Dubreton, *Machine Infernale*, 188; (Cuvillier-Fleury, II, 111 (13 April 1834); Maillé, *Mémoires*, 93 (April 1834).

44. Rémusat, *Mémoires*, III, 394; Duc d'Orléans, *Lettres 1825–1842* (1889), 128 (to Queen Louise, 21 April 1834).

45. Apponyi, II, 414 (17 April 1834); Lucas-Dubreton, *Machine Infernale*, 190.

46. Orléans, *Lettres*, 130 (Orléans to Queen Louise, 21 April 1834).

47. Apponyi, II, 413 (14 April 1834).

48. Marie Amélie, 462 (14 April 1834).

49. Lucas-Dubreton, *Machine Infernale*, 233.

50. Douglas Johnson, 165.

51. *Louis-Philippe*, 98–9; Lucas-Dubreton, *Machine Infernale*, 240, 251, 274–5, 350, 360–1; Cuvillier-Fleury, II, 143 (letter from Trognon, 30 July 1835); Orléans, *Lettres*, 155 (to Duchesse de Dino, 28 July 1835).

52. Apponyi, III, 109–11 (30 July 1835); cf. Viennet, 170 (1 August 1835).

53. Orléans, *Lettres*, 155 (to Duchesse de Dino, 28 July 1835).

54. Rumigny, 266–7 (28 July 1835).

55. Henry Greville, I, 153 (15 November 1841); Granville, II, 121 (12 February 1832).

56. Cuvillier-Fleury, II, 139–41 (letters of Trognon, 28, 29 July 1835?); Apponyi, III, 111–12 (30 July 1835).

57. Henry Greville, I, 66 (9 August 1835); Lucas-Dubreton, *Machine Infernale*, 297; Viennet, 170–2 (5 August 1835); André Gayot (ed.), *François Guizot et Madame Laure de Gasparin (fragments inédits)* (1934), 26 (Guizot to Madame de Gasparin, 6 August 1835).

58. Cuvillier-Fleury, II, 143 (letter from Trognon, 30 July 1835); Lucas-Dubreton, *Machine Infernale*, 311.

59. Collingham, 165–7; Schroeder, 719; Balzac, *Correspondance*, IV, 73n; Dennis Mack Smith, *Mazzini* (New Haven, Conn., 1994), 20, 31.

60. *Louis-Philippe*, 98–9; Dino, II, 75 (29 July 1836).

61. Fontaine, II, 866 (20 October 1830).

62. Heine, *De la France*, 41–5 (28 December 1831).

63. Fontaine, II, 910 (1 October 1831).

64. Castellane, II, 421, 427 (12 March, 25 April 1831); M. Guizot, *Mémoires pour servir à l'histoire de mon temps* (8 vols, 1858–67), II, 187.

65. Pinkney, 301; Castellane, III, 76–7 (5 May 1833); Jean Delmas (ed.), *Histoire militaire de la France* (4 vols, 1992–8), II, 427.

66. Antonetti, 731–2.

67. Ibid., 797.

68. Ibid., 727–9; *Louis-Philippe*, 18, 84, 90–2; Hugo, *Choses vues 1847–48*, 197 (1847).

69. Antonetti, 683.

70. Rémusat, *Mémoires*, III, 34–5; Apponyi, III, 50 (15 March 1835); Cuvillier-Fleury, II, 125 (6 December 1834).

71. Viennet, 144 (11 November 1834).

72. Cuvillier-Fleury, II, 80–1 (June 1833), 129 (18 February 1835).

73. Antonetti, 764–5; Douglas Johnson, 173.

74. Laffitte, 211; Mansel, *The Court of France 1789–1830*, 185.

75. F.H.G. Castil-Blaze, *Chapelle musique des rois de France* (1832), 259, 280; Comte de Mérode-Westerloo, *Souvenirs* (2 vols, 1864), II, 182; Berlioz, 25; Archives Historiques du Ministère de la Guerre XAE11, 9 (Baron de Gressot Aide-Major-Général de la Garde Royale to Comte de Bordessoulle, 7 November 1829).

76. Duc Pasquier, *Souvenirs sur la révolution de 1848* (1948), 292.

77. Soubiès, 75.

78. AN 565 AP FL7 120/2 (to Madame de Flahaut, 14 August 1830).

79. Gérard, 366; Viennet, 195 (12 January 1837).

80. Fontaine, II, 908 (27 August 1831); Michael Marrinan, *Painting Politics for Louis-Philippe* (Yale, 1988), 12 and ill. 15.

81. Apponyi, II, 65 (20 September 1831); Castellane, II, 455 (2, 3 October 1831).

82. Fontaine, II, 911 (1 October 1831).

83. Castellane, II, 392, 425 (15 November 1830, 3 April 1831), III, 67 (3 March 1833).

84. Ibid., II, 455 (2 October 1831).

85. Comte de Montalivet, *Fragments et souvenirs* (2 vols, 1900), II, 25.

86. Ibid., II, 25, 293; Apponyi, III, 425 (17 October 1840); Rémusat, *Mémoires*, III, 11; Granville, II, 249 (Lady Granville to Duke of Devonshire, 21 November 1837).

87. Balabine, 93 (20 January 1843).

88. Jane Ridley, *The Young Disraeli 1804–46* (1995), 270–1. In 1832, however, Disraeli had published an apocalyptic booklet denouncing the ambition of France and Louis-Philippe: *England and France; or, a Cure for the Ministerial Gallomania* (1832).

89. Montalivet, II, 25; Prince de Joinville, *Vieux Souvenirs* (1970 ed.), 274–5; Apponyi, II, 322–4 (23 January 1833); Rumigny, 283 (20 September 1836); Hugo, *Choses vues 1830–46*, 199 (23 December 1846).

90. De Kock, II, 101.

91. Dino, I, 237, 297, 314 (30 August 1834, 12 December 1834, 8 January 1835); cf. Rémusat, *Mémoires*, III, 490.

92. Girardin, *Correspondance parisienne* (1853), 325 (1 June 1844); Hugo, *Choses vues 1830–46*, 283, 297 (June 1844, 6 September 1844).

93. Hugo, *Choses vues 1830–46*, 301 (16 November 1844).

94. Ibid., 282, 301 (28 June, 16 November 1844).

95. Ibid., 291–4 (4 August 1844).

96. Marie Amélie, 451, 467 (2 January 1833, 1835); cf. Castellane, II, 231 (2 March 1828).

97. Charles Greville, III, 341 (25 January 1837).

98. Ibid., III, 342–3 (27 January, 2 February 1837). After a ball in the state apartments and theatre at the Tuileries in 1833, although he sneered at the guests, Rodolphe Apponyi con-

ceded that it was one of the finest *fêtes* he had seen: Apponyi, II, 329 (31 January 1833); cf. Fontaine, II, 960 (31 January 1833).

99. Ticknor, II, 126 (diary for 10 January 1838); cf. Edward Boykin (ed.), *Victoria, Albert and Mrs Stevenson* (1957), 125 (letter of Mrs Stevenson, February 1838).

100. Orléans, *Souvenirs*, 71; Montalivet, II, 291.

101. Cf. Gayot, 231 (Guizot to Madame Laure de Gasparin, 14 November 1842): *c'est un assez grand ennui que ces courses continuelles à Saint-Cloud. Mais je n'ai pas le courage d'insister pour que le Roi revienne plus tôt à Paris, c'est à dire dans sa prison. A Saint-Cloud il est libre et il se promène.*

102. J. Vatout, *Souvenirs historiques des résidences royales de France* (7 vols, 1845), V, 370; Rémusat, *Mémoires*, III, 409; Paul Viallaneix, *Michelet* (1998), 217.

103. Martin-Fugier, *La Vie élégante*, 337.

104. Joinville, 144; Jean-Marie Moulin, *Le Château de Compiègne* (1987), 46.

105. Françoise Maison, 'Les Camps sous Louis-Philippe vus du Château', *Bulletin de la Société Historique de Compiègne*, XXXVI, 1999, 168.

106. Viennet, 239–42 (9 October 1839).

107. Dino, II, 152 (3 June 1837).

108. Boigne, II, 330.

109. Granville, II, 168–71 (to Lady Carlisle, 7, 14 October 1834); Apponyi, II, 469, 490, 510 (9 October, 20 November 1834); cf. Cuvillier-Fleury, II, 120 (29 September–8 October 1834).

110. Henry Greville, I, 38 (15 November 1834); cf. Heine, *De la France*, 102 (25 March 1832).

111. AN 565 AP FL11/275 (letter of 30 August 1833); cf. Castellane, II, 503 (14 April 1832).

112. Orléans, *Souvenirs*, 53, 65, 92.

113. Antonetti, 755, 758, 782.

114. Dino, I, 313 (23 January 1835); Laffitte, 320.

115. Boigne, II, 343; Ticknor, II, 121 (28 December 1837); Granville, II, 234 (to Duke of Devonshire, 12 June 1837).

116. Boigne, II, 350–1; Dino, II, 153–4 (5, 6 June 1837).

117. Montalivet, II, 264; Thomas W. Gaetghens, *Versailles, de la résidence royale au musée historique* (Antwerp, 1984), 104, 115, 116. The best description remains Alexandre de Laborde, *Versailles ancien et moderne* (1839).

118. *Juillet 1830*, 77; Fontaine, II, 1008 (24 December 1841); Gaetghens, 310, 313.

119. Gaetghens, 321–2.

120. Viennet, 203–6 (11 June 1837); Delacroix, *CG*, I, 436 (letter to Feuillet, 7 June 1837); Boigne, II, 351; cf. for a full contemporary account, Jules Janin, *Fontainebleau, Versailles, Paris* (1837).

121. Girardin 1, 38 (30 November 1836); Balzac, *Lettres à Madame Hanska*, III, 130 (5 January 1846).

122. Gaetghens, 333.

123. AN CC (Archives de la Chambre des Pairs) 496 (letter of 8 January 1832).

124. Antonetti, 626; Maillé, *Mémoires*, 141.

125. Moré, 294, 311 (letters of 18 July 1831, 24 June 1832); Maillé, *Mémoires*, 201 (December 1837).

126. Neuilly, 402.

127. Norfolk County Record Office, Bulwer Papers BUL 1/2/1 (diary for 6 October 1832); cf. for similar sentiments, Maillé, *Mémoires*, 109–10 (December 1834).

128. Cf. Rousseau, 1179 (police report of 8 June 1821, quoting him as saying *qu'il n'y a dans la famille que la duchesse de Berry qui ait un grand caractère*).

129. Clément, *Chateaubriand*, 347, 366; Chateaubriand, *Mémoires d'outre-tombe*, III, 192, 203.
130. *Mémoires d'outre-tombe*, III, 658, 660.
131. Ibid., III, 659, 427.
132. Maillé, *Souvenirs*, 52.
133. Ferdinand de Bertier de Sauvigny, *Souvenirs d'un ultra-royaliste (1815–1832)* (1993), 561.
134. Apponyi, II, 315 (5 January 1833); Maillé, *Mémoires*, 179 (February 1837), cf. Raikes, III, 143 (17 March 1837).
135. Girardin 1, 607 (8 February 1840); cf. Apponyi, III, 247 (19 May 1836); Gautier, *Paris*, 214–15.
136. Aumale, I, 192 (Cuvillier-Fleury to Aumale, 6 December 1843); Yriarte, 29, 147, 165.
137. Lacour-Gayet, III, 283 (Talleyrand to Princesse de Vaudémont, 26 November 1831).
138. Girardin, *Correspondance parisienne*, 4 (17 January 1840).
139. Balzac, *Correspondance*, II, 58n, 537n, 556 (Duc de Fitzjames to Balzac, 7 October 1834).
140. Graham Robb, *Balzac* (1995 ed.), 335; Z. Marcas, in *L'Illustre Gaudissart* (Livres de Poche, 1971), 90.
141. *Memoranda. Journal intime 1836–1864* (1993), 10, 117, 119, 232 (26 July 1837, 2 August 1837, 28 July 1838).
142. Baron d'Eckstein, *Lettres inédites*, ed. Louis le Guillou (1984), 26 (letter to Comtesse Valérie de Menthon, 14 April 1838).
143. Henry Greville, I, 58 (10 May 1835).
144. Vicomte Armand de Melun, *Mémoires* (2 vols, 1891), I, 158–9.
145. Ernest Legouvé, *Soixante ans de souvenirs* (2 vols, 1886–7), I, 356; cf. Xavier Marmier, I, 190 (January 1861).
146. Gronow, I, 258; J.-L. Bory, *Eugenè Sue. Le roi du roman populaire* (1962), 133, 233; Legouvé, I, 357.
147. Castellane, II, 489–90 (1, 6 February 1832); Raikes, II, 208 (9 January 1834).
148. Apponyi, I, 234 (25 February 1830); Cuvillier-Fleury, I, 180 (30 May 1830); NLS MSS 6243 f262 (Stuart to Aberdeen, 30 August 1830: the estates were Saint–Leu, Boissy, Mortefontaine and the forêt de Montmorency); Cornut-Gentille, 164, 240. This manoeuvre had been in part directed by Talleyrand, who needed the silence of the Duc de Bourbon, father of the Duc d'Enghien, in order to mask his part in Enghien's execution in 1804. Talleyrand had helped arrange the marriage of one of his cousins, the Marquis de Chabannes, to a niece of the Baronne de Feuchères, Mathilde Dawes, in 1827.
149. Castellane, II, 484, 488 (18, 31 January 1832).
150. Martin-Fugier, *La Vie élégante*, 85; Dino, III, 25 (15 February 1841).
151. Apponyi, II, 317, III, 12, 17 (16 January 1833, 19 January, 3 February 1835).
152. Du Montet, 395.
153. Heine, *De la France*, 168–9 (16 June 1832), 315.
154. Apponyi, II, 399, 407 (19 March, 2 April 1834); Dino, II, 35 (10 April 1836).
155. Douglas Johnson, 206; Girardin 1, 781; Mérimée, *CG*, III, 357n; Balabine, 123 (19 May 1843); cf. for the rise in Easter communions, Daumard, 350.
156. Mérimé, *CG*, III, 333 (to Madame de Montijo, 11 March 1843); cf. ibid., 2e série, VI, 376 (Mérimée to Panizzi, 14 March 1865: *toutes les femmes les plus catins sont dévotes à present*).
157. A.J.B. Whyte, *The Early Life and Letters of Cavour 1810–1848* (1925), 279–80 (Cavour to Pietro di Santarosa, 1843).
158. Collingham, 118, 308, 350, 354; Inès Murat, *La IIe République* (1987), 20.

159. Harriet Raikes (ed.), *Private Correspondence of Thomas Raikes with the Duke of Wellington* (1861), 356 (to Wellington, 19 October 1843).

160. Lacour-Gayet, III, 353, 381, 388, 393–400; Talleyrand, V, 482–3.

161. Lord Sudley, *The Lieven–Palmerston Correspondence 1828–1856* (1943), 151 (Lieven to Lady Cowper, 24 May 1838).

162. Castellane, III, 249 (9 April 1841).

10   City of Ink *1830–1848*

1. Ledré, 105.

2. *Mémoires d'outre-tombe*, III, 202.

3. Rumigny, 251 (20 August 1830); Smith Allen, 128.

4. Sédillot, 106; Paul Johnson, 881.

5. Anik Devries, 'La musique à bon marché', in Peter Bloom (ed.), *Music in Paris in the Eighteen Thirties* (New York, 1987), 232.

6. Adalbert von Bornstedt, *Fragments de silhouettes de Paris* (2 vols, 1837), I, 7, 336.

7. Bertier de Sauvigny, *Nouvelle Histoire de Paris*, 344.

8. Delacroix, *Journal*, I, 55 (24 January 1824); Récamier, II, 543.

9. Morgan, *France in 1829–30*, I, 383–4; Gronow, II, 59; cf. Parent-Lardeur, 187, quoting a catalogue of 1823; *aujourd'hui tout le monde veut écrire, tout le monde veut lire.*

10. Raikes, *Journal*, III, 231 (14 August 1837).

11. Smith Allen, 55, 277.

12. Hortense, III, 17; Martin-Fugier, 270 and id., *Les Romantiques*, 110–11; Rémusat, *Mémoires*, II, 148; Balzac, 'Des salons littéraires', in *Les Journalistes* (1998), 147–56.

13. Legouvé, I, 353, 355; Sainte-Beuve, *Mes poisons* (1965), 76.

14. Julien Frédéric Tarn, *Le Marquis de Custine* (1985), 152, 688.

15. Henri-Jean Martin and Roger Chartier, *Histoire de l'édition française* (4 vols, 1983–7), II, 554.

16. Sédillot, 106.

17. Nicole Felkay, *Balzac et ses éditeurs 1822–1837, Essai sur la librairie romantique* (1987), 260.

18. *Chateaubriand, le voyageur et l'homme politique* (1969), 203 (contract of 22 March 1836).

19. Balzac, *Correspondance*, III, 189n; Hugo, I, 570 (Madame Victor Hugo to General Hugo, 2 December 1823).

20. Mérimée, *CG*, II, 248n, IV, 262n; cf. for a table of authors' earnings, Martin and Chartier, III, 152–3.

21. Jean-Claude Yon, *Eugène Scribe, la fortune et la liberté* (2000), 16; Neil Cole Arvin, *Eugène Scribe and the French Theatre 1815–1830* (Harvard, 1824), 52; Janin, *The American in Paris*, I, 175, 206–8; Gerhard, 125.

22. Norfolk County Record Office, Bulwer Papers BUL 1/2/1 (diary for 6 October 1831).

23. Anne Uberfeld, *Théophile Gautier* (1992), 221–3; Hugo, *Choses vues 1847–48*, 438 (1848).

24. Martin-Fugier, *Les Romantiques*, 144; Daumard, 502; Gerhard, 38.

25. Norfolk County Record Office, Bulwer Papers BUL 1/2/1 (diary for 6 October 1832).

26. AN F4 2696 (*Ministère de l'Intérieur. Etat des sommes à payer pour le mois de janvier 1825*); Kruse, 159, 551.

27. Guillemin, 261.

28. Aumale, I, 206 (Cuvillier-Fleury to Aumale, 26 December 1843); Frank Lestringant, *Alfred de Musset* (1999), 47, 384.

29. Fontaney, *Journal intime*, 25 (2 September 1831).

30. Viallaneix, 203, 263.

31. Lacour-Gayet, III, 44 (Talleyrand to Duchesse de Courland, 27 September 1815).

32. Rossi, 11.

33. Maillé, *Souvenirs*, 313 (May 1830).

34. Robb, *Balzac*, 123, 131.

35. *Molé*, II, 13–14, III, 379, 155; Rémusat, *Mémoires*, II, 111.

36. Rémusat, *Mémoires*, III, 167–70; François Guizot, *Lettres de . . . et de la princesse de Lieven* (hereafter *Guizot/Lieven*) (3 vols, 1963–4), I, 107 (Lieven to Guizot, 19 September 1837); Hugo, *Choses Vues 1847–48*, 78 (10 April 1847).

37. *Molé*, VI, 280–1 (note of August 1847). The Duchesse de Dino also played a part in the composition of the memoirs of her lover, Talleyrand: *Molé*, V, 48 (note of December 1822).

38. Rémusat, *Mémoires*, I, 193, II, 110, III, 170.

39. *Molé*, I, 272, 287–9; cf. for another brilliant physical description by a memoir-writer, Charles de Rémusat on Madame de Staël, *Mémoires*, I, 357.

40. Barante, III, 148 (Rémusat to Barante, 7 December 1823).

41. Foy, III, 158, 160 (19, 23 December 1824).

42. Stanley Mellon, *The Political Uses of History. A Study of Historians in the French Restoration* (Stanford, 1958), 1.

43. Rosanvallon, 229.

44. Bronne, *La Comtesse Le Hon*, *passim*; Heine, *De la France*, 92 (25 March 1832).

45. Girardin 1, 457, 524 (3 May, 13 September 1839); Apponyi, II, 380 (28 January 1834). His brother Montpensier also visited antique-dealers, in disguise in order to bargain better: Boigne, II, 442.

46. Heine, *Lutèce*, 212 (11 December 1841); cf. Musset, *La Confession d'un enfant du siècle*, 56: *notre siècle n'a point de formes . . . l'antique, le gothique, le goût de la Renaissance, celui de Louis XIII tout est pêle-mêle. Enfin nous avons de tous les siècles hors du nôtre – chose qui ne s'est jamais vue à une autre époque.*

47. Norfolk County Record Office, Bulwer Papers BUL 1/2/1 (diary for 6 October 1832).

48. See e.g. Balzac, *Lettres à Madame Hanska*, III, 583–4 (30 December 1846).

49. Paul Jarry, *Cénacles et vieux logis parisiens* (1929), 202. Among its first inhabitants was one of the most celebrated courtesans of the century, Esther Lachmann, later Madame Herz, later still Marquise de Paiva, finally Countess Henckel von Donnersmarck.

50. Stendhal, *Paris–Londres*, 660 (March 1826); Sédillot, 83–4; Daumard, 358 and n.

51. Orléans, *Souvenirs*, 275.

52. Foy, II, 106 (4 July 1822); *Molé*, III, 304.

53. Dino, II, 16 (11 February 1836). In addition the Duchesse de Massa would be Minister of the Marine; the Duchesse de Montmorency Minister of Finance; the Marquise de Caraman Minister of Commerce.

54. Barry, 123, 143.

55. Dino, I, 299 (12 December 1834); Rémusat, *Mémoires*, III, 97; Duc Albert de Broglie, *Mémoires* (2 vols, 1938–43), I, 77; cf. Marmier, *Journal*, I, 190 (January 1861).

56. Montalivet, II, 18; see e.g. *Lettres à Madame Récamier*, 375 (letter of Chateaubriand, 14 May 1833).

57. Apponyi, II, 186 (20 April 1832).

58. Albert de Broglie, *Mémoires*, I, 78. I am grateful for this reference to Stuart Preston.

59. Françoise Wagener, *La Comtesse de Boigne* (1997), 117, 165, 192, 267.

60. Ibid., 414; Boigne, II, 146, 225.

61. See e.g. Ley, 340n; Staël, *Dix années d'exil*, 207n.

62. Rossi, 454.

63. Boigne, II, 462.

64. Gautier, *Paris et les Parisiens*, 408, 462.

65. *Paris ou le livre des Cent et un*, I, vi.

66. Henry Murger, *Scènes de la vie de bohème* (Gallimard, 1988), 438–9; Girardin 1, 802.

67. Fontaney, 30.

68. Apponyi, II, 369, 428 (15 March 1833, 8 May 1834).

69. Citron, II, 185; Gerhard, 244.

70. *Ferragus* (Presses Pocket, 1992), 34–5.

71. Citron, II, 96–9; *La Fille aux yeux d'or* (Presses Pocket, 1992), 340.

72. Tarn, 353; Citron, II, 196.

73. *Le Cabinet des antiques* (Calmann Levy, 1895), 221; cf. Stéphanie de Longueville, 'La grande dame de 1830', in *Les Français peints par eux-mêmes*, I, 165: *l'or est le seul dieu du jour.*

74. Chevalier, 643; Citron, II, 196.

75. Citron, II, 194.

76. *Correspondance*, III, 32 (to Louise, February 1836).

77. *Le Père Goriot* (Booking International, 1993), 315.

78. Vigier, 449.

79. Maurice Reclus, *Emile de Girardin*, 29; Ledré, 243–7.

80. A.H. Johnson (ed.), *The Letters of Charles Greville and Henry Reeve 1836–1865* (1924), 29 (Reeve to Greville, 12 October 1840).

81. Tarn, 350.

82. Girardin 1, 448 (12 April 1839); cf. Edmond Got, *Journal* (2 vols, 1910), I, 175 (29 June 1845): *Ah les journaux! Le journalisme! C'est le mot, c'est la puissance d'à présent.*

83. De Musset, *Correspondance*, I (*1826–1839*, 1985), 163, 180 (to Alfred Tattet, 8 August 1835; to Princess Belgiojoso, 15 May 1839).

84. Balzac, *Les Journalistes* (Arlea, 1998), 9, 27.

85. Daniel Halévy, *Le Courrier de Monsieur Thiers* (1921), 206 (Bugeaud to Thiers, n.d.).

86. Barbey d'Aurevilly, *Memoranda*, 131 (22 August 1837).

87. Robb, *Balzac*, 278, 374; *Correspondance*, IV, 671 (Pierre Hetzel to Balzac, 3 February 1844), V, 60 (Emile de Girardin to Balzac, 27 November 1845).

88. Paul Johnson, 166.

89. Roger Chartier (ed.), *La Correspondance. Les usages de la lettre au XIXe siècle* (1991), 86–8.

90. Jean-Henri Marlet, *Tableaux de Paris* (Paris–Geneva, 1979), ed. Guillaume de Bertier de Sauvigny, 34.

91. Tarn, 426.

92. In *Autre Etude de femme* (Folio, 1971), 79.

93. Duchesse de Broglie, 87 (Duchesse de Broglie to Madame de Castellane, 15 February 1821); Daudet, *Police politique, passim* and 197, 290; *Guizot/Lieven*, II, 26 (Lieven to Guizot, 14 March 1840).

94. Hence, for example, Napoleon's gift to King Joseph during the Hundred Days, of his letters from Marie-Louise in 1813–14, their removal in 1823 from Paris to the Bernadotte Archives in Stockholm by Joseph's sister-in-law Queen Désirée, and eventual publication in 1955: *Marie-Louise et Napoléon 1813–1814. Lettres inédites*, ed. C.F. Palmstierna, 14–15;

Notes

cf. Maurice Lescure, *Madame Hamelin* (1995), 120, 121, for Hortense Allart's use of the letters she had received from Chateaubriand to challenge Madame Récamier's version of his life.

95. *Correspondance de Fauriel et Mary Clarke* (1911), frontispiece (letter of Mary Clarke, 3 April 1855).

96. Thomas (ed.), *Correspondance générale de Chateaubriand*, V, 6, 48 (letters of 12 September, 24 October 1823).

97. Ibid., V, 6, 16 (letters of 12, 20 September 1823).

98. Rousseau, 1166 (note of 20 December 1820); cf. Chateaubriand, *CG*, IV, 227 (Chateaubriand to Duchesse de Duras, 17 or 18 December 1821: *votre billet est brûlé*), 233 (id. to id., December 1821: *Brûlez ce billet*).

99. Lacour-Gayet, II, 348 (letter of 20 March 1814).

100. Balzac, *Illusions perdues*, 319: *nous devons à la paix, aux Bourbons, une littérature jeune et originale*; Mellon, 129–49, 154, 157, 168. The defences of the Terror included Thiers' history of the revolution and J.C. Bailleul, *Examen critique de l'ouvrage posthume de Mme la baronne de Staël* (2 vols, 1818).

101. Goethe, *Conversations with Eckermann and Soret* (2 vols, 1850), I, 406–8. I am grateful for this reference to Laure Murat.

102. L.T.C. Rolt, *Isambard Kingdom Brunel* (1970 ed.), 37; cf. A.J. Tudesq, *Les Grands Notables en France, 1840–49* (2 vols, 1964), I, 337, for notables' preference for educating their children in Paris.

103. Morgan, *France in 1829–30*, II, 289.

104. Vigier, 424.

105. Mercer, II, 243 (7 August 1815); Stanley, 124 (8 July 1814); Stendhal, *Paris–Londres*, 859 (22 May 1828); Legouvé, I, 111, 113.

106. Airlie, I, 166 (Palmerston to Lady Cowper, 15 December 1829).

107. Shepherd, 272; cf. Jerzy Skowronok, *Adam Czartoryski 1770–1861* (Warsaw, 1994), 230; Kruse, 117.

108. Alphonse Esquiros, *Paris ou les sciences, les institutions et les moeurs au XIXe siècle* (2 vols, 1847), I, 1.

109. See John Harley Warner, *Against the Spirit of System. The French Impulse in Nineteenth-Century American Medicine* (1998); Ackerknecht, xiii, 18, 151, 176, 191–3.

110. Cairns, II, 365.

111. Ibid., I, 246, 285–9; Reclus, 55–6.

112. Berlioz, 77–8.

113. James H. Johnson, 257.

114. Ibid., 31.

115. AN 234 AP [papers of Baron Mounier] 2 (police report of 13 March 1821).

116. See e.g. Viennet, 143 (10 November 1834: *le foyer était plein d'hommes politiques, de journalistes, d'oisifs . . .*).

117. Decin State Archives, Czech Republic, Prince Clary, unpublished diary (25 April 1822).

118. Guest, 28; Comte d'Alton-Shée, *Souvenirs de 1847 et de 1848* (1879), 297; Castellane, III, 73 (27 March 1833); Raikes, *Journal*, IV, 422 (1 March 1845); cf. Rupert Christiansen, *Tales of the New Babylon* (Minerva ed., 1995), 64–5. A similar case was that of the last Prince Kaunitz, a famous *boulevardier* who was found, on his death in 1849, to own 300 miniatures of women: Apponyi, IV, 229 (20 January 1849).

Notes

119. James H. Johnson, 81, 189–91.
120. Pueckler-Muskau, 357 (7 January 1829); cf. Maillé, *Mémoires*, 43 (March 1832).
121. *Rossini à Paris*, 91, 92, 95; Philip Gossett, 'Music at the Théâtre Italien', in Peter Bloom (ed.), *Music in Paris*, 332; Gerhard, 70.
122. *Rossini à Paris*, 95.
123. Guest, 17, 73–9, 86.
124. *Rossini à Paris*, 100; Guest, 106; James H. Johnson, 241–2, 245; Apponyi, II, 20 (23 June 1831); Gerhard, 29.
125. James H. Johnson, 250, 256; Apponyi, II, 87 (30 November 1831).
126. Heine, *Lutèce*, 93 (12 June 1840).
127. Granier, 241, 257 (Prince Wilhelm to Princess Charlotte of Prussia, 20 April, 19 May 1814); Peter Bloom, 'A Review of Fétis's Revue Musicale', in *Music in Paris*, 76.
128. Granville, II, 18 (letter to Duke of Devonshire, 21 March 1828).
129. James H. Johnson, 250–1; Fauré, 47n; Castellane, III, 73 (27 March 1833).
130. Apponyi, I, 3 (30 February [sic] 1826).
131. F. Grillparzer, *Journal de mon voyage en France (1836)* (1942), 59, 75 (20, 24 April 1836); Ilsa Barea, *Vienna. Legend and Reality* (1966), 35.
132. Marie Amélie, 311 (28 December 1823).
133. Jean-Claude Yon, *Offenbach* (1996), 17.
134. Herbert Weinstock, *Vincenzo Bellini. His Life and his Operas* (1971), 311: Karin Pendle, *Eugène Scribe and French Opera of the Nineteenth Century* (1979), 3; Marcello Conati, 'Verdi et la culture parisienne des années 1830', in Peter Bloom (ed.), *Music in Paris*, 210–15.
135. Cairns, II, 97; Helga Jeanblanc, *Des Allemands dans l'industrie et le commerce du livre à Paris 1811–1870* (1994), 256–7; Heine, *Lutèce*, 306 (20 March 1843).
136. Citron, II, 104–8, 151.
137. Pierre Gaissier and Juliet Wilson, *The Life and Complete Works of Goya* (New York, 1981), 343.
138. Cairns, II, 46; Herbert Weinstock, *Donizetti and the World of Opera in Italy, Paris and Vienna in the first Half of the Nineteenth Century* (1964), 108, 142 (letter of 8 April 1839), 147 (letter of 6 December 1839).
139. James H. Johnson, 252–3.
140. Wagner, 169; *Marianne et Germania*, 244.
141. Wagner, 193, 197, 216, 234. Berlioz, too, felt better appreciated in Weimar than in Paris: Cairns, II, 277, 279.

11   Nationalists and Europeans *1838–1840*

1. P. Alessandra Maccioni Ruju and Marco Mosteri, *The Life and Times of Gugliemo Libri (1802–1869)* (Hilversum, 1998); Guichen, 282.
2. Bloom, 333.
3. Rosanvallon, 286; Balabine, 76 (31 December 1842).
4. Beth Archer Brombert, *Cristina. Portraits of a Princess* (1978), 27, 29.
5. Ibid., 55–7, 59.
6. Ibid., 244, 316.
7. Ibid., 75, 81, 94.
8. Ibid., 52.
9. Ibid., 124–7.

10. Ibid., 359–61, 340. Another version of her remark is: *Thalberg est le premier pianiste du monde; Liszt est le seul.*

11. Ibid., 309, 311; Apponyi, III, 371 (26 March 1839).

12. Ticknor, II, 126 (diary for 10 January 1838).

13. Musset, *Correspondance*, I (1985), 180 (letter of 15 May 1836).

14. Brombert, 273, 287; Lestringant, 464–5.

15. Marie-Louise Pailleron, *François Buloz et ses amis. La vie littéraire sous Louis-Philippe* (n.d.), 324; Brombert, 239, 244, 255, 257; cf. Ulrike Reuter, 'Entre fascination et sollicitude, une amitié. Christine de Belgiojoso et Heinrich Heine, patriotes et compagnons de la liberté', in Kruse, 157–61.

16. Reuter, 154 (Heine to Belgiojoso, 18 April 1834).

17. Ibid., 157; Lestringant, 431.

18. Jeffrey L. Sammons, *Heinrich Heine* (Princeton, 1979), 204; Kruse, 159, 551; Brombert, 72.

19. Brombert, 91, 93.

20. Ibid., 73, 88, 163, 183.

21. Ibid., 164, 173, 336–7; (Princesse Belgiojoso), *Etude* (2nd ed., 1847), 209; Cracow, Czartoryski Archive MSS 7032 (Princesse Belgiojoso to Princesse Czartoryska, 7 February 1839).

22. Whyte, 115, 166, 179, 281, 107 (to Paul Emile Maurice, 10 March 1835).

23. Ibid., 182–4 (letter of May 1838).

24. Ibid., 279.

25. Ernest Daudet, *Une vie d'ambassadrice au siècle dernier* (1903), 105; Mérimée, *CG*, II, 351 (to Madame de Montijo, 18 June 1840); Chateaubriand, *Mémoires d'outre-tombe*, II, 465.

26. Daudet, *Ambassadrice*, 130, 184.

27. Ibid., 198–200; H. Montgomery Hyde, *Princess Lieven* (1938), 218.

28. Hyde, 223 (letter to Earl Grey, 14 November 1835); E. Jones Parry (ed.), *The Correspondence of Lord Aberdeen and Princess Lieven* (hereafter *Aberdeen/Lieven*) (2 vols, 1938), I, 43–4 (Lieven to Aberdeen, 6 December 1835).

29. *Guizot/Lieven*, I, 119 (Lieven to Guizot, 24 September 1837), II, 198 (Lieven to Guizot, 12 September 1840).

30. Sudley, 191 (to Lady Palmerston, 8 October 1840).

31. *Guizot/Lieven*, I, 6.

32. Gayot, 59, 82 (Guizot to Madame Laure de Gasparin, 6 June, 14 August 1836).

33. Hyde, 230, 234.

34. Girardin 1, 47–8 (15 December 1836); cf. Comte de Hübner, *Une année de ma vie* (1891), 213 (23 February 1854).

35. Balabine, 104–5 (15 March 1843); cf. Castellane, III, 384 (24 March 1847); Mérimée, *CG*, IV, 211 (to Madame de Montijo, 23 November 1844); Comte de Hübner, *Neuf ans de souvenirs d'un ambassadeur d'Autriche à Paris sous le Second Empire* (2 vols, 1904), I, 368 (3 December 1855).

36. Granville, II, 221 (letter to Lady Carlisle, January 1837).

37. Earl of Malmesbury, *Memoirs of an Ex-Minister* (2nd ed., 2 vols, 1884), I, 78–9 (diary for 3 May 1837).

38. Hyde, 239; Harold Temperley, *The Unpublished Diary and Political Sketches of Princess Lieven* (1925), 197; cf. *Guizot/Lieven*, II, 257 (Lieven to Guizot, 13 October 1840 *re: mes ambassadeurs*).

39. Apponyi, III, 283 (2 October 1836).

40. *Guizot/Lieven*, II, 161 (Lieven to Guizot, 2 June 1840).

41. Temperley, 197.

42. Sudley, 184 (to Lady Cowper, 8 March 1840), cf. 180 (letter of 18 January 1840) *re* her 'profound scorn and dislike for French people'.

43. *Aberdeen/Lieven*, I, 44 (to Lord Aberdeen, 6 December 1835); Charles Greville, I, 337 (19 January 1837).

44. Hyde, 251; *Aberdeen/Lieven*, I, 103 (Aberdeen to Lieven, 13 March 1838).

45. Apponyi, III, 228 (8 April 1836); Sudley, 156 (Lieven to Lady Cowper, 1 October 1838); Hübner, I, 215 (23 February 1854); Daudet, *Ambassadrice*, 372; Halévy, 139–40 (Bresson to Thiers, 14 June 1840). A letter to her brother of 16 October 1840, protesting her loyalty to Russia, is in *Guizot/Lieven*, II, 264–6.

46. Sudley, 199, 238 (Lieven to Lady Palmerston, 16 November 1840, 25 October 1842); Princesse de Ligne, *Souvenirs* (1923), 257 (Prince de Ligne to van Praet, n.d.).

47. Daudet, *Ambassadrice*, 234; Sudley, 129 (Lieven to Cowper, 22 May 1836).

48. Dino, II, 120 (20 April 1837); *Molé*, V, 242–9.

49. Mrs Gore, *Paris in 1841*, 72; see e.g. BL MSS 51638 f42vo (A. Bourke to Lady Holland, 21 December 1837): *on dit que cet hiver sera très brillant; il y a une foule énorme d'étrangers.*

50. Louis Desnoyers et al., *Les Etrangers à Paris* (1844), v, xxiv–v.

51. A.-J. Meindre, *Histoire de Paris et de son influence en Europe depuis les temps les plus reculés jusqu'à nos jours* (5 vols, 1854–5), I, 4.

52. Henry Greville, I, 80 (20 December 1836); Apponyi, III, 149 (15 November 1835); Apponyi, IV, 51 (26 December 1844); cf. G. de Bertier de Sauvigny, *La France et les Français vus par les voyageurs américains 1814–1848* (1982), 21, where the number of full-time American residents *c.* 1840 is estimated at 300.

53. *La Rue Saint-Dominique* (Musée Rodin, 1984), 136–45; Castellane, II, 161 (20 February 1877); Yriarte, 175–7.

54. Castellane, II, 58 (26 January 1825), 215 (8 January 1828); cf. Apponyi, III, 186 (18 February 1836); Girardin, I, 143 (30 May 1837); Martin-Fugier, *La Vie élégante*, 113.

55. *Aumale/Cuvillier-Fleury*, I, 126–7 (Cuvillier-Fleury to Aumale, 2 March 1843).

56. Archives du Château de Dauboeuf, Normandy (consulted by kind permission of Alexandre Pradère), unsigned diary, 20 February 1838.

57. *Passages from my Autobiography*, 204 (letter to Lady Clarke, November 1818), cf. 247 (id. to id., 20 December 1818).

58. Cracow, Czartoryski Archives, MSS 7032 (undated letter).

59. Thomas R. Palfrey, *Le Panorama littéraire de l'Europe (1833–1834). Une revue légitimiste sous la monarchie de juillet* (Evanston, 1950), 49; *Marianne et Germania*, 54–5; Robert Marquant, 'Un essai de création d'un Institut allemand à Paris en 1826', *Etudes germaniques*, XII, 1957, 105.

60. *Galignani's Paris Guide* (1822), 589.

61. Jeanblanc, 125–8, 232, 237; Boulenger, 19, 176.

62. Monchoux, 177, 211. Baudry's books were printed by J. Smith, 16, rue Montmorency.

63. Palfrey, *Le Panorama littéraire*, 32 and *passim*.

64. Thomas R. Palfrey, *L'Europe littéraire. Un essai de périodique cosmopolite* (1927), *passim*; Balzac, *Correspondance*, II, 212, 279 (contract of 27 March 1833).

65. *Cent ans de vie française à la Revue des deux mondes* (1929), 12; cf. A. Wilson Server, *L'Espagne dans la Revue des deux mondes 1829–1848* (1939), *passim*.

66. Brombert, 53; Monchoux, 148; Marquis de Custine, *La Russie en 1839, second édition, revue, corrigée et augmentée* (4 vols, 1843), III, 242; Heine, *De la France*, 394 (November 1832). Other

short-lived European reviews were the *Courier de l'Europe* (1830–4), *L'Européen* (1831–2 and 1835–8), and the *Nouvelle Revue encyclopédique* (London, Paris and Rome, 1837–8).

67. Heine, *De l'Allemagne*, 280 (7 July 1830); Eve Sourian, *Madame de Staël et Henri Heine* (1974), 151; Dresch, 55; *Heine à Paris* (1981), 99, 109 (will of 7 March 1843).

68. *Lettres à Madame Hanska*, I, 57 (1 August 1833).

69. Vigny, *Correspondance*, II, 22n; Delacroix, *CG*, I, 354 (March 1833); Balzac, *Correspondance*, III, 71n; Lestringant, 480.

70. *Lettres à Madame Hanska*, I, 448 (22 October 1836), 488 (10 April 1837), 550 (20 October 1837), 625 (15 November 1838); II, 243 (7 July 1843), 578 (15 February 1845); III, 274 (14 July 1846).

71. *Correspondance*, III, 839.

72. Ibid., II, 392 (to Laure Surville, 12 October 1833); *Lettres à Madame Hanska*, I, 99 (26 October 1833).

73. *Correspondance*, II, 35 (to Zulma Carraud, 2 July 1832).

74. *Balzac dans l'empire russe* (Maison de Balzac, 1993), 57, 84–7, 103; *Correspondance*, III, 11n.

75. Smirnov, 213 (Stepan Chevyriov, 'Une visite à Balzac en 1839').

76. *Correspondance*, II, 625 (letter from Marquis de Salvo, 27 January 1835).

77. Ibid., II, 345 (to Zulma Carraud, 27 August 1833); *Lettres à Madame Hanska*, II, 240 (July 1843), 280 (20 November 1843); III, 608 (10 January 1847); IV, 289 (27 March 1848).

78. Etienne de Jouy, *L'Hermite de la Guiane*, II, 101 (9 October 1815).

79. I owe this point to Professor Christopher Thompson, Oxford, lecture at Egyptian Cultural Centre, London, 13 November 1999.

80. *Lettres à Madame Hanska*, I, 74 (13 September 1833); *Correspondance*, III, 676 (to editor of *La Presse*, 17 August 1839), cf. IV, 571 (to Hans Christian Andersen, 25 March 1843); Cairns, II, 264; Lestringant, 25.

81. Odile Nouvel-Kammerer, *Papiers peints romantiques* (1991), 293 and *passim*; Lemoine, 146, 148; Dresch, 78.

82. Ticknor, I, 140 (diary for 16 June 1817).

83. Waresquiel, 381; Swetchine, 59 (Madame Swetchine to Edouard de La Grange, 16 December 1823): *à aucune époque l'Italie n'a vu autant de Français voyageurs.* Other French travel books on Italy include Antoine Laurent Castellan, *Lettres d'Italie* (1819); Jules Janin, *Voyage en Italie* (1839); Alexandre Dumas, *Une année à Florence* (1840).

84. E.g. Louis Dupré, *Voyage à Athènes et à Constantinople* (1825); Baron Renouard de Bussières, *Lettres sur l'Orient* (2 vols, 1829); V. Fontanier, *Voyages en Orient, entrepris par ordre du gouvernement français de l'année 1821 à l'année 1829* (3 vols, 1829); Léon de Laborde, *Voyage de la Syrie* (1837) and *Voyage de l'Asie Mineure* (1838); Maréchal Marmont, *Voyage en Hongrie, en Transylvanie, dans la Russie méridionale, à Constantinople . . . en Syrie, en Palestine, en Egypte* (5 vols, 1839); Comte de Marcellus (the embassy secretary who had seized the Venus de Milo for the Louvre from Miletus in 1820), *Souvenirs de l'Orient* (1839); Edmond de Cadalvène, director of the French post office at Alexandria and Constantinople, *L'Egypte et la Turquie de 1829 à 1836* (1837), and *Deux années de l'histoire de l'Orient* (2 vols, 1839–40); Comte Joseph d'Estourmel, *Journal d'un voyage en Orient* (1844); Xavier Marmier, *Du Rhin au Nil* (2 vols, 1846); Alexis de Valon, *Une année dans le Levant* (1846); Antoine de Latour, *Voyage de S.A.R. Mgr. le duc de Montpensier à Tunis, en Egypte, en Turquie et en Grèce. 1847.*

85. Luppé, *Lamartine*, 151; Lamartine, *CG*, I, 62 (to Molé, 16 September 1830), 100 (to Comte de Sercey, 31 December 1830), 205 (to Comte de Virieu, 8 October 1831).

86. Lamartine, *CG*, I, 290, 301 (to Virieu, 24 July; to Madame de Cessiat, 6 September 1832).

87. Ibid., I, 304 (to Edmond de Cazalès, 6 September 1832), 319 (to Edmond de Cazalès, 12 November 1832), 343 (to Virieu, 5 September 1833).

88. Ubersfeld, 88.

89. Ibid., 136; Jeanblanc, 110–11.

90. Delacroix, *CG*, I, 299, 317 (to Fr Villot, 29 February 1832).

91. L. Finot, *Le Livre du centenaire de la Société Asiatique (1822–1922)* (1922), 6–7; Margaret Lesser, *Clarkey. A Portrait in Letters of Mary Clarke Mohl 1793–1883* (1984), 68, 118; M.C.M. Simpson, *Julius and Mary Mohl* (1887), 13–14.

92. Anouar Louca, *Voyageurs et écrivains égyptiens en France au XIXe siècle* (1970), 39, 45–6.

93. Louca (ed.), *L'Or de Paris*, 119, 122, 158.

94. Susan Gilson Miller, *Disorienting Encounters. Travels of a Moroccan Scholar in France 1845–6* (Berkeley, 1992), 153.

95. Louca, *Voyageurs*, 76, 70.

96. James Etmekjian, *The French Influence on the Western Armenian Renaissance 1843–1915* (New York, 1964), 104–10.

97. P. Mansel, *Constantinople. City of the World's Desire 1453–1924* (1995), 255–6; Marcello Conati, 'Verdi et Paris', in Bloom (ed.), *Music in Paris*, 214.

98. Mansel, *Constantinople*, 255–6.

99. Marie Pascale Marcia Widemann, 'Le Comité Philhellénique et la politique intérieure française 1824–1829', *Revue de la Société d'Histoire de la Restauration et de la Monarchie Constitutionelle*, 1991, V, 27–41.

100. William St Clair, *That Greece might still be free* (1972), 245, 266–7; *Campagne d'un jeune Français en Grèce envoyé par M. le duc de Choiseul* (1827), 205.

101. Nina Athanassoglou-Kallmyer, *French Images from the Greek War of Independence 1821–1830* (Yale, 1989), 107; Eugène Lovinesco, *Les Voyageurs français en Grèce au XIXe siècle* (1909), 60–73n, 82–90. Other books published in Paris on the newly independent country included F.-C.-H.-L. Pouqueville, *Voyage de la Grèce* (2e éd., 6 vols, 1826–7); G.B. Depping, *La Grèce ou Description topographique de la Livadie, de la Morée et de l'Archipel* (6 vols, 1830); B.A. Buchon, *La Grèce continentale et la Morée. Voyage, séjour et études historiques en 1840 et 1841* (1843).

102. Tudesq, I, 217; see e.g. A. de Jouffroy, *Charles X à Holyrood* (1833); Sosthènes de La Rochefoucauld, *Pèlerinage à Gorizia* (1839); Théodore Muret, *Album de l'exil. Résidences de la branche aînée des Bourbons depuis 1830* (1850).

103. Françoise Melonio, *Tocqueville et les Français* (1993), 340; Benoit Yvert, *Politique libérale. Bibliographie sélective du libéralisme politique français* (1994), number 74.

104. Balzac, *Correspondance*, III, 426 (to Custine, August 1838).

105. *La Russie en 1839*, II, 61, IV, 333.

106. Tarn, 433.

107. Ibid., 69, 243–4, 260, 294.

108. Custine, *Lettres inédites*, 76 (Custine to La Grange, 29 October 1818); Luppé, 47 (to La Grange).

109. Custine, *La Russie en 1839*, III, 13.

110. Custine, *Lettres à Varnhagen d'Ense et à Rahel Varnhagen d'Ense*, 51, 317 (to Rahel, 9 September 1816, 21 July 1829); Zamoyski, *Chopin*, 126; Tarn, 253, 442, 445, 447 (letter to Manzoni, April 1842); Muhlstein, 316.

111. Gautier, *Voyage en Espagne* (Gallimard, 1981), 7; id., *Paris et les Parisiens*, 203.

112. Other French books on Spain included *Madrid, ou observations sur les moeurs et usages des*

Espagnols au commencement du XIXe siècle (2 vols, 1825); Alfred de Musset, *Contes d'Espagne et d'Italie* (1830); A. de Bourgoing, *L'Espagne. Souvenirs de 1823 et de 1833* (1834); Antoine Fontaney, *Scènes de la vie castillane et andalouse* (1835); Alexandre Dumas, *De Paris à Cadix* (1841); Théophile Gautier, *Voyage en Espagne* (1843); Edgar Quinet, *Mes vacances en Espagne* (1846).

113. *L'Espagne sous Ferdinand VII* (2 vols, Brussels, 1838), II, 285; Custine, *Lettres à Varnhagen d'Ense*, 361 (4 February 1831).

114. *L'Espagne sous Ferdinand VII*, I, 47, 147, 160, 225, 271.

115. Anka Muhlstein, *Astolphe de Custine* (1996), 244.

116. Apponyi, III, 91 (1 June 1835); Dino, II, 84 (28 August 1836), quoting a letter of Madame Adélaïde to Talleyrand; Antonetti, 764–5; Bury and Tombs, 59.

117. *Louis-Philippe*, 127; Jeannine Baticle et Cristina Marinas, *La Galerie espagnole de Louis-Philippe au Louvre 1838–1848* (1981), 6.

118. Pailleron, 253.

119. Boulenger, 136; Alfred Destrez, *Le Faubourg Saint-Honoré de Louis XIV au Second Empire* (1953), 257; *Rossini à Paris*, 100; Viennet, 263 (2 May 1842). Another Spanish Parisian was Juan Maria Maury Castaneda, born in Malaga in 1773, died in Paris 1845, author of *L'Espagne poétique, choix de poésies castillanes depuis Charles-Quint jusqu'à nos jours* (2 vols, 1826–7).

120. Apponyi, III, 437 (20 November 1840); Rémusat, *Mémoires*, III, 387; Dino, III, 260 (5 May 1843). In addition many Bourbons of Naples visited, or resided in, Paris, including King Ferdinand II, the Prince of Capua and the Count of Syracuse.

121. Douglas Hill, *The Troubled Trinity. Godoy and the Spanish Monarchs* (Tuscaloosa, 1987), 268–79.

122. Jean Sarrailh, *Martinez de la Rosa* (1930), 243n, 284.

123. For a full survey of its defects, and French and European impact, see Michel Cadot, *La Russie dans la vie intellectuelle française (1839–1856)* (1967), 173–278; cf. Luppé, 236.

124. Tarn, 533; Luppé, *Custine*, 235; Custine, *La Russie en 1839*, I, xix, IV, 376.

125. Custine, *La Russie en 1839*, III, 377, II, 309.

126. Luppé, *Custine*, 232.

127. *La Russie en 1839*, III, 272, 374.

128. Ibid., I, 322, II, 330n; cf. Custine, *L'Espagne sous Ferdinand VII*, I, 139.

129. Tarn, 527–9.

130. *La Russie en 1839*, II, 103.

131. Muhlstein, *Custine*, 235–7; Tarn, 480.

132. Cracow, Czartoryski Archives MSS 5452 ff249, 260 (Custine to Czartoryski, 9 May, 11 September 1843).

133. Tarn, 41, 48–9, 509.

134. Custine, *La Russie en 1839*, I, 5, 362–3.

135. Ibid., I, 274, 322.

136. Tarn, 520.

137. Staël, *Oeuvres complètes* (1820), I, 7; Heine, *De l'Allemagne*, 152–5.

138. *Marianne et Germania*, 38, 217–18; Viallaneix, 92; Hugo, *Le Rhin*, I, 22. In 1832, however, Eugène Lerminier, foreseeing the rise of German power, asked: *Comment cette religieuse et méditative Germanie deviendra-t'elle politique et active?: Lettres philosophiques adressées à un Berlinois* (1832), 397 (17 November 1832).

139. In 1831 the *Revue britannique* wrote that Germany did not exist as a nation: Monchoux, 333.

Notes

140. Heine, *De l'Allemagne*, 153–4; Monchoux, 392.
141. Guichen, 417 (Bresson to Sébastiani, 9 November 1831); cf. for contemporary awareness of this French retreat, Apponyi, II, 422 (2 May 1834); Hübner, *Neuf ans*, I, 14 (19 February 1851); Anna Owinska, *La Politique de la France envers l'Allemagne à l'époque de la monarchie de juillet 1830–1848* (Wroclaw, 1974), 47, citing a mémoire of the Baron de Bourgoing (3 December 1840).
142. La Maisonfort, 242; Ludwig Boerne, *Fragments politiques et littéraires* (1842), 211.
143. Fergusson, 224, 236, 239, 247, 259, 273, 284, 414.
144. Ibid., 251, 259, 266.
145. Ibid., 346–9; Prévost-Marcilhacy, 36.
146. Fergusson, 360, 362.
147. Antonetti, 480 (letter to Comte de Broval).
148. Viennet, 154, 183 (27 December 1834, 24 February 1836).
149. Alan Sked, *The Decline and Fall of the Habsburg Empire 1815–1918* (1989), 23 (Robert Gordon to Aberdeen, 13 December 1842); Heine, *Lutèce*, 175 (13 February 1841); Ledré, 176; Guyot, 293–5.
150. Sked, *Decline and Fall*, 107.
151. Guyot, 115 (Granville to Palmerston, 30 September 1833).
152. BL Add. MSS 51524 ff157, 160–1 (to Lord Holland, 9 March 1831, 28 May–6 July 1837).
153. Paddy Griffith, *Military Thought in the French Army 1815–1851* (Manchester, 1989), 41; Hugo, *Choses vues 1830–46*, 293 (August 1844).
154. Got, I, 145 (11 November 1843); cf. Griffith, 41.
155. Orléans, *Souvenirs*, 65, 69, 325.
156. Ibid., 19, 22 (Orléans to Queen Louise, 14 January 1842).
157. Id., *Lettres*, 265, 312 (to General Schneider, 27 December 1839; will of 9 April 1840).
158. Ibid., 30 (to Madame Adélaïde, 19 June 1831), 33, 36 (to General Marbot, 24 June 1831); Rémusat, *Mémoires*, III, 462.
159. De Vigny, *Servitude et grandeur militaires* (Nelson ed. n.d.), 19.
160. *Mémoires d'outre-tombe*, III, 471, 602, 612, 641.
161. Rossi, 468; Comtesse R. Rzewuska, *Mémoires* (3 vols, Rome, 1939–50), II, 259.
162. Zamoyski, *Holy Madness*, 309.
163. Granville, II, 234 (to Duke of Devonshire, 12 June 1837); Girardin 1, 45 (15 December 1836).
164. Heine, *De l'Allemagne*, 446–7; Kathleen Jones, 159.
165. *Lettres à Madame Récamier*, 505 (letter of 25 November 1843); cf. for similar complaints of mutual ignorance, Mérimée, *CG* (2e série), II, 518 (to Edward Ellice, 9 May 1858).
166. Jules Michelet, *Cours au Collège de France* (2 vols, 1995), II, 170, 173.
167. Gérard de Puymège, *Chauvin le soldat laboureur. Contribution à l'étude des nationalismes* (1993), 15, 34, 39, 43 (1845).
168. *Aberdeen/Lieven*, I, 128 (Lieven to Aberdeen, 28 May 1839).
169. *Lutèce*, 79, 179 (3 June 1840, 31 March 1841), cf. 152 (12 November 1840).
170. Schroeder, 729, 736, 738.
171. Guyot, 160, 168.
172. Jean-Marie Carré, *Voyageurs et écrivains français en Egypte* (2nd ed., 2 vols, Cairo, 1956), II, 37.
173. Antonetti, 768–9; Girardin 1, 23 (27 October 1836).
174. Antonetti, 811.

175. *Lutèce*, 129, 175 (7 October 1840, 13 February 1841).

176. Daudet, *Ambassadrice*, 288.

177. André Karamzine, 'Le Paris d'il y a cent ans', *Revue hebdomadaire*, July 1937, 537 (André to Madame Karamzine, 15 January 1848).

178. François Charles-Roux, *Thiers et Mehemet Ali* (1951), 33; Bury and Tombs, 65.

179. Charles-Roux, 226 (Thiers to Walewski, 8 October 1840).

180. Afaf Lutfi al-Sayyid Marsot, *Egypt in the Reign of Muhammad Ali* (Cambridge, 1984), 243.

181. Guyot, 203.

182. Antonetti, 822.

183. Schroeder, 740–7.

184. Dino, II, 347 (10 August 1840).

185. Girardin 1, 720 (31 July 1840); Apponyi, III, 411 (31 July 1840); Collingham, 229.

186. Guyot, 195.

187. Bury and Tombs, 70.

188. Rémusat, *Mémoires*, III, 464; Guyot, 202.

189. T. Raikes, *Journal*, IV, 42 (11 August 1840).

190. Antonetti, 823; Pasquier, *La Révolution de 1848*, 46; Heine, *Lutèce*, 100 (27 July 1840); Delmas, II, 475–6; Rémusat, *Mémoires*, III, 467.

191. Françoise de Bernardy, *Alexandre Walewski le fils polonais de Napoléon* (1976), 40; Charles-Roux, 178, 180 (Thiers to Walewski, 7 September 1840).

192. Rémusat, *Mémoires*, III, 462; *Le Siècle*, 30 August 1840.

193. Henry Lytton Bulwer, *The Monarchy of the Middle Classes* (2 vols, 1836), II, 103, 307.

194. Heydon MSS BUL 1/19/6 (Hortense Allart to Bulwer, January 1841; Madame de Castellane to Bulwer, June 1842).

195. Sudley, 173 (to Lady Cowper, 29 September 1839); Lady Granville also found him 'extremely agreeable and efficient': Granville, II, 293 (to Lady Carlisle, 23 July 1839).

196. Guyot, 159.

197. Ibid., 310 (Bulwer to Aberdeen, 10 September 1841).

198. Jane Preston, 'That Odd Rich Old Woman', unpublished typescript, 172, 185, 214; Mérimée, *CG*, III, 444 (to Madame de Montijo, 20 October 1843).

199. PRO FO 27/604 (Bulwer to Palmerston, 27 July 1840, 'most confidential'); Guyot, 197.

200. Antonetti, 823.

201. Guyot, 201.

202. Ibid., 202 (Thiers to Leopold I, 14 September 1840).

203. PRO FO 27/605 (Bulwer to Palmerston, 14 September 1840); Guyot, 202–3.

204. PRO FO 27/605 (Bulwer to Palmerston, 28 August 1840); Bury and Tombs, 72.

205. Lloyd S. Kramer, *Threshold of a New World. Intellectuals and the Exile Experience in Paris 1830–1848* (Ithaca, NY, 1988), 25.

206. NLS MSS 6242 f345 (report to Lord Stuart de Rothesay, morning 28 July 1830).

207. Rambuteau, 286.

208. Kruse, 441; Hugo, *Le Rhin*, II, 228, 292, 294, 297, 309, 338–9.

209. Orléans, *Lettres*, 33 (to Marbot, 24 June 1831); Halévy, 109 (Mérode to Thiers, 16 January 1839).

210. Viallaneix, 247; Owinska, 45, citing a mémoire of the Baron de Bourgoing (3 December 1840).

211. *Lutèce*, 6, 120 (21 September 1840).

212. Kruse, 442; *Marianne et Germania*, 225–6; Sheehan, 622.

213. Musset, *Confession d'un enfant du siècle*, 107; *Marianne et Germania*, 225–6.

214. Monchoux, 85–9; Ledré, 174.

215. Bury and Tombs, 72–3.

216. Harriet Raikes (ed.), 163 (letter of 11 October 1840); Heine, *Lutèce*, 126, 131 (3, 7 October 1840); cf. *The Letters of Charles Greville and Henry Reeve 1836–1865* (1924), 16 (Reeve to Greville, 8 October 1840).

217. Guichen, 396.

218. Dino, II, 365 (4 September 1840); Harriet Raikes (ed.), 165 (letters of 13 October 1840).

219. Collingham, 235; Harriet Raikes (ed.), 167 (to Wellington, 17 October 1840).

220. *Guizot/Lieven*, II, 235 (to Guizot, 29 September 1840); Hyde, 248.

221. Barante, VI, 10 (Duchesse de Broglie to Barante, 2 May 1837); René de Chambrun (ed.), *Les 5 Cercueils de l'Empereur. Souvenirs inédits de Philippe de Rohan-Chabot* (1985), 144 (letter of Madame de Rohan-Chabot, 16 December 1840).

222. Fergusson, 328–9, 367, 372–3; Heine, *Lutèce*, 332 (5 March 1843).

223. Heine, *Lutèce*, 183, 332 (31 March 1841, 5 March 1843).

224. Fergusson, 233, 421–2; Collingham, 231; Tudesq, I, 495.

225. Fergusson, 423–4; Collingham, 234.

226. Tudesq, I, 503, 519.

227. Bury and Tombs, 74–5; Guyot, 213.

228. Rémusat, *Mémoires*, III, 484; Charles-Roux, 263–4; *Revue rétrospective ou Archives secrètes du dernier gouvernement* (1848), 516 (journal sent to Prince de Joinville).

229. Harriet Raikes (ed.), 182 (to Wellington, 5 November 1840).

230. M.S. Anderson, *The Eastern Question 1774–1923* (1983 ed.), 104.

231. Bury and Tombs, 77.

232. Citron, II, 219; Balabine, 117 (19 May 1843); Karamzine, 540 (Karamzine to Madame Karamzine, 30 January 1848).

233. Gautier, *Paris*, 204–7; Mérimée, *CG*, IV, 420 (to Madame de Montijo, 31 January 1846).

234. Girardin 1, 72 (11 January 1837).

235. Ibid., 89 (26 January 1837), 778; Boulenger, 117–20; Fauré, 76–9, 90–1; Gasnault, 162.

236. Daumard, 177; Gasnault, 83.

237. Gasnault, 95–103; Raikes, *Journal*, II, 323 (13 February 1836).

238. Eugène Briffault, 'Le Palais-Royal', in Lurine (ed.), I, 203–4; Boulenger, 1–4, 12; Balzac, *Lettres à Madame Hanska*, I, 534 (1 September 1837).

239. Jean-Paul Aron, *Le Mangeur du XIXe siècle* (1973), 59; Paul Ariste, *La Vie et le monde du boulevard 1830–1870* (1930), 32–3; *An Englishman in Paris*, I, 42.

240. Boulenger, 37.

241. Balzac, *A Paris!* (1993 ed.), 39; Balzac, *Lettres à Madame Hanska*, II, 9 (15 March 1841). Even Princess Lieven was amused: *Guizot/Lieven*, II, 235 (Lieven to Guizot, 29 September 1840).

242. F. Hebbel, *Journal* (1943), 165 (Hebbel to Elise, 19 September 1843).

243. *Les Français peints par eux–mêmes*, III, 67.

244. Decin State Archives, Czech Republic, Prince Clary, unpublished journal (25 April 1822): *On ne fait pas de pas à Paris sans rencontrer des gens qu'on croit aux Antipodes*.

245. Franz Liszt, *Selected Letters* (Oxford, 1998), 149 (to Princess Belgiojoso, 20 October 1840).

246. *Hittorff*, 153–62, 355.

247. Balzac, *Lettres à Madame Hanska*, III, 365 (23 September 1846).

248. Reclus, 128.

249. Morgan, *France in 1829–30*, II, 280–2.

250. Balzac, *Lettres à Madame Hanska*, I, 578 (22 January 1838).

251. Girardin 1, 659–60 (17 April 1840), II, 151 (6 March 1841).

252. David van Zanten, *Building Paris. Architectural Institutions and the Transformation of the French Capital 1830–1870* (Cambridge, 1994), 92, 97.

253. J. Kneppelhout, *Souvenirs d'un voyage à Paris* (Leyden, 1839), I, 127–9; cf. for similar reactions, Decin State Archives, Czech Republic, Prince Clary, unpublished diary (2 May 1822): *j'interromps ma lettre pour sortir et me donner la fête des rues de Paris et c'est une fête véritable que de les parcourir*; Apponyi, IV, 66 (3 February 1845).

254. Mrs Gore, *Paris in 1841*, 8; cf. Fontaine, II, 926 (31 March 1832).

255. Apponyi, III, 453, 460 (4 January, 6 February 1841).

12 Funerals *1840–1844*

1. Hugo, *Choses vues 1830–46*, 183–5 (15 December 1840).

2. Heine, *Lutèce*, 159 (11 January 1841).

3. Marc Gaillard, *L'Arc de Triomphe* (1998), 24, 66 and *passim*; *Moniteur*, 16 December 1840, 2445.

4. Hugo, *Choses vues 1830–46*, 180, 190, 196 (15 December 1840); Apponyi, III, 448–9 (26 December 1840).

5. Chambrun, 143–4 (letter of Olivia de Rohan-Chabot, 16 December 1840).

6. Gaillard, 106.

7. Lucas-Dubreton, *Culte de Napoléon*, 377 and n.

8. Chambrun, 143–4 (letter of Olivia de Rohan-Chabot, 16 December 1840).

9. *Moniteur*, 11 December 1840, 2422.

10. Hugo, *Choses vues 1830–46*, 179 (15 December 1840).

11. Tarn, 164–5; Custine, *Lettres à Varnhagen d'Ense*, 393–5 (letter of 17 December 1840).

12. Comtesse d'Armaillé, 49; Dino, II, 437 (19 December 1840).

13. Harriet Raikes (ed.), 204 (to Wellington, 16 December 1840); Apponyi, III, 446 (26 December 1840).

14. Collingham, 318–19; Apponyi, III, 447 (26 December 1840); Nesselrode, VIII, 89 (Cômtesse to Comte Charles de Nesselrode, 17 December 1840).

15. Maurice Descôtes, *La Légende de Napoléon et les écrivains français au XIXe siècle* (1967), 201.

16. Hugo, *Choses vues 1830–1846*, 180, 181, 184 (15 December 1846).

17. Citron, II, 315.

18. Marie Amélie, 496.

19. Lucas-Dubreton, *Culte de Napoléon*, 355.

20. Daumard, 634.

21. E.g. Girardin I, 750 (20 December 1840).

22. Adrien Dansette, *Louis-Napoléon à la conquête du pouvoir* (1961), 72, 81.

23. Pinkney, *The French Revolution of 1830*, 50; Odile Krakovich, *Les Pièces de théâtre soumises à la Censure (1800–1830)* (1982), 32; Lucas-Dubreton, *Culte de Napoléon*, 288–90.

24. Edgar Newman, 'What the crowd wanted in the French revolution of 1830', in John M. Merriman, *1830 in France* (New York, 1975), 28–9.

25. Talleyrand, IV, 169 (Dalberg to Talleyrand, 3 May 1831).
26. Heine, *De la France*, 99 (25 March 1832).
27. *Mémoires d'outre-tombe*, II, 269, 359–60.
28. Ibid., II, 388; cf. Descôtes, 107.
29. Dino, III, 435 (17 December 1840).
30. Apponyi, III, 445 (26 December 1840).
31. Hyde, 245; *Guizot/Lieven*, II, 153 (to Guizot, 27 May 1840).
32. Vicomte E. de Grenville, *Histoire du journal La Mode* (1861), 541 (article of 15 December 1840).
33. Nesselrode, VIII, 82 (Comtesse to Comte Charles de Nesselrode, 7 December 1840).
34. Girardin 1, 747 (5 December 1840), II, 124 (24 January 1841).
35. Lamartine, *CG*, II, 23, 153 (to Virieu, 17 February 1834, 1 October 1835).
36. *Lamartine. Le poète et l'homme d'état* (Bibliothèque Nationale, 1969), 163.
37. Antonetti, 816; Alton-Shée, II, 46–52.
38. Pailleron, 76–7.
39. Viennet, 251–2 (16 December 1840).
40. Dino, I, 331 (19 August 1835).
41. Dansette, 87, 106.
42. Bernardy, *Charles de Flahaut*, 189, 191; cf. 'Madame de Sousa's death has had very little effect on M. de Flahault and none at all on Marguerite': Sudley, 123 (Princess Lieven to Lady Cowper, 25 April 1836).
43. Rémusat, *Mémoires*, III, 403–8; Viennet, 251 (29 September 1840); Apponyi, III, 424 (13 October 1840).
44. Apponyi, III, 309, 311 (12, 26 February 1838). Similarly the *airs de supériorité* of his son Morny would contribute to his dismissal as Minister of the Interior fourteen years later: M. de Maupas, *Mémoires sur le Second Empire* (2 vols, 1884), I, 560.
45. AN 565 AP FL 354, 355, 357 (letters of 8, 11 August 1840).
46. Antonetti, 818–19.
47. Ibid., 817; Dansette, 165.
48. Dansette, 178, 199; Louis-Napoléon Bonaparte, *Oeuvres* (3 vols, 1848), I, 319–21.
49. *Aberdeen/Lieven*, I, 45 (Lieven to Aberdeen, 25 January 1836); Ordioni, 260–1.
50. Révérend, V, 425–6; Ordioni, 258; Granville, II, 116 (Lady Granville to Duke of Devonshire, November 1831).
51. Daudet, *Ambassadrice*, 263–4 (letter of 12 July 1839); cf. Apponyi, III, 384, 415 (16 June, 4 July 1839, 28 August 1840).
52. Sudley, 224 (to Lady Palmerston, 21 February 1842).
53. Castellane, IV, 420 (25 December 1852); *Rue de l'Université*, 94.
54. Heine, *Lutèce*, 22 (25 February 1840).
55. Orléans, *Lettres*, 183 (to Queen Louise, 2 March 1837).
56. Boigne, II, 420.
57. Hugo, *Choses vues 1830–1846*, 237 (July 1842); Boigne, II, 397–9.
58. Hugo, *Choses vues 1830–1846*, 280 (26 February 1844); Apponyi, III, 477 (26 July 1842).
59. Hervé Robert, 'Les funérailles du duc d'Orléans. Une "fête royale" sous la monarchie de juillet', *Revue historique*, 602, April–June 1997, 458.
60. Griffith, 74; Robert, 'Les funérailles', 462–3, 469, 471.
61. Robert, 'Les funérailles', 473.

62. Heine, *Lutèce*, 266 (19 July 1842); Balabine, 24, 31 (25 July, 18 August 1842).

63. Robert, 'Les funérailles', 479–80 (letter of 30 July 1842).

64. Ibid., 483–5; cf. for public reaction, Tudesq, II, 672, 685.

65. Hugo, *Choses vues 1830–1846*, 240 (21 July 1842).

66. Heine, *Lutèce*, 275 (29 July 1842).

67. Viennet, 267 (15 July 1842).

68. Viallaneix, 296; *Lamartine. L'homme et le poète*, 171; *Revue des deux mondes*, 15 December 1948, 580 (Aumale to Queen Louise, 26 September 1847); cf. Joinville, 199.

69. Paul Benichou, *Le Temps des prophètes. Doctrines de l'âge romantique* (1977), 450.

70. Zamoyski, *Holy Madness*, 310–11.

71. Ibid., 285–6.

72. *Le Diable à Paris*, I, 261: *de mémoire d'auditeur ces cours n'ont jamais compté plus de quatre auditeurs*; Alexander Herzen, *My Past and Thoughts* (4 vols, 1960), II, 666; Jean Borrily, 'Mickiewicz and France', in Waclaw Lednicki (ed.), *Adam Mickiewicz in World Literature* (Berkeley, 1956), 259–60; Zofia Mitosek, *Adam Mickiewicz aux yeux des Français* (Warsaw, 1992), 189, 195; cf. Balabine, 77 (31 December 1842).

73. Mitosek, 97.

74. Wiktor Weintraub, 'Mickiewicz: a Biographical Sketch', in Lednicki, 598–9.

75. Mitrowski, 222, 231, 245, 254, 300n; cf. Mérimée, *CG*, IV, 67–8 and note (to Madame de Montijo, 23 March 1844).

13   The People *1844–1852*

1. *La Confession d'un enfant du siècle*, 107.

2. *Correspondence parisienne*, 407 (21 December 1844).

3. *Journal des débats*, 27 November 1828, 1.

4. Chevalier, 129, quoting *Un hiver à Paris* (1845).

5. Vigier, 82.

6. Chevalier, 129, 235, 597n, 603.

7. Collingham, 66.

8. Chevalier, 38, 41, 157.

9. Charles Simond, *Paris de 1800 à 1900* (3 vols, 1900–1), I, 564–6.

10. See e.g. Orléans, *Lettres*, 149 (letter to Queen Louise, 29 May 1835): *la classe que la révolution a élevée au pouvoir fait comme les castes qui triomphent: elle s'isole en s'épurant et s'amollit par le succès.*

11. Mansel, *Louis XVIII*, 115.

12. Isaiah Berlin, *Karl Marx. His Life and Environment* (Fontana, 1995), 66–9.

13. Rosanvallon, 179; Antonetti, 893; Collingham, 71.

14. Chateaubriand, *Mémoires d'outre-tombe*, III, 217.

15. Heine, *Lutèce*, 183 (31 March 1841).

16. Rossi, 76.

17. Martin-Fugier, *Les Romantiques*, 200–2.

18. David H. Pinkney, *Decisive Years in France 1840–1847* (1986), 31.

19. Ibid., 16.

20. *Journal*, 116 (2 May 1834).

21. Inès Murat, *La IIe République*, 30. (References to Murat hereafter are to this work unless otherwise stated.)

22. *Louis-Philippe*, 119.

23. Cf. Mérimée, *CG*, IV, 429 (letter of 14 March 1846); *l'on ne pense qu'à gagner sur les actions des chemins de fer.*

24. Fergusson, 451.

25. Sir Edward Blount, *Memoirs* (1902), 46, 58, 61, 69, 83.

26. Normanby Papers, Mulgrave Castle, Whitby, Yorkshire (hereafter referred to as NP) P (Normanby to Palmerston, 29 February 1848).

27. Fergusson, 455; Mérimée, *CG*, IV, 464 (letter to Madame de Montijo, 13 June 1846).

28. François Loyer (ed.), *Autour de l'Opéra. Naissance de la ville moderne* (1995), 53.

29. Daumard, 416, 437, 444.

30. Edgar L. Newman, *Historical Dictionary of France from the 1815 Restoration to the Second Empire* (2 vols, 1987), II, 771. (References to Newman hereafter are to this work unless otherwise stated.)

31. Ibid., II, 772.

32. Newman, II, 770; Daumard, 66, 217, 317; Vigier, 267.

33. Daumard, 11.

34. Chevalier, 587–8n.

35. Daumard, 8–9.

36. Bulwer, *The Monarchy of the Middle Classes*, II, 113.

37. Chevalier, 440.

38. Archives Rohan-Chabot, Chabrol memoirs, ff26v, 35–7; Chevalier, 588.

39. Vigier, 228, 305.

40. Chevalier, 436–7, 442; Benichou, 411.

41. Murat, 48.

42. *Louis-Philippe*, 94; Jean-Pierre Aguet, *Les Grèves sous la monarchie de juillet (1830–1848)* (Geneva, 1954), 4, 19–22, 365, 374, 384, 390.

43. PRO FO 27/605 (despatches of Bulwer to Palmerston, 4, 5, 7 September 1840).

44. Comte d'Haussonville, *Femmes d'autrefois, hommes d'aujourd'hui* (1912), 204 (letter of 1 September 1815).

45. Fauré, 57.

46. Collingham, 135–6.

47. Luppé, *Lamartine*, 273.

48. Chevalier, 221, 244, 254.

49. Berlin, 71; Collingham, 367.

50. Pinkney, 90–7; Collingham, 374–6; Murat, 53, 64.

51. Custine, *Lettres à Varnhagen d'Ense*, 430 (letter of 1 December 1841).

52. Chevalier, 236.

53. Barry, 267; Cairns, II, 305; Bory, 225, 243, 246, 256–7, 272; Chevalier, 666–9.

54. Rosanvallon, 268.

55. David McLellan, *Karl Marx. His Life and Thought* (1973), 79.

56. Arnold Ruge, *Zwei Jahre in Paris* (2 vols, Leipzig, 1846), I, 4; McLellan, 77; Zamoyski, *Holy Madness*, 314; Sheehan, 583.

57. Kramer, 26.

58. Herzen, II, 673; Kramer, 51.

59. For German accounts of Paris, see e.g. G.B. Depping, *Erinnerungen aus dem Leben eines Deutschen in Paris* (Leipzig, 1832); August Lewald, *Album aus Paris* (2 vols, Hamburg, 1832); Victor Lang, *Paris wie es ist, oder gemälde dieser hauptstadt und ihrer nächstenumgebung* (Paris, 1835); Adalbert von Bornstedt, *Pariser Silhouetten* (2 vols, Leipzig, 1836); Eduard Kolloff, *Schilderungern*

Notes

aus Paris (2 vols, Hamburg, 1839); Paul Guger, *Wegweiser für Deutsche in Paris oder ausführliches gemälde diesere hauptstadt und ihrer umgebung* (Stuttgart, 1841); Carl Ferdinand Gutzkow, *Briefe aus Paris* (1842); Ida Kohl, *Paris und die Französen* (3 vols, Dresden and Leipzig, 1843).

60. Jeanblanc, 11.

61. Pinkney, 99; Desnoyers, 166.

62. Pinkney, 100–1; McClellan, 86–7.

63. McLellan, 97, 103–4, Heine, *Lutèce*, 258 (20 June 1842).

64. William H. Sewell Jr, *Work and Revolution in France. The Language of Labor from the Old Regime to 1848* (Cambridge, 1980), 145.

65. *Le Palais-Royal*, 204; McLellan, 131.

66. Jean Salem (ed.), *Manuscrits de 1844* (Flammarion, 1996 ed.), 149, 185, 187.

67. Berlin, 85.

68. McLellan, 135–6.

69. A. Toussenel, *Les Juifs rois de l'époque. Histoire de la féodalité financière* (2 vols, 1847).

70. Rémusat, *Mémoires*, III, 449 (speech of Tocqueville, 2 July 1839); cf. Heine, *Lutèce*, 156 (article of 6 January 1841).

71. Harriet Raikes (ed.), 225 (6 January 1841); Berlioz, *Memoirs*, 358.

72. Collingham, 323; Schroeder, 770–1; Guyot, 272, 291.

73. Antonetti, 878.

74. Ibid., 877.

75. Apponyi, IV, 100 (9 September 1846); Hugo, *Choses vues 1847–48* (1972), 43 (January 1847).

76. Balabine, 279 (21 February 1847); cf. Barante, VII, 201 (letter of 21 February 1847).

77. Roger Bullen, *Palmerston, Guizot and the Collapse of the Entente Cordiale* (1974), 192–3; Apponyi, IV, 105 (8 February 1847); NP PP 206 (undated letter of Thiers).

78. Guyot, 301.

79. Fergusson, 468; Antonetti, 873; Collingham, 361.

80. Daumard, 428; Hugo, *Choses vues 1847–48*, 152 (12 August 1847).

81. Antonetti, 898–9; Collingham, 389.

82. Antonetti, 892.

83. *Correspondance parisienne*, 513 (11 July 1847).

84. Balabine, 309 (13 July 1847); Hugo, *Choses vues 1847–48*, 101–6 (7 July 1847); Castellane, III, 397 (7 July 1847); Gautier, *Paris et les Parisiens*, 328–31.

85. Hugo, *Choses vues 1847–48*, 154–61 (21–7 August 1847); Mérimée, *CG*, V, 145 (to Madame de Montijo, 19 August 1847).

86. Antonetti, 886–7, 890; Collingham, 390–5; Murat, 38.

87. Ledré, 193.

88. Barante, VII, 225 (letter of 28 August 1847); NP P (Normanby to Palmerston, 23 July 1847).

89. Girardin I, 724 (31 July 1840).

90. Antonetti, 830, 887; Castellane, III, 388 (23 March 1847); Sainte-Beuve, *Mes poisons*, 83, 90.

91. Vigier, 553.

92. Murat, 48–9; Mérimée, *CG*, V, 403n; Viallaneix, 295.

93. *Guizot/Lieven*, III, 243 (Guizot to Lieven, 5 August 1846).

94. Gronow, I, 246; cf. Heine, *Lutèce*, 232 (24 January 1842).

95. Apponyi, IV, 20.

96. Nesselrode, VIII, 346 (letter of Countess Nesselrode, 20 September 1846).

97. Collingham, 97; Antonetti, 904; Auguste Nougarède, *La Vérité sur la révolution de février 1848* (1850), 160.

98. Gayot, 231 (Guizot to Madame Laure de Gasparin, 14 November 1842); *Moniteur*, 22 December 1847, 2989; Pasquier, *Souvenirs de 1848*, 51–2, 160; Fontaine, II, 992 (24 December 1841).

99. NP N (Normanby to Palmerston, 7 February, 16 July 1847, 17 February 1848); cf. Boigne, II, 443 *re* Louis-Philippe's *tristes symptômes d'affaiblissement moral* in 1847.

100. Bullen, 325.

101. Antonetti, 905; Viennet, 291; cf. Rambuteau, 288, 297.

102. Antonetti, 902, 910–11 (Joinville to Nemours, 7 November 1847; to Aumale, 24 January 1848).

103. Collingham, 403; Gronow, I, 245; Pasquier, *Souvenirs de 1848*, 160; Hugo, *Choses vues 1847–48*, 195–6 (31 December 1847).

104. Tocqueville, 734.

105. Harold Acton, *The Last Bourbons of Naples* (1961), 206.

106. Apponyi, IV, 134 (18 February 1848).

107. Karamzine, 542 (André Karamzine to Madame Karamzine, 12 February 1848); cf. Barante, VII, 279 (Barante to Ernest de Barante, 20 February 1848).

108. Antonetti, 912; Collingham, 405–6; Ledré, 202.

109. NLS MSS 9269 f29 ('journal of my life' by John Dunlop, 25 October 1845); cf. Guyot, 314 (Bulwer to Aberdeen, 10 September 1841): Louis-Philippe 'relies and leans upon the Army, not merely as a means of government, sanctioned by temporary expediency, but as a permanent system of civil policy'.

110. Murat, 76; Collingham, 300; Merriman, 198.

111. Antonetti, 914–15.

112. Ligne, 126; Karamzine, 547 (letter of 23 February 1848).

113. Apponyi, IV, 136 (22 February 1848); Vigier, 553; Antonetti, 915.

114. NP P (Normanby to Palmerston, 22 February 1848).

115. Pasquier, *Souvenirs de 1848*, 207; Ligne, 128.

116. Apponyi, IV, 136–7 (23 February 1848).

117. Karamzine, 548 (letter of 23 February 1848).

118. Apponyi, IV, 136 (22 February 1848); Viennet, 293 (26 February 1848); cf. Chevalier, 209, 217n.

119. *Louis-Philippe*, 143.

120. Antonetti, 808.

121. Rémusat, *Mémoires*, III, 394, 401.

122. Ledré, 172; Antonetti, 915–16; cf. Mérimée, *CG*, VI, 256 (to Madame de Montijo, 8 March 1848).

123. Antonetti, 917; Balzac, *Lettres à Madame Hanska*, II, 716 (letter of 23 February 1848, 11 p.m.); NP PP 155 (Molé to Normanby, *mercredi 8h du soir*); Nougarède, 169.

124. Balzac, *Lettres à Madame Hanska*, II, 713 (letter of 23 February 1848).

125. Maurice Agulhon, *Les Quarante-Huitards* (1992 ed.), 39, 41.

126. Ibid., 43; *Louis-Philippe*, 145 (depositions of Sergeant Giacomoni, 8 March 1848; of Pierre Unieau, 15 March 1848); Viennet, 295 (26 February 1848); Antonetti, 918.

127. Ledré, 205; *Mémoires d'outre-tombe*, III, 202.

128. Hugo, *Choses vues 1846–48*, 275 (24 February 1848).

Notes

129. Nougarède, 158.

130. Alton-Shée, *Souvenirs*, 263; Pasquier, *Souvenirs de 1848*, 222, 225.

131. Nougarède, 214.

132. Antonetti, 918–19.

133. Murat, 86; Pasquier, *Souvenirs de 1848*, 228; Tocqueville, 748; Normanby, *A Year of Revolution* (2 vols, 1857), I, 92 (diary for 24 February 1848).

134. Tocqueville, 746.

135. Hugo, *Choses vues 1847–48*, 279 (24 February 1848); Murat, 87.

136. Pasquier, *Souvenirs de 1848*, 223; *Louis-Philippe*, 146.

137. Tocqueville, 748; Murat, 87.

138. Montalivet, II, 159.

139. Antonetti, 920–1; Montalivet, II, 160.

140. Nougarède, 217.

141. Antonetti, 921–2; *Louis-Philippe*, 146; Viennet, 296 (6 March 1848).

142. Reclus, 158.

143. *Louis-Philippe*, 146.

144. Antonetti, 922; Montalivet, II, 167, 170.

145. Montalivet, II, 171–2; Antonetti, 923–7.

146. Alton-Shée, *Souvenirs*, 284; Castellane, V, 47 (7 March 1848).

147. Antonetti, 923–7; Pasquier, *Souvenirs de 1848*, 249.

148. Boigne, II, 444, 476.

149. Normanby, I, 164n; NP P (Normanby to Palmerston, 29 February 1848).

150. Hugo, *Choses vues 1847–48*, 301 (March 1848); Mérimée, *CG*, V, 254 (to Madame de Montijo, 3 March 1848); cf. for similar views Comte Horace de Vielcastel, *Mémoires . . . sur le règne de Napoléon III* (6 vols, 1883–4), I, 114 (5 November 1850); Pasquier, *Souvenirs de 1848*, 249.

151. Balzac, *Lettres à Madame Hanska*, II, 729 (letter of 3 March 1848).

152. *Louis-Philippe*, 151–2.

153. Tocqueville, 748.

154. Pasquier, *Souvenirs de 1848*, 253; Alton-Shée, *Souvenirs*, 289; Tocqueville, 753–4; Apponyi, IV, 149, 207 (1 December 1848).

155. Hugo, *Choses vues 1847–48*, 52, 284 (14 February 1847, 1848).

156. Pasquier, *Souvenirs de 1848*, 259; Murat, 91–2.

157. Hugo, *Choses vues 1847–48*, 286 (24 February 1848); Luppé, *Lamartine*, 349; Tocqueville, 751.

158. Pasquier, *Souvenirs de 1848*, 237.

159. Viennet, 299 (6 March 1848); Apponyi, IV, 140 (24 February 1848).

160. Ligne, 135, 137.

161. Hugo, *Choses vues 1847–48*, 280 (24 February 1848); Tocqueville, 759–60.

162. Henry Greville, I, 234 (diary for 3 March 1848); Hyde, 255.

163. Bury and Tombs, 100–1; Douglas Johnson, 261; Fergusson, 477; NP P (Normanby to Palmerston, 28 February 1848).

164. Cairns, II, 379, 383, 390.

165. Apponyi, IV, 207 (1 December 1848); Pasquier, *Souvenirs de 1848*, 162.

166. *Le Palais Royal*, 238.

167. Fauré, 116–18; Teresa Ransom, *Fanny Trollope. A Remarkable Life* (1995), 177.

168. Agulhon, *Les Quarante-Huitards*, 44–5; Fauré, 118–19.

169. *Lettres à Madame Hanska*, IV, 211 (26 February 1848).

170. Ibid., IV, 220, 260 (1 March, March 1848); *Correspondance*, V, 479 (to Eugène Surville, 9 February 1849).

171. Normanby, I, 208-9.

172. Ibid., I, 206; Castellane, IV, 49 (9 March 1848).

173. Agulhon, *Les Quarante-Huitards*, 48-50.

174. NP P (Normanby to Palmerston, 28 February 1848).

175. Luppé, *Lamartine*, 354.

176. Lawrence C. Jennings, *France and Europe in 1848* (Oxford, 1973), 12-13.

177. Ledré, 212, 214.

178. Louis Girard, *Nouvelle Histoire de Paris. La Deuxième République et le Second Empire 1848-1870* (1981), 16-17; Apponyi, IV, 153 (27 February 1848); Murat, 113-14.

179. Tocqueville, 767.

180. Apponyi, IV, 158 (1 March 1848); Murat, 207.

181. Chevalier, 131-2n.

182. Murat, 125; R. Limouzin-Lamothe, *Mgr Denys-Auguste Affre archévêque de Paris (1793-1848)* (1971), 303-5.

183. Zamoyski, *Holy Madness*, 335.

184. Murat, 158.

185. Ibid., 189.

186. Mérimée, *CG*, VI, 315 (to Théodore Lagrenée, 25 May 1848).

187. A.J. de Marnay, *Mémoires secrets et témoignages authentiques* (1875), 288 (entry for 8 April 1848); Girardin, *Correspondance parisienne*, 537 (13 May 1848).

188. Mérimée, *CG*, V, 269n; Murat, 251.

189. Murat, 116-17, 120-1.

190. Sewell, 245; Girard, *Nouvelle Histoire de Paris*, 40; Murat, 265.

191. Ligne, 140; Normanby, I, 213.

192. Girard, *Nouvelle Histoire de Paris*, 19-20.

193. NP O 153 (Clarendon to Palmerston, n.d.), P (Normanby to Palmerston, 22 March 1848).

194. Hübner, *Une année de ma vie*, 51; Brombert, 176-7 (to Thierry, 13 February 1848).

195. Brombert, 180-1; Acton, 222.

196. Brombert, 184, 194-5.

197. Jean Sigmann, *1848. Les révolutions romantiques et démocratiques de l'Europe* (1970), 69.

198. NP P (Normanby to Palmerston, 24 February 1848).

199. Murat, 233-9. Failed candidates included Balzac (who for electoral purposes dropped the noble particle), Michelet, Dumas, de Vigny, Victor Huo and Eugène Sue.

200. Normanby, I, 449 (8 June 1848).

201. Tocqueville, 803.

202. Normanby, I, 257.

203. NP P (Normanby to Palmerston, 23 March 1848); *Marianne et Germania*, 7; Jennings, 67.

204. Cracow, Czartoryski Archive MSS 5479 I ff1053-5.

205. Jennings, 47.

206. Zamoyski, *Holy Madness*, 354; Normanby, I, 393 (diary for 16 May 1848).

207. Normanby, I, 393; Murat, 250-4.

208. Tocqueville, 770, 806; Murat, 268-9.

209. Tocqueville, 810.

210. Murat, 271; cf. Mérimée, *CG* (2e série), V, 347 (to Viollet Leduc, 28 February 1863): *j'ai entendu parler polonais sur toutes les barricades*.

211. Normanby, II, 14; cf. Citron, II, 474.

212. Hugo, *Choses vues 1847–48*, 340–1 (24 June 1848); NP P (Normanby to Palmerston, 11 June 1848).

213. Pinkney, 58–9; Tocqueville, 793; NP P (Normanby to Palmerston, 25 June 1848).

214. Normanby, II, 41, 89; Murat, 280.

215. Murat, 283.

216. Ibid., 284–5, 291; Agulhon, 32; Dansette, 227.

217. Murat, 292; Castellane, IV, 89 (6 July 1848).

218. Murat, 296–300.

219. Mérimée, *CG*, V, 335–8 (to Madame de Boigne, 27 June 1848); Roots, 96; Jessop, 42; James Simpson, 108, cf. Normanby, II, 51, 57.

220. *CG*, V, 338 (to Jenny Dacquin, 27 June 1848).

221. Ibid., V, 343 (28 June 1848).

222. Henri Lecouturier, *Paris incompatible avec la République* . . . (1848), 6, 15, 35, 60; cf. Lucien Davésiès, *Paris tuera la France. Nécessité de déplacer le siège du gouvernement* (1850); Citron, II, 28–30.

223. Chevalier, 280; cf. Citron, II, 148–9 for other specimens of anti-Parisianism.

224. Balzac, *Illusions perdues*, 267.

225. Tocqueville, 777.

226. Mérimée, *CG*, V, 273 (25 March 1848 to Madame de Montijo); cf. Castellane, IV, 51 (22 March 1848).

227. Hugo, *Choses vues 1847–48*, 48, 214, 346 (11 February 1847, 4 July 1848); Tocqueville, 824.

228. Got, I, 241 (18 July 1848).

229. Murat, 261–2; Castellane, IV, 79 (12 June 1848).

230. NP P (Normanby to Palmerston, 15 June 1848).

231. Murat, 339; Barante, VII, 484 (Sainte-Aulaire to Barante, 11 November 1849); Hugo, *Choses vues 1847–48*, 407 (11 December 1848).

232. Murat, 351; Louis Girard, *Napoléon III* (1986 ed.), 93, 97; Normanby, II, 259, 361.

233. Murat, 357, 337; Apponyi, IV, 210 (17 December 1848).

234. NP N 896 (Normanby to Lady Normanby, 2 December 1848): Maupas, I, 51, 115.

235. Earl of Kerry (ed.), *The Secret of the Coup d'état* (1924), 78 (Flahaut to Madame de Flahaut, 6 March 1850); Dansette, 237; cf. NP N 907 (Normanby to Lady Normanby, 22 December 1848).

236. Girard, *Napoléon III*, 108; Morny, 520.

237. Tocqueville, 846–7; Girard, *Napoleon III*, 106–7; Castellane, IV, 135 (16 February 1849); Apponyi, IV, 262 (4 April 1849).

238. Castellane, IV, 200, 205 (30 November 1849, 14 January 1850); Murat, 377.

239. Hübner, *Neuf ans*, II, 9 (10 February 1851).

240. Morny, 526–33 (account written in July 1854).

241. Bronne, 191.

242. Dansette, 311, 339; Mérimée, *CG*, VI, 155n; J. Quero Molares, 'Spain in 1848', in F. Fetjö (ed.), *1848. The Opening of an Era* (1948), 144; NP P (Normanby to Palmerston, 20 November 1851).

243. Heine, *Lutèce*, 228–9 (28 December 1841); cf. Alfred de Vigny, *Servitude et grandeur militaires* (1835; Nelson ed., n. d.), 19, 21, 24.

244. Vielcastel, I, 219 (18 November 1851); AN 565 AP FL14 (Flahaut to Madame de Flahaut, 1 December 1851).

245. Maupas, I, 219, 444; cf. *Lieven/Aberdeen*, II, 608 (Lieven to Aberdeen, 23 December 1851), reporting words of the Prince President to the Comte de Montalembert: *si en 1789 j'avais eu l'honneur d'être soldat de la garde française, j'aurais donné ma vie pour défendre Louis XVI et Marie-Antoinette*.

246. M. Quatrelles de l'Epine, *Le Maréchal de Saint-Arnaud* (2 vols, 1939), II, 117; Kerry, 113, 114 (Flahaut to Madame de Flahaut, 13, 14 November 1851).

247. Castellane, IV, 162 (28 May 1849).

248. AN 565 AP FL14.

249. Maricourt, 375.

250. Maupas, I, 321, 405.

251. AN 565 AP FL14.

252. Hübner, *Neuf ans*, I, 38 (3 December 1851); Maupas, I, 403; Dansette, 355, 357; NP P (Normanby to Palmerston, 3 December 1851).

253. Hübner, *Neuf ans*, I, 40–2 (4 December 1851); Gronow, II, 181; Girard, *Nouvelle Histoire de Paris*, 76; Girard, *Napoléon III*, 147–53; Mérimée, *CG*, VI, 263 (to Jenny Dacquin, 3 December 1851).

254. AN 341 AP I 6 [*papiers Le Hon*] II (*dossier du coup d'état*), consulted by kind permission of Prince Poniatowski.

255. AN 565 AP FL14 (Flahaut to Baroness Keith).

256. Kerry, 124–5.

257. NP P (Normanby to Lord John Russell, 14 December 1851).

258. AN 565 AP (letter of 11 January 1852).

259. Kerry, 210, 229 (Flahaut to Morny, 3 March 1852; to Louis-Napoleon, 30 January 1852). Marie Amélie's letters are referred to in a despatch of Stuart de Rothesay to Lord Aberdeen of 27 August 1830: NLS MSS 6243 f197.

260. Maupas, I, 349; Bory, 359; Girard, *Napoléon III*, 155.

261. Nassau William Senior, *Journals kept in France and Italy from 1848 to 1852* (2 vols, 1871), II, 227 (22 December 1851).

262. Vielcastel, I, 230 (6 December 1851).

263. Halévy, 289 (Mignet to Thiers, 9 January 1852); Hübner, *Neuf ans*, II, 99 (30 February 1857); NP P (Normanby to Palmerston, 6 December 1851); cf. for government/salon antagonism, Apponyi, IV, 413, 448 (10 February, 5 April 1854); Mérimée, *CG* (2e série), V, 90 (Mérimée to Madame de Montijo, 28 April 1862).

264. Vielcastel, I, 234 (9 December 1851); Hubner, I, 75 (16 September 1852).

265. Girard, *Napoleon III*, 69; Apponyi, IV, 342, 344, 378 (4, 18 December 1851).

266. NP P (Normanby to Palmerston 7, 11 December 1851).

267. Hübner, I, 33, 37–8, 40, 44 (2, 3, 7 December 1851).

268. *Lieven/Aberdeen*, II, 605 (Lieven to Aberdeen, 9 December 1851).

269. Kerry, 149 (Flahaut to Madame de Flahaut, 9 November 1851, 20 December 1852).

270. Ibid., 158 (Morny to Flahaut, 26 December 1851), 159 (Flahaut to Morny, 28 December 1851), 206n, 238 (Flahaut to Madame de Flahaut, November 1852); Lord Edmund Fitzmaurice, *Life of Lord Granville* (2 vols, 1905), I, 66 (memorandum of interview between Monsieur de Flahaut and Lord Granville, 3 January 1852).

271. Kerry, 256n. However, he had opposed the confiscation of the Orléans properties in 1852.

272. Vielcastel, II, 2, 12, 216 (1, 12 January, 27 July 1852).

273. Fergusson, 561.
274. Joinville, 271.
275. Murat, 474; Girard, *Napoléon III*, 156–7.
276. Hübner, *Neuf ans*, II, 50 (7, 8 January 1852).
277. Ibid., I, 63 (29 March 1852).
278. Vielcastel, II, 54 (10 April 1852).
279. Girard, *Napoléon III*, 183: Castellane, IV, 405 (7 November 1852).
280. Girard, *Napoléon III*, 184; Castellane, IV, 415 (letter of Madame de Contades, 2 December 1852); NP W 98 (Andrew O'Reilly to Normanby, 2 December 1852); Van Zanten, 102; photograph in Girard, *Nouvelle Histoire de Paris*, 87.

Conclusion   Birth of an Empire *Versailles, 17 January 1871*

1. Girard, *Napoléon III*, 239; Chevalier, 355; Jean des Cars and Pierre Pinon (eds.), *Paris–Haussmann* (1991), 52–4.
2. Girard, *Napoléon III*, 177; David H. Pinkney, *Napoleon III and the Rebuilding of Paris* (1958), 88, 239, 341–3; des Cars and Pinon, 126–30; Van Zanten, 86–7.
3. Pinkney, *Napoleon III*, 30; Girard, *Napoléon III*, 239, 269; Pinon, 203–4, 218.
4. Gautier, *Paris et les Parisiens*, 131, 176; cf. for a similar view, Edmond Texier et Albert Kaempfen, *Paris capitale du monde* (1867), 2: *qui s'en souvient encore de ce Paris d'hier?*
5. Scott Haine, 155.
6. Pinon, 190–2; Pinkney, *Napoleon III*, 36.
7. Girard, *Nouvelle Histoire de Paris*, 85.
8. Alistair Horne, *The Fall of Paris. The Siege and the Commune 1870–1* (1965), 24; Queen Victoria, *Leaves from a Journal* (1961), 98 (22 August 1855).
9. *Letters of Queen Victoria*, ed. A.C. Benson and Viscount Esher (3 vols, 1908), III, 137 (to Leopold III, 23 August 1855).
10. Vielcastel, II, 85, 86 (16 July, 12 October 1851); Moulin, 51–69.
11. Mérimée, *CG* (2e série), V, 9 (Mérimée to Léon de Laborde, 12 January 1862), 513 (to Jenny Dacquin, 16 November 1863).
12. Hugo, *Les Misérables* (Garnier Flammarion, 1967), II, 362; *Choses vues 1846–48*, 423 (24 December 1848).
13. Jennings, 142, 210.
14. Vielcastel, V, 9 (25 January 1859); Hübner, *Neuf ans*, II, 323, 350, 425 (12, 28 March 1859, 30 April 1859).
15. Mérimée, *CG* (2e série), III, 103–5 (Mérimée to Panizzi, 29 April 1859), 137 (to Madame de Montijo, 10 June 1859).
16. Harold Kurtz, *The Empress Eugenie* (1964), 128; Girard, *Napoléon III*, 285; cf. Mérimée, *CG* (2e série), III, 115 (to Panizzi, 10 May 1859); Vielcastel, V, 50 (10 May 1859). The army was received with equal enthusiasm, and showers of flowers, on its return to Paris three months later: Vielcastel, V, 145 (15 August 1859).
17. Sewell, 148.
18. Halévy, 379 (Guizot to Thiers, 24 May 1866), 382 (Thiers to Cousin, 10 May 1866), 388n.
19. Girard, *Napoléon III*, 383–5, 393.
20. Arthur Gould Lee (ed.), *The Empress Frederick writes to Sophie* (1955), 130 (to Queen Sophie of the Hellenes, 1892); Girard, *Nouvelle Histoire de Paris*, 380–3, 398, 418; Marmier, *Journal*, II, 121 (August 1869).

21. Delmas, II, 420, 551, 571.
22. Girard, *Nouvelle Histoire de Paris*, 137.
23. PRO FO 27/1806 (despatches from Lord Lyons, 12, 14 July 1870).
24. PRO FO 27/606 (despatch of Lord Granville, 'secret and confidential').
25. Girard, *Napoléon III*, 413, 447, 458, 461–6; Mérimée, *CG* (2e série), IX 135 (to Jenny Dacquin, 18 July 1870).
26. Gautier, *Correspondance générale* (12 vols, Geneva, 1985–2000), XI, 109, 110 (to Carlotta Grisi, 14, 27 July 1870), 112n; Christiansen, 137–8.
27. Thomas J. Adriance, *The Last Gaiter Button. A Study of the Mobilization and Concentration of the French Army in the War of 1870* (New York, 1987), 3.
28. Chalmin, 323; Delmas, II, 450.
29. Girard, *Napoléon III*, 484, 487; id., *Nouvelle Histoire de Paris*, 413.
30. Horne, 73, 178.
31. *Heine à Paris* (Goethe Institute, 1981), 99, 109 (will of 7 March 1843).
32. *Henri Lehmann 1814–1882* (Musée Carnavalet, 1983), 31, 35.
33. Polovtsov, III, 143 (despatch of Pozzo, 14 July 1819); R.B. Mowat, *The Concert of Europe* (1930), 364.
34. Mérimée, *CG* (2e série), VI, 2, 50 (Mérimée to Viollet le Duc, 2 January 1864; to Madame de Montijo, 9 February 1864).
35. Ibid., IX, 170 (Mérimée to Madame de Beaulaincourt, 13 September 1870).
36. General J. von Verdy du Vernois, *With the Royal Headquarters in 1870–71* (1897), 184–6 (15 October 1870).
37. W.H. Russell, *My Diary during the last great war* (1874), 333, 363 (25–26 September, 9 October 1870); Frederick III, *War Diary*, ed. A.R. Allinson (1927), 181 (6 November 1870).
38. Frederick III, 165 (21 October 1870), 226.
39. Russell, 200, 212 (24 November, 3 December 1870); Michael Howard, *The Franco-Prussian War* (1981 ed.), 347.
40. Frederick III, 269.
41. Russell, 553 (18 January 1871).
42. Granier, 228 (to Princess Charlotte, 30 March 1814).
43. Russell, 554–8 (18 January 1871).
44. Frederick III, 269–73 (18 January 1871); Robert Baldick (ed.), *Pages from the Goncourt Journal* (1962), 183 (30 January 1871).
45. Horne, 259, 295; William Serman, *La Commune de Paris 1871* (1986), 176, 245, 440.
46. Serman, 121, 204.
47. Horne, 274.
48. Ibid., 351–2.
49. Robert Tombs, *The War against Paris 1871* (Cambridge, 1981), 169; Horne, 389.
50. Tombs, 162.
51. Ibid., 171, 185; Horne, 417–18.

Bibliography

Primary Sources

Brünnsee, Schloss, Austria, diaries and correspondence of the Duchesse de Berri

Carlisle, Cumbria County Record Office, diaries of Lord Lonsdale, 1817

Châteauroux, Château de La Ferrière, letters from and to the Duchesse d'Escars

Cracow, Czartoryski Library, Czartoryski MSS 5479, 3102, 2775, 2777, 5294, 5444, 5452, 5462, 5469, 6454, 6465, 6487–90, 7032

Decin, Czech Republic, Statni oblasti archiv, Litomerice Pobocka Decin, Archivu Clary-Aldringen, diary of Prince Clary's visit to Paris, 1822

Edinburgh, National Library of Scotland, MSS 6399, journal of a visit to France by the Hon. W.F. Mackenzie of Seaforth, April–May 1814

——19424, diary of Sir Thomas Frederick Elliot, September 1827

——9269, Journals of my Life by John Dunlop MD, 1845

——Stuart de Rothesay papers, MSS 21307–8, 21318–28, 21262–8, 21285, 21288, 15386–9, 6160, 6163, 6198, 6200, 6201, 6208, 6228, 6242–4

Rulegas House, Moray, Ayrshire, diary of Lady Dalrymple Hamilton, 1814–18

Heydon Hall, Norfolk, papers of Henry Lytton Bulwer

La Grange, Château de, memoirs of Comtesse de Chabot

Lamb Papers, Wiltshire, letters of John Bowes Wright to J. Lamb, 1815–26

London, British Library, MSS 47375, Lieven papers, letters of Comtesse de Flahaut to Princess Lieven

——Holland House papers, letters to Lord and Lady Holland from Comte and Comtesse de Flahaut (51717–18), Comtesse de Bourke and Madame de Coigny (51638), Louis-Philippe (51524), James Mackintosh (52441), Prince de Talleyrand (51635), Henry Lytton Bulwer (51614)

——Public Record Office, FO 27/604–7, despatches of Henry Lytton Bulwer and Lord Granville to Palmerston, 1840

New York Public Library, Berg Collection, diary of John Cam Hobhouse, April–May 1814, April–July 1815

Norwich, Norfolk County Record Office, Bulwer papers BUL 1/2/1, diary of Henry Lytton Bulwer, 1832

Oxford, Bodleian Library, 'Memorandums of Paris in 1815', MSS by Edward Mangin

Paris, Bibliothèque Thiers, Fonds Masson, MSS 236, 246, 1247, 1248 La Bédoyère papers

——MSS 667, Martin Doisy, album journal

Paris, Archives Nationales

——F7 3783–6, police reports, 1814–30

——03, papers of the Maison du Roi, 1814–30

——40AP8–14, reports of Comte Beugnot to Louis XVIII, 1814
——104AP3, Cahier de la Comtesse Amable d'Ecquevilly
——115AP, Mounier papers, account of July revolution by Marquis de Sémonville
——197AP, La Châtre papers, letters of Louis XVIII
——300AP III 16, Archives de la Maison de France, letters of Duc d'Orléans
——340AP5, Papiers Le Hon
——349AP23, Montesquiou papers, *Garde nationale, ordres du jour, 1814–15*
——384AP (Suchet papers) 207, 1, *Listes pour les invitations au Bal du Dimanche gras de 1819*
——565AP, Flahaut papers, FL5 Flahaut to Madame de Souza, FL8–14 Flahaut to Comtesse de Flahaut, FL6–7 Madame de Souza to Flahaut
Lady Elizabeth Foster Dormer MSS, Journal of Elizabeth Duchess of Devonshire
Private collection, diary of Anne Lister 1825–8
Rohan-Chabot, Comte Jean de, collection of memoirs of and letters to Comte de Chabrol
Turin, Archivio di Stato, Lettere Ministri Francia 1829 in 1830
Whitby, Mulgrave Castle, Normanby Papers, including letters of Lord Normanby to Lord Palmerston, 1846–52, and letters from French correspondents

Secondary Sources

Unless otherwise stated, books in English are published in London, books in French in Paris

'A Visitor', *A Slight sketch of Paris; or some account of the French capital and its improved state, since 1802*, 1814
Ackerknecht, Erwin, H., *Medicine at the Paris Hospital 1794–1848*, Baltimore, 1967
Acton, Harold, *The Last Bourbons of Naples*, 1961
Adburgham, Alison, *Silver Fork Society. Fashionable Life and Literature 1814–1840*, 1983
Adriance, Thomas J., *The Last Gaiter Button. A Study of the Mobilization and Concentration of the French Army in the War of 1870*, New York, 1987

Agoult, Comtesse d', *Mémoires, souvenirs et portraits*, 2 vols, 1990
Aguet, Jean-Pierre, *Les Grèves sous la monarchie de juillet (1830–1848)*, Geneva, 1954
Agulhon, Maurice, *Le Cercle dans la France bourgeoise 1810–1848. Etude d'une mutation de sociabilité*, 1977
——*Les Quarante-Huitards*, 1992 ed.
Airlie, Mabell Countess of, ed., *Lady Palmerston and her Times*, 2 vols, 1922
Albemarle, George Thomas Earl of, *Fifty Years of My Life*, 2 vols, 1876
Alexander, R. S., *Bonapartism and Revolutionary Tradition in France. The Fédérés of 1815*, Cambridge, 1991
Alexandre Théodore Brongniart, Musée Carnavalet, 1986
Allen, Ian, *L'Allemagne de Mme de Staël et la polémique romantique*, 1929
Allen, James Smith, *In the Public Eye. A History of Reading in Modern France 1800–1940*, Princeton, 1991
Al-Sayyid Marsot, Afaf Lutfi, *Egypt in the Reign of Muhammad Ali*, Cambridge, 1984
Altick, Richard D., *Punch. The Lively Youth of a British Institution 1841–1851*, Columbus, Ohio, 1997
Alton-Shée, Comte d', *Mes mémoires 1826–1848*, 2 vols, 1869
——*Souvenirs de 1847 et de 1848*, 1879
Anderson, M.S., *The Eastern Question 1774–1923*, 1981 ed.
André, Roger, *L'Occupation de la France par les alliés, juillet–novembre 1815*, 1924
Anglaisiana ou les Anglais, les Ecossais et les Irlandais à Londres et à Paris, 1815
Anne, Théodore, *Mémoires, souvenirs et anecdotes sur l'intérieur du palais de Charles X, et les événements de 1815 à 1830*, 3 vols, 1831
Anon., *Impressions and Observations of a Young Person during a Residence in Paris*, 3rd ed., 1845
Anon., *Le Palais Royal ou les filles en bonne fortune*, 1815
Anon., *Memorandums of a Residence in France*, 1816
Anon., *The Englishman's Mentor. The Picture of the Palais Royal; describing its Spectacles, Gaming Rooms, Coffee Houses, Restaurateurs, Tabagies, Reading Rooms, Milliners' Shops, Gamesters . . . and That High Change of Fashionable Dissipation and Vice of Paris*, 1819

Anon., *The Picture of the Palais Royal*, 1815

Antonetti, Guy, *Louis-Philippe*, 1994

Apponyi, Comte Rodolphe, *Journal*, 4 vols, 1913–26

Ariste, Paul d', *La Vie et le monde du boulevard 1830–1870*, 1930

Ariste, Paul d' et Maurice Arnety, *Les Champs Elysées. Etude topographique, historique et anecdotique*, 1913

Armaillé, Comtesse d', *Quand on savait vivre heureux (1830–1860). Souvenirs de jeunesse*, 1934

Aron, Jean-Paul, *Le Mangeur du XIXe siècle*, 1973

Arvin, Neil Cole, *Eugène Scribe and the French Theatre 1815–1830*, Harvard, 1924

Athanassoglou-Kallmyer, Nina, *French Images from the Greek War of Independence 1821–1830*, Yale, 1989

——*Eugène Delacroix. Print, Politics and Satire 1814–1822*, New Haven, 1991

Aumale, Duc d', *Correspondance du . . . et de Cuvillier-Fleury*, 4 vols, 1910–14

Babboneix, L., 'Lamartine Garde du Corps', *Revue d'histoire littéraire*, XXII, 1925, 344–70

Baden und Württemberg im Zeitalter Napoleons, 2 vols, Stuttgart, 1987

Bailleul, J.C., *Examen critique de l'ouvrage post-hume de Mme la baronne de Staël*, 2 vols, 1818

Bain, Margaret I., *Les Voyageurs français en Ecosse 1770–1830 et leurs curiosités intellec-tuelles*, 1931

Balabine, Victor de, *Journal*, 1914

Balayé, Simone, ed. *Les Carnets de voyage de Madame de Staël*, Geneva, 1971

Balzac dans l'empire russe, Maison de Balzac, 1993

Balzac et la Révolution française, Maison de Balzac, 1988

Balzac, Honoré de, *A Paris!*, 1993

——*Autre Etude de femme*, Folio, 1971 ed.

——*Correspondance*, 5 vols, 1960–9

——*Ferragus*, Presses Pocket, 1992

——*Illusions perdues*, Booking International, 1993

——*L'Illustre Gaudissart*, Livres de Poche, 1971

——*La Fille aux yeux d'or*, Presses Pocket, 1992

——*Le Cabinet des antiques*, Calman Lévy, 1895

——*Le Père Goriot*, 1993, Booking International

——*Les Journalistes*, Arléa, 1998

——*Lettres à Madame Hanska*, 4 vols, 1967–8

——*Mémoires de deux jeunes mariées*, Garnier Flammarion, 1979

——*Splendeurs et misères des courtisanes*, Booking International, 1993

Barante, Baron de, *Souvenirs*, 8 vols, 1892

Barberis, Pierre, *Balzac et le mal du siècle*, 2 vols, 1970

Barbey d'Aurevilly, J., *Memoranda. Journal intime 1836–1864*, 1993

Bardoux, A., *La Duchesse de Duras*, 1888

Barea, Ilsa, *Vienna. Legend and Reality*, 1966

Baring, Sir Francis Thornhill (afterwards Lord Northbrook), *Journal and correspon-dence from 1808 to 1852*, 2 vols, 1905

Barry, Joseph, *George Sand ou le scandale de la liberté*, 1982

Bary, Emile, *Les Cahiers d'un rhétoricien de 1815*, 1890

Bassanville, Comtesse de, *Les Salons d'autre-fois. Souvenirs intimes*, 1862

Baticle, Jeannine et Cristina Marinas, *La Galerie espagnole de Louis-Philippe au Louvre 1838–1848*, 1981

Batty, Robert, *French Scenery from Drawings made in 1819*, 1822

Beal, Mary and John Cornforth, *British Embassy, Paris*, 1992

Bellenger, Sylvain et Françoise Hamon, *Duban. Les couleurs de l'architecte*, 1996

Belliard, Comte, *Mémoires*, 3 vols, 1842

Benichou, Paul, *Le Temps des prophètes. Doctrines de l'âge romantique*, 1977

Béraud, F.-F.-A., *Les Filles publiques de Paris, et la police qui les régit*, 2 vols, Paris and Leipzig, 1839

Bergeron, Louis, *Paris. Genèse d'un paysage*, 1989

Berlin, Isaiah, *Karl Marx. His Life and Environment*, Fontana, 1995

Berlioz, Hector, *Memoirs from 1803 to 1865*, New York, 1966

Bernardy, Françoise de, *Alexandre Walewski, le fils polonais de Napoléon*, 1976

——*Charles de Flahaut*, 1954

——*Flahaut fils de Talleyrand, père de Morny*, 1974

Berry, Mary, *Social Life in England and France, from the French Revolution of 1789 to that of July*

1830, 1831

——*Extracts of the Journals and Correspondence*, 3 vols, 1865

Bertier de Sauvigny, Ferdinand de, *Souvenirs d'un ultra-royaliste (1815–1832)*, 1993

Bertier de Sauvigny, Guillaume de, *La France et les Français vus par les voyageurs américains 1814–1840*, 1982

——*Metternich*, 1986

——*Metternich et la France après le Congrès de Vienne*, 3 vols, 1968–72

——*Nouvelle Histoire de Paris. La Restauration 1815–1830*, 1977

Beugnot, Comte, *Mémoires*, 2 vols, 1866

Beurdeley, Michel, *La France à l'encan. L'exode des objets d'art dans la Révolution 1789–1799*, 1981

Biver, Marie-Louise, *Le Paris de Napoléon*, 1963

Blake, Mrs Warenne, ed., *An Irish Beauty of the Regency, compiled from 'Mes Souvenirs', the unpublished Journals of the Hon. Mrs Calvert 1789–1822*, 1911

Blanch, Lesley, ed., *The Game of Hearts. Harriet Wilson and her Memoirs*, 1957

Blessington, Countess of, *Journal of a Tour through the Netherlands to Paris in 1821*, 1822

——*The Idler in France*, 2 vols, 1841

Blomac, Nicole de, *La Gloire et le jeu. Des hommes et des chevaux 1766–1866*, 1991

Bloom, Peter, ed., *Music in Paris in the Eighteen Thirties*, New York, 1987

Blount, Sir Edward, *Memoirs*, 1902

Bluche, Frédéric, *Le Plébiscite des Cent Jours*, Geneva, 1974

Boerne, Ludwig, *Fragments politiques et littéraires*, 1842

——*Lettres écrites de Paris pendant les années 1830 et 1831*, 1832

Boigne, Comtesse de, *Mémoires*, 2 vols, 1979 ed.

Bonald, Vicomte de, *Réflexions sur l'intérêt général de l'Europe, suivies de quelques considérations sur la noblesse*, 1815

Bonaparte, Louis-Napoléon, *Oeuvres*, 3 vols, 1848

Bornstedt, Adalbert von, *Pariser Silhouetten*, 2 vols, Leipzig, 1836

Borrily, Jean, 'Mickiewicz and France', in Waclaw Lednicki (ed.), *Adam Mickiewicz in World Literature*, Berkeley, 1956

Bory, J.-L., *Eugène Sue. Le roi du roman populaire*, 1962

Bouchot, Henri, *Le Luxe français. La Restauration*, 1894

Boulenger, Jacques, *Sous Louis-Philippe. Le boulevard*, 1933

Bourbon-Parme, Prince Sixte de, *La Dernière Conquête du roi. Alger 1830*, 2 vols, 1930

Bourgoing, A. de, *L'Espagne. Souvenirs de 1823 et de 1833*, 1834

Bourjon, Michel and Bruno Pons, *Le Quai Voltaire*, 1990

Bourset, Madeleine, *Casimir Périer. Un prince financier au temps du Romantisme*, 1994

Boutet de Monvel, Roger, *Les Anglais à Paris 1800–1850*, 1911

Bowie, Karen, ed., *Les Grandes Gares parisiennes au XIX siècle*, n.d.

Bowring, Sir John, *Autobiographical Recollections*, 1877

Bowron, Edgar Peters and Joseph J. Rishel, eds., *Art in Rome in the Eighteenth Century*, Philadelphia, 2000

Boykin, Edward, ed., *Victoria, Albert and Mrs Stevenson*, 1957

Bro, Général de, *Memoires*, 1914

Broglie, Duc Albert de, *Mémoires*, 2 vols, 1938–43

Broglie, Duc Victor de, *Souvenirs 1785–1870*, 4 vols, 1886

Broglie, Duchesse de, *Lettres*, 1896

Brombert, Beth Archer, *Cristina. Portraits of a Princess*, 1978

Bronne, Carlo, *Les Abeilles du manteau*, Brussels, 1944

——*La Comtesse Le Hon et la première ambassade de Belgique à Paris*, Brussels, 1952

Broughton, Lord, *Recollections of a Long Life*, 6 vols, 1909

Brown, Mark, 'The Comité Franco-Polonais and the French reaction to the Polish uprising of November 1830', *English Historical Review*, XCIII, 1978, 774–93

Brownlow, Emma Sophia Countess, *The Eve of Victorianism*, 1940

Bruce, Ian, *Lavallette Bruce*, 1953

Buckingham, James Silk, *France, Piedmont, Italy, Lombardy, the Tyrol and Bavaria. An Autumnal Tour*, 2 vols, 1847

Bullen, Roger, *Palmerston, Guizot and the Collapse of the Entente Cordiale*, 1974

Bulwer, Henry Lytton, *The Life of Viscount Palmerston*, 3 vols, 1870–4

——*The Monarchy of the Middle Classes*, 2 vols,

1836

Burdett, Allen, *Thomas Moore en France. Contribution à l'histoire de la fortune des oeuvres de Thomas Moore dans la littérature française 1819–1830*, 1911

Burghersh, Lady, *Letters . . . from Germany and France during the Campaign of 1813–14*, 1893

Burney, Fanny, *Journals and Letters*, 13 vols, Oxford, 1972–84

Bury, Lady Charlotte, *Diary Illustrative of the Times of George the Fourth*, 3rd ed., 2 vols, 1838

Bury, J.P.T. and R.R. Tombs, *Thiers 1797–1877. A Political Life*, 1986

Byron, Lord, *Letters and Journals*, 12 vols, 1973–82

Cadot, Michel, *La Russie dans la vie intellectuelle française (1839–1856)*, 1967

Cairns, David, *Berlioz*, 2 vols, 1989–99

Campagne d'un jeune Français en Grèce envoyé par M. le duc de Choiseul, 1827

Carey, David, *Life in Paris*, 1822

Caricatures politiques 1829–1848. De l'éteignoir à la poire, Maison de Chateaubriand, 1994

Carlton House. The Past Glories of George IV's Palace, The Queen's Gallery, 1991

Carné, Comte L. de, *Souvenirs de ma jeunesse au temps de la Restauration*, 1872

Caron, Jean-Claude, *Générations romantiques. Les étudiants de Paris et le Quartier Latin 1814–1851*, 1991

Carracioli, F., *Paris, le modèle des nations étrangères, ou l'Europe française*, Vienna and Paris, 1777

——*Paris métropole de l'Univers*, 1802

Carré, Jean-Marie, *Voyageurs et écrivains français en Egypte*, 2nd ed., 2 vols, Cairo, 1956

Cars, Jean des and Pierre Pinon, eds., *Paris–Haussmann*, 1991

Cassaigneau, Jean et Jean Rilliet, *Marc-Auguste Pictet ou le rendez-vous de l'Europe universelle*, Geneva, 1995

Castellane, Maréchal de, *Journal*, 5 vols, 1896–7

Castil-Blaze, F.H.G., *Chapelle-musique des rois de France*, 1832

Castlereagh, Viscount, *Correspondence, Despatches and other Papers*, 12 vols, 1848–53

Caulaincourt, Comte du, *Mémoires*, 3 vols, 1933

Cent ans de vie française à la Revue des deux mondes, 1929

Chagniot, Jean, *Paris au XVIII siècle*, 1988

Chalmin, Pierre, *L'Officier français de 1815 à 1870*, 1957

Chambrun, René de, ed., *Les 5 Cercueils de l'Empereur. Souvenirs inédits de Philippe de Rohan-Chabot*, 1985

Champier, Victor et Roger Sandoz, *Le Palais Royal d'après des documents inédits, 1629–1900*, 2 vols, 1900

Charles, Jacques, ed., *De Versailles à Paris. Le destin des collections royales*, 1989

Charles-Roux, François, *Thiers et Mehemet Ali*, 1951

Chartier, Roger, ed., *La Correspondance. Les usages de la lettre au XIXe siècle*, 1991

Chastenay, Madame de, *Mémoires*, 2 vols, 1896–7

Chateaubriand, *Congrès de Vérone*, Geneva, 1979

——*Correspondance générale* (in publication)

——*De Buonaparte et des Bourbons et de la nécessité de se rallier à nos princes légitimes pour le bonheur de la France et celui de l'Europe*, 1814

——*Lettres à Madame Récamier*, ed. Maurice Levaillant, 1988 ed.

——*Mémoires d'outre-tombe*, 3 vols, 1951

——*Mémoires . . . sur le duc de Berri*, 1820

——*Réflexions politiques sur quelques écrits du jour et sur les intérêts de tous les Français*, 1814

Chateaubriand. Le voyageur et l'homme politique, Bibliothèque Nationale, 1969

Chaudonneret, Marie-Claude, *L'Etat et les artistes. De la Restauration à la monarchie de juillet (1815–1833)*, 2000

Chevalier, Louis, *Classes laborieuses et classes dangereuses à Paris pendant la première moitié du dix-neuvième siècle*, 1984 ed.

Christiansen, Rupert ed., *Tales of the New Babylon*, Minerva, 1995 ed.

Chroust, Anton, *Die Berichte der Französichen Gesandten*, Munich, 1935

Chuquet, Arthur, *L'Année 1814*, 1914

Church, Clive H., *Europe in 1830*, 1983

Citron, Pierre, *La Poésie de Paris dans la littérature française, de Rousseau à Baudelaire*, 2 vols, 1961

Clark, Peter and Bernard Lepetit, eds., *Capital Cities and their Hinterlands in Early Modern Europe*, 1996

Claudin, Gustave, *Mes souvenirs. Les boulevards de 1840 à 1879*, 1884

Clayden, P.W., *Rogers and his Contemporaries*, 2 vols, 1889

Clément Jean-Paul, *Chateaubriand. Biographie morale et intellectuelle*, 1998
——ed., *Madame de Chateaubriand*, 1990

Clerc, Catherine, *La Caricature contre Napoléon*, 1985

Cochelet, Mlle, *Mémoires sur la reine Hortense et la famille impériale*, 2 vols, 1836

Colchester, Lord, *Diary and Correspondence*, 3 vols, 1861

Coleman, William, *Death is a Social Disease*, Madison, Wisconsin, 1982

Collingham, Hugh with R.S. Alexander, *The July Monarchy*, 1988

Collins, Herbert F., *Talma. A Biography of an Actor*, 1964

Colvin, Christina, ed., *Maria Edgeworth in France and Switzerland*, Oxford, 1979

Connelly, Willard, *Count D'Orsay*, 1952

Constant, Benjamin, *Journaux intimes*, 1951

Constant, Benjamin et Rosalie de, *Correspondance 1786–1830*, 1955

Contamine, Henry, *Diplomatie et diplomates sous la Restauration 1814–1830*, 1970

Cooper, J. Fenimore, *Recollections of Europe*, Paris, 1837

Corbet, Charles, *L'Opinion française face à l'inconnu russe 1799–1894*, 1967

Cornut-Gentille, Pierre, *La Baronne de Feuchères (1790–1840)*, 2000

Correspondance de Fauriel et de Mary Clarke, 1911

Corti, Egon Conte, *Ludwig I of Bavaria*, 1938

Corvisier, André, ed., *Histoire militaire de la France*, 4 vols, 1992–8

Cowley, Lord, *Diaries and Letters*, 1927

Croker, J.W., *Correspondence and Diaries*, 3 vols, 1884

Crouzet, François, *Britain Ascendant. Comparative Studies in Franco-British Economic History*, Cambridge–Paris, 1990

Cuisin, J.P.R., *Les Nymphes du Palais-Royal*, 1815

Custine, Marquis de, *La Russie en 1839*, 2e éd. revue et corrigée, 4 vols, 1843
——*Lettres à Varnhagen d'Ense et à Rahel Varnhagen d'Ense*, Brussels, 1870
——*Lettres inédites . . . au marquis de La Grange*, n.d.
——*Mémoires et voyages ou lettres écrites à diverses époques pendant des courses en Suisse, en Calabre, en Angleterre et en Ecosse*, 2 vols, 1830

Cuvillier-Fleury, Alfred, *Journal intime*, 2 vols, 1900–3

Dallas, Gregor, *1815. The Roads to Waterloo*, 1997

Dansette, Adrien, *Louis-Napoléon à la conquête du pouvoir*, 1961

Dard, Emile, *Un rival de Fersen. Quintin Crawford*, 1947

Daudet, Ernest, *Histoire de l'Emigration*, 3 vols, 1905–7
——*L'Ambassade du duc Decazes en Angleterre (1820–1821)*, 1910
——*La Police politique. Chroniques des temps de la Restauration*, 1912
——*Louis XVIII et le duc Decazes*, 1899
——*Une vie d'ambassadrice au siècle dernier*, 1903

Daumard, Adeline, *La Bourgeoisie parisienne de 1815 à 1848*, 1996 ed.
——'La vie de salon en France dans la première moitié du XIXe siècle', in Etienne François, ed., *Sociabilité et société bourgeoise en France, en Allemagne et en Suisse (1750–1850)*, 1986
——'Noblesse et aristocratie en France au XIXe siècle', in *Les Noblesses européennes au XIXe siècle*, Ecole Française de Rome, 1988

Davésiès, Lucien, *Paris tuera la France. Nécessité de déplacer le siège du gouvernement*, 1850

Davidoff, Leonore, *The Best Circles*, 1986 ed.

Decours, Cathérine, *La Dernière Favorite*, 1993

Dedem de Gelder, Général Baron de, *Mémoires*, 1900

Delacroix, Eugène, *Correspondance générale*, 5 vols, 1935
——*Journal*, 3 vols, 1893–5

Délécluze, E.J., *Journal 1824–1828*, 1948

Depping, G.B., *Erinnerungen aus dem Leben eines Deutschen in Paris*, Leipzig, 1832

Descôtes, Maurice, *La Légende de Napoléon et les écrivains français au XIXe siècle*, 1967

Desnoyers, Louis et al., *Les Etrangers à Paris*, 1844

Destrez, Alfred, *Le Faubourg Saint-Honoré de Louis XIV au Second Empire*, 1953

Déterville, H., *Le Palais Royal ou les filles en bonne fortune*, 1815

Devonshire, M.G., *The English Novel in France 1830–1870*, 1929

Bibliography

Dibdin, Revd Thomas Frognall, *A Bibliographical, Antiquarian and Picturesque Tour in France and Germany*, 3 vols, 1821

Dino, Duchesse de, *Chronique de 1831 à 1862*, 4 vols, 1909

Dipper, Christophe, 'La noblesse allemande à l'époque de la bourgeoisie', in *Les Noblesses européennes au XIXe siècle*, Ecole Française de Rome, 1988

Doudeauville, Duc de, *Mémoires*, 15 vols, 1861–4

Dresch, Joseph, *Heine à Paris 1831–1856*, 1956

Du Montet, Baronne, *Souvenirs*, 1914

Dugon, Marquis, *Au service du roi en exil*, 1968

Dumas, Alexandre, *De Paris à Cadix*, 1841

Dupré, Lóuis, *Voyage à Athènes et à Constantinople*, 1825

Dupuis, Charles, *Le Ministère de Talleyrand en 1814*, 2 vols, 1919

Duras, Duchesse de, *Olivier ou le secret*, ed. Denise Virieux, 1971

——*Ourika*, Ladvocat ed. 1824

Duvergier de Hauranne, Prosper, *Histoire du gouvernement parlementaire en France*, 10 vols, 1857–72

Eckstein, Baron d', *Lettres inédites*, ed. Louis le Guillou, 1984

Englishman in Paris, An, *Notes and Recollections*, 2 vols, 1892

Esquiros, Alphonse, *Paris ou les sciences, les institutions et les moeurs au XIXe siècle*, 2 vols, 1847

Esterhazy, Comte François, *Journal*, Budapest, 1940

Estève, Edmond, *Byron et le romantisme français*, 1907

Estourmel, Comte Joseph d', *Journal d'un Voyage en Orient*, 1844

Etmekjian, James, *French Influence on the Western Armenian Renaissance 1843–1915*, New York, 1964

Etudes sur les mouvements libéraux et nationaux de l'Europe, 1930

Eustace, Revd John Chetwode, *A Letter from Paris, to George Petre Esq.*, 1814

Fauré, Alain, *Paris Carême-prenant. Du carnaval à Paris au XIXe siècle 1800–1914*, 1978

Fayol, Amédée, *La Vie et l'oeuvre d'Orfila*, 1930

Fejtö, F., ed., *1848. The Opening of an Era*, 1948

Felkay, Nicole, *Balzac et ses éditeurs 1822–1837.*

Essai sur la librairie romantique, 1987

Fellowes, W.D., *Paris during the interesting month of July 1815*, 1815

Fergusson, Niall, *The World's Banker. The Rise of the House of Rothschild*, 1999

Fierro, Alfred, *Histoire et Dictionnaire de Paris*, 1996

Firmin-Didot, G. Georges, *Royauté ou empire. La France en 1814 d'après les rapports inédits du Comte Anglès*, n.d.

Fitzmaurice, Lord Edmund, *Life of Lord Granville*, 2 vols, 1905

Fleury, Comte, *La Palais de Saint-Cloud. Ses origines – ses hôtes – ses ruines*, 1902

Fontaine, Pierre-François-Léonard, *Journal*, 2 vols, 1987

Fontaney, Antoine, *Journal intime*, 1925

——*Scènes de la vie castillane et andalouse*, 1835

Forgues, E., *Le Dossier secret de Fouché*, 1908

Forster, Charles de, *Quinze ans à Paris (1832–1848). Paris et les Parisiens*, 2 vols, 1848

Fox, Henry Edward, *Journal*, 1923

Foy, Général, *Notes autobiographiques*, 3 vols, 1926

Franklin, Robert, *Lord Stuart de Rothesay*, 1993

Frazer, Colonel Sir Augustus Simon, *Letters . . . written during the Peninsular and Waterloo Campaigns*, 1859

Frederick III, *War Diary*, ed. A.R. Allinson, 1927

Frénilly, Baron de, *Souvenirs*, 1908

Frye, Major W.E., *After Waterloo. Reminiscences of European Travel 1815–1819*, 1908

Gachot, Edouard, *Marie Louise intime*, 2 vols, 1911

Gaetghens, Thomas W., *Versailles, de la résidence royale au musée historique*, Antwerp, 1984

Gaillard, Marc, *L'Arc de Triomphe*, 1998

Gaissier, Pierre and Juliet Wilson, *The Life and Complete Works of Goya*, New York, 1981

Galignani's New Paris Guide, 1842

Galignani's Paris Guide or Stranger's Guide through the French Metropolis, 10th ed., Paris–Calais–London, 1822

Gardie, Comte de la, 'Mémoires. Séjour en France', *Revue d'histoire diplomatique*, October 1933, 492–515

Gasnault, François, *Guinguettes et lorettes. Bals publics et danse sociale à Paris entre 1830 et*

1870, 1986

Gautier, Théophile, *Paris et les Parisiens*, 1996 ed.

——*Voyage en Espagne*, Gallimard, 1981 ed.

Gayot, André, ed. *François Guizot et Madame Laure de Gasparin (fragments inédits)*, 1934

Genlis, Madame de, *Dernières Lettres d'amour. Correspondance inédite avec le comte Anatole de Montesquiou*, 1954

Gérando, Baronne de, *Lettres*, 1880

Gérard, François, *Correspondance*, 1867

Géraud, Edmond, *Un homme de lettres sous l'Empire et la Restauration*, 1893

——*Un témoin des deux Restaurations*, 1893

Gerhard, Anselm, *The Urbanisation of Opera. Music Theatre in Paris in the Nineteenth Century*, Chicago, 1998

Girard, Louis, *La Garde nationale 1814–1871*, 1964

——*Napoléon III*, 1986 ed.

——*Nouvelle Histoire de Paris. La Deuxième République et le Second Empire 1848–1870*, 1981

Girardin, Madame de, *Correspondance parisienne*, 1853

——*Lettres parisiennes du Vicomte de Launay*, 1986 ed.

Giraud, P.-F.-F., *Campagne de Paris, en 1814, precédée d'un coup d'oeil sur celle de 1813*, 1814

Girod de l'Ain, Maurice, *Vie militaire du Général Foy*, 1900

Glenbervie, Lord, *Diaries*, 2 vols, 1928

Godechot, Jacques, 'Nation, patrie, nationalisme et patriotisme en France au XVIIIe siècle', *Annales historiques de la Révolution française*, 1971

Goethe, *Conversations with Eckermann and Soret*, 2 vols, 1850

Gomm, Field Marshal Sir William Maynard, *Letters and Journals*, 1881

Gore, Mrs, *Greville; or, A season in Paris*, Paris, 1841

——*Paris in 1841*, 1842

Gossez, Rémi, *Un ouvrier en 1820. Manuscrit inédit de Jacques Etienne Bedé*, 1984

Got, Edmond, *Journal*, 2 vols, 1910

Gould, Cecil, *Trophy of Conquest*, 1967

Gourgaud, General Baron, *Sainte-Hélène. Journal inédit de 1815 à 1822*, 2 vols, 1899

Gower, Lord Granville Leveson, *Private Correspondence 1781 to 1821*, 2 vols, 1916

Graham, Peter W., ed., *Byron's Bulldog. The Letters of John Cam Hobhouse to Lord Byron*, Columbus, Ohio, 1989

Granier, Hermann, ed., *Hohenzollernbriefe aus den Freiheitskriegen 1813–1815*, Leipzig, 1913

Grant, James, *Paris and its People*, 2 vols, 1844

Granville, Harriet Countess, *Letters*, 2 vols, 1894

Grenville, Vicomte E. de, *Histoire du journal La Mode*, 1861

Greville, Charles, *Memoirs*, 8 vols, 1938 ed.

Greville, Henry, *Leaves from the Diary*, 1883

Griffith, Paddy, *Military Thought in the French Army 1815–1851*, Manchester, 1989

Grillparzer, Franz, *Journal de mon voyage en France (1836)*, 1942

Griscom, John, *A Year in Europe*, 2 vols, New York, 1823

Gronow, Captain, *Reminiscences and Recollections*, 2 vols, 1892 ed.

Grosjean, Georges, *La Politique extérieure de la Restauration et l'Allemagne*, 2e éd., 1930

Guest, Ivor, *The Romantic Ballet in Paris*, 1966

Guichen, Vicomte de, *La Crise d'orient de 1839 à 1841 et l'Europe*, 1921

——*La Révolution de juillet 1830 et l'Europe*, 1917

Guillemin, Henri, *L'Homme des Mémoires d'outre-tombe*, 1964

Guizot, François, *Lettres de . . . et de la princesse de Lieven*, 3 vols, 1963–4

——*Mémoires pour servir à l'histoire de mon temps*, 8 vols, 1858–67

Gunnell, Doris, *Sutton Sharpe et ses amis français*, 1925

Guyot, Raymond, *La Première Entente Cordiale*, 1926

Haine, W. Scott, *The World of the Paris Cafe. Sociability among the French Working Class 1789–1814*, Baltimore, 1996

Halévy, Daniel, *Le Courrier de Monsieur Thiers*, 1921

Hall, Lt Francis, *Travels in France in 1818*, 1819

Hammer, Karl, *Hôtel Beauharnais, Paris*, Munich–Zurich, 1983

Hamon, Françoise et Charles MacCullum, *Louis Visconti 1791–1853*, 1991

Hapdé, J.B.A., *Relation historique . . . de la nuit du 13 février 1820*, 1820

Harpaz, Ephraim, *L'Ecole libérale sous la Restauration*, Geneva, 1968

Harsin, Jill, *Policing Prostitution in Nineteenth-Century Paris*, Princeton, 1985

Hartley, Janet, *Alexander I*, 1994

Haussonville, Comte d', *Ma jeunesse*

1814–1830, 1883

——*Femmes d'autrefois, hommes d'aujourd'hui*, 1912

Haydon, Benjamin Robert, *Autobiography and Memoirs*, 2 vols, 1926

Hazlitt, William, *Notes of a Journey through France and Italy*, 1826

Heine à Paris, Goethe Institute, Paris, 1981

Heine, Heinrich, *De l'Allemagne*, 1998 ed.

——*De la France*, 1994 ed.

——*Lutèce*, Geneva, 1979 ed.

Hennet de Goutel, Baron, 'Les derniers jours de l'Empire racontés par un Cent-suisse, d'après le journal inédit de M. de Marsilly (1811–1816)', *Revue des études napoléoniennes*, January 1918, XIII, 175–200, 271–95

Henri Lehmann 1814–1882, Musée Carnavalet, 1983

Heriot de Vroil, A.H., *Mémoires d'un officier de la Garde Royale*, 1904

Herzen, Alexander, *My Past and Thoughts*, 4 vols, 1960

Heuberger, Georg, *The Rothschilds. Essays in the History of a European Family*, Frankfurt, 1994

Higgs, David, *Nobles in Nineteenth-Century France*, 1992

Hill, Douglas, *The Troubled Trinity. Godoy and the Spanish Monarchs*, Tuscaloosa, 1987

Hittorff. Un architecte du XIXe siècle, Musée Carnavalet, 1986

Hobhouse, J.C., *The Substance of some Letters, written by an Englishman resident at Paris during the Last Reign of the Emperor Napoleon*, 2 vols, 1816

Holohan, Renagh, *The Irish Chateaux*, Dublin, 1989

Horne, Alistair, *The Fall of Paris. The Siege and the Commune 1870–1*, 1965

Horner, Francis, *Memoirs and Correspondence*, 2 vols, 1843

Hortense, Queen, 'Lettres à Alexandre Ier', *Revue de Paris*, 15 October 1897, 673–710

——*Mémoires*, 3 vols, 1927

Howard, Michael, *The Franco-Prussian War*, 1981 ed.

Hübner, Count von, *Neuf ans de souvenirs d'un ambassadeur d'Autriche à Paris sous le Second Empire*, 2 vols, 1904

——*Une année de ma vie*, 1891

Hugo, Victor, *Choses Vues 1830–46*, 1972 ed.

——*Choses Vues 1847–48*, 1972 ed.

——*Correspondance familiale et écrits intimes*, 4 vols, 1988

——*Le Rhin*, 2 vols, 1912 ed.

——*Les Misérables*, Garnier Flammarion, 1967

Hyde, H. Montgomery, *Princess Lieven*, 1938

Janin, Jules, *The American in Paris*, 2 vols, 1843

——*Fontainebleau, Versailles, Paris*, 1837

Jarry, Paul, *Cénacles et vieux logis parisiens*, 1929

Jaucourt, Comte de, *Correspondance . . . avec le prince de Talleyrand*, 1905

Jeanblanc, Helga, *Des Allemands dans l'industrie et le commerce du livre à Paris 1811–1870*, 1994

Jennings, Lawrence, C., *France and Europe in 1848*, Oxford, 1973

Jessop, Thomas, *Journal d'un voyage à Paris en septembre–octobre 1820*, 1928

Johns, Christopher M.S., *Antonio Canova and the Politics of Patronage in Revolutionary and Napoleonic Europe*, Berkeley, 1999

Johnson, A.H., ed., *The Letters of Charles Greville and Henry Reeve 1836–1865*, 1924

Johnson, Douglas, *Guizot*, 1963

Johnson, James H., *Listening in Paris*, 1995

Johnson, Paul, *The Birth of the Modern. World Society 1825–1830*, 1996 ed.

Joinville, Prince de, *Vieux Souvenirs*, 1970 ed.

Jones, Ethel, *Les Voyageurs français en Angleterre de 1815 à 1830*, 1930

Jones, Kathleen, *La Revue britannique. Son histoire et son action littéraire 1825–1840*, 1939

Jouffroy, A. de, *Charles X à Holyrood*, 1833

Jouy, Etienne de, *Guillaume le franc-parleur*, 2 vols, 1816

——*L'Hermite de la Guiane*, 3 vols, 1816–18

Juillet 1830, Musée Carnavalet, 1980

Karamzine, André, 'Le Paris d'il y a cent ans', *Revue hebdomadaire*, July 1937, 531–65

Kastner, Georges, *Les Voix de Paris. Essai d'une histoire littéraire et musicale des cris populaires de la capitale*, 1857

Kaye, John William, *The Life and Correspondence of Major-General Sir John Malcolm GCB*, 2 vols, 1856

Keates, Jonathan, *Stendhal*, 1995 ed.

Kendall, Alan, *Gioacchino Rossini the Reluctant Hero*, 1992

Kerry, Earl of, ed., *The First Napoleon. Some unpublished documents from the Bowood Papers*, 1925

——*The Secret of the Coup d'état*, 1924

King, Helen Maxwell, *Les Doctrines littéraires de la Quotidienne 1814–1830*, 1920

King, Norman, *Correspondances suédoises de Germaine de Staël 1812–1816*, 1988

Kneppelhout, J., *Souvenirs d'un voyage à Paris*, Leyden, 1839

Knight, Cornelia, *Autobiography*, 2 vols, 1861

Kock, Paul de, ed., *La Grande Ville. Nouveau Tableau de Paris comique, critique et philosophique*, 2 vols, 1844

Kohl, Ida, *Paris und die Französen*, 3 vols, Dresden and Leipzig, 1843

Kohler, Pierre, *Madame de Staël et la Suisse. Etude biographique et littéraire*, Lausanne, 1916

Kozlowski, Piotr, *Diorama social de Paris par un étranger qui y a séjourné l'hiver de l'année 1823 et une partie de l'année 1824*, 1997

Kozmian, A.E., 'Le carnet d'un mondain sous la Restauration', *Revue de Paris*, 15 January 1900, 311–53

Krakovich, Odile, *Les Pièces de théâtre soumises à la Censure (1800–1830)*, 1982

Kramer, Lloyd, S., *Threshold of a New World. Intellectuals and the Exile Experience in Paris 1830–1848*, Ithaca, NY, 1988

Krone und Verfassung. König Max I Joseph und der neue Staat, 2 vols, Munich, 1980

Kruse, Joseph, A., ed., *La Loreley et la liberté. Heinrich Heine (1797–1856). Un poète allemand de Paris*, 1997

Kukiel, M., *Czartoryski and European Unity 1770–1861*, Princeton, 1955

Kurtz, Harold, *The Empress Eugénie*, 1964

La Boulaye, Vicomte de, *Mémoires*, 1975

La Fayette, Général de, *Mémoires, correspondance et manuscrits*, 6 vols, 1838

La Garde Royale pendant les événements du 26 juillet au 4 août 1830, par un officier employé à l'état major, 1830

La Maisonfort, Marquis de, *Mémoires d'un royaliste*, 1999

La Reine Hortense. Une femme artiste, Malmaison, 1993

La Rochefoucauld, Sosthènes de, *Pèlerinage à Gorizia*, 1839

La Rue de Lille, 1983

La Rue du Bac, 1990

La Rue Saint-Dominique, Musée Rodin, 1984

[Laborde, Alexandre de], *Quarante-huit heures de garde au château des Tuileries*, 1816

——*Versailles ancien et moderne*, 1839

Lacour-Gayet, G., *Talleyrand*, 4 vols, 1928–34

Laffitte, Jacques, *Mémoires*, 1932

Lamarque, Général, *Mémoires et souvenirs*, 3 vols, 1835–6

Lamartine, Alphonse de, *Correspondance générale de 1830 à 1848*, 2 vols, 1943–8

Lamartine. Le poète et l'homme d'état, Bibliothèque Nationale, 1969

Langeron, Général de, *Mémoires*, 1902

Langeron, Roger, *Decazes ministre du roi*, 1960

Langle, Henry-Melchior de, *Le Petit Monde des cafés et débits parisiens au XIXe siècle. Evolution de la sociabilité citadine*, 1990

Langlois, Gilles Antoine, *Folies, tivolis et attractions. Les premier parcs de loisir parisiens*, n.d.

Lannoy, Fl. De, 'L'idée favorite de Talleyrand', *Revue d'histoire moderne*, VI, 1931, 440–54

L'Attaque de Paris par les troupes alliées le 18[30] mars 1814, 1814 (an official Russian campaign journal)

Lavallette, Count, *Memoirs*, 2 vols, 1831

Le Diable à Paris, 2 vols, 1845–6

Le Gallo, Emile, *Les Cent-Jours*, 1924

Le Guide des dîneurs ou Statistique des principaux restaurants de Paris, 1815

Le Palais Royal, Musée Carnavalet, 1988

Le Sur, C.L., *La France et les Français en 1817. Tableau moral et politique*, 1817

Lechner, André, *1812–1814*, 4 vols, Moscow, 1992

Ledré, Charles, *La Presse à l'assaut de la monarchie*, 1960

Lefebvre de Behaine, Comte, *Le Comte d'Artois sur la route de Paris en 1814*, 1921

Legouvé, Ernest, *Soixante ans de souvenirs*, 2 vols, 1886–7

Lemoine, Bertrand, *Les Passages couverts en France*, 1990

Lenôtre, Georges, *Le Jardin de Picpus*, 1928

Léopold avant Léopold Ier, ed. Gilbert Kirschen, Brussels, 1990

Léribault, Christophe, *Les Anglais à Paris au XIX siècle*, 1994

Lescure, Maurice, *Madame Hamelin*, 1995

Lesser, Margaret, *Clarkey. A Portrait in Letters of Mary Clarke Mohl 1793–1883*, 1984

Lestringant, Frank, *Alfred de Musset*, 1999

Levaillant, Maurice, ed., *Chateaubriand. Lettres à Madame Récamier*, 1998 ed.

Ley, Francis, *Madame de Kruedener 1764–1824. Romantisme et sainte alliance*, 1994

Liautard, Abbé, *Mémoires*, ed. Abbé Denys, 2

vols, 1844

Lieven, Dominic, *The Aristocracy in Europe 1815–1914*, 1992

Ligne, Princesse de, *Souvenirs*, 1923

Limouzin-Lamothe, R., *Mgr Denys-Auguste Affre archévêque de Paris (1793–1848)*, 1971

Liszt, Franz, *Selected Letters*, Oxford, 1998

Loliée, Frédéric, *Le Duc de Morny et la société du Second Empire*, 1909

Lomuller, L.M., *Guillaume Ternaux 1763–1833*, 1978

Louca, Anouar, *Voyageurs et écrivains égyptiens en France au XIXe siècle*, 1970

——ed., *L'Or de Paris*, 1988

Louis-Philippe, l'homme et le roi 1773–1850, Archives Nationales, 1974

Lovinesco, Eugène, *Les Voyageurs français en Grèce au XIXe siècle*, 1909

Löwenstern, Baron de, *Mémoires*, 2 vols, 1903

Loyer, François, ed., *Autour de l'Opéra. Naissance de la ville moderne*, 1995

Lucas-Dubreton, J., *Le Culte de Napoléon 1815–1848*, 1959

——*Louis-Philippe et la Machine Infernale*, 1951

——*Louvel le régicide*, 1925

Luppé, Marquis de, *Astolphe de Custine*, Monaco, 1957

——*Les Travaux et les jours d'Alphonse de Lamartine*, 1942

Lurine, Louis, *Les Rues de Paris*, 2 vols, 1844

Lyons, Marvin, *Le Triomphe du livre. Une histoire sociologique du livre en France au XIX siècle*, 1987

——'The Audience for Romanticism. Walter Scott in France 1815–51', *European History Quarterly*, XIV, 1984, 21–46

Macaulay, Neill, *Dom Pedro. The Struggle for Liberty in Brazil and Portugal 1798–1834*, Durham, NY, 1986

Macé de Lépinay, François, 'Un monument parisien éphémère. La chapelle expiatoire du duc de Berry', *Bulletin de la Société de l'Histoire de l'Art Français*, 1973

Mack Smith, Dennis, *Mazzini*, New Haven, Conn., 1994

Madrid, ou observations sur les moeurs et usages des Espagnols au commencement du XIXe siècle, 2 vols, 1825

Magny, Françoise, ed., *Palais Bourbon. Sa place*, 1987

——*Rue de l'Université*, 1987

Maigron, Louis, *Le Roman historique à l'époque romantique. Essai sur l'influence de Walter Scott*, 1896

Maillé, Duchesse de, *Mémoires 1832–1851*, 1989

——*Souvenirs des deux restaurations*, 1984

Maine de Biran, M.F.P.G., *Journal*, 3 vols, Neuchâtel, 1954–7

Maison, Françoise, 'Les camps sous Louis-Philippe vus du château', *Bulletin de la Société Historique de Compiègne*, XXXVI, 1999, 167–77

Maistre, Comte Joseph de, *Lettres et opuscules inédits*, 2 vols, 1851

Malmesbury, Earl of, *Memoirs of an Ex-Minister*, 2nd ed., 2 vols, 1889

Mansel, Philip, *Louis XVIII*, 1981

——*Pillars of Monarchy. An Outline of the Political and Social History of Royal Guards 1400–1984*, 1984

——*The Court of France 1789–1830*, 1989

Marc, Edmond, *Mes journées de juillet 1830*, 1930

Marcellus, Comte de, *Souvenirs de l'Orient*, 1839

Marchal, Charles, *Physiologie de l'Anglais à Paris*, 1844

Marchant, M., *Nouveau Conducteur de Paris*, 1822

Marchant de Beaumont, F.M., *Manuel et itinéraire du curieux dans le cimetière de Père La Chaise*, 1828

Marianne et Germania 1789–1889. Un siècle de passions franco-allemandes, Petit Palais, 1997

Maricourt, Baron de, *Madame de Souza et sa famille*, 1907

Marie Amélie, *Journal*, ed. Suzanne d'Huart, 1987

Marigny, Madame de, *Journal inédit*, 1907

Marlet, Jean-Henri, *Tableaux de Paris*, ed. Guillaume de Bertier de Sauvigny, Paris–Geneva, 1979

Marmier, Xavier, *Journal 1848–1890*, 2 vols, Geneva, 1968

Marmont, Maréchal, *Mémoires*, 9 vols, 1857

——*Voyage en Hongrie, en Transylvanie, dans la Russie méridionale, à Constantinople . . . en Syrie, en Palestine, en Egypte*, 5 vols, 1839

Marnay, A.J. de, *Mémoires secrets et témoignages authentiques*, 1875

Marquant, Robert, *Thiers et le baron Cotta*, 1959

——'Un essai de création d'un Institut allemand à Paris en 1826', *Etudes germaniques*,

XII, 1957, 97–118

Marrinan, Michael, *Painting Politics for Louis-Philippe*, Yale, 1988

Martin, Henri-Jean et Roger Chartier, *Histoire de l'édition française*, 4 vols, 1983–7

Martin-Fugier, Anne, *La Vie élégante ou la formation du Tout-Paris 1815–1848*, 1990 ed.

——*Les Romantiques 1820–1848*, 1998

Massa, Marquis Philippe de, *Souvenirs et impressions 1840–1871*, 1897

Mathieu, Caroline et Sylvain Bellenger, *Paris 1837. Vues de quelques monuments de Paris achevés sous le règne de Louis-Philippe Ier. Aquarelles de Félix Duban*, 1999

Maupas, M. de, *Mémoires sur le Second Empire*, 2 vols, 1884

Mayne, John, *Journal . . . during a Tour on the Continent*, 1909

Mazas, Alexandre, *Saint-Cloud, Paris et Cherbourg*, 1832

Mazier du Heaume, M., *Observations d'un Français sur l'enlèvement des chefs-d'oeuvre du Muséum de Paris en réponse à la lettre du duc de Wellington au Lord Castlereagh sous la date du 23 septembre 1815*, 1815

McClellan, David, *Karl Marx. His Life and Thought*, 1973

McGuigan, Dorothy Gies, *Metternich and the Duchess*, 1975

Meindre, A.-J., *Histoire de Paris et de son influence en Europe depuis les temps les plus reculés jusqu'à nos jours*, 5 vols, 1854–5

Mellon, Stanley, *The Political Uses of History. A Study of Historians in the French Restoration*, Stanford, 1958

Melonio, Françoise, *Tocqueville et les Français*, 1993

Melun, Vicomte Armand de, *Mémoires*, 2 vols, 1891

Mercer, General Cavalié, *Journal of the Waterloo Campaign*, 2 vols, 1870

Mérimée, Prosper, *Carmen*, 1965 ed.

——*Correspondance générale*, 16 vols, Paris–Toulouse, 1941–61

Mérode-Westerloo, Comte de, *Souvenirs*, 2 vols, 1864

Merriman, John M., *1830 in France*, New York, 1975

Metternich, Prince, *Mémoires, documents et écrits divers*, 8 vols, 1880–4

Michelet, Jules, *Cours au Collège de France*, 2 vols, 1995

——*Journal*, Gallimard, 1959

Mikhailofsky-Danilefsky, A., *History of the Campaign in France in the Year 1814*, 1839

Miller, Susan Gilson, ed., *Disorienting Encounters. Travels of a Moroccan Scholar in France 1845–6*, Berkeley, 1992

Milton, Henry, *Letters on the Fine Arts written from Paris in the Year 1815*, 1816

Mirkine-Guetzevitch, B., '1830 dans l'évolution constitutionnelle de l'Europe', in *Etudes sur les mouvements libéraux et nationaux de l'Europe*, 1930

Mitosek, Zofia, *Adam Mickiewicz aux yeux des Français*, Warsaw, 1992

Moisy, Pierre, *Les Séjours en France de Sulpice Boisserée (1820–1825)*, 1956

Monchoux, André, *L'Allemagne devant les lettres françaises, de 1814 à 1835*, 1953

Montalivet, Comte de, *Fragments et souvenirs*, 2 vols, 1900

Montcalm, Marquise de, *Correspondance*, 1949

——*Mon journal pendant le premier ministère de mon frère*, 1934

Montclos, Brigitte de, *Les Russes à Paris au XIXe siècle*, 1996

Montesquiou, Comte Anatole de, *Souvenirs sur la Révolution, l'Empire, la Restauration et le règne de Louis-Philippe*, 1961

Montfort, Denys de, *Petit Vocabulaire à l'usage des Français et des Alliés* (Klein Wordenbuch), 1815

Moore, Thomas, *Journal*, 6 vols, 1983

Moré, Comte de, *Mémoires (1758–1837)*, 1898

Morgan, Lady, *France*, 3rd ed., 2 vols, 1818

——*France in 1829–30*, 2 vols, 1830

——*Passages from my Autobiography*, New York, 1859

Morin, Marie-Renée, ed., *Correspondance Lamartine–Virieu*, 2 vols, 1987

Morny, Duc de, 'La genèse du coup d'état', *Revue des deux mondes*, 1 December 1925, 512–48

Morritt, J.B.S., *A Grand Tour*, 1985 ed.

Mortemart, Duc de, 'Trois journées, avant, pendant et après mon ministère', *Le Correspondant*, CCCXXI, 10 December 1930, 643–58, 25 December 1930, 801–23

Moulin, Jean-Marie, *Le Château de Compiègne*, 1987

Mowat, R.B., *The Concert of Europe*, 1930

Muffat, Adrien-Jean-Baptiste, *Arts, métiers et cris de Paris*, c. 1815

Müffling, Baron von, *Passages from my Life*

and Writings, 2nd ed. rev., 1858

Muhlstein, Anka, *Astolphe de Custine*, 1996

——*Baron James. The Rise of the French Rothschilds*, 1984

Murat, Inès, *La IIe République*, 1987

Murat, Laure, *Paris des écrivains*, 1996

Muret, Théodore, *Album de l'exil. Résidences de la branche aînée des Bourbons depuis 1830*, 1850

Murger, Henry, *Scènes de la vie de bohème*, Gallimard, 1988

Musset, Alfred de, *Contes d'Espagne et d'Italie*, 1830

——*Correspondance*, I, *1826–1839*, 1985

——*La Confession d'un enfant du siècle*, 1993 ed.

Napoléon I, *Correspondance générale*, 32 vols, 1858–70

Nesselrode, Chancelier Comte de, *Lettres et papiers*, 11 vols, 1904–11

Netter, Lucienne, *Heine et la peinture de la vie parisienne*, Frankfurt, 1980

Neuilly, Comte de, *Dix années d'émigration. Souvenirs et correspondance*, 1865

Newman, Edgar Leon, *Historical Dictionary of France from the 1815 Restoration to the Second Empire*, 2 vols, 1987

——'The Blouse and the Frock Coat. The Alliance of the Common People of Paris with the Liberal Leadership and Middle Class during the Last Years of the Bourbon Restoration', *Journal of Modern History*, XLVI, 3, 1974, 26–39

Niepovic, Gaëtan, *Etudes physiologiques sur les grandes métropoles de l'Europe occidentale*, 1840

Noailles, Marquis de, *Le Comte Molé 1781–1855. Sa vie, ses mémoires*, 6 vols, 1922–30

Noailles, Vicomtesse de, *Vie de la princesse de Poix née Beauvau*, 1855

Normanby, Marquess of, *A Year of Revolution*, 2 vols, 1857

Nougarède, Auguste, *La Vérité sur la révolution de février 1848*, 1850

Nouvel-Kammerer, Odile, *Papiers peints romantiques*, 1991

Olivier, Juste, *Paris en 1830. Journal*, 1951

Ordioni, Pierre, *Pozzo di Borgo diplomate de l'Europe française*, 1935

Orléans, Duc d', *Lettres 1825–1842*, 1889

Orléans, Ferdinand-Philippe Duc d', *Souvenirs 1810–1830*, Geneva, 1993

Orléans, Louis-Philippe d', *Extraits de mon journal du mois de mars 1815*, Twickenham, 1816

Owinska, Anna, *La Politique de la France envers l'Allemagne à l'époque de la monarchie de juillet 1830–1848*, Wroclaw, 1974

Pailhès, G., *La Duchesse de Duras et Chateaubriand*, 1910

Pailleron, Marie-Louise, *François Buloz et ses amis. La vie littéraire sous Louis-Philippe*, n.d.

Palfrey, Thomas R., *L'Europe littéraire. Un essai de périodique cosmopolite*, 1927

——*Le Panorama littéraire de l'Europe (1833–1834). Une revue légitimiste sous la monarchie de juillet*, Evanston, 1950

Palmstierna, C.F., *Marie-Louise et Napoléon 1813–1814. Lettres inédites*, 1955

Pange, Victor de, *Le plus beau de toutes les fêtes. La correspondance inédite de Madame de Staël et d'Elizabeth Hervey duchesse de Devonshire*, 1980

Parent-Lardeur, Françoise, *Les Cabinets de lecture. La lecture publique à Paris sous la Restauration*, 1982

Paris et le phénomène des capitales littéraires. Recherches actuelles en littérature comparée, 1984

Paris, fonctions d'une capitale, 1962

Paris ou le livre des cent et un, 15 vols, 1831–5

Paris révolutionnaire, 4 vols, 1838

Parry, E. Jones, ed., *The Correspondence of Lord Aberdeen and Princess Lieven*, 2 vols, 1938

Pasquier, Duc, *Histoire de mon temps*, 6 vols, 1893–5

——*Souvenirs sur la révolution de 1848*, 1948

Pélissier, Léon-G., *Le Portefeuille de la comtesse d'Albany, 1806–1824*, 1902

Pendle, Karin, *Eugène Scribe and French Opera of the Nineteenth Century*, 1979

Perey, Lucien, *La Comtesse Hélène Potocka*, n.d.

Perret, Edouard, *Le Château de Saint-Ouen*, 1940

Petiteau, Natalie, *Elites et mobilité. La Noblesse d'Empire au XIXe siècle (1808–1914)*, 1997

Picard, M. et M. Mazères, *Les Trois Quartiers*, Comédie en Trois Actes et en Prose, 3e éd., 1827

Pichot, Amédée, *Voyage historique et littéraire en Angleterre et en Ecosse*, 3 vols, 1825

Piette, Christine, *Les Juifs de Paris (1808–1840). La marche vers l'assimilation*, Quebec, 1983

Pigeory, Félix, *Les Monuments de Paris*.

Histoire de l'architecture civile, politique et religieuse sous le règne de Louis-Philippe, 1847

Pinkney, David H., *Decisive Years in France 1840–1847*, 1986

——*Napoleon III and the Rebuilding of Paris*, 1958

——*The French Revolution of 1830*, Princeton, 1972

Pinon, Pierre, *Paris, biographie d'une capitale*, 1999

Planta, Edward, *A New Picture of Paris*, 1814

Playfair, William, *France as it is, not Lady Morgan's France*, 2 vols, 1818

Poirier, Jean, 'Lycéens impériaux 1814–1815', *Revue de Paris*, 15 May 1921, 380–401

Polovtsov, A., ed., *Correspondance diplomatique des ambassadeurs et ministres de Russie en France et de France en Russie avec leurs gouvernements de 1814 à 1830*, 3 vols, St Petersburg, 1902–7

Poniatowski, Michel, *Louis-Philippe et Louis XVIII*, 1982

Potocka, Comtesse, *Mémoires*, 1897

Powell, Anthony, ed., *Barnard Letters 1778–1824*, 1928

Pradère, Alexandre, 'Du style troubadour au style Boulle', *Connaissance des arts*, June 1991

Pradt, Mgr de, *L'Europe et l'Amérique en 1822 et 1823*, 2 vols, 1824

——*Récit historique sur la Restauration de la royauté en France le 31 mars 1814*, 1816

Preston, Jane, 'That Odd Rich Old Woman', unpublished life of Mrs Lytton

Pueckler-Muskau, Prince von, *Tour in England, Ireland and France, in the Years 1826, 1827, 1828 and 1829*, Zurich, 1940

Pugin, A., *Paris and its Environs displayed in a series of two hundred picturesque views*, 2 vols, 1831

Puraye, Jean et Hans-Otto Lang, eds., *Lettres de Léopold Ier . . . 1804–1864*, Liège, 1973

Puymège, Gérard de, *Chauvin le soldat laboureur. Contribution à l'étude des nationalismes*, 1993

Quatrelles de L'Epine, M., *Le Maréchal de Saint-Arnaud*, 2 vols, 1939

Quinet, Edgar, *Mes vacances en Espagne*, 1846

Raczynski, Comte Athanase, 'Le dernier hiver d'un règne. Paris 1824', *Revue d'histoire diplomatique*, 1903, 124–47

Raffles, Thomas, *Letters during a Tour through some Parts of France . . . in the Summer of 1817*, Liverpool, 1818

Raikes, Harriet, ed., *Private Correspondence of Thomas Raikes with the Duke of Wellington*, 1861

Raikes, Thomas, *France since 1830*, 2 vols, 1841

——*A Portion of the Journal*, 4 vols, 1857

Rambuteau, Comte de, *Mémoires*, 1903

Ransom, Teresa, *Fanny Trollope. A Remarkable Life*, 1995

Ray, Gordon N., *Thackeray. The Uses of Adversity*, 1955

Récamier, Madame, *Souvenirs et correspondance*, 2e éd., 1860

Reclus, Maurice, *Emile de Girardin*, 1934

Rees van Tets, Henrica, *Voyage d'une Hollandaise en France en 1819*, 1966

Reinhard, Madame, *Lettres . . . à sa mère*, 1901

Reiset, Vicomte de, *Marie-Caroline duchesse de Berri 1816–1830*, 1906

Rémusat, Charles de, *Correspondance pendant les premières années de la Restauration*, 6 vols, 1883–6

——*Mémoires de ma vie*, 5 vols, 1958–67

Renan, Ernest, *Cahiers de jeunesse 1845–6*, 2 vols, 1906–7

Révérend, Vicomte A., *Titres, anoblissements et pairies de la Restauration 1814–1830*, 7 vols, 1901–8

Revue rétrospective ou Archives secrètes du dernier gouvernement, 1848

Reymondin de Bex, M., *Histoire de la première quinzaine de juin 1820*, 1820

Richelieu, Duc de, *Lettres . . . au marquis d'Osmond 1816–1818*, 1939

Richemont, Pictet de et François d'Ivernois, *Correspondance diplomatique*, 2 vols, 1914

Ridley, Jane, *The Young Disraeli 1804–46*, 1995

Rivaz, Charles-Emmanuel de, *Mes souvenirs de Paris 1810–1814*, Martigny, 1967

Robb, Graham, *Balzac*, 1995 ed.

——*Victor Hugo*, 1997

Robert, Hervé, 'Les funérailles du duc d'Orléans. Une "fête royale" sous la monarchie de juillet', *Revue historique*, 602, April–June 1997, 457–88

——'Louis-Philippe duc d'Orléans et la Révolution de juillet 1830. Hasard et nécessité', *Revue de la Société d'Histoire de la Restauration et de la Monarchie Constitutionelle*, VI, 1992, 37–56

Robinson, J.M., *Buckingham Palace*, 1995

——*Windsor Castle*, 1997

Rochechouart, Comte de, *Souvenirs de la Révolution, l'Empire et la Restauration*, 1933

Rodriguez, Julien Antoine, *Relation historique de ce qui s'est passé à Paris, à la mémorable époque de la déchéance de Napoléon Buonaparte*, 1814

Rolt, L.T.C., *Isambard Kingdom Brunel*, 1970 ed.

Roots, William, *Paris in 1814: or a Tour in France after the First Fall of Napoleon*, Newcastle, 1909

Rosanvallon, Pierre, *Le Moment Guizot*, 1985

Rossi, Henri, *Mémoires aristocratiques féminins 1789–1848*, 1998

Rossini à Paris, Musée Carnavalet, 1992

Rostopchine, André, *Matériaux en grande partie inédits pour la biographie future du comte Théodore Rostopchine*, Brussels, 1864

Rousseau, François, 'Un observateur secret de M. de Chateaubriand (1820–1821). Documents inédits', *Le Correspondant*, 25 March 1912, 1159–85

Roussier, Michel, 'Le Conseil Municipal de Paris et le Retour des Bourbons (1814–1815)', *Bulletin de la Société de l'Histoire de Paris*, 1962, 91–109

Rue de l'Université, 1987

Ruge, Arnold, *Zwei Jahre in Paris*, 2 vols, Leipzig, 1846

Rumigny, Comte de, *Souvenirs*, 1921

Rush, Richard, *A Residence at the Court of London*, 1987 ed.

Russell, W.H., *My Diary during the last great war*, 1874

Rutland, Duke and Duchess of, *Journal of a Trip to Paris*, July 1814

Rzewuska, Comtesse R., *Mémoires*, 3 vols, Rome, 1939–50

Sackville-West, V., *Knole and the Sackvilles*, 1958 ed.

Sainte-Aulaire, Comtesse de, *Souvenirs*, Périgueux, 1875

Sainte-Beuve, *Mes poisons*, 1965 ed.

Saint-Exupéry, S. de and Chantal de Tourtier, *Les Archives du Maréchal Ney et de sa famille conservées aux Archives Nationales*, 1962

Saint-Marc, Pierre, *Le Maréchal Marmont duc de Raguse*, 1957

Saint-Simon, Comte de, et A. Thierry son élève, *De la réorganisation de la société européenne ou de la nécessité de rassembler les peuples de l'Europe en un seul corps politique en conservant à chacun son indépendance nationale*, October 1814

Salem, Jean, ed., *Manuscrits de 1844*, Flammarion, 1996 ed.

Sammons, Jeffrey L., *Heinrich Heine*, Princeton, 1979

Sarrailh, Jean, *Martinez de la Rosa*, 1930

Saule, Béatrix, *Visite du Musée des Carosses*, Versailles, 1997

Schaller, H. de, *Souvenirs d'un officier fribourgeois 1798–1848*, Fribourg, 1890

Schroeder, Paul W., *The Transformation of European Politics 1763–1848*, 1994

Schwarzenberg, Fürst, *Briefe . . . an Seine Frau 1799–1816*, Vienna, 1913

Scott, John, of Gala, *Journal of a Tour to Waterloo and Paris in company with Sir Walter Scott in 1815*, 1842

Scott, John, *Paris Revisited in 1815, by Way of Brussels*, 2nd ed., 1816

——with Frederick Nash, *Picturesque Views of the City of Paris and its Environs*, 1820

[Scott, Walter], *Paul's Letters to his Kinsfolk*, Edinburgh, 1816

Sédillot, René, *Le Coût de la Révolution française*, 1987

Sémallé, Comte de, *Souvenirs*, 1898

Senior, Nassau William, *Journals kept in France and Italy from 1848 to 1852*, 2 vols, 1871

Serman, William, *La Commune de Paris 1871*, 1986

Sermoneta, Duchess of, ed., *The Locks of Norbury*, 1940

Serre, Comte de, *Correspondance*, 6 vols, 1876

Sevrin, Abbé Ernest, *Les Missions religieuses en France sous la Restauration 1815–1830*, 2 vols, Saint-Mandé, 1948–57

Sewell Jr, William H., *Work and Revolution in France. The Language of Labor from the Old Regime to 1848*, Cambridge, 1980

Sewrin, M. et M. Dumersan, *Les Anglaises pour rire ou la Table et le Logement*, 1815

Sheehan, James J., *German History 1770–1866*, 1989

Shelley, Frances Lady, *Diary*, 2 vols, 1912–13

Shepherd, Revd William, *Paris in 1802 and in 1814*, 1814

Sigmann, Jean, *1848. Les révolutions romantiques et démocratiques de l'Europe*, 1970

Silvestre de Sacy, J., *Le Faubourg Saint-Germain*, 1966

Simond, Charles, *Paris de 1800 à 1900*, 3 vols, 1900–1

Simpson, James, *Paris after Waterloo*, 1853

Simpson, M.C.M., *Julius and Mary Mohl*, 1887

Sismondi, S. de, 'Lettres écrites pendant les cent jours', *Revue historique*, January 1877, III, 86–106, 319–45; May 1877, IV, 139–53, V, 347–61; September 1877, VI, 347–60; January 1878, X, 106–29

Sked, Alan, *Europe's Balance of Power 1815–48*, 1979

——*The Decline and Fall of the Habsburg Empire 1815–1918*, 1989

Skowronok, Jerzy, *Adam Czartoryski 1770–1861*, Warsaw, 1994

Smirnov, A. et al., *Les Russes découvrent la France au XVIIIe et au XIXe siècle*, Moscow, 1990

Solovieff, Georges, ed., *Madame de Staël. Ses amis, ses correspondants. Choix de lettres*, 1970

Sorel, Albert, *L'Europe et la Révolution française*, 8 vols, 1885–1904

Sourian, Eve, *Madame de Staël et Henri Heine*, 1974

Spang, Rebecca L., *The Invention of the Restaurant. Paris and Modern Gastronomic Culture*, Harvard, 2000

Spitzer, Alan B., *The French Generation of 1820*, Princeton, 1987

St Clair, William, *That Greece might still be free*, 1972

Staël, Madame de, *Considérations sur la Révolution française*, ed. Jacques Godechot, 1983

——*Dix années d'exil*, ed. Simone Balayé, 1996

——*Oeuvres complètes*, 1820

Stanley, Edward, *Before and After Waterloo*, 1907

Stendhal, *Oeuvres intimes*, 1955

——*Paris–Londres. Chroniques*, ed. Renée Denier, 1997

——*Promenades dans Rome*, Gallimard, 1997

——*Rome, Naples et Florence en 1817*, 1964 ed.

——*Vie de Napoléon*, 1929

Stevenson, Seth William, *Journal of a Tour through Part of France, Flanders and Holland, including a Visit to Paris . . . made in the summer of 1816*, Norwich, 1817

Sudley, Lord, ed., *The Lieven–Palmerston Correspondence 1828–1856*, 1943

Sultana, Donald, *From Abbotsford to Paris and Back. Sir Walter Scott's Journey of 1815*, Stroud, 1993

Sussman, George D., *Selling Mothers' Milk. The Wetnursing Business in France 1715–1914*, Urbana, Ill., 1982

Talleyrand intime d'après sa correspondance avec la duchesse de Courlande, 1894

Talleyrand, Prince de, *Mémoires*, 5 vols, 1891

Tanski, Joseph, *Souvenirs d'un soldat journaliste à Paris*, 1869

Tarn, Julien Frédéric, *Le Marquis de Custine*, 1985

Taylor, Tom, ed., *The Life of Benjamin Robert Haydon*, 2nd ed., 3 vols, 1853

Temperley, Harold, *The Unpublished Diary and Political Sketches of Princess Lieven*, 1925

Texier, Edmond, *Tableau de Paris*, 2 vols, 1853

——et Albert Kaempfen, *Paris capitale du monde*, 1867

Thackeray, William Makepeace, *The Paris Sketch-book*, 1868 ed.

The Letters of Charles Greville and Henry Reeve 1836–1865, 1924

Thomas, Louis, ed. *Correspondance générale de Chateaubriand*, 5 vols, 1912–24

Tibéri, Jean, *La Nouvelle Athènes. Paris capitale de l'esprit*, 1992

Ticknor, George, *Life, Letters and Journals*, 3 vols, Boston, 1876

Tocqueville, Comte de, *Souvenirs*, ed. Bouquins, 1986

Tombs, Robert, *The War against Paris 1871*, Cambridge, 1981

Tomkinson, Lt-Col. William, *The Diary of a Cavalry Officer in the Peninsular and Waterloo Campaigns*, 1894

Toussenel, A., *Les Juifs rois de l'époque. Histoire de la féodalité financière*, 2 vols, 1847

Toustain, Marquis de, *Mémoires*, 1933

Trollope, Fanny, *Fashionable Life in Paris and London*, 3 vols, 1856

——*Hargrave or the Addiction of a Man of Fashion*, 3 vols, 1843

——*Paris and the Parisians in 1835*, 2 vols, 1836

Tronchet, Louis, *Picture of Paris. Being a Complete Guide to all the Public buildings, Places of Amusement and Curiosities in that Metropolis*, May 1814

Tudesq, A.J., *Les Grands Notables en France, 1840–49*, 2 vols, 1964

Tulard, Jean, ed., *Napoléon*, 1977

——*Napoléon à Sainte-Hélène*, 1981

——*Paris et son administration (1800–1830)*, 1976

Turnbull, D., *The French Revolution of 1830; the Events which produced it, and the scenes by which it was accompanied*, 1830

Ubersfeld, Anne, *Théophile Gautier*, 1992

Ullrichova, Maria, ed., *Clemens Metternich–Wilhelmine von Sagan. Ein Briefwechsel, 1813–1815*, Graz, 1966

Un âge d'or des arts décoratifs 1814–1848, Grand Palais, 1891

Underwood, T.R., *A Narrative of Memorable Events in Paris, preceding the capitulation and during the occupancy of that city by the Allied Armies in 1814*, 1828

Uxkull, Boris, *Arms and the Woman. The Intimate Journal of a Baltic Nobleman during the Napoleonic Wars*, 1966

Valon, Alexis de, *Une année dans le Levant*, 1846

Van Zanten, David, *Building Paris. Architectural Institutions and the Transformation of the French Capital 1830–1870*, Cambridge, 1994

Vansittart, Jane, ed., *Surgeon James's Journal 1815*, 1964

Vatout, J., *Souvenirs historiques des résidences royales de France*, 7 vols, 1845

Vaudreuil, Comte de, *Correspondance avec le comte d'Artois*, 2 vols, 1890

Verdy du Vernois, General J. von, *With the Royal Headquarters in 1870–71*, 1897

Viallaneix, Paul, *Michelet, les travaux et les jours 1798–1874*, 1998

Victoria, Queen, *Leaves from a Journal*, 1961

Vidal, C., *Louis-Philippe, Metternich et la crise italienne de 1830–1831*, 1931

Vielcastel, Comte Horace de, *Mémoires . . . sur le règne de Napoléon III*, 6 vols, 1883–4

Viennet, J.P.F., *Journal*, 1955

Vigier, Philippe, *Paris pendant la monarchie de juillet*, 1991

Vigny, Alfred de, *Cinq-Mars*, Livres de Poche, 1970

——*Correspondance*, I, ed. Madeleine Ambrière, 1989

——*Journal d'un poète*, 1928

——*Servitude et grandeur militaires*, 1835

Villèle, Comte de, *Mémoires et correspondance*, 5 vols, 1888–96

Villeneuve, Marquis de, *Charles X et Louis XIX en exil*, 1889

Villien, Bruno, *Vie de Talma*, unpublished manuscript, 1999

Vitrolles, Baron de, *Mémoires*, 2 vols, 1950–2

Wagener, Françoise, *La Comtesse de Boigne*, 1997

Wagner, Richard, *My Life*, 1983 ed.

Walsh, Comte Théobald, *Voyage en Suisse, en Lombardie, et en Piémont*, 2 vols, 1834

Wansey, Henry, *A Visit to Paris in June 1814*, 1814

Waquet, Françoise, *Les Fêtes royales sous la Restauration ou l'ancien régime retrouvé*, Geneva, 1981

Waresquiel, Emmanuel de, *La Vie de Richelieu*, 1990

——et Benoit Yvert, *Histoire de la Restauration 1814–1830. Naissance de la France moderne*, 1996

Warner, John Harley, *Against the Spirit of System. The French Impulse in Nineteenth-Century American Medicine*, 1998

Webster, C.K., *The Foreign Policy of Castlereagh 1815–1822*, 1925

Weinstock, Herbert, *Donizetti and the World of Opera in Italy, Paris and Vienna in the first Half of the Nineteenth Century*, 1964

——*Vincenzo Bellini. His Life and his Operas*, 1971

Wellington, Duke of, *Supplementary Despatches*, 15 vols, 1858–72

Welvert, Eugène, *Napoléon et la police sous la première restauration*, n.d.

[Westmoreland, Earl of,] *Memoir of the Operations of the Allied Armies under Prince Schwarzenberg and Marshal Blücher*, 1822

Whyte, A.J.B., *The Early Life and Letters of Cavour 1810–1848*, Oxford, 1925

Widemann, Marie Pascale Marcia, 'Le Comité Philhellénique et la politique intérieure française (1824–1829)', *Revue de la Société d'Histoire de la Restauration et de la Monarchie Constitutionelle*, 1991, 27–41

Willard, Emma, *Journal and letters from France and Great-Britain*, Troy, NY, 1833

Williams, Helen Maria, *A Narrative of the Events which have taken place in France from the landing of Napoleon Bonaparte on the 1st of March 1815, till the Restoration of Louis XVIII*, 1815

Willms, Johann, *Paris, Capital of Europe. From the Revolution to the Belle Epoque*, New York, 1997

Wilmot, Martha, *Impressions of Vienna 1816–1829*, 1935

Bibliography

Wilmot Ormsby, James, *Letters from the Continent during the Months of October, November and December 1818*, 1819

Wilson Server, A., *L'Espagne dans la Revue des deux mondes 1829–1848*, 1939

Wilson-Smith, Timothy, *Delacroix. A Life*, 1992

Wolzogen, Wilhelm von, *Journal de voyage à Paris 1788–1791*, 1998

Wortman, Richard S., *Scenarios of Power. Myth and Ceremony in Russian Monarchy*, I, Princeton, 1995

Yon, Jean-Claude, *Eugène Scribe, la fortune et la liberté*, 2000

——*Offenbach*, 1996

Yriarte, Charles, *Les Cercles de Paris 1828–1864*, 1864

Yvert, Benoit, *Politique libérale. Bibliographie sélective du libéralisme politique français*, 1994

Zamoyski, Adam, *Chopin*, 1979

——*Holy Madness. Romantics, Patriots and Revolutionaries 1776–1871*, 1999

Zawadski, W.M., *A Man of Honour. Adam Czartoryski as a Statesman of Russia and Poland 1795–1831*, Oxford, 1993

Index

Index

Cabello Felix, Don, 172
Cabet, Etienne, 388
Cadiz, Duke of, 392
Café de Paris, 366
Calvert, Mrs, 124
Cambacérès, Duc, 425
Cambacérès, Jean-Jacques-Régis de, 29
Cambronne, General, 91, 175
Campana, Marquise, 416
Canning, George, 147, 231
Canova, Antonio, 93
Caradoc, Colonel John (*later* 1st Lord Howden), 263–4
Carême, Marie-Antoine, 43, 188
Carey, David: *Life in Paris*, 149
Carlos, Don, 349
Carlyle, Thomas, 327
Carné, Comte de, 123
carnival, 165–6, 283, 365, 383, 388
Carnot, Hippolyte, 406
Carnot, Lazare, Count, 33, 76, 90
Caroline, Queen of George IV, 142
Carrel, Armand, 238
Castellane, Maréchal Boniface, Comte de, 52, 78, 108, 117, 137, 191, 206, 230, 277, 282, 291, 293, 301, 313, 338, 403, 415
Castellane, Cordélia, Comtesse de (*née* Greffuhle), 206, 214, 265, 312–13, 321, 336
Castellane-Majastres, Gabrielle-Ernestine de: marries Fouché, 85
Castlereagh, Robert Stewart, Viscount, 11, 20, 87, 90, 98–9
Castries, Marquise de, 303, 319
Catalani, Madame (singer), 96
Catel, Charles-Simon: *Sémiramis*, 96; *Les Bayadères*, 190
Cathcart, Charles Murray, 2nd Earl, 84
Catherine II (the Great), Empress of Russia, 39
Catherine de Médicis, Queen of France, 4–5
Catholic Church: re-establishment and revival of, 210–17, 305–6
Caulaincourt, Armand Augustin Louis, Comte de, 8, 12, 16, 23, 56, 60, 70–1, 74, 81
Cavaignac, Godefroy, 264, 286–8, 290
Cavaignac, General Louis Eugène, 411–12, 419
Cavour, Count Camille, 305, 332–3, 429
Cayla, Comtesse du (*née* Zoë Talon), 181, 191–3, 197, 204, 308
Celnart, Madame, 123
Censeur européen, Le (journal), 116, 339
censorship, 217, 219–20, 262, 290, 307, 321
Cercle Anglais, 157
Cercle de l'Union, 157, 420
Cercle des Etrangers (*later* Cercle de l'Europe), 157

Chabannes, Comte de, 302
Chabot, Comte de, 254
Chabrol, Comte de, 9, 86, 144, 249, 387
Chalais, Prince de, 137, 405
Chamber of Deputies: debates in, 105–6; ultra-royalism, 108; dissolved and re-elected (1816), 110–11; and franchise, 113; as model in Europe, 114; growing importance, 116, 233; 1819 elections to, 119–20; electoral reform of, 120, 173, 178; disorder in, 176; forces resignation of Richelieu, 181; nobles in, 207–8, 229; dispute with Charles X over Charte, 232; dissolved by Charles X's *ordonnance*, 237; shares legislation with Louis-Philippe, 262–3; influence in London, 336; 1846 elections, 395–6; in 1848 revolution, 404–5
Chamber of Peers: Napoleon makes hereditary, 80, 202; reconstituted, 105–7; as model in Europe, 114; importance, 116; requests new electoral law, 117; likened to salon, 120; rejects Villèle's financial law, 186; debates in, 201; and inheritance laws, 201–2; popularity, 201–2; composition, 207–8, 229; shares legislation with Louis-Philippe, 262–3; and accession of Louis-Philippe, 264–5; resignations from, 300
Chambord, Henri-Dieudonné, Comte de (Duc de Bordeaux; 'Henri V'): born, 179–80, 184, 191; baptism, 196; refuses throne of France (1873), 237; and July revolution, 252, 255; as prospective king, 261, 264, 301, 303, 404–5; Stuart insists on remaining in France, 263; leaves for exile in England, 264; court in London, 375; represents nobility, 414
Changarnier, General Nicolas Anne Théodule, 417, 419
Chantilly, Château de, 296
Chapelle Expiatoire, 193–4, 267, 281, 432
Charivari, Le (journal), 286, 289
Charles I, King of England, 162
Charles II, King of England, 162, 164
Charles X, King of France (*earlier* Comte d'Artois): and Sémallé, 14; returns from exile, 20–1; cedes French conquests to Allies, 26; meets royalists, 29; and discontent with government, 31; painted by Gérard, 37; and revival of Household troops, 56; backs Soult as Minister of War, 65; and Louis XVIII's acceptance of Charte, 72; Fouché corresponds with, 81; invites Duchess of Devonshire to visit Chamber of Deputies, 106; political influence and ambitions, 117–19; qualities, 117–18; finances Piet's salon, 121; Anglophilia, 143, 151; accession, 164, 197–8; at Berri's assassination, 167, 171;

543

Index

Index

Ferdinand I, Emperor of Austria, 260
Ferdinand II, King of the Two Sicilies, 329
Ferdinand IV, King of Naples, 183
Ferdinand VII, King of Spain, 174, 182–3, 234, 348, 350
Ferrand, Comte, 27, 31
Fersen, Count Axel, 244n
Fesch, Cardinal, 154
Feuchères, Baron de, 151
Feval, Paul: *Le Fils du Diable*, 389
Fieschi, Joseph, 288
Fiévée (politician), 48, 97
Fife, James Duff, 4th Earl of, 147–8
Fitzjames, Duc de, 14, 118, 163, 230, 300, 303, 324, 346
Fitzjames, Marquis de, 301, 314
Flahaut, General Comte Charles de:
  background and character, 22–4; life in Paris, 61, 75, 223; as Hortense's lover, 62; dispute with Pozzo, 63; as émigré, 67; and Napoleon's return to Paris, 70, 74–5, 77, 82; favours Napoleon II, 81; withdraws to Lyon, 90; mother writes to in England, 116, 152–3; mother's devotion to, 130, 154; on Duchesse de Broglie's salon, 138; meets Thomas Moore, 149; affair with Queen Hortense ends, 152; marriage, 153–4; disparages Rothschild, 187; home as political centre, 227–8; seeks post under Louis-Philippe, 265; on July revolution, 268; and *entente cordiale*, 269; hopes for ambassadorship in London, 270; and conflict in Belgium, 272; accompanies Louis-Philippe on review, 288; on loss of royal posts, 292; visits Louis-Philippe, 293; appointed Premier Ecuyer to Duc d'Orléans, 297; and Prince de Léon's insult to Orléans, 305; and Princess Lieven, 334; at Napoleon's funeral, 371; at Hortense's funeral, 375; and trial of Louis-Napoleon, 376; as ambassador to Austria, 398–9; advises Louis-Napoleon, 415–17; and 1851 coup, 419–21; moves to England, 421; death, 428
Flahaut, Comte de (d. 1793), 23
Flahaut, Louisa de, 421
Flahaut, Margaret Mercer Nairne, Comtesse de, 153, 227–8, 233, 234, 267, 270, 305, 314–15, 320, 335, 359, 367, 371, 417–19
Flauguergues, M. (deputy), 77
Fontaine, Pierre, 65, 80–1, 200, 254, 267, 298
Fontainebleau, Château de, 8, 13, 17, 23–4, 71, 224, 296–7, 425
Fontaney, Antoine-Etienne, 129, 311, 318
Forbin, Comte de: *Voyage dans le Levant*, 343
Foster, Augustus, 48
Foucauld, Vicomte de, 217, 260
Fouché, Joseph, Duc d'Otrante, 70, 76–7, 81–2,

84–5, 89–90, 96–7, 133, 149, 187, 242, 313
Foulkes, Mr: killed in 1830 revolution, 240
Fourier, Charles, 388
Fournier (bookseller), 310
Foy, General Maximilien Sébastien: on Mme de Souza, 23; regrets losing war, 59–60; on Napoleon's approach to Paris, 102; as liberal in Chamber of Deputies, 117, 173–4, 178, 180, 183, 204; painted by Gérard, 135; on Suchet's salon, 136; fights duel, 173; attacks 1823 expedition to Spain, 182; on preoccupation with business and railways, 185; at Rothschild ball, 188; Orléans complains to, 195; and royalist revival, 200; on nobility, 204; religious indifference, 211; funeral, 215–16, 372; nationalism, 227
Fraguier, Marquis de, 208
France: agreements under 1814 Treaty of Paris, 26–7; position in Europe, 26–7, 35, 55–6; constitution, 27–8; power of royal patronage in, 31–3; war casualties, 38; territorial losses under Second Treaty of Paris, 98–9; joins Holy Alliance, 99; new army formed, 100; financial dealings, 186–7, 364; population, 202; loss of empire and territories, 226–8, 231–3; and *entente cordiale* with Britain, 269; Polish refugees in, 274; overseas military campaigns, 355–6; nationalism in, 356–9, 380–2; and Ottoman crisis, 358–61; claims on Rhine, 361–3; religious worship of, 380–1; railway development in, 385–6; voting franchise, 385, 411; Republic proclaimed (1848), 405; first election by universal male suffrage (1848), 409; and Louis-Napoleon's *coup d'état* (1851), 417–19; war with Prussia (1870–1), 428–9
Francis I, Emperor of Austria, 84, 88, 93, 99
Francis I, King of the Two Sicilies, 234–5
Francis Joseph, Emperor of Austria, 260
Frascati café, Paris, 206
Frayssinous, Monseigneur Denis Antoine Luc, Comte de, Bishop of Hermopolis, 211–12
Frazer, General Augustus, 88
Frederick, Crown Prince of Prussia (*later* German Kaiser), 430–1
Frederick William III, King of Prussia, 10, 13, 18, 37, 40, 89, 93, 156, 224, 231 & n
French language: status of, 39–40, 346, 354
French Revolution: English influence on, 162; memorials to, 193–4; arouses repugnance, 268; praised, 395
Frye, Major, 93
furniture *see* interior decoration

Galignani, Giovanni Antonio, 145–6, 149, 160, 339

Index

Humboldt, Alexander von, 129, 135, 182, 293, 297, 322, 338, 391
Hume, David: *History of the Stuarts*, 162
Hundred Days (1815), 66–79, 86, 98
Hunt, Leigh, 142
Huvé, Jean-Jacques-Marie, 191
Hyde de Neuville, M., 121

inheritance laws, 201–2
interior decoration, 314, 353–4
Irving, Washington, 129
Isabella II, Queen of Spain, 348–9, 392
Isabelle-Ferdinande, Infanta of Spain, 351
Isabey, Jean-Baptiste, 43, 135
Ismail Pasha, 345
Italy: cultural influence, 39; affected by July revolution, 271; divisions, 329; nationalism in, 329, 409; political exiles in Paris, 329–33; French travellers in, 342–3; French war against Austria in, 426

Jacob (furniture makers), 155
Jacob, Georges, 191
Jacqueminot, General, 398–9
James II, King of England: reburial, 163–4
James, Surgeon Haddy, 92, 101
Janin, Jules, 383–4
Jardin de Picpus, 194
Jardin des Plantes, 51
Jardin du Luxembourg, 432
Jaucourt, Comte de, 17, 64–5
Jena, battle of (1806), 11n
Jerome-Bonaparte, King of Westphalia, 46, 94
Jesuits, 212, 217–18
Jews: community in Paris, 188; Thiers criticises, 364; anti-Semitism, 391
Joachim, King of Naples *see* Murat, Joachim
João, King of Portugal, 261
Jockey Club (Paris), 158
Johnson, Samuel, 40
Joinville, François d'Orléans, Prince de, 288, 293n, 369, 397 & n, 421
Jordan, Camille, 120
Jordan, Dorothea, 148
Joseph Bonaparte, King of Spain, 6–7, 227
Josephine, Empress of Napoleon I, 28, 154
Journal de Paris, 160
Journal des chasses du roi, 248
Journal des débats, 186, 210, 229, 238, 364, 383–4, 389
Journal du commerce, Le (newspaper), 239
journalists and journalism, 307, 319–20
Jouy, Etienne de, 135, 342
Julie Bonaparte, Queen of Spain, 80
July revolution (1830), 238–54, 261, 265, 268–9, 280; influence abroad, 271–2, 276;

commemorated, 280–2

Kant, Immanuel, 333
Karr, Alphonse, 413
Keate, John, 93
Keith, Admiral George Keith Elphinstone, Viscount, 153
Kellermann, Marshal François Christophe de, 20
Kemble, Charles, 161
Kératry, M. de (deputy), 176
Kinnaird, Charles, 8th Baron, 77, 149
Kinnaird, Douglas, 133
Kleist, General, 10
Klincksieck (publishers), 339
Kneppelhout, J., 367
Kock, Paul de: *La Grande Ville*, 317
Komierowski, Colonel, 245
Kossuth, Lajos, 391
Kozlovski, Piotr, 123
Krüdener, Baroness Julie de, 96–7, 99

Labédoyère, Angélique François Huguet, Comte de, 68, 70, 81, 90–1, 194
Labédoyère, Comtesse de, 9, 91
Lablache, Louis, 134
Laborde, Alexandre de, 74–5, 273, 346
Laborde, Léon de, 343
La Bourdonnaye, Comte de ('the White Jacobin'), 166, 229
La Briche, Madame de, 139, 168, 170, 223, 312
Lacordaire, Jean Baptiste Henri, Abbé, 305, 407
Lacretelle, Charles de, 40, 206
Lacroix, Auguste de, 366
Ladvocat (publisher), 309–10
Lafarge, Marie Fortunée, 376
Lafayette, Georges, 410
La Fayette, Marie-Joseph Paul-Roch-Yves-Gilbert Motier, Marquis de: in Mme de Staël's salon, 52; speech on French sacrifices for Napoleon, 81; elected to Chamber, 119; and death of Berri, 172; and electoral reform, 173; invokes nationalism, 174; threatened in Chamber, 176; and popular disorder, 177; benefits from émigré indemnities, 200; popularity, 205; deserts revolutionary army, 207; on effect of Charte, 219; arrest ordered (1830), 247; in July revolution, 249, 252, 269; reappointed to command Garde Nationale, 249; Louis-Philippe visits in Hôtel de Ville, 258–9; regrets lack of revolutionary constitution, 264; relations with Louis-Philippe, 266; speeches supporting Poland, 273, 275; speech during cholera epidemic, 285; relations with Princess Belgiojoso, 330; visits Prussia, 352

Index

Laffitte & Blount (bankers), 386, 408

Laffitte, Charles, 386

Laffitte, Jacques: and fall of Paris (1814), 8; converts to Bonapartism, 77, 111, 113; elected to Chamber of Deputies (1816), 111; salon, 121, 137; and unrest in June 1820, 177–8; defeated (1824), 183; wealth, 188, 245; Orléans complains to, 195; and indemnities to émigrés, 200; subscribes to Foy fund, 215; re-elected (1827), 219; near-bankruptcy, 237; in opposition to Charles X, 245–7, 249–56; supports Orléans (Louis-Philippe) for throne, 254–6, 258, 263, 267; urges reunion of Belgium with France, 272; resigns, 279, 282, 355; heads deputation to Louis-Philippe in 1832 rising, 285; dress, 297; Rothschild opposes, 353; at Duc d'Orléans' funeral, 380

Lagrenée, Théodore de, 413

Lainé, Joseph-Henri-Joachim, 72, 90, 207, 301

Lallemand, Nicholas, 176–7

La Maisonfort, Marquis de, 221

Lamarque, General, 285, 372

Lamartine, Alphonse de: serves in Gardes du Corps, 33, 134; on Mme de Montcalm, 122; in diplomatic service, 134; on Mlle Noblet, 147; marriage, 152; praises Byron, 160; popularity, 205; refuses office, 234; on Chamber of Deputies, 235; poem on Polish uprising, 273; at Notre Dame, 305; on adulation of Chateaubriand, 309; literary success, 309, 311; political activities, 312; writes on Paris, 317; travels in Italy, 343; on ending of Ottoman crisis, 365; oratory, 365, 373–4, 396, 410; anti-Bonapartism, 373–4; on death of Duc d'Orléans, 380; predicts class warfare, 388; insists on attending reform banquet, 398; advocates republic on fall of Louis-Philippe, 405; in provisional government (1848), 406–8, 411; elected in 1848 election, 409–10; supposedly blackmailed by Ledru-Rollin, 411; loses presidential election, 414; *Histoire des Girondins*, 395; *Méditations*, 184, 308; *Voyage en Orient*, 344

Lamartine, Eliza (*née* Birch), 152

Lamb, Lady Caroline, 92

Lamb, Charles, 161

Lamb, Frederick, 96

Lamennais, Félicité Robert de, 273

Langeron, General, Comte de, 8

Lannes, Maréchal Jean, Duc de Montebello, 203

La Rochefoucauld, Jules de, 254

La Rochefoucauld, Vicomte Sosthènes de, 14, 118, 181, 184, 191, 193, 208, 215, 326

La Rochejaquelein, Félicie, Comtesse de (*née*

Duras; *then* Princesse de Talmont), 130–1, 281

Las Cases, Emmanuel, Comte de, 67; *Mémorial de Sainte-Hélène*, 241, 252

Lassailly, Charles: *Le Cadavre*, 387

Lasteyrie, M. de, 254

La Tour du Pin, Marquise de, 315, 316n

Latour-Maubourg (Minister of War), 120

La Trémoille, Princesse de, 122

Lavallette, Antoine-Marie, Comte de, 62, 70–1, 133

Lawrence, Sir Thomas, 155, 198

League of the Just, 389

Leclerq, Théodore, 48

Lecouturier, Henri, 413

Ledru-Rollin, Auguste, 411, 414

Lefebvre, Maréchal François, 18, 136

legitimists: oppose Louis-Philippe, 300–5

Legouvé, Ernest, 303, 309

Lehmann, Henri, 332, 390, 429

Le Hon, Comtesse, 314, 367, 375n, 398, 415–18

Le Hon, Léopold, 417–18

Leipzig, battle of (1813; 'Battle of the Nations'), 2

Lemercier, Népomucène, 346

Léon, Prince de, 305

Leopardi, Giacomo, Count, 40

Leopold I, King of the Belgians, 10, 47, 230, 272, 296, 361, 397

Leopold, Prince of Hohenzollern, 427

Le Raincy (park), 35, 254, 256

Leroux, Pierre, 388

Le Sueur, Jean-François, 33, 324, 326

Le Sur, C.L., 100

letter-writing, 320–1

Lévis, Duc de, 129, 160

Liancourt, Duc de, 208

Liberté, La (newspaper), 428

Librairie Hispano-Américaine, 339

Libri, Guglielmus Brutus, Count, 329

Lichtenstein, Prince, 13

Lieven, Count, 40

Lieven, Princess Dorothea von (*née* von Benckendorff), 125, 306, 321, 329, 333–7, 353, 357–60, 363, 373, 377, 395–6, 405, 420–1

Ligne, Prince de, 399

Lister, Anne, 146, 215, 218

Liszt, Franz, 327, 330–1, 366, 385

Liverpool, Robert Banks Jenkinson, 2nd Earl of, 90, 93, 105, 142, 187

Lobau, Maréchal, Comte de, 245, 249, 285–6, 288, 399

Lobau, Maréchale de, 420

Lock family (of Norbury), 242

London: rebuilding and improvements in, 48–9; dominance, 143–4; Custine on horror of, 150; fog in, 222; as revolutionary centre,

Index

Index

Index

Virginie, Mlle (actress), 167
Visconti, Louis, 189
Vitrolles, Baron de, 3, 251
Voltaire, François Marie Arouet de, 211, 220, 352; *La Henriade*, 14
Vorwärts (German newspaper), 389–91

Wagner, Richard, 223, 327–8, 340, 429
Waldor, Mélanie, 332
Walewska, Marie, 228
Walewski, Alexandre, Comte, 228, 244, 360
Wall, Comte de, 239
Wallace, Richard, 156
Warsaw: 1830–1 insurrection, 273–4; *see also* Poland
Waterloo, battle of (1815), 80–1, 227
Weitling, Wilhelm, 390
Wellesley, Richard Colley, Marquess, 137
Wellington, Arthur Wellesley, 1st Duke of: on royal patronage in France, 32; painted by Gérard, 37; and Chateaubriand, 40; entertains in Paris, 53, 89, 92; unpopularity in Paris, 59–60, 96; attends Congress of Vienna, 60; Orléans corresponds with, 76; commands allied armies in Netherlands, 80; Waterloo victory, 80; advances on Paris, 82; suggested as French king, 83; forms government in Paris, 84; cheered in Paris, 87; shocked at Prussian troops' behaviour, 88; given Canova statue of Napoleon, 93; orders removal of art treasures, 94–6; and government of France, 99; attends conferences of ambassadors in Paris, 109; on Comte d'Artois, 117–18; visits Princesse de Vaudémont's salon, 132; art collection, 137; sees satirical plays, 146;

carriage, 210; Polignac's friendship with, 231
Wellington, Catherine, Duchess of (*née* Pakenham), 71
Westmorland, Countess of, 43
Wilhelm I, German Kaiser and King of Prussia, 428, 430–1
Wilhelm, Prince of Prussia, 6, 11, 51, 326
William I, King of the Netherlands, 271
William III (of Orange), King of England, 163–4
William IV, King of England, 148, 270
Williams, Helen Maria, 41, 79, 83, 87
Wilmot, Martha, 128
Wilson, Harriette: *Paris Lions and London Tigers*, 150
Windischgraetz, Prince, 260
Winsor, F.A., 143
Winterhalter, Franz, 390
Wolzogen, Baron von, 268
women: royalist sentiments, 79; constitutional restrictions on, 121; maintain salons, 121–2, 315; respect for, 140; religious faith, 211, 213, 305–6; changing status of, 314–15; letter-writing, 320–1; orientals' view of, 345
Wrede, Marshal, 18
Wright, John Bowes, 69, 139–40
Württemberg, Crown Prince (*later* King) of, 10, 231

Yonne, Dufay de l', 375
York, Frederick Augustus, Duke of, 83, 153

Zamoyski, Count Ladislaus, 274n